THE GOSPEL OF MATTHEW

Writer - The Holy Spirit
Illustrator - Simon Amadeus Pillario
Colors - Leslie Simonin Wilmer
Ryan Esch

ILLUSTRATION AND LETTERING

Simon Amadeus Pillario

COLORS

Ryan Esch, Leslie Simonin Wilmer and Simon Amadeus Pillario

QUALITY CHECKING

Ryan Esch and Bruce Nicole

BIBLE AND THEOLOGICAL CONSULTANT

Rev. Dr. Christopher R. Smith

ANCIENT CULTURE AND HISTORY CONSULTANTS

Dr. Mark Woolmer
Professor Lloyd Llewellyn-Jones
Arkan Amin Zaki Al-Amin

KICKSTARTER BACKERS

See page at the back of this publication.

TRANSLATION

Holy Bible, New International Version TM, NIV TM Copyright © 1973, 1978, 1984, 2011 by Biblica, Inc. Used with permission. All rights reserved worldwide.The "New International Version" is a trademark registered in the European Union Intellectual Property Office (EUIPO) and United States Patent and Trademark Office by Biblica, Inc. The "NIV", "Biblica", "International Bible Society" and the Biblica Logo are trademarks registered in the United States Patent and Trademark Office by Biblica, Inc.
Used with permission.

Featuring:

In association with:

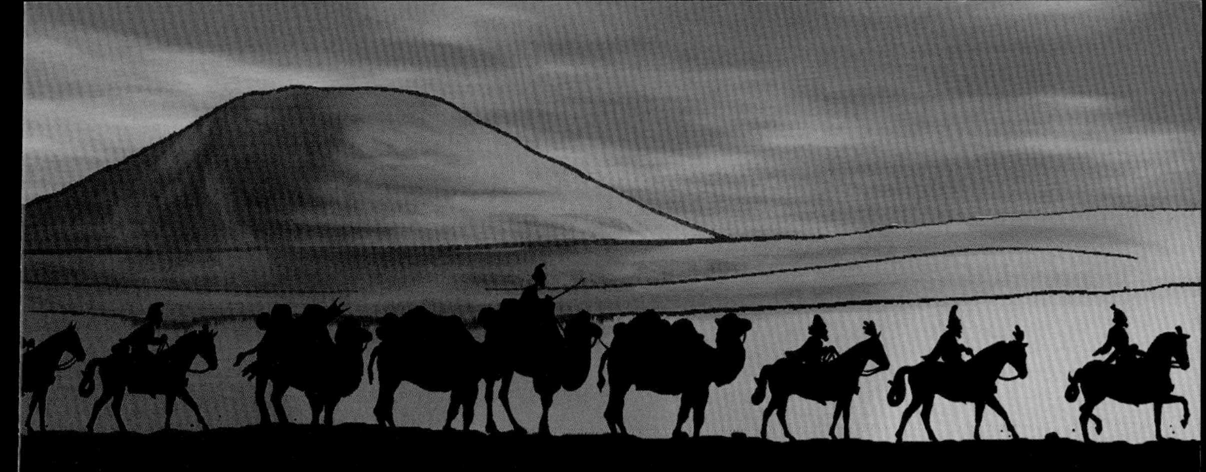

INTRODUCTION

Throughout the books of Moses and the prophets, God has promised a messiah, a king to come and liberate his people, Israel, and rule the earth with peace and justice.

But what will be the fulfilment of this prophesied royal conqueror from heaven? The story begins in a sheep's feeding trough...

INTERPRETATION

The Word for Word Bible Comic has avoided, as far as possible, creating a new interpretation, version or re-telling of the text. Using research to ensure the narrative is represented as authentically as possible, the pictures in the comic aim to represent what the text plainly illustrates. In the case of ambiguity, a multitude of qualified and respected Bible Commentaries (including Bailey, Lange, Archer and a range of others cross referenced with Biblehub.com) have been deferred to.

Text is clear.	=	Draw it clearly.
Text is ambiguous but the Bible clarifies it elsewhere.	=	Draw it clearly.
Text is ambiguous but good commentators agree.	=	Interpretation strongly implied by the images.
Text is ambiguous and commentators divided.	=	Draw the images to be as ambiguous as the text.

While this graphic novel is only the events and words of the Gospel of Matthew, we fully utilise the other gospels which paint in many details, contextual and setting elements that are not in the text alone. We study biblical and historical accounts in depth and present a visual which is harmonized and consistent with all four gospels. For example, scene changes that are not obvious from the text alone, or a list of people who are also present in a scene can easily be illuminated effortlessly with images.

TREATMENT OF THE TEXT

All the words from the translation are used. Where the pictorial format makes some words redundant, these are featured in the gutter spaces between the panels. The only "words" added are sound effects or words in other languages that you don't need to read.

Minor punctuation (for example speech marks, some commas and semi-colons within speech) are rendered redundant where speech bubbles and breaks between panels indicate the pauses or changes in speaker, and have therefore been excluded. An ellipsis has been used where a sentence continues over two or more panels to indicate the continuity of thought. Exclamation marks and question marks have remained in accordance with the translation.

One of the advantages to a pictorial version is the ability to render emotion visually, and in accordance with common use, capitalisation has been used to indicate shouting. Large numbers have been converted to digits to save space and aid readability.

Example: From Matthew 12:23 . How it appears in the Bible...
"23 All the people were astonished and said, "Could this be the Son of David?"

How it appears on the comic:

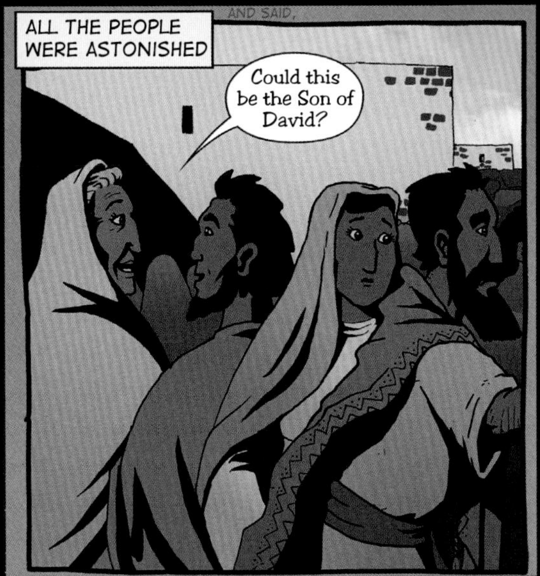
AND SAID,
ALL THE PEOPLE WERE ASTONISHED
Could this be the Son of David?

"The days are coming," declares the Lord, "when I will fulfill the good promise I made to the people of Israel and Judah. In those days and at that time I will make a righteous Branch sprout from David's line; he will do what is just and right in the land."

Jeremiah 33:14-15

The Word for Word
Bible Comic presents...

The Gospel of

Matthew

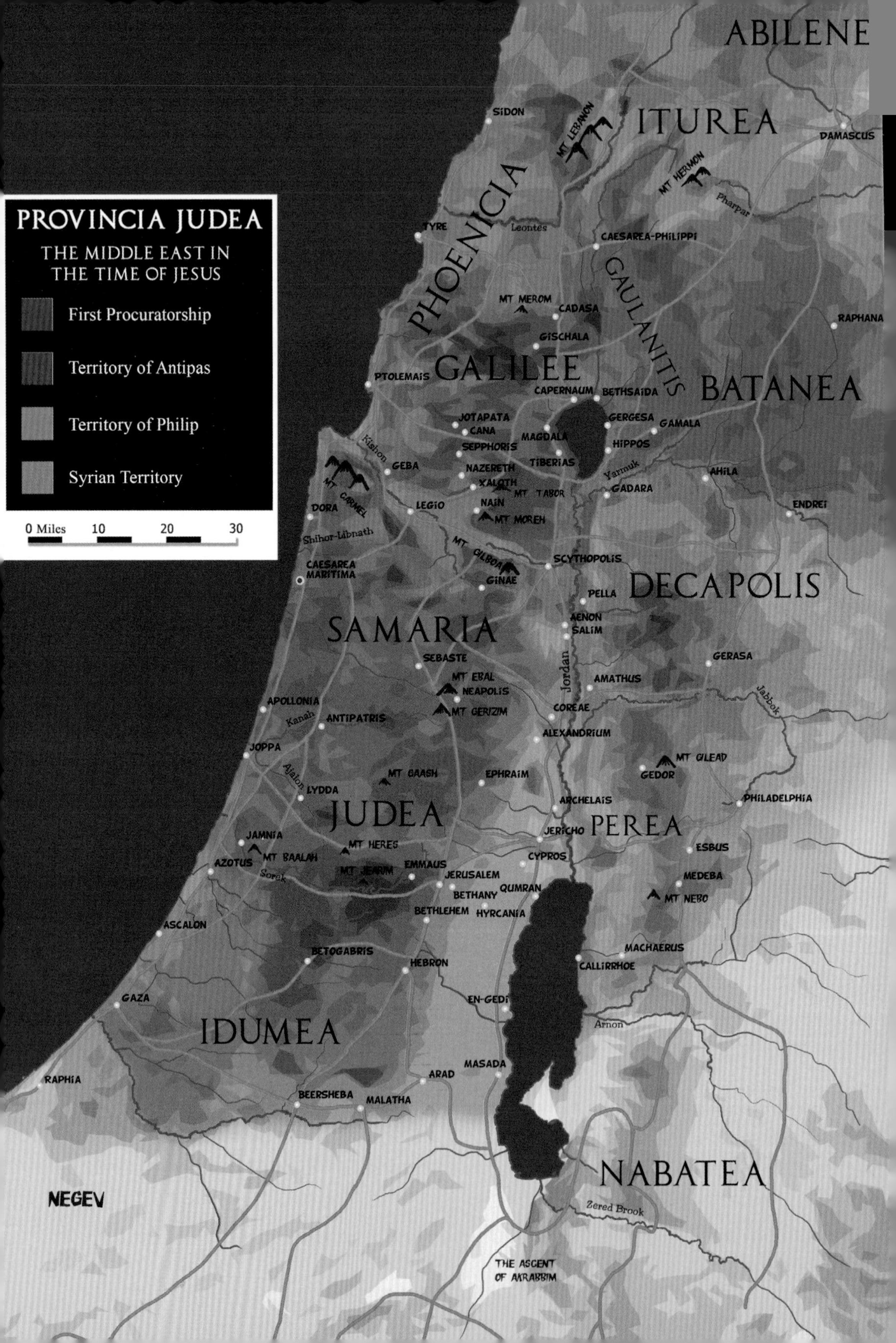
PROVINCIA JUDEA
THE MIDDLE EAST IN THE TIME OF JESUS
First Procuratorship
Territory of Antipas
Territory of Philip
Syrian Territory
0 Miles 10 20 30
ABILENE
ITUREA
SIDON
MT LEBANON
DAMASCUS
MT HERMON
PHOENICIA
Pharpar
TYRE
Leontes
CAESAREA-PHILIPPI
GAULANITIS
MT MEROM
CADASA
RAPHANA
GISCHALA
GALILEE
PTOLEMAIS
BATANEA
CAPERNAUM
BETHSAIDA
JOTAPATA
GERGESA
GAMALA
CANA
MAGDALA
Kishon
SEPPHORIS
HIPPOS
TIBERIAS
GEBA
NAZERETH
Yarmuk
AHILA
MT CARMEL
XALOTH
MT TABOR
GADARA
DORA
LEGIO
NAIN
MT MOREH
ENDREI
Shihor-Libnath
MT GILBOA
SCYTHOPOLIS
CAESAREA MARITIMA
GINAE
DECAPOLIS
PELLA
AENON
SAMARIA
SALIM
SEBASTE
GERASA
Jordan
MT EBAL
AMATHUS
NEAPOLIS
Jabbok
APOLLONIA
MT GERIZIM
COREAE
Kanah
ANTIPATRIS
ALEXANDRIUM
JOPPA
MT GILEAD
Ajalon
MT GAASH
EPHRAIM
GEDOR
LYDDA
ARCHELAIS
PHILADELPHIA
JUDEA
PEREA
JAMNIA
JERICHO
MT HERES
ESBUS
MT BAALAH
CYPROS
AZOTUS
Sorek
MT JEARIM
EMMAUS
JERUSALEM
MEDEBA
BETHANY
QUMRAN
MT NEBO
BETHLEHEM
HYRCANIA
ASCALON
MACHAERUS
BETOGABRIS
HEBRON
CALLIRRHOE
GAZA
EN-GEDI
Arnon
IDUMEA
MASADA
RAPHIA
ARAD
BEERSHEBA
MALATHA
NABATEA
NEGEV
Zered Brook
THE ASCENT OF AKRABBIM

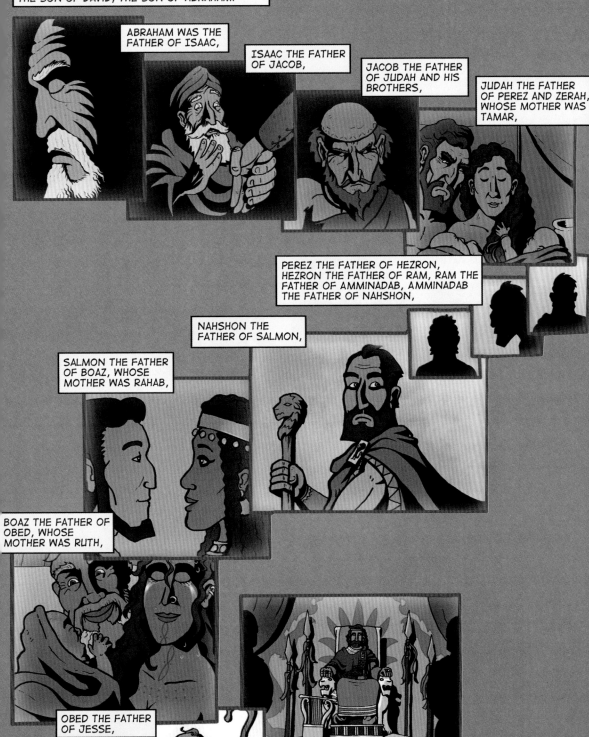

THIS IS THE GENEALOGY OF JESUS THE MESSIAH THE SON OF DAVID, THE SON OF ABRAHAM:

ABRAHAM WAS THE FATHER OF ISAAC,

ISAAC THE FATHER OF JACOB,

JACOB THE FATHER OF JUDAH AND HIS BROTHERS,

JUDAH THE FATHER OF PEREZ AND ZERAH, WHOSE MOTHER WAS TAMAR,

PEREZ THE FATHER OF HEZRON, HEZRON THE FATHER OF RAM, RAM THE FATHER OF AMMINADAB, AMMINADAB THE FATHER OF NAHSHON,

NAHSHON THE FATHER OF SALMON,

SALMON THE FATHER OF BOAZ, WHOSE MOTHER WAS RAHAB,

BOAZ THE FATHER OF OBED, WHOSE MOTHER WAS RUTH,

OBED THE FATHER OF JESSE,

AND JESSE THE FATHER OF KING DAVID.

DAVID WAS THE FATHER OF SOLOMON, WHOSE MOTHER HAD BEEN URIAH'S WIFE...

MATTHEW 1:1-6

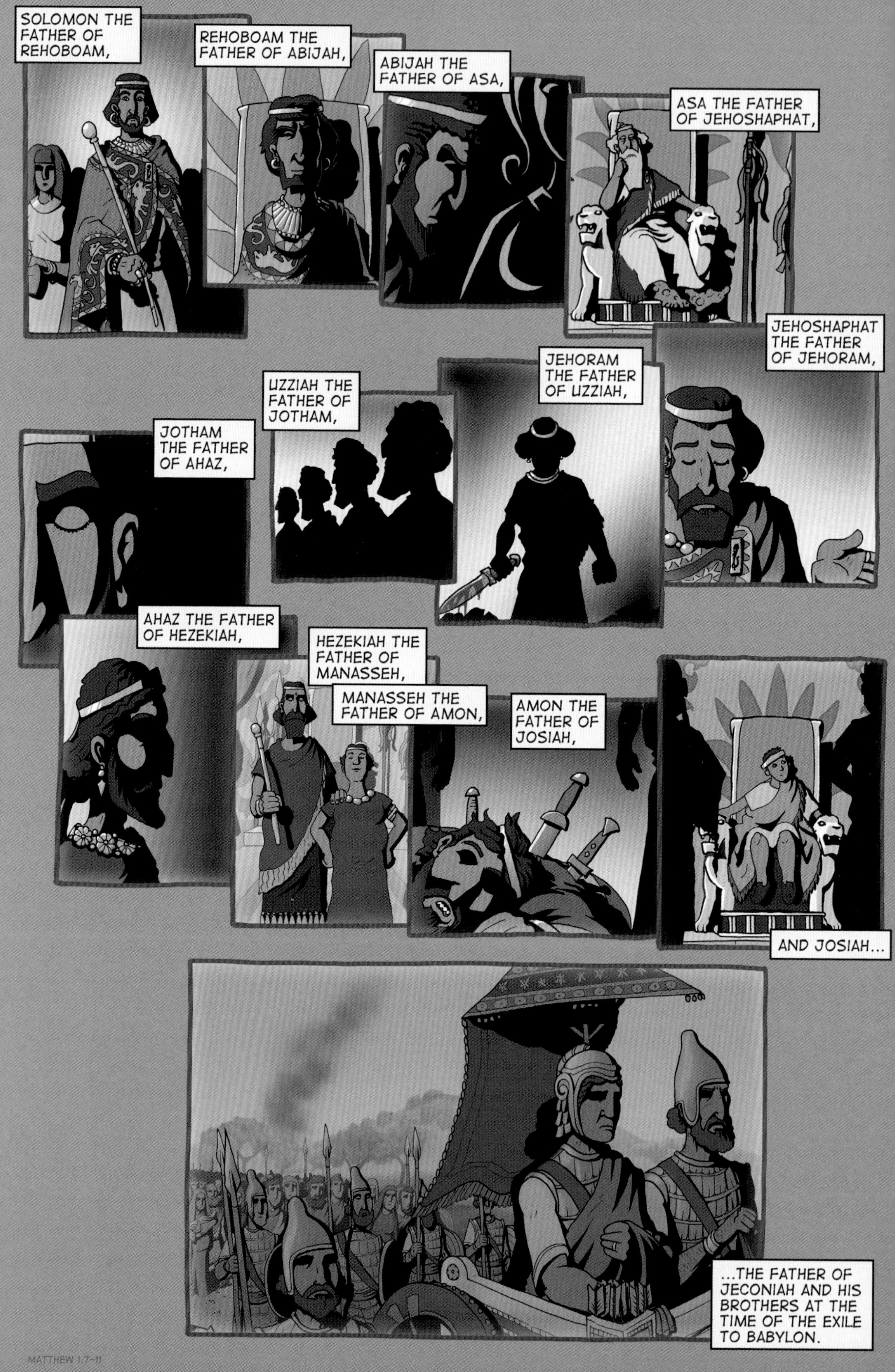
SOLOMON THE FATHER OF REHOBOAM,
REHOBOAM THE FATHER OF ABIJAH,
ABIJAH THE FATHER OF ASA,
ASA THE FATHER OF JEHOSHAPHAT,
JEHOSHAPHAT THE FATHER OF JEHORAM,
JEHORAM THE FATHER OF UZZIAH,
UZZIAH THE FATHER OF JOTHAM,
JOTHAM THE FATHER OF AHAZ,
AHAZ THE FATHER OF HEZEKIAH,
HEZEKIAH THE FATHER OF MANASSEH,
MANASSEH THE FATHER OF AMON,
AMON THE FATHER OF JOSIAH,
AND JOSIAH...
...THE FATHER OF JECONIAH AND HIS BROTHERS AT THE TIME OF THE EXILE TO BABYLON.

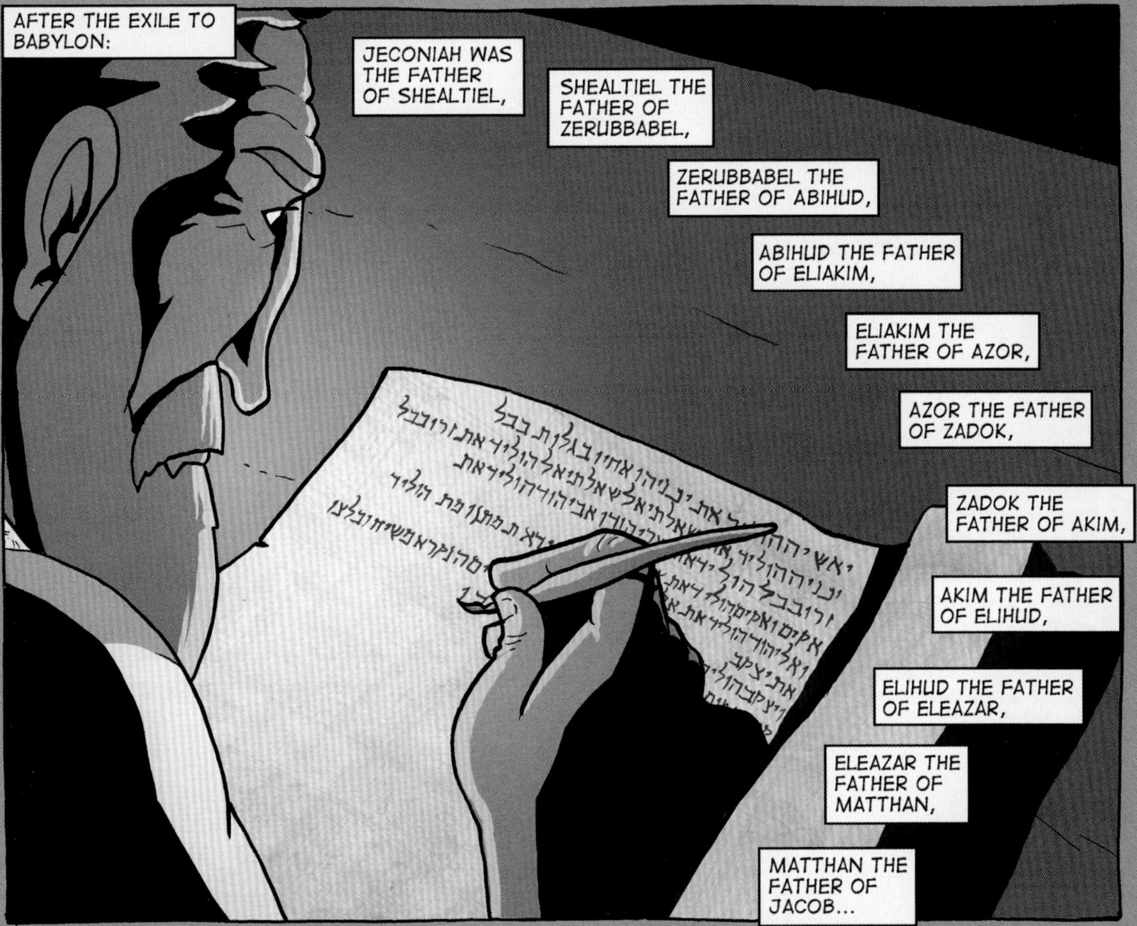
AFTER THE EXILE TO BABYLON:
JECONIAH WAS THE FATHER OF SHEALTIEL,
SHEALTIEL THE FATHER OF ZERUBBABEL,
ZERUBBABEL THE FATHER OF ABIHUD,
ABIHUD THE FATHER OF ELIAKIM,
ELIAKIM THE FATHER OF AZOR,
AZOR THE FATHER OF ZADOK,
ZADOK THE FATHER OF AKIM,
AKIM THE FATHER OF ELIHUD,
ELIHUD THE FATHER OF ELEAZAR,
ELEAZAR THE FATHER OF MATTHAN,
MATTHAN THE FATHER OF JACOB...

HE HUSBAND OF MARY, AND MARY WAS THE MOTHER OF JESUS WHO IS CALLED THE MESSIAH.

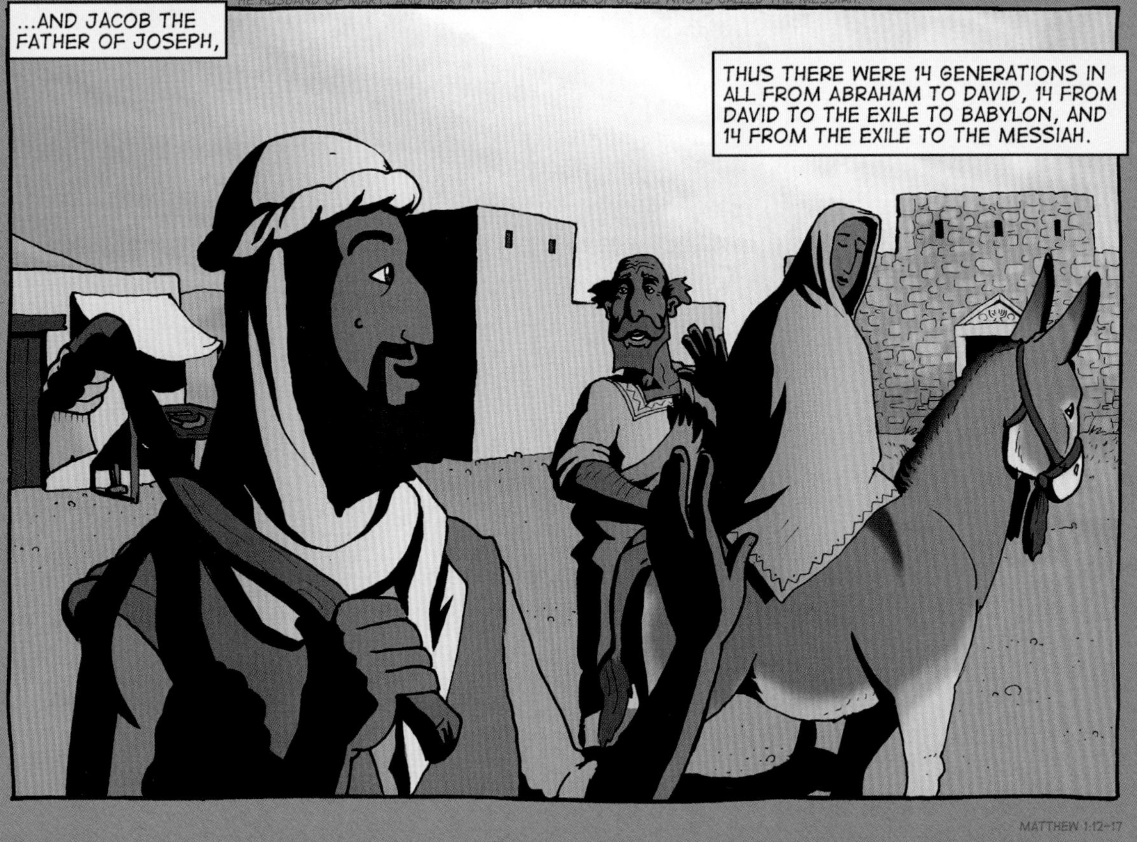
...AND JACOB THE FATHER OF JOSEPH,
THUS THERE WERE 14 GENERATIONS IN ALL FROM ABRAHAM TO DAVID, 14 FROM DAVID TO THE EXILE TO BABYLON, AND 14 FROM THE EXILE TO THE MESSIAH.

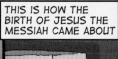

THIS IS HOW THE BIRTH OF JESUS THE MESSIAH CAME ABOUT

BUT BEFORE THEY CAME TOGETHER, SHE WAS...

...pregnant through the Holy Spirit.

HIS MOTHER MARY WAS PLEDGED TO BE MARRIED TO JOSEPH

BECAUSE JOSEPH HER HUSBAND WAS FAITHFUL TO THE LAW...

...AND YET WAS A RIGHTEOUS MAN AND DID NOT WANT TO EXPOSE HER TO PUBLIC DISGRACE...

...HE HAD IN MIND TO DIVORCE HER QUIETLY.

BUT AFTER HE HAD CONSIDERED THIS, AND SAID,

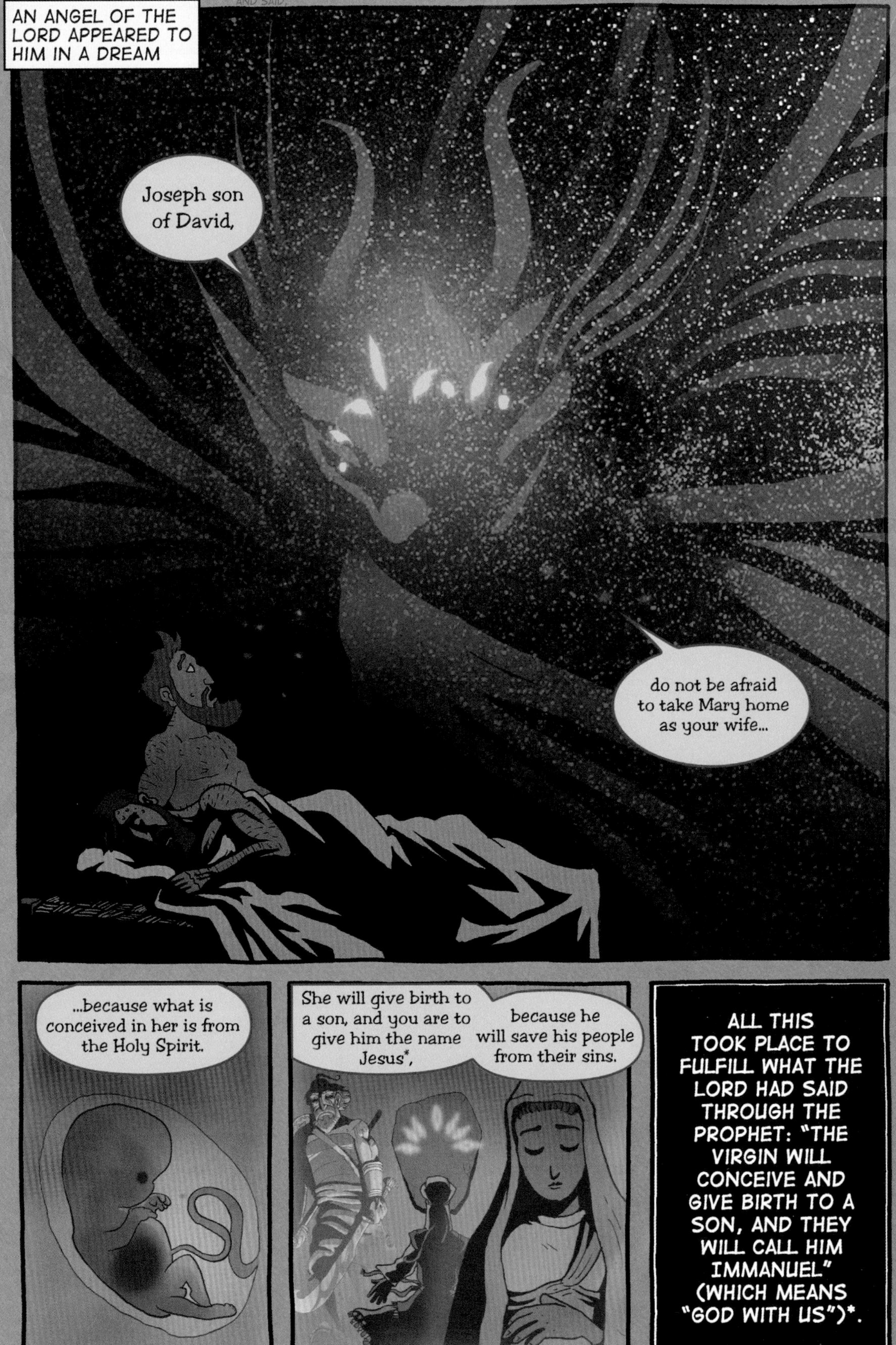

AN ANGEL OF THE LORD APPEARED TO HIM IN A DREAM
Joseph son of David,
do not be afraid to take Mary home as your wife...
...because what is conceived in her is from the Holy Spirit.
She will give birth to a son, and you are to give him the name Jesus*,
because he will save his people from their sins.
ALL THIS TOOK PLACE TO FULFILL WHAT THE LORD HAD SAID THROUGH THE PROPHET: "THE VIRGIN WILL CONCEIVE AND GIVE BIRTH TO A SON, AND THEY WILL CALL HIM IMMANUEL" (WHICH MEANS "GOD WITH US")*.

*JESUS IS THE GREEK FORM OF JOSHUA, WHICH MEANS THE LORD SAVES.

*ISAIAH 7:14

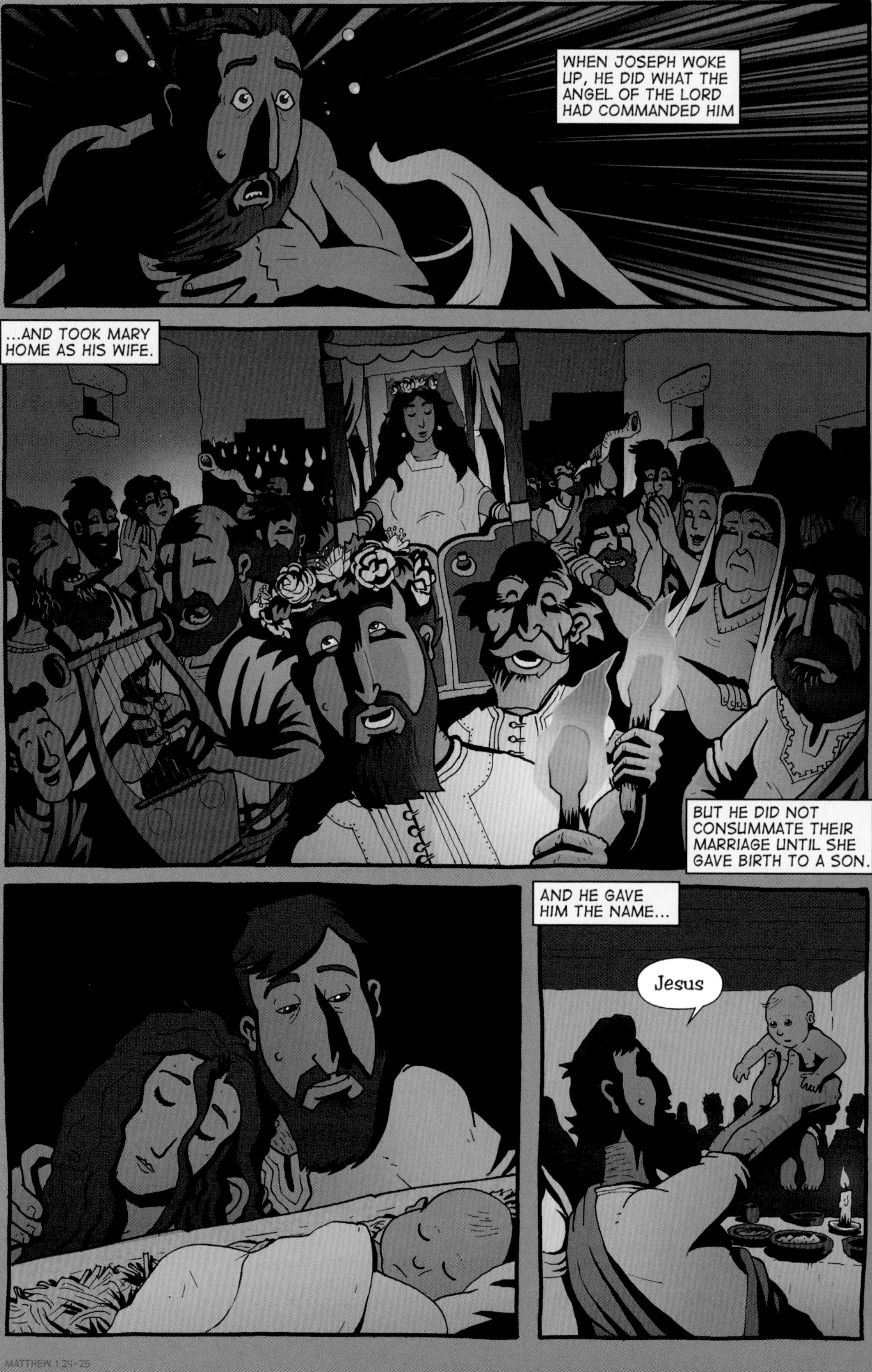
WHEN JOSEPH WOKE UP, HE DID WHAT THE ANGEL OF THE LORD HAD COMMANDED HIM
...AND TOOK MARY HOME AS HIS WIFE.
BUT HE DID NOT CONSUMMATE THEIR MARRIAGE UNTIL SHE GAVE BIRTH TO A SON.
AND HE GAVE HIM THE NAME...
Jesus

WORD FOR WORD
BIBLE COMIC

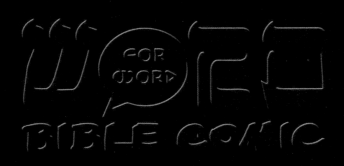

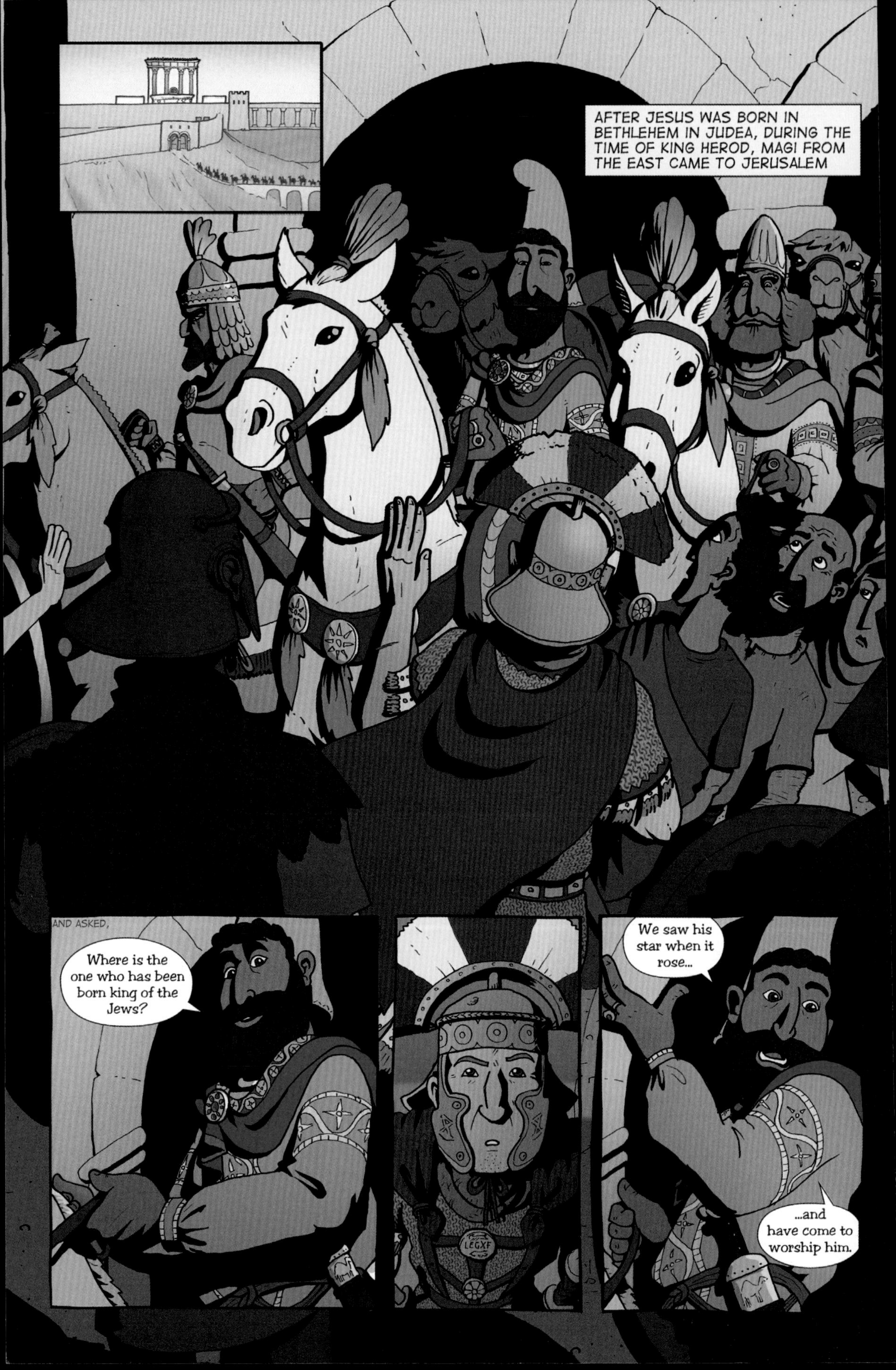
AFTER JESUS WAS BORN IN BETHLEHEM IN JUDEA, DURING THE TIME OF KING HEROD, MAGI FROM THE EAST CAME TO JERUSALEM
AND ASKED,
Where is the one who has been born king of the Jews?
We saw his star when it rose...
...and have come to worship him.

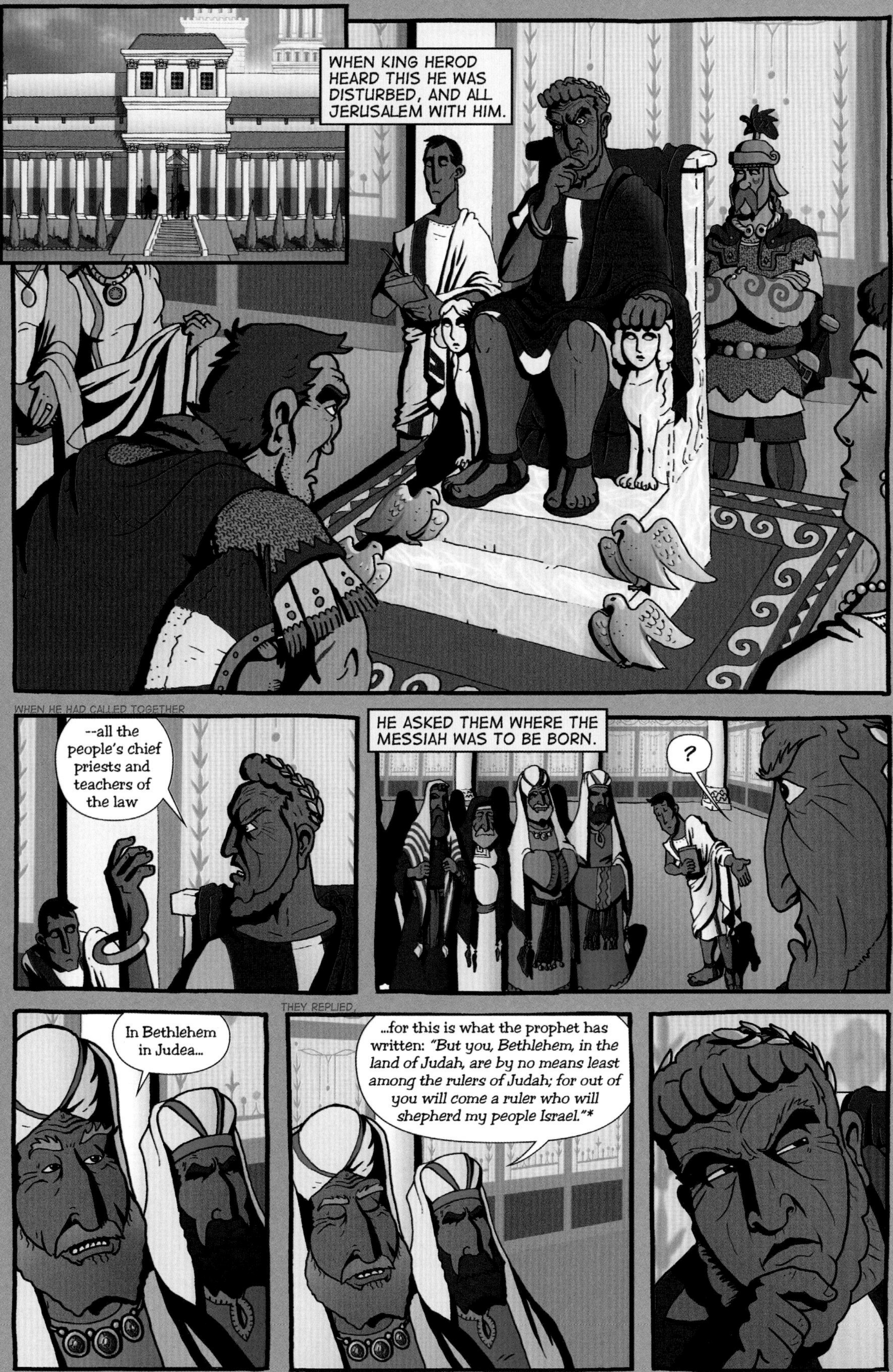
WHEN KING HEROD HEARD THIS HE WAS DISTURBED, AND ALL JERUSALEM WITH HIM.
WHEN HE HAD CALLED TOGETHER
--all the people's chief priests and teachers of the law
HE ASKED THEM WHERE THE MESSIAH WAS TO BE BORN.
?
THEY REPLIED,
In Bethlehem in Judea...
...for this is what the prophet has written: *"But you, Bethlehem, in the land of Judah, are by no means least among the rulers of Judah; for out of you will come a ruler who will shepherd my people Israel."**

*MICAH 5:2,4

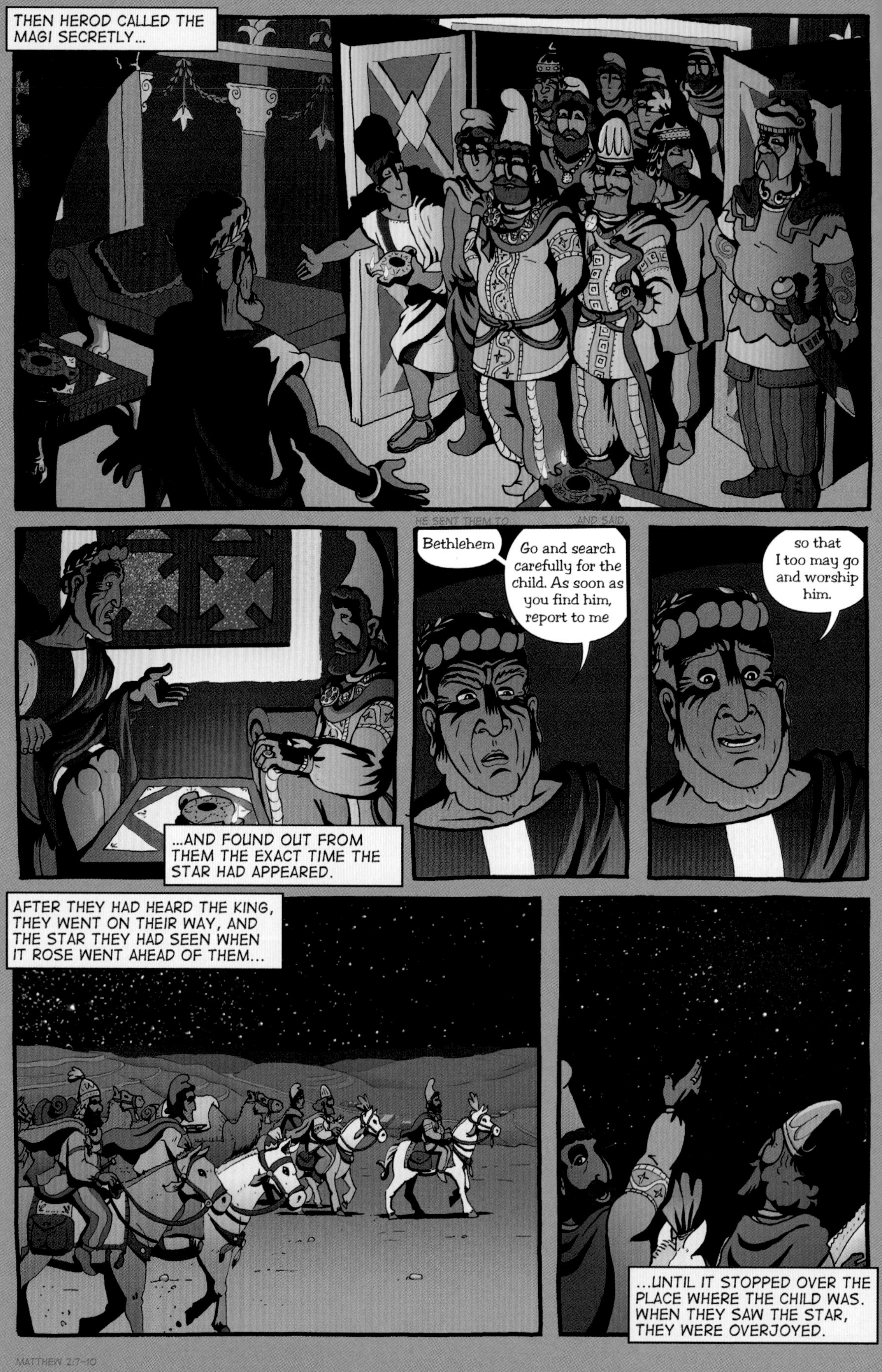
THEN HEROD CALLED THE MAGI SECRETLY...
...AND FOUND OUT FROM THEM THE EXACT TIME THE STAR HAD APPEARED.
HE SENT THEM TO
Bethlehem
AND SAID,
Go and search carefully for the child. As soon as you find him, report to me
so that I too may go and worship him.
AFTER THEY HAD HEARD THE KING, THEY WENT ON THEIR WAY, AND THE STAR THEY HAD SEEN WHEN IT ROSE WENT AHEAD OF THEM...
...UNTIL IT STOPPED OVER THE PLACE WHERE THE CHILD WAS. WHEN THEY SAW THE STAR, THEY WERE OVERJOYED.

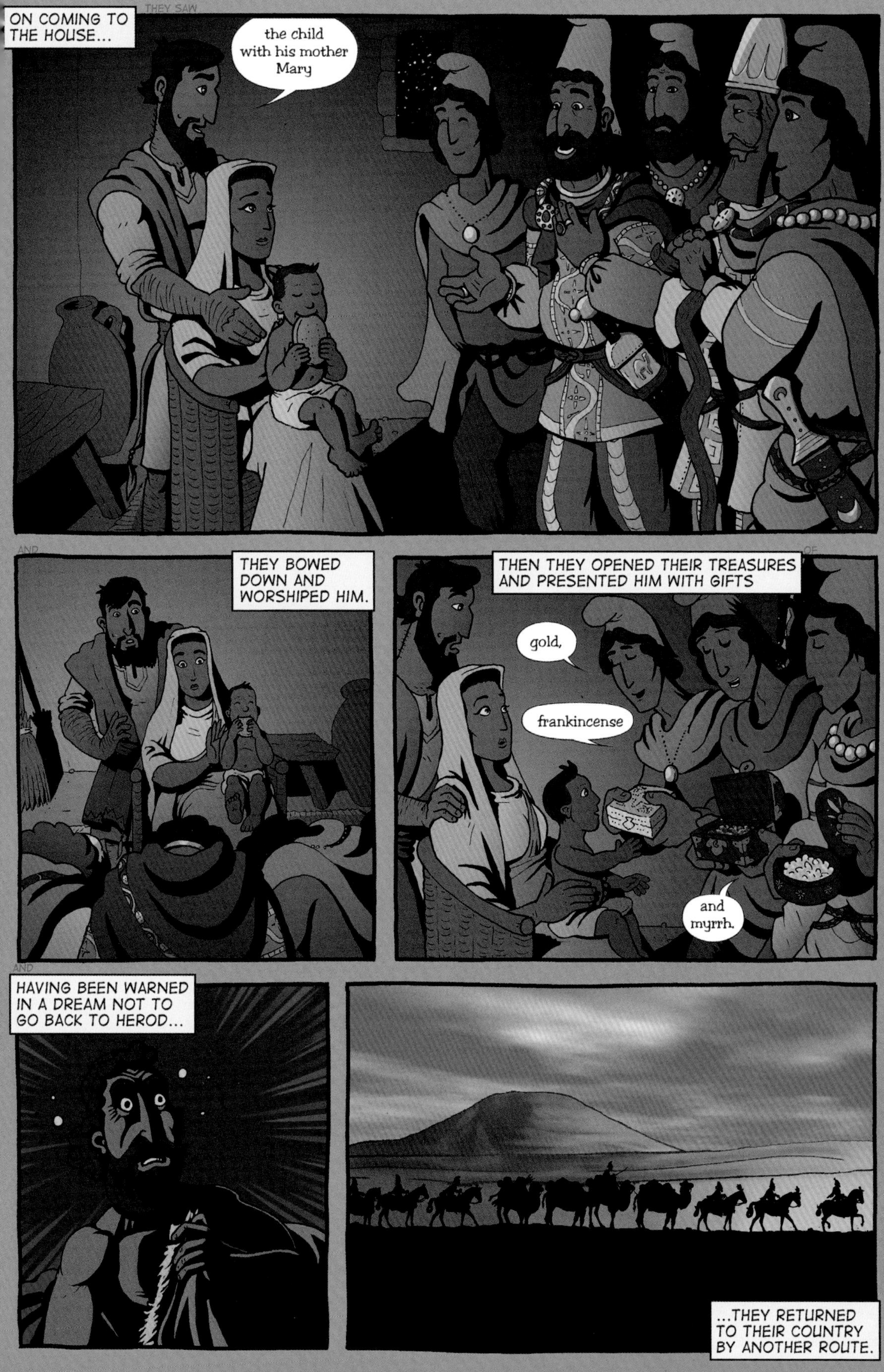
ON COMING TO THE HOUSE...
THEY SAW
the child with his mother Mary
AND
THEY BOWED DOWN AND WORSHIPED HIM.
THEN THEY OPENED THEIR TREASURES AND PRESENTED HIM WITH GIFTS
OF
gold,
frankincense
and myrrh.
AND
HAVING BEEN WARNED IN A DREAM NOT TO GO BACK TO HEROD...
...THEY RETURNED TO THEIR COUNTRY BY ANOTHER ROUTE.

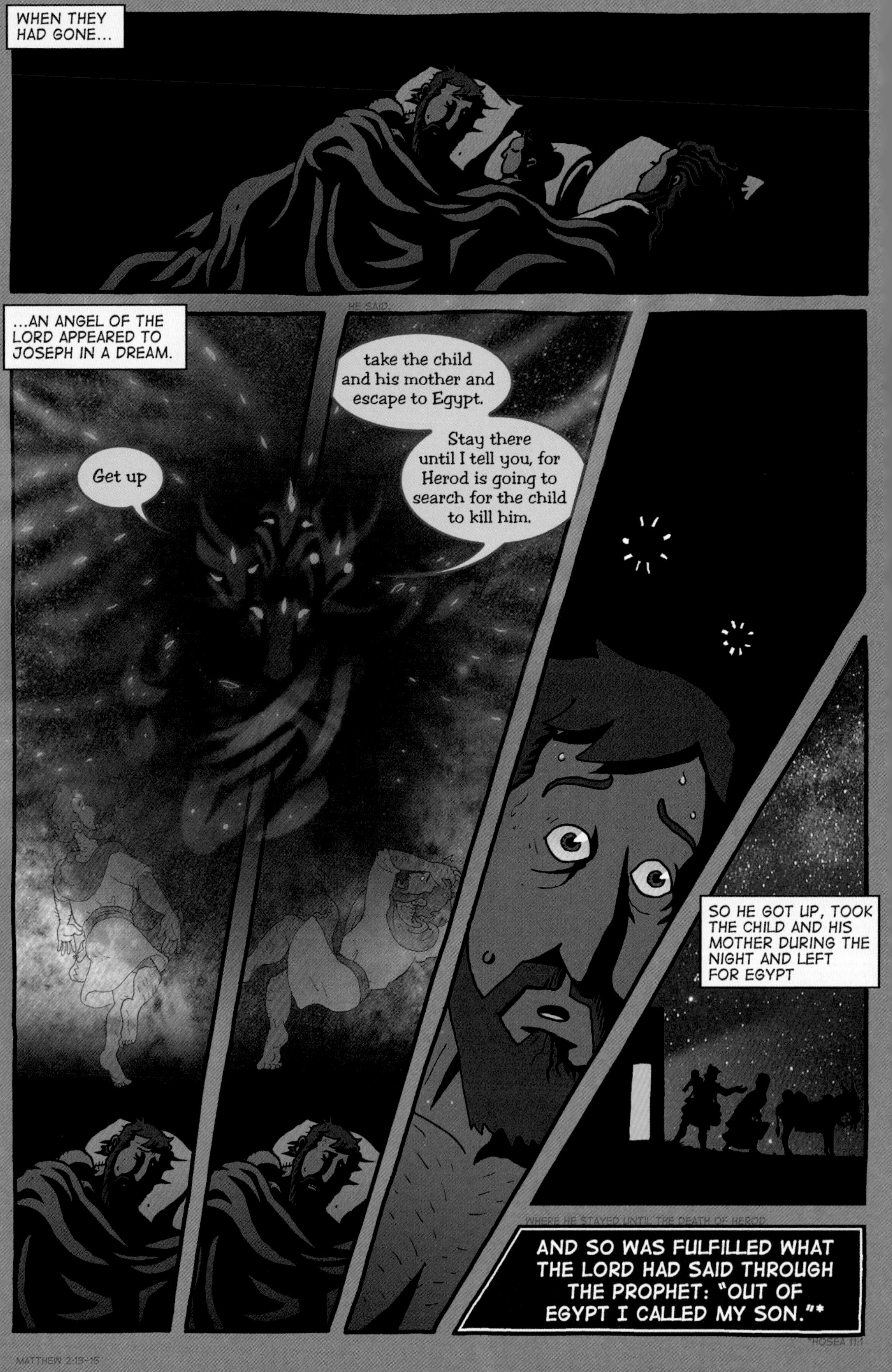
WHEN THEY HAD GONE...
...AN ANGEL OF THE LORD APPEARED TO JOSEPH IN A DREAM.
HE SAID,
Get up
take the child and his mother and escape to Egypt.
Stay there until I tell you, for Herod is going to search for the child to kill him.
SO HE GOT UP, TOOK THE CHILD AND HIS MOTHER DURING THE NIGHT AND LEFT FOR EGYPT
WHERE HE STAYED UNTIL THE DEATH OF HEROD.
AND SO WAS FULFILLED WHAT THE LORD HAD SAID THROUGH THE PROPHET: "OUT OF EGYPT I CALLED MY SON."*
*HOSEA 11:1

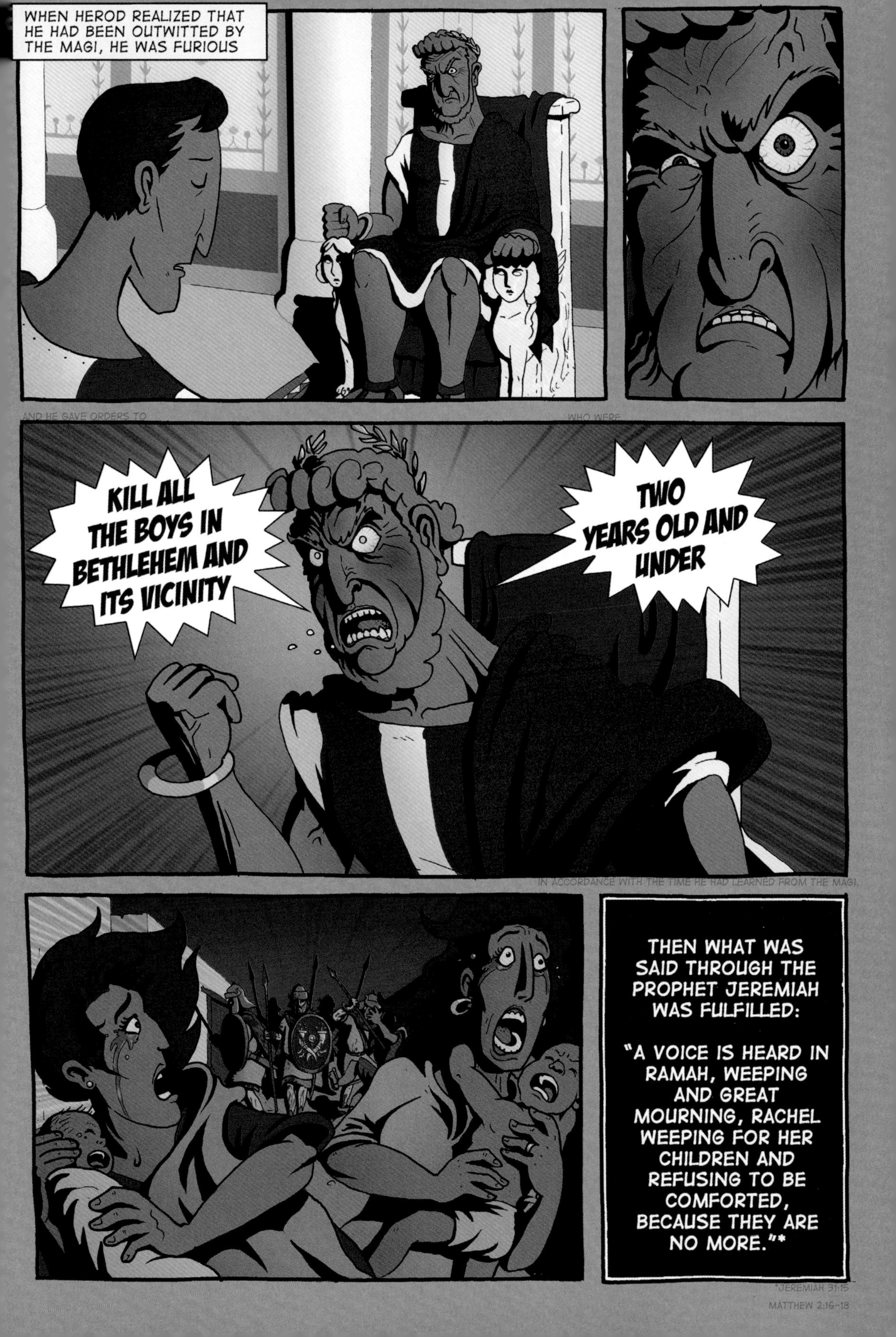
WHEN HEROD REALIZED THAT HE HAD BEEN OUTWITTED BY THE MAGI, HE WAS FURIOUS
AND HE GAVE ORDERS TO
KILL ALL THE BOYS IN BETHLEHEM AND ITS VICINITY
WHO WERE
TWO YEARS OLD AND UNDER
IN ACCORDANCE WITH THE TIME HE HAD LEARNED FROM THE MAGI.
THEN WHAT WAS SAID THROUGH THE PROPHET JEREMIAH WAS FULFILLED:
"A VOICE IS HEARD IN RAMAH, WEEPING AND GREAT MOURNING, RACHEL WEEPING FOR HER CHILDREN AND REFUSING TO BE COMFORTED, BECAUSE THEY ARE NO MORE."*

*JEREMIAH 31:15

MATTHEW 2:16-18

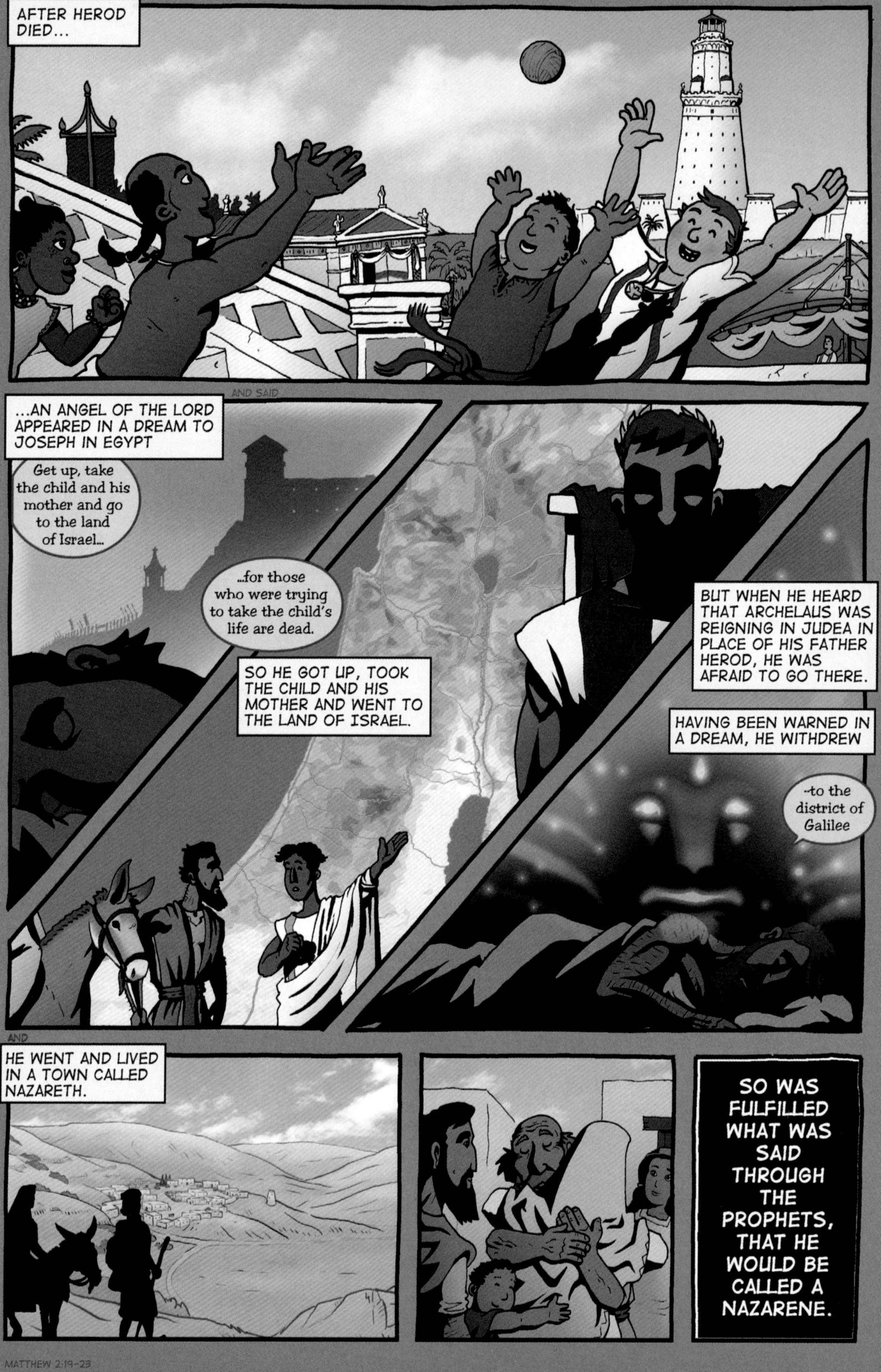
AFTER HEROD DIED...
AND SAID
...AN ANGEL OF THE LORD APPEARED IN A DREAM TO JOSEPH IN EGYPT
Get up, take the child and his mother and go to the land of Israel...
...for those who were trying to take the child's life are dead.
SO HE GOT UP, TOOK THE CHILD AND HIS MOTHER AND WENT TO THE LAND OF ISRAEL.
BUT WHEN HE HEARD THAT ARCHELAUS WAS REIGNING IN JUDEA IN PLACE OF HIS FATHER HEROD, HE WAS AFRAID TO GO THERE.
HAVING BEEN WARNED IN A DREAM, HE WITHDREW
--to the district of Galilee
AND
HE WENT AND LIVED IN A TOWN CALLED NAZARETH.
SO WAS FULFILLED WHAT WAS SAID THROUGH THE PROPHETS, THAT HE WOULD BE CALLED A NAZARENE.

WORD
FOR WORD
BIBLE COMIC

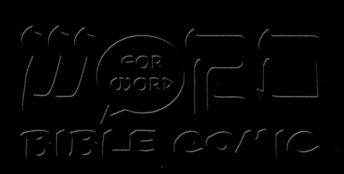

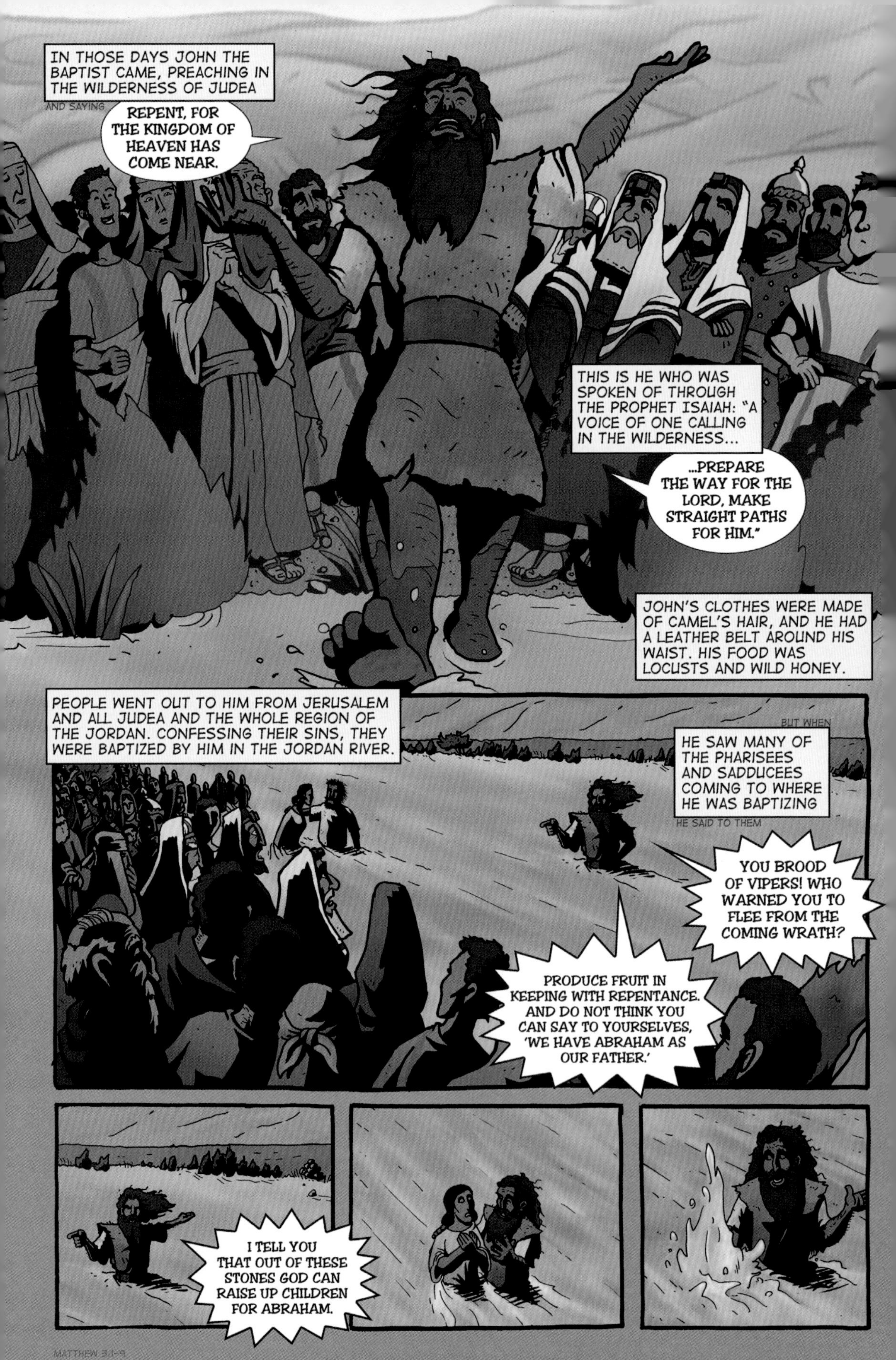

IN THOSE DAYS JOHN THE BAPTIST CAME, PREACHING IN THE WILDERNESS OF JUDEA
AND SAYING
REPENT, FOR THE KINGDOM OF HEAVEN HAS COME NEAR.
THIS IS HE WHO WAS SPOKEN OF THROUGH THE PROPHET ISAIAH: "A VOICE OF ONE CALLING IN THE WILDERNESS...
...PREPARE THE WAY FOR THE LORD, MAKE STRAIGHT PATHS FOR HIM."
JOHN'S CLOTHES WERE MADE OF CAMEL'S HAIR, AND HE HAD A LEATHER BELT AROUND HIS WAIST. HIS FOOD WAS LOCUSTS AND WILD HONEY.
PEOPLE WENT OUT TO HIM FROM JERUSALEM AND ALL JUDEA AND THE WHOLE REGION OF THE JORDAN. CONFESSING THEIR SINS, THEY WERE BAPTIZED BY HIM IN THE JORDAN RIVER.
BUT WHEN
HE SAW MANY OF THE PHARISEES AND SADDUCEES COMING TO WHERE HE WAS BAPTIZING
HE SAID TO THEM
YOU BROOD OF VIPERS! WHO WARNED YOU TO FLEE FROM THE COMING WRATH?
PRODUCE FRUIT IN KEEPING WITH REPENTANCE. AND DO NOT THINK YOU CAN SAY TO YOURSELVES, 'WE HAVE ABRAHAM AS OUR FATHER.'
I TELL YOU THAT OUT OF THESE STONES GOD CAN RAISE UP CHILDREN FOR ABRAHAM.

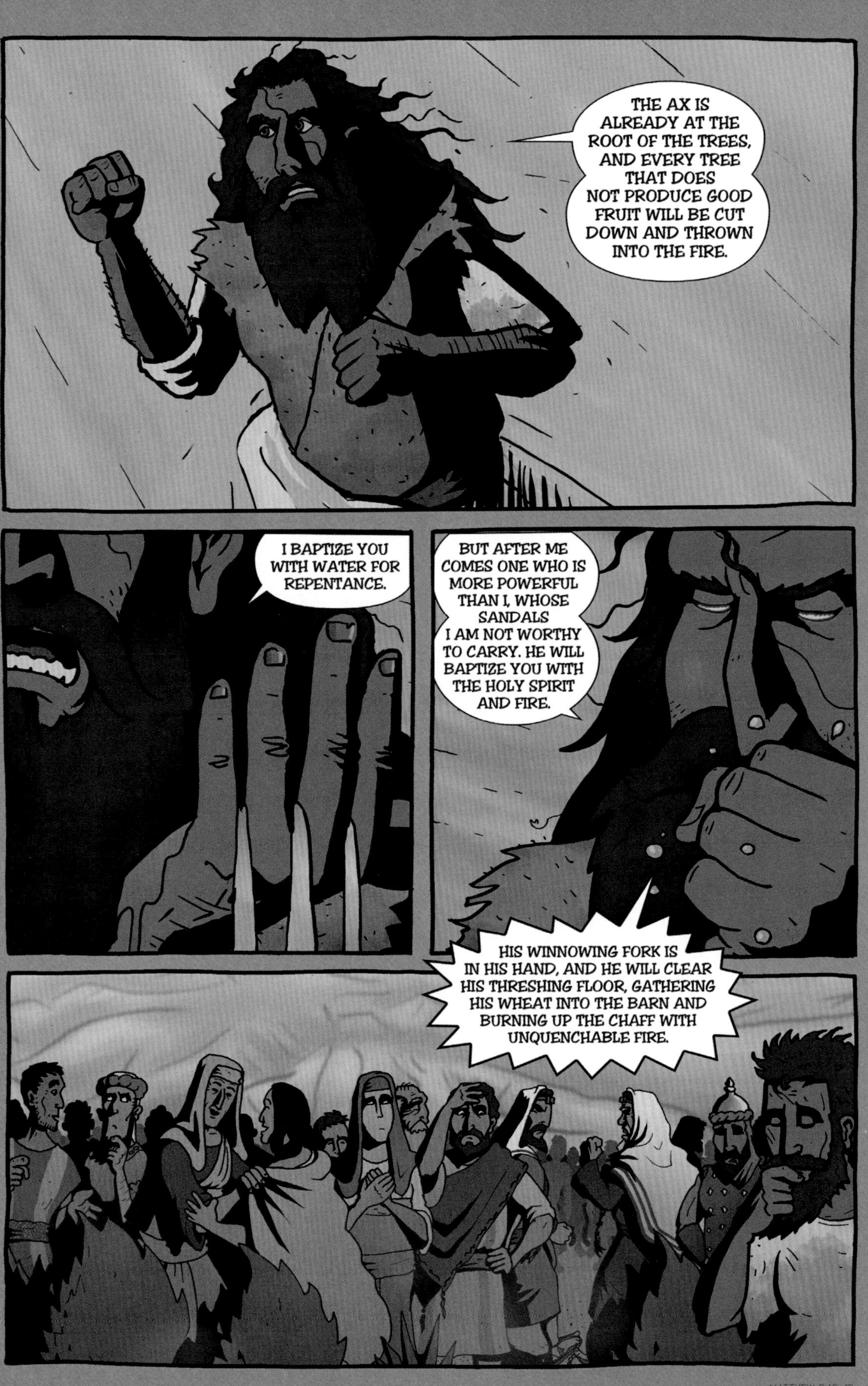
THE AX IS ALREADY AT THE ROOT OF THE TREES, AND EVERY TREE THAT DOES NOT PRODUCE GOOD FRUIT WILL BE CUT DOWN AND THROWN INTO THE FIRE.
I BAPTIZE YOU WITH WATER FOR REPENTANCE.
BUT AFTER ME COMES ONE WHO IS MORE POWERFUL THAN I, WHOSE SANDALS I AM NOT WORTHY TO CARRY. HE WILL BAPTIZE YOU WITH THE HOLY SPIRIT AND FIRE.
HIS WINNOWING FORK IS IN HIS HAND, AND HE WILL CLEAR HIS THRESHING FLOOR, GATHERING HIS WHEAT INTO THE BARN AND BURNING UP THE CHAFF WITH UNQUENCHABLE FIRE.

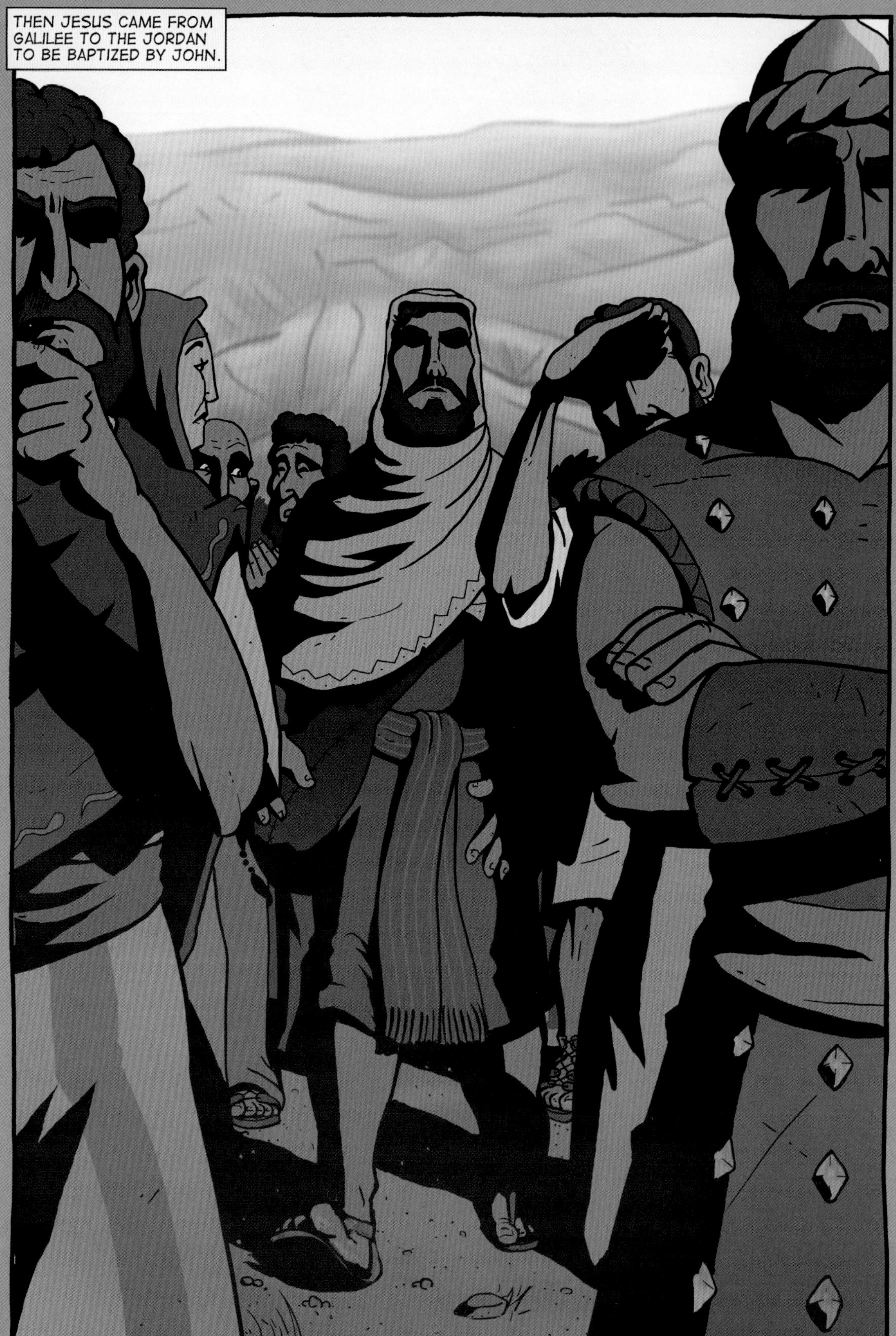
THEN JESUS CAME FROM GALILEE TO THE JORDAN TO BE BAPTIZED BY JOHN.

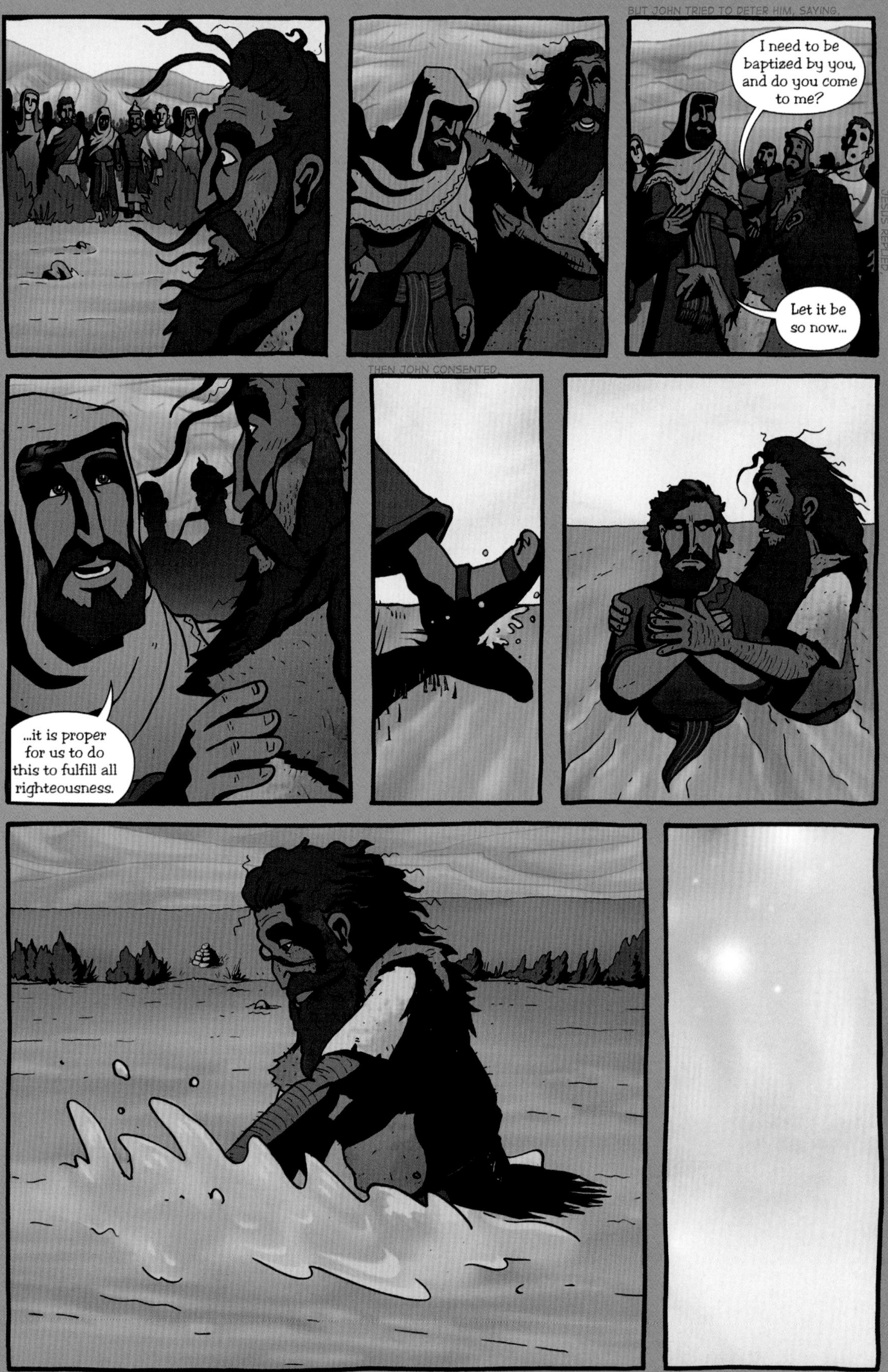
BUT JOHN TRIED TO DETER HIM, SAYING,
I need to be baptized by you, and do you come to me?
JESUS REPLIED,
Let it be so now...
...it is proper for us to do this to fulfill all righteousness.
THEN JOHN CONSENTED.

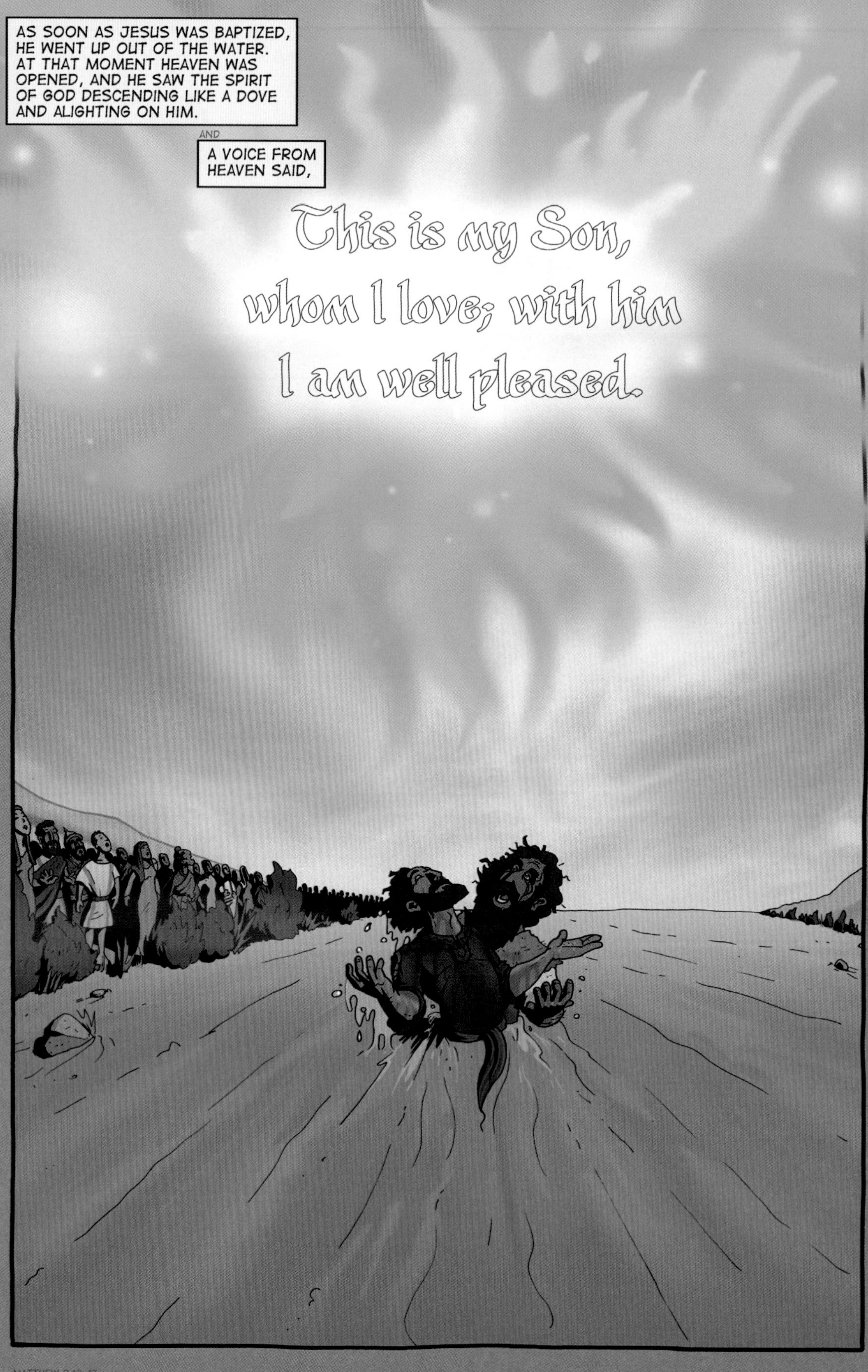
AS SOON AS JESUS WAS BAPTIZED, HE WENT UP OUT OF THE WATER. AT THAT MOMENT HEAVEN WAS OPENED, AND HE SAW THE SPIRIT OF GOD DESCENDING LIKE A DOVE AND ALIGHTING ON HIM.
AND
A VOICE FROM HEAVEN SAID,
This is my Son, whom I love; with him I am well pleased.

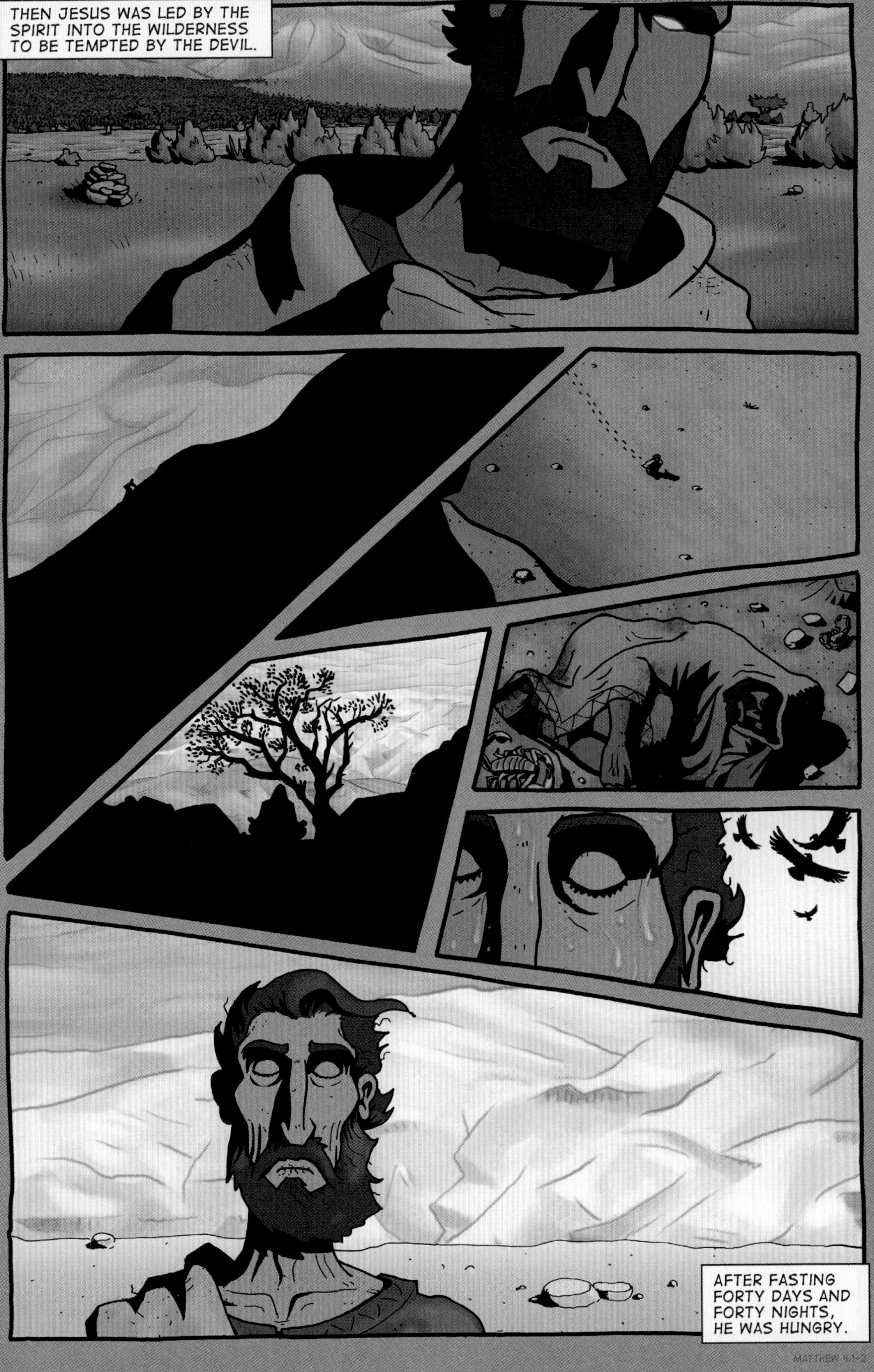
THEN JESUS WAS LED BY THE SPIRIT INTO THE WILDERNESS TO BE TEMPTED BY THE DEVIL.
AFTER FASTING FORTY DAYS AND FORTY NIGHTS, HE WAS HUNGRY.

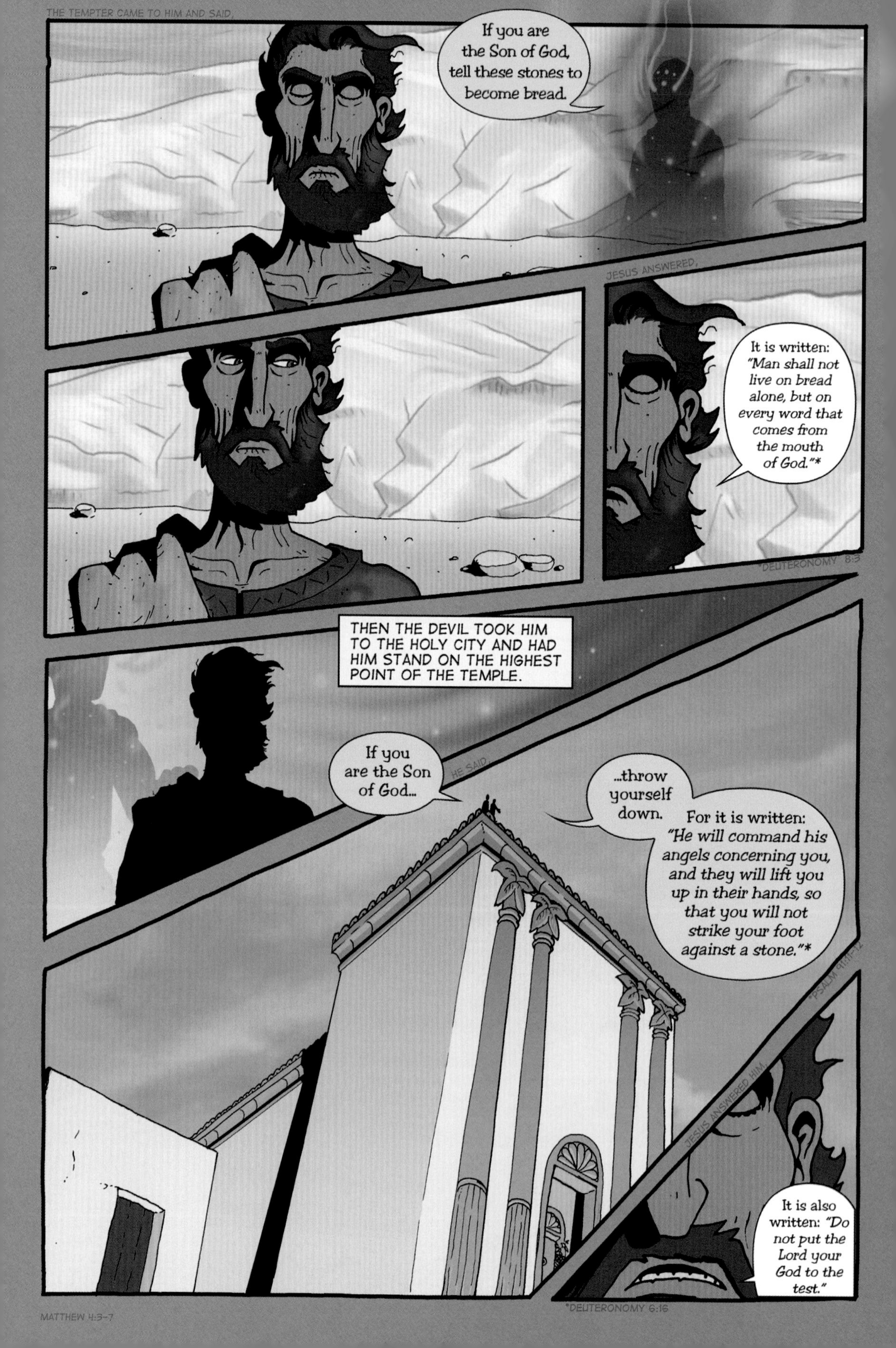
THE TEMPTER CAME TO HIM AND SAID,
If you are the Son of God, tell these stones to become bread.
JESUS ANSWERED,
It is written: "Man shall not live on bread alone, but on every word that comes from the mouth of God."*
*DEUTERONOMY 8:3
THEN THE DEVIL TOOK HIM TO THE HOLY CITY AND HAD HIM STAND ON THE HIGHEST POINT OF THE TEMPLE.
If you are the Son of God...
HE SAID,
...throw yourself down.
For it is written: "He will command his angels concerning you, and they will lift you up in their hands, so that you will not strike your foot against a stone."*
*PSALM 91:11-12
JESUS ANSWERED HIM,
It is also written: "Do not put the Lord your God to the test."
*DEUTERONOMY 6:16

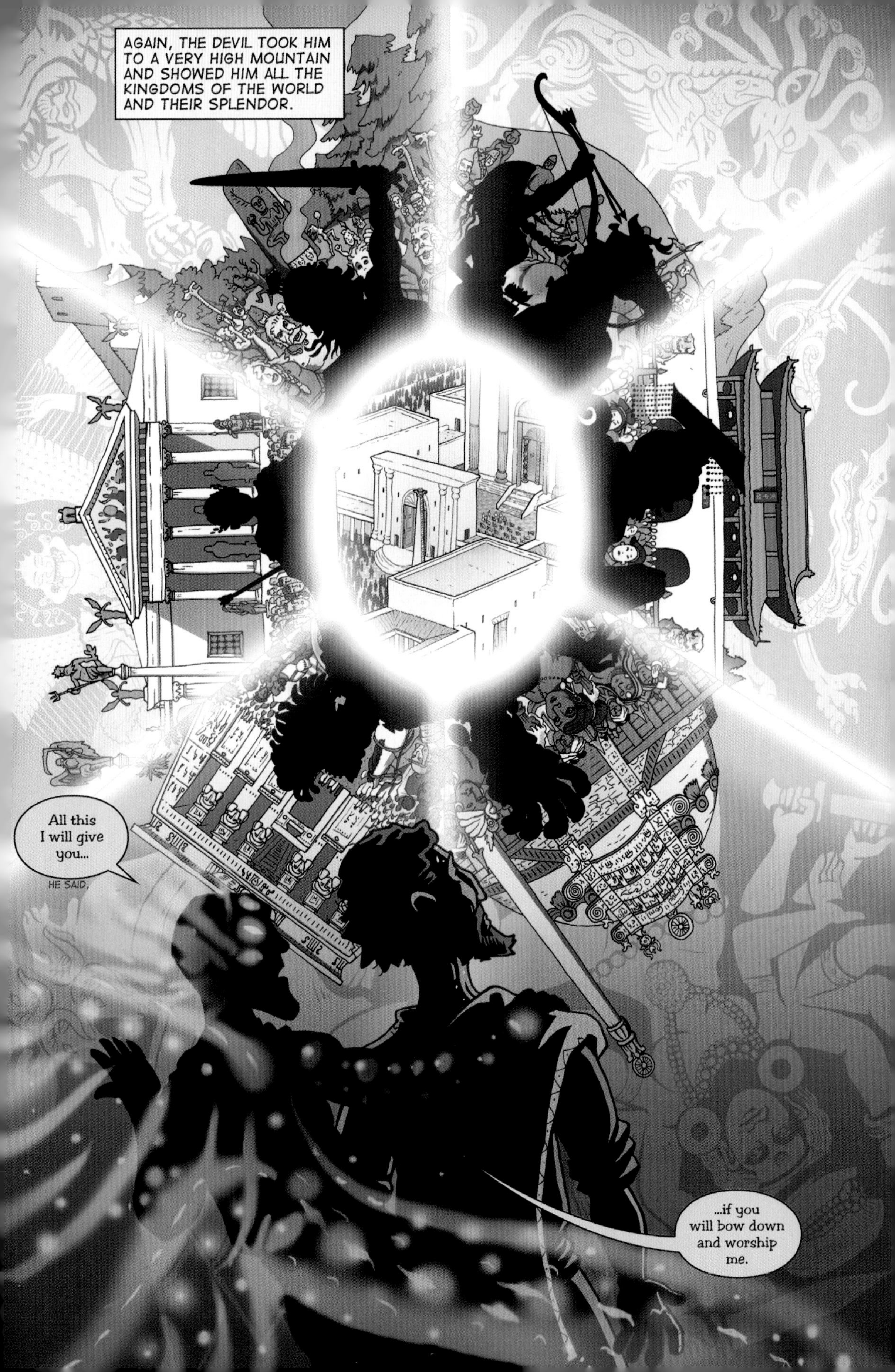
AGAIN, THE DEVIL TOOK HIM TO A VERY HIGH MOUNTAIN AND SHOWED HIM ALL THE KINGDOMS OF THE WORLD AND THEIR SPLENDOR.
All this I will give you...
HE SAID,
...if you will bow down and worship me.

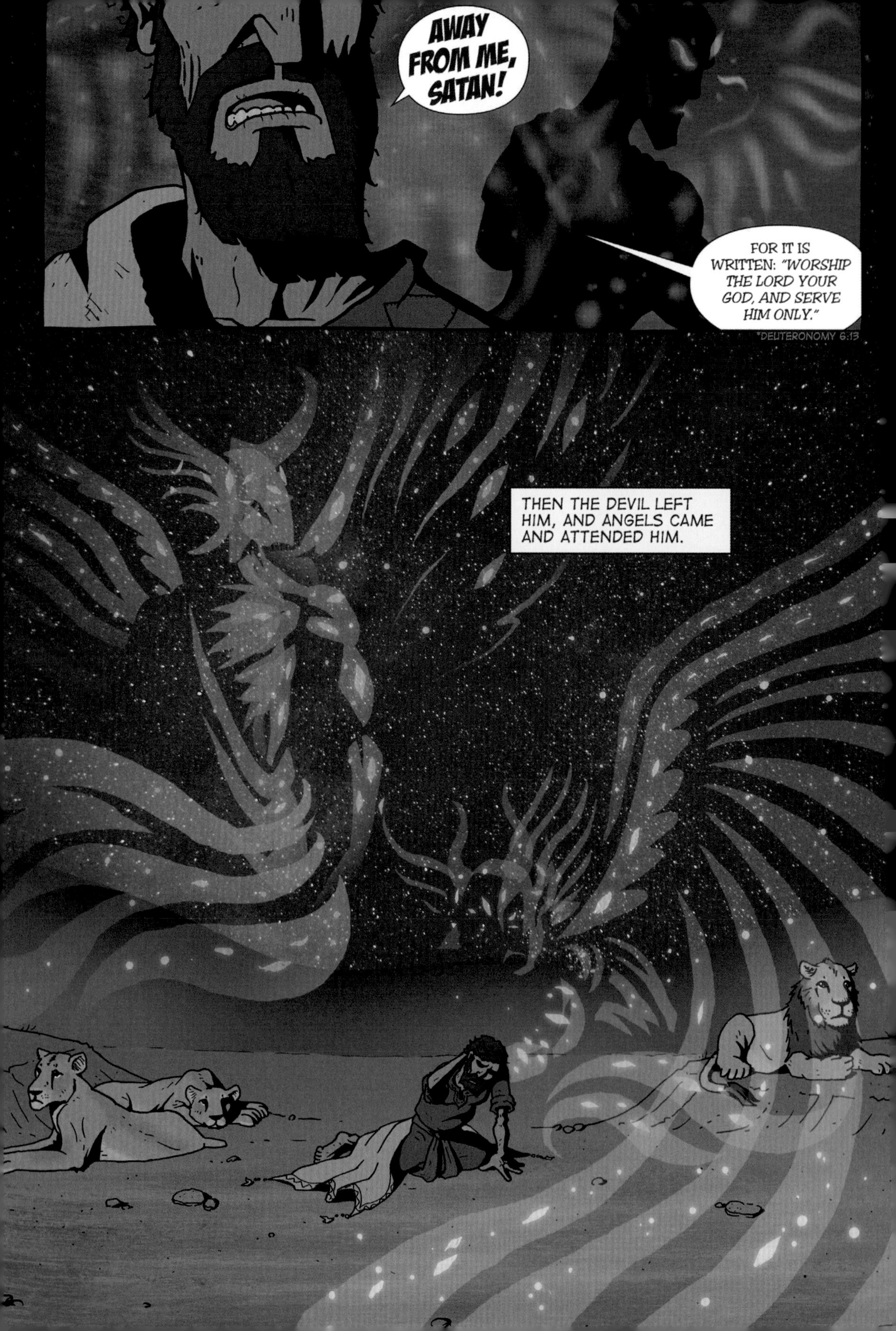
AWAY FROM ME, SATAN!
FOR IT IS WRITTEN: "WORSHIP THE LORD YOUR GOD, AND SERVE HIM ONLY."
*DEUTERONOMY 6:13
THEN THE DEVIL LEFT HIM, AND ANGELS CAME AND ATTENDED HIM.

WORD FOR WORD
BIBLE COMIC

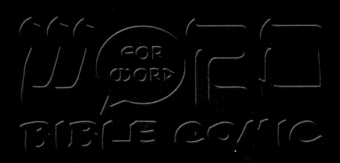

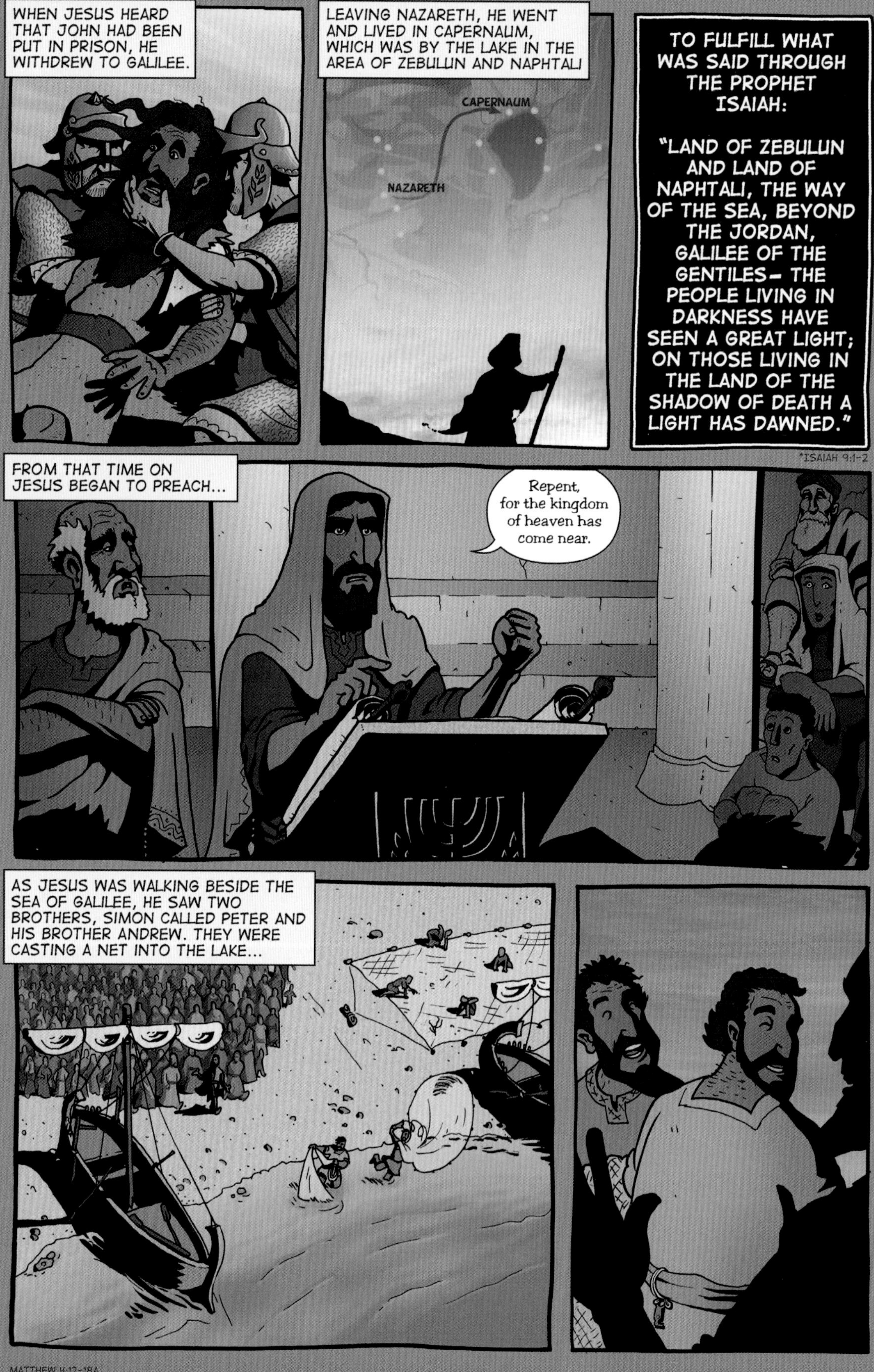
WHEN JESUS HEARD THAT JOHN HAD BEEN PUT IN PRISON, HE WITHDREW TO GALILEE.
LEAVING NAZARETH, HE WENT AND LIVED IN CAPERNAUM, WHICH WAS BY THE LAKE IN THE AREA OF ZEBULUN AND NAPHTALI
CAPERNAUM
NAZARETH
TO FULFILL WHAT WAS SAID THROUGH THE PROPHET ISAIAH:
"LAND OF ZEBULUN AND LAND OF NAPHTALI, THE WAY OF THE SEA, BEYOND THE JORDAN, GALILEE OF THE GENTILES– THE PEOPLE LIVING IN DARKNESS HAVE SEEN A GREAT LIGHT; ON THOSE LIVING IN THE LAND OF THE SHADOW OF DEATH A LIGHT HAS DAWNED."
*ISAIAH 9:1–2
FROM THAT TIME ON JESUS BEGAN TO PREACH...
Repent, for the kingdom of heaven has come near.
AS JESUS WAS WALKING BESIDE THE SEA OF GALILEE, HE SAW TWO BROTHERS, SIMON CALLED PETER AND HIS BROTHER ANDREW. THEY WERE CASTING A NET INTO THE LAKE...

JESUS SAID,

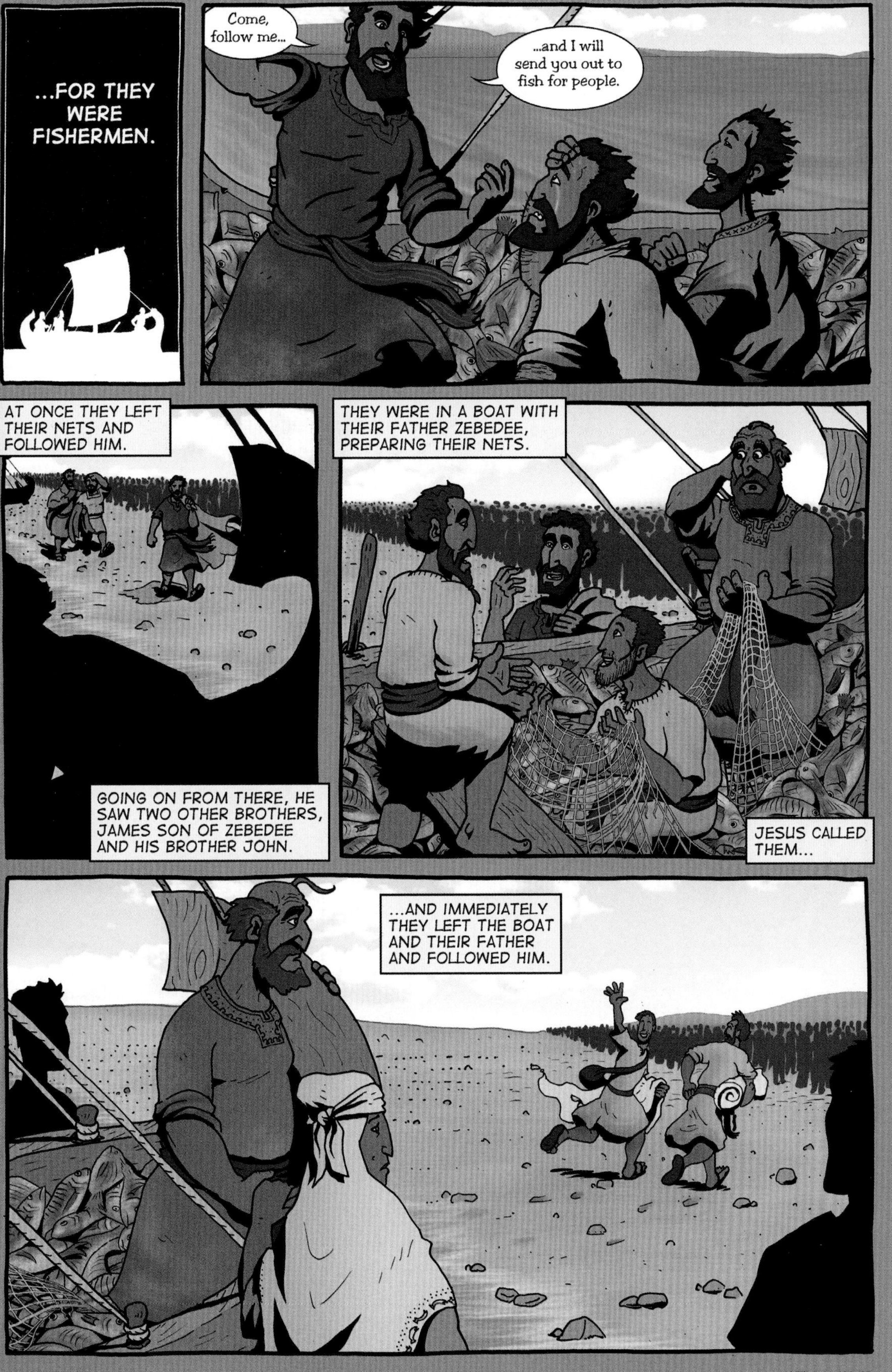
...FOR THEY WERE FISHERMEN.
Come, follow me...
...and I will send you out to fish for people.
AT ONCE THEY LEFT THEIR NETS AND FOLLOWED HIM.
GOING ON FROM THERE, HE SAW TWO OTHER BROTHERS, JAMES SON OF ZEBEDEE AND HIS BROTHER JOHN.
THEY WERE IN A BOAT WITH THEIR FATHER ZEBEDEE, PREPARING THEIR NETS.
JESUS CALLED THEM...
...AND IMMEDIATELY THEY LEFT THE BOAT AND THEIR FATHER AND FOLLOWED HIM.

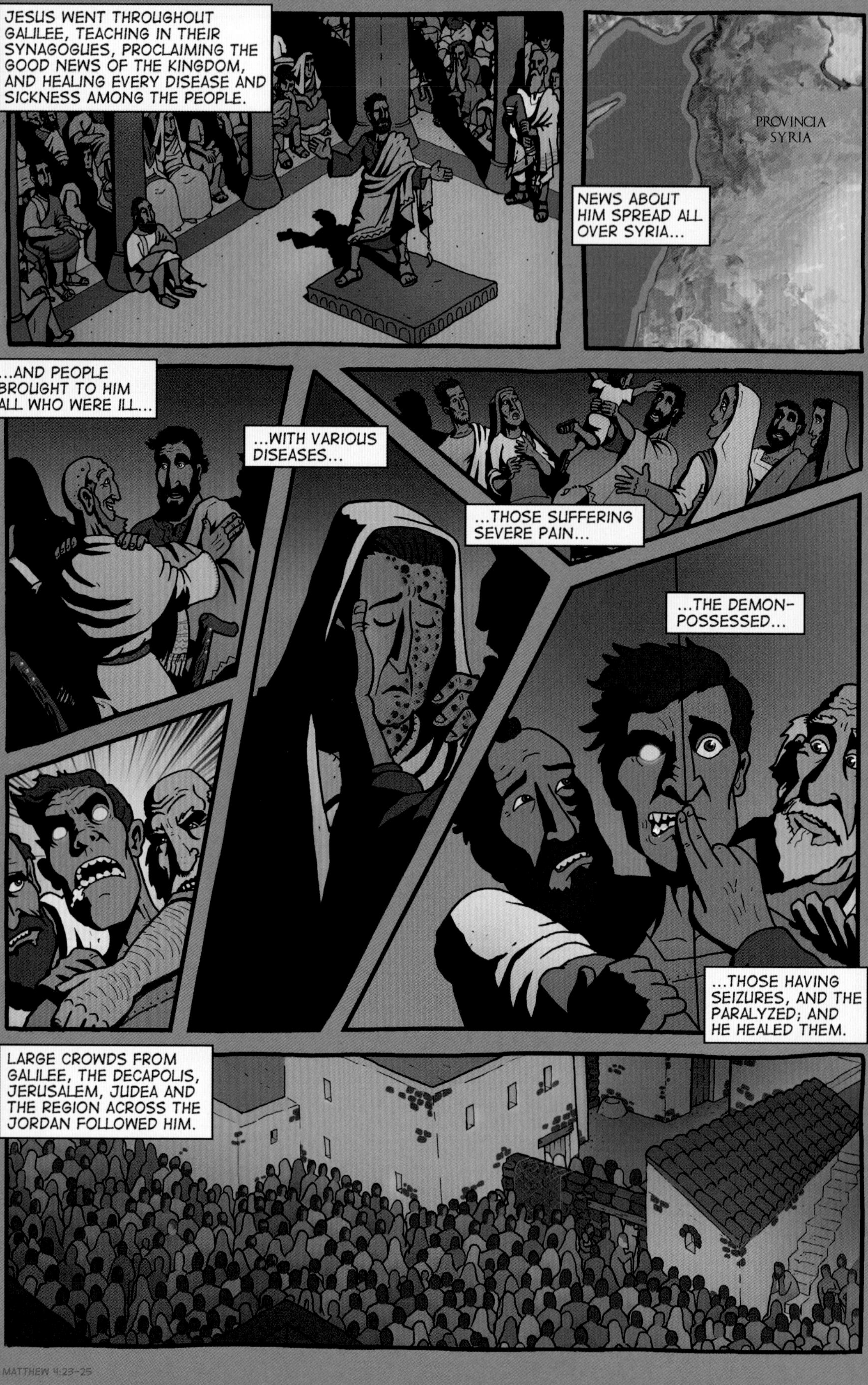
JESUS WENT THROUGHOUT GALILEE, TEACHING IN THEIR SYNAGOGUES, PROCLAIMING THE GOOD NEWS OF THE KINGDOM, AND HEALING EVERY DISEASE AND SICKNESS AMONG THE PEOPLE.
PROVINCIA SYRIA
NEWS ABOUT HIM SPREAD ALL OVER SYRIA...
...AND PEOPLE BROUGHT TO HIM ALL WHO WERE ILL...
...WITH VARIOUS DISEASES...
...THOSE SUFFERING SEVERE PAIN...
...THE DEMON-POSSESSED...
...THOSE HAVING SEIZURES, AND THE PARALYZED; AND HE HEALED THEM.
LARGE CROWDS FROM GALILEE, THE DECAPOLIS, JERUSALEM, JUDEA AND THE REGION ACROSS THE JORDAN FOLLOWED HIM.

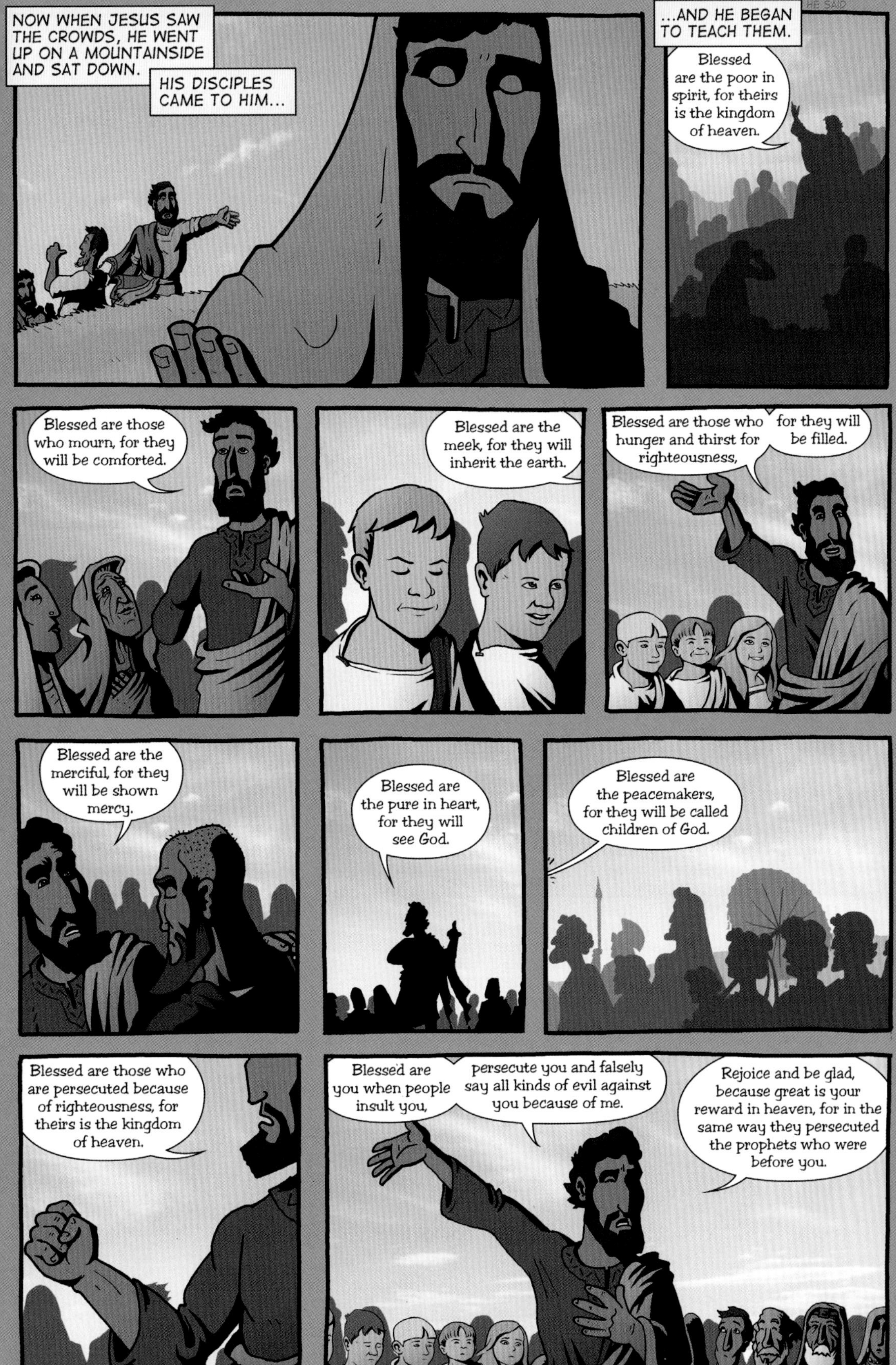
NOW WHEN JESUS SAW THE CROWDS, HE WENT UP ON A MOUNTAINSIDE AND SAT DOWN.
HIS DISCIPLES CAME TO HIM...
...AND HE BEGAN TO TEACH THEM.
Blessed are the poor in spirit, for theirs is the kingdom of heaven.
Blessed are those who mourn, for they will be comforted.
Blessed are the meek, for they will inherit the earth.
Blessed are those who hunger and thirst for righteousness,
for they will be filled.
Blessed are the merciful, for they will be shown mercy.
Blessed are the pure in heart, for they will see God.
Blessed are the peacemakers, for they will be called children of God.
Blessed are those who are persecuted because of righteousness, for theirs is the kingdom of heaven.
Blessed are you when people insult you,
persecute you and falsely say all kinds of evil against you because of me.
Rejoice and be glad, because great is your reward in heaven, for in the same way they persecuted the prophets who were before you.

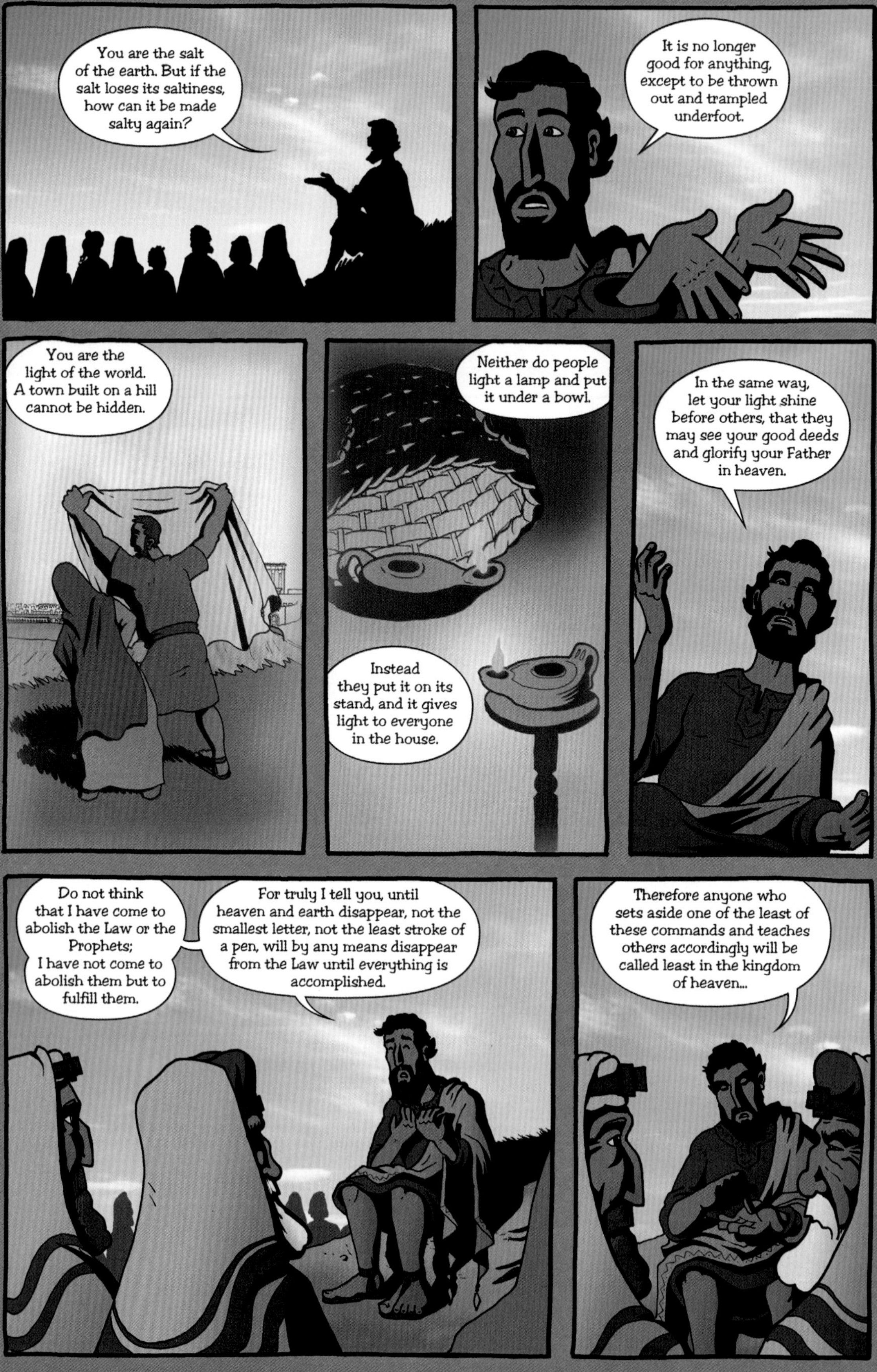
You are the salt of the earth. But if the salt loses its saltiness, how can it be made salty again?
It is no longer good for anything, except to be thrown out and trampled underfoot.
You are the light of the world. A town built on a hill cannot be hidden.
Neither do people light a lamp and put it under a bowl.
Instead they put it on its stand, and it gives light to everyone in the house.
In the same way, let your light shine before others, that they may see your good deeds and glorify your Father in heaven.
Do not think that I have come to abolish the Law or the Prophets; I have not come to abolish them but to fulfill them.
For truly I tell you, until heaven and earth disappear, not the smallest letter, not the least stroke of a pen, will by any means disappear from the Law until everything is accomplished.
Therefore anyone who sets aside one of the least of these commands and teaches others accordingly will be called least in the kingdom of heaven...

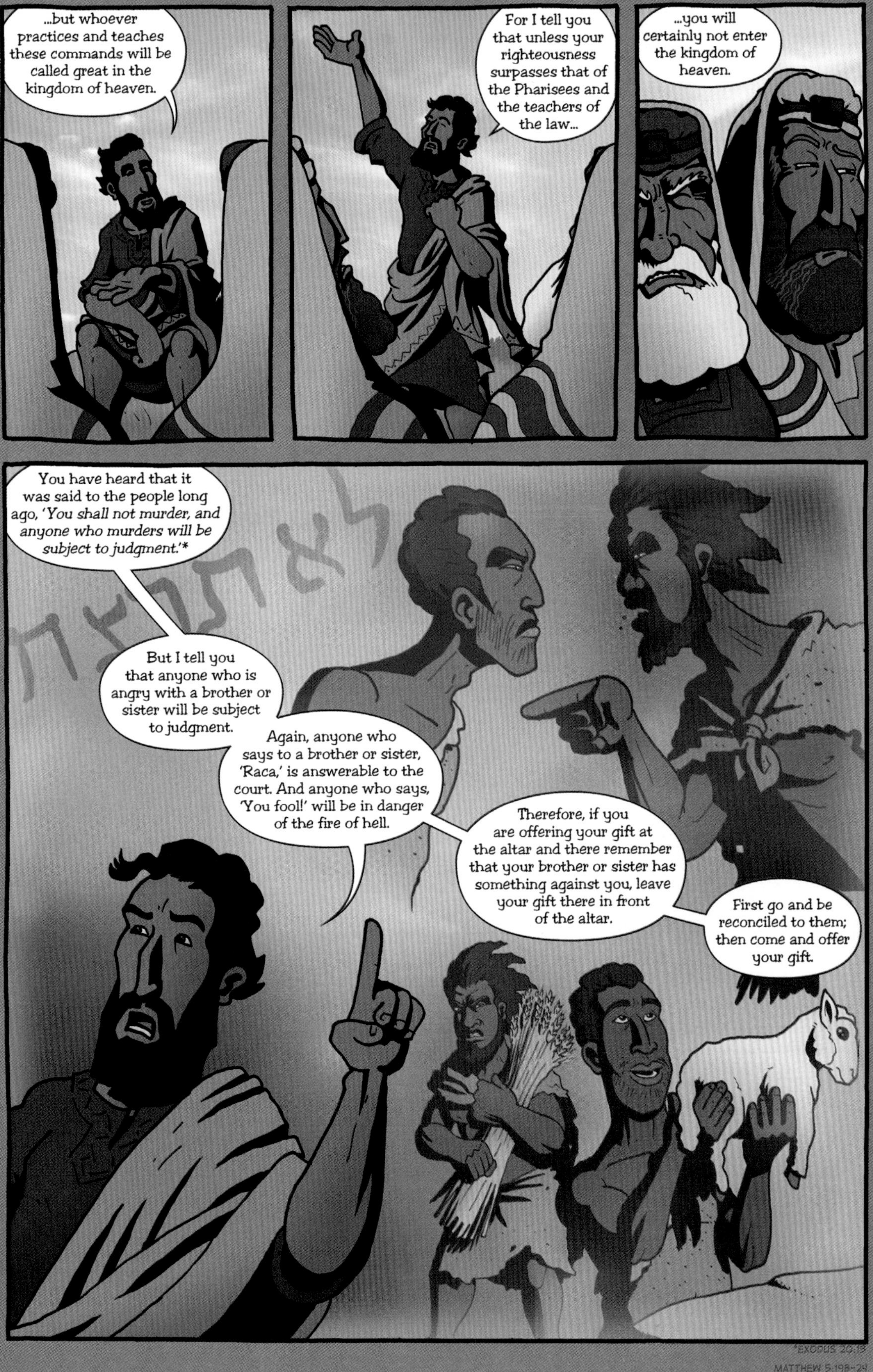
...but whoever practices and teaches these commands will be called great in the kingdom of heaven.
For I tell you that unless your righteousness surpasses that of the Pharisees and the teachers of the law...
...you will certainly not enter the kingdom of heaven.
You have heard that it was said to the people long ago, '*You shall not murder, and anyone who murders will be subject to judgment.*'*
But I tell you that anyone who is angry with a brother or sister will be subject to judgment.
Again, anyone who says to a brother or sister, 'Raca,' is answerable to the court. And anyone who says, 'You fool!' will be in danger of the fire of hell.
Therefore, if you are offering your gift at the altar and there remember that your brother or sister has something against you, leave your gift there in front of the altar.
First go and be reconciled to them; then come and offer your gift.

*EXODUS 20:13

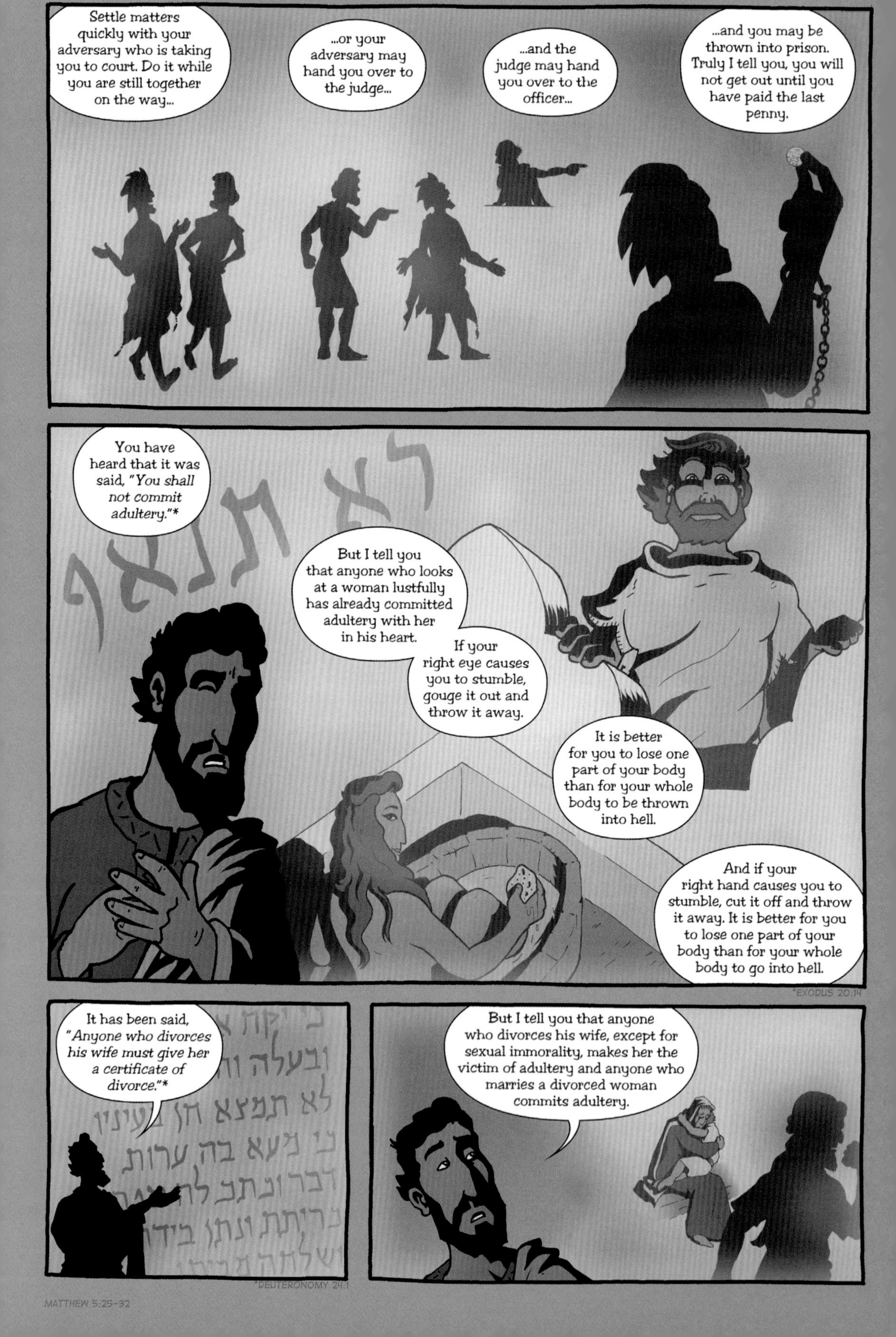
Settle matters quickly with your adversary who is taking you to court. Do it while you are still together on the way...
...or your adversary may hand you over to the judge...
...and the judge may hand you over to the officer...
...and you may be thrown into prison. Truly I tell you, you will not get out until you have paid the last penny.
You have heard that it was said, "You shall not commit adultery."*
לא תנאף
But I tell you that anyone who looks at a woman lustfully has already committed adultery with her in his heart.
If your right eye causes you to stumble, gouge it out and throw it away.
It is better for you to lose one part of your body than for your whole body to be thrown into hell.
And if your right hand causes you to stumble, cut it off and throw it away. It is better for you to lose one part of your body than for your whole body to go into hell.
It has been said, "Anyone who divorces his wife must give her a certificate of divorce."*
But I tell you that anyone who divorces his wife, except for sexual immorality, makes her the victim of adultery and anyone who marries a divorced woman commits adultery.

*EXODUS 20:14

*DEUTERONOMY 24:1

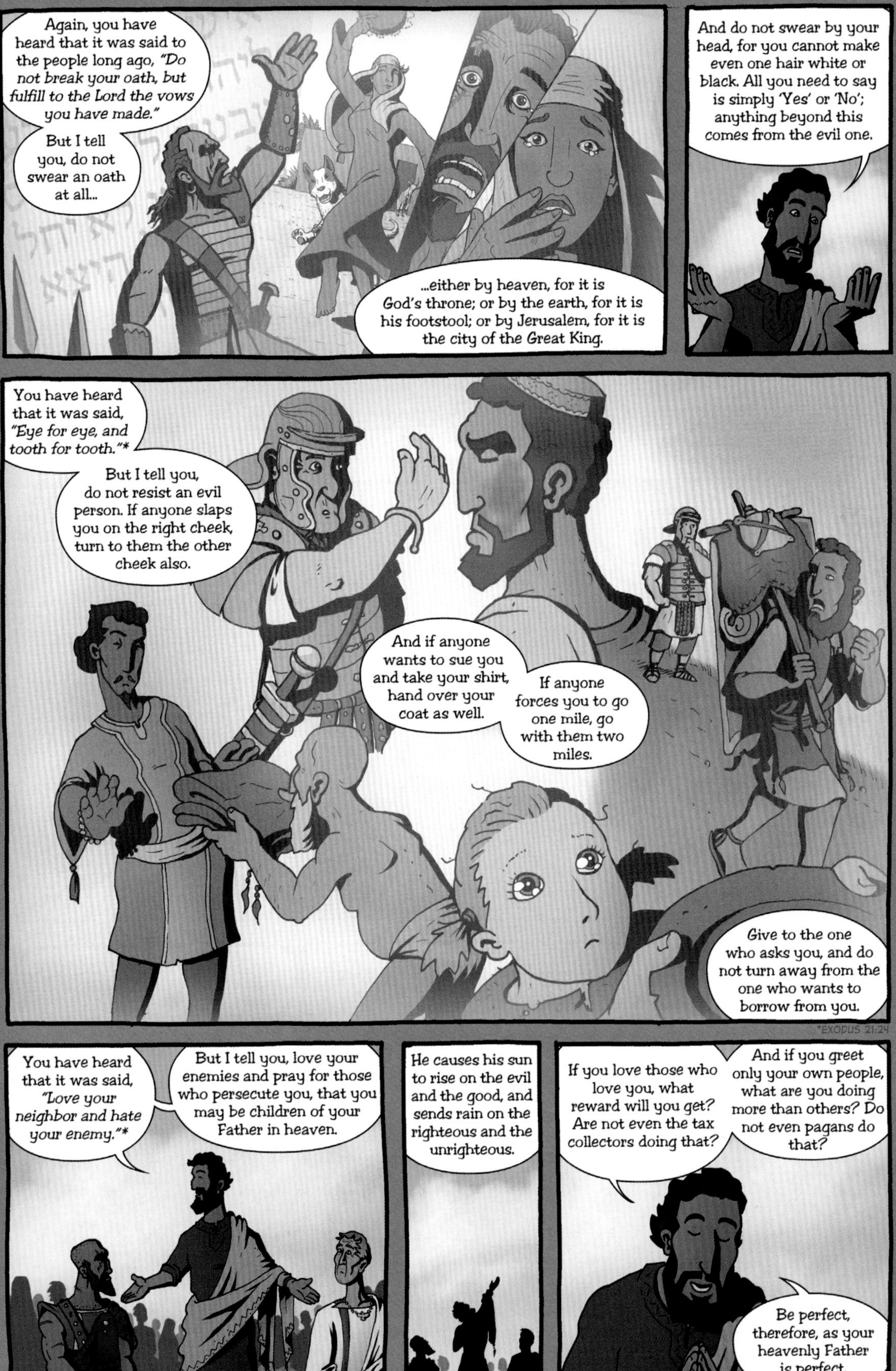
Again, you have heard that it was said to the people long ago, *"Do not break your oath, but fulfill to the Lord the vows you have made."*
But I tell you, do not swear an oath at all...
...either by heaven, for it is God's throne; or by the earth, for it is his footstool; or by Jerusalem, for it is the city of the Great King.
And do not swear by your head, for you cannot make even one hair white or black. All you need to say is simply 'Yes' or 'No'; anything beyond this comes from the evil one.
You have heard that it was said, *"Eye for eye, and tooth for tooth."**
But I tell you, do not resist an evil person. If anyone slaps you on the right cheek, turn to them the other cheek also.
And if anyone wants to sue you and take your shirt, hand over your coat as well.
If anyone forces you to go one mile, go with them two miles.
Give to the one who asks you, and do not turn away from the one who wants to borrow from you.
You have heard that it was said, *"Love your neighbor and hate your enemy."**
But I tell you, love your enemies and pray for those who persecute you, that you may be children of your Father in heaven.
He causes his sun to rise on the evil and the good, and sends rain on the righteous and the unrighteous.
If you love those who love you, what reward will you get? Are not even the tax collectors doing that?
And if you greet only your own people, what are you doing more than others? Do not even pagans do that?
Be perfect, therefore, as your heavenly Father is perfect.

*EXODUS 21:24

*LEVITICUS 19:18

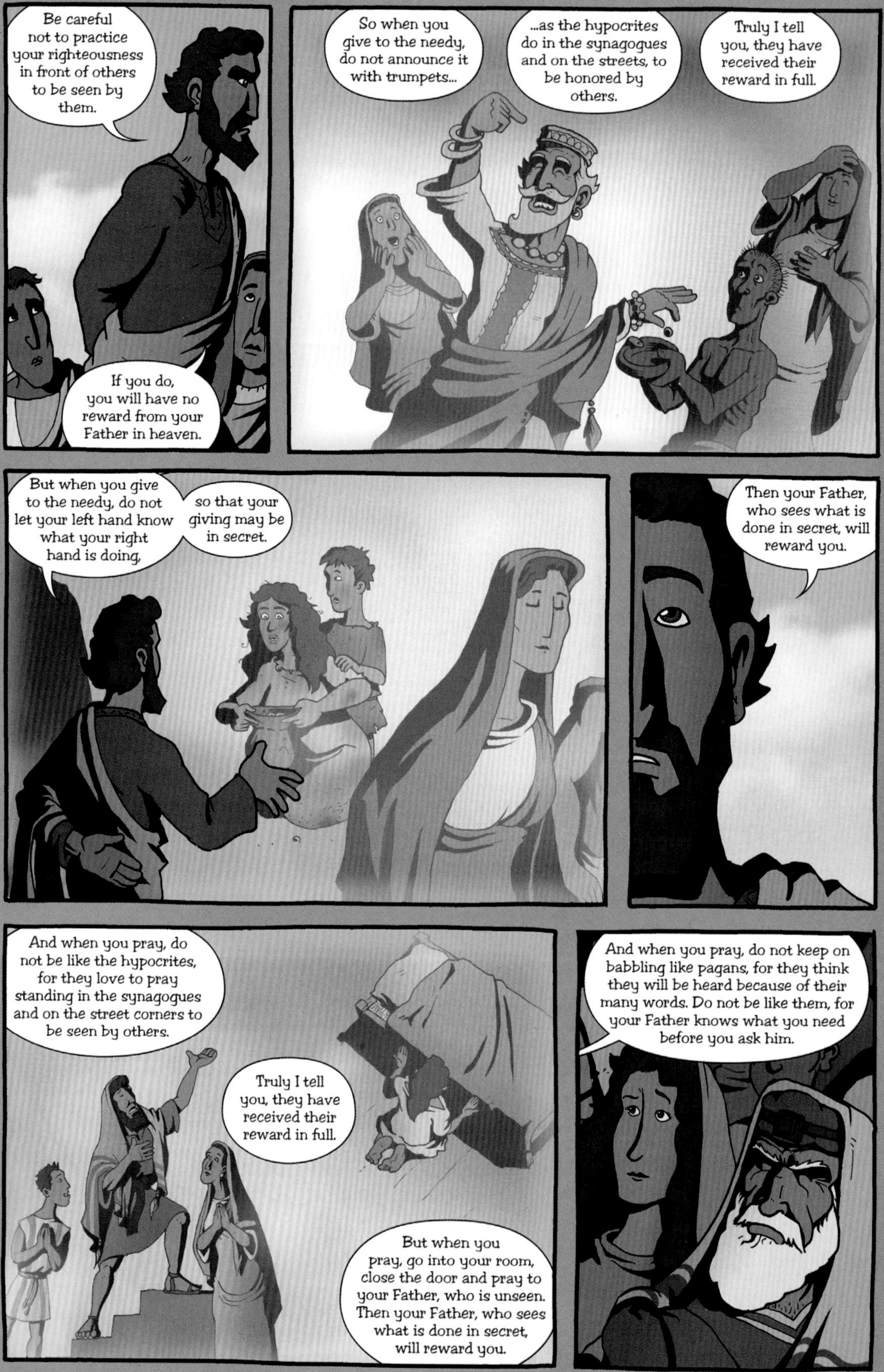
Be careful not to practice your righteousness in front of others to be seen by them.
If you do, you will have no reward from your Father in heaven.
So when you give to the needy, do not announce it with trumpets...
...as the hypocrites do in the synagogues and on the streets, to be honored by others.
Truly I tell you, they have received their reward in full.
But when you give to the needy, do not let your left hand know what your right hand is doing,
so that your giving may be in secret.
Then your Father, who sees what is done in secret, will reward you.
And when you pray, do not be like the hypocrites, for they love to pray standing in the synagogues and on the street corners to be seen by others.
Truly I tell you, they have received their reward in full.
But when you pray, go into your room, close the door and pray to your Father, who is unseen. Then your Father, who sees what is done in secret, will reward you.
And when you pray, do not keep on babbling like pagans, for they think they will be heard because of their many words. Do not be like them, for your Father knows what you need before you ask him.

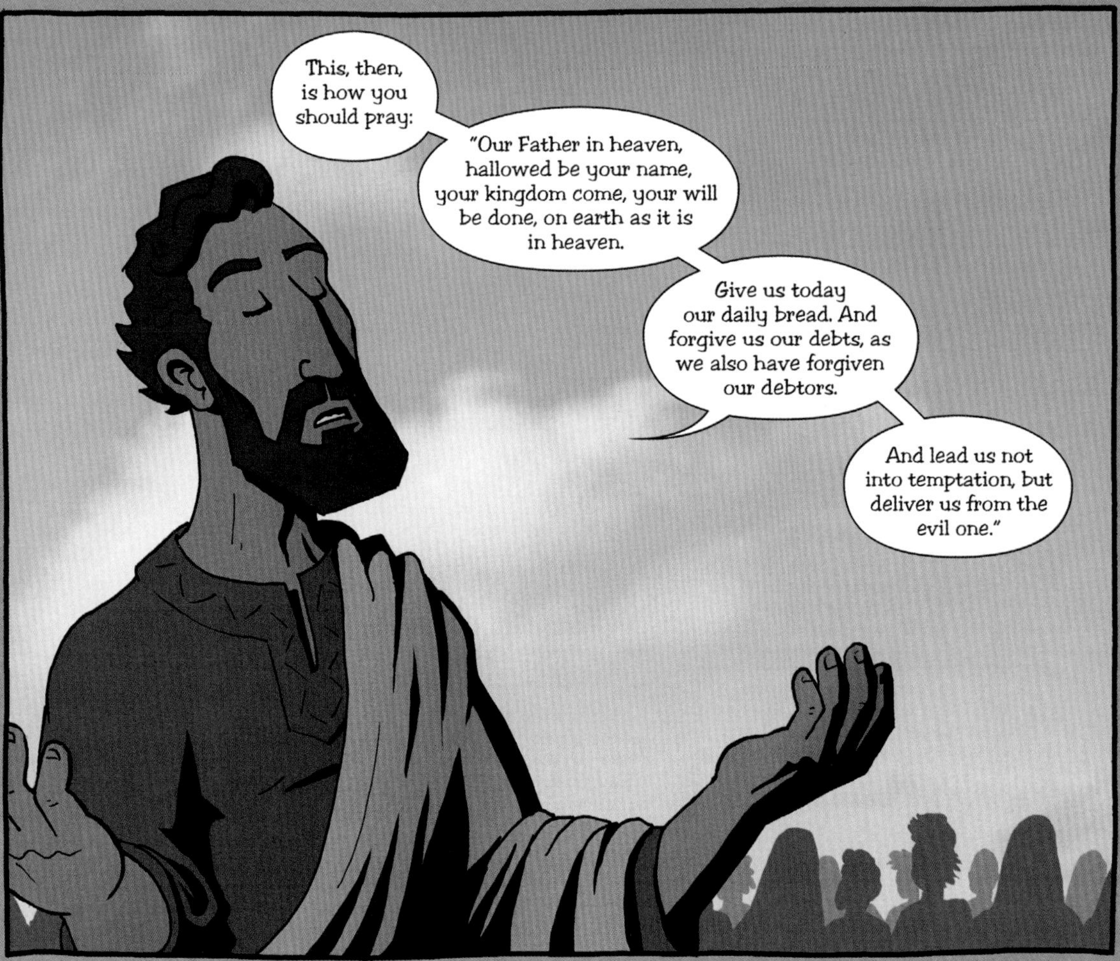

This, then, is how you should pray:
"Our Father in heaven, hallowed be your name, your kingdom come, your will be done, on earth as it is in heaven.
Give us today our daily bread. And forgive us our debts, as we also have forgiven our debtors.
And lead us not into temptation, but deliver us from the evil one."

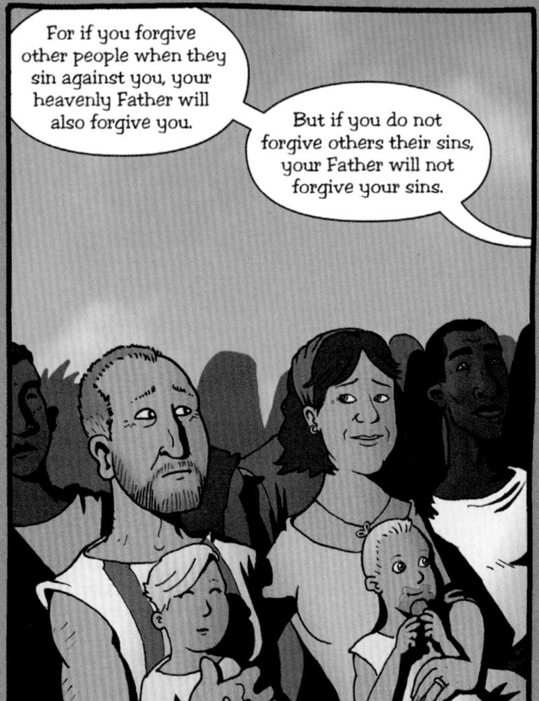

For if you forgive other people when they sin against you, your heavenly Father will also forgive you.
But if you do not forgive others their sins, your Father will not forgive your sins.

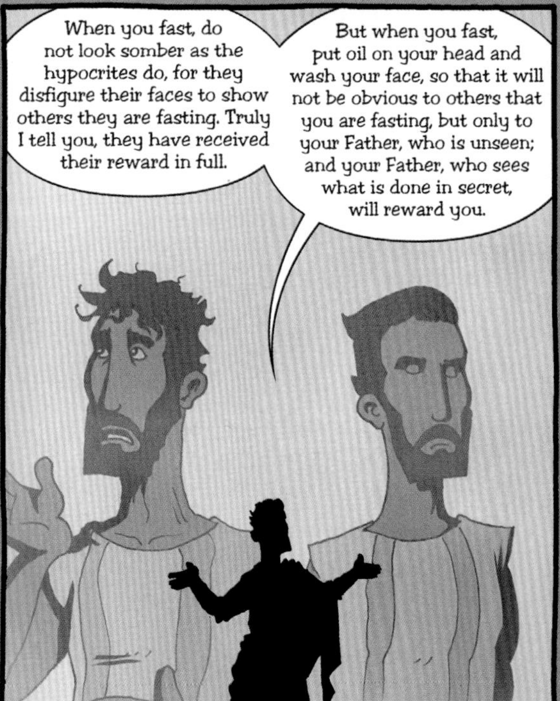

When you fast, do not look somber as the hypocrites do, for they disfigure their faces to show others they are fasting. Truly I tell you, they have received their reward in full.
But when you fast, put oil on your head and wash your face, so that it will not be obvious to others that you are fasting, but only to your Father, who is unseen; and your Father, who sees what is done in secret, will reward you.

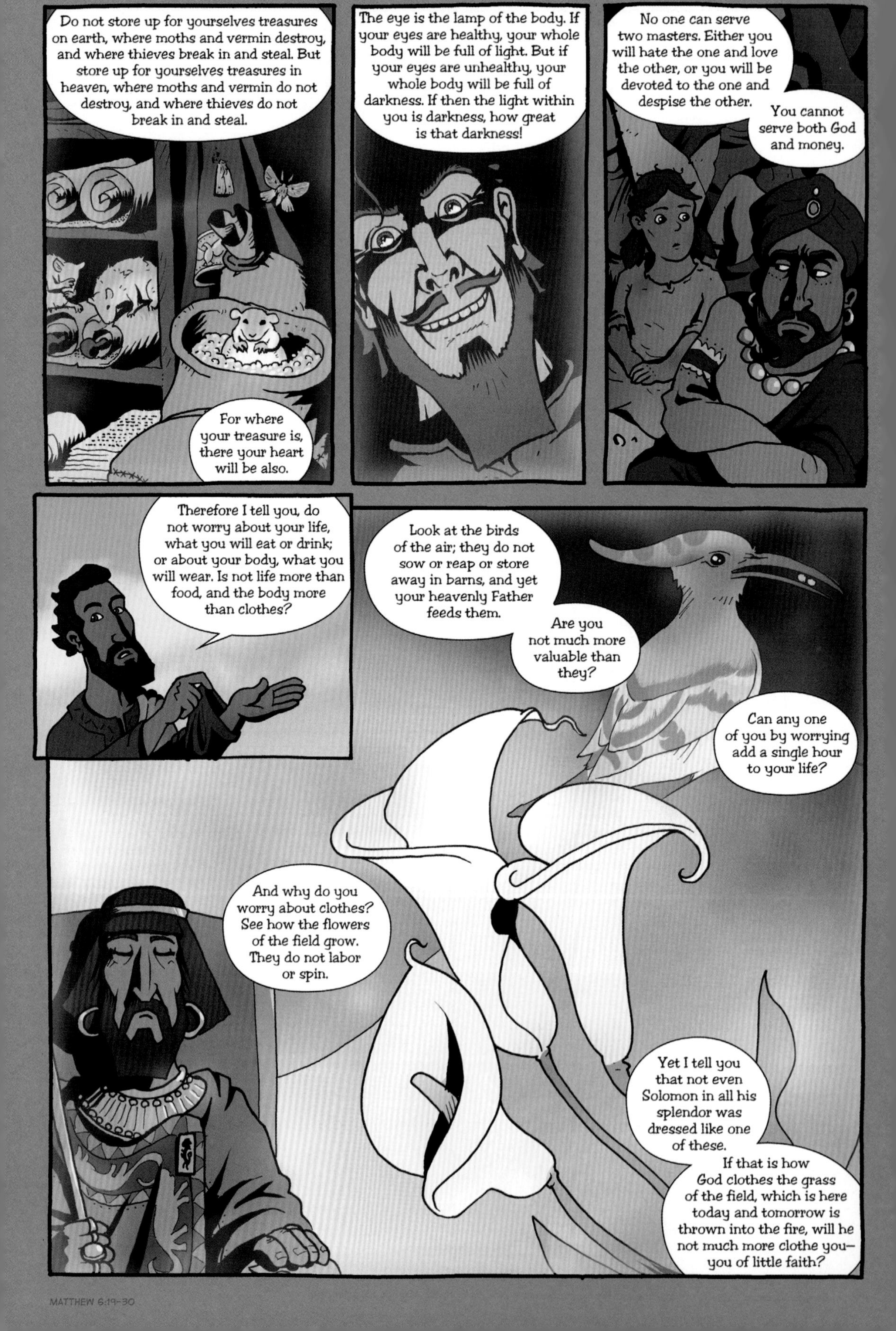
Do not store up for yourselves treasures on earth, where moths and vermin destroy, and where thieves break in and steal. But store up for yourselves treasures in heaven, where moths and vermin do not destroy, and where thieves do not break in and steal.
For where your treasure is, there your heart will be also.
The eye is the lamp of the body. If your eyes are healthy, your whole body will be full of light. But if your eyes are unhealthy, your whole body will be full of darkness. If then the light within you is darkness, how great is that darkness!
No one can serve two masters. Either you will hate the one and love the other, or you will be devoted to the one and despise the other.
You cannot serve both God and money.
Therefore I tell you, do not worry about your life, what you will eat or drink; or about your body, what you will wear. Is not life more than food, and the body more than clothes?
Look at the birds of the air; they do not sow or reap or store away in barns, and yet your heavenly Father feeds them.
Are you not much more valuable than they?
Can any one of you by worrying add a single hour to your life?
And why do you worry about clothes? See how the flowers of the field grow. They do not labor or spin.
Yet I tell you that not even Solomon in all his splendor was dressed like one of these.
If that is how God clothes the grass of the field, which is here today and tomorrow is thrown into the fire, will he not much more clothe you—you of little faith?

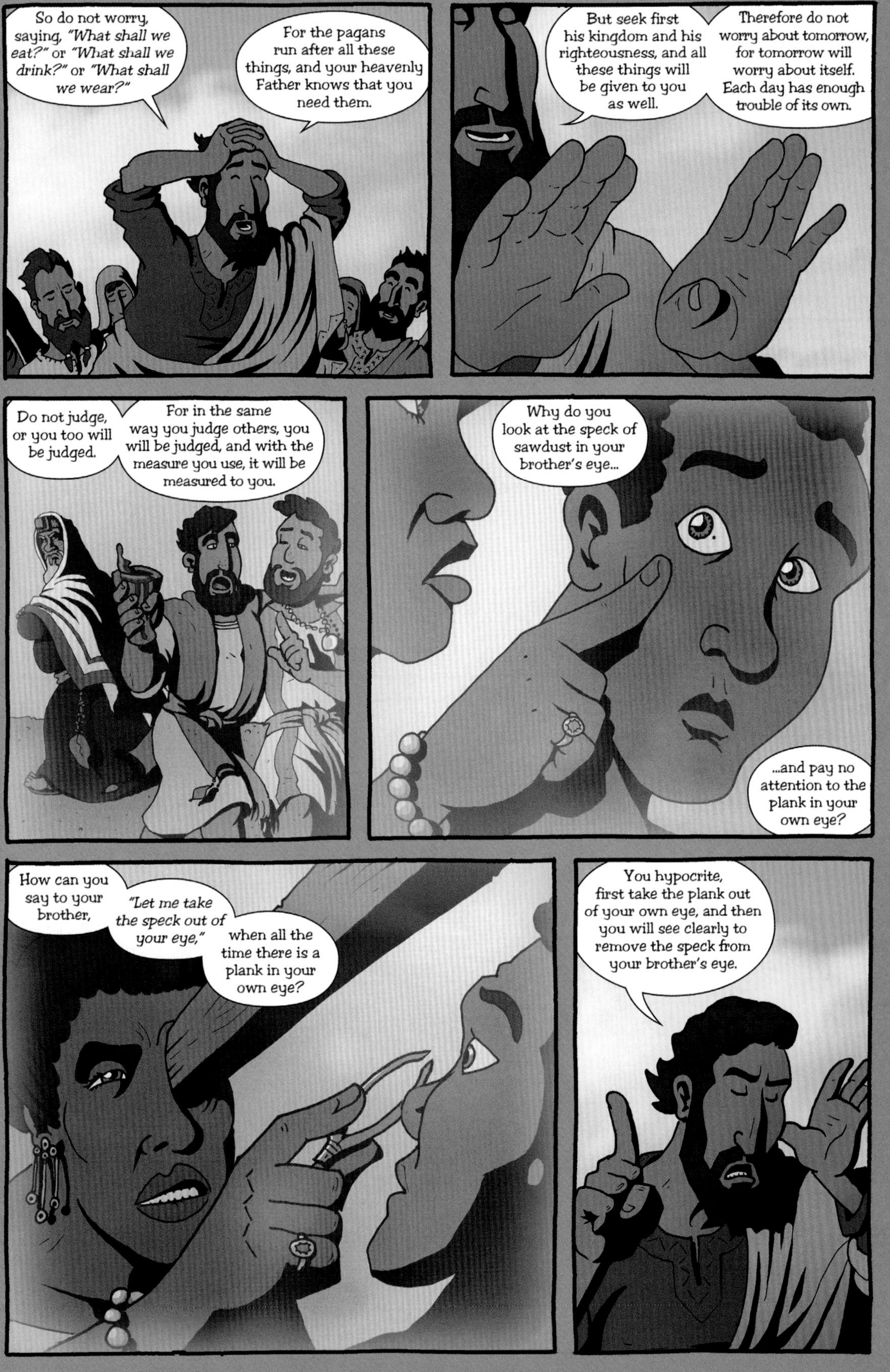
So do not worry, saying, "What shall we eat?" or "What shall we drink?" or "What shall we wear?"
For the pagans run after all these things, and your heavenly Father knows that you need them.
But seek first his kingdom and his righteousness, and all these things will be given to you as well.
Therefore do not worry about tomorrow, for tomorrow will worry about itself. Each day has enough trouble of its own.
Do not judge, or you too will be judged.
For in the same way you judge others, you will be judged, and with the measure you use, it will be measured to you.
Why do you look at the speck of sawdust in your brother's eye...
...and pay no attention to the plank in your own eye?
How can you say to your brother,
"Let me take the speck out of your eye,"
when all the time there is a plank in your own eye?
You hypocrite, first take the plank out of your own eye, and then you will see clearly to remove the speck from your brother's eye.

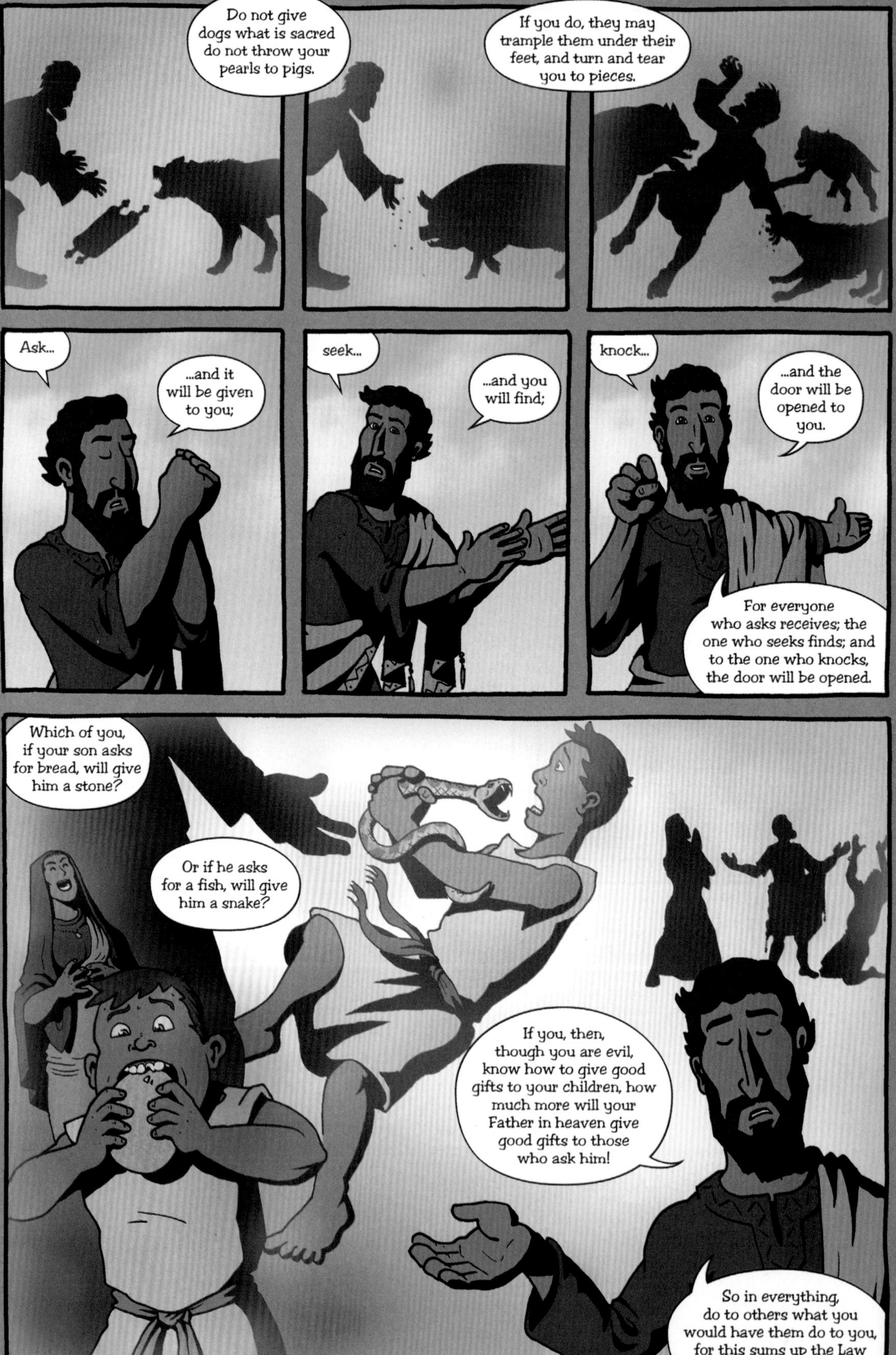
Do not give dogs what is sacred do not throw your pearls to pigs.
If you do, they may trample them under their feet, and turn and tear you to pieces.
Ask...
...and it will be given to you;
seek...
...and you will find;
knock...
...and the door will be opened to you.
For everyone who asks receives; the one who seeks finds; and to the one who knocks, the door will be opened.
Which of you, if your son asks for bread, will give him a stone?
Or if he asks for a fish, will give him a snake?
If you, then, though you are evil, know how to give good gifts to your children, how much more will your Father in heaven give good gifts to those who ask him!
So in everything, do to others what you would have them do to you, for this sums up the Law and the Prophets.

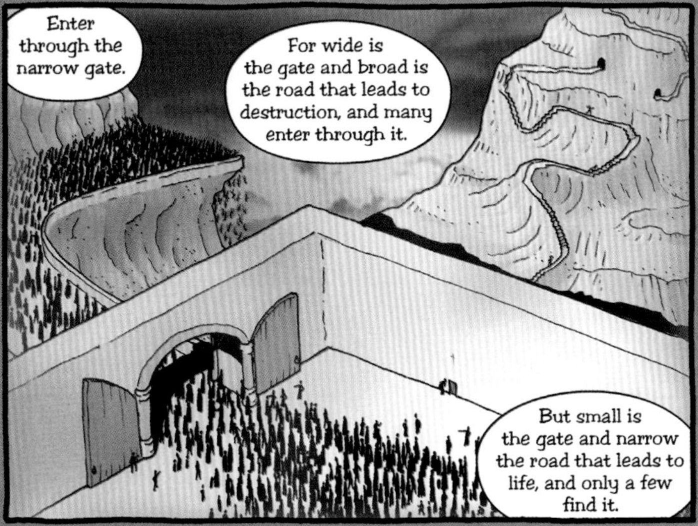
Enter through the narrow gate.
For wide is the gate and broad is the road that leads to destruction, and many enter through it.
But small is the gate and narrow the road that leads to life, and only a few find it.

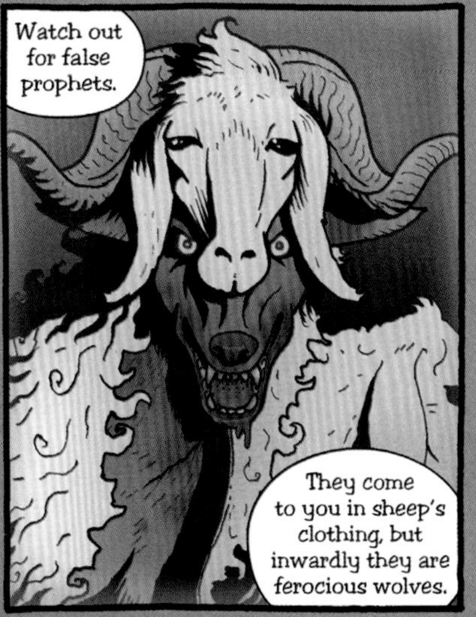
Watch out for false prophets.
They come to you in sheep's clothing, but inwardly they are ferocious wolves.

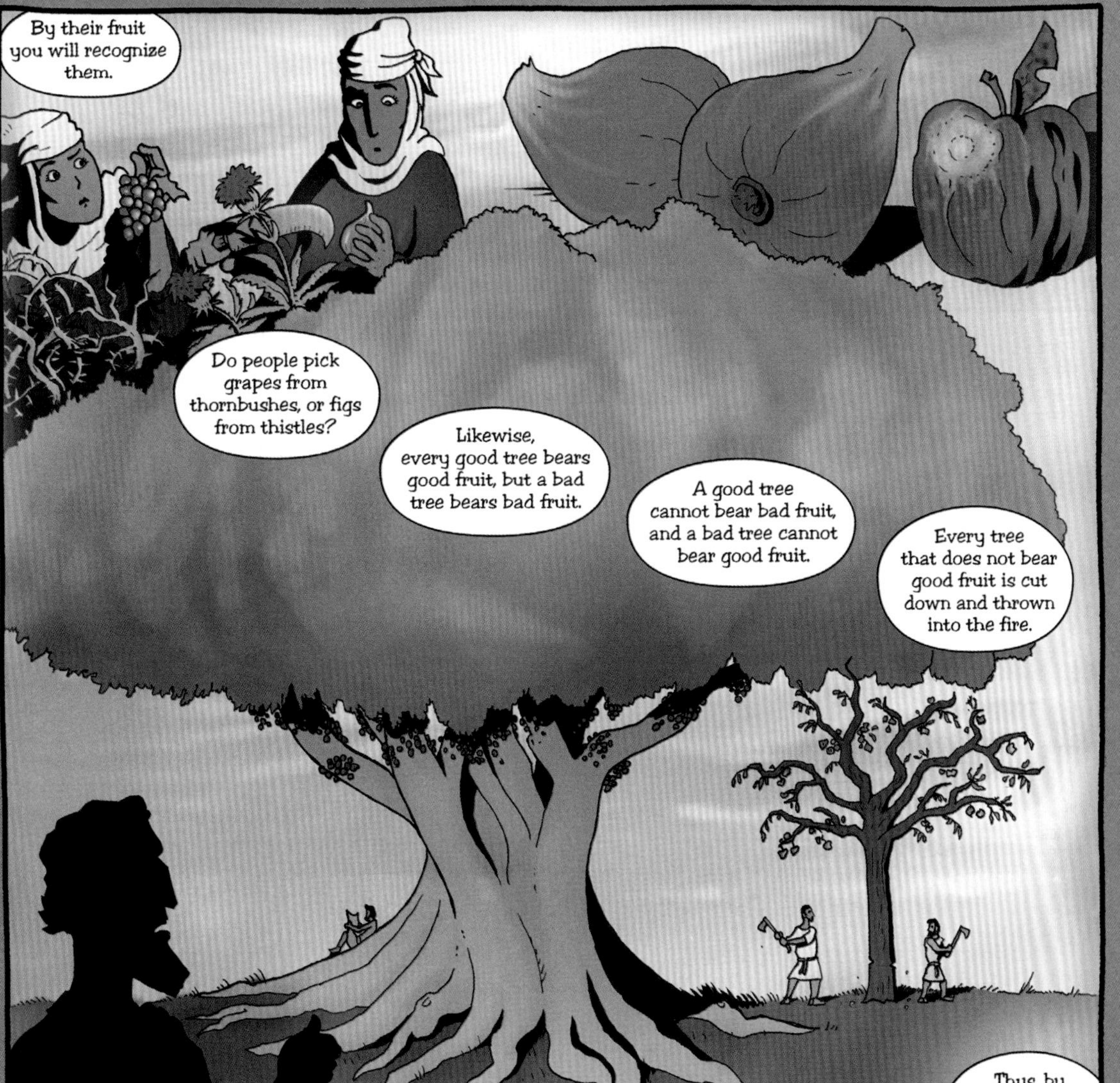
By their fruit you will recognize them.
Do people pick grapes from thornbushes, or figs from thistles?
Likewise, every good tree bears good fruit, but a bad tree bears bad fruit.
A good tree cannot bear bad fruit, and a bad tree cannot bear good fruit.
Every tree that does not bear good fruit is cut down and thrown into the fire.
Thus, by their fruit you will recognize them.

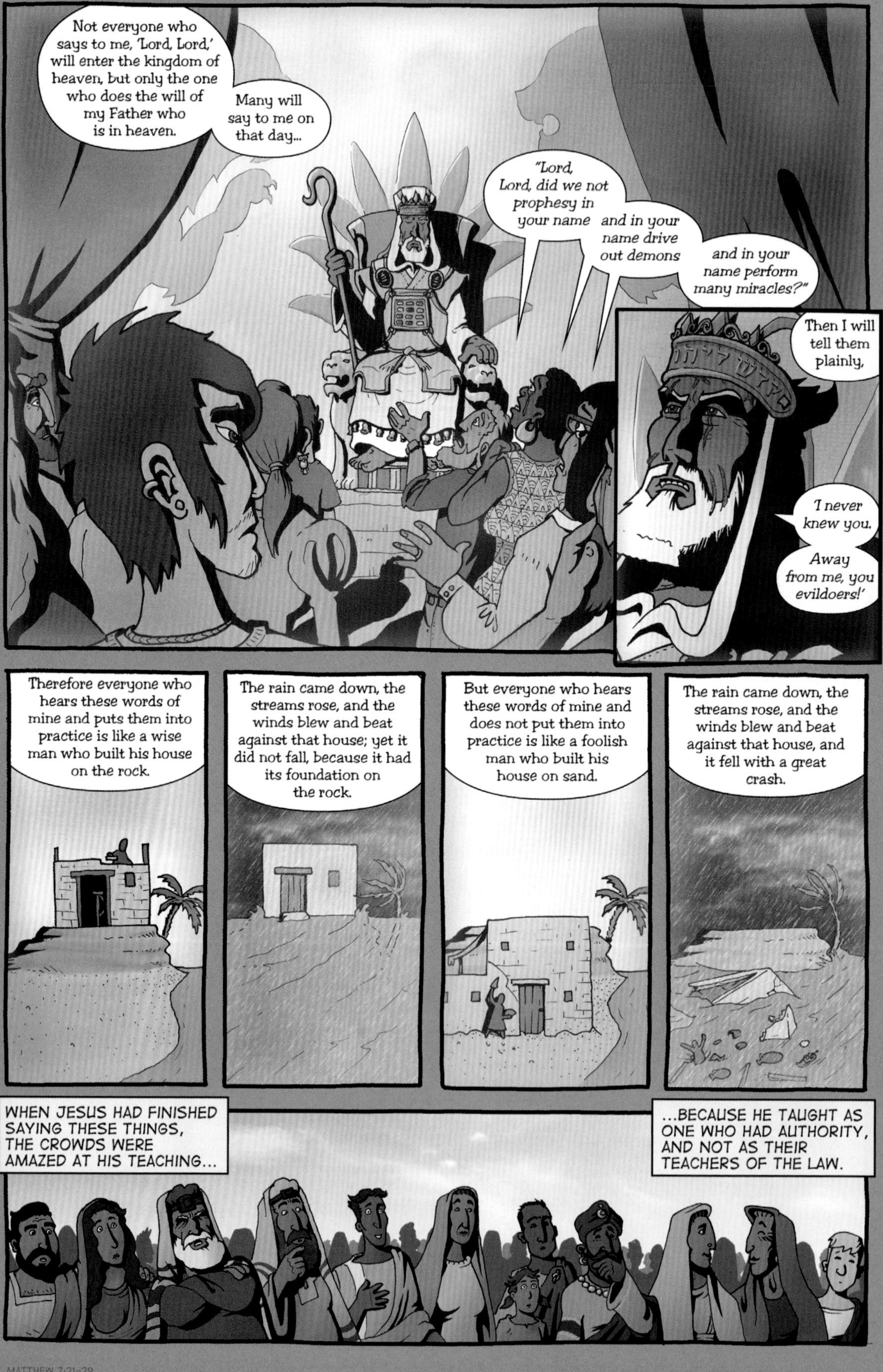
Not everyone who says to me, 'Lord, Lord,' will enter the kingdom of heaven, but only the one who does the will of my Father who is in heaven.
Many will say to me on that day...
"Lord, Lord, did we not prophesy in your name
and in your name drive out demons
and in your name perform many miracles?"
Then I will tell them plainly,
'I never knew you.
Away from me, you evildoers!'
Therefore everyone who hears these words of mine and puts them into practice is like a wise man who built his house on the rock.
The rain came down, the streams rose, and the winds blew and beat against that house; yet it did not fall, because it had its foundation on the rock.
But everyone who hears these words of mine and does not put them into practice is like a foolish man who built his house on sand.
The rain came down, the streams rose, and the winds blew and beat against that house, and it fell with a great crash.
WHEN JESUS HAD FINISHED SAYING THESE THINGS, THE CROWDS WERE AMAZED AT HIS TEACHING...
...BECAUSE HE TAUGHT AS ONE WHO HAD AUTHORITY, AND NOT AS THEIR TEACHERS OF THE LAW.

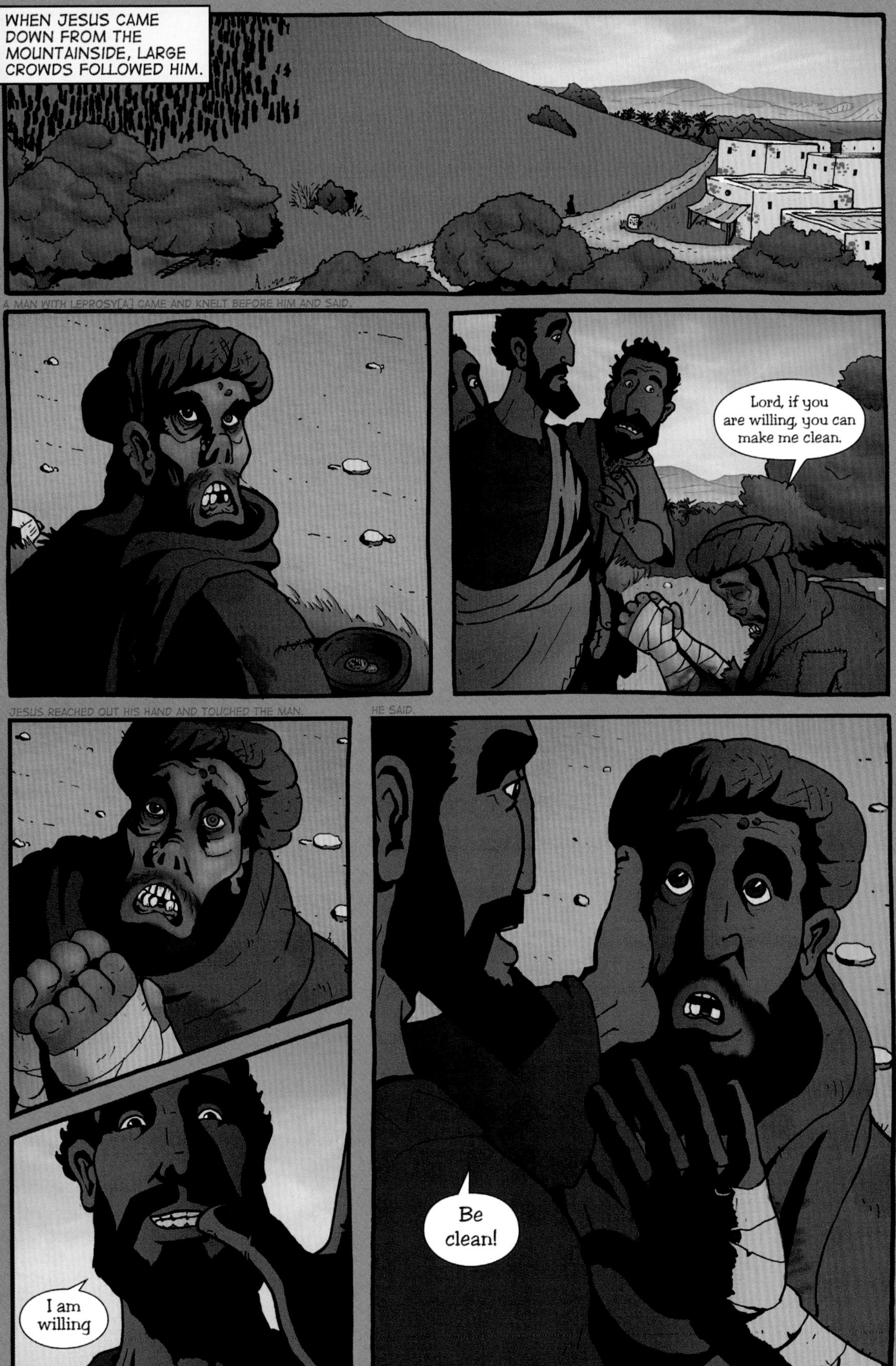
WHEN JESUS CAME DOWN FROM THE MOUNTAINSIDE, LARGE CROWDS FOLLOWED HIM.
A MAN WITH LEPROSY[A] CAME AND KNELT BEFORE HIM AND SAID,
Lord, if you are willing, you can make me clean.
JESUS REACHED OUT HIS HAND AND TOUCHED THE MAN.
I am willing
HE SAID.
Be clean!
IMMEDIATELY HE WAS CLEANSED OF HIS LEPROSY.

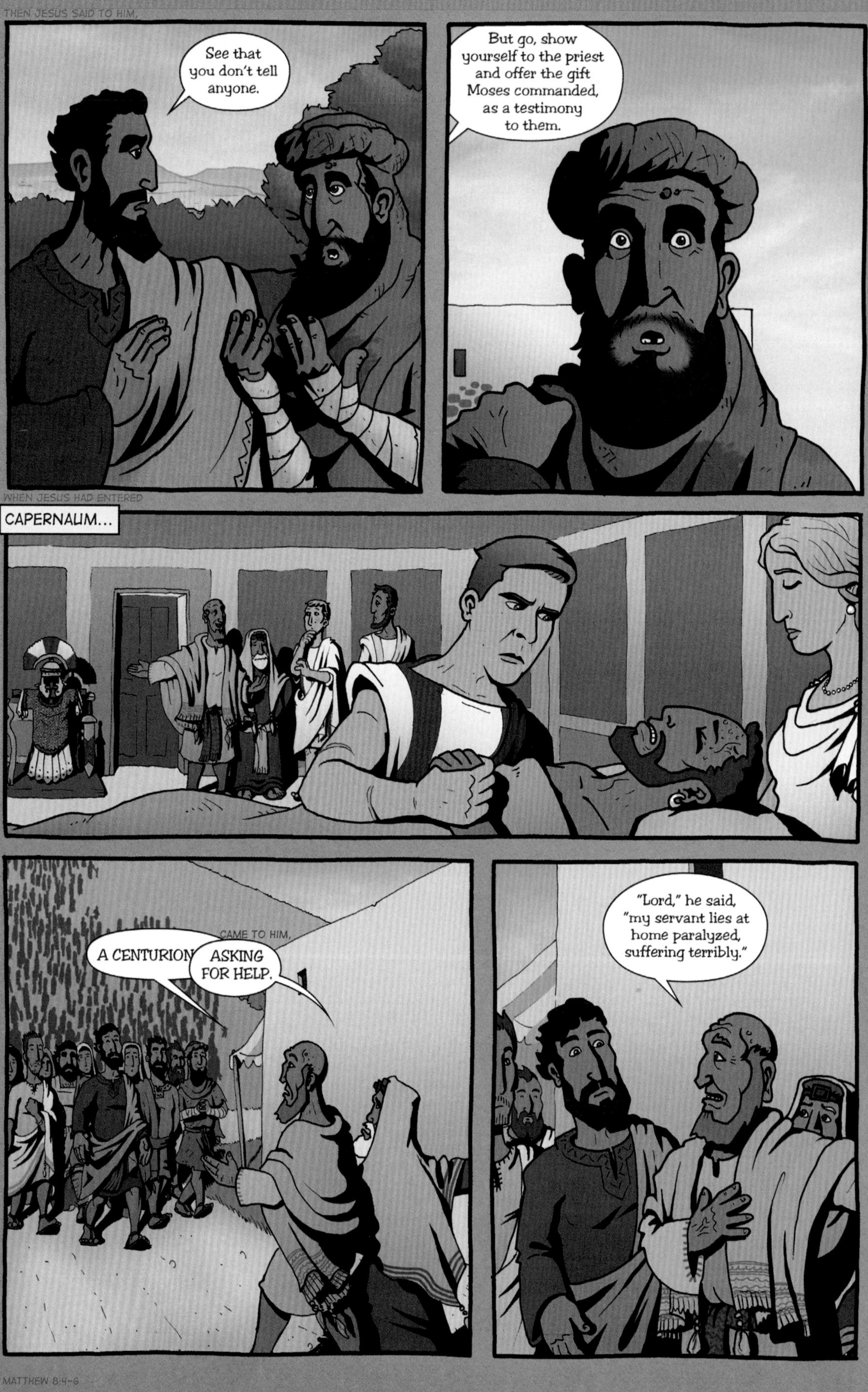
THEN JESUS SAID TO HIM,
See that you don't tell anyone.
But go, show yourself to the priest and offer the gift Moses commanded, as a testimony to them.
WHEN JESUS HAD ENTERED
CAPERNAUM...
A CENTURION
CAME TO HIM,
ASKING FOR HELP.
"Lord," he said, "my servant lies at home paralyzed, suffering terribly."

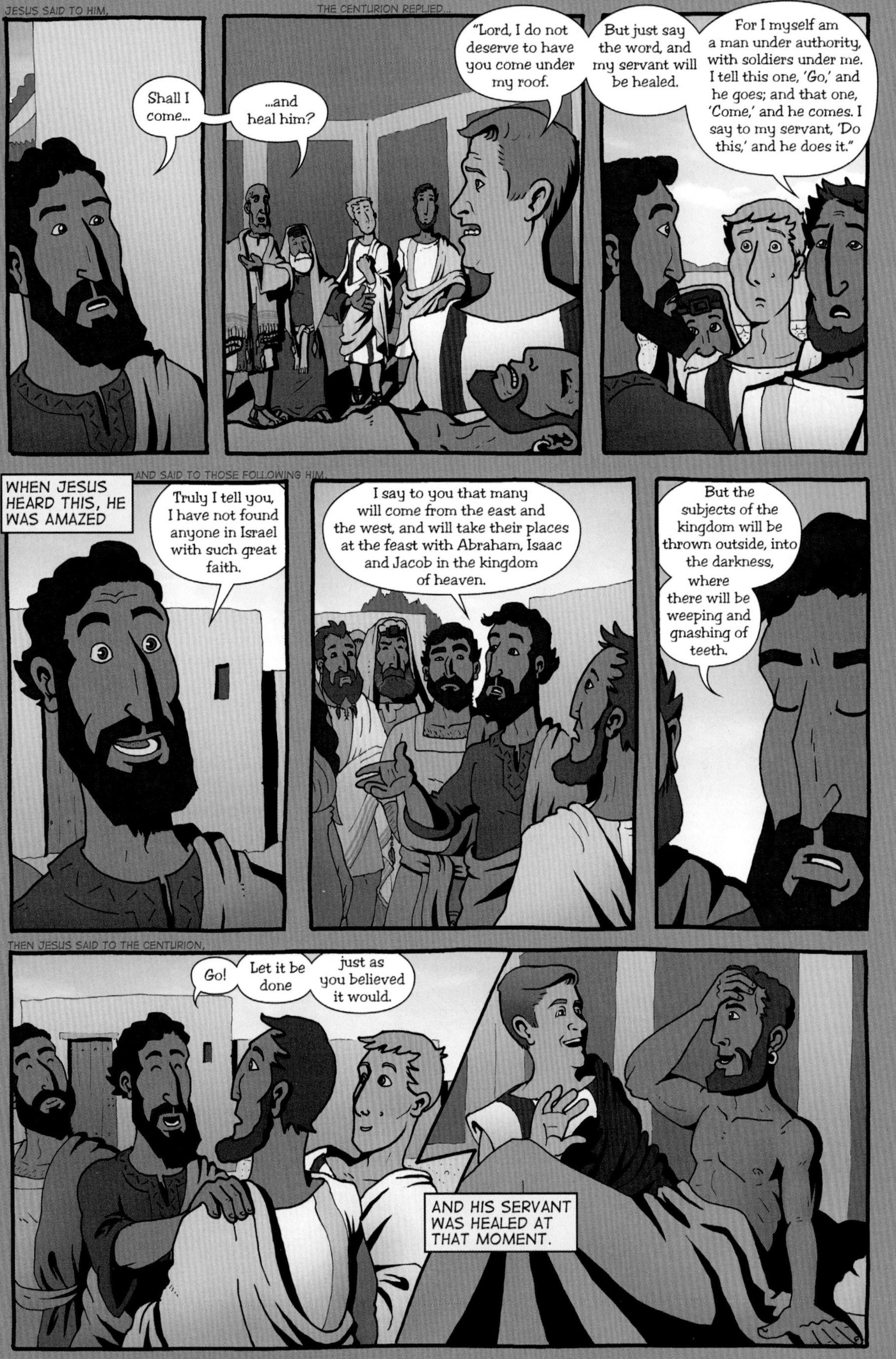
JESUS SAID TO HIM,
Shall I come...
...and heal him?
THE CENTURION REPLIED...
"Lord, I do not deserve to have you come under my roof.
But just say the word, and my servant will be healed.
For I myself am a man under authority, with soldiers under me. I tell this one, 'Go,' and he goes; and that one, 'Come,' and he comes. I say to my servant, 'Do this,' and he does it."
WHEN JESUS HEARD THIS, HE WAS AMAZED
AND SAID TO THOSE FOLLOWING HIM,
Truly I tell you, I have not found anyone in Israel with such great faith.
I say to you that many will come from the east and the west, and will take their places at the feast with Abraham, Isaac and Jacob in the kingdom of heaven.
But the subjects of the kingdom will be thrown outside, into the darkness, where there will be weeping and gnashing of teeth.
THEN JESUS SAID TO THE CENTURION,
Go!
Let it be done
just as you believed it would.
AND HIS SERVANT WAS HEALED AT THAT MOMENT.

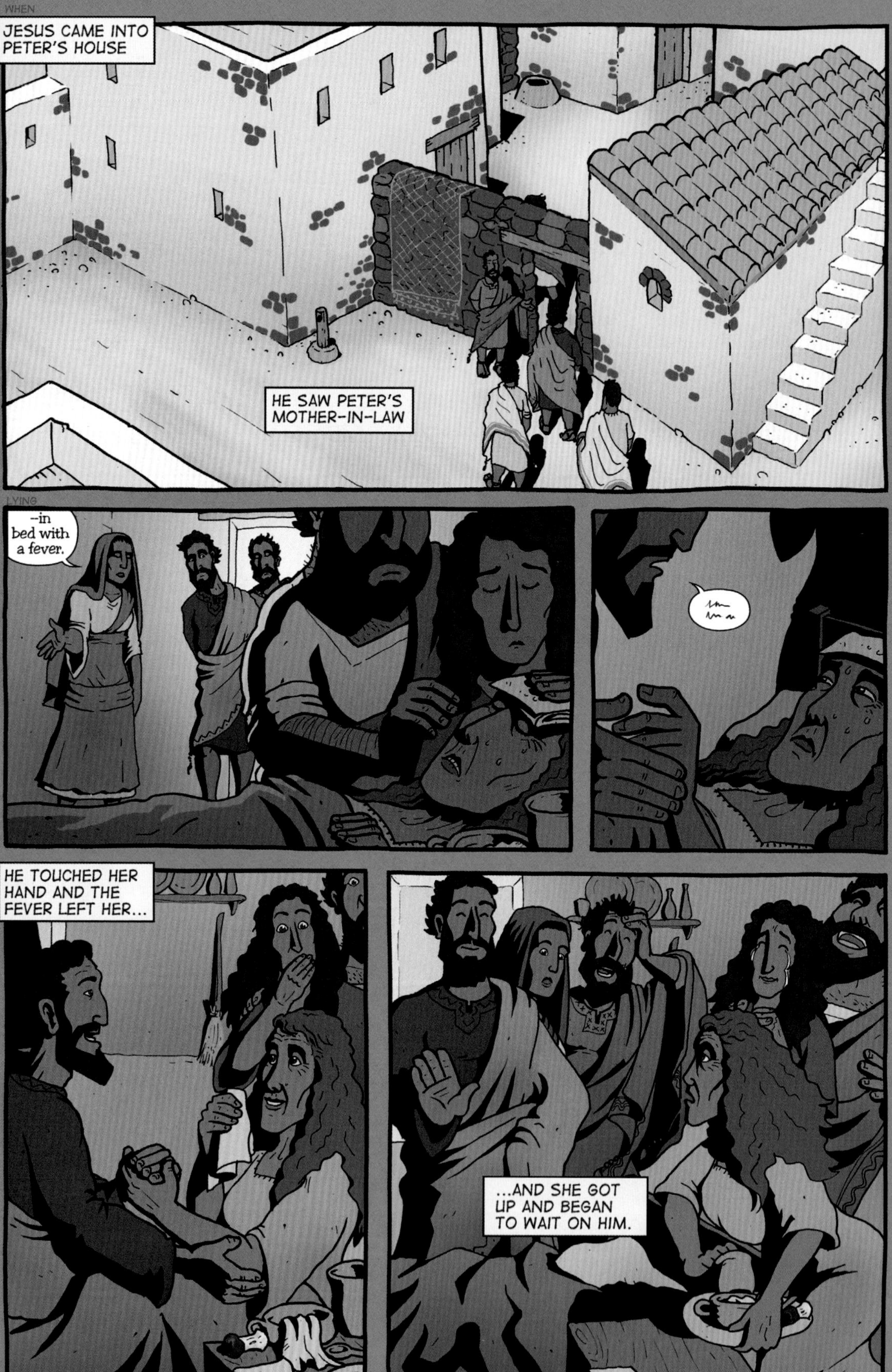
WHEN
JESUS CAME INTO PETER'S HOUSE
HE SAW PETER'S MOTHER-IN-LAW
LYING
--in bed with a fever.
HE TOUCHED HER HAND AND THE FEVER LEFT HER...
...AND SHE GOT UP AND BEGAN TO WAIT ON HIM.

MATTHEW 8:14–15

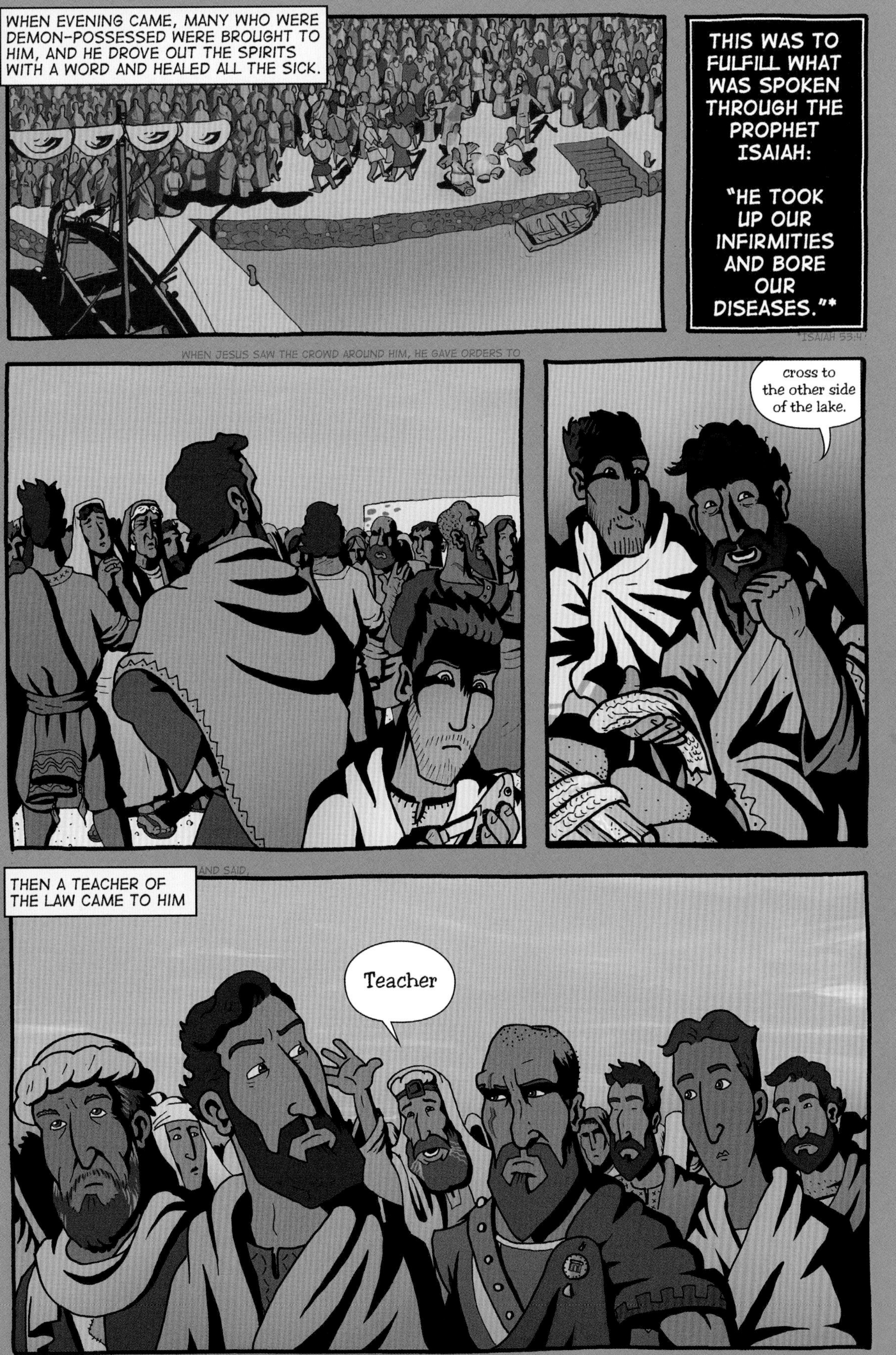
WHEN EVENING CAME, MANY WHO WERE DEMON-POSSESSED WERE BROUGHT TO HIM, AND HE DROVE OUT THE SPIRITS WITH A WORD AND HEALED ALL THE SICK.
THIS WAS TO FULFILL WHAT WAS SPOKEN THROUGH THE PROPHET ISAIAH:
"HE TOOK UP OUR INFIRMITIES AND BORE OUR DISEASES."*
*ISAIAH 53:4
WHEN JESUS SAW THE CROWD AROUND HIM, HE GAVE ORDERS TO
cross to the other side of the lake.
THEN A TEACHER OF THE LAW CAME TO HIM
AND SAID,
Teacher

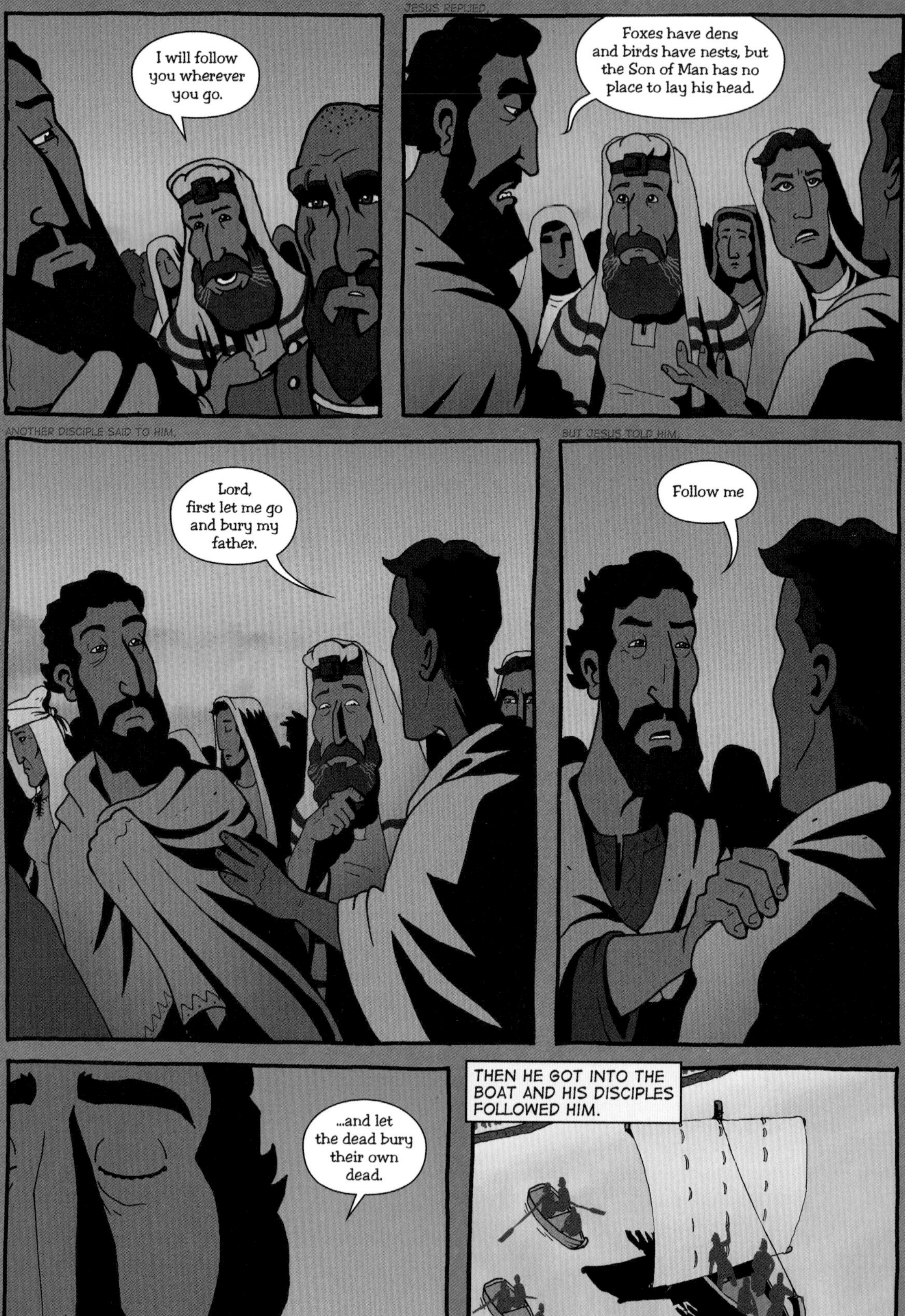
I will follow you wherever you go.
JESUS REPLIED,
Foxes have dens and birds have nests, but the Son of Man has no place to lay his head.
ANOTHER DISCIPLE SAID TO HIM,
Lord, first let me go and bury my father.
BUT JESUS TOLD HIM,
Follow me
...and let the dead bury their own dead.
THEN HE GOT INTO THE BOAT AND HIS DISCIPLES FOLLOWED HIM.

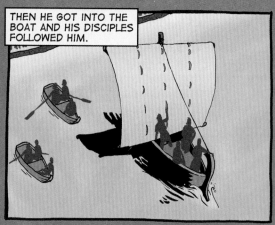

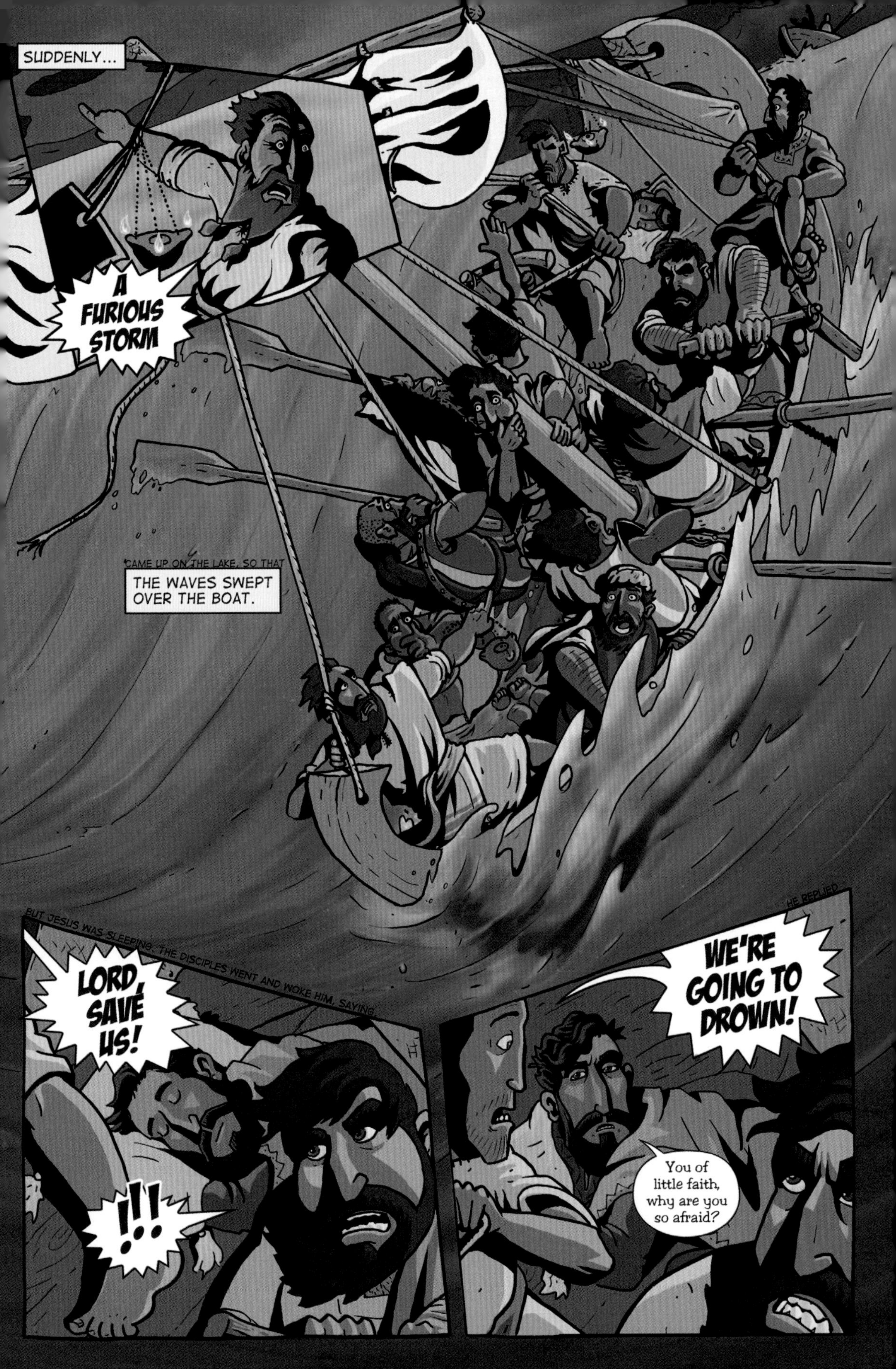
SUDDENLY...
A FURIOUS STORM
CAME UP ON THE LAKE, SO THAT
THE WAVES SWEPT OVER THE BOAT.
BUT JESUS WAS SLEEPING. THE DISCIPLES WENT AND WOKE HIM, SAYING,
LORD, SAVE US!
!!!
WE'RE GOING TO DROWN!
HE REPLIED
You of little faith, why are you so afraid?

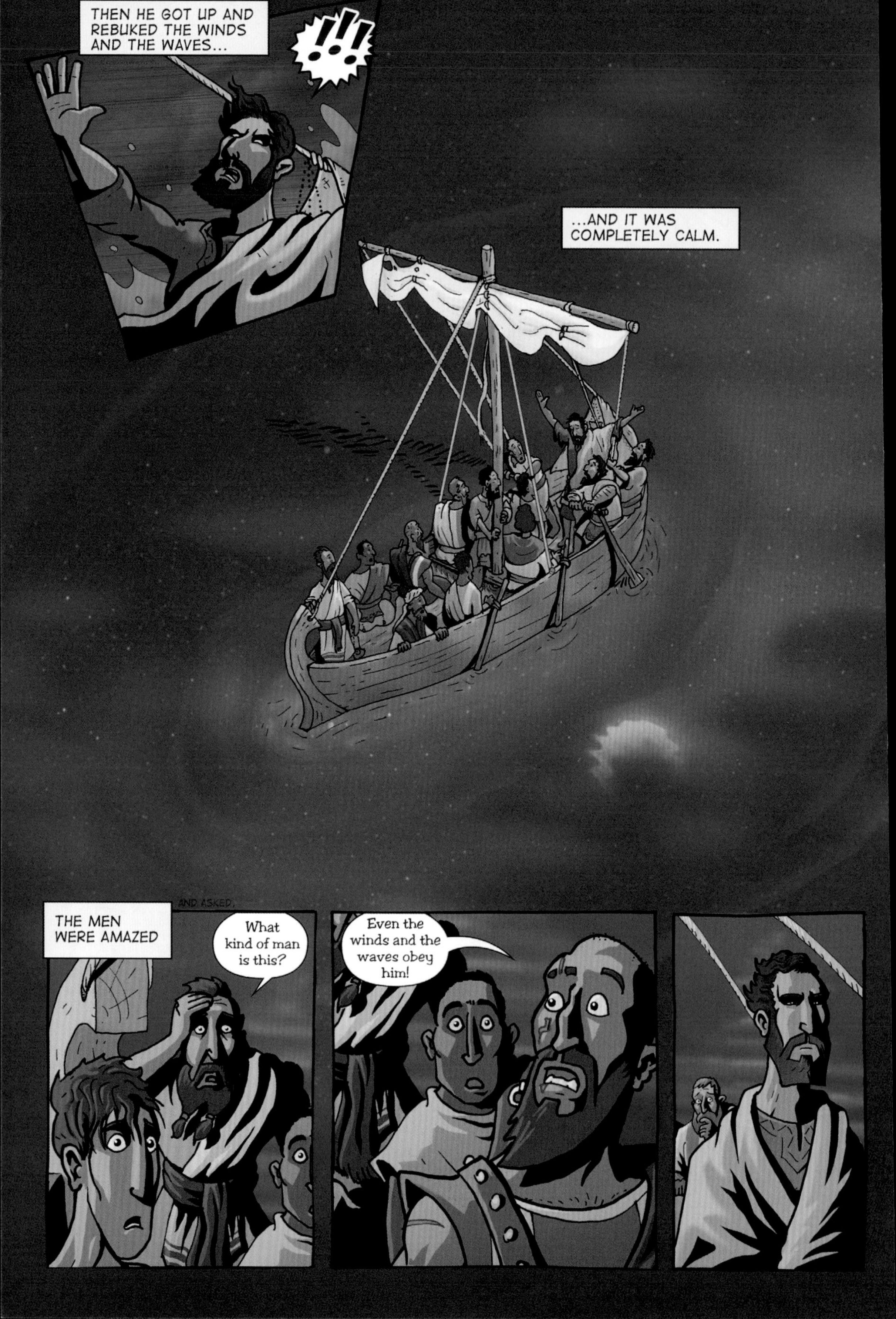
THEN HE GOT UP AND REBUKED THE WINDS AND THE WAVES...
!!!
...AND IT WAS COMPLETELY CALM.
THE MEN WERE AMAZED
AND ASKED,
What kind of man is this?
Even the winds and the waves obey him!

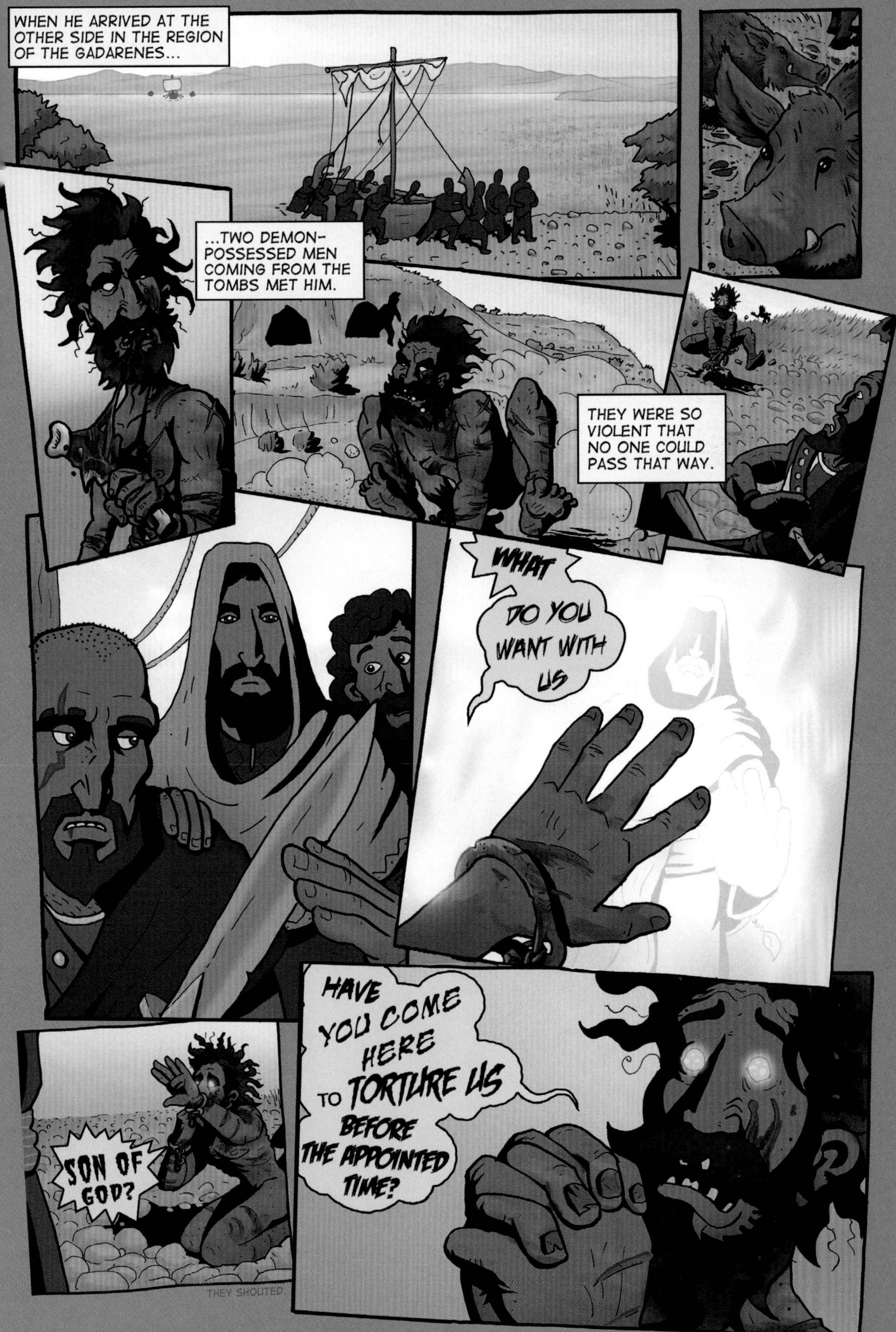

WHEN HE ARRIVED AT THE OTHER SIDE IN THE REGION OF THE GADARENES...
...TWO DEMON-POSSESSED MEN COMING FROM THE TOMBS MET HIM.
THEY WERE SO VIOLENT THAT NO ONE COULD PASS THAT WAY.
WHAT DO YOU WANT WITH US
SON OF GOD?
HAVE YOU COME HERE TO TORTURE US BEFORE THE APPOINTED TIME?
THEY SHOUTED

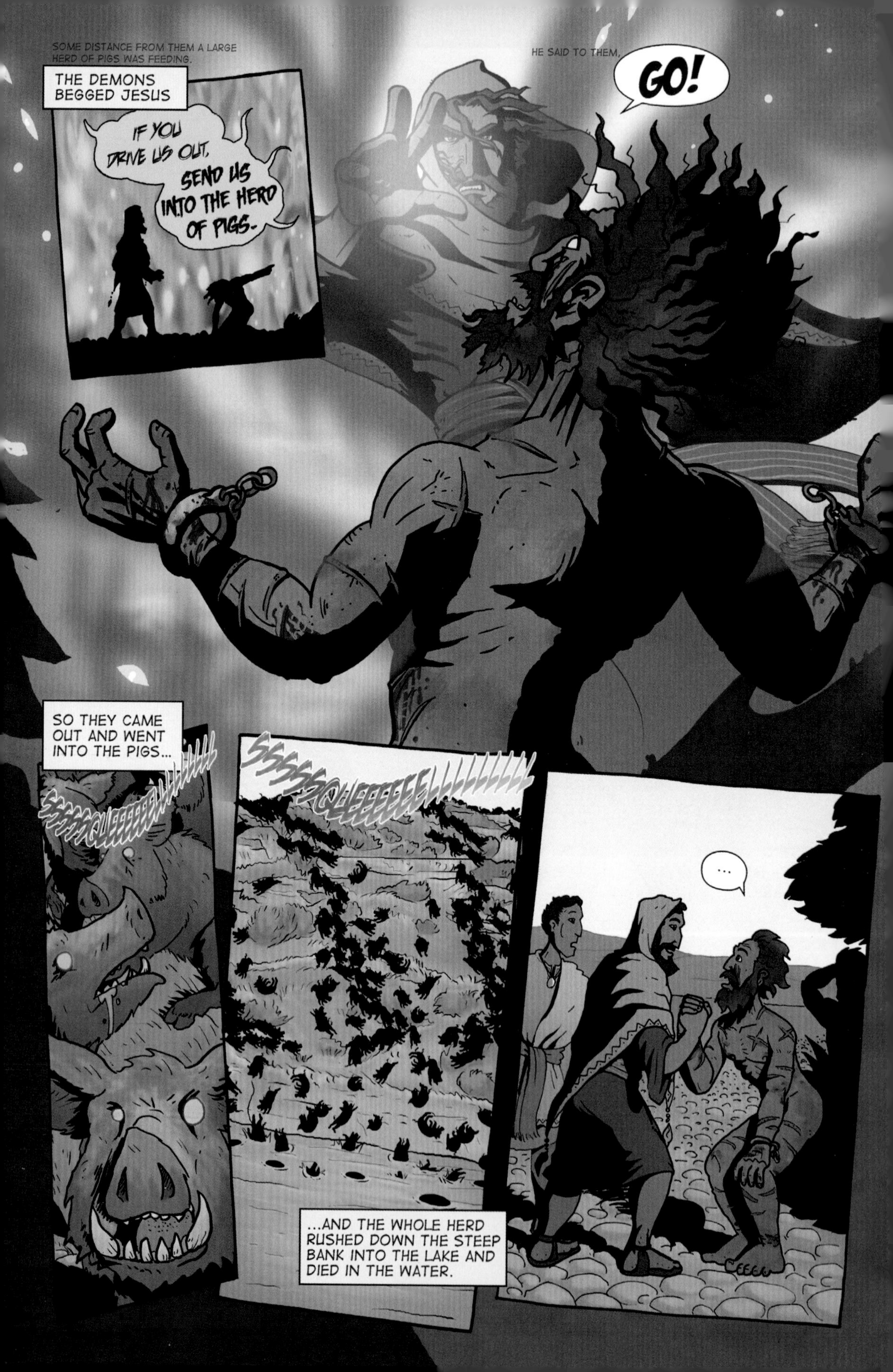
SOME DISTANCE FROM THEM A LARGE HERD OF PIGS WAS FEEDING.
THE DEMONS BEGGED JESUS
IF YOU DRIVE US OUT, SEND US INTO THE HERD OF PIGS.
HE SAID TO THEM,
GO!
SO THEY CAME OUT AND WENT INTO THE PIGS...
SSSSSQUEEEEEEELLLLLLL
SSSSSQUEEEEEEELLLLLLLLL
...AND THE WHOLE HERD RUSHED DOWN THE STEEP BANK INTO THE LAKE AND DIED IN THE WATER.
...

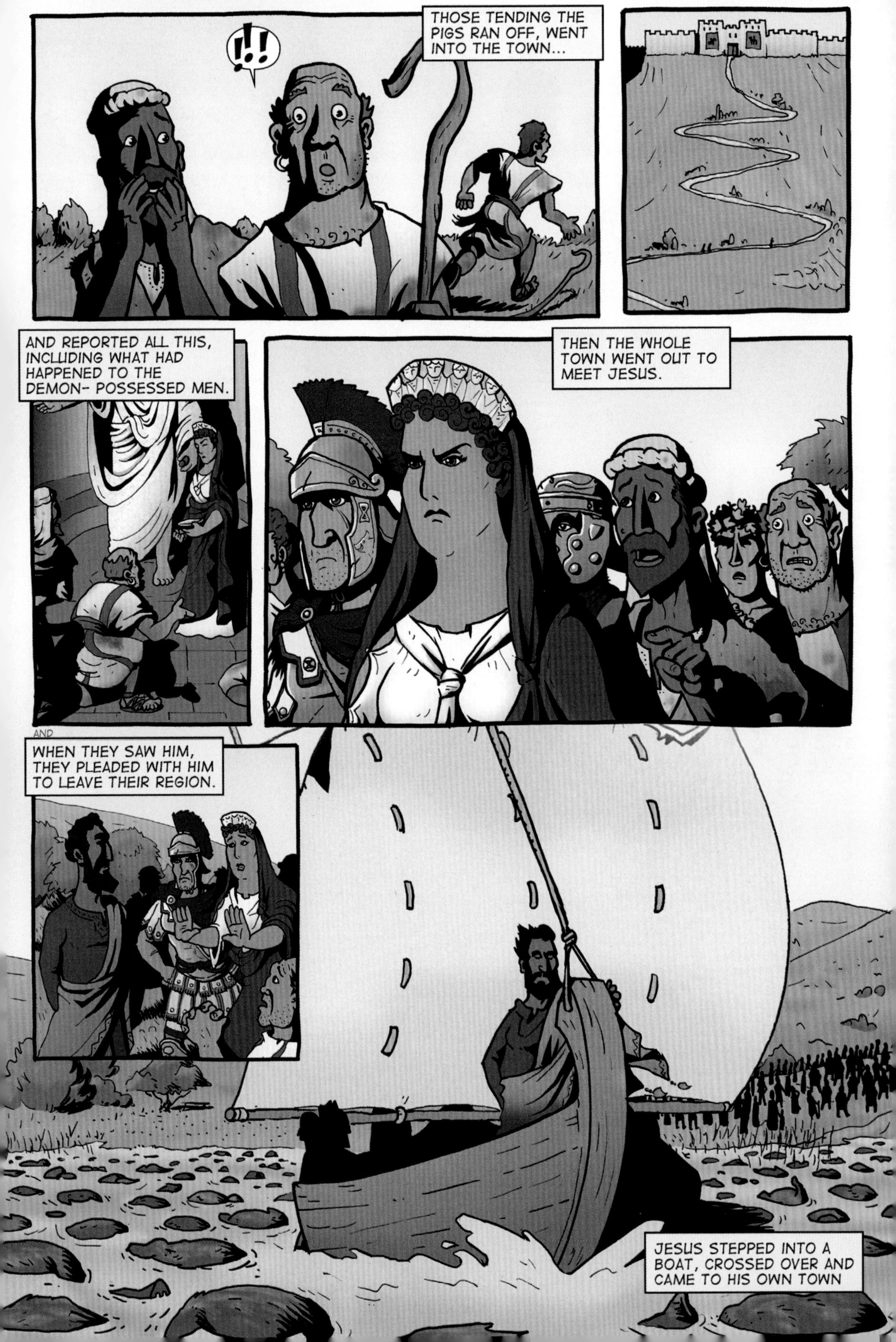
!!!
THOSE TENDING THE PIGS RAN OFF, WENT INTO THE TOWN...
AND REPORTED ALL THIS, INCLUDING WHAT HAD HAPPENED TO THE DEMON- POSSESSED MEN.
THEN THE WHOLE TOWN WENT OUT TO MEET JESUS.
AND
WHEN THEY SAW HIM, THEY PLEADED WITH HIM TO LEAVE THEIR REGION.
JESUS STEPPED INTO A BOAT, CROSSED OVER AND CAME TO HIS OWN TOWN

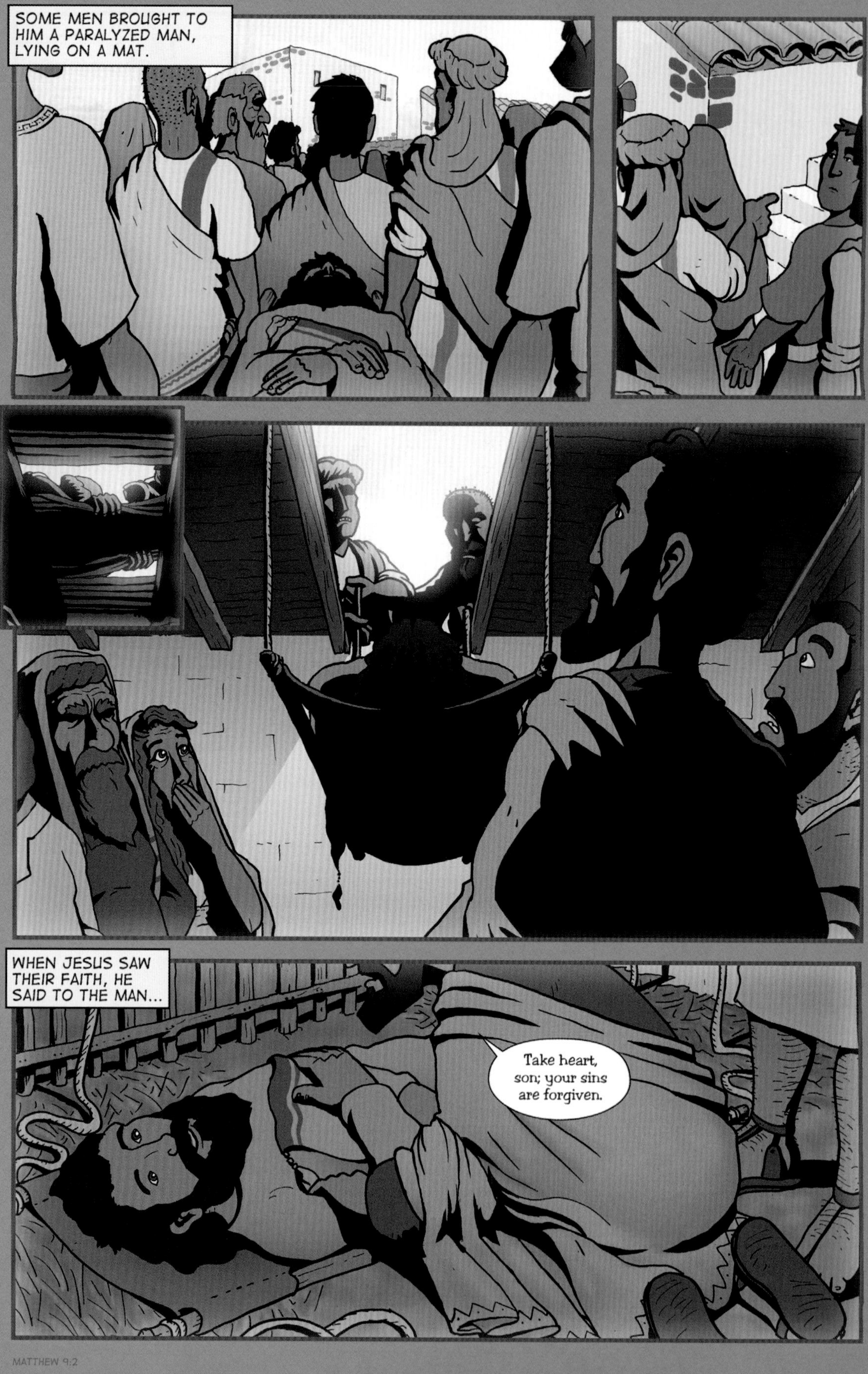
SOME MEN BROUGHT TO HIM A PARALYZED MAN, LYING ON A MAT.
WHEN JESUS SAW THEIR FAITH, HE SAID TO THE MAN...
Take heart, son; your sins are forgiven.

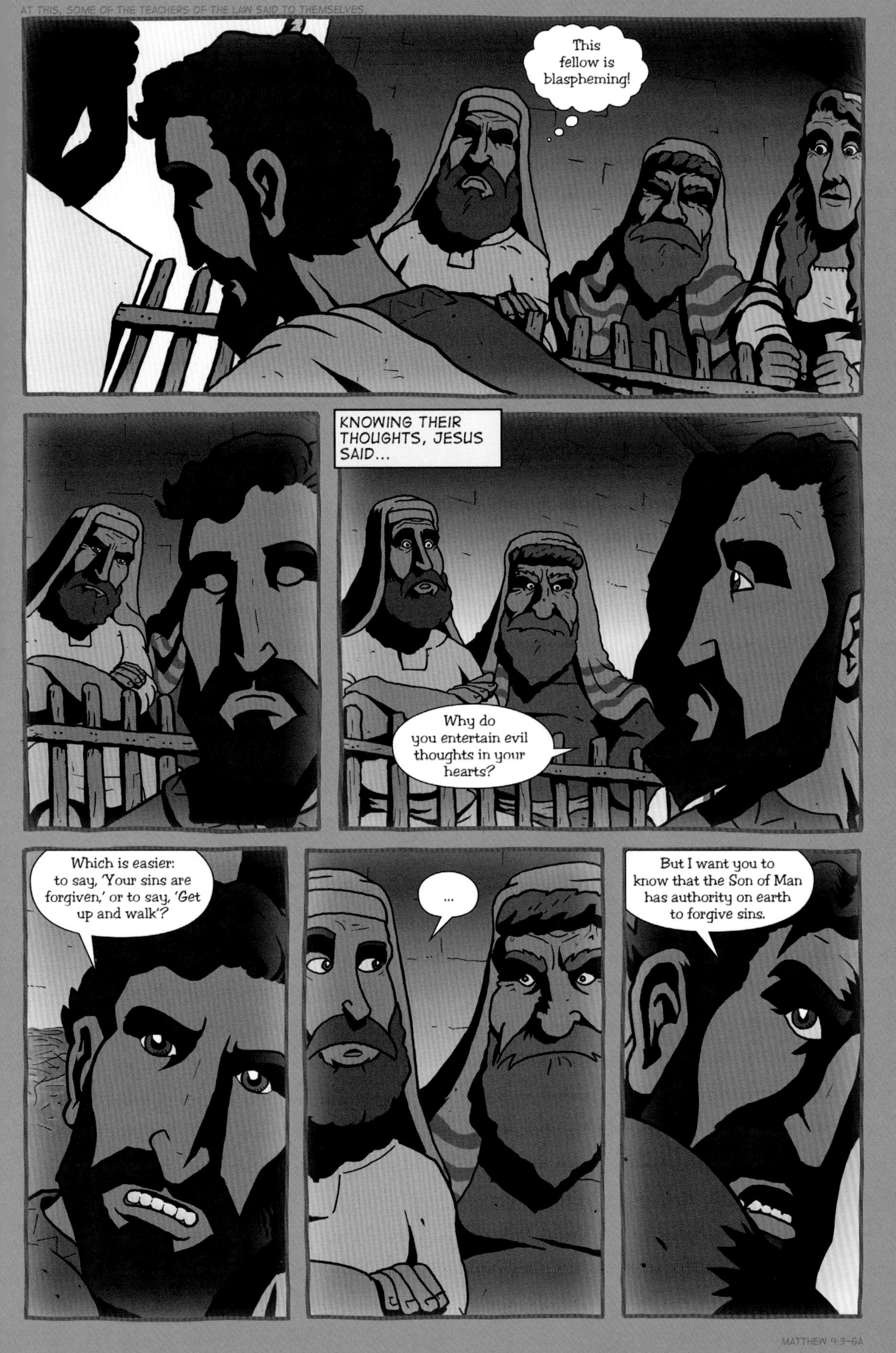
AT THIS, SOME OF THE TEACHERS OF THE LAW SAID TO THEMSELVES,
This fellow is blaspheming!
KNOWING THEIR THOUGHTS, JESUS SAID...
Why do you entertain evil thoughts in your hearts?
Which is easier: to say, 'Your sins are forgiven,' or to say, 'Get up and walk'?
...
But I want you to know that the Son of Man has authority on earth to forgive sins.

SO HE SAID TO THE PARALYZED MAN,

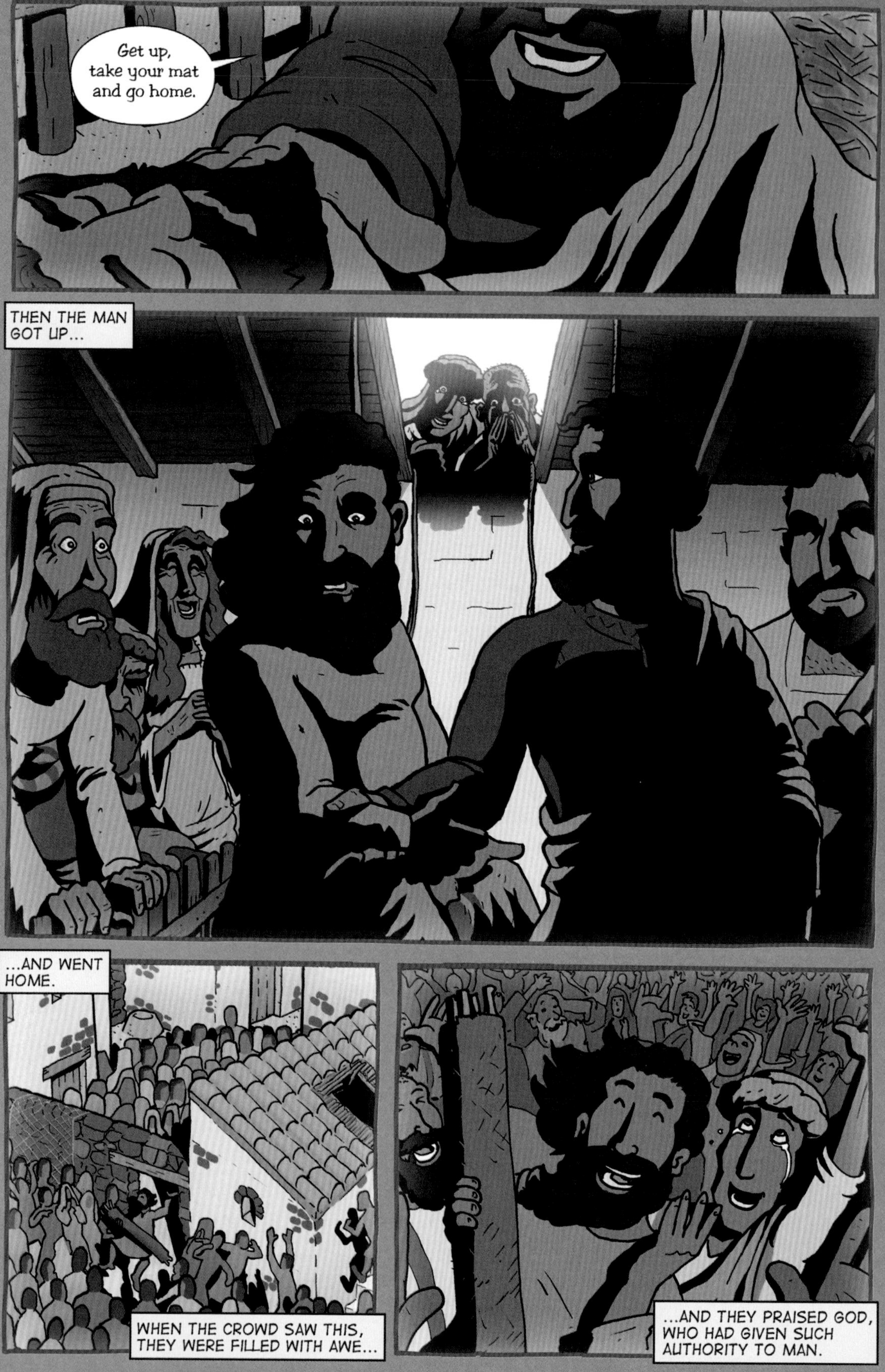
Get up, take your mat and go home.
THEN THE MAN GOT UP...
...AND WENT HOME.
WHEN THE CROWD SAW THIS, THEY WERE FILLED WITH AWE...
...AND THEY PRAISED GOD, WHO HAD GIVEN SUCH AUTHORITY TO MAN.

MATTHEW 9:6B-8

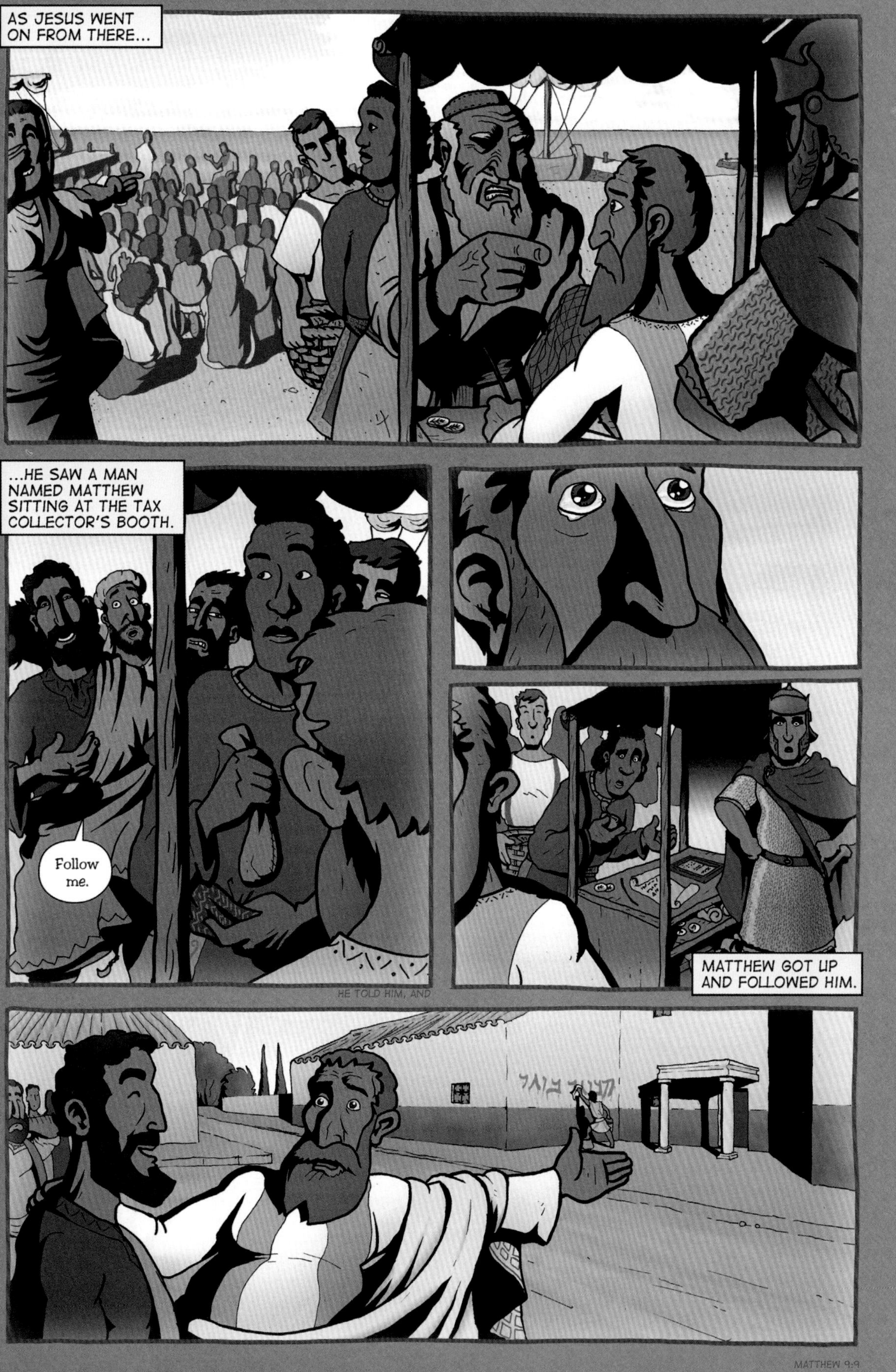
AS JESUS WENT ON FROM THERE...
...HE SAW A MAN NAMED MATTHEW SITTING AT THE TAX COLLECTOR'S BOOTH.
Follow me.
HE TOLD HIM, AND
MATTHEW GOT UP AND FOLLOWED HIM.

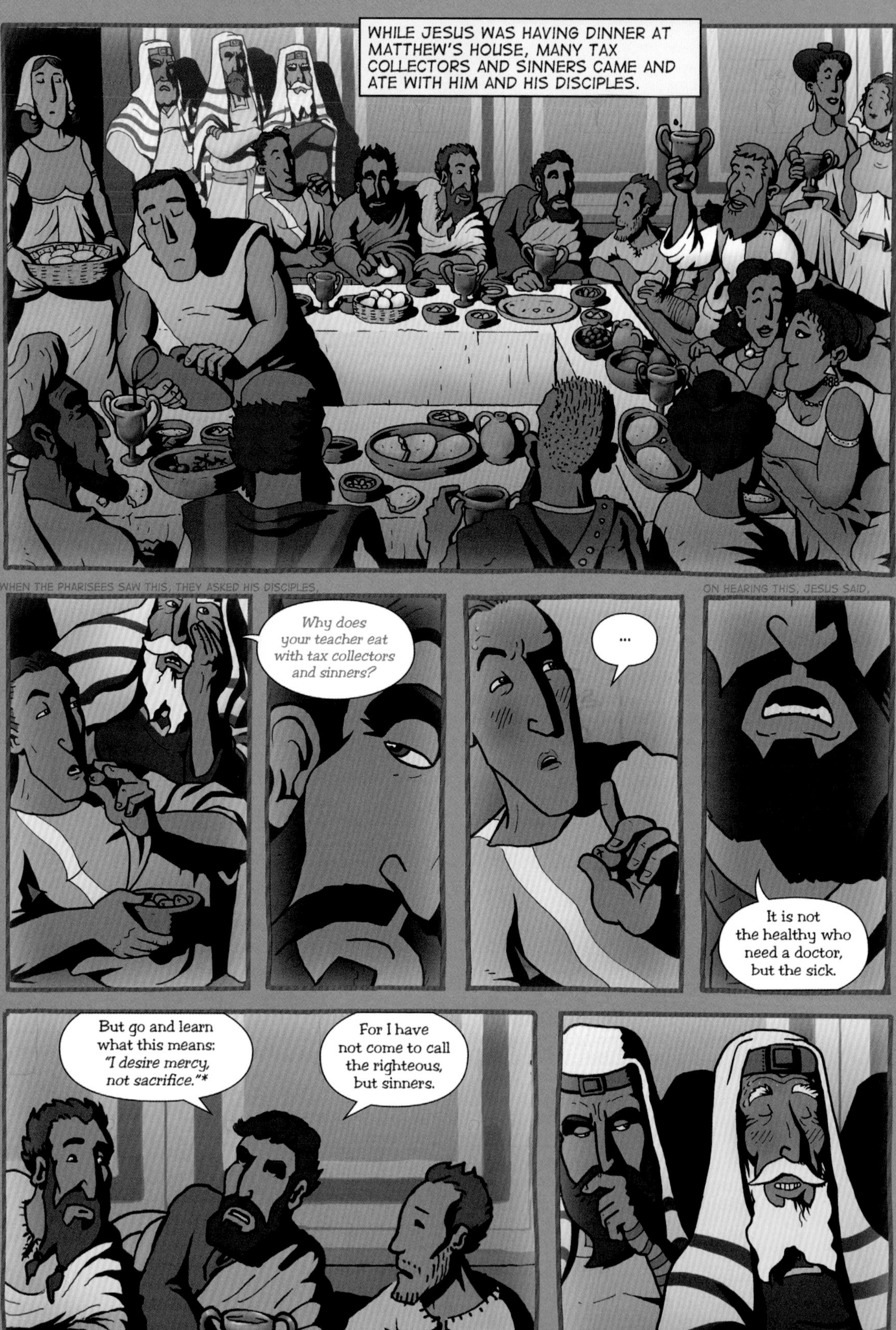
WHILE JESUS WAS HAVING DINNER AT MATTHEW'S HOUSE, MANY TAX COLLECTORS AND SINNERS CAME AND ATE WITH HIM AND HIS DISCIPLES.
WHEN THE PHARISEES SAW THIS, THEY ASKED HIS DISCIPLES,
Why does your teacher eat with tax collectors and sinners?
...
ON HEARING THIS, JESUS SAID,
It is not the healthy who need a doctor, but the sick.
But go and learn what this means: "I desire mercy, not sacrifice."*
For I have not come to call the righteous, but sinners.

*HOSEA 6:6

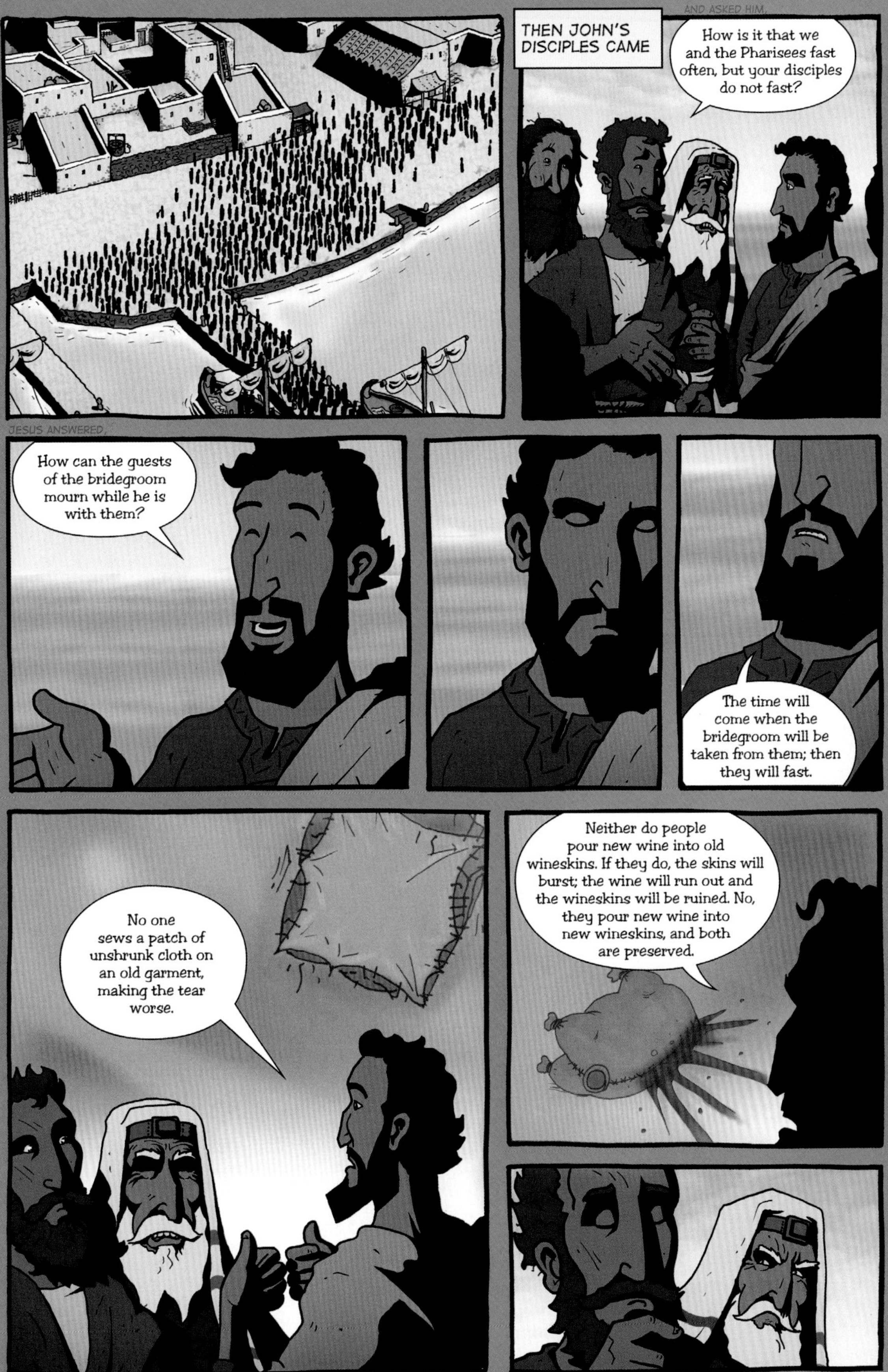
THEN JOHN'S DISCIPLES CAME
AND ASKED HIM,
How is it that we and the Pharisees fast often, but your disciples do not fast?
JESUS ANSWERED,
How can the guests of the bridegroom mourn while he is with them?
The time will come when the bridegroom will be taken from them; then they will fast.
No one sews a patch of unshrunk cloth on an old garment, making the tear worse.
Neither do people pour new wine into old wineskins. If they do, the skins will burst; the wine will run out and the wineskins will be ruined. No, they pour new wine into new wineskins, and both are preserved.

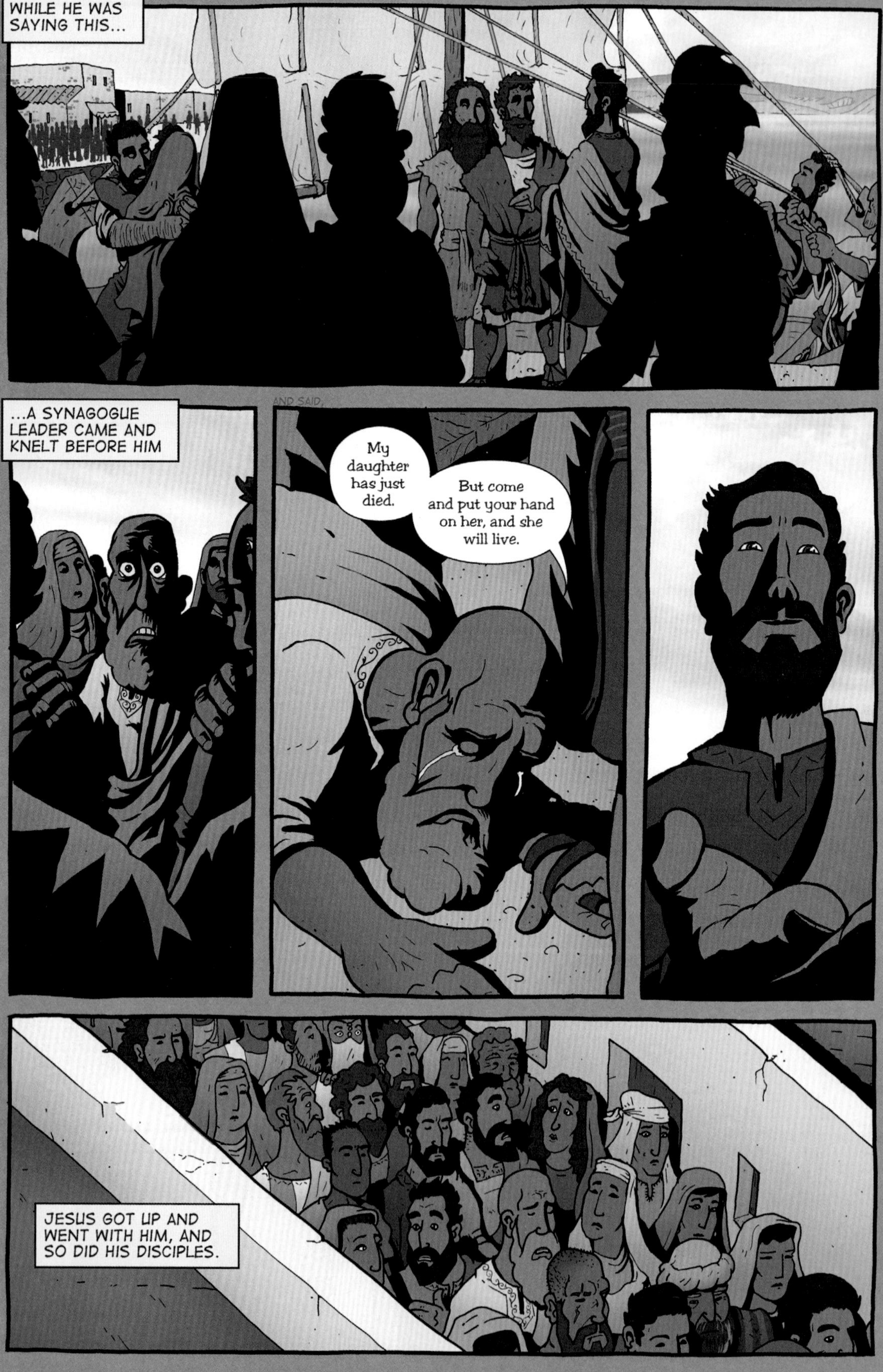
WHILE HE WAS SAYING THIS...
...A SYNAGOGUE LEADER CAME AND KNELT BEFORE HIM
AND SAID,
My daughter has just died.
But come and put your hand on her, and she will live.
JESUS GOT UP AND WENT WITH HIM, AND SO DID HIS DISCIPLES.

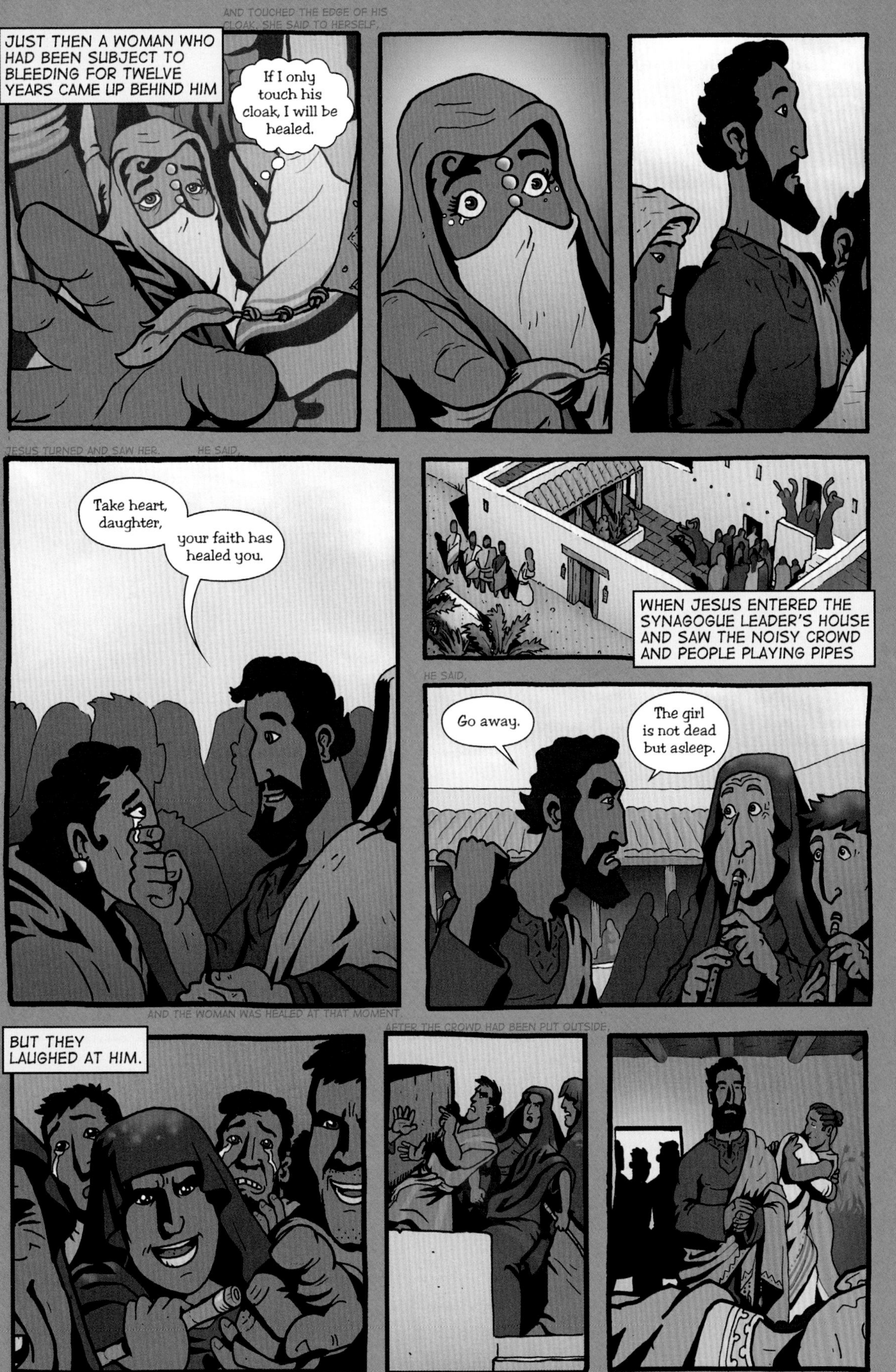
JUST THEN A WOMAN WHO HAD BEEN SUBJECT TO BLEEDING FOR TWELVE YEARS CAME UP BEHIND HIM
AND TOUCHED THE EDGE OF HIS CLOAK. SHE SAID TO HERSELF,
If I only touch his cloak, I will be healed.
JESUS TURNED AND SAW HER.
HE SAID,
Take heart, daughter,
your faith has healed you.
AND THE WOMAN WAS HEALED AT THAT MOMENT.
WHEN JESUS ENTERED THE SYNAGOGUE LEADER'S HOUSE AND SAW THE NOISY CROWD AND PEOPLE PLAYING PIPES
HE SAID,
Go away.
The girl is not dead but asleep.
BUT THEY LAUGHED AT HIM.
AFTER THE CROWD HAD BEEN PUT OUTSIDE,

MATTHEW 9:20-25A

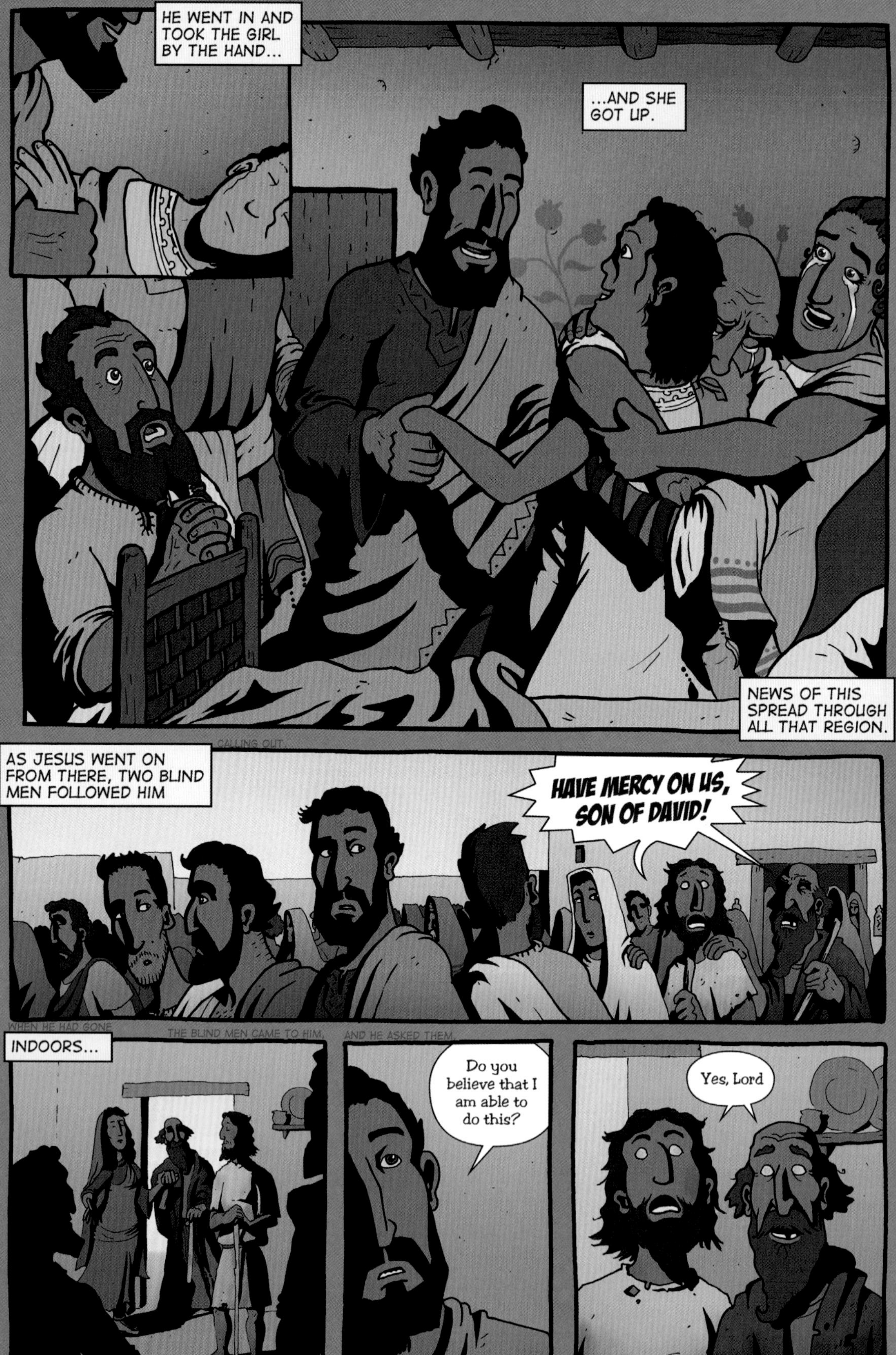
HE WENT IN AND TOOK THE GIRL BY THE HAND...
...AND SHE GOT UP.
NEWS OF THIS SPREAD THROUGH ALL THAT REGION.
CALLING OUT.
AS JESUS WENT ON FROM THERE, TWO BLIND MEN FOLLOWED HIM
HAVE MERCY ON US, SON OF DAVID!
WHEN HE HAD GONE
INDOORS...
THE BLIND MEN CAME TO HIM.
AND HE ASKED THEM.
Do you believe that I am able to do this?
Yes, Lord
THEY REPLIED.

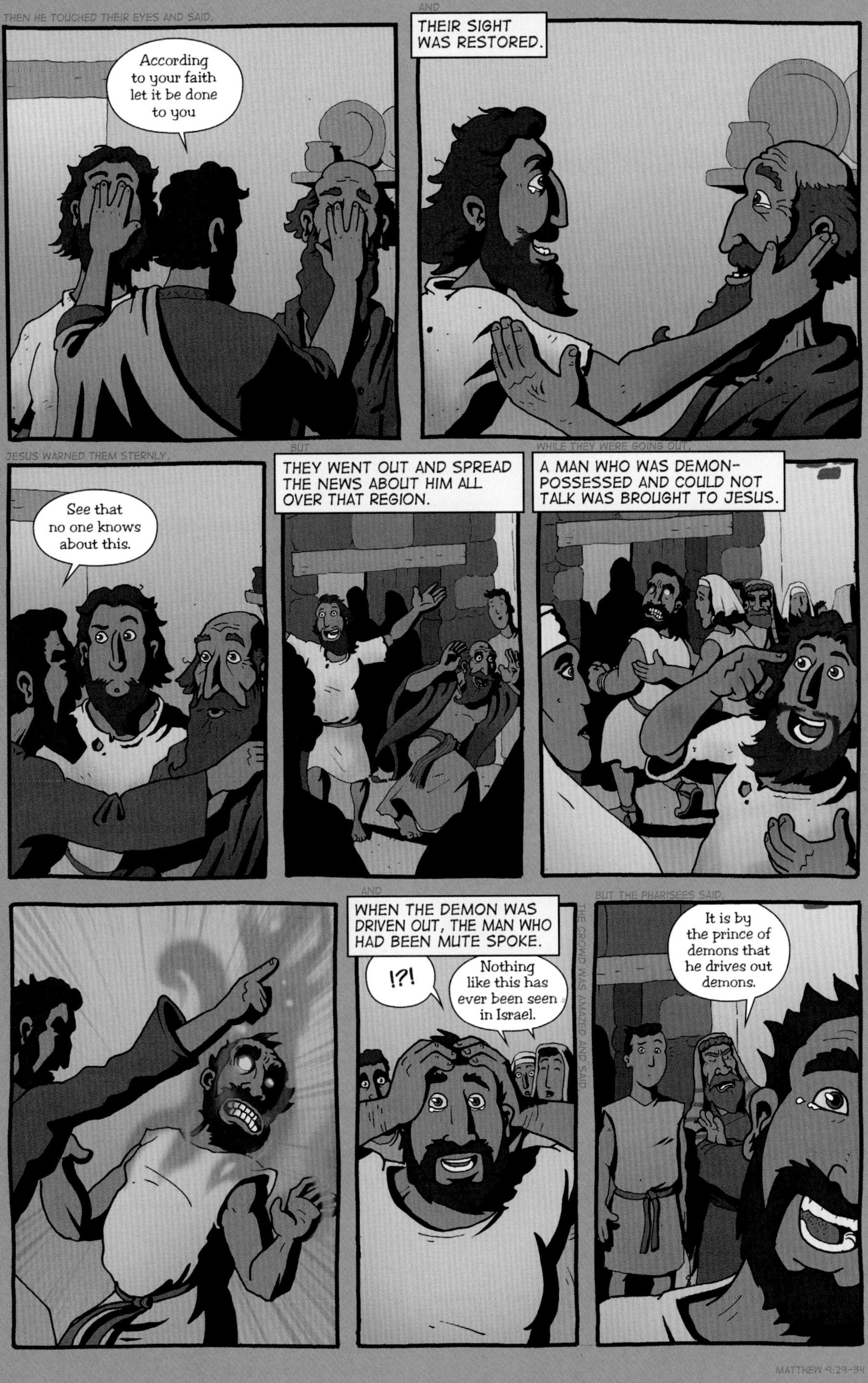
THEN HE TOUCHED THEIR EYES AND SAID,
According to your faith let it be done to you
AND
THEIR SIGHT WAS RESTORED.
JESUS WARNED THEM STERNLY,
See that no one knows about this.
BUT
THEY WENT OUT AND SPREAD THE NEWS ABOUT HIM ALL OVER THAT REGION.
WHILE THEY WERE GOING OUT,
A MAN WHO WAS DEMON-POSSESSED AND COULD NOT TALK WAS BROUGHT TO JESUS.
AND
WHEN THE DEMON WAS DRIVEN OUT, THE MAN WHO HAD BEEN MUTE SPOKE.
THE CROWD WAS AMAZED AND SAID,
!?!
Nothing like this has ever been seen in Israel.
BUT THE PHARISEES SAID,
It is by the prince of demons that he drives out demons.

MATTHEW 9:29-34

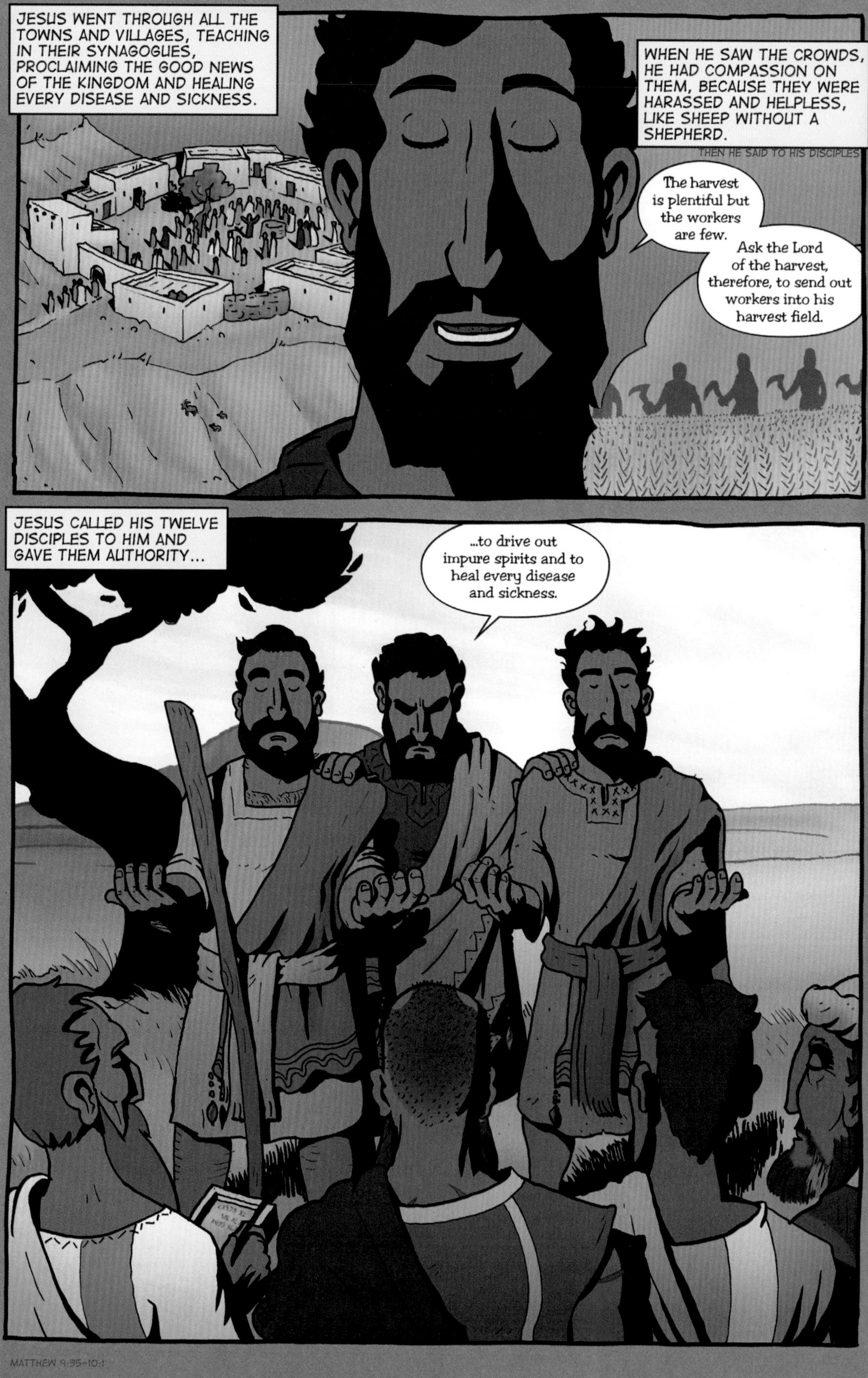
JESUS WENT THROUGH ALL THE TOWNS AND VILLAGES, TEACHING IN THEIR SYNAGOGUES, PROCLAIMING THE GOOD NEWS OF THE KINGDOM AND HEALING EVERY DISEASE AND SICKNESS.
WHEN HE SAW THE CROWDS, HE HAD COMPASSION ON THEM, BECAUSE THEY WERE HARASSED AND HELPLESS, LIKE SHEEP WITHOUT A SHEPHERD.
THEN HE SAID TO HIS DISCIPLES
The harvest is plentiful but the workers are few.
Ask the Lord of the harvest, therefore, to send out workers into his harvest field.
JESUS CALLED HIS TWELVE DISCIPLES TO HIM AND GAVE THEM AUTHORITY...
...to drive out impure spirits and to heal every disease and sickness.

THESE ARE THE NAMES OF THE TWELVE APOSTLES:

FIRST, SIMON (WHO IS CALLED PETER) AND HIS BROTHER ANDREW

JAMES SON OF ZEBEDEE, AND HIS BROTHER JOHN;

PHILIP AND BARTHOLOMEW;

THOMAS...

...AND MATTHEW THE TAX COLLECTOR;

JAMES SON OF ALPHAEUS, AND THADDAEUS;

SIMON THE ZEALOT AND JUDAS ISCARIOT

WHO BETRAYED HIM.

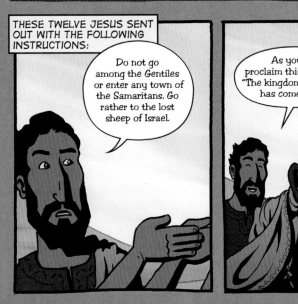

THESE TWELVE JESUS SENT OUT WITH THE FOLLOWING INSTRUCTIONS:

Do not go among the Gentiles or enter any town of the Samaritans. Go rather to the lost sheep of Israel.

As you go, proclaim this message: "The kingdom of heaven has come near."

Heal the sick, raise the dead, cleanse those who have leprosy, drive out demons.

Freely you have received; freely give.

MATTHEW 10:2-8

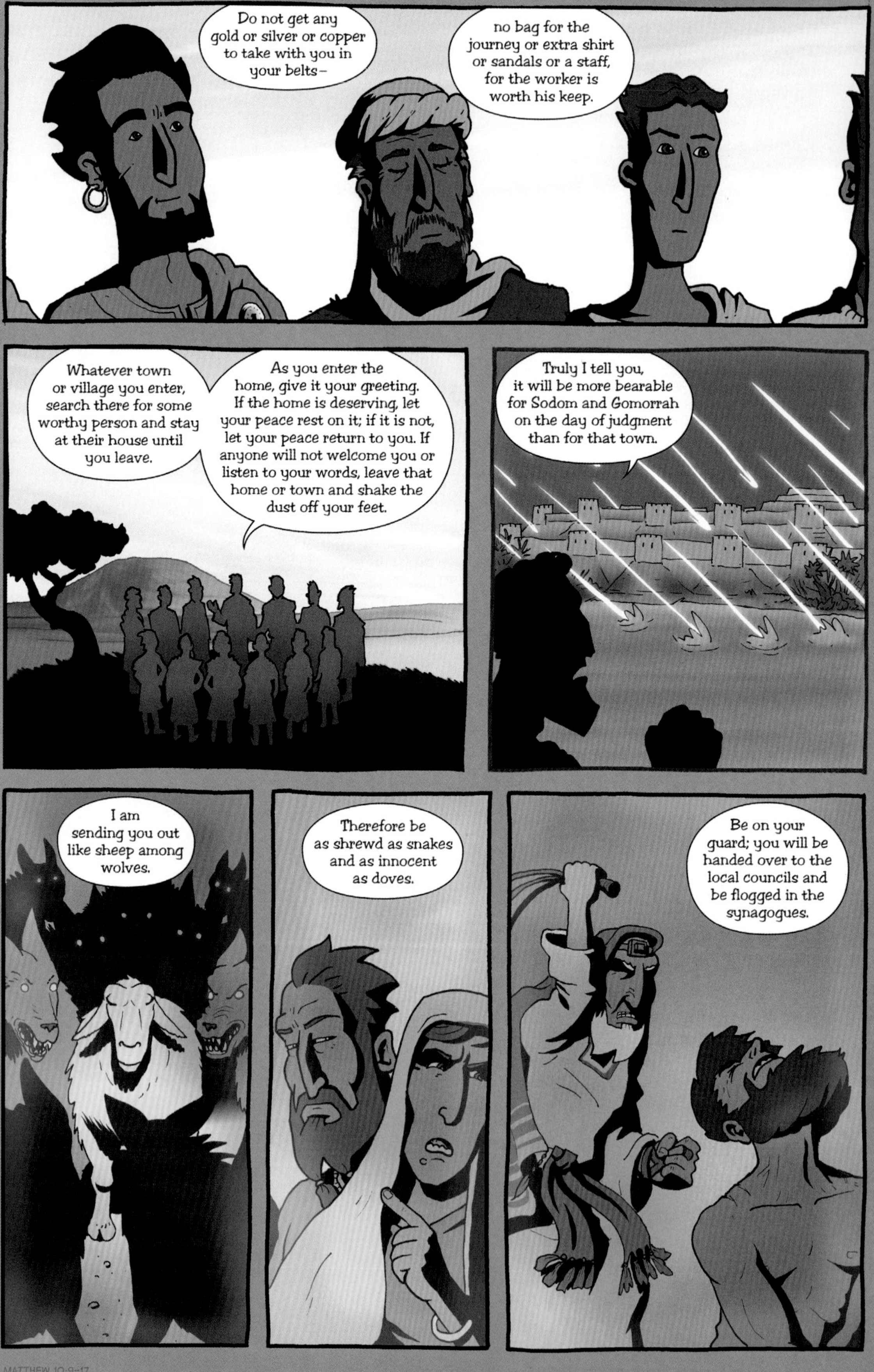

Do not get any gold or silver or copper to take with you in your belts–
no bag for the journey or extra shirt or sandals or a staff, for the worker is worth his keep.
Whatever town or village you enter, search there for some worthy person and stay at their house until you leave.
As you enter the home, give it your greeting. If the home is deserving, let your peace rest on it; if it is not, let your peace return to you. If anyone will not welcome you or listen to your words, leave that home or town and shake the dust off your feet.
Truly I tell you, it will be more bearable for Sodom and Gomorrah on the day of judgment than for that town.
I am sending you out like sheep among wolves.
Therefore be as shrewd as snakes and as innocent as doves.
Be on your guard; you will be handed over to the local councils and be flogged in the synagogues.

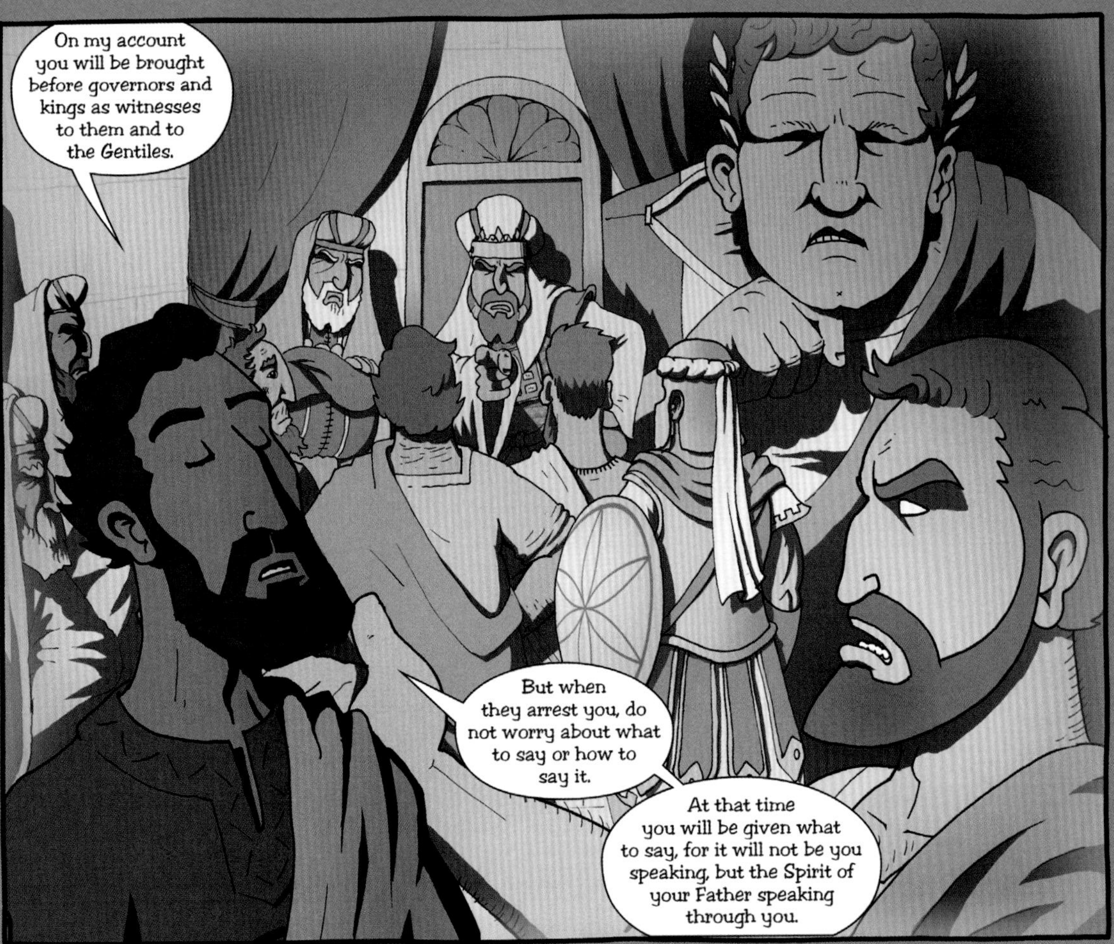
On my account you will be brought before governors and kings as witnesses to them and to the Gentiles.
But when they arrest you, do not worry about what to say or how to say it.
At that time you will be given what to say, for it will not be you speaking, but the Spirit of your Father speaking through you.

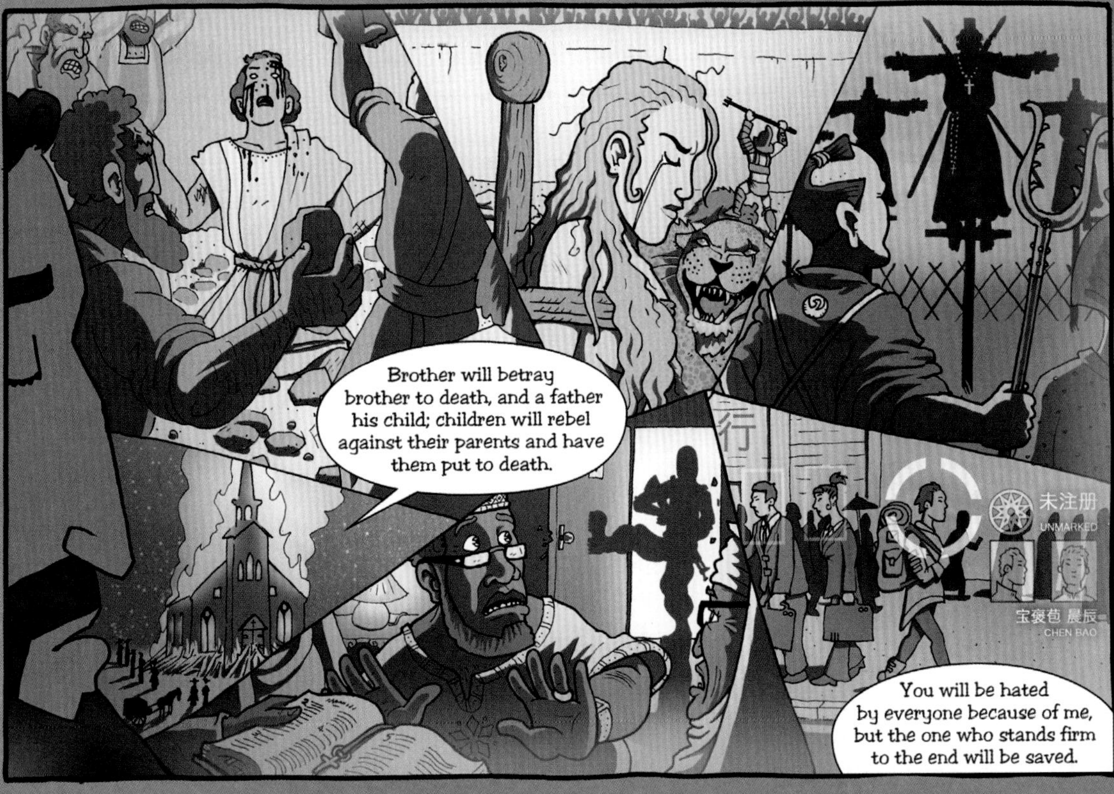
Brother will betray brother to death, and a father his child; children will rebel against their parents and have them put to death.
未注册
UNMARKED
CHEN BAO
You will be hated by everyone because of me, but the one who stands firm to the end will be saved.

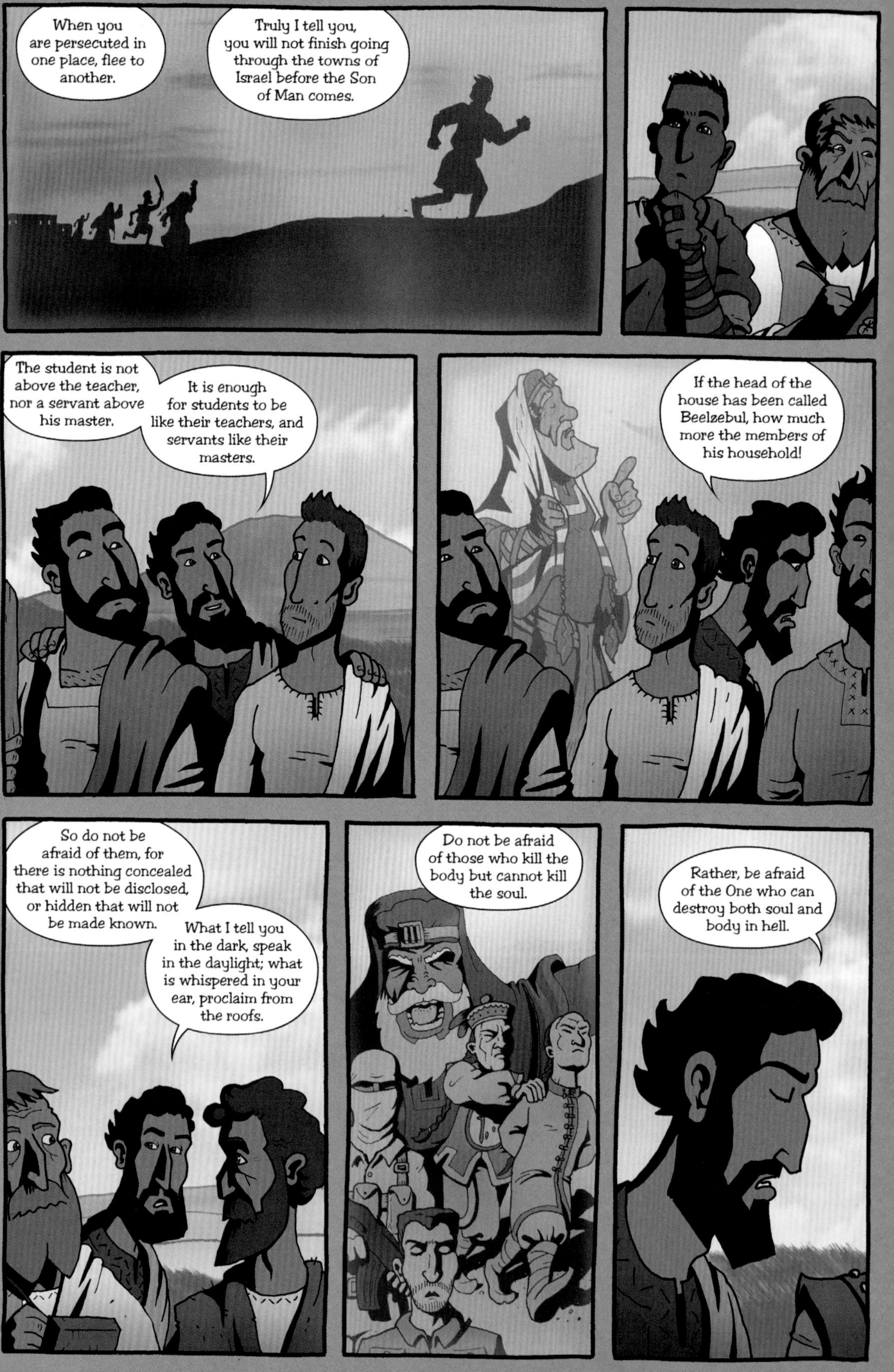
When you are persecuted in one place, flee to another.
Truly I tell you, you will not finish going through the towns of Israel before the Son of Man comes.
The student is not above the teacher, nor a servant above his master.
It is enough for students to be like their teachers, and servants like their masters.
If the head of the house has been called Beelzebul, how much more the members of his household!
So do not be afraid of them, for there is nothing concealed that will not be disclosed, or hidden that will not be made known.
What I tell you in the dark, speak in the daylight; what is whispered in your ear, proclaim from the roofs.
Do not be afraid of those who kill the body but cannot kill the soul.
Rather, be afraid of the One who can destroy both soul and body in hell.

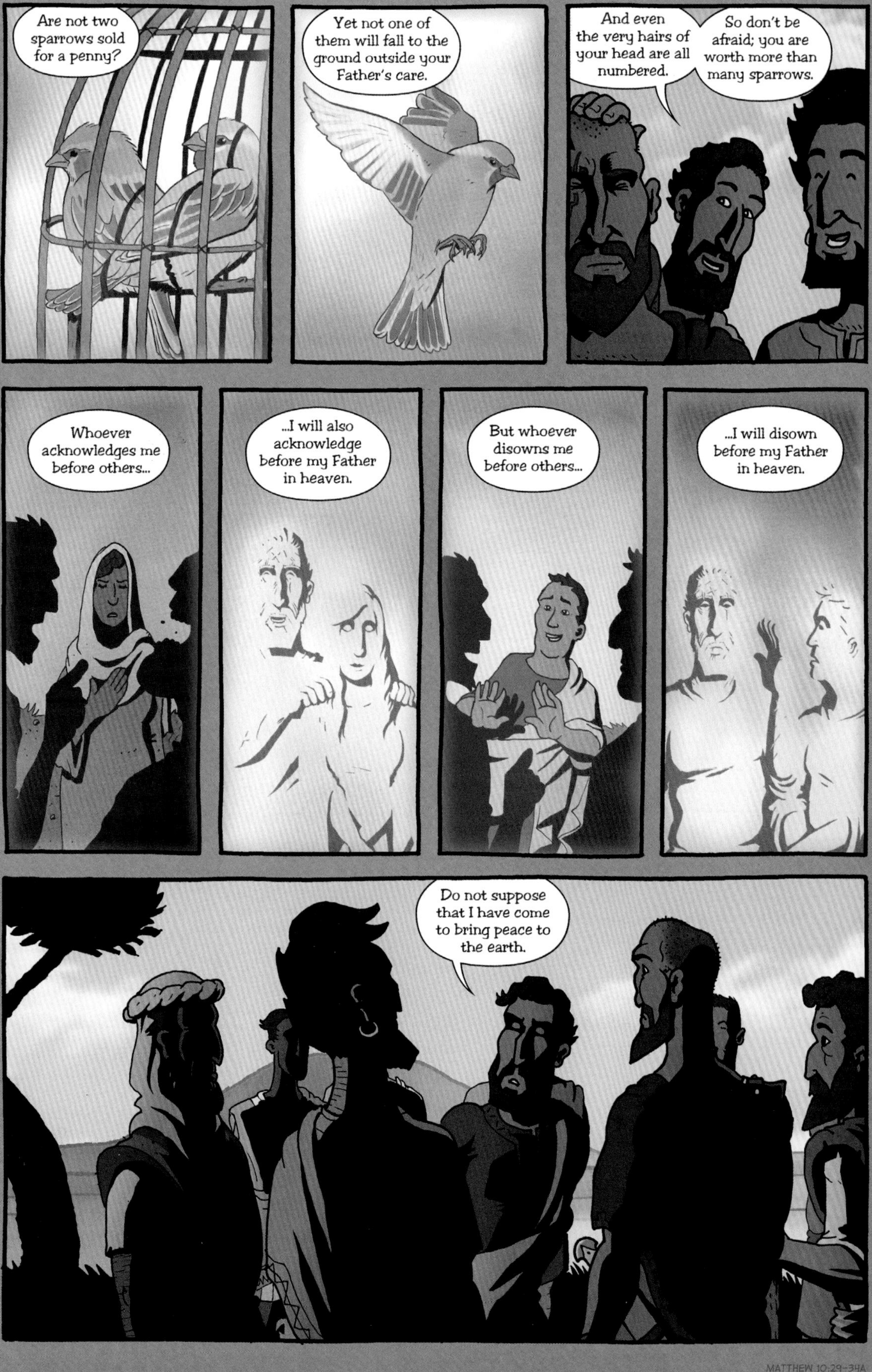
Are not two sparrows sold for a penny?
Yet not one of them will fall to the ground outside your Father's care.
And even the very hairs of your head are all numbered.
So don't be afraid; you are worth more than many sparrows.
Whoever acknowledges me before others...
...I will also acknowledge before my Father in heaven.
But whoever disowns me before others...
...I will disown before my Father in heaven.
Do not suppose that I have come to bring peace to the earth.

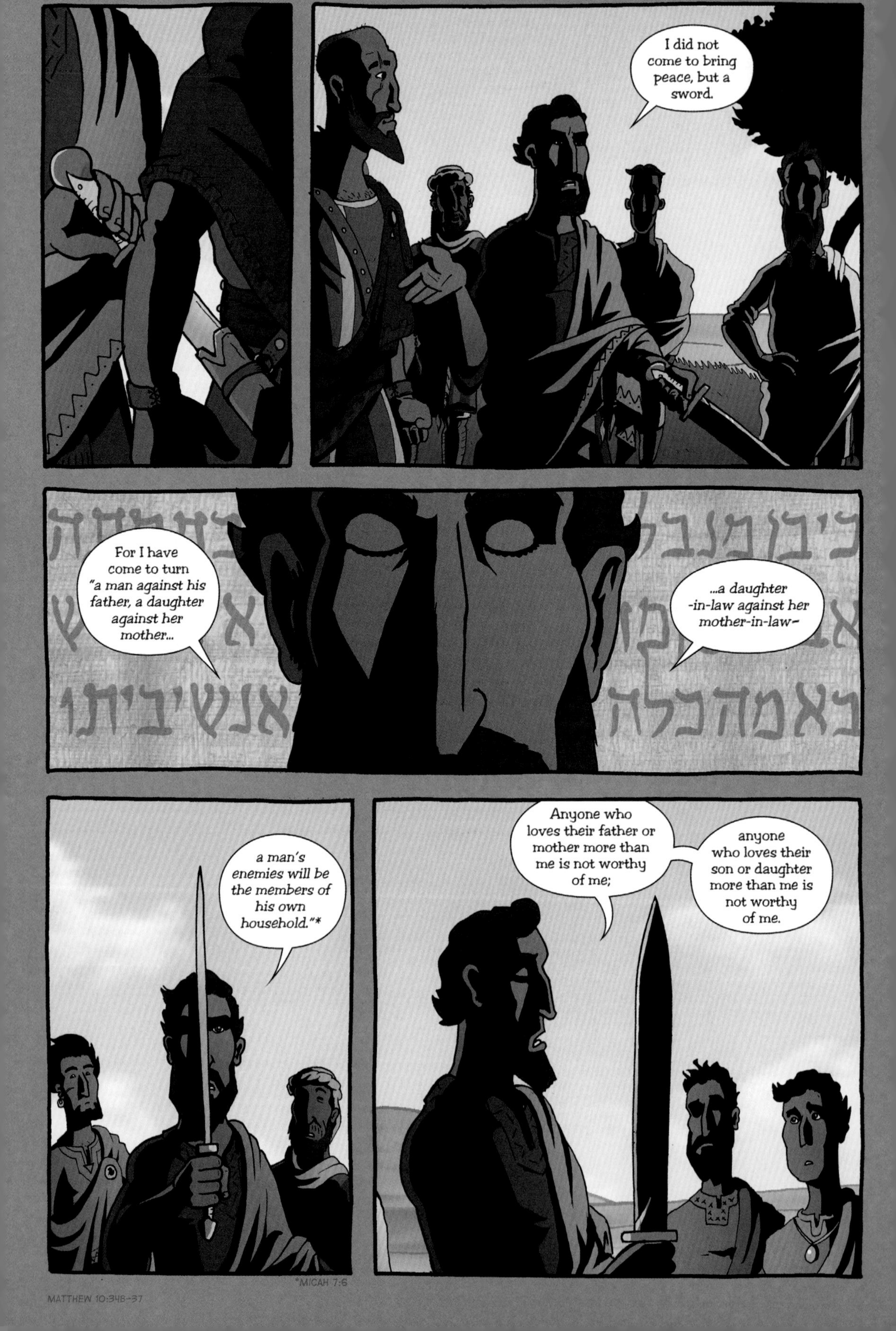
I did not come to bring peace, but a sword.
For I have come to turn "a man against his father, a daughter against her mother...
...a daughter -in-law against her mother-in-law–
a man's enemies will be the members of his own household."*
Anyone who loves their father or mother more than me is not worthy of me;
anyone who loves their son or daughter more than me is not worthy of me.

*MICAH 7:6

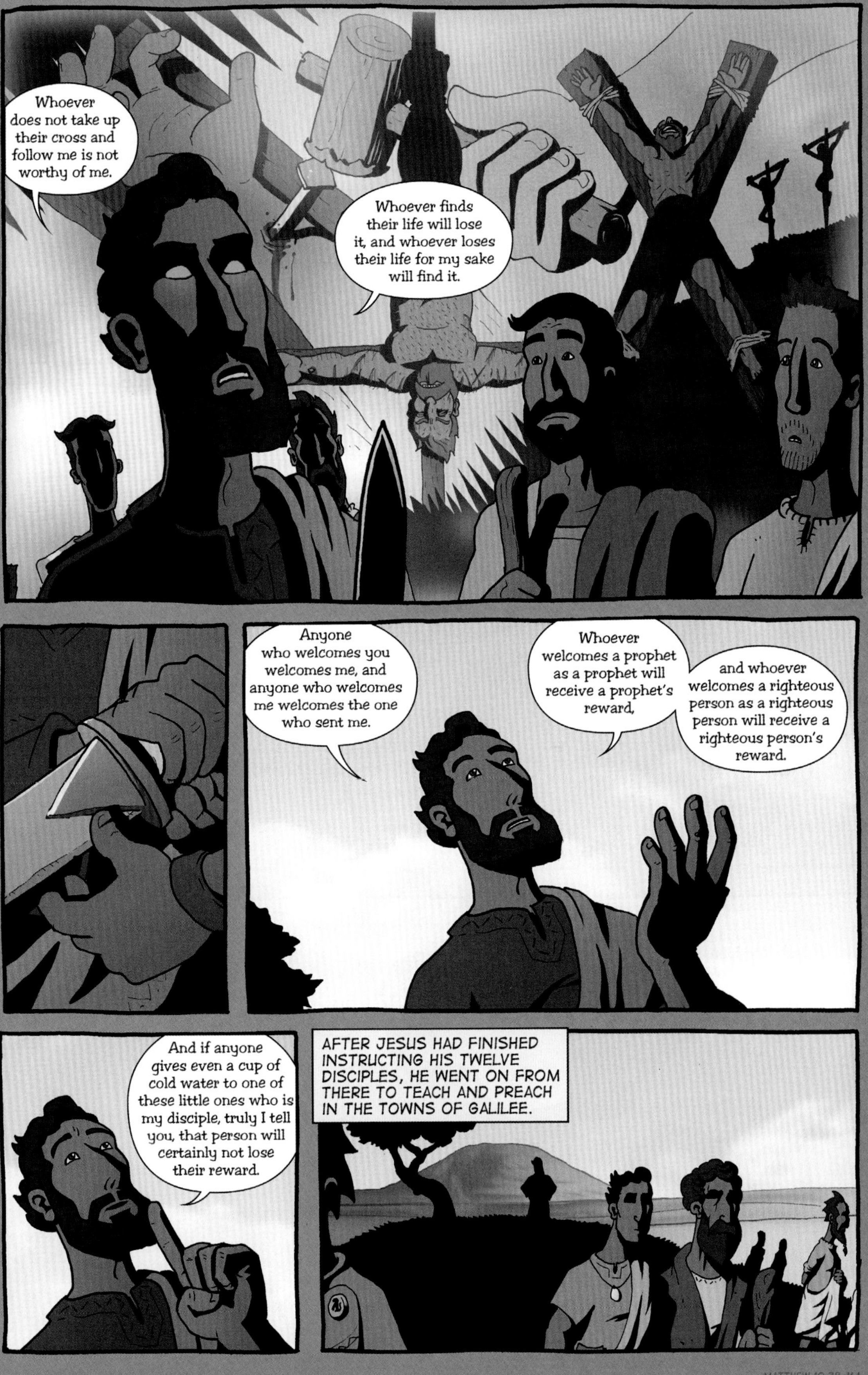
Whoever does not take up their cross and follow me is not worthy of me.
Whoever finds their life will lose it, and whoever loses their life for my sake will find it.
Anyone who welcomes you welcomes me, and anyone who welcomes me welcomes the one who sent me.
Whoever welcomes a prophet as a prophet will receive a prophet's reward,
and whoever welcomes a righteous person as a righteous person will receive a righteous person's reward.
And if anyone gives even a cup of cold water to one of these little ones who is my disciple, truly I tell you, that person will certainly not lose their reward.
AFTER JESUS HAD FINISHED INSTRUCTING HIS TWELVE DISCIPLES, HE WENT ON FROM THERE TO TEACH AND PREACH IN THE TOWNS OF GALILEE.

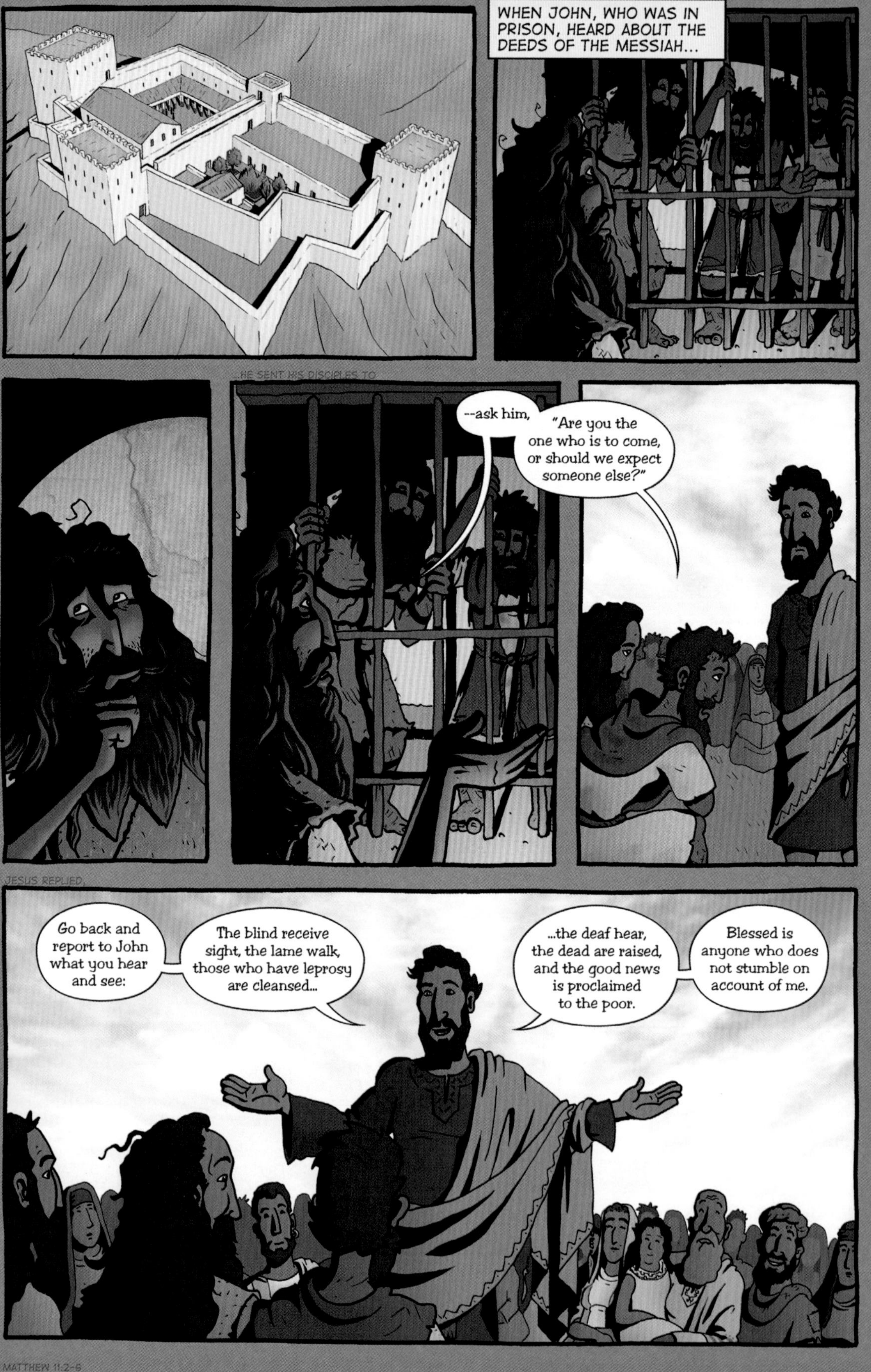
WHEN JOHN, WHO WAS IN PRISON, HEARD ABOUT THE DEEDS OF THE MESSIAH...
...HE SENT HIS DISCIPLES TO
--ask him,
"Are you the one who is to come, or should we expect someone else?"
JESUS REPLIED,
Go back and report to John what you hear and see:
The blind receive sight, the lame walk, those who have leprosy are cleansed...
...the deaf hear, the dead are raised, and the good news is proclaimed to the poor.
Blessed is anyone who does not stumble on account of me.

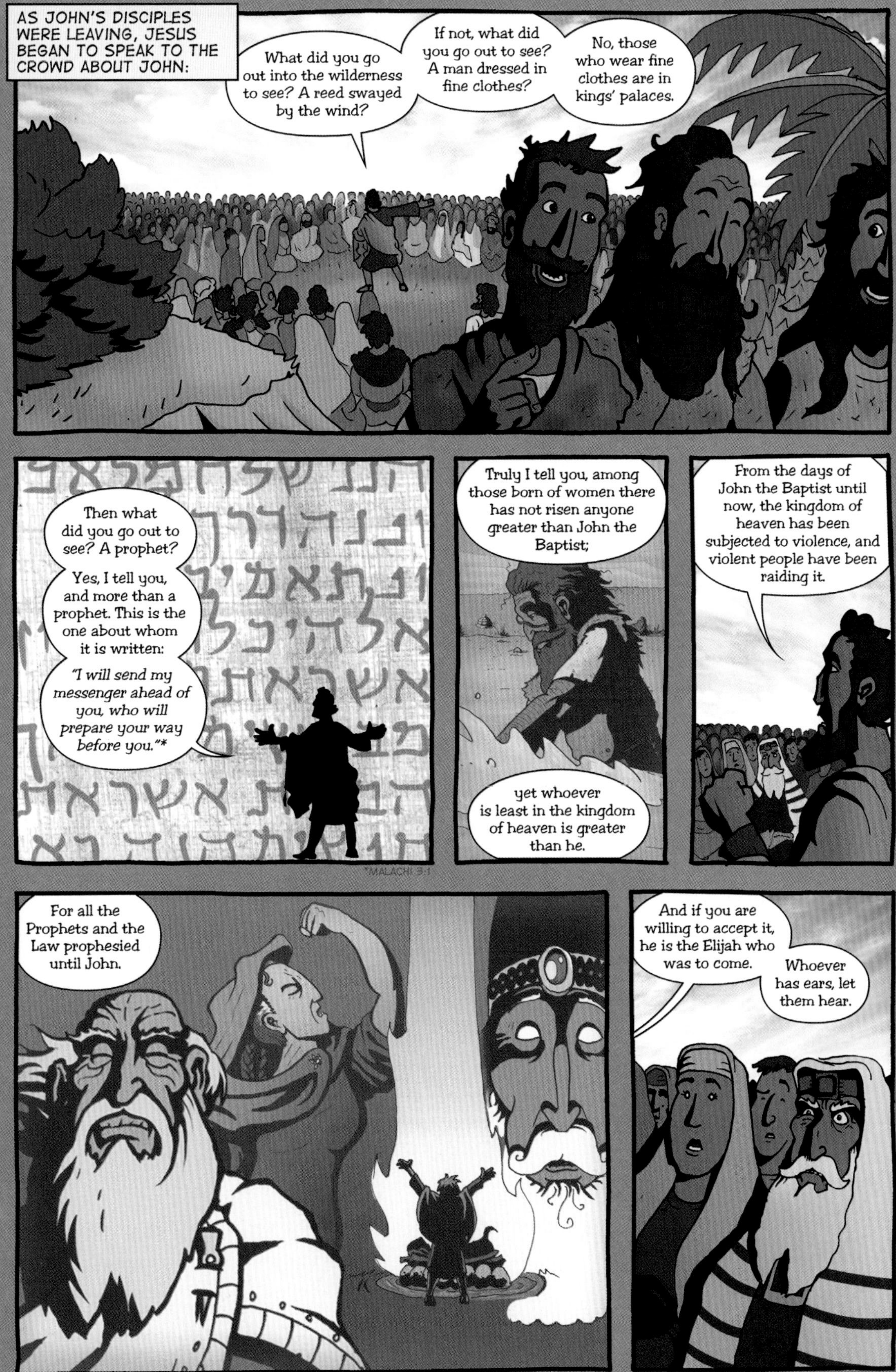
AS JOHN'S DISCIPLES WERE LEAVING, JESUS BEGAN TO SPEAK TO THE CROWD ABOUT JOHN:
What did you go out into the wilderness to see? A reed swayed by the wind?
If not, what did you go out to see? A man dressed in fine clothes?
No, those who wear fine clothes are in kings' palaces.
Then what did you go out to see? A prophet?
Yes, I tell you, and more than a prophet. This is the one about whom it is written:
"I will send my messenger ahead of you, who will prepare your way before you."*
Truly I tell you, among those born of women there has not risen anyone greater than John the Baptist;
yet whoever is least in the kingdom of heaven is greater than he.
From the days of John the Baptist until now, the kingdom of heaven has been subjected to violence, and violent people have been raiding it.
*MALACHI 3:1
For all the Prophets and the Law prophesied until John.
And if you are willing to accept it, he is the Elijah who was to come.
Whoever has ears, let them hear.

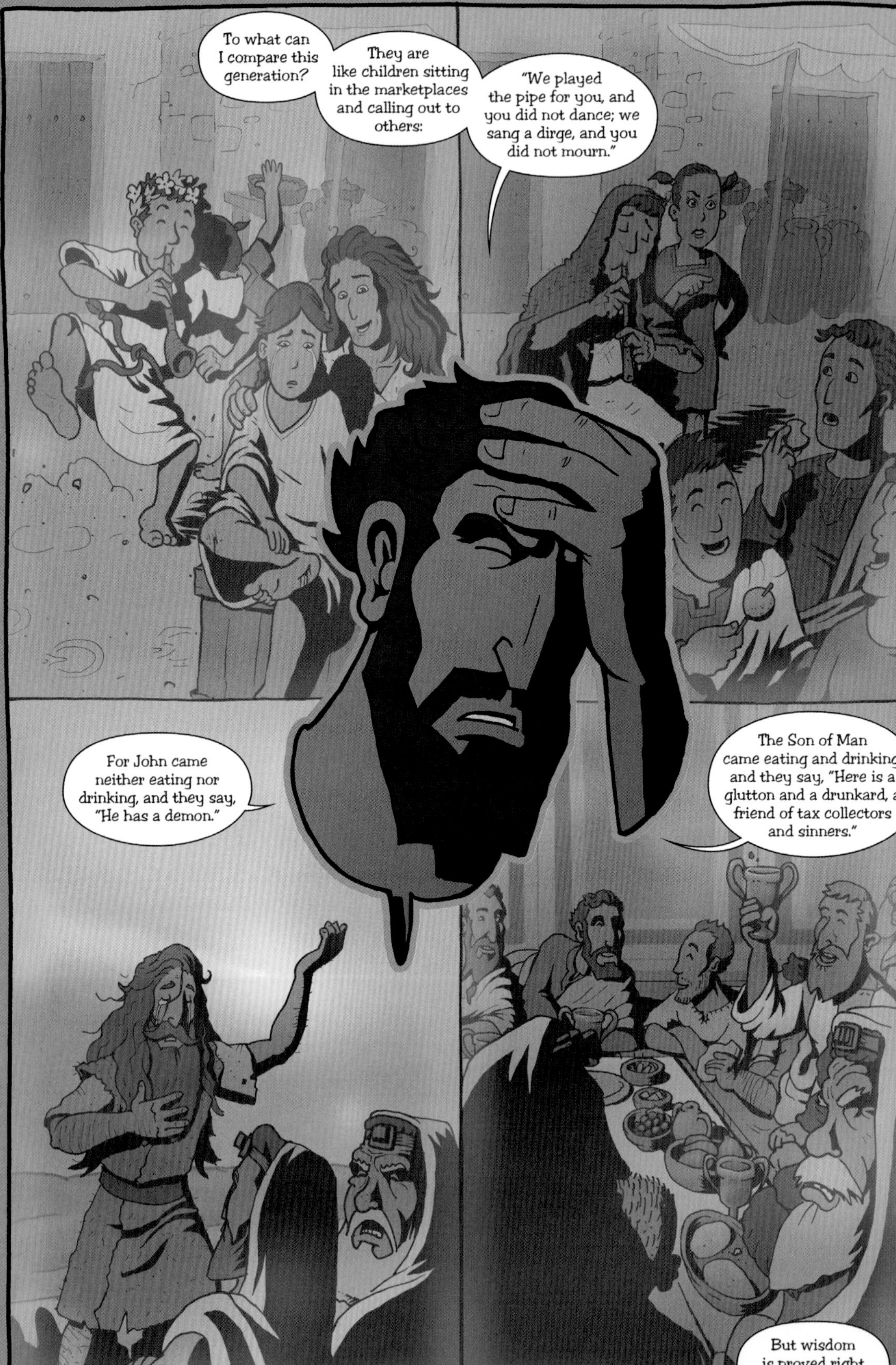
To what can I compare this generation?
They are like children sitting in the marketplaces and calling out to others:
"We played the pipe for you, and you did not dance; we sang a dirge, and you did not mourn."
For John came neither eating nor drinking, and they say, "He has a demon."
The Son of Man came eating and drinking, and they say, "Here is a glutton and a drunkard, a friend of tax collectors and sinners."
But wisdom is proved right by her deeds.

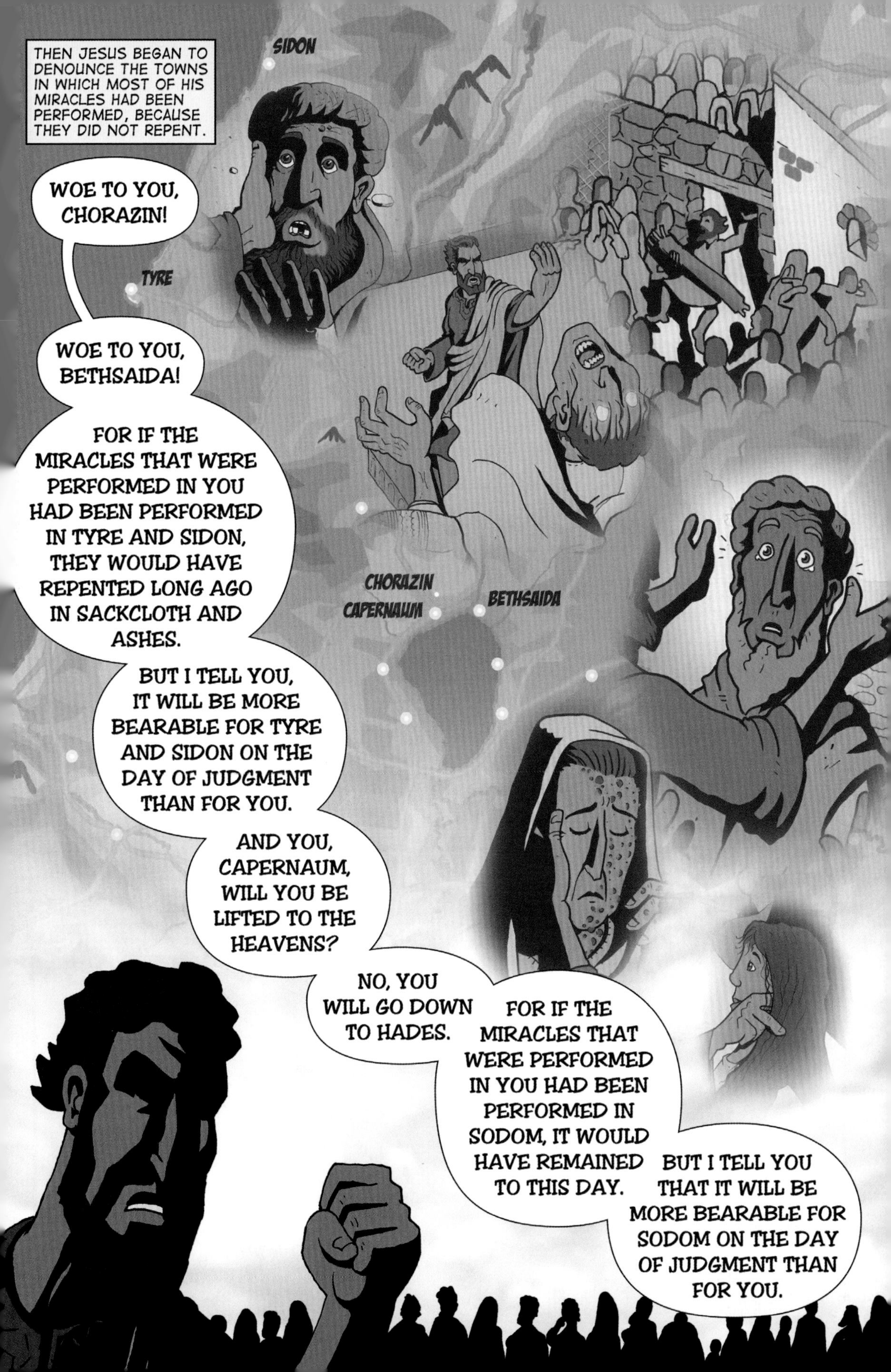
THEN JESUS BEGAN TO DENOUNCE THE TOWNS IN WHICH MOST OF HIS MIRACLES HAD BEEN PERFORMED, BECAUSE THEY DID NOT REPENT.
SIDON
TYRE
WOE TO YOU, CHORAZIN!
WOE TO YOU, BETHSAIDA!
FOR IF THE MIRACLES THAT WERE PERFORMED IN YOU HAD BEEN PERFORMED IN TYRE AND SIDON, THEY WOULD HAVE REPENTED LONG AGO IN SACKCLOTH AND ASHES.
CHORAZIN
CAPERNAUM
BETHSAIDA
BUT I TELL YOU, IT WILL BE MORE BEARABLE FOR TYRE AND SIDON ON THE DAY OF JUDGMENT THAN FOR YOU.
AND YOU, CAPERNAUM, WILL YOU BE LIFTED TO THE HEAVENS?
NO, YOU WILL GO DOWN TO HADES.
FOR IF THE MIRACLES THAT WERE PERFORMED IN YOU HAD BEEN PERFORMED IN SODOM, IT WOULD HAVE REMAINED TO THIS DAY.
BUT I TELL YOU THAT IT WILL BE MORE BEARABLE FOR SODOM ON THE DAY OF JUDGMENT THAN FOR YOU.

AT THAT TIME JESUS SAID,

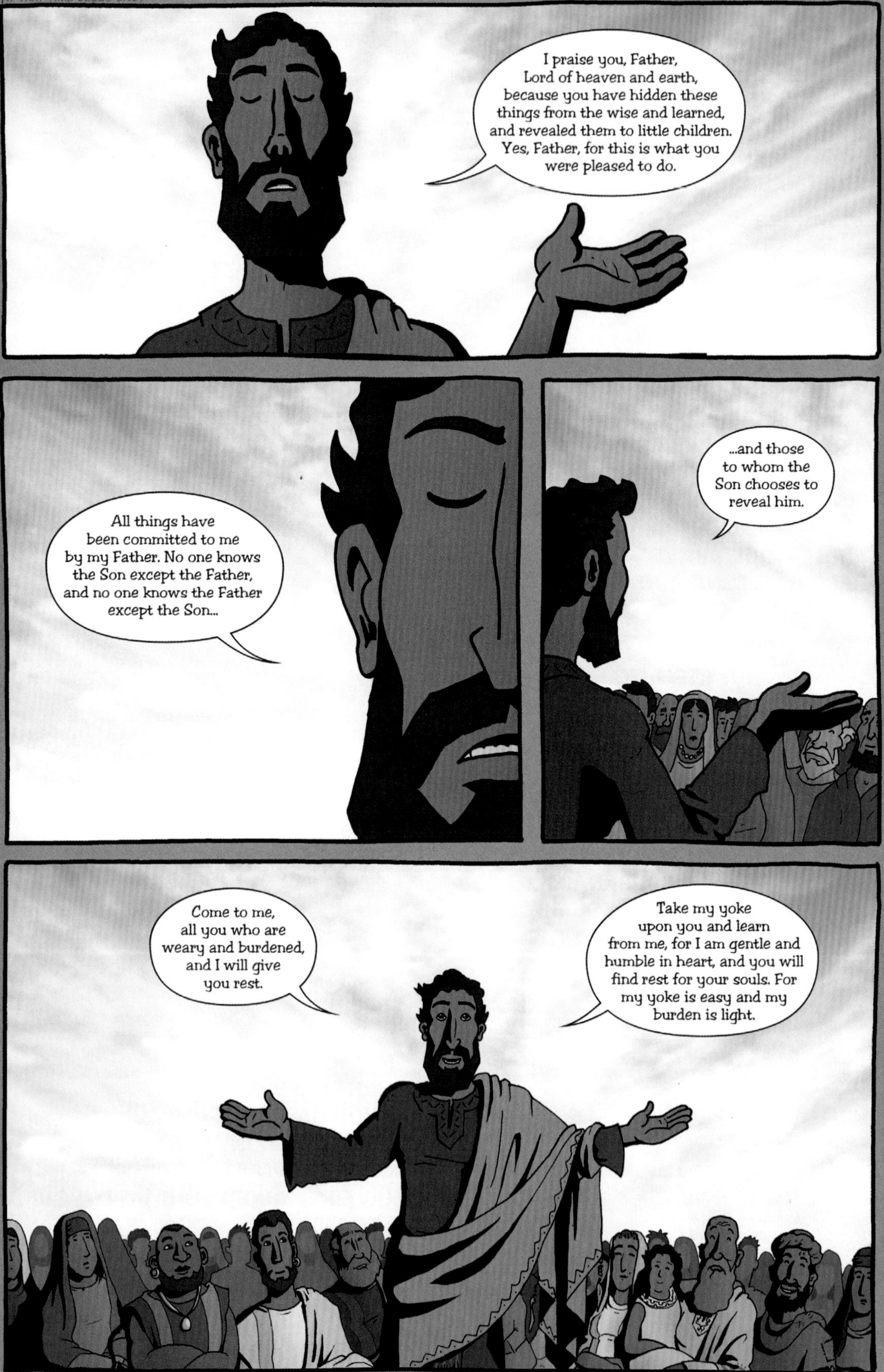
I praise you, Father, Lord of heaven and earth, because you have hidden these things from the wise and learned, and revealed them to little children. Yes, Father, for this is what you were pleased to do.
All things have been committed to me by my Father. No one knows the Son except the Father, and no one knows the Father except the Son...
...and those to whom the Son chooses to reveal him.
Come to me, all you who are weary and burdened, and I will give you rest.
Take my yoke upon you and learn from me, for I am gentle and humble in heart, and you will find rest for your souls. For my yoke is easy and my burden is light.

MATTHEW 11:25–30

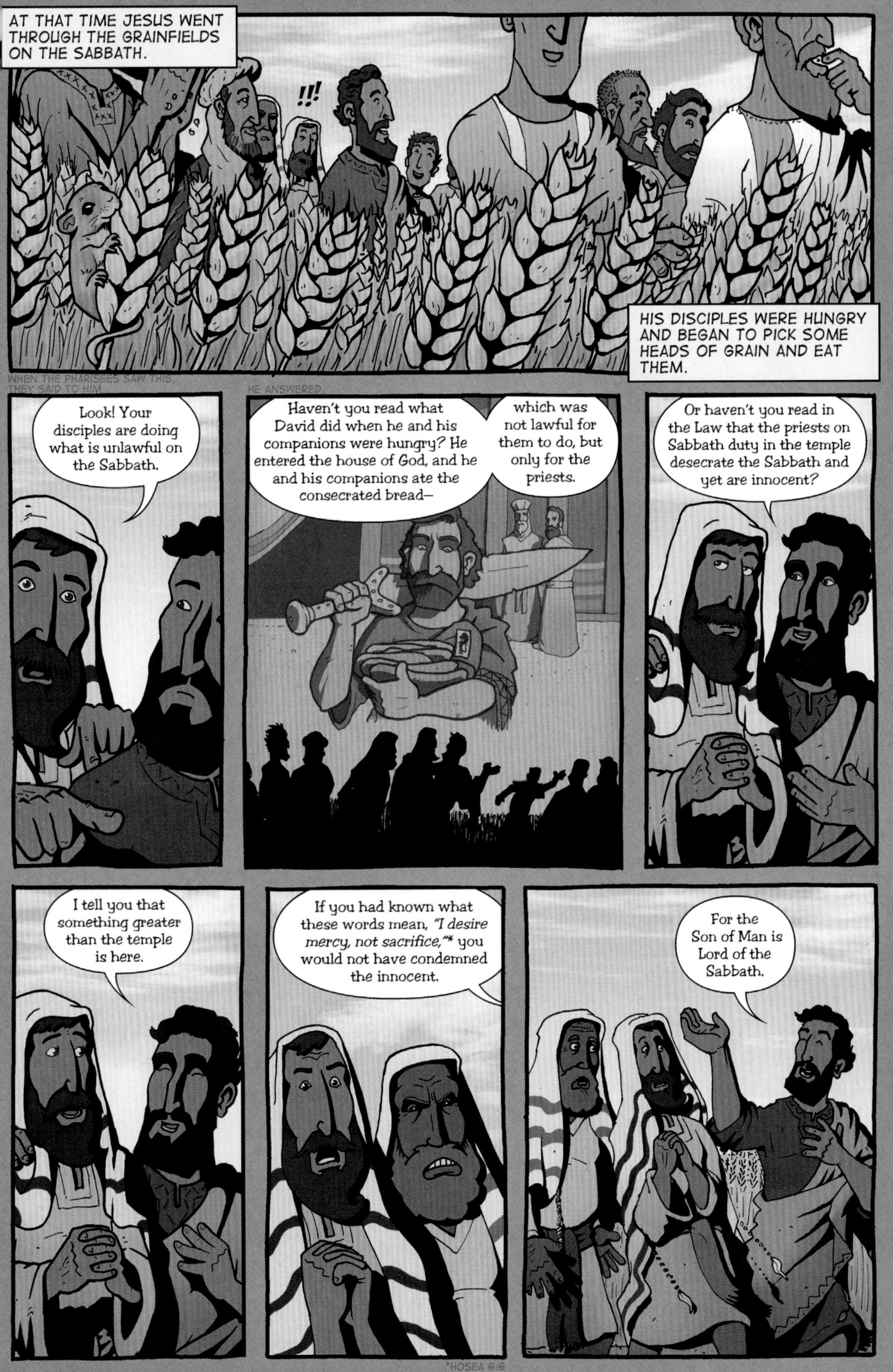
AT THAT TIME JESUS WENT THROUGH THE GRAINFIELDS ON THE SABBATH.
!!!
HIS DISCIPLES WERE HUNGRY AND BEGAN TO PICK SOME HEADS OF GRAIN AND EAT THEM.
WHEN THE PHARISEES SAW THIS, THEY SAID TO HIM
Look! Your disciples are doing what is unlawful on the Sabbath.
HE ANSWERED,
Haven't you read what David did when he and his companions were hungry? He entered the house of God, and he and his companions ate the consecrated bread–
which was not lawful for them to do, but only for the priests.
Or haven't you read in the Law that the priests on Sabbath duty in the temple desecrate the Sabbath and yet are innocent?
I tell you that something greater than the temple is here.
If you had known what these words mean, *"I desire mercy, not sacrifice,"** you would not have condemned the innocent.
For the Son of Man is Lord of the Sabbath.

*HOSEA 6:6

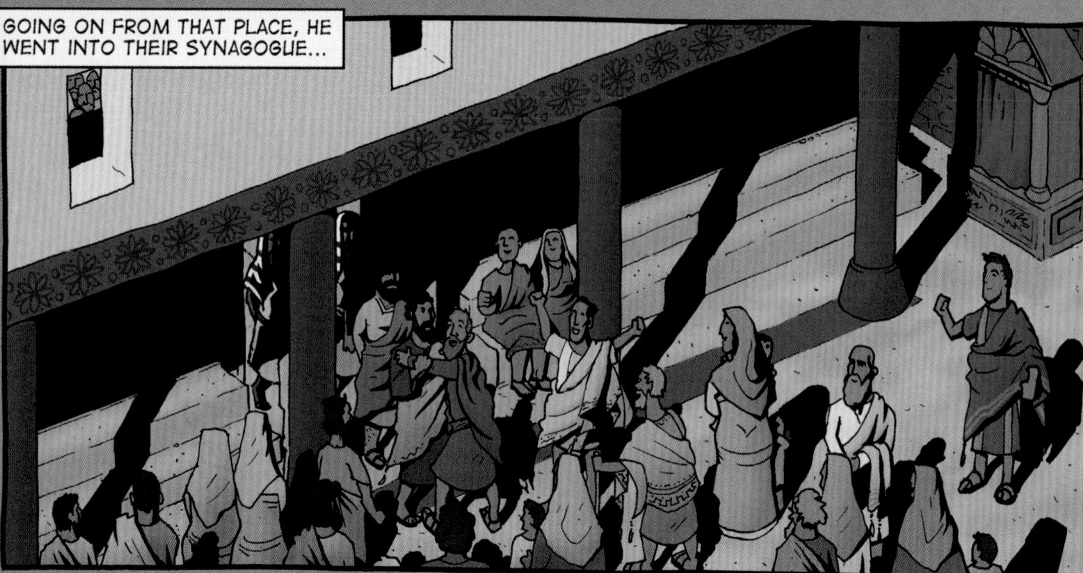
GOING ON FROM THAT PLACE, HE WENT INTO THEIR SYNAGOGUE...

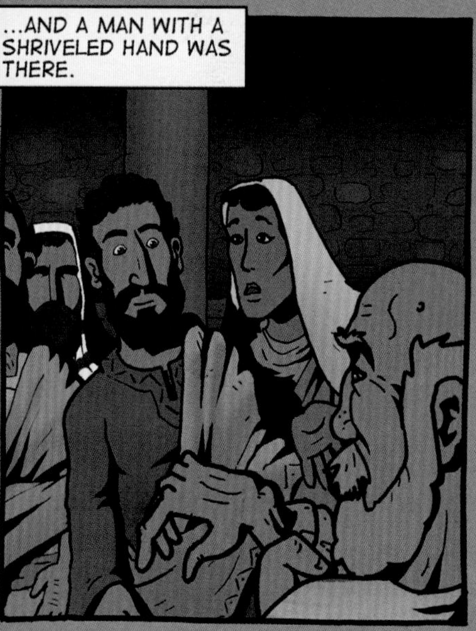
...AND A MAN WITH A SHRIVELED HAND WAS THERE.

LOOKING FOR A REASON TO BRING CHARGES AGAINST JESUS, THEY ASKED HIM,

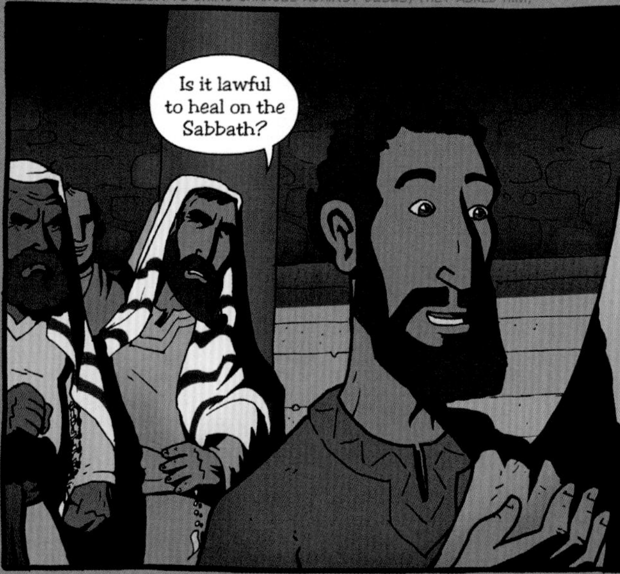
Is it lawful to heal on the Sabbath?

HE SAID TO THEM,

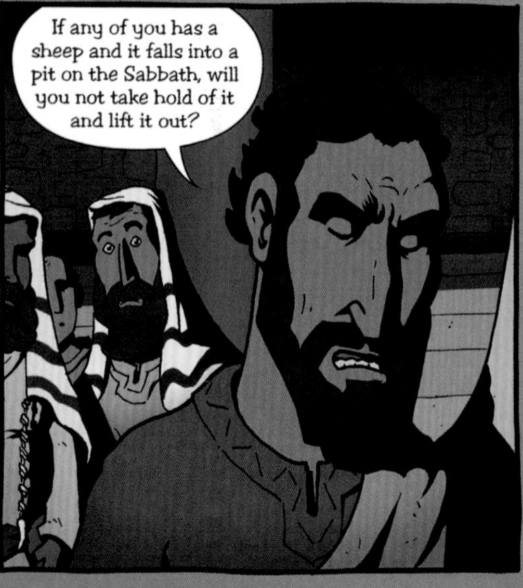
If any of you has a sheep and it falls into a pit on the Sabbath, will you not take hold of it and lift it out?

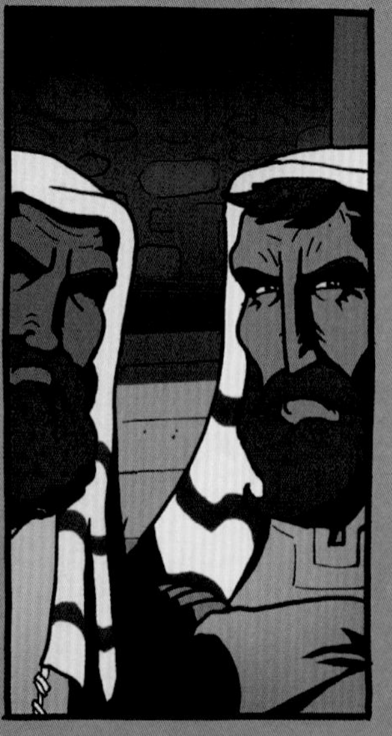

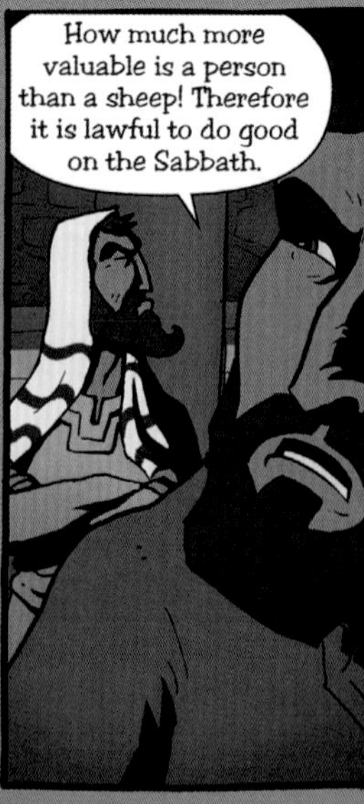
How much more valuable is a person than a sheep! Therefore it is lawful to do good on the Sabbath.

THEN HE SAID TO THE MAN,

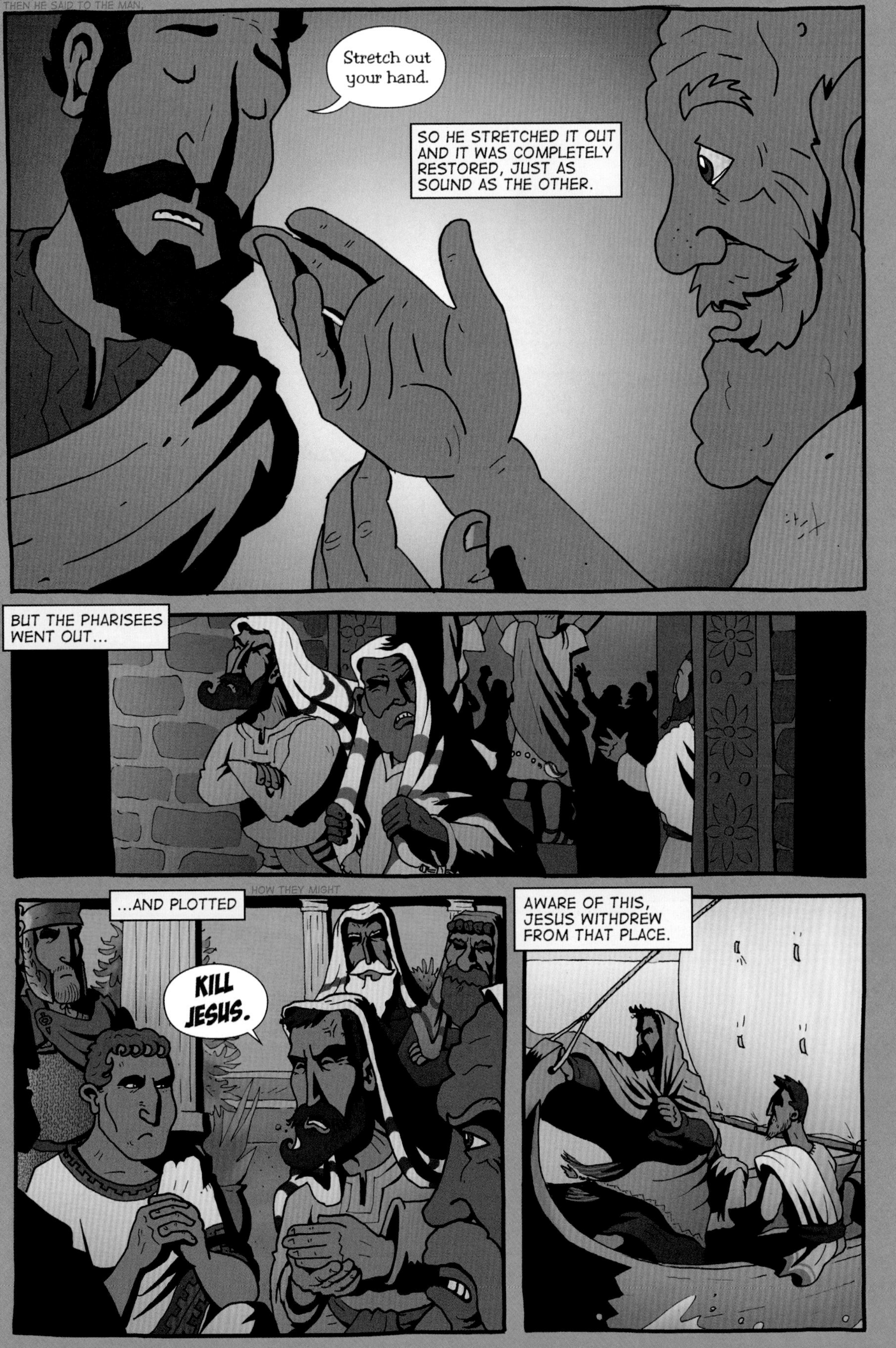

Stretch out your hand.
SO HE STRETCHED IT OUT AND IT WAS COMPLETELY RESTORED, JUST AS SOUND AS THE OTHER.
BUT THE PHARISEES WENT OUT...
...AND PLOTTED
HOW THEY MIGHT
KILL JESUS.
AWARE OF THIS, JESUS WITHDREW FROM THAT PLACE.

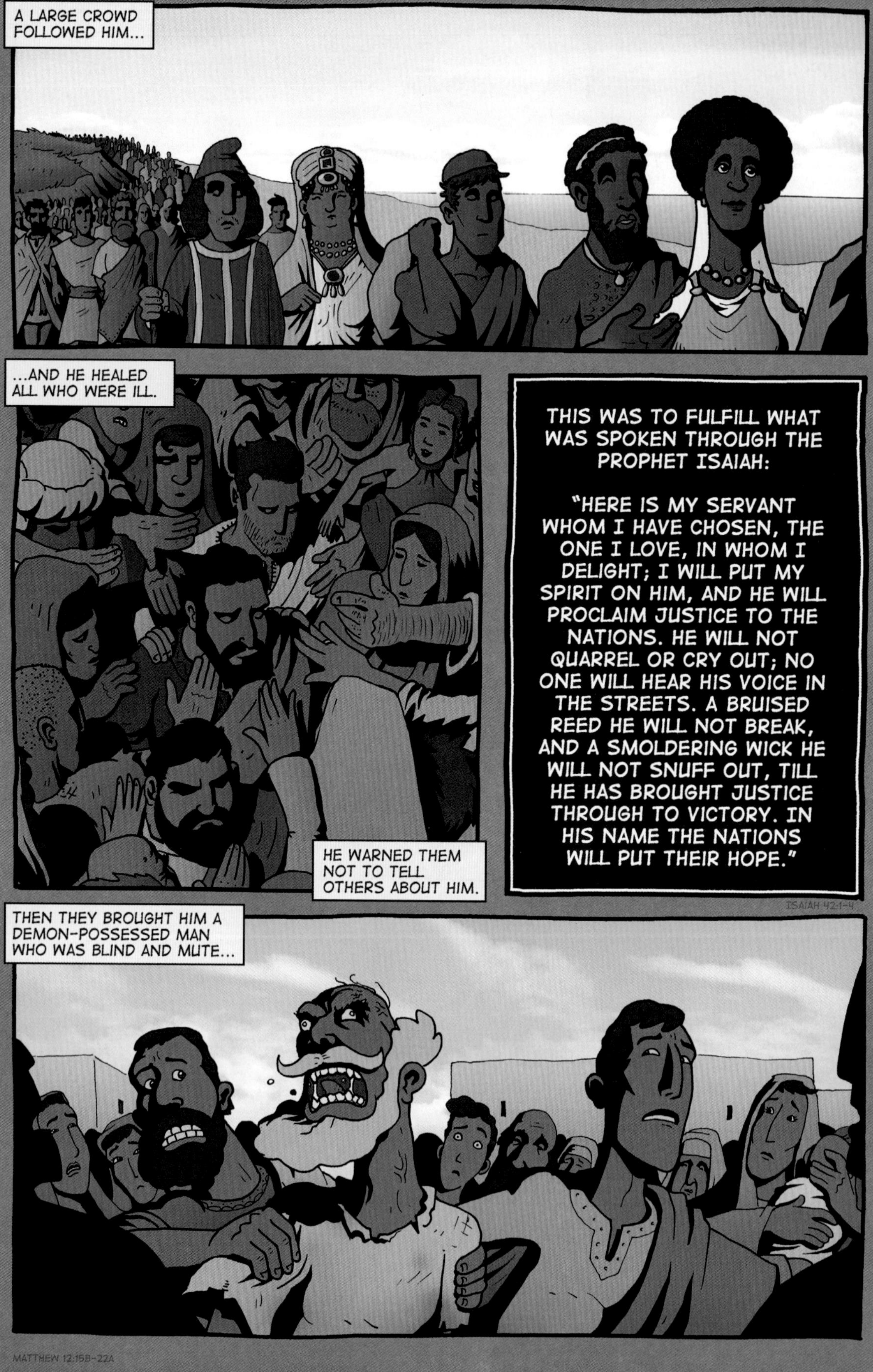
A LARGE CROWD FOLLOWED HIM...
...AND HE HEALED ALL WHO WERE ILL.
HE WARNED THEM NOT TO TELL OTHERS ABOUT HIM.
THIS WAS TO FULFILL WHAT WAS SPOKEN THROUGH THE PROPHET ISAIAH:
"HERE IS MY SERVANT WHOM I HAVE CHOSEN, THE ONE I LOVE, IN WHOM I DELIGHT; I WILL PUT MY SPIRIT ON HIM, AND HE WILL PROCLAIM JUSTICE TO THE NATIONS. HE WILL NOT QUARREL OR CRY OUT; NO ONE WILL HEAR HIS VOICE IN THE STREETS. A BRUISED REED HE WILL NOT BREAK, AND A SMOLDERING WICK HE WILL NOT SNUFF OUT, TILL HE HAS BROUGHT JUSTICE THROUGH TO VICTORY. IN HIS NAME THE NATIONS WILL PUT THEIR HOPE."
ISAIAH 42:1-4
THEN THEY BROUGHT HIM A DEMON-POSSESSED MAN WHO WAS BLIND AND MUTE...

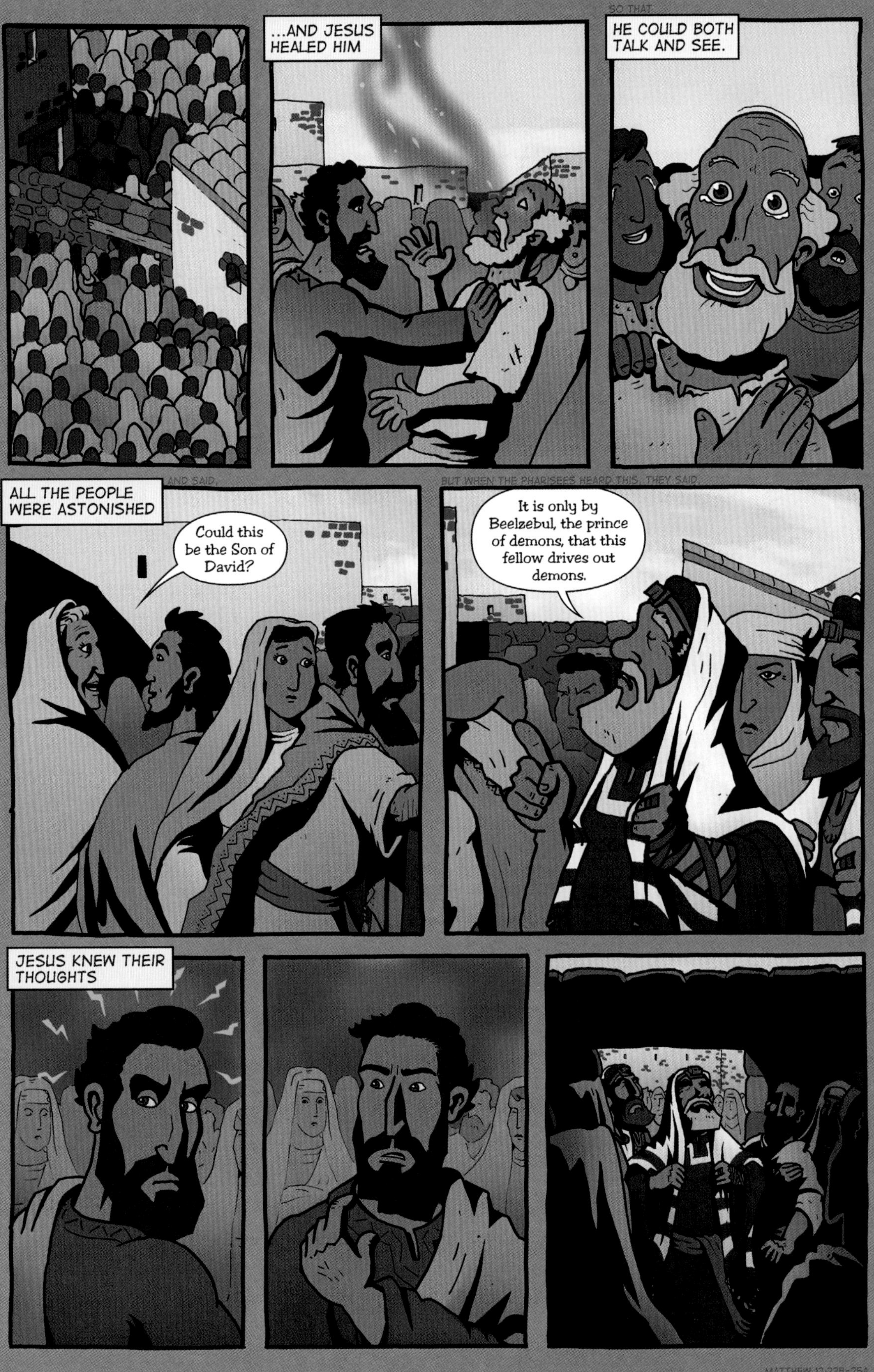
...AND JESUS HEALED HIM
SO THAT
HE COULD BOTH TALK AND SEE.
ALL THE PEOPLE WERE ASTONISHED
AND SAID,
Could this be the Son of David?
BUT WHEN THE PHARISEES HEARD THIS, THEY SAID,
It is only by Beelzebul, the prince of demons, that this fellow drives out demons.
JESUS KNEW THEIR THOUGHTS

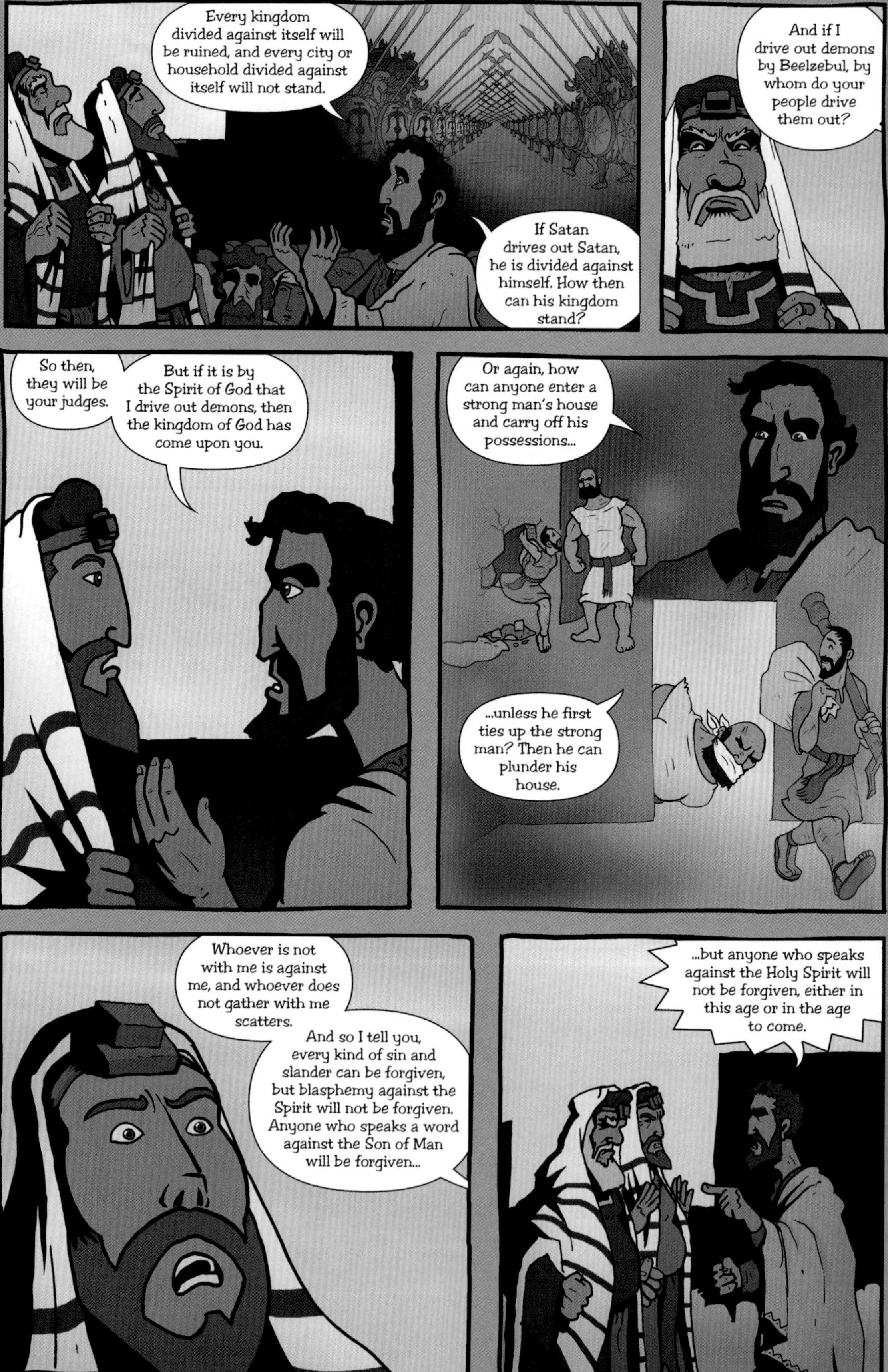
Every kingdom divided against itself will be ruined, and every city or household divided against itself will not stand.
If Satan drives out Satan, he is divided against himself. How then can his kingdom stand?
And if I drive out demons by Beelzebul, by whom do your people drive them out?
So then, they will be your judges.
But if it is by the Spirit of God that I drive out demons, then the kingdom of God has come upon you.
Or again, how can anyone enter a strong man's house and carry off his possessions...
...unless he first ties up the strong man? Then he can plunder his house.
Whoever is not with me is against me, and whoever does not gather with me scatters.
And so I tell you, every kind of sin and slander can be forgiven, but blasphemy against the Spirit will not be forgiven. Anyone who speaks a word against the Son of Man will be forgiven...
...but anyone who speaks against the Holy Spirit will not be forgiven, either in this age or in the age to come.

Make a tree good and its fruit will be good...

...or make a tree bad and its fruit will be bad, for a tree is recognized by its fruit.

You brood of vipers, how can you who are evil say anything good?

For the mouth speaks what the heart is full of.

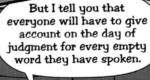

But I tell you that everyone will have to give account on the day of judgment for every empty word they have spoken.

A good man brings good things out of the good stored up in him, and an evil man brings evil things out of the evil stored up in him.

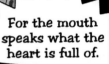

For by your words you will be acquitted, and by your words you will be condemned.

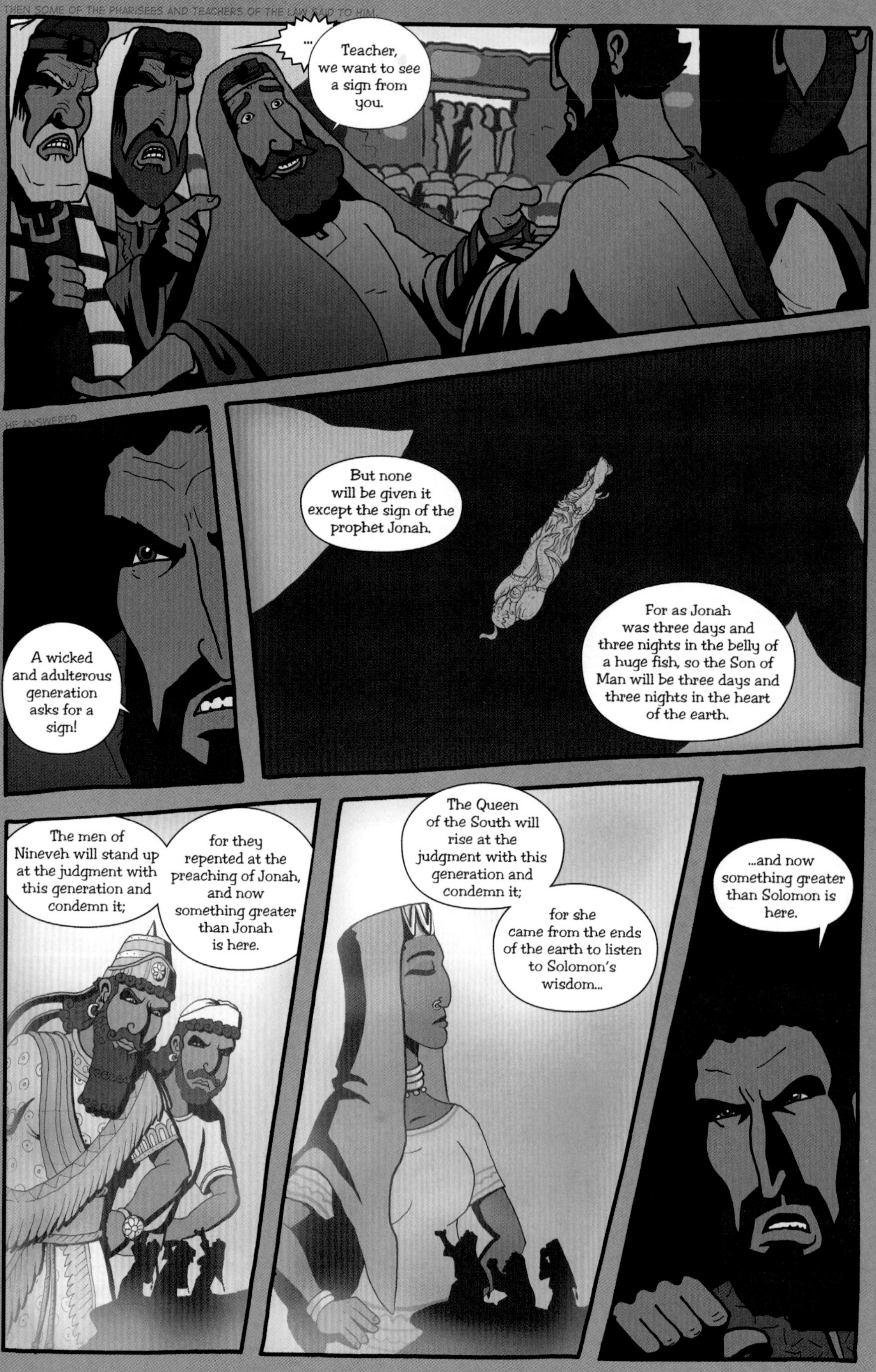
THEN SOME OF THE PHARISEES AND TEACHERS OF THE LAW SAID TO HIM
...
Teacher, we want to see a sign from you.
HE ANSWERED
A wicked and adulterous generation asks for a sign!
But none will be given it except the sign of the prophet Jonah.
For as Jonah was three days and three nights in the belly of a huge fish, so the Son of Man will be three days and three nights in the heart of the earth.
The men of Nineveh will stand up at the judgment with this generation and condemn it;
for they repented at the preaching of Jonah, and now something greater than Jonah is here.
The Queen of the South will rise at the judgment with this generation and condemn it;
for she came from the ends of the earth to listen to Solomon's wisdom...
...and now something greater than Solomon is here.

When an impure spirit comes out of a person, it goes through arid places seeking rest and does not find it.

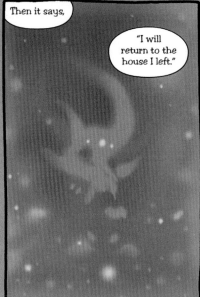

Then it says,

"I will return to the house I left."

When it arrives, it finds the house unoccupied, swept clean and put in order.

Then it goes and takes with it seven other spirits more wicked than itself, and they go in and live there.

And the final condition of that person is worse than the first.

That is how it will be with this wicked generation.

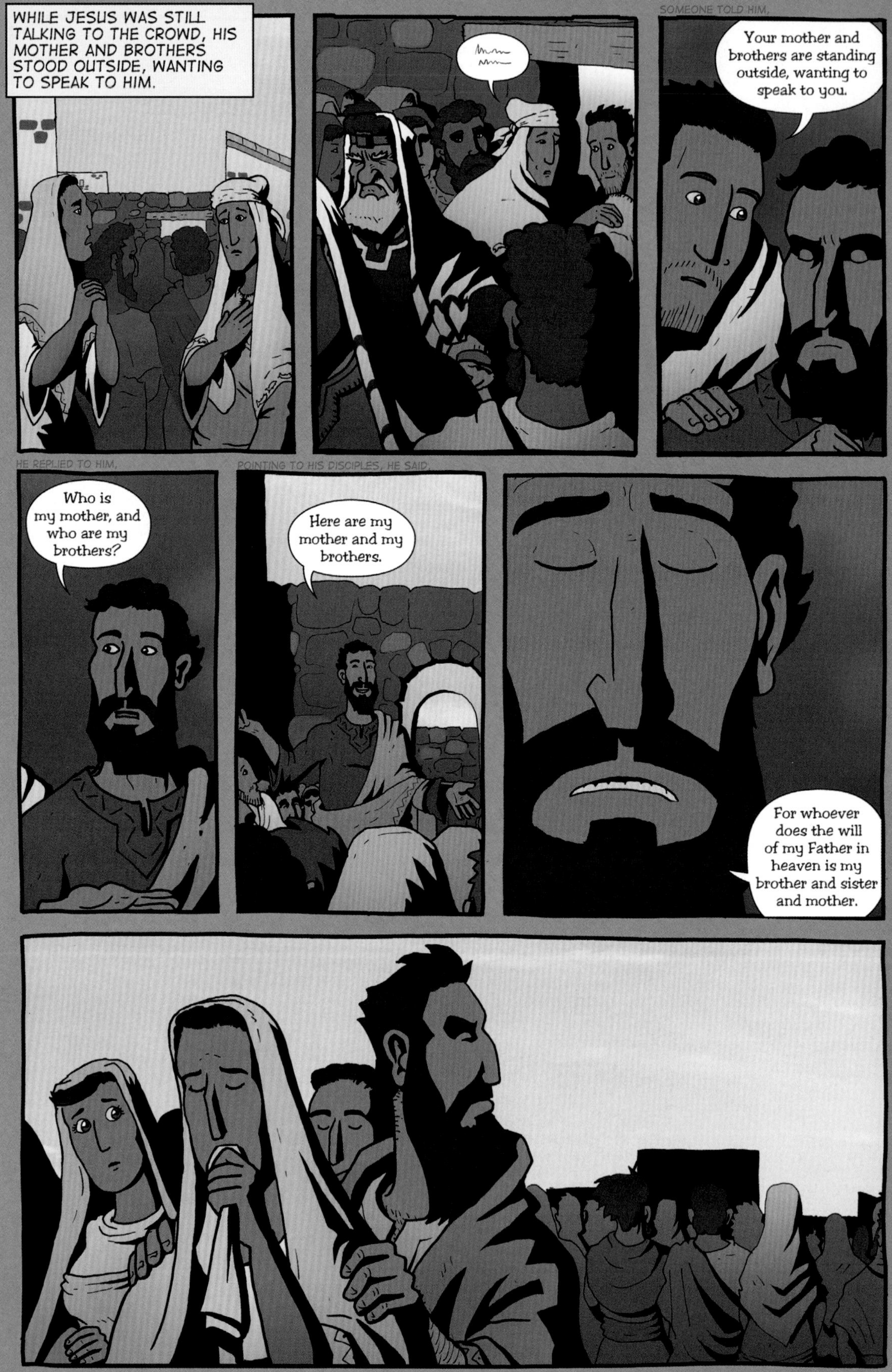

WHILE JESUS WAS STILL TALKING TO THE CROWD, HIS MOTHER AND BROTHERS STOOD OUTSIDE, WANTING TO SPEAK TO HIM.
SOMEONE TOLD HIM,
Your mother and brothers are standing outside, wanting to speak to you.
HE REPLIED TO HIM,
Who is my mother, and who are my brothers?
POINTING TO HIS DISCIPLES, HE SAID,
Here are my mother and my brothers.
For whoever does the will of my Father in heaven is my brother and sister and mother.

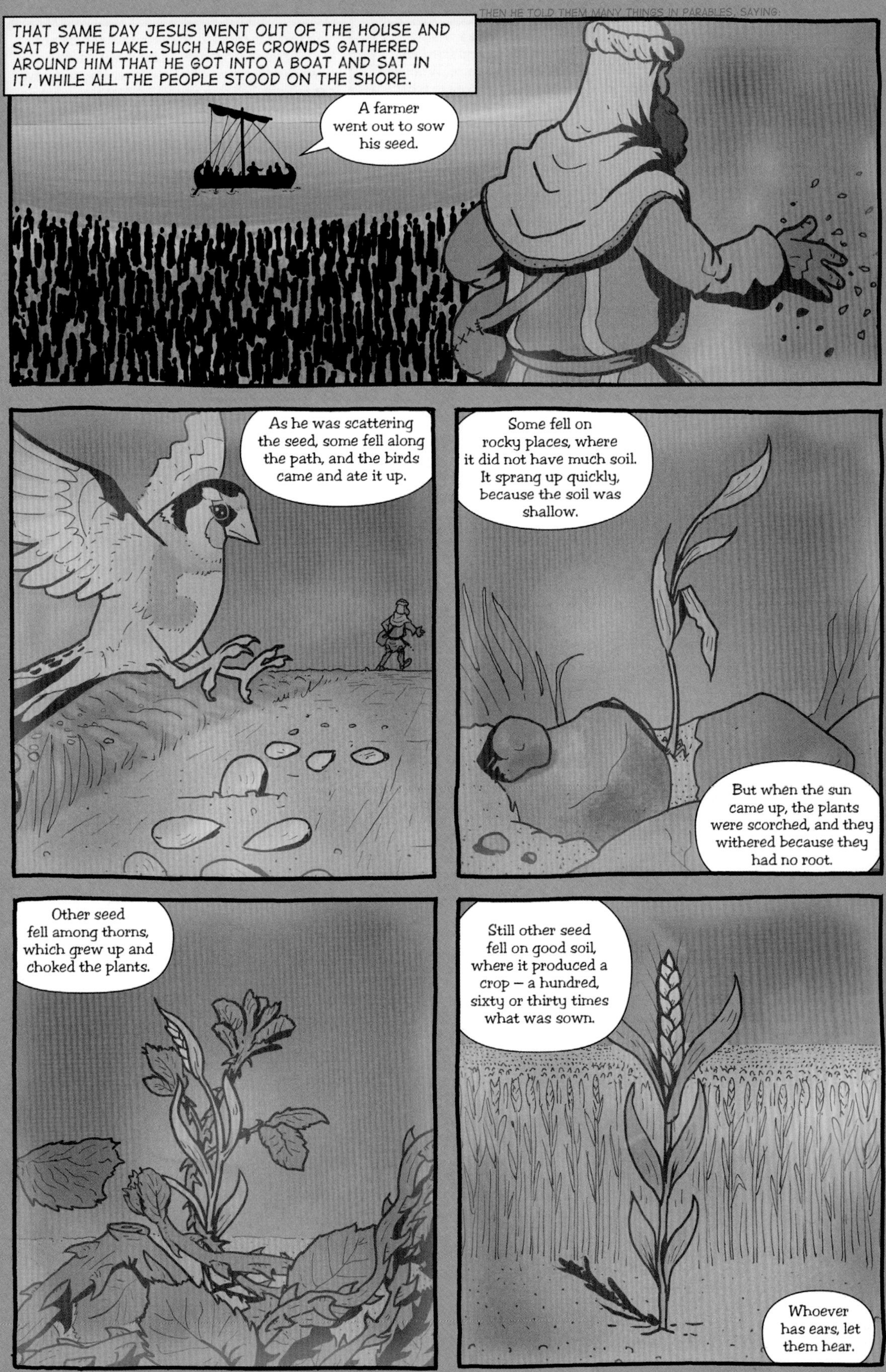

THEN HE TOLD THEM MANY THINGS IN PARABLES, SAYING:
THAT SAME DAY JESUS WENT OUT OF THE HOUSE AND SAT BY THE LAKE. SUCH LARGE CROWDS GATHERED AROUND HIM THAT HE GOT INTO A BOAT AND SAT IN IT, WHILE ALL THE PEOPLE STOOD ON THE SHORE.
A farmer went out to sow his seed.
As he was scattering the seed, some fell along the path, and the birds came and ate it up.
Some fell on rocky places, where it did not have much soil. It sprang up quickly, because the soil was shallow.
But when the sun came up, the plants were scorched, and they withered because they had no root.
Other seed fell among thorns, which grew up and choked the plants.
Still other seed fell on good soil, where it produced a crop – a hundred, sixty or thirty times what was sown.
Whoever has ears, let them hear.

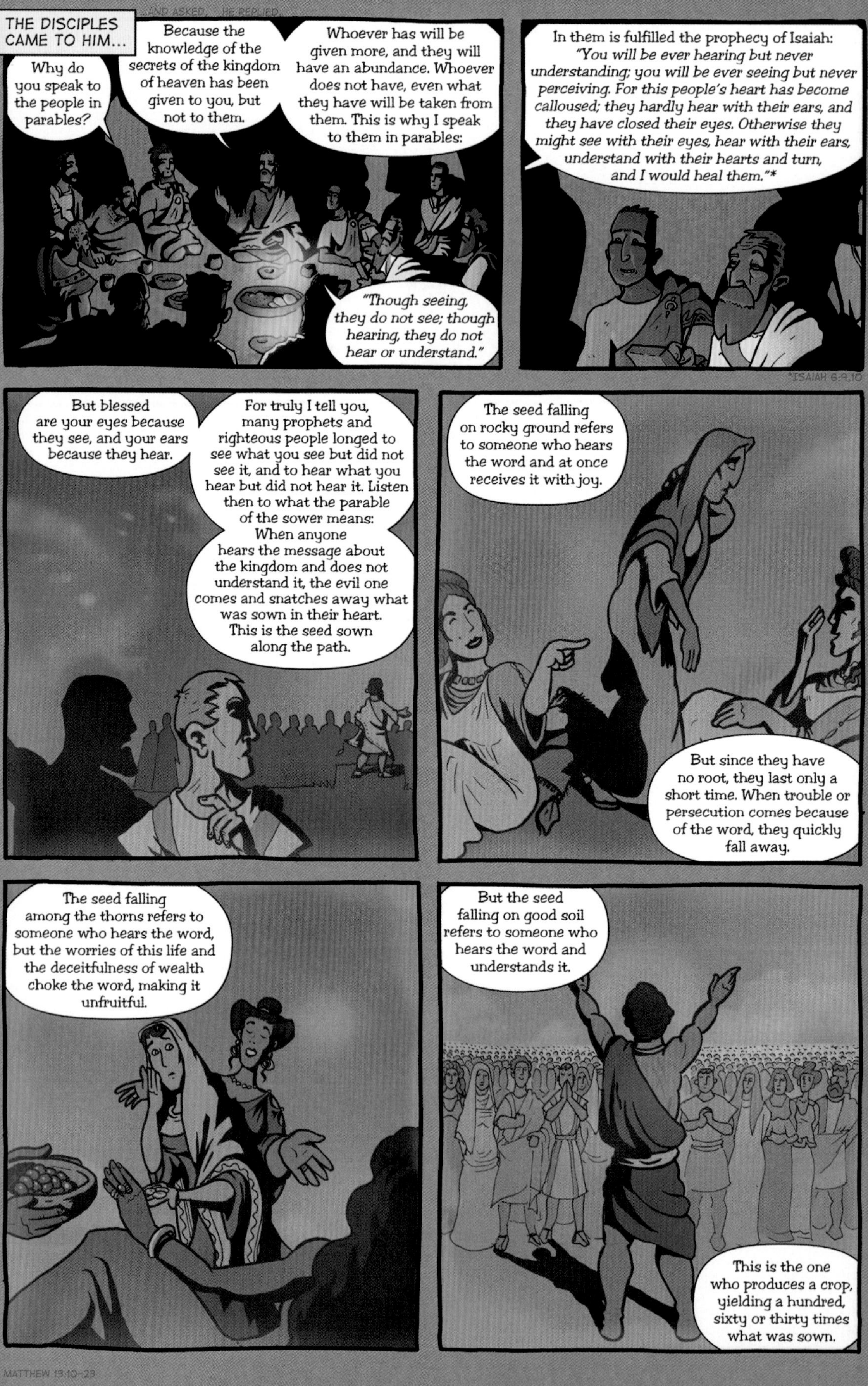
THE DISCIPLES CAME TO HIM…
…AND ASKED, HE REPLIED.
Why do you speak to the people in parables?
Because the knowledge of the secrets of the kingdom of heaven has been given to you, but not to them.
Whoever has will be given more, and they will have an abundance. Whoever does not have, even what they have will be taken from them. This is why I speak to them in parables:
"Though seeing, they do not see; though hearing, they do not hear or understand."
In them is fulfilled the prophecy of Isaiah: *"You will be ever hearing but never understanding; you will be ever seeing but never perceiving. For this people's heart has become calloused; they hardly hear with their ears, and they have closed their eyes. Otherwise they might see with their eyes, hear with their ears, understand with their hearts and turn, and I would heal them."**
*ISAIAH 6:9,10
But blessed are your eyes because they see, and your ears because they hear.
For truly I tell you, many prophets and righteous people longed to see what you see but did not see it, and to hear what you hear but did not hear it. Listen then to what the parable of the sower means:
When anyone hears the message about the kingdom and does not understand it, the evil one comes and snatches away what was sown in their heart. This is the seed sown along the path.
The seed falling on rocky ground refers to someone who hears the word and at once receives it with joy.
But since they have no root, they last only a short time. When trouble or persecution comes because of the word, they quickly fall away.
The seed falling among the thorns refers to someone who hears the word, but the worries of this life and the deceitfulness of wealth choke the word, making it unfruitful.
But the seed falling on good soil refers to someone who hears the word and understands it.
This is the one who produces a crop, yielding a hundred, sixty or thirty times what was sown.

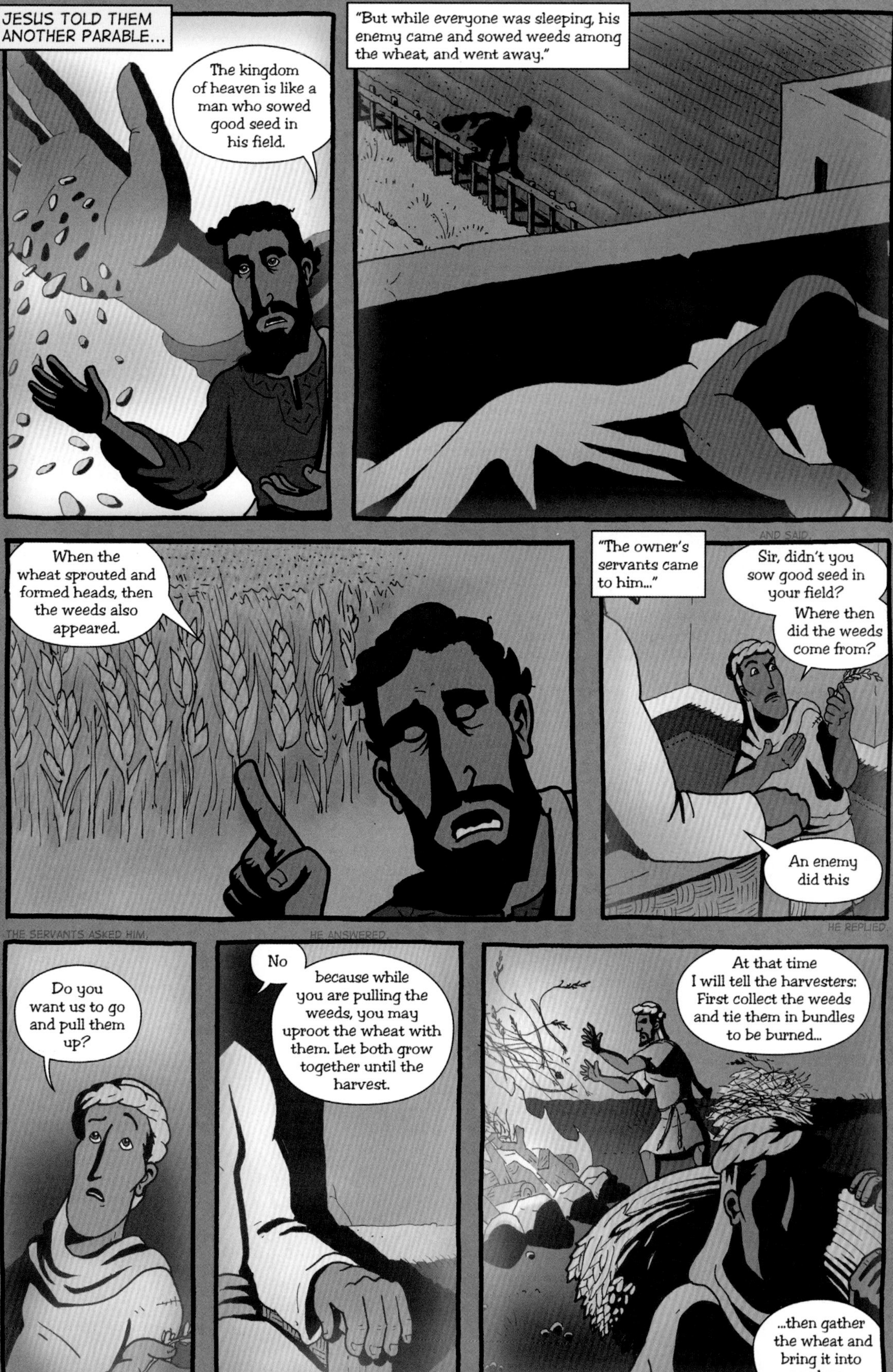
JESUS TOLD THEM ANOTHER PARABLE...
The kingdom of heaven is like a man who sowed good seed in his field.
"But while everyone was sleeping, his enemy came and sowed weeds among the wheat, and went away."
When the wheat sprouted and formed heads, then the weeds also appeared.
"The owner's servants came to him..."
AND SAID,
Sir, didn't you sow good seed in your field?
Where then did the weeds come from?
An enemy did this
HE REPLIED.
THE SERVANTS ASKED HIM,
Do you want us to go and pull them up?
HE ANSWERED,
No
because while you are pulling the weeds, you may uproot the wheat with them. Let both grow together until the harvest.
At that time I will tell the harvesters: First collect the weeds and tie them in bundles to be burned...
...then gather the wheat and bring it into my barn.

MATTHEW 13:24–30

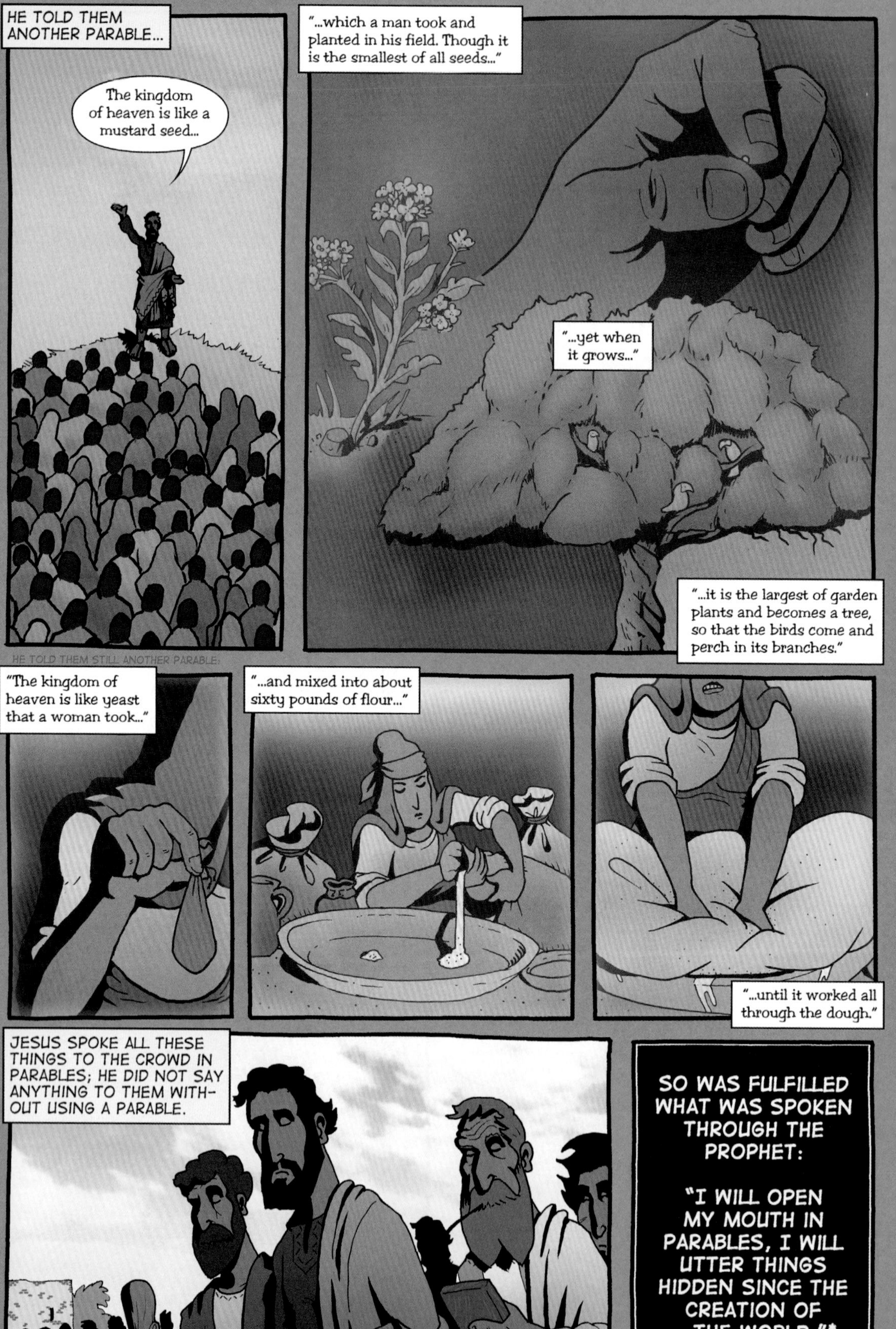
HE TOLD THEM ANOTHER PARABLE...
The kingdom of heaven is like a mustard seed...
"...which a man took and planted in his field. Though it is the smallest of all seeds..."
"...yet when it grows..."
"...it is the largest of garden plants and becomes a tree, so that the birds come and perch in its branches."
HE TOLD THEM STILL ANOTHER PARABLE:
"The kingdom of heaven is like yeast that a woman took..."
"...and mixed into about sixty pounds of flour..."
"...until it worked all through the dough."
JESUS SPOKE ALL THESE THINGS TO THE CROWD IN PARABLES; HE DID NOT SAY ANYTHING TO THEM WITHOUT USING A PARABLE.
SO WAS FULFILLED WHAT WAS SPOKEN THROUGH THE PROPHET:
"I WILL OPEN MY MOUTH IN PARABLES, I WILL UTTER THINGS HIDDEN SINCE THE CREATION OF THE WORLD."*

*PSALM 78:2

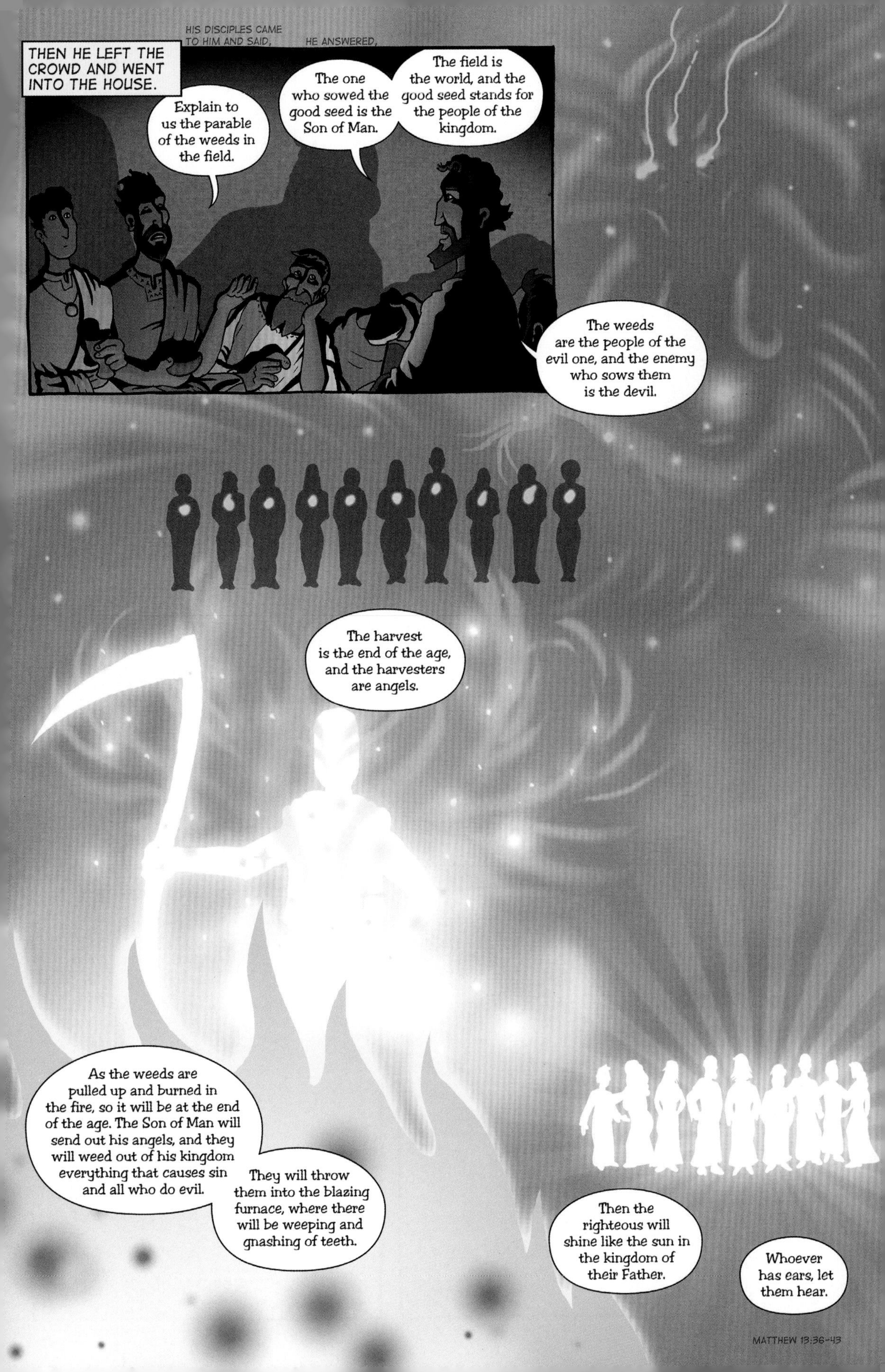
THEN HE LEFT THE CROWD AND WENT INTO THE HOUSE.
HIS DISCIPLES CAME TO HIM AND SAID,
Explain to us the parable of the weeds in the field.
HE ANSWERED,
The one who sowed the good seed is the Son of Man.
The field is the world, and the good seed stands for the people of the kingdom.
The weeds are the people of the evil one, and the enemy who sows them is the devil.
The harvest is the end of the age, and the harvesters are angels.
As the weeds are pulled up and burned in the fire, so it will be at the end of the age. The Son of Man will send out his angels, and they will weed out of his kingdom everything that causes sin and all who do evil.
They will throw them into the blazing furnace, where there will be weeping and gnashing of teeth.
Then the righteous will shine like the sun in the kingdom of their Father.
Whoever has ears, let them hear.
MATTHEW 13:36-43

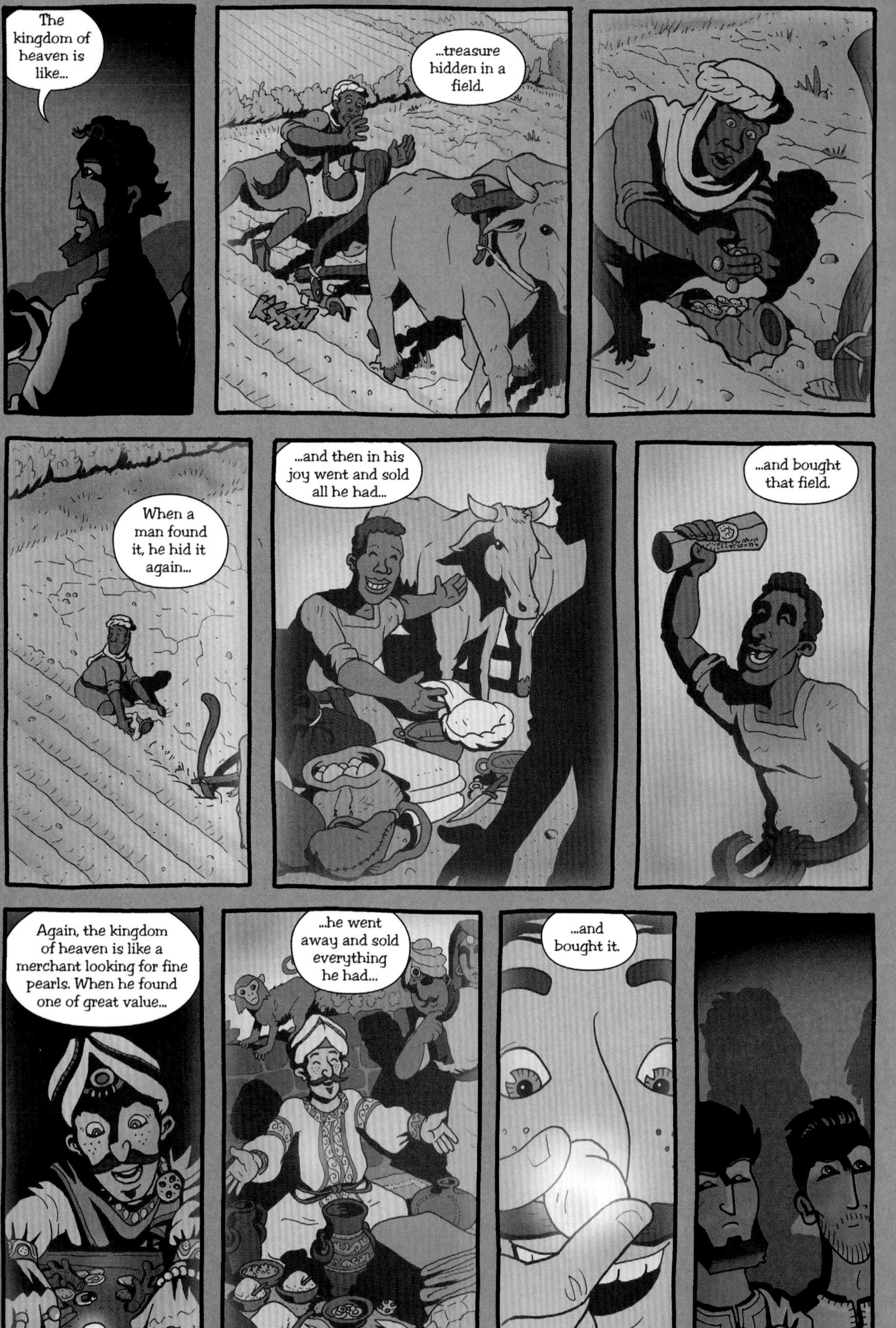
The kingdom of heaven is like...
...treasure hidden in a field.
KSSH
When a man found it, he hid it again...
...and then in his joy went and sold all he had...
...and bought that field.
Again, the kingdom of heaven is like a merchant looking for fine pearls. When he found one of great value...
...he went away and sold everything he had...
...and bought it.

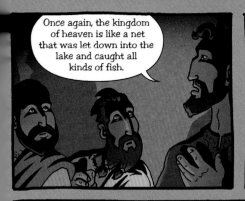

Once again, the kingdom of heaven is like a net that was let down into the lake and caught all kinds of fish.

When it was full, the fishermen pulled it up on the shore.

Then they sat down and collected the good fish in baskets,

but threw the bad away.

This is how it will be at the end of the age.

The angels will come and separate the wicked from the righteous

and throw them into the blazing furnace, where there will be weeping and gnashing of teeth.

JESUS ASKED.

Have you understood all these things?

Yes

THEY REPLIED.

HE SAID TO THEM.

Therefore every teacher of the law who has become a disciple in the kingdom of heaven...

...is like the owner of a house who brings out of his storeroom new treasures as well as old.

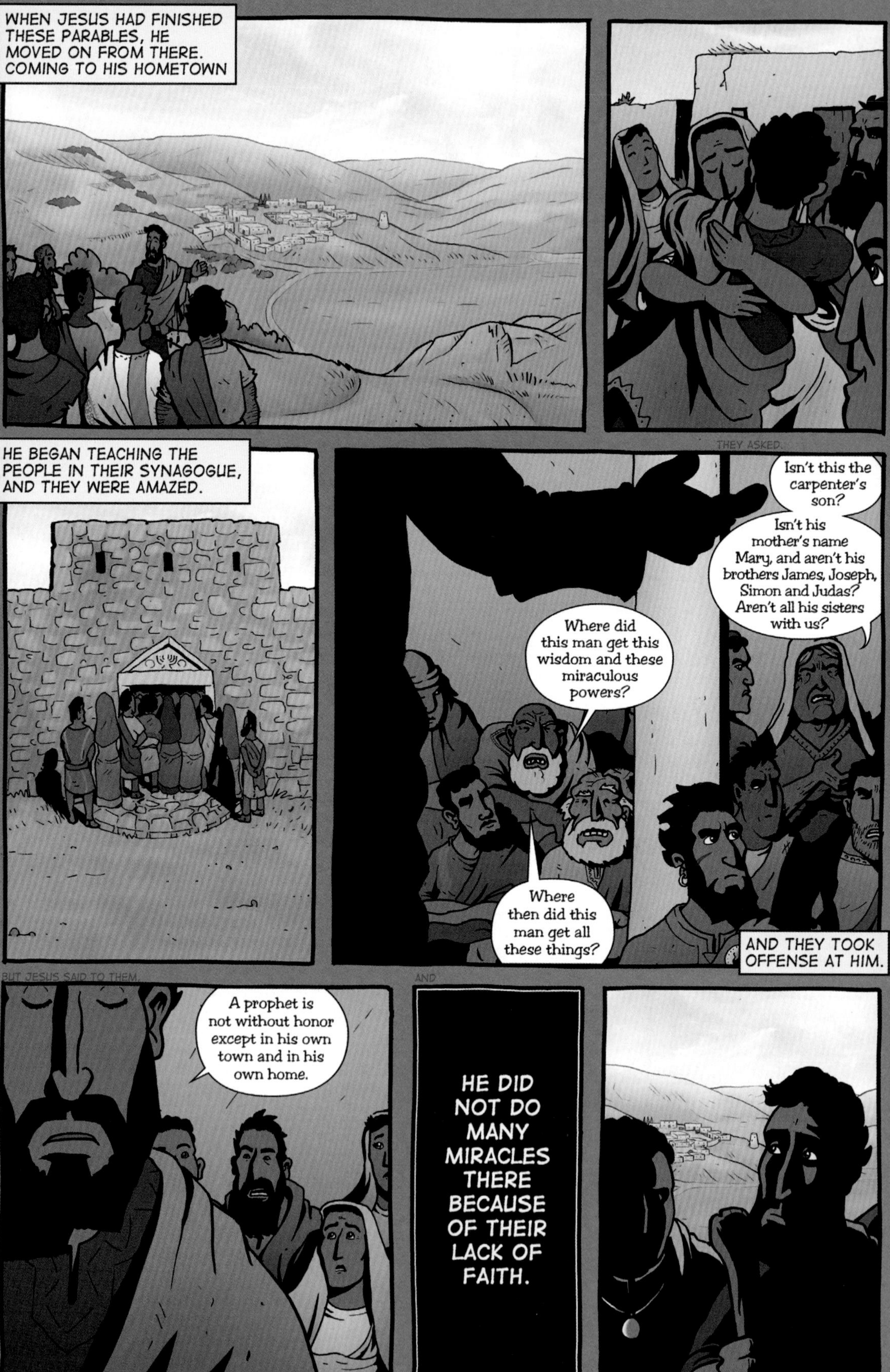
WHEN JESUS HAD FINISHED THESE PARABLES, HE MOVED ON FROM THERE. COMING TO HIS HOMETOWN
HE BEGAN TEACHING THE PEOPLE IN THEIR SYNAGOGUE, AND THEY WERE AMAZED.
THEY ASKED,
Where did this man get this wisdom and these miraculous powers?
Isn't this the carpenter's son?
Isn't his mother's name Mary, and aren't his brothers James, Joseph, Simon and Judas? Aren't all his sisters with us?
Where then did this man get all these things?
AND THEY TOOK OFFENSE AT HIM.
BUT JESUS SAID TO THEM,
A prophet is not without honor except in his own town and in his own home.
AND
HE DID NOT DO MANY MIRACLES THERE BECAUSE OF THEIR LACK OF FAITH.

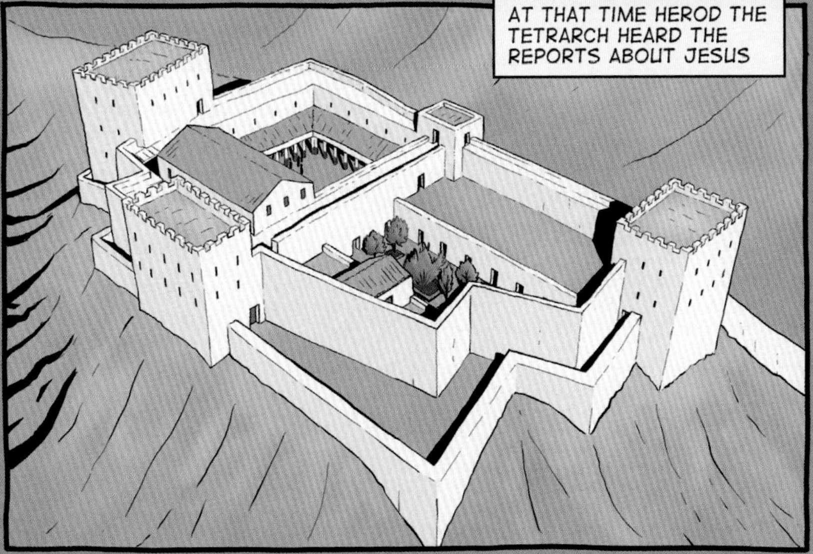
AT THAT TIME HEROD THE TETRARCH HEARD THE REPORTS ABOUT JESUS

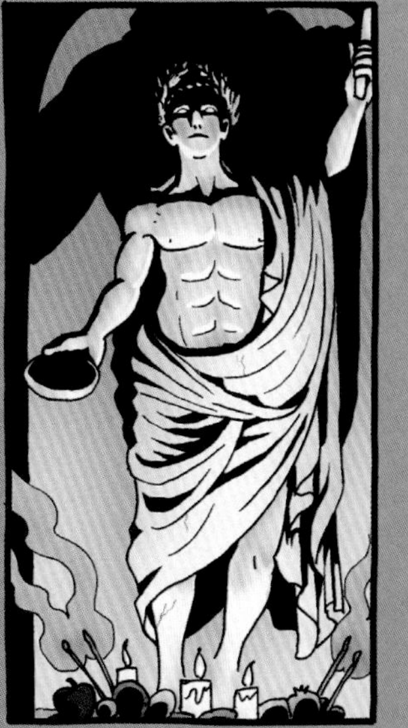

AND HE SAID TO HIS ATTENDANTS,

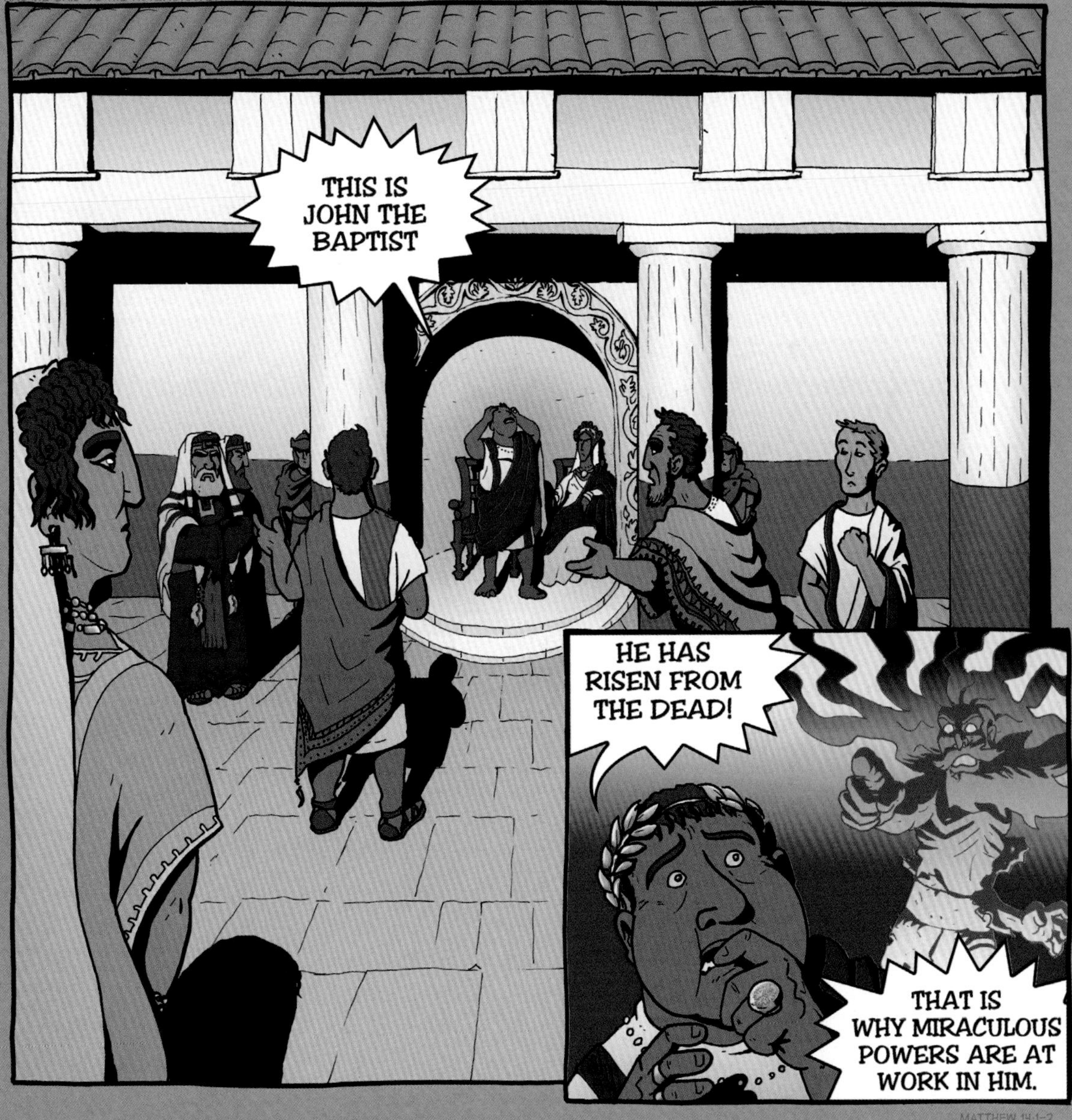
THIS IS JOHN THE BAPTIST
HE HAS RISEN FROM THE DEAD!
THAT IS WHY MIRACULOUS POWERS ARE AT WORK IN HIM.

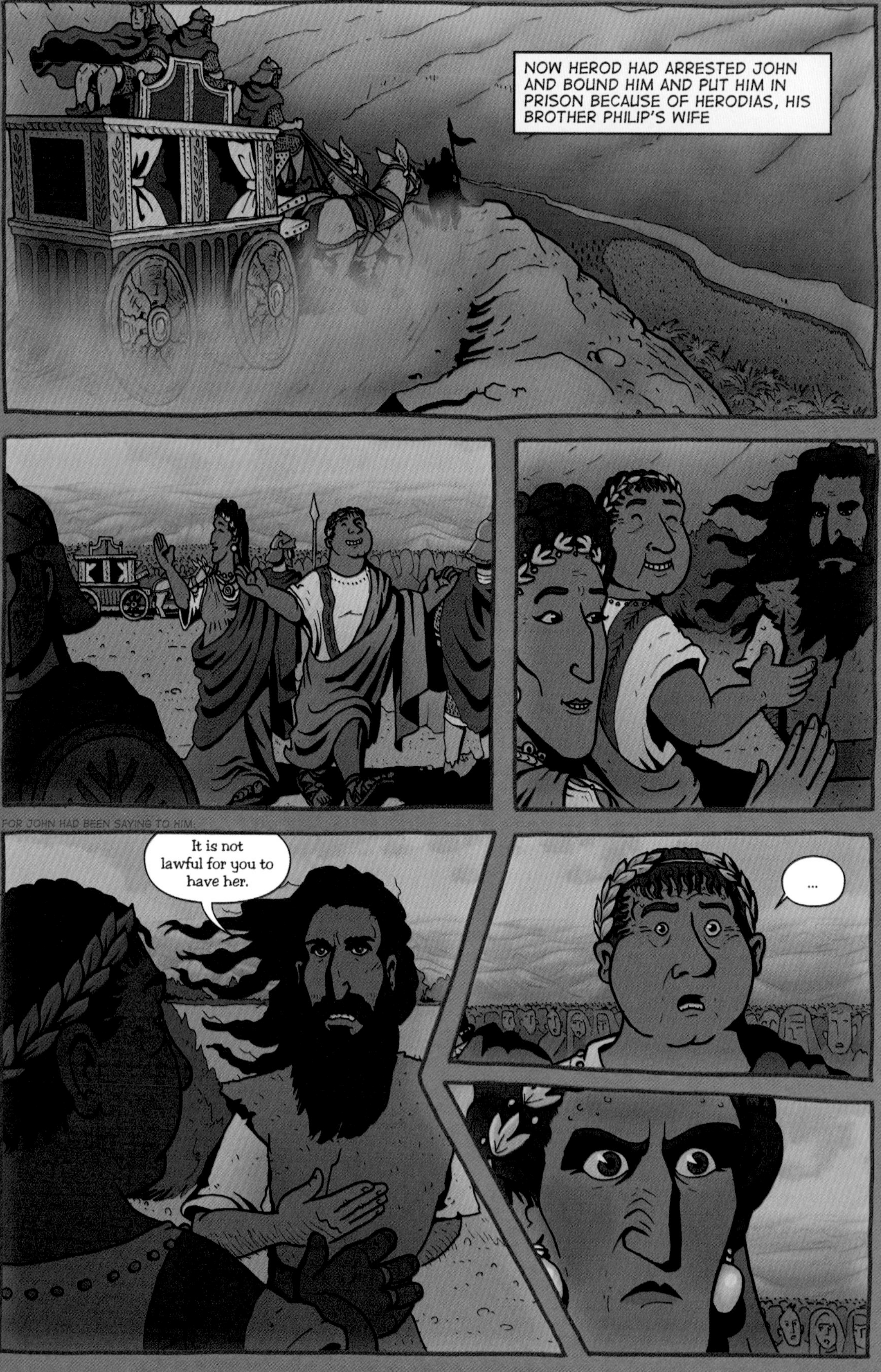
NOW HEROD HAD ARRESTED JOHN AND BOUND HIM AND PUT HIM IN PRISON BECAUSE OF HERODIAS, HIS BROTHER PHILIP'S WIFE
FOR JOHN HAD BEEN SAYING TO HIM:
It is not lawful for you to have her.
...

HEROD WANTED TO KILL JOHN, BUT HE WAS AFRAID OF THE PEOPLE...

...BECAUSE THEY CONSIDERED JOHN A PROPHET.

!!!

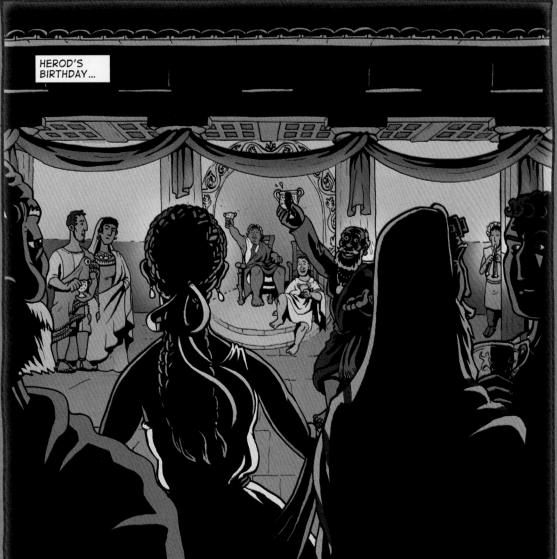

HEROD'S BIRTHDAY...

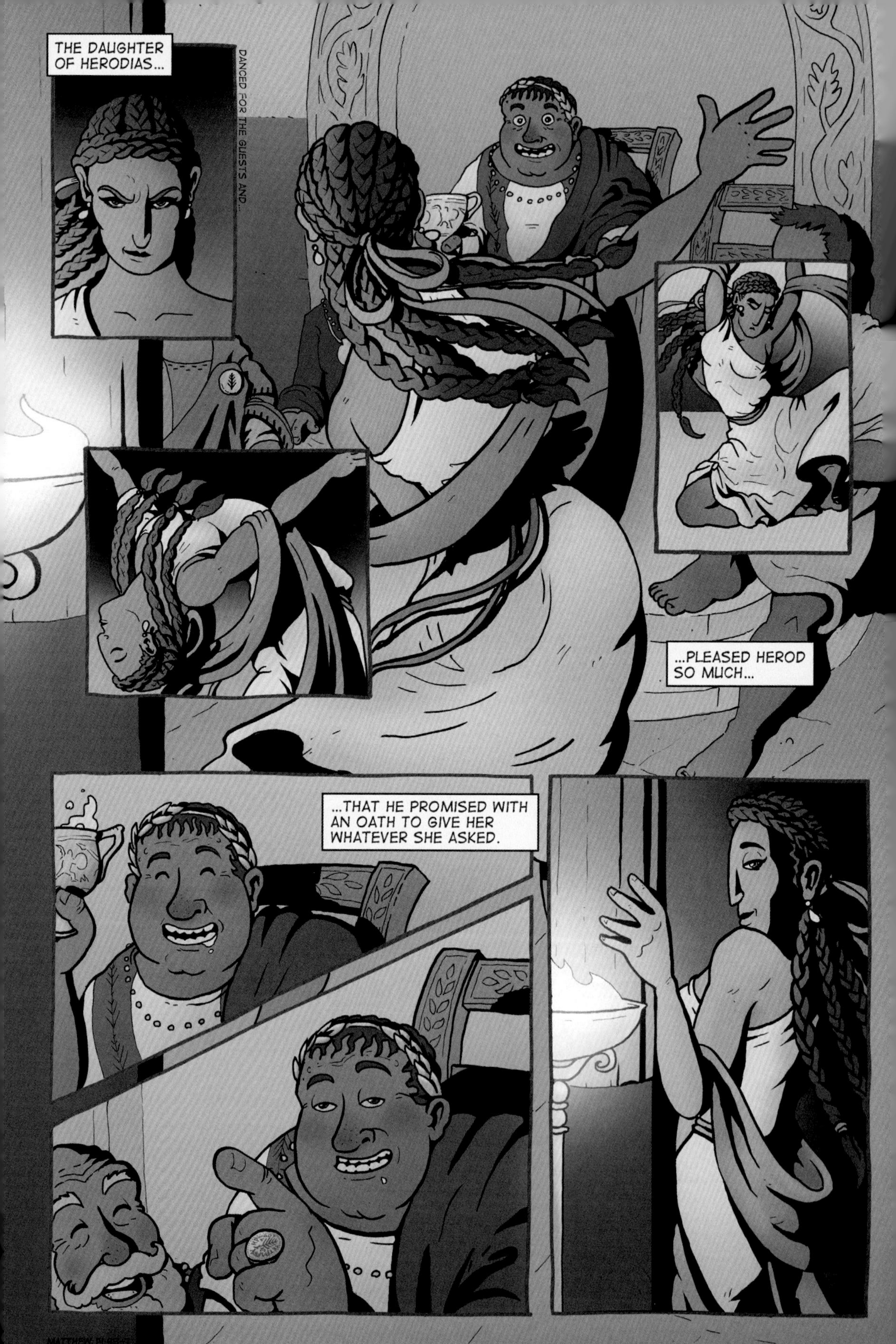
THE DAUGHTER OF HERODIAS...
DANCED FOR THE GUESTS AND...
...PLEASED HEROD SO MUCH...
...THAT HE PROMISED WITH AN OATH TO GIVE HER WHATEVER SHE ASKED.

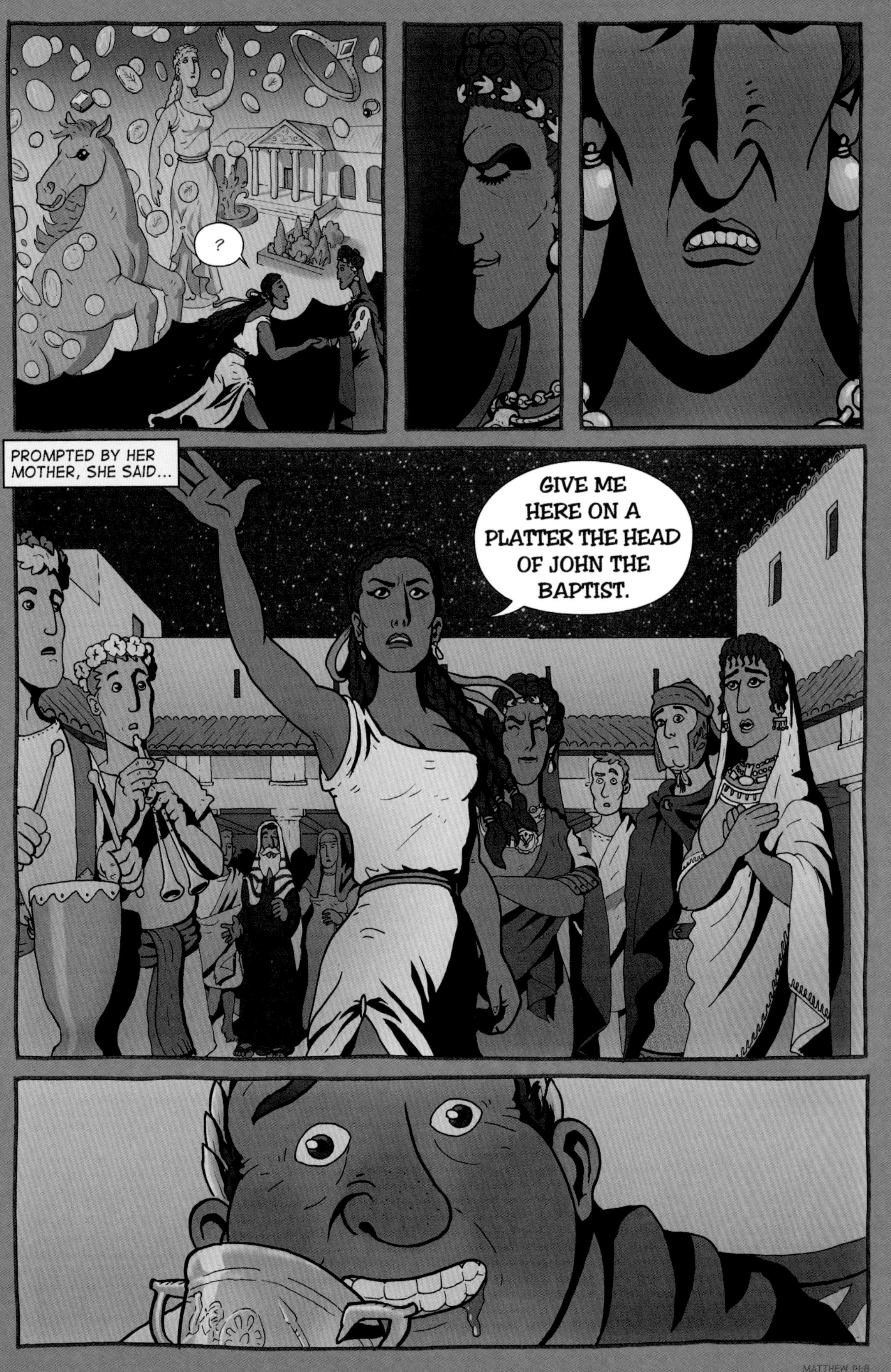
?
PROMPTED BY HER MOTHER, SHE SAID...
GIVE ME HERE ON A PLATTER THE HEAD OF JOHN THE BAPTIST.

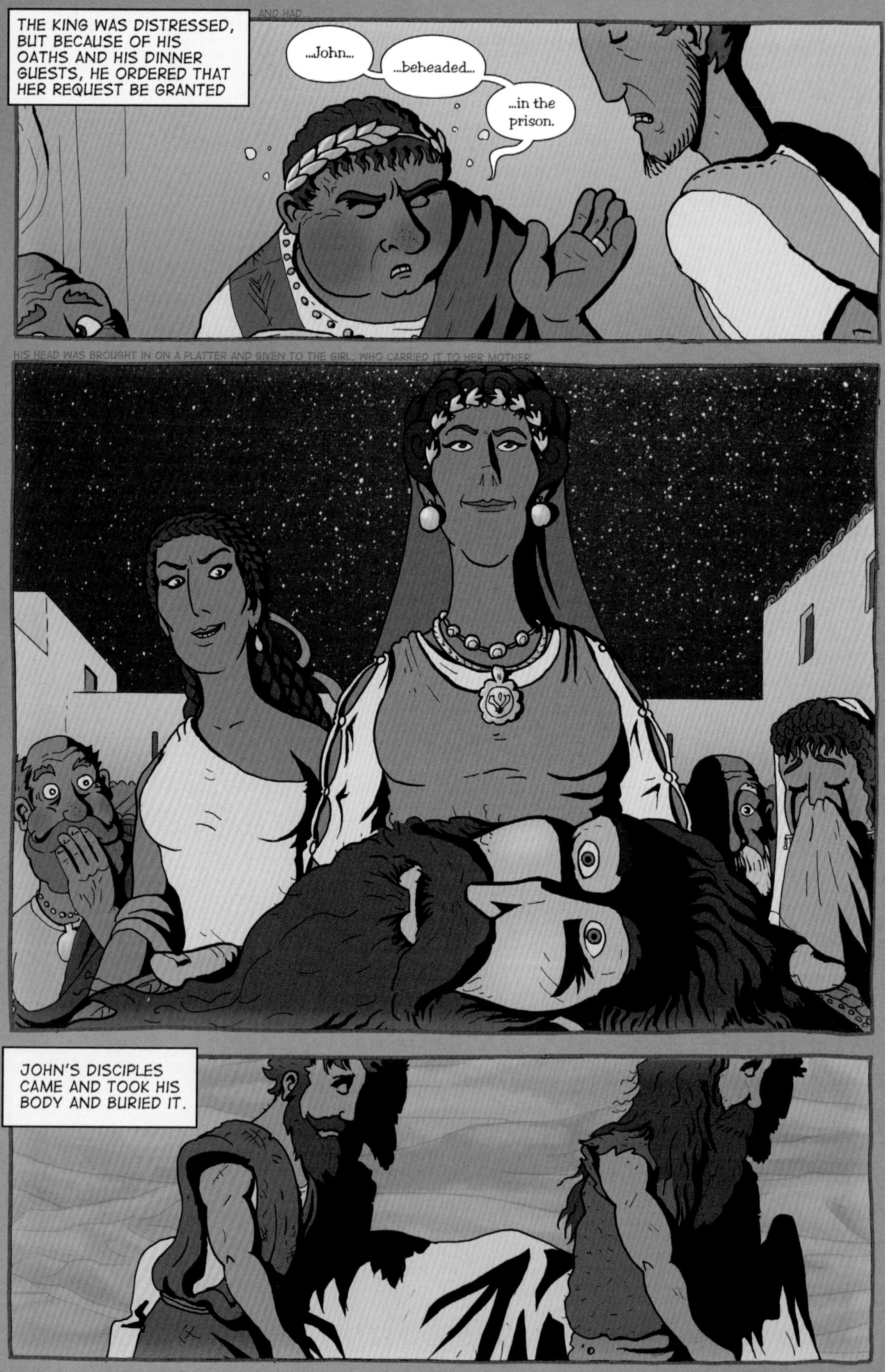
THE KING WAS DISTRESSED, BUT BECAUSE OF HIS OATHS AND HIS DINNER GUESTS, HE ORDERED THAT HER REQUEST BE GRANTED
AND HAD...
...John...
...beheaded...
...in the prison.
HIS HEAD WAS BROUGHT IN ON A PLATTER AND GIVEN TO THE GIRL, WHO CARRIED IT TO HER MOTHER.
JOHN'S DISCIPLES CAME AND TOOK HIS BODY AND BURIED IT.

THEN THEY WENT AND TOLD JESUS.

WHEN JESUS HEARD WHAT HAD HAPPENED, HE WITHDREW BY BOAT PRIVATELY TO A SOLITARY PLACE.

WHEN JESUS LANDED AND SAW A LARGE CROWD.

HE HAD COMPASSION ON THEM...

HEARING OF THIS, THE CROWDS FOLLOWED HIM ON FOOT FROM THE TOWNS.

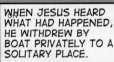

...AND HEALED THEIR SICK.

AS EVENING APPROACHED, THE DISCIPLES CAME TO HIM AND SAID,

This is a remote place, and it's already getting late.

Send the crowds away, so they can go to the villages and buy themselves some food.

JESUS REPLIED,

They do not need to go away.

You give them something to eat.

THEY ANSWERED.

We have here only five loaves of bread and two fish

Bring them here to me

HE SAID.

MATTHEW 14:12B–18

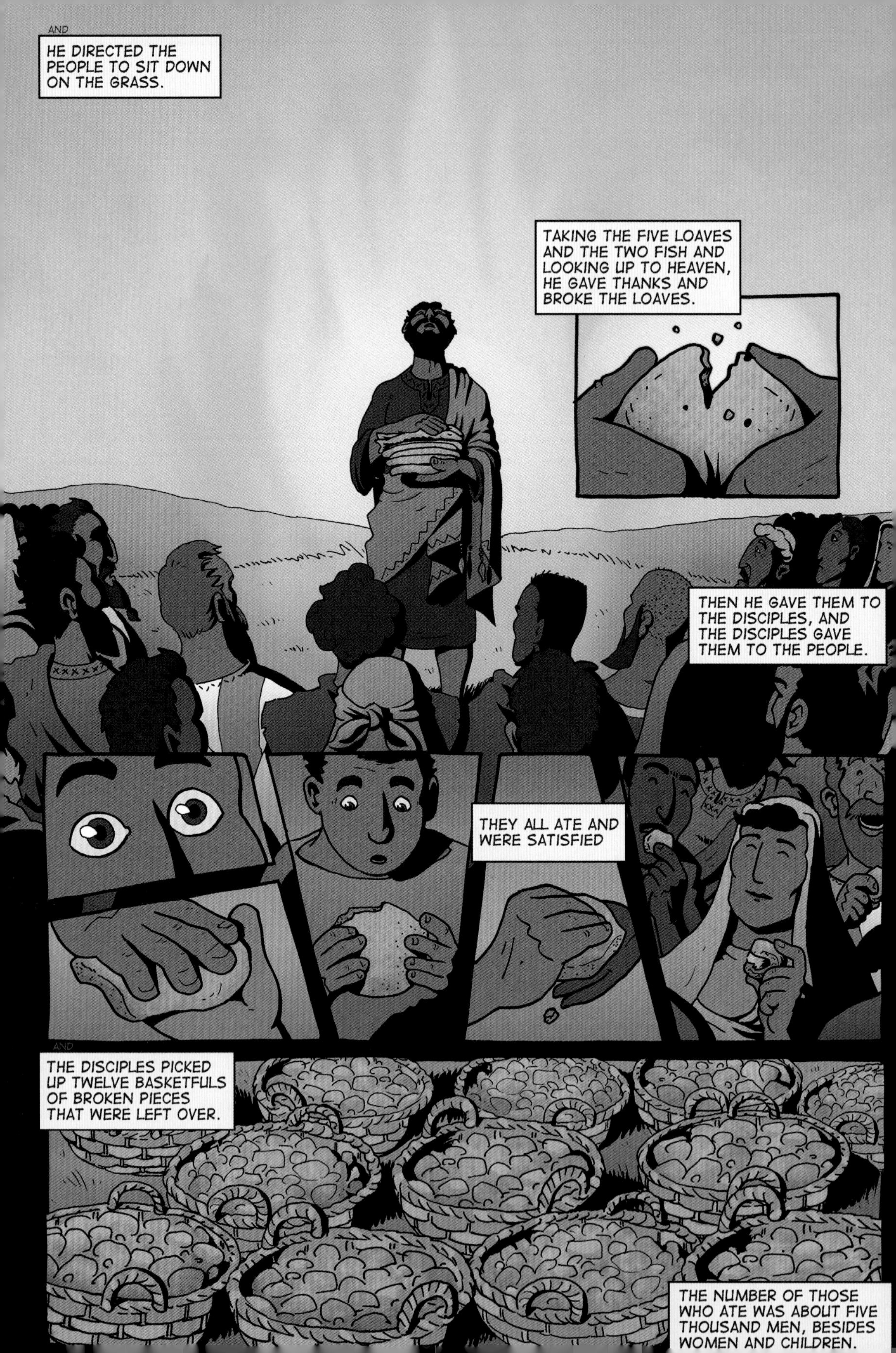
AND
HE DIRECTED THE PEOPLE TO SIT DOWN ON THE GRASS.
TAKING THE FIVE LOAVES AND THE TWO FISH AND LOOKING UP TO HEAVEN, HE GAVE THANKS AND BROKE THE LOAVES.
THEN HE GAVE THEM TO THE DISCIPLES, AND THE DISCIPLES GAVE THEM TO THE PEOPLE.
THEY ALL ATE AND WERE SATISFIED
AND
THE DISCIPLES PICKED UP TWELVE BASKETFULS OF BROKEN PIECES THAT WERE LEFT OVER.
THE NUMBER OF THOSE WHO ATE WAS ABOUT FIVE THOUSAND MEN, BESIDES WOMEN AND CHILDREN.

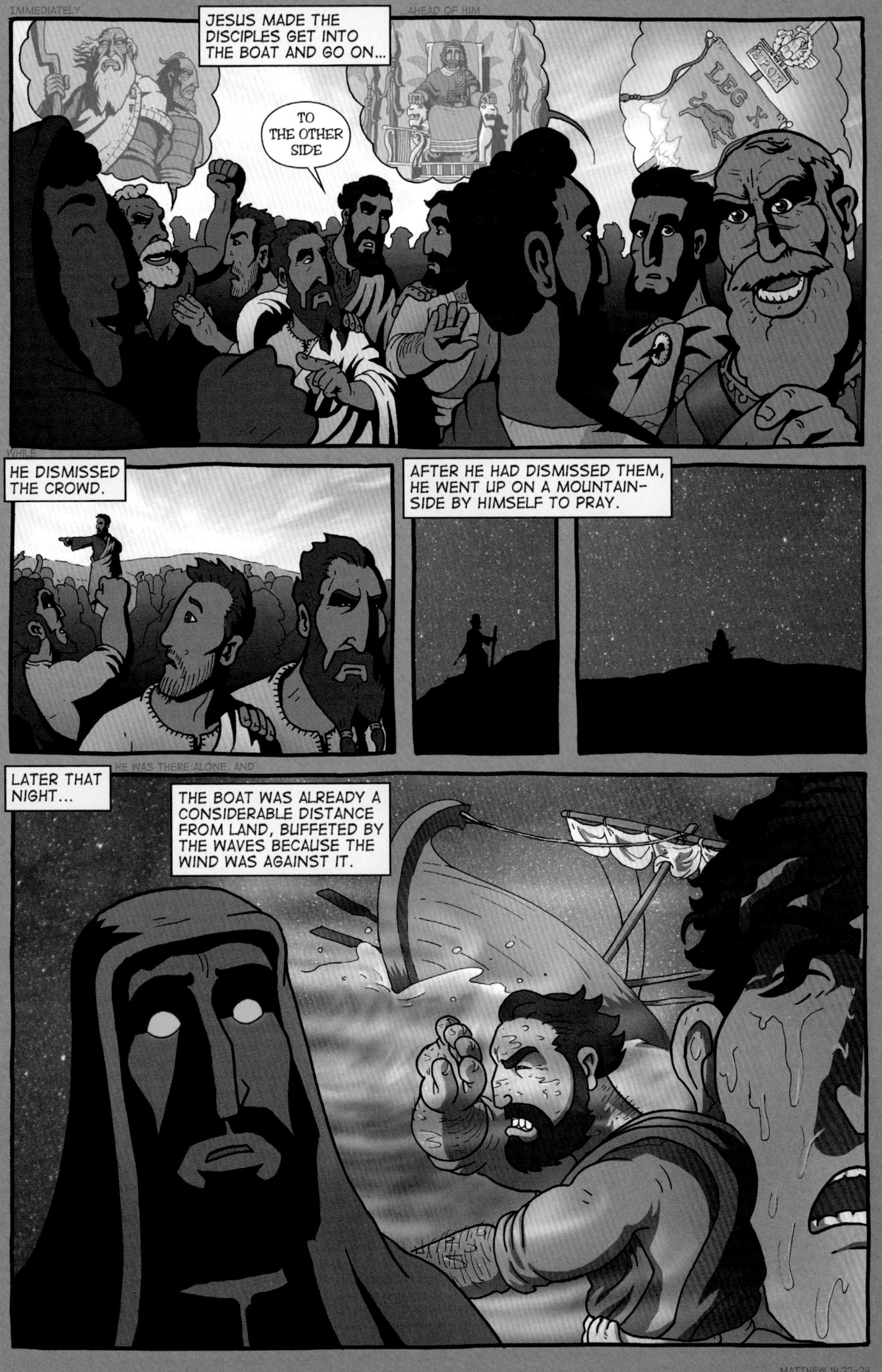

IMMEDIATELY
JESUS MADE THE DISCIPLES GET INTO THE BOAT AND GO ON...
...AHEAD OF HIM
SPQR
LEG X
TO THE OTHER SIDE
WHILE
HE DISMISSED THE CROWD.
AFTER HE HAD DISMISSED THEM, HE WENT UP ON A MOUNTAIN-SIDE BY HIMSELF TO PRAY.
HE WAS THERE ALONE, AND
LATER THAT NIGHT...
THE BOAT WAS ALREADY A CONSIDERABLE DISTANCE FROM LAND, BUFFETED BY THE WAVES BECAUSE THE WIND WAS AGAINST IT.

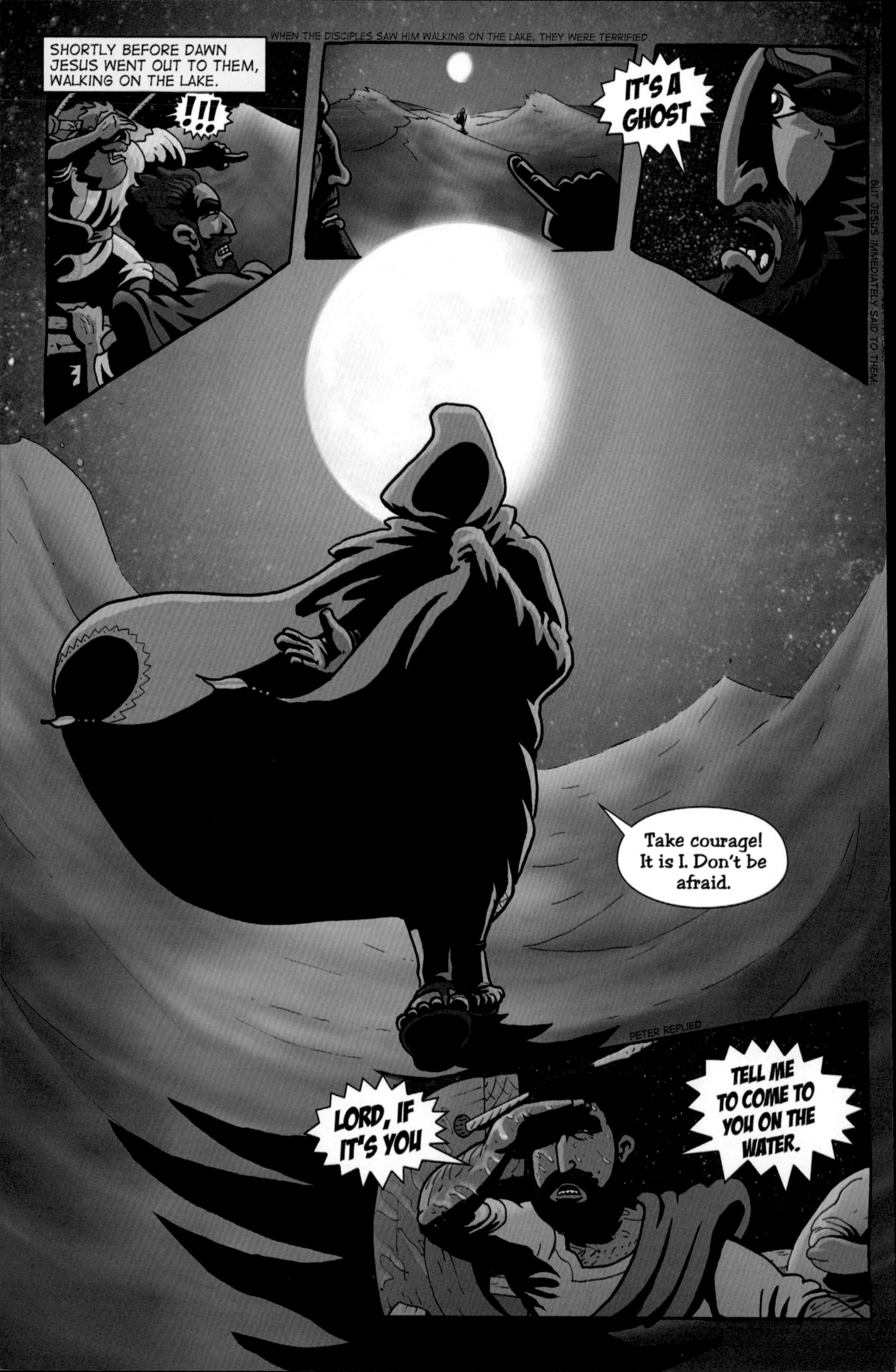

SHORTLY BEFORE DAWN JESUS WENT OUT TO THEM, WALKING ON THE LAKE.
!!!
WHEN THE DISCIPLES SAW HIM WALKING ON THE LAKE, THEY WERE TERRIFIED.
IT'S A GHOST
BUT JESUS IMMEDIATELY SAID TO THEM:
Take courage! It is I. Don't be afraid.
PETER REPLIED
LORD, IF IT'S YOU
TELL ME TO COME TO YOU ON THE WATER.

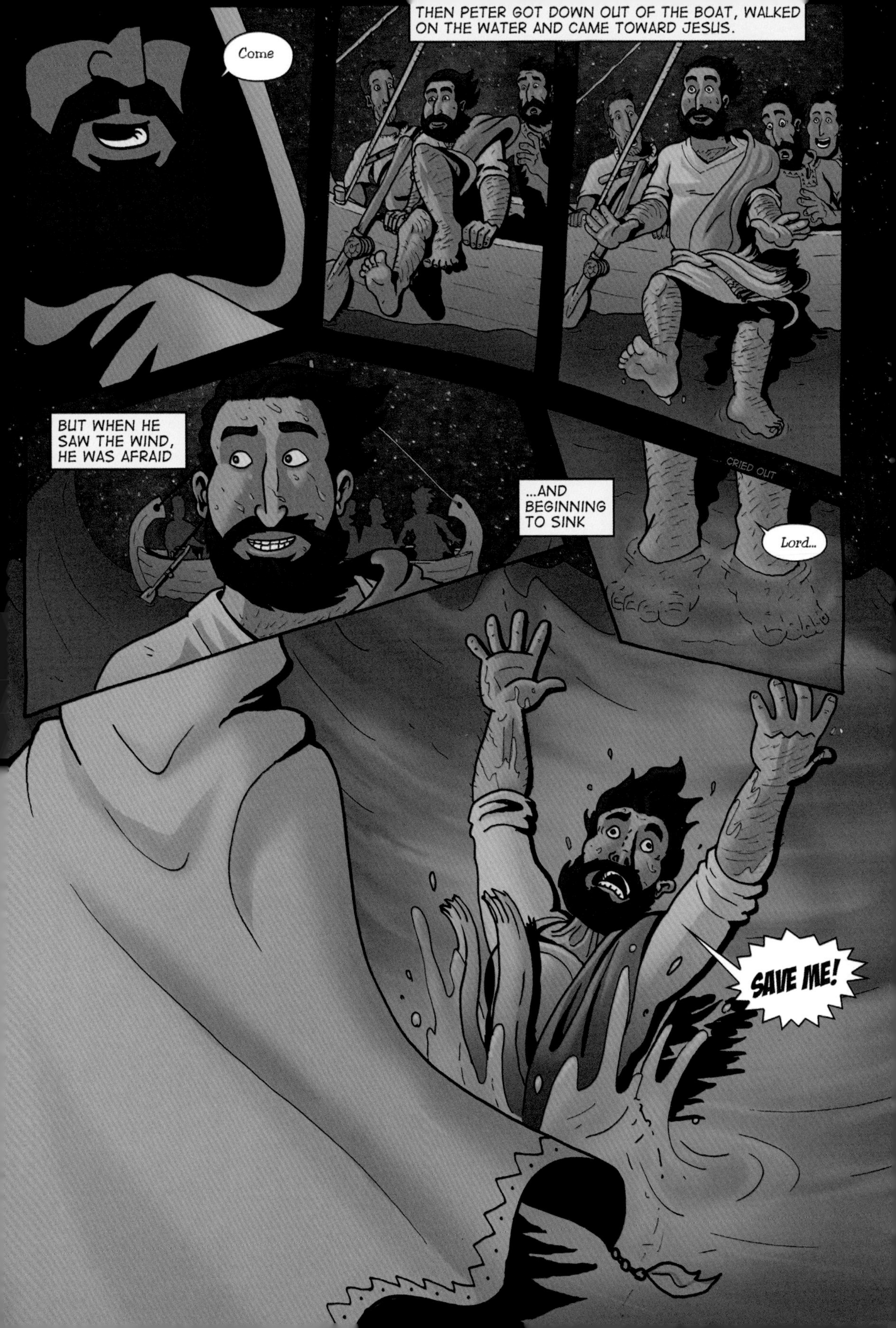
Come
THEN PETER GOT DOWN OUT OF THE BOAT, WALKED ON THE WATER AND CAME TOWARD JESUS.
BUT WHEN HE SAW THE WIND, HE WAS AFRAID
...AND BEGINNING TO SINK
... CRIED OUT
Lord...
SAVE ME!

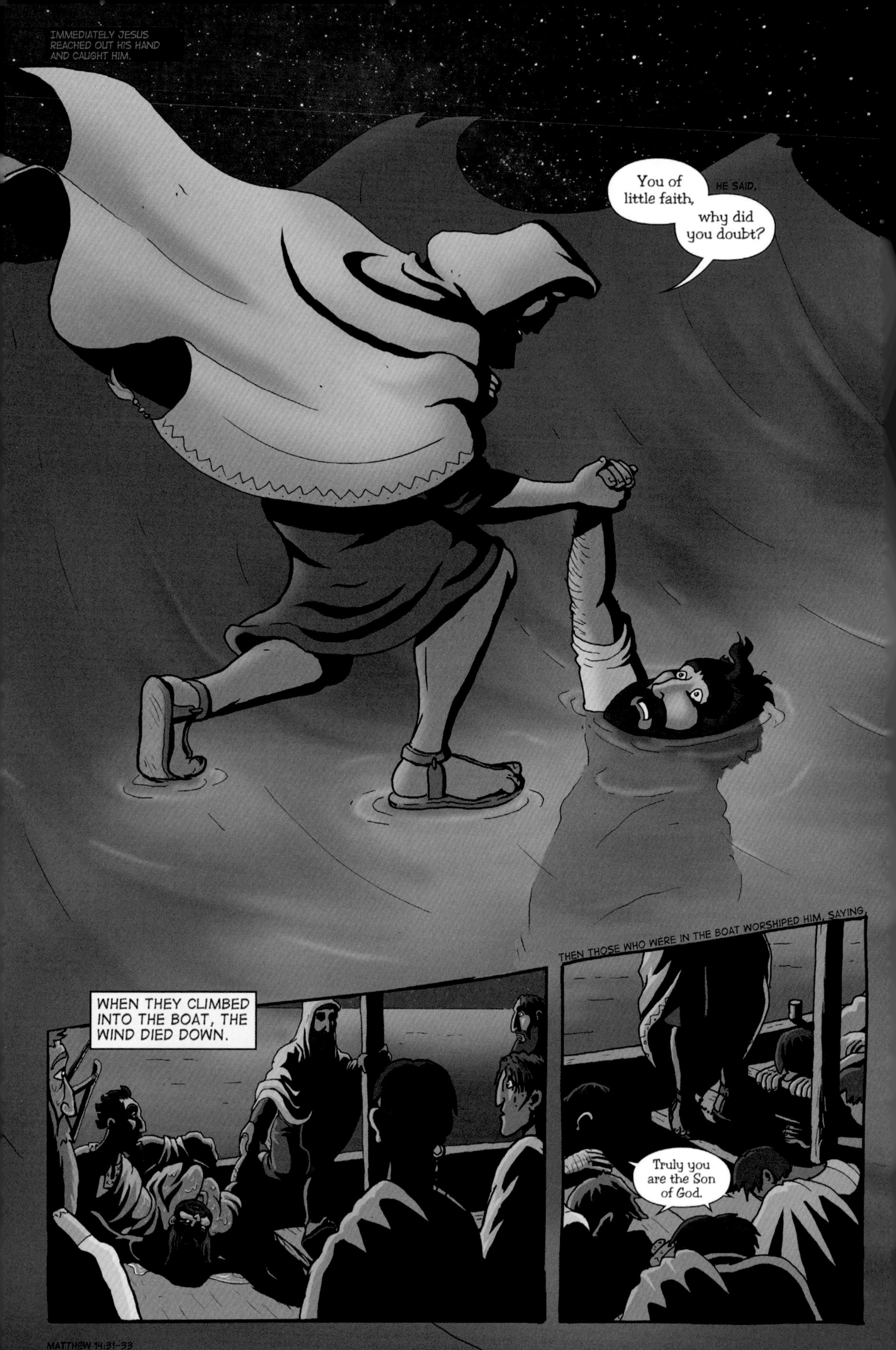
IMMEDIATELY JESUS REACHED OUT HIS HAND AND CAUGHT HIM.
You of little faith,
HE SAID,
why did you doubt?
WHEN THEY CLIMBED INTO THE BOAT, THE WIND DIED DOWN.
THEN THOSE WHO WERE IN THE BOAT WORSHIPED HIM, SAYING,
Truly you are the Son of God.

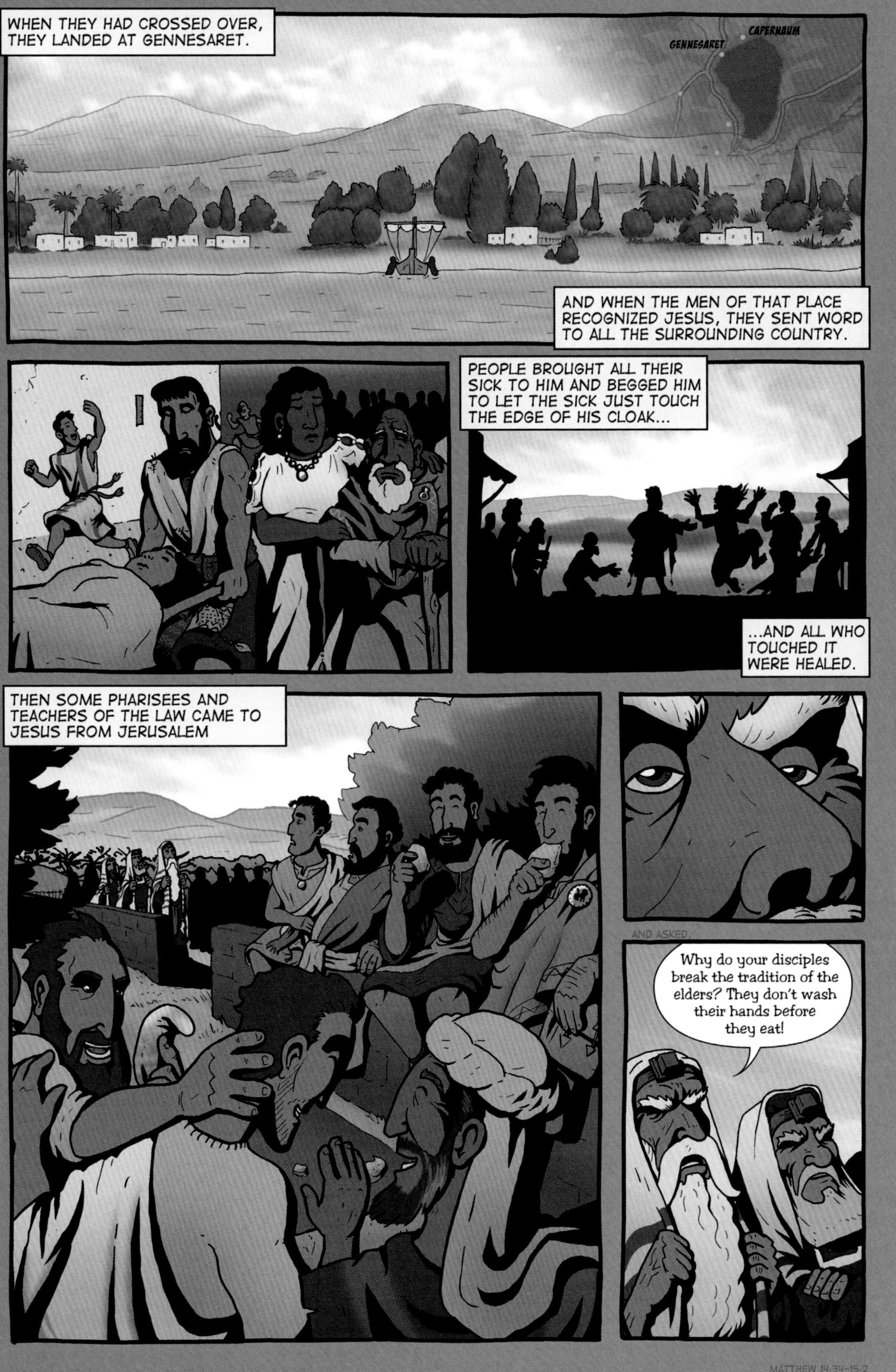
WHEN THEY HAD CROSSED OVER, THEY LANDED AT GENNESARET.
GENNESARET
CAPERNAUM
AND WHEN THE MEN OF THAT PLACE RECOGNIZED JESUS, THEY SENT WORD TO ALL THE SURROUNDING COUNTRY.
PEOPLE BROUGHT ALL THEIR SICK TO HIM AND BEGGED HIM TO LET THE SICK JUST TOUCH THE EDGE OF HIS CLOAK...
...AND ALL WHO TOUCHED IT WERE HEALED.
THEN SOME PHARISEES AND TEACHERS OF THE LAW CAME TO JESUS FROM JERUSALEM
AND ASKED,
Why do your disciples break the tradition of the elders? They don't wash their hands before they eat!

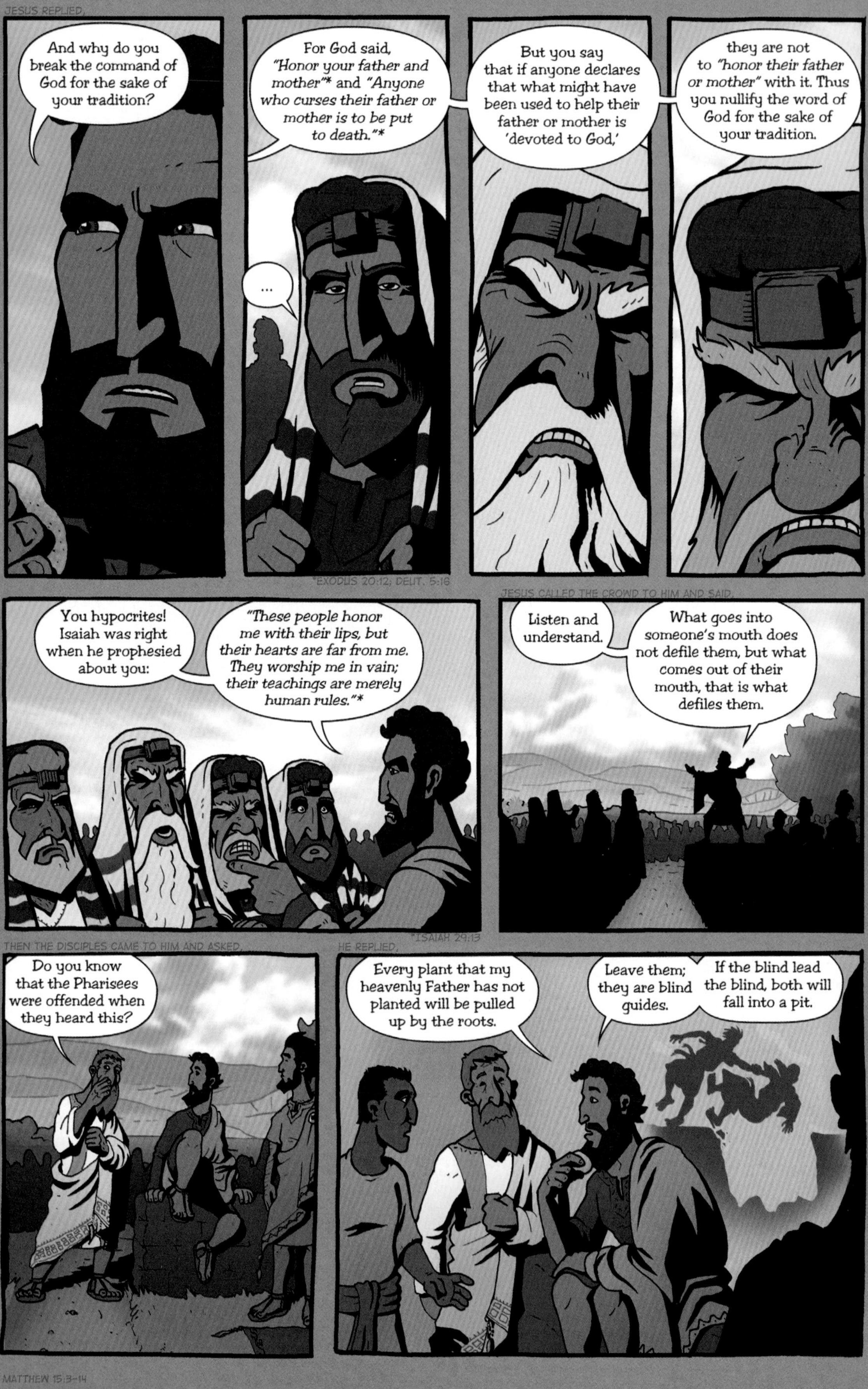
JESUS REPLIED,
And why do you break the command of God for the sake of your tradition?
For God said, "Honor your father and mother"* and "Anyone who curses their father or mother is to be put to death."*
...
But you say that if anyone declares that what might have been used to help their father or mother is 'devoted to God,'
they are not to "honor their father or mother" with it. Thus you nullify the word of God for the sake of your tradition.
*EXODUS 20:12; DEUT. 5:16
You hypocrites! Isaiah was right when he prophesied about you:
"These people honor me with their lips, but their hearts are far from me. They worship me in vain; their teachings are merely human rules."*
*ISAIAH 29:13
JESUS CALLED THE CROWD TO HIM AND SAID,
Listen and understand.
What goes into someone's mouth does not defile them, but what comes out of their mouth, that is what defiles them.
THEN THE DISCIPLES CAME TO HIM AND ASKED,
Do you know that the Pharisees were offended when they heard this?
HE REPLIED,
Every plant that my heavenly Father has not planted will be pulled up by the roots.
Leave them; they are blind guides.
If the blind lead the blind, both will fall into a pit.

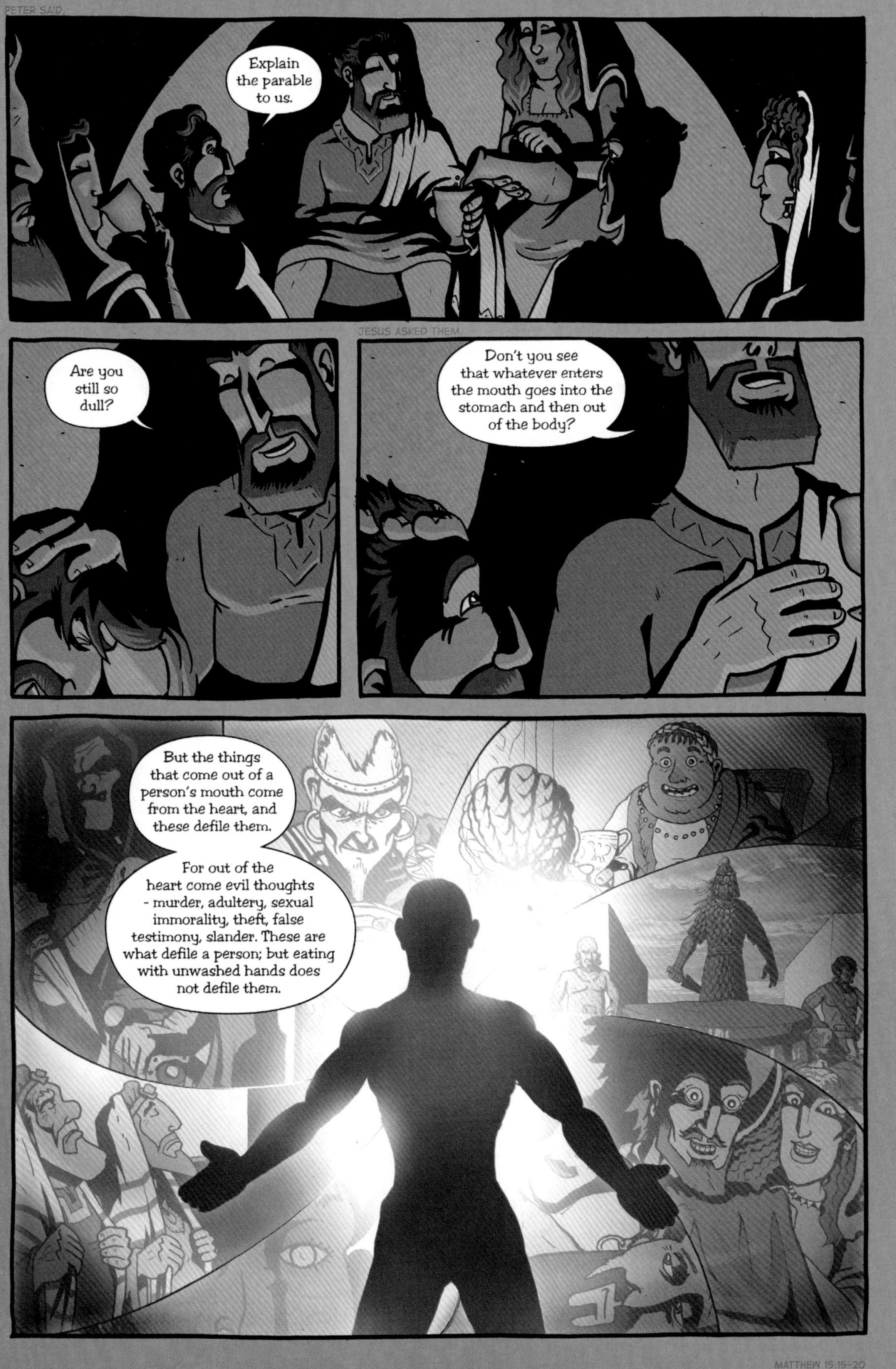
PETER SAID,
Explain the parable to us.
JESUS ASKED THEM,
Are you still so dull?
Don't you see that whatever enters the mouth goes into the stomach and then out of the body?
But the things that come out of a person's mouth come from the heart, and these defile them.
For out of the heart come evil thoughts - murder, adultery, sexual immorality, theft, false testimony, slander. These are what defile a person; but eating with unwashed hands does not defile them.

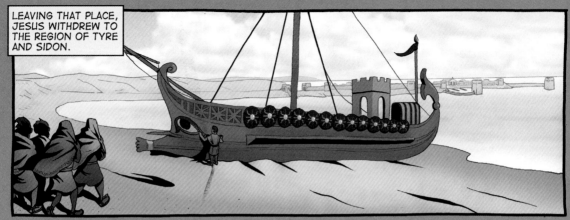

LEAVING THAT PLACE, JESUS WITHDREW TO THE REGION OF TYRE AND SIDON.

A CANAANITE WOMAN FROM THAT VICINITY CAME TO HIM

LORD, SON OF DAVID, HAVE MERCY ON ME! MY DAUGHTER IS DEMON-POSSESSED AND SUFFERING TERRIBLY.

JESUS DID NOT ANSWER A WORD.

SO HIS DISCIPLES CAME TO HIM AND URGED HIM,

Send her away

for she keeps crying out after us.

HE ANSWERED.

I WAS SENT ONLY TO THE LOST SHEEP OF ISRAEL.

THE WOMAN CAME AND KNELT BEFORE HIM.

LORD, HELP ME!

HE REPLIED.

IT IS NOT RIGHT TO TAKE THE CHILDREN'S BREAD AND TOSS IT TO THE DOGS.

SHE SAID.

YES IT IS, LORD.

EVEN THE DOGS EAT THE CRUMBS THAT FALL FROM THEIR MASTER'S TABLE.

SHE SAID.

THEN JESUS SAID TO HER,

WOMAN, YOU HAVE GREAT FAITH! YOUR REQUEST IS GRANTED.

AND HER DAUGHTER WAS HEALED AT THAT MOMENT.

MATTHEW 15:21-28

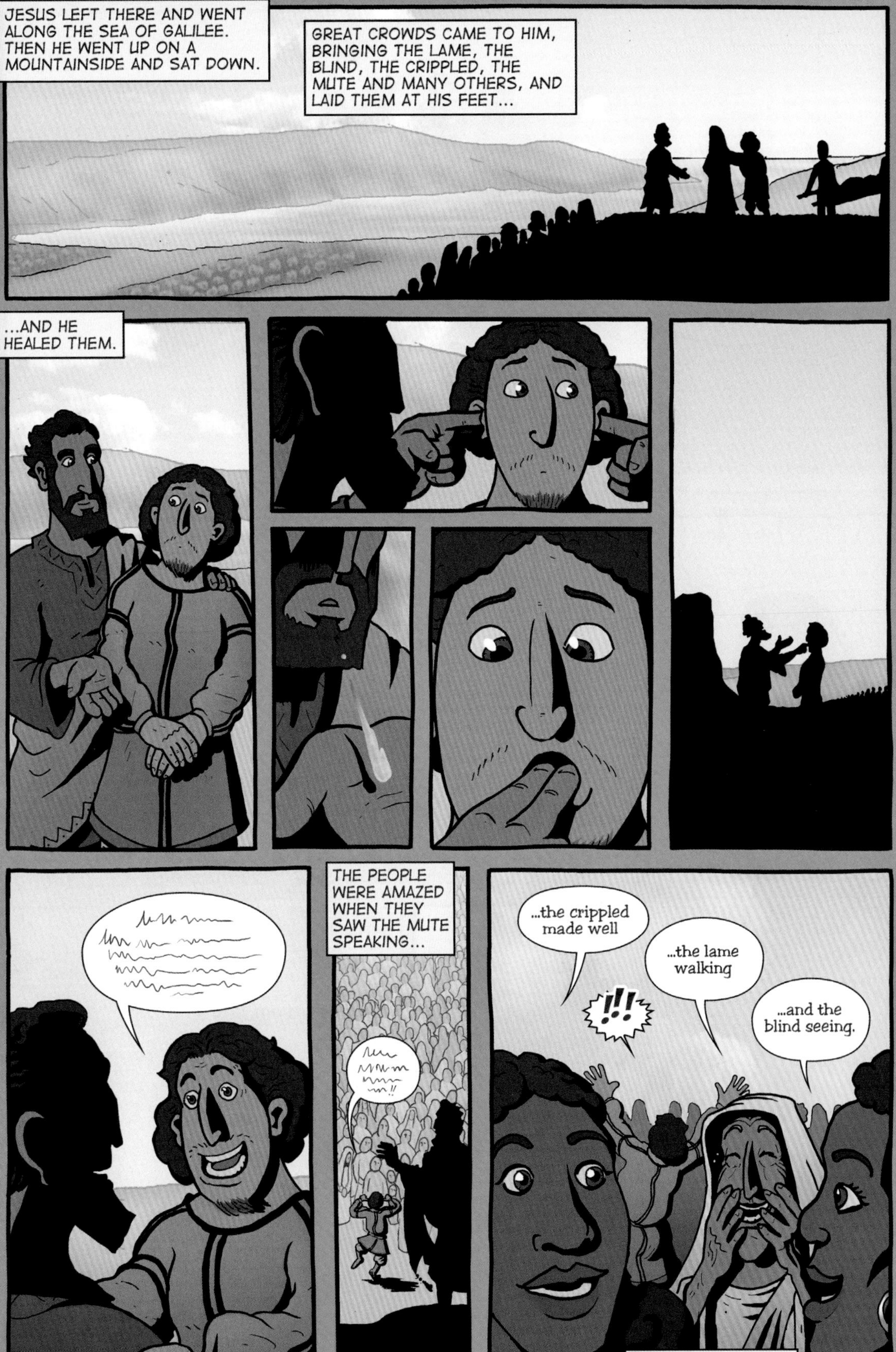

JESUS LEFT THERE AND WENT ALONG THE SEA OF GALILEE. THEN HE WENT UP ON A MOUNTAINSIDE AND SAT DOWN.
GREAT CROWDS CAME TO HIM, BRINGING THE LAME, THE BLIND, THE CRIPPLED, THE MUTE AND MANY OTHERS, AND LAID THEM AT HIS FEET...
...AND HE HEALED THEM.
THE PEOPLE WERE AMAZED WHEN THEY SAW THE MUTE SPEAKING...
...the crippled made well
...the lame walking
!!!
...and the blind seeing.
AND THEY PRAISED THE GOD OF ISRAEL.

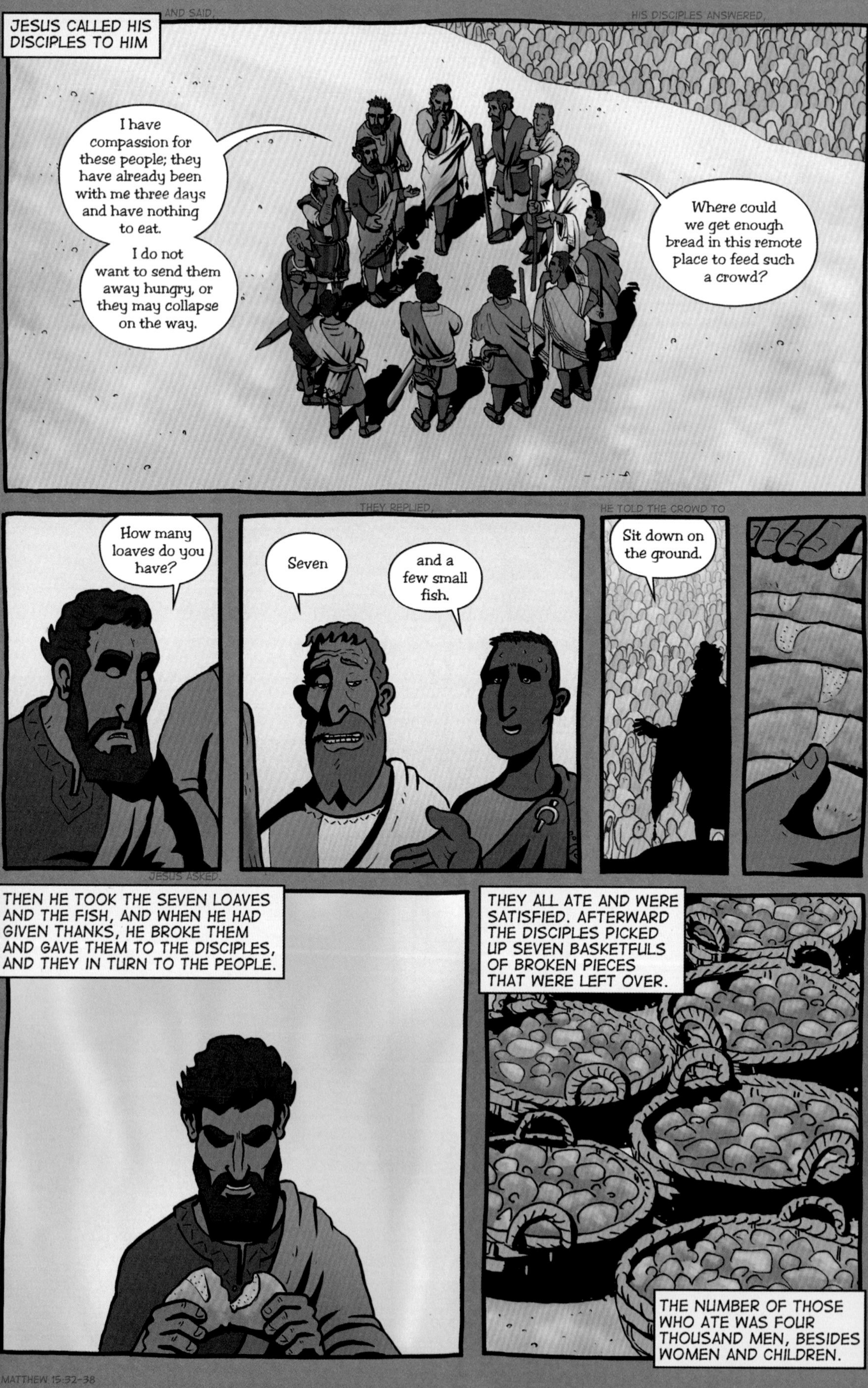
JESUS CALLED HIS DISCIPLES TO HIM
AND SAID,
I have compassion for these people; they have already been with me three days and have nothing to eat.
I do not want to send them away hungry, or they may collapse on the way.
HIS DISCIPLES ANSWERED,
Where could we get enough bread in this remote place to feed such a crowd?
How many loaves do you have?
JESUS ASKED.
THEY REPLIED,
Seven
and a few small fish.
HE TOLD THE CROWD TO
Sit down on the ground.
THEN HE TOOK THE SEVEN LOAVES AND THE FISH, AND WHEN HE HAD GIVEN THANKS, HE BROKE THEM AND GAVE THEM TO THE DISCIPLES, AND THEY IN TURN TO THE PEOPLE.
THEY ALL ATE AND WERE SATISFIED. AFTERWARD THE DISCIPLES PICKED UP SEVEN BASKETFULS OF BROKEN PIECES THAT WERE LEFT OVER.
THE NUMBER OF THOSE WHO ATE WAS FOUR THOUSAND MEN, BESIDES WOMEN AND CHILDREN.

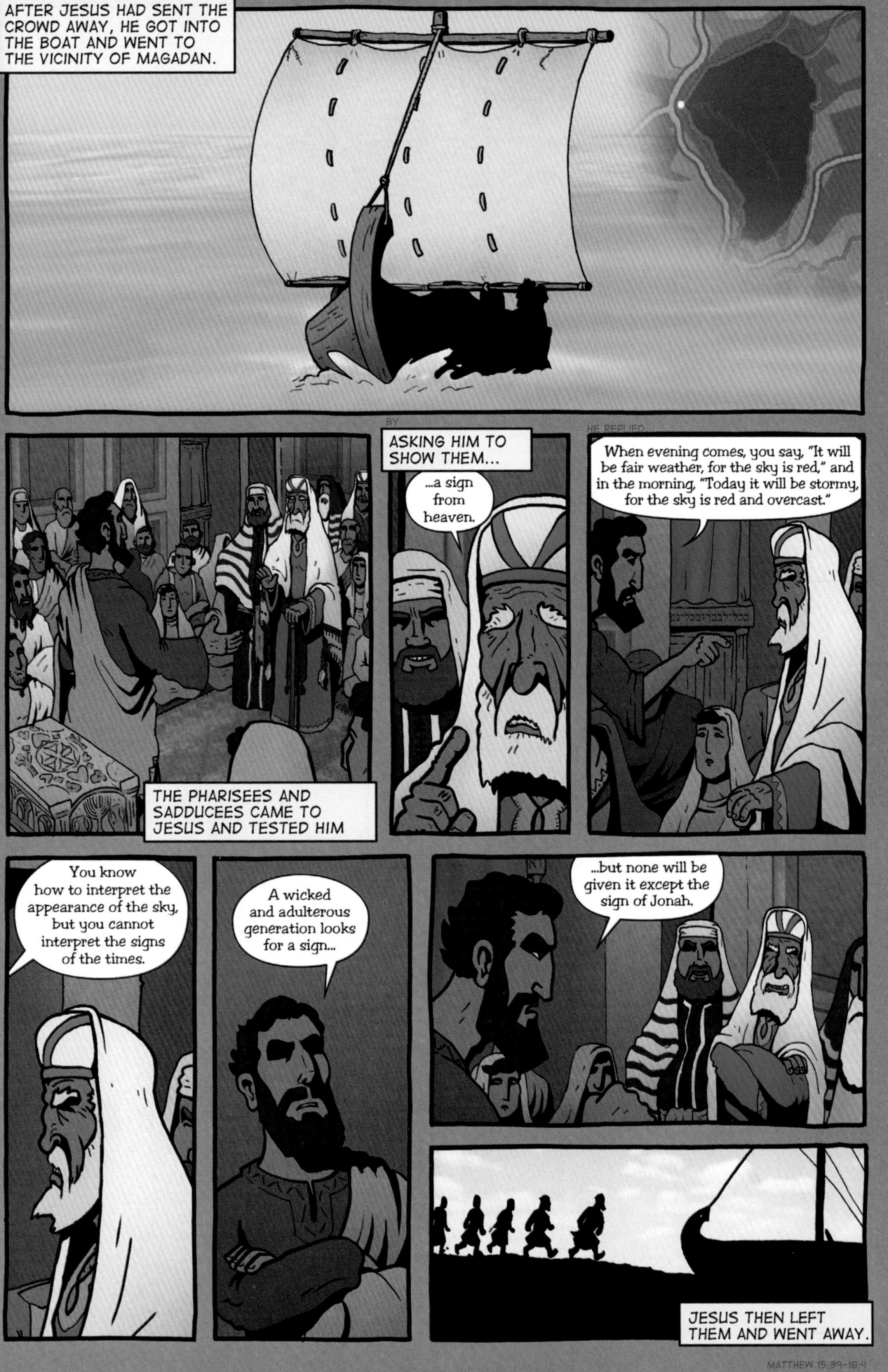
AFTER JESUS HAD SENT THE CROWD AWAY, HE GOT INTO THE BOAT AND WENT TO THE VICINITY OF MAGADAN.
THE PHARISEES AND SADDUCEES CAME TO JESUS AND TESTED HIM
ASKING HIM TO SHOW THEM...
...a sign from heaven.
When evening comes, you say, "It will be fair weather, for the sky is red," and in the morning, "Today it will be stormy, for the sky is red and overcast."
You know how to interpret the appearance of the sky, but you cannot interpret the signs of the times.
A wicked and adulterous generation looks for a sign...
...but none will be given it except the sign of Jonah.
JESUS THEN LEFT THEM AND WENT AWAY.

WHEN THEY WENT ACROSS THE LAKE, THE DISCIPLES FORGOT TO TAKE BREAD.

JESUS SAID TO THEM

AND SAID,

THEY DISCUSSED AMONG THEMSELVES

AWARE OF THEIR DISCUSSION, JESUS ASKED,

Be careful

Be on your guard against the yeast of the Pharisees and Sadducees.

It is because we didn't bring any bread.

You of little faith, why are you talking among yourselves about having no bread?

Do you still not understand?

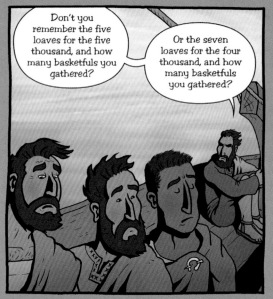

Don't you remember the five loaves for the five thousand, and how many basketfuls you gathered?

Or the seven loaves for the four thousand, and how many basketfuls you gathered?

How is it you don't understand that I was not talking to you about bread? But be on your guard against the yeast of the Pharisees and Sadducees.

THEN THEY UNDERSTOOD THAT HE WAS NOT TELLING THEM TO GUARD AGAINST THE YEAST USED IN BREAD, BUT AGAINST THE TEACHING OF THE PHARISEES AND SADDUCEES.

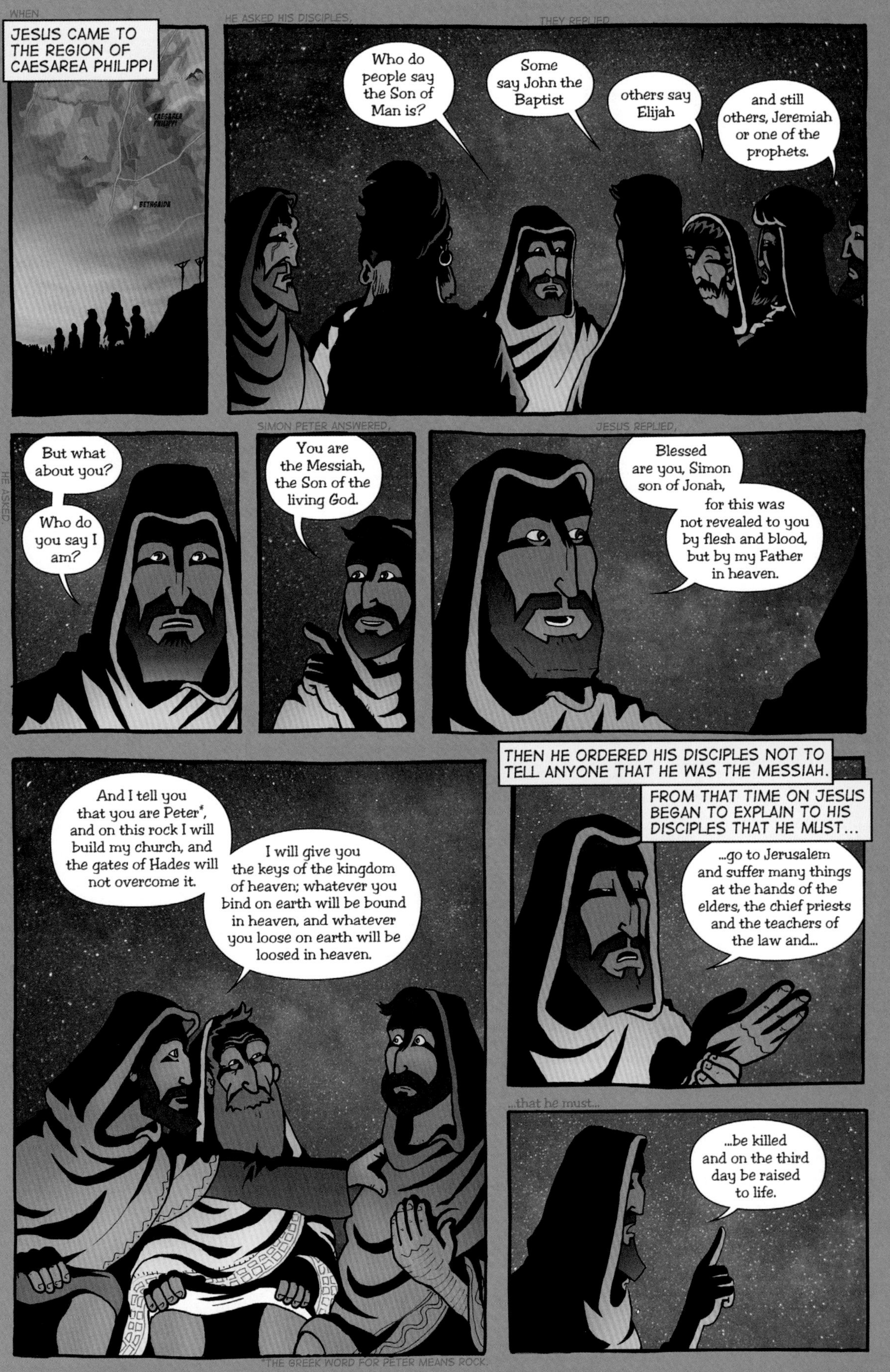
WHEN
JESUS CAME TO THE REGION OF CAESAREA PHILIPPI
CAESAREA PHILIPPI
BETHSAIDA
HE ASKED HIS DISCIPLES,
Who do people say the Son of Man is?
THEY REPLIED
Some say John the Baptist
others say Elijah
and still others, Jeremiah or one of the prophets.
HE ASKED
But what about you?
Who do you say I am?
SIMON PETER ANSWERED,
You are the Messiah, the Son of the living God.
JESUS REPLIED,
Blessed are you, Simon son of Jonah, for this was not revealed to you by flesh and blood, but by my Father in heaven.
And I tell you that you are Peter*, and on this rock I will build my church, and the gates of Hades will not overcome it.
I will give you the keys of the kingdom of heaven; whatever you bind on earth will be bound in heaven, and whatever you loose on earth will be loosed in heaven.
*THE GREEK WORD FOR PETER MEANS ROCK.
THEN HE ORDERED HIS DISCIPLES NOT TO TELL ANYONE THAT HE WAS THE MESSIAH.
FROM THAT TIME ON JESUS BEGAN TO EXPLAIN TO HIS DISCIPLES THAT HE MUST...
...go to Jerusalem and suffer many things at the hands of the elders, the chief priests and the teachers of the law and...
...that he must...
...be killed and on the third day be raised to life.

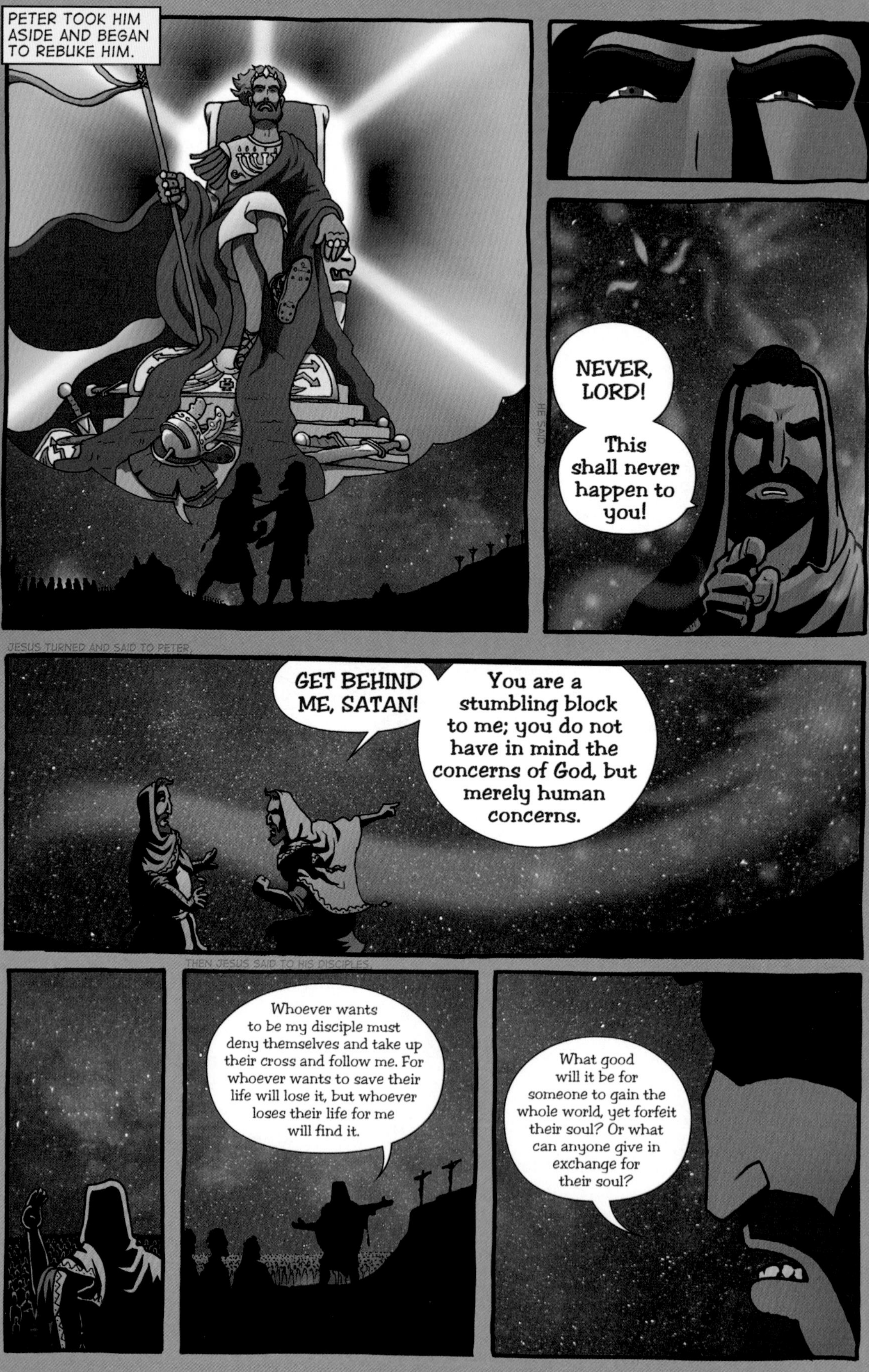
PETER TOOK HIM ASIDE AND BEGAN TO REBUKE HIM.
HE SAID,
NEVER, LORD!
This shall never happen to you!
JESUS TURNED AND SAID TO PETER,
GET BEHIND ME, SATAN!
You are a stumbling block to me; you do not have in mind the concerns of God, but merely human concerns.
THEN JESUS SAID TO HIS DISCIPLES,
Whoever wants to be my disciple must deny themselves and take up their cross and follow me. For whoever wants to save their life will lose it, but whoever loses their life for me will find it.
What good will it be for someone to gain the whole world, yet forfeit their soul? Or what can anyone give in exchange for their soul?

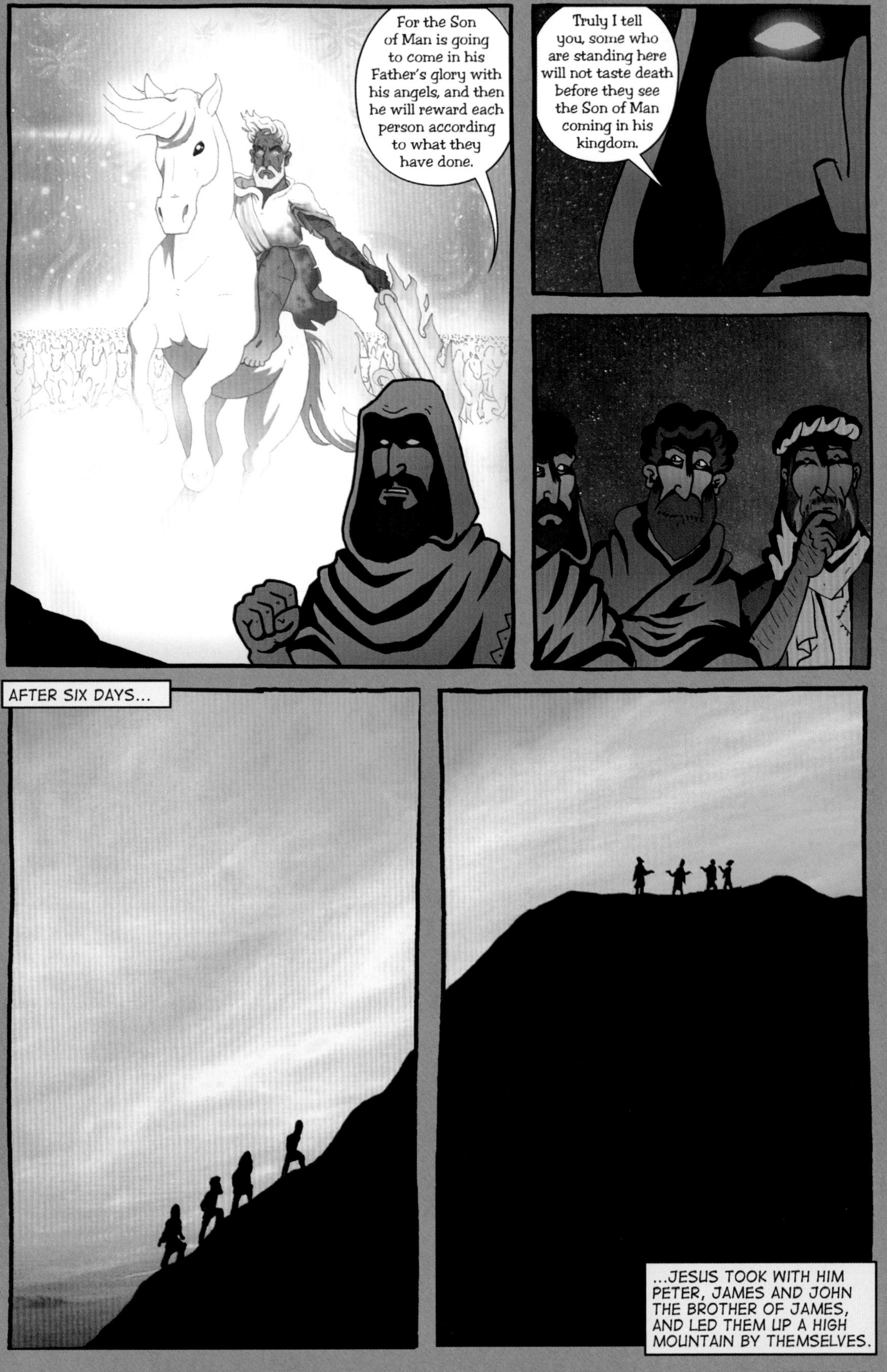
For the Son of Man is going to come in his Father's glory with his angels, and then he will reward each person according to what they have done.
Truly I tell you, some who are standing here will not taste death before they see the Son of Man coming in his kingdom.
AFTER SIX DAYS...
...JESUS TOOK WITH HIM PETER, JAMES AND JOHN THE BROTHER OF JAMES, AND LED THEM UP A HIGH MOUNTAIN BY THEMSELVES.

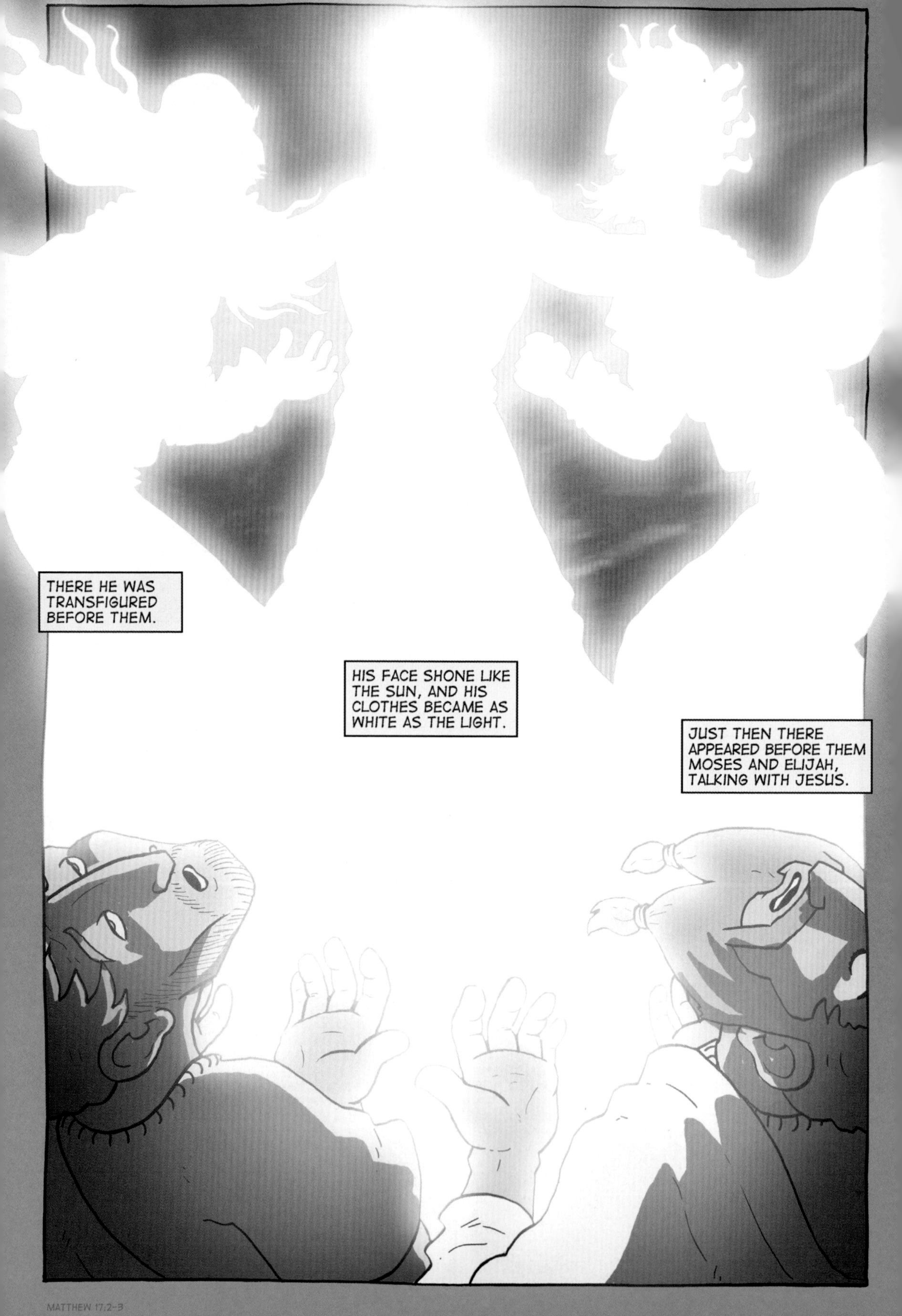
THERE HE WAS TRANSFIGURED BEFORE THEM.
HIS FACE SHONE LIKE THE SUN, AND HIS CLOTHES BECAME AS WHITE AS THE LIGHT.
JUST THEN THERE APPEARED BEFORE THEM MOSES AND ELIJAH, TALKING WITH JESUS.

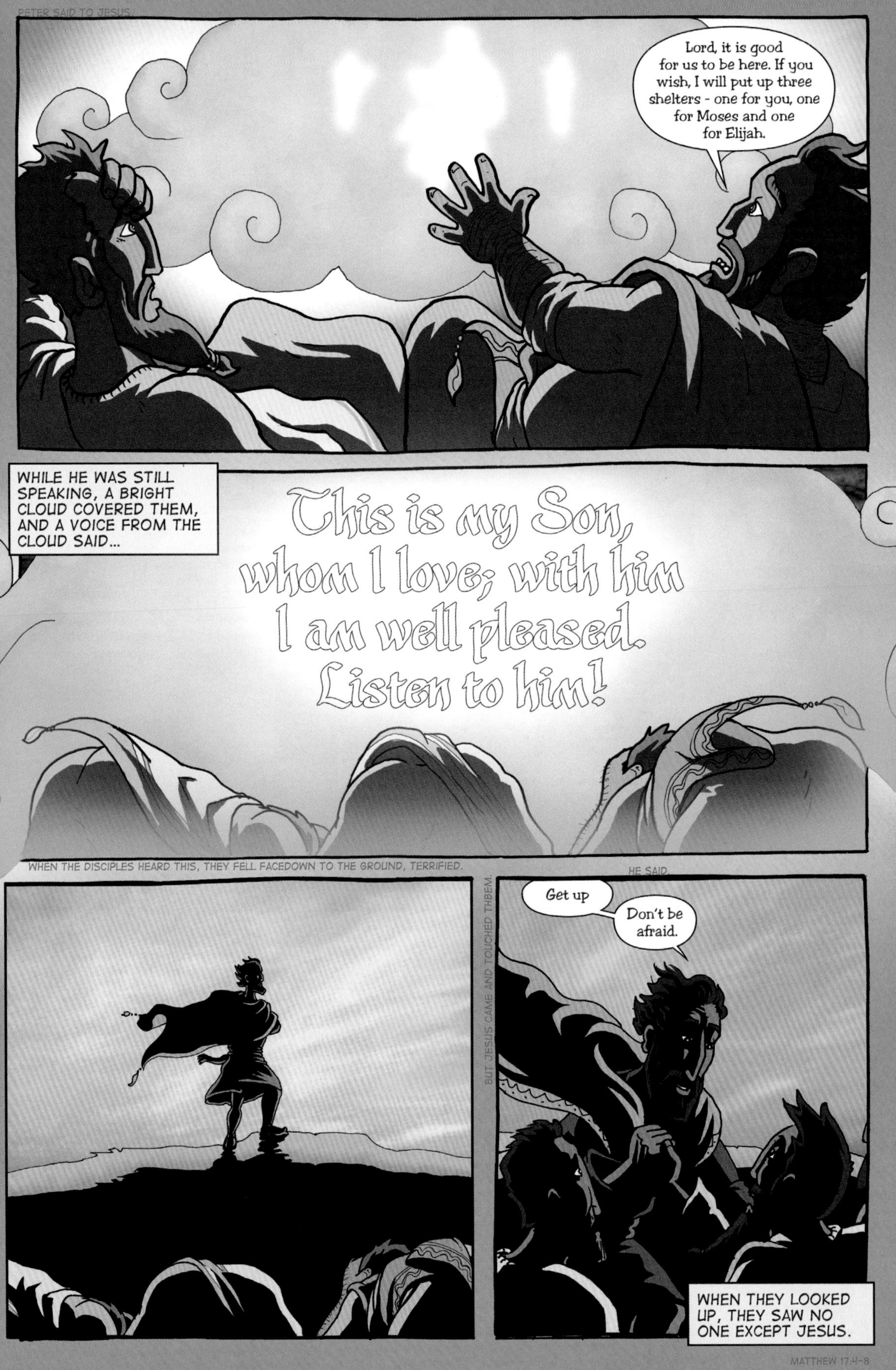
PETER SAID TO JESUS,
Lord, it is good for us to be here. If you wish, I will put up three shelters - one for you, one for Moses and one for Elijah.
WHILE HE WAS STILL SPEAKING, A BRIGHT CLOUD COVERED THEM, AND A VOICE FROM THE CLOUD SAID...
This is my Son, whom I love; with him I am well pleased. Listen to him!
WHEN THE DISCIPLES HEARD THIS, THEY FELL FACEDOWN TO THE GROUND, TERRIFIED.
BUT JESUS CAME AND TOUCHED THEM.
HE SAID,
Get up
Don't be afraid.
WHEN THEY LOOKED UP, THEY SAW NO ONE EXCEPT JESUS.

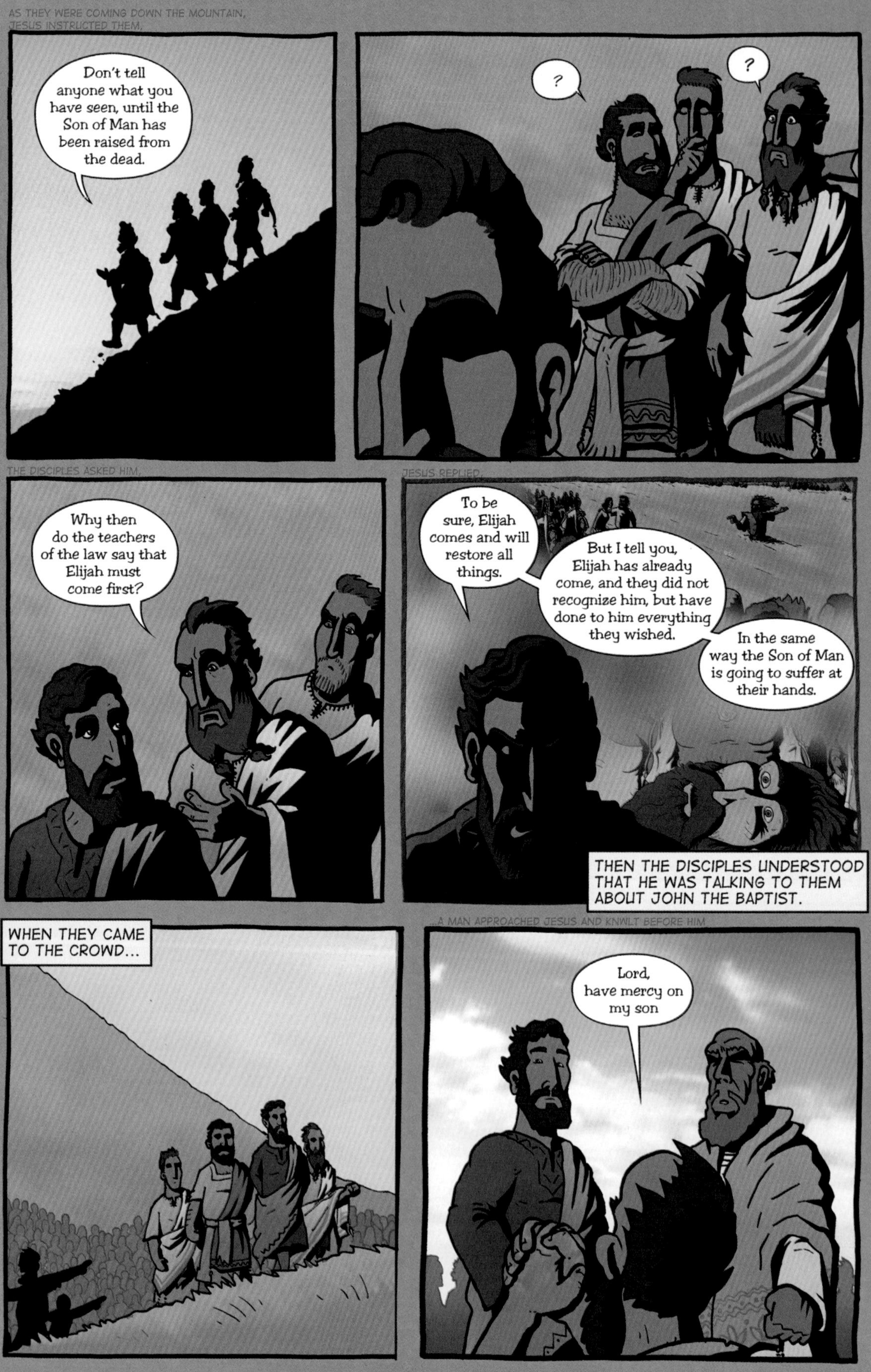
AS THEY WERE COMING DOWN THE MOUNTAIN, JESUS INSTRUCTED THEM,
Don't tell anyone what you have seen, until the Son of Man has been raised from the dead.
?
?
THE DISCIPLES ASKED HIM,
Why then do the teachers of the law say that Elijah must come first?
JESUS REPLIED,
To be sure, Elijah comes and will restore all things.
But I tell you, Elijah has already come, and they did not recognize him, but have done to him everything they wished.
In the same way the Son of Man is going to suffer at their hands.
THEN THE DISCIPLES UNDERSTOOD THAT HE WAS TALKING TO THEM ABOUT JOHN THE BAPTIST.
WHEN THEY CAME TO THE CROWD...
...A MAN APPROACHED JESUS AND KNWLT BEFORE HIM
Lord, have mercy on my son

"He has seizures and is suffering greatly. He often falls into the fire or into the water."

"I brought him to your disciples, but they could not heal him."

"You unbelieving and perverse generation, how long shall I stay with you? How long shall I put up with you? Bring the boy here to me."

"AAAAAA"

JESUS REBUKED THE DEMON AND IT CAME

"OUT OF THE BOY"

HE WAS HEALED AT THAT MOMENT.

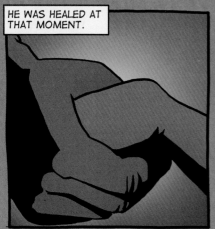

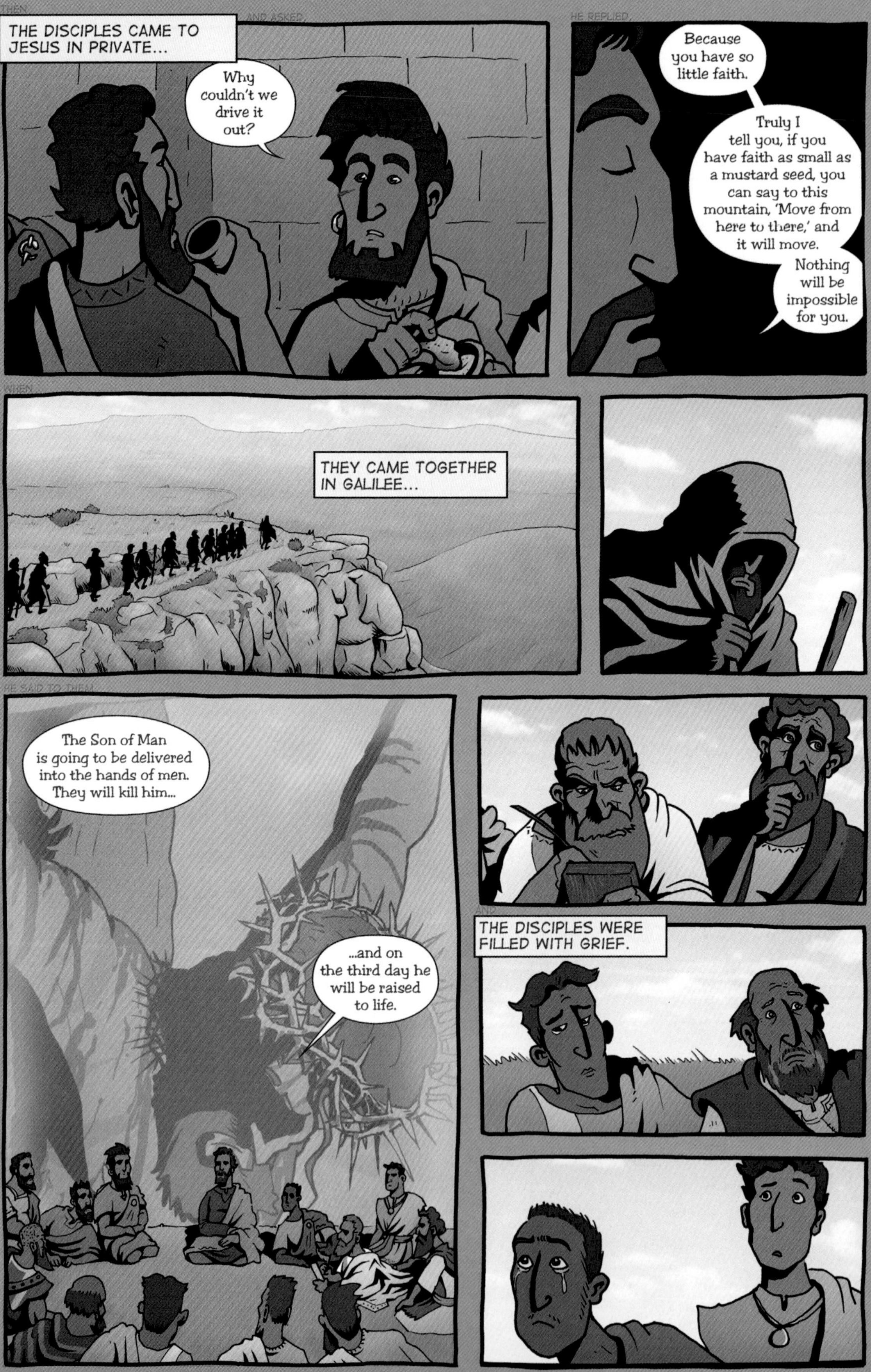
THEN
THE DISCIPLES CAME TO JESUS IN PRIVATE...
AND ASKED,
Why couldn't we drive it out?
HE REPLIED,
Because you have so little faith.
Truly I tell you, if you have faith as small as a mustard seed, you can say to this mountain, 'Move from here to there,' and it will move.
Nothing will be impossible for you.
WHEN
THEY CAME TOGETHER IN GALILEE...
HE SAID TO THEM,
The Son of Man is going to be delivered into the hands of men. They will kill him...
...and on the third day he will be raised to life.
AND
THE DISCIPLES WERE FILLED WITH GRIEF.

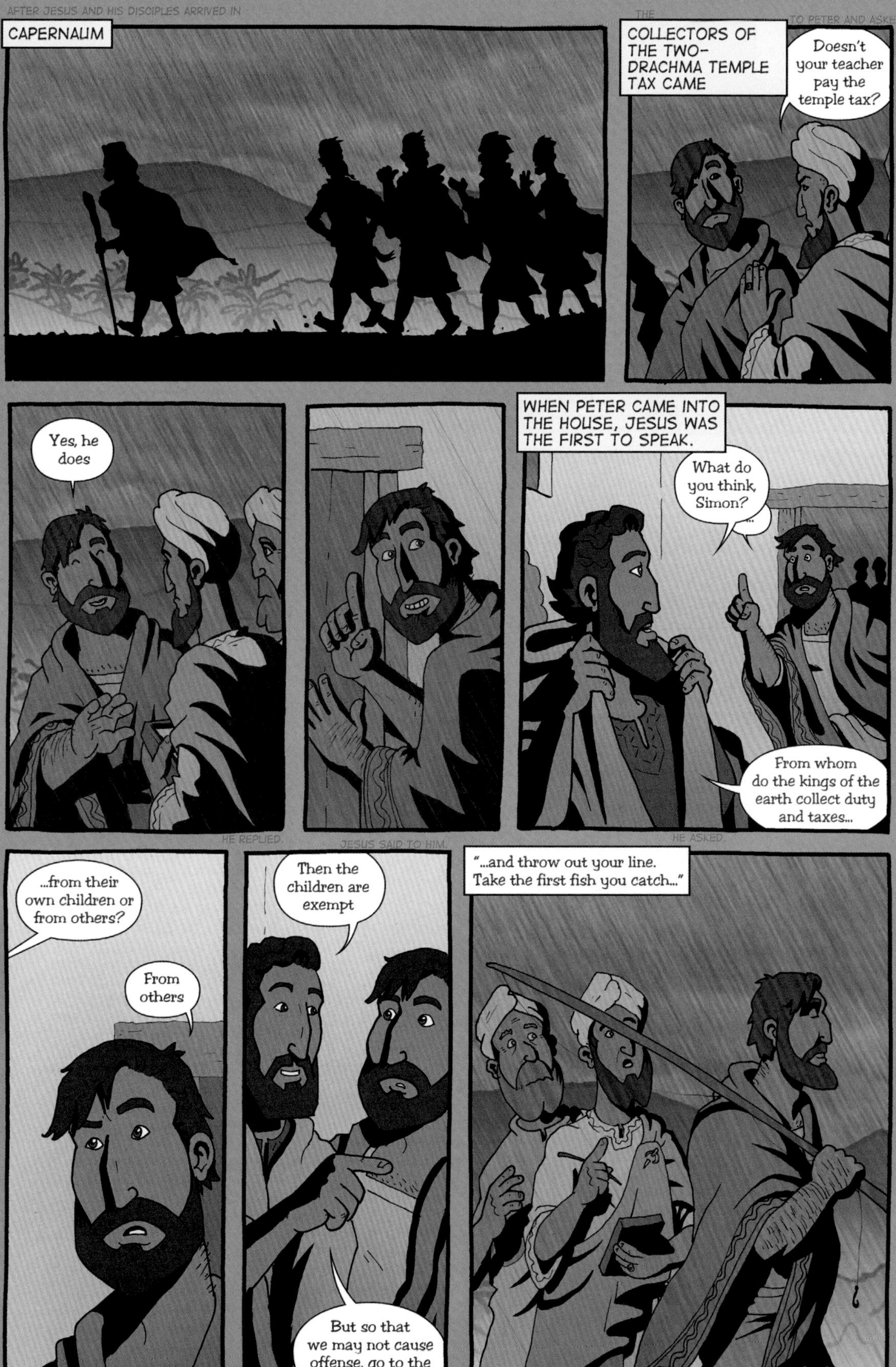

AFTER JESUS AND HIS DISCIPLES ARRIVED IN
CAPERNAUM
THE
COLLECTORS OF THE TWO-DRACHMA TEMPLE TAX CAME
TO PETER AND ASKED,
Doesn't your teacher pay the temple tax?
Yes, he does
HE REPLIED.
WHEN PETER CAME INTO THE HOUSE, JESUS WAS THE FIRST TO SPEAK.
What do you think, Simon?
JESUS SAID TO HIM.
...
From whom do the kings of the earth collect duty and taxes...
HE ASKED.
...from their own children or from others?
From others
PETER ANSWERED.
Then the children are exempt
But so that we may not cause offense, go to the lake...
"...and throw out your line. Take the first fish you catch..."

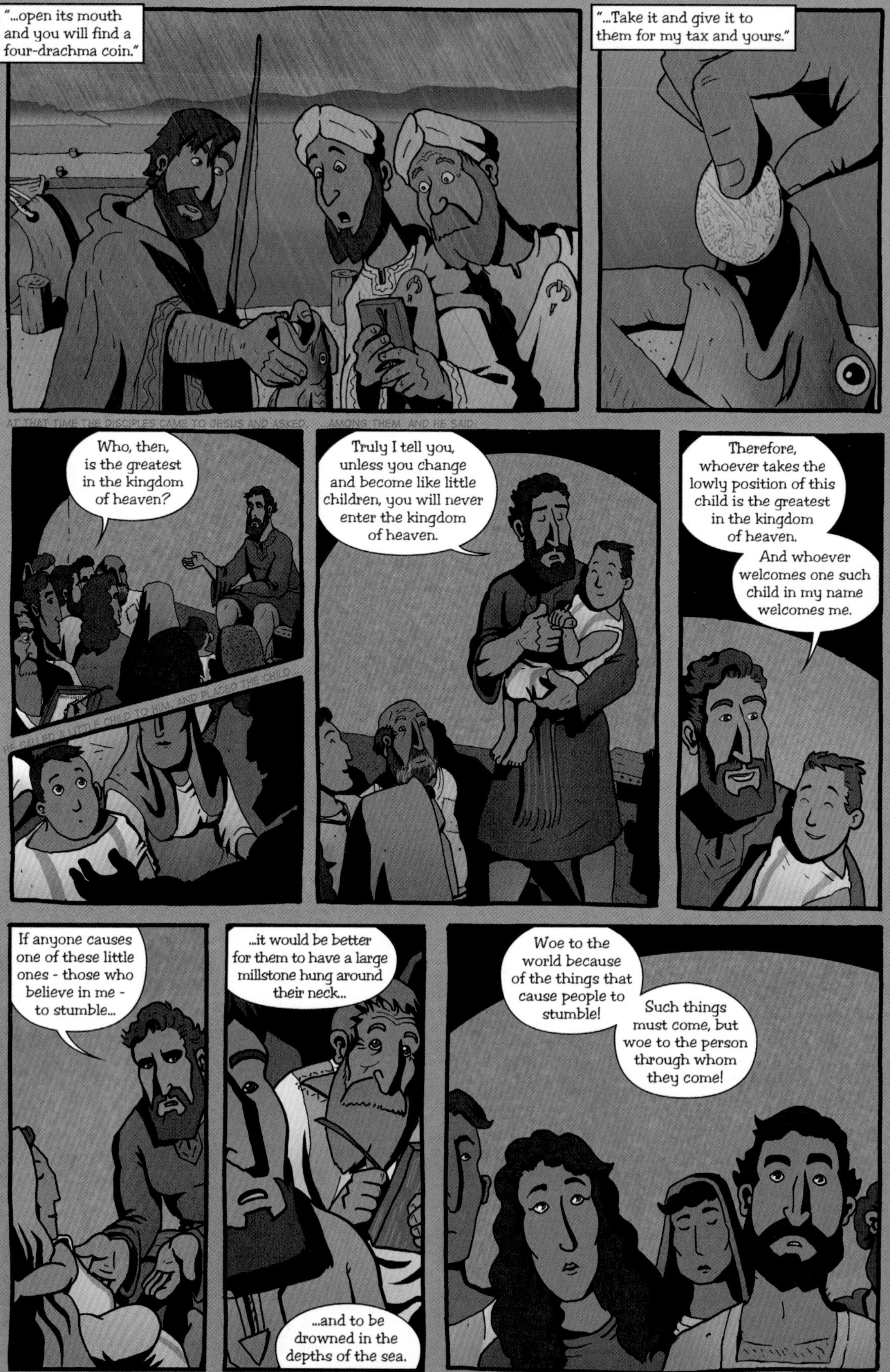

"...open its mouth and you will find a four-drachma coin."
"...Take it and give it to them for my tax and yours."
AT THAT TIME THE DISCIPLES CAME TO JESUS AND ASKED,
Who, then, is the greatest in the kingdom of heaven?
HE CALLED A LITTLE CHILD TO HIM, AND PLACED THE CHILD...
...AMONG THEM. AND HE SAID:
Truly I tell you, unless you change and become like little children, you will never enter the kingdom of heaven.
Therefore, whoever takes the lowly position of this child is the greatest in the kingdom of heaven.
And whoever welcomes one such child in my name welcomes me.
If anyone causes one of these little ones - those who believe in me - to stumble...
...it would be better for them to have a large millstone hung around their neck...
...and to be drowned in the depths of the sea.
Woe to the world because of the things that cause people to stumble!
Such things must come, but woe to the person through whom they come!

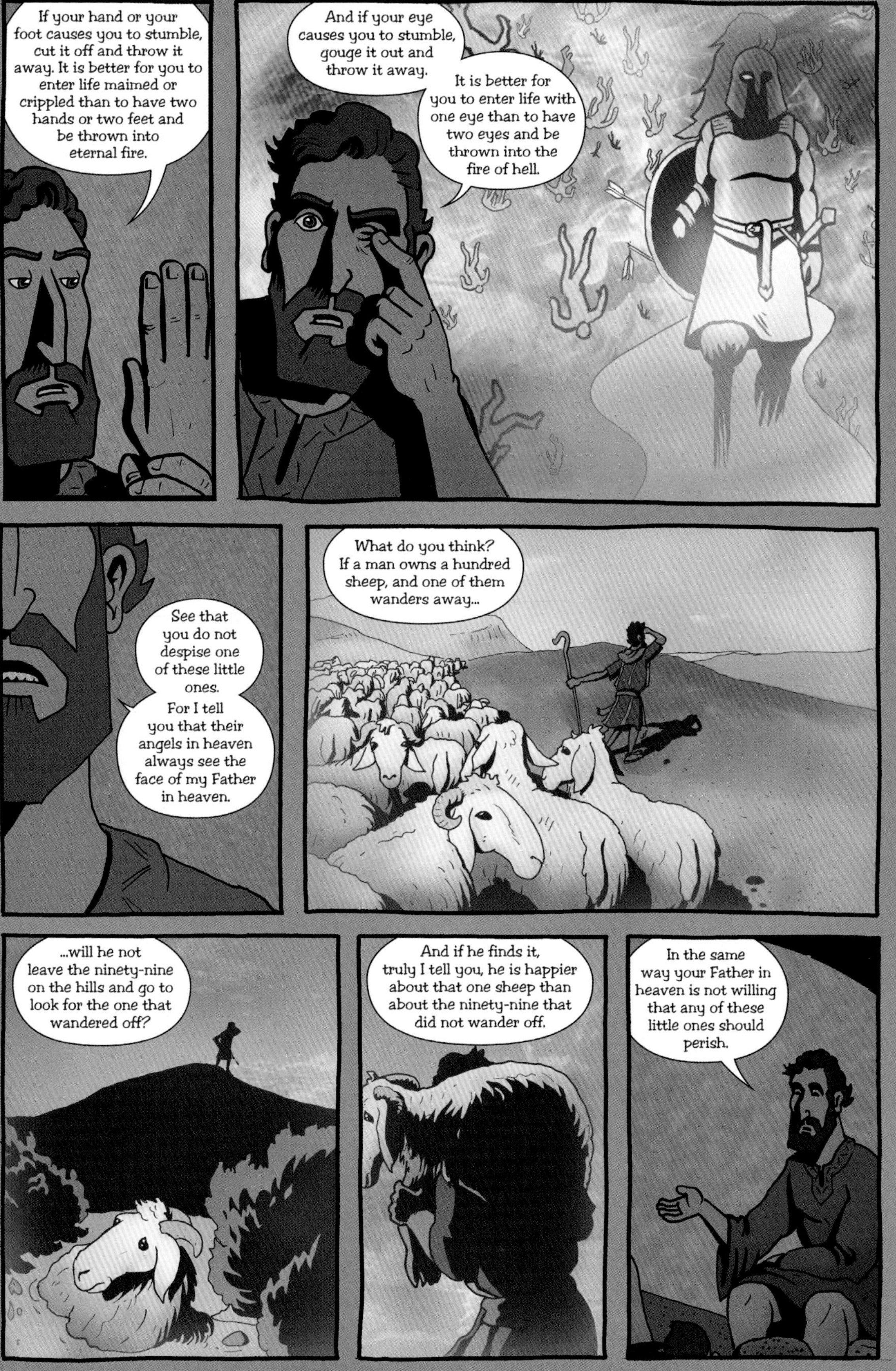
If your hand or your foot causes you to stumble, cut it off and throw it away. It is better for you to enter life maimed or crippled than to have two hands or two feet and be thrown into eternal fire.
And if your eye causes you to stumble, gouge it out and throw it away.
It is better for you to enter life with one eye than to have two eyes and be thrown into the fire of hell.
See that you do not despise one of these little ones.
For I tell you that their angels in heaven always see the face of my Father in heaven.
What do you think? If a man owns a hundred sheep, and one of them wanders away...
...will he not leave the ninety-nine on the hills and go to look for the one that wandered off?
And if he finds it, truly I tell you, he is happier about that one sheep than about the ninety-nine that did not wander off.
In the same way your Father in heaven is not willing that any of these little ones should perish.

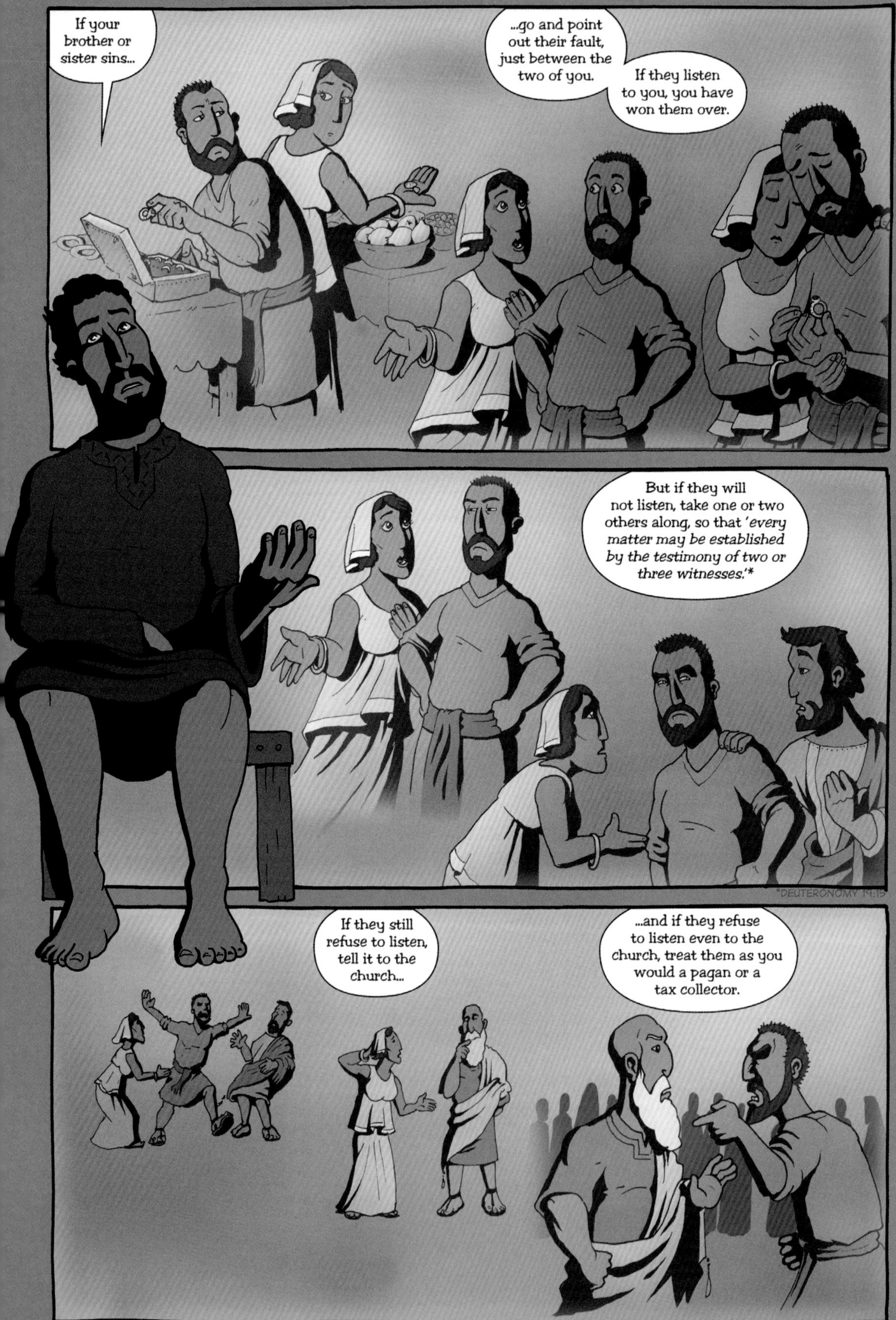
If your brother or sister sins...
...go and point out their fault, just between the two of you.
If they listen to you, you have won them over.
But if they will not listen, take one or two others along, so that *'every matter may be established by the testimony of two or three witnesses.'**
*DEUTERONOMY 19:15
If they still refuse to listen, tell it to the church...
...and if they refuse to listen even to the church, treat them as you would a pagan or a tax collector.

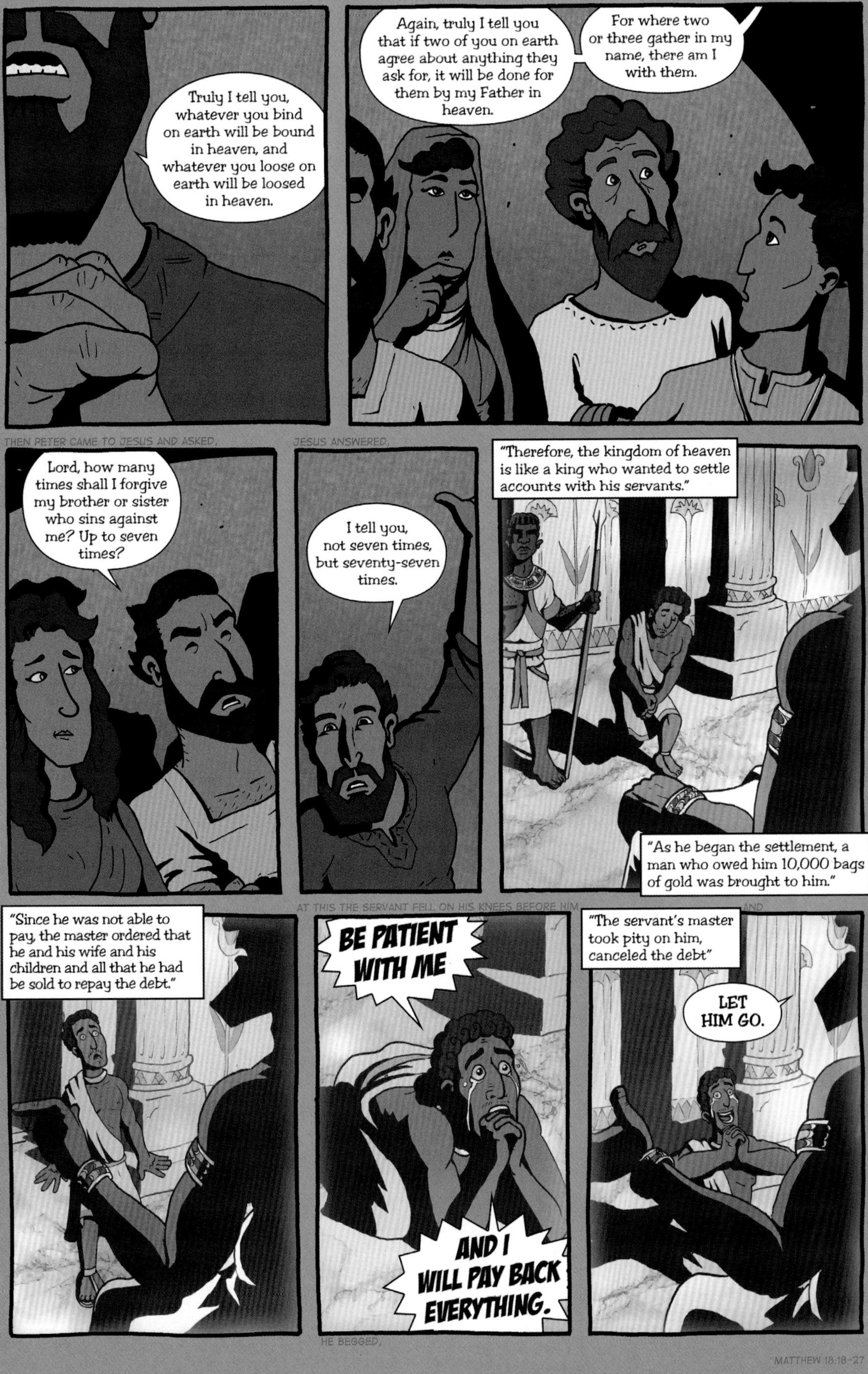
Truly I tell you, whatever you bind on earth will be bound in heaven, and whatever you loose on earth will be loosed in heaven.
Again, truly I tell you that if two of you on earth agree about anything they ask for, it will be done for them by my Father in heaven.
For where two or three gather in my name, there am I with them.
THEN PETER CAME TO JESUS AND ASKED,
Lord, how many times shall I forgive my brother or sister who sins against me? Up to seven times?
JESUS ANSWERED,
I tell you, not seven times, but seventy-seven times.
"Therefore, the kingdom of heaven is like a king who wanted to settle accounts with his servants."
"As he began the settlement, a man who owed him 10,000 bags of gold was brought to him."
"Since he was not able to pay, the master ordered that he and his wife and his children and all that he had be sold to repay the debt."
AT THIS THE SERVANT FELL ON HIS KNEES BEFORE HIM.
BE PATIENT WITH ME
HE BEGGED,
AND I WILL PAY BACK EVERYTHING.
AND
"The servant's master took pity on him, canceled the debt"
LET HIM GO.

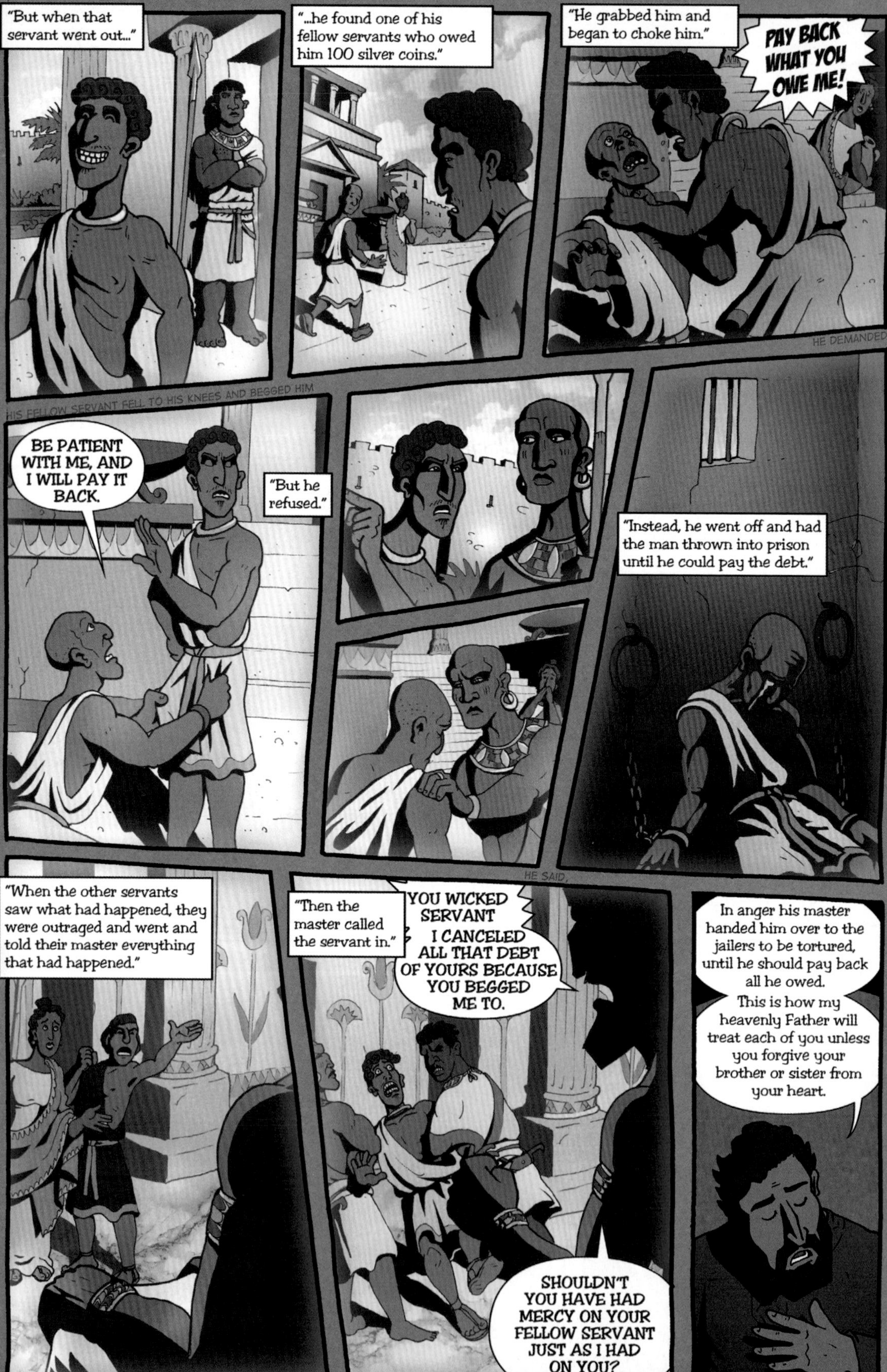
"But when that servant went out..."
"...he found one of his fellow servants who owed him 100 silver coins."
"He grabbed him and began to choke him."
PAY BACK WHAT YOU OWE ME!
HE DEMANDED.
HIS FELLOW SERVANT FELL TO HIS KNEES AND BEGGED HIM
BE PATIENT WITH ME, AND I WILL PAY IT BACK.
"But he refused."
"Instead, he went off and had the man thrown into prison until he could pay the debt."
"When the other servants saw what had happened, they were outraged and went and told their master everything that had happened."
HE SAID,
"Then the master called the servant in."
YOU WICKED SERVANT
I CANCELED ALL THAT DEBT OF YOURS BECAUSE YOU BEGGED ME TO.
SHOULDN'T YOU HAVE HAD MERCY ON YOUR FELLOW SERVANT JUST AS I HAD ON YOU?
In anger his master handed him over to the jailers to be tortured, until he should pay back all he owed.
This is how my heavenly Father will treat each of you unless you forgive your brother or sister from your heart.

MATTHEW 18:28-35

WORD FOR WORD
BIBLE COMIC

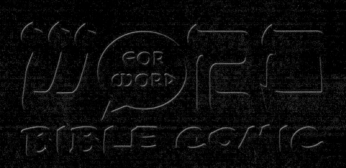

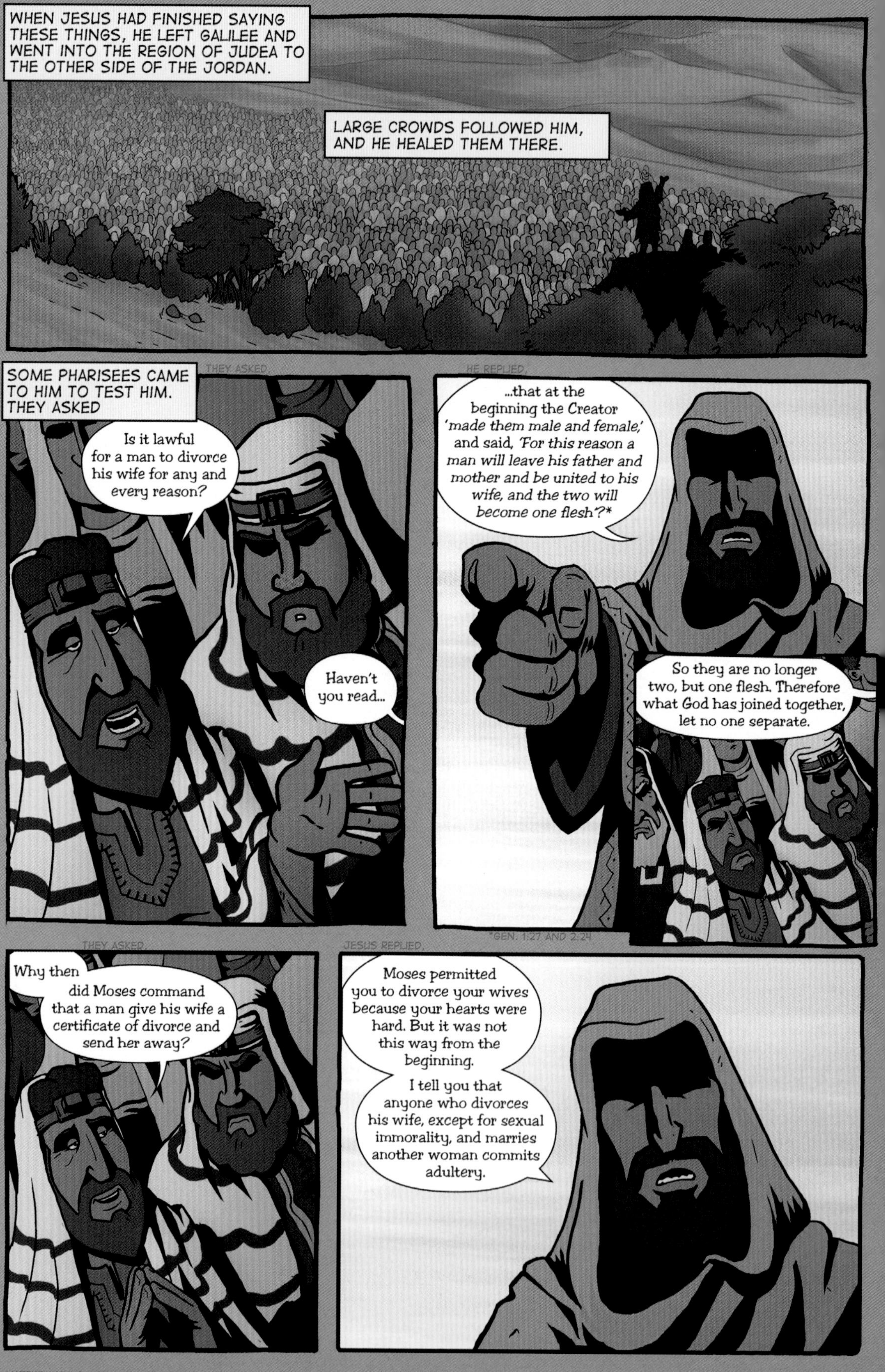
WHEN JESUS HAD FINISHED SAYING THESE THINGS, HE LEFT GALILEE AND WENT INTO THE REGION OF JUDEA TO THE OTHER SIDE OF THE JORDAN.
LARGE CROWDS FOLLOWED HIM, AND HE HEALED THEM THERE.
SOME PHARISEES CAME TO HIM TO TEST HIM. THEY ASKED
THEY ASKED,
Is it lawful for a man to divorce his wife for any and every reason?
Haven't you read...
HE REPLIED,
...that at the beginning the Creator *'made them male and female,'* and said, *'For this reason a man will leave his father and mother and be united to his wife, and the two will become one flesh'*?*
So they are no longer two, but one flesh. Therefore what God has joined together, let no one separate.
*GEN. 1:27 AND 2:24
THEY ASKED,
Why then did Moses command that a man give his wife a certificate of divorce and send her away?
JESUS REPLIED,
Moses permitted you to divorce your wives because your hearts were hard. But it was not this way from the beginning.
I tell you that anyone who divorces his wife, except for sexual immorality, and marries another woman commits adultery.

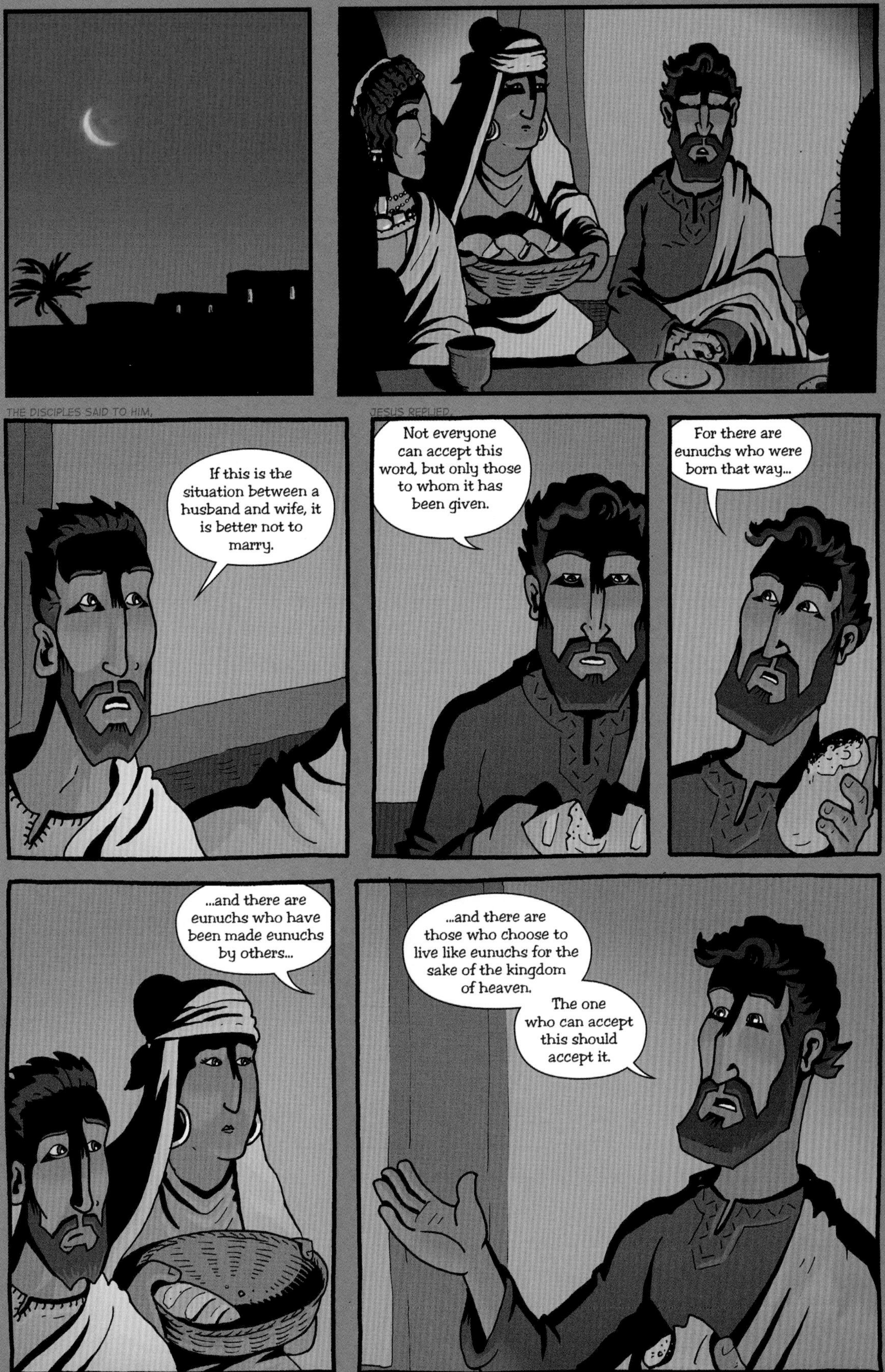
THE DISCIPLES SAID TO HIM,
If this is the situation between a husband and wife, it is better not to marry.
JESUS REPLIED,
Not everyone can accept this word, but only those to whom it has been given.
For there are eunuchs who were born that way...
...and there are eunuchs who have been made eunuchs by others...
...and there are those who choose to live like eunuchs for the sake of the kingdom of heaven.
The one who can accept this should accept it.

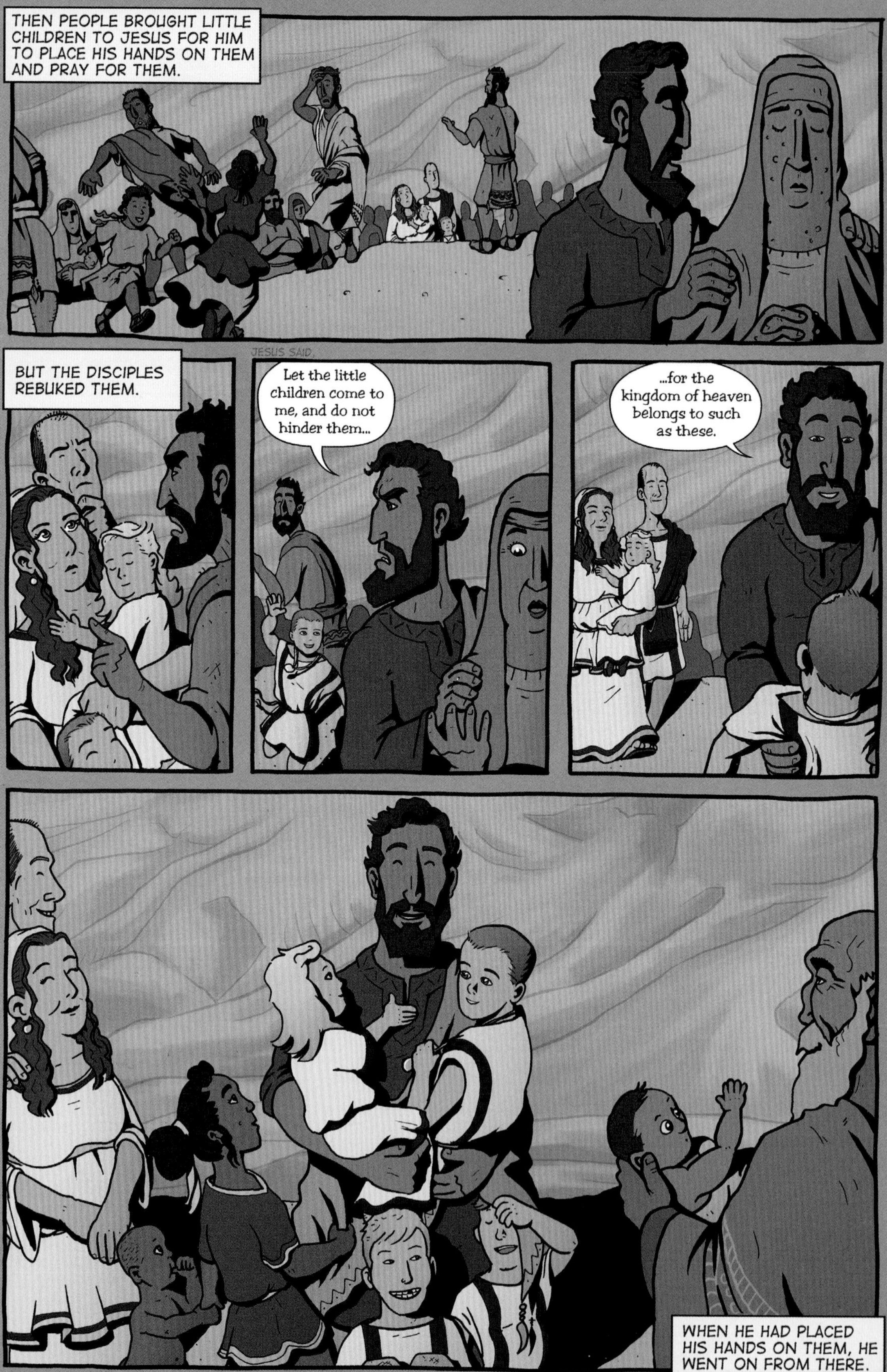
THEN PEOPLE BROUGHT LITTLE CHILDREN TO JESUS FOR HIM TO PLACE HIS HANDS ON THEM AND PRAY FOR THEM.
BUT THE DISCIPLES REBUKED THEM.
JESUS SAID,
Let the little children come to me, and do not hinder them...
...for the kingdom of heaven belongs to such as these.
WHEN HE HAD PLACED HIS HANDS ON THEM, HE WENT ON FROM THERE.

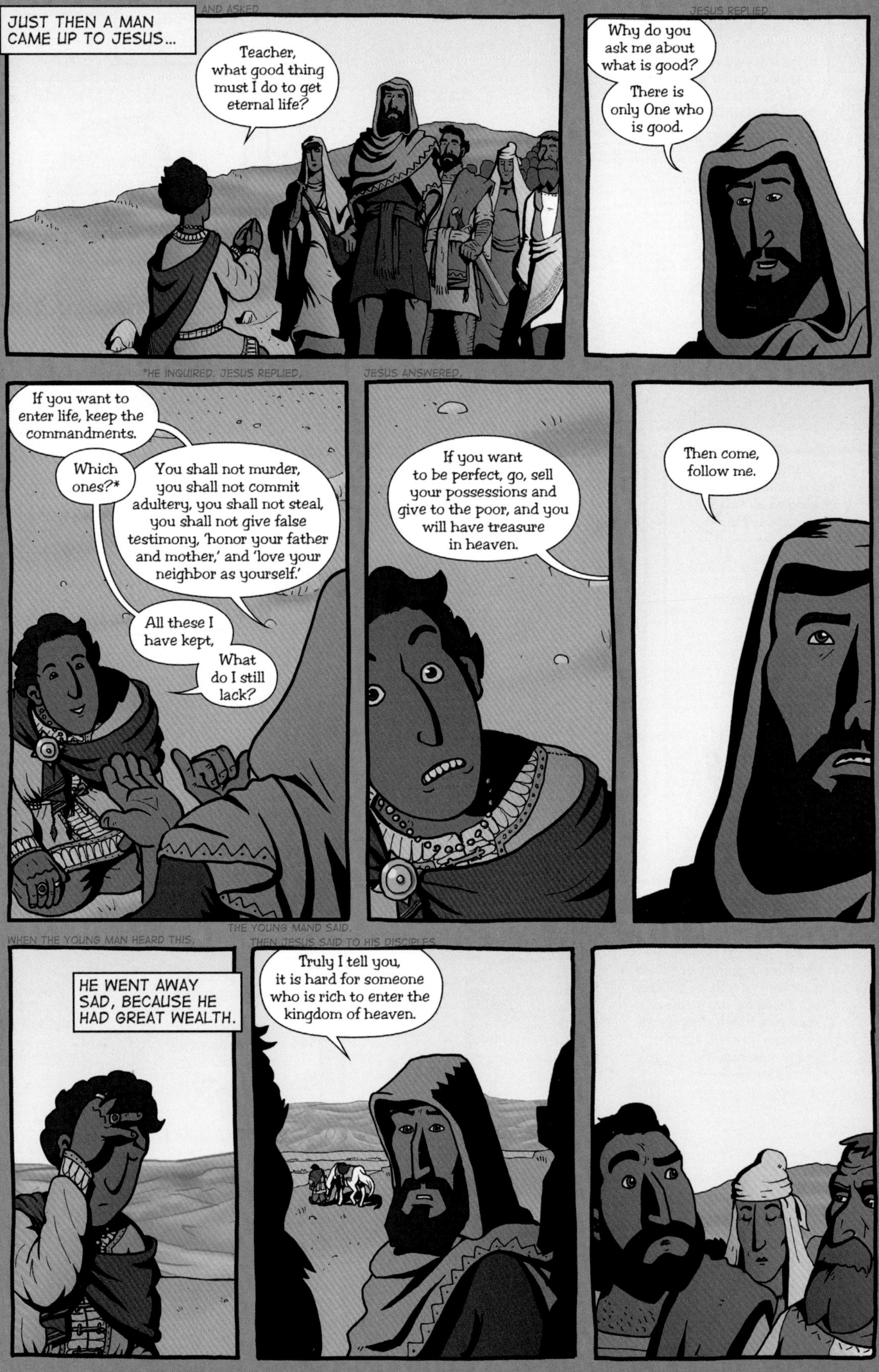
JUST THEN A MAN CAME UP TO JESUS...
AND ASKED
Teacher, what good thing must I do to get eternal life?
JESUS REPLIED
Why do you ask me about what is good?
There is only One who is good.
*HE INQUIRED. JESUS REPLIED,
If you want to enter life, keep the commandments.
Which ones?*
You shall not murder, you shall not commit adultery, you shall not steal, you shall not give false testimony, 'honor your father and mother,' and 'love your neighbor as yourself.'
THE YOUNG MAND SAID.
All these I have kept,
What do I still lack?
JESUS ANSWERED,
If you want to be perfect, go, sell your possessions and give to the poor, and you will have treasure in heaven.
Then come, follow me.
WHEN THE YOUNG MAN HEARD THIS,
HE WENT AWAY SAD, BECAUSE HE HAD GREAT WEALTH.
THEN JESUS SAID TO HIS DISCIPLES,
Truly I tell you, it is hard for someone who is rich to enter the kingdom of heaven.

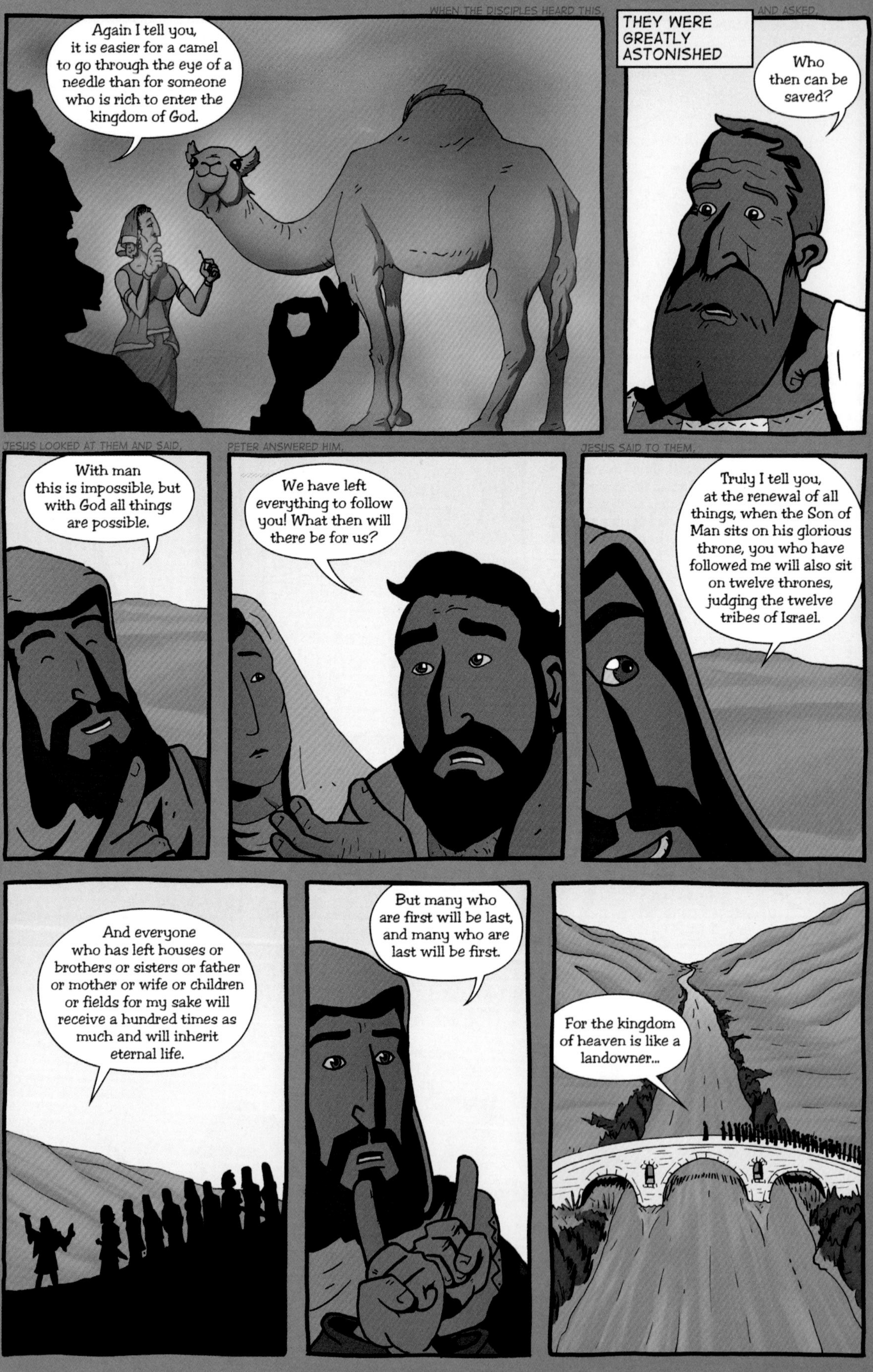
Again I tell you, it is easier for a camel to go through the eye of a needle than for someone who is rich to enter the kingdom of God.
WHEN THE DISCIPLES HEARD THIS,
THEY WERE GREATLY ASTONISHED
AND ASKED,
Who then can be saved?
JESUS LOOKED AT THEM AND SAID,
With man this is impossible, but with God all things are possible.
PETER ANSWERED HIM,
We have left everything to follow you! What then will there be for us?
JESUS SAID TO THEM,
Truly I tell you, at the renewal of all things, when the Son of Man sits on his glorious throne, you who have followed me will also sit on twelve thrones, judging the twelve tribes of Israel.
And everyone who has left houses or brothers or sisters or father or mother or wife or children or fields for my sake will receive a hundred times as much and will inherit eternal life.
But many who are first will be last, and many who are last will be first.
For the kingdom of heaven is like a landowner...

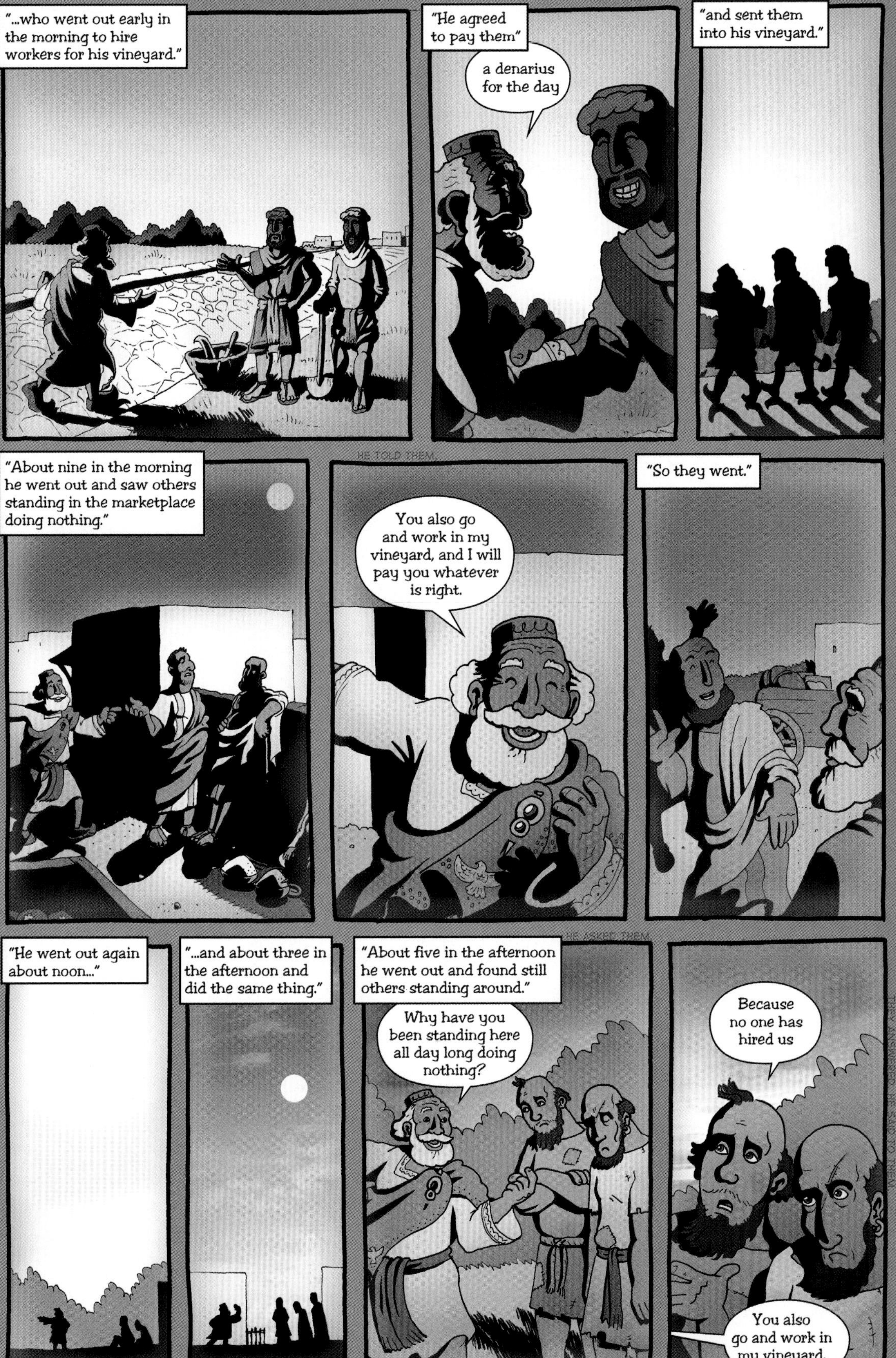
"...who went out early in the morning to hire workers for his vineyard."
"He agreed to pay them"
a denarius for the day
"and sent them into his vineyard."
HE TOLD THEM,
"About nine in the morning he went out and saw others standing in the marketplace doing nothing."
You also go and work in my vineyard, and I will pay you whatever is right.
"So they went."
"He went out again about noon..."
"...and about three in the afternoon and did the same thing."
"About five in the afternoon he went out and found still others standing around."
HE ASKED THEM
Why have you been standing here all day long doing nothing?
THEY ANSWERED. HE SAID TO THEM,
Because no one has hired us
You also go and work in my vineyard.

"When evening came..." THE OWNER OF THE VINEYARD SAID TO HIS FOREMAN,

Call the workers and pay them their wages,

beginning with the last ones hired and going on to the first.

"The workers who were hired about five in the afternoon came and each received..."

a denarius

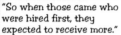

"So when those came who were hired first, they expected to receive more."

BUT EACH ONE OF THEM ALSO RECEIVED

a denarius.

*AGAINST THE LANDOWNER.

GRUMBLE

These who were hired last worked only one hour

WHEN THEY RECEIVED IT, THEY BEGAN TO*

THEY SAID...

...and you have made them equal to us who have borne the burden of the work and the heat of the day.

BUT HE ANSWERED ONE OF THEM,

I am not being unfair to you, friend. Didn't you agree to work for a denarius?

Take your pay and go.

I want to give the one who was hired last the same as I gave you.

Don't I have the right to do what I want with my own money?

Or are you envious because I am generous?

So the last will be first, and the first will be last.

MATTHEW 20:8-16

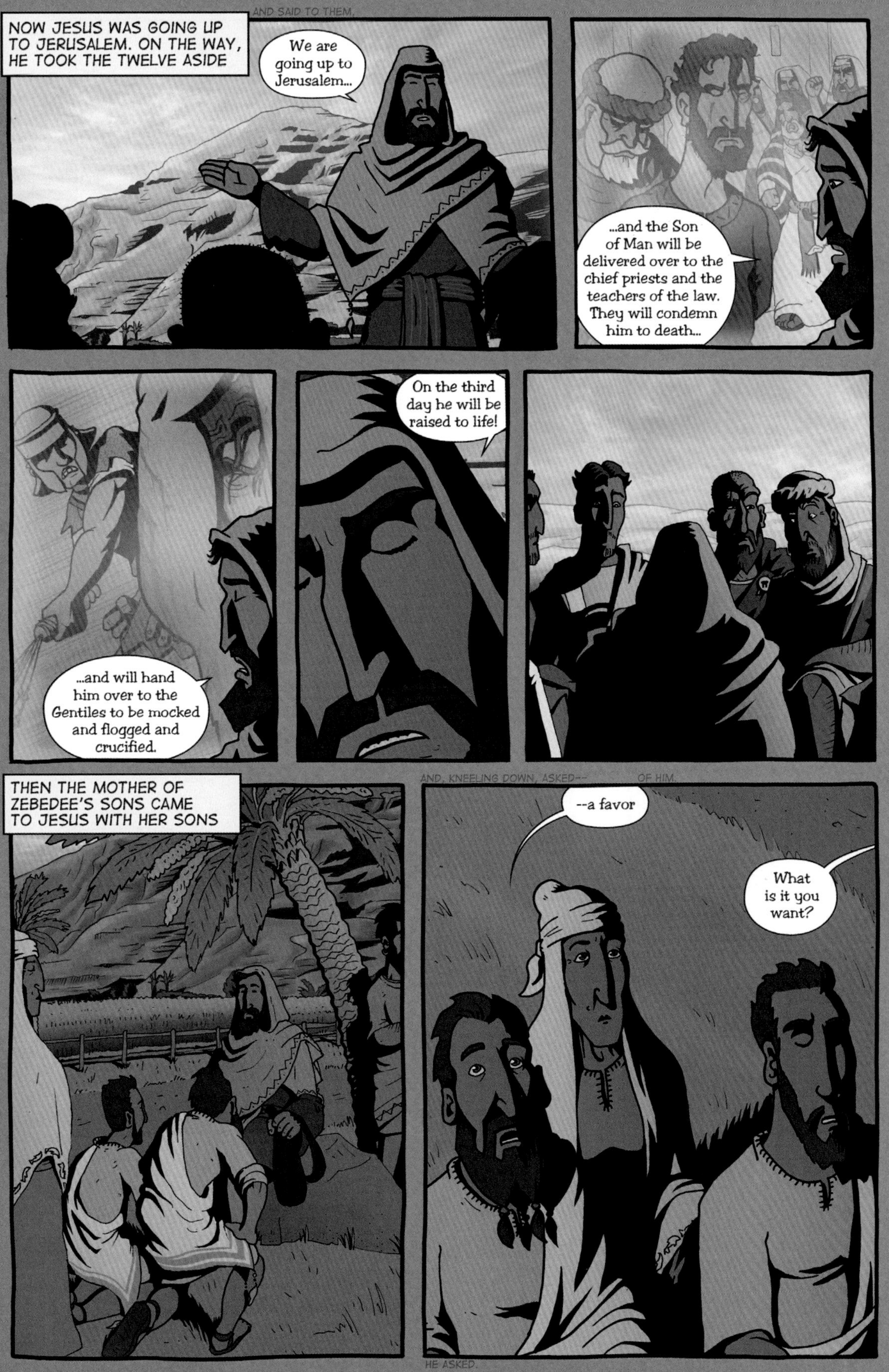
NOW JESUS WAS GOING UP TO JERUSALEM. ON THE WAY, HE TOOK THE TWELVE ASIDE
AND SAID TO THEM,
We are going up to Jerusalem...
...and the Son of Man will be delivered over to the chief priests and the teachers of the law. They will condemn him to death...
...and will hand him over to the Gentiles to be mocked and flogged and crucified.
On the third day he will be raised to life!
THEN THE MOTHER OF ZEBEDEE'S SONS CAME TO JESUS WITH HER SONS
AND, KNEELING DOWN, ASKED--
--a favor
OF HIM.
What is it you want?
HE ASKED.

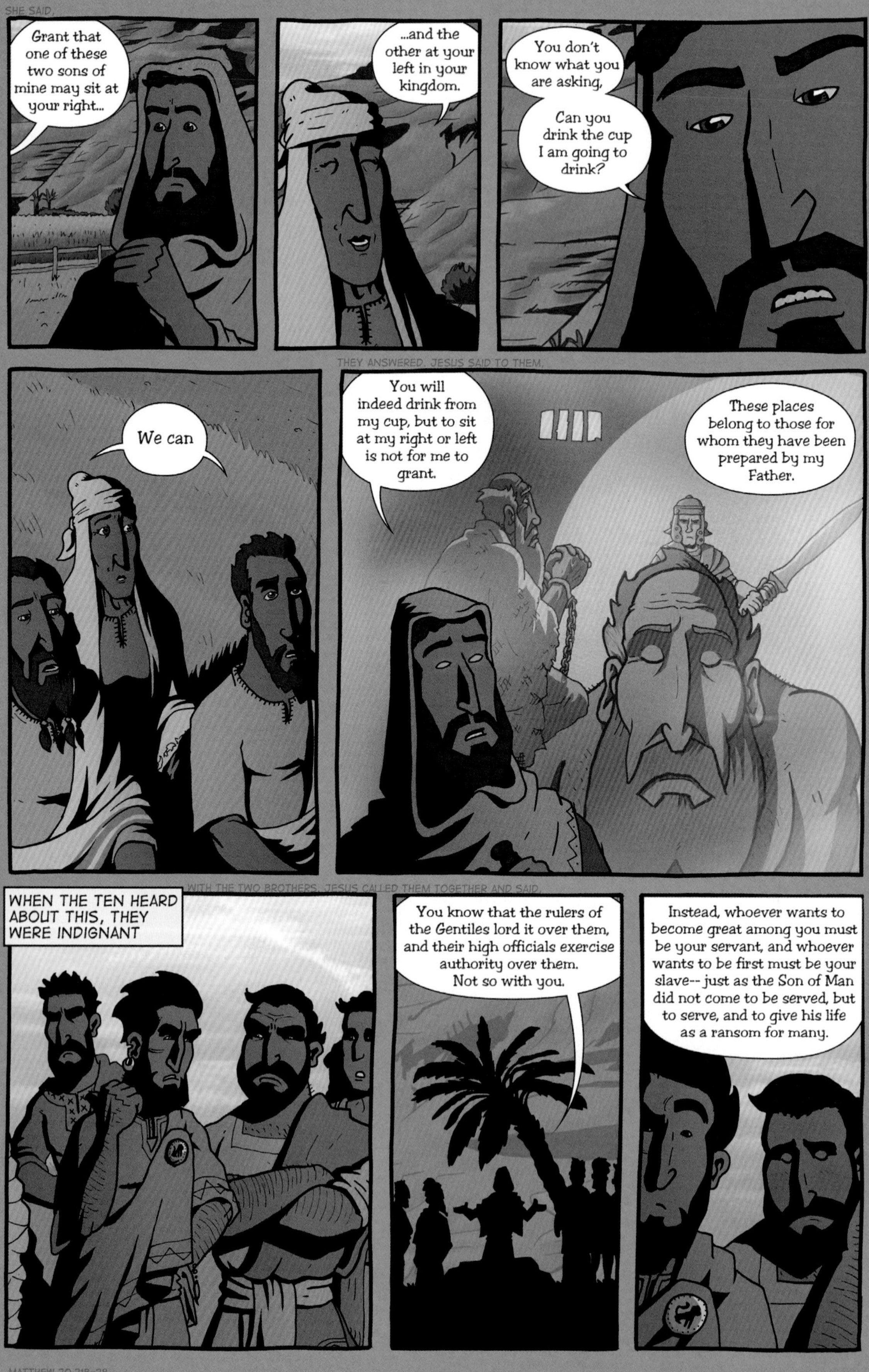
SHE SAID,
Grant that one of these two sons of mine may sit at your right...
...and the other at your left in your kingdom.
You don't know what you are asking,
Can you drink the cup I am going to drink?
THEY ANSWERED. JESUS SAID TO THEM,
We can
You will indeed drink from my cup, but to sit at my right or left is not for me to grant.
These places belong to those for whom they have been prepared by my Father.
WITH THE TWO BROTHERS, JESUS CALLED THEM TOGETHER AND SAID
WHEN THE TEN HEARD ABOUT THIS, THEY WERE INDIGNANT
You know that the rulers of the Gentiles lord it over them, and their high officials exercise authority over them. Not so with you.
Instead, whoever wants to become great among you must be your servant, and whoever wants to be first must be your slave-- just as the Son of Man did not come to be served, but to serve, and to give his life as a ransom for many.

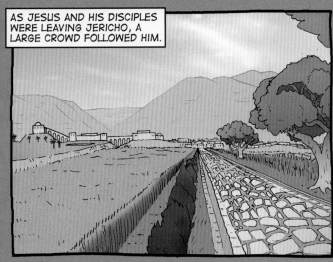

AS JESUS AND HIS DISCIPLES WERE LEAVING JERICHO, A LARGE CROWD FOLLOWED HIM.

TWO BLIND MEN WERE SITTING BY THE ROADSIDE...

...AND WHEN THEY HEARD THAT

???

Jesus was going by

THEY SHOUTED,

LORD, SON OF DAVID, HAVE MERCY ON US!

THE CROWD REBUKED THEM AND TOLD THEM TO

BE QUIET

BUT THEY SHOUTED ALL THE LOUDER,

LORD....

...SON OF DAVID, HAVE MERCY ON US!

JESUS STOPPED AND CALLED THEM.

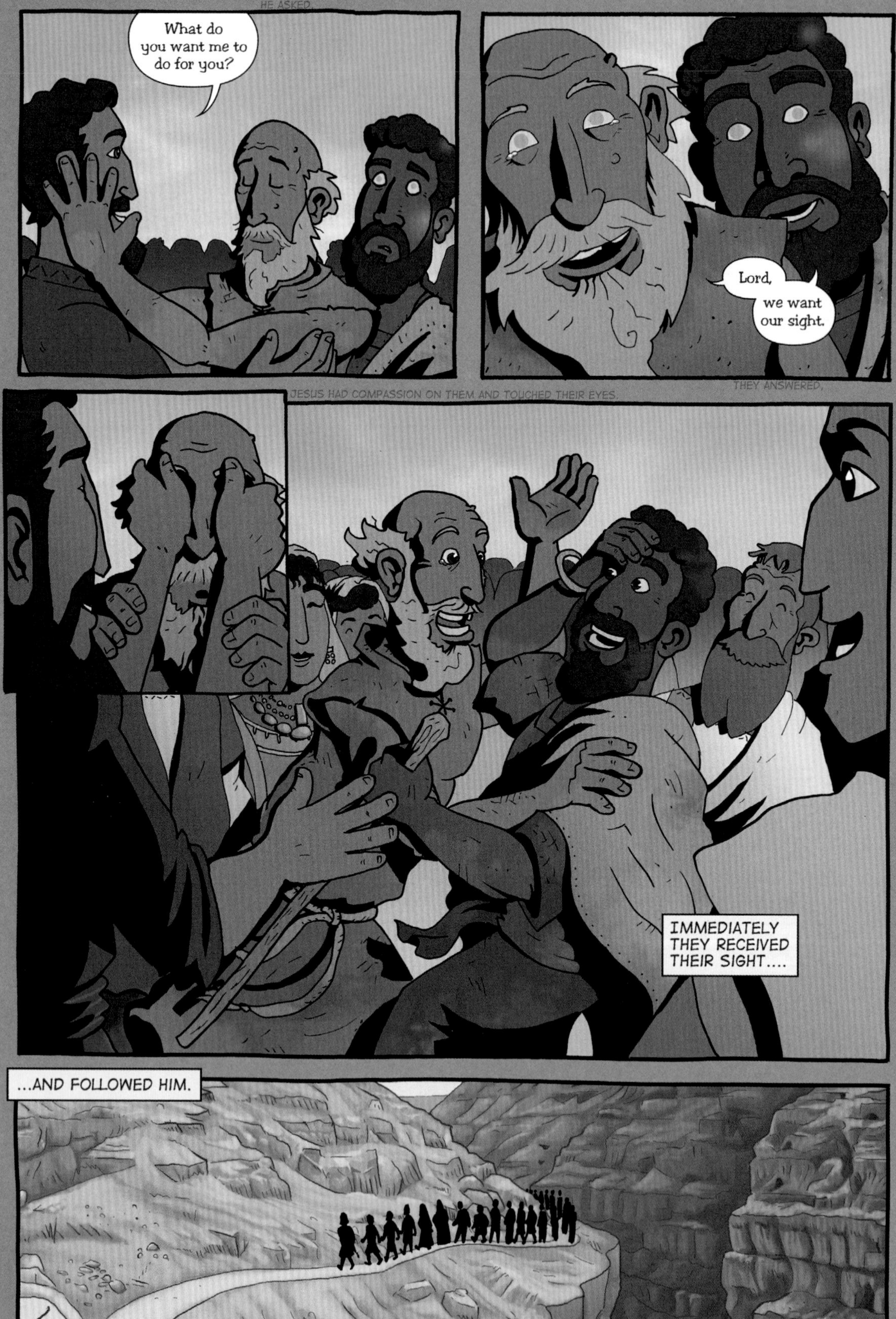
HE ASKED,
What do you want me to do for you?
THEY ANSWERED,
Lord, we want our sight.
JESUS HAD COMPASSION ON THEM AND TOUCHED THEIR EYES.
IMMEDIATELY THEY RECEIVED THEIR SIGHT....
...AND FOLLOWED HIM.

MATTHEW 20:32B-34

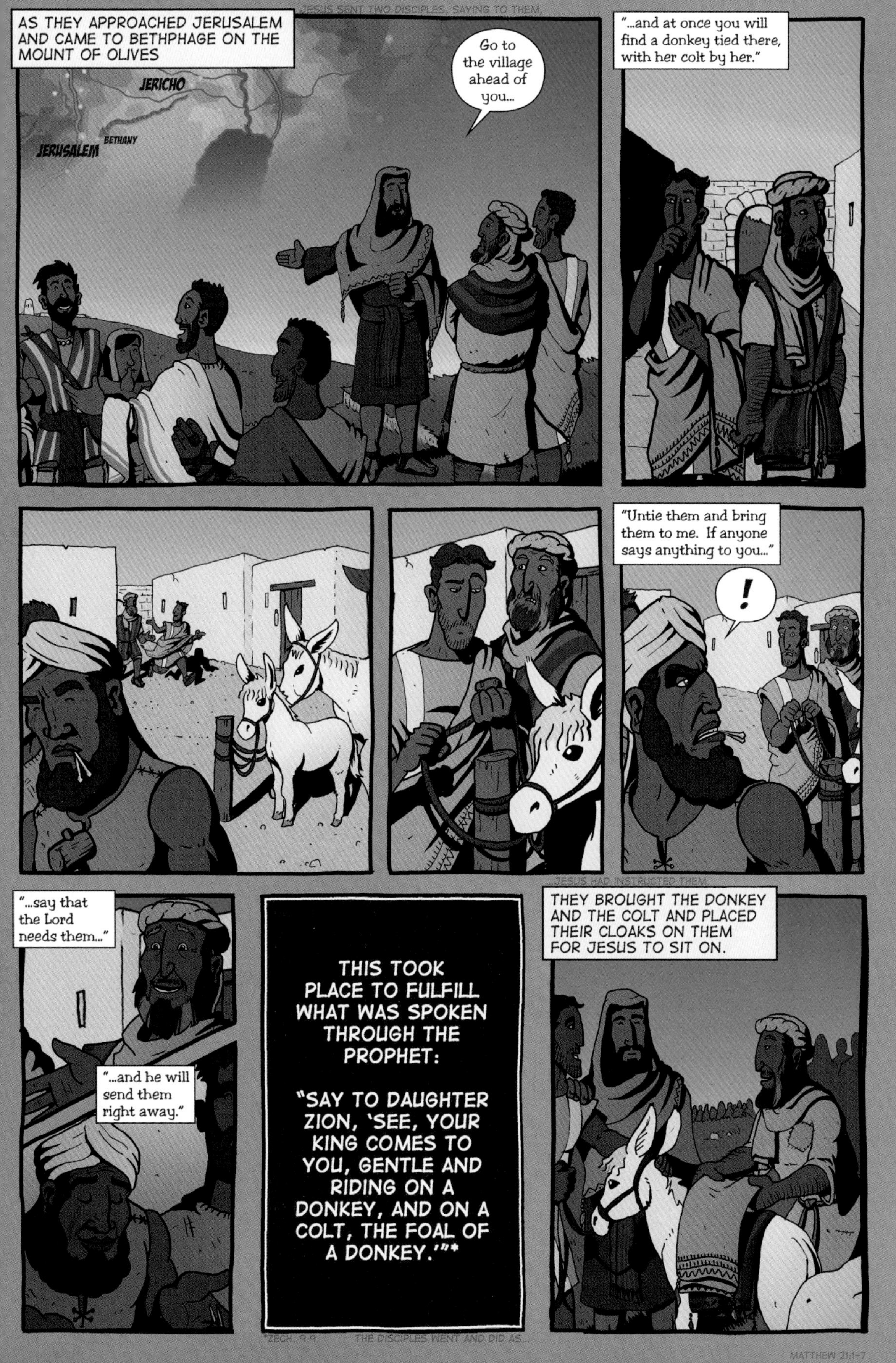
AS THEY APPROACHED JERUSALEM AND CAME TO BETHPHAGE ON THE MOUNT OF OLIVES
JESUS SENT TWO DISCIPLES, SAYING TO THEM,
JERICHO
JERUSALEM
BETHANY
Go to the village ahead of you...
"...and at once you will find a donkey tied there, with her colt by her."
"Untie them and bring them to me. If anyone says anything to you..."
!
...JESUS HAD INSTRUCTED THEM.
"...say that the Lord needs them..."
"...and he will send them right away."
THIS TOOK PLACE TO FULFILL WHAT WAS SPOKEN THROUGH THE PROPHET:
"SAY TO DAUGHTER ZION, 'SEE, YOUR KING COMES TO YOU, GENTLE AND RIDING ON A DONKEY, AND ON A COLT, THE FOAL OF A DONKEY.'"*
*ZECH. 9:9
THE DISCIPLES WENT AND DID AS...
THEY BROUGHT THE DONKEY AND THE COLT AND PLACED THEIR CLOAKS ON THEM FOR JESUS TO SIT ON.

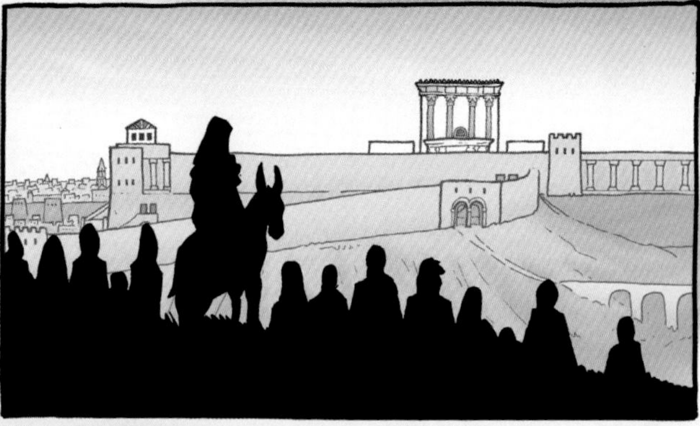
A VERY LARGE CROWD SPREAD THEIR CLOAKS ON THE ROAD, WHILE OTHERS CUT BRANCHES FROM THE TREES AND SPREAD THEM ON THE ROAD.
THE CROWDS THAT WENT AHEAD OF HIM AND THOSE THAT FOLLOWED SHOUTED,

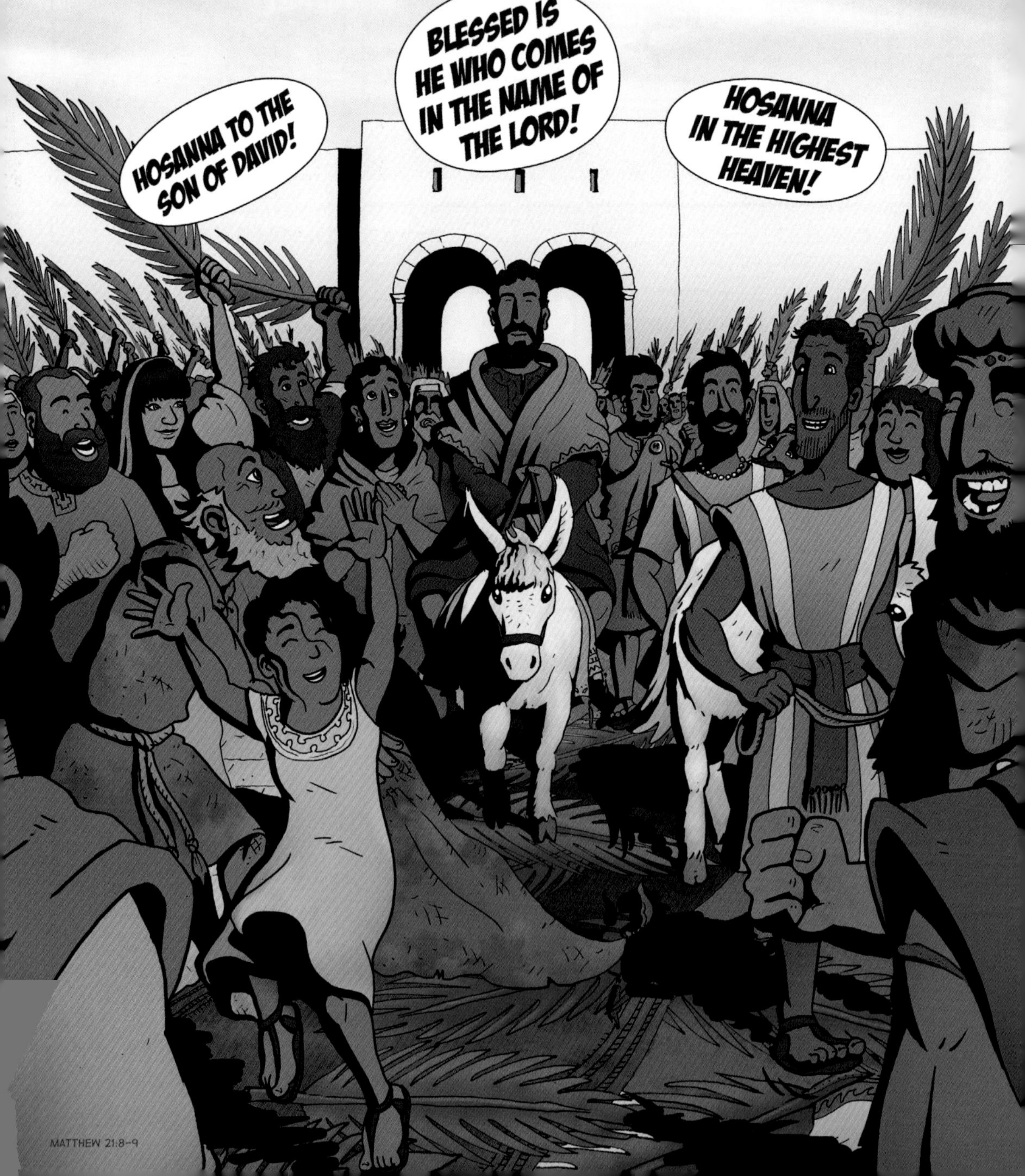
HOSANNA TO THE SON OF DAVID!
BLESSED IS HE WHO COMES IN THE NAME OF THE LORD!
HOSANNA IN THE HIGHEST HEAVEN!

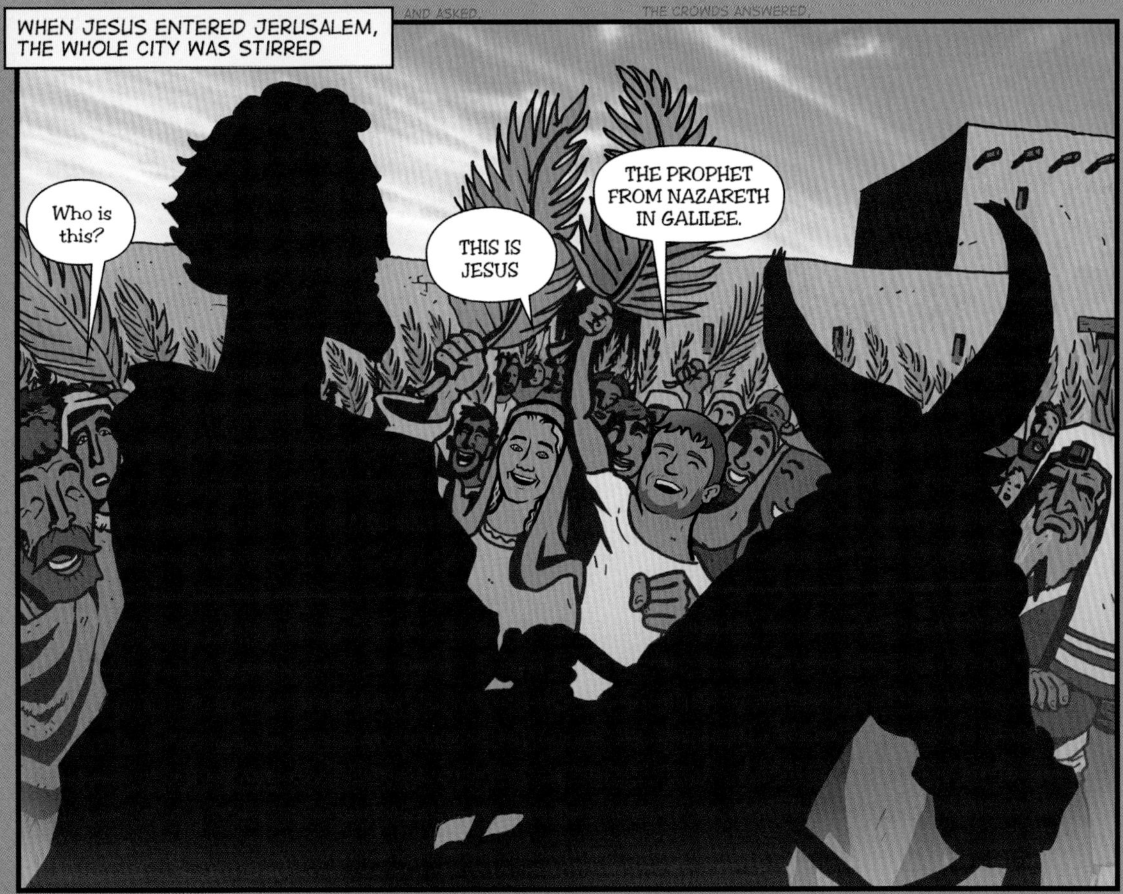
WHEN JESUS ENTERED JERUSALEM, THE WHOLE CITY WAS STIRRED
AND ASKED,
Who is this?
THE CROWDS ANSWERED,
THIS IS JESUS
THE PROPHET FROM NAZARETH IN GALILEE.

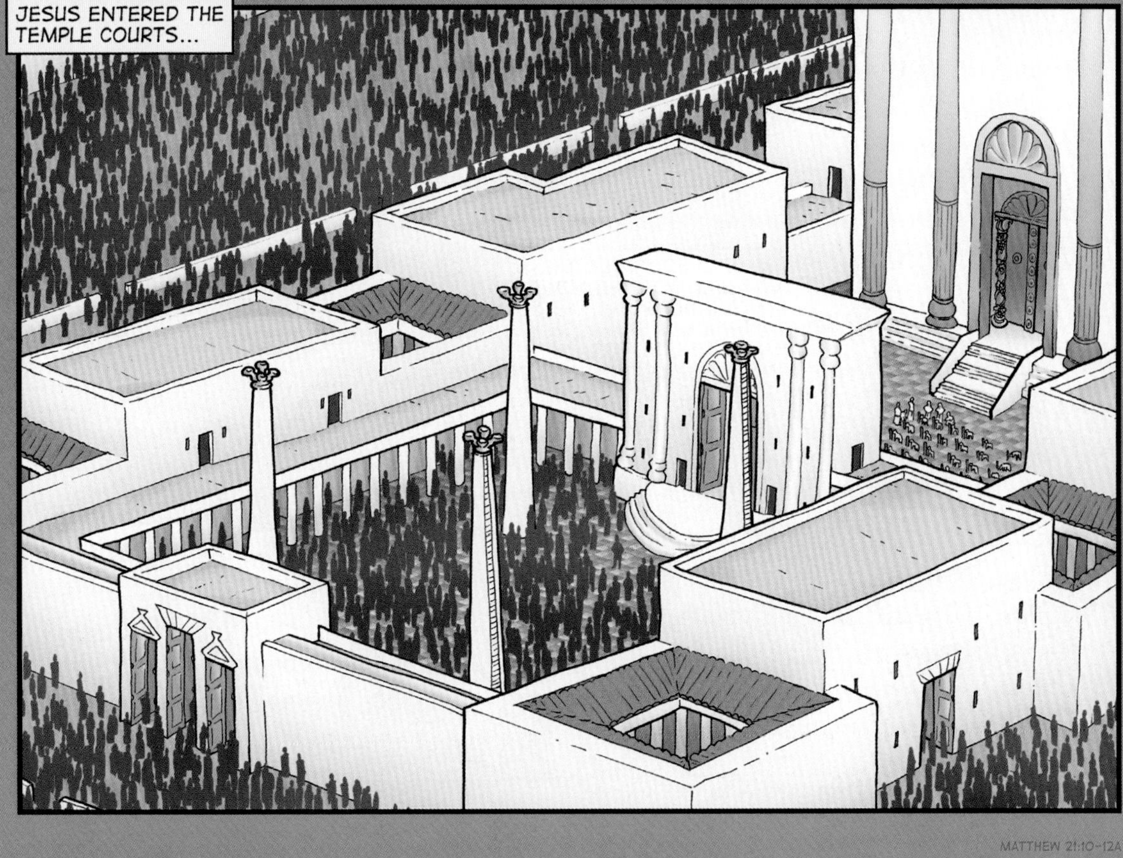
JESUS ENTERED THE TEMPLE COURTS...

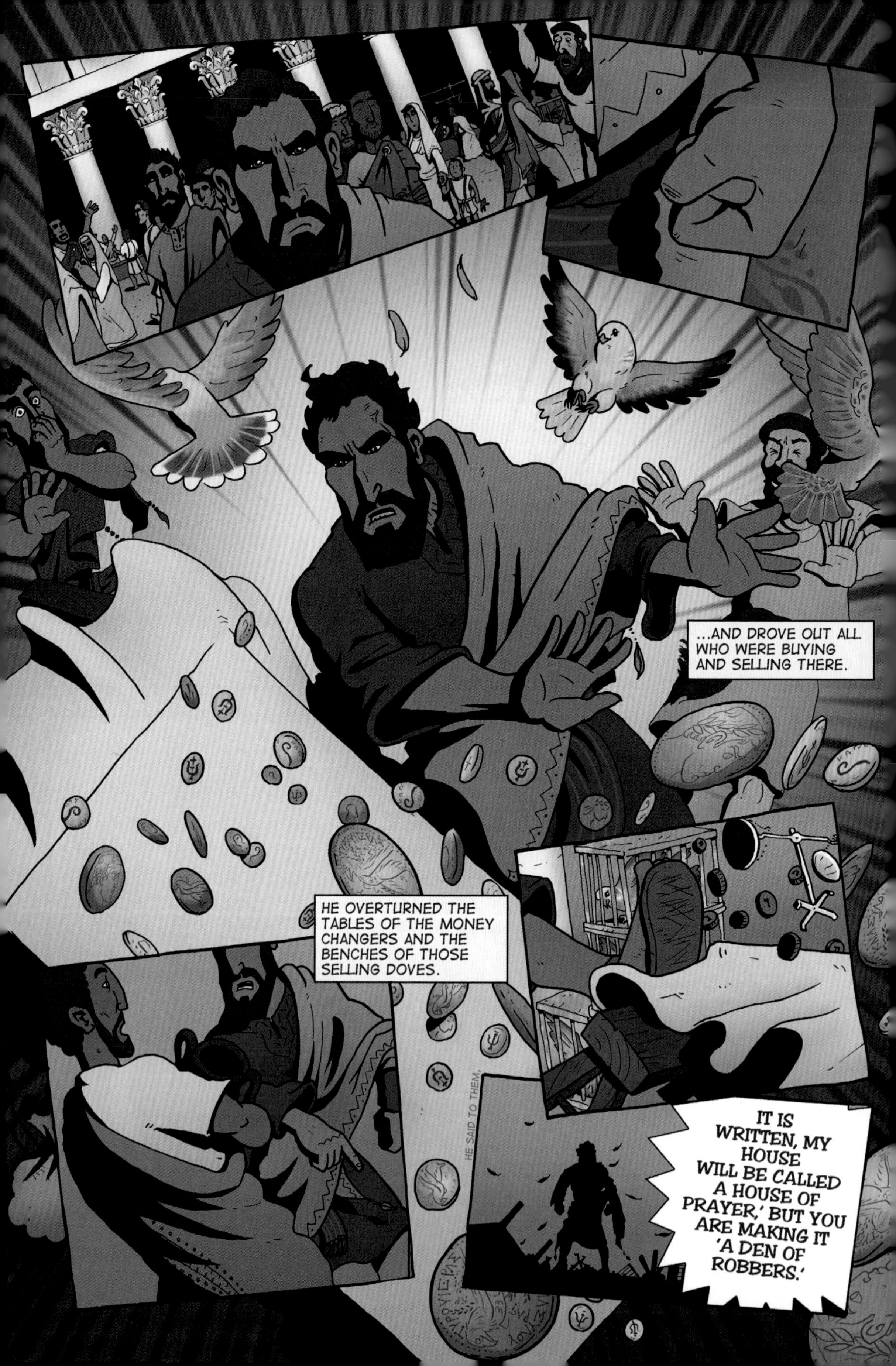
...AND DROVE OUT ALL WHO WERE BUYING AND SELLING THERE.
HE OVERTURNED THE TABLES OF THE MONEY CHANGERS AND THE BENCHES OF THOSE SELLING DOVES.
HE SAID TO THEM,
'IT IS WRITTEN, MY HOUSE WILL BE CALLED A HOUSE OF PRAYER,' BUT YOU ARE MAKING IT 'A DEN OF ROBBERS.'

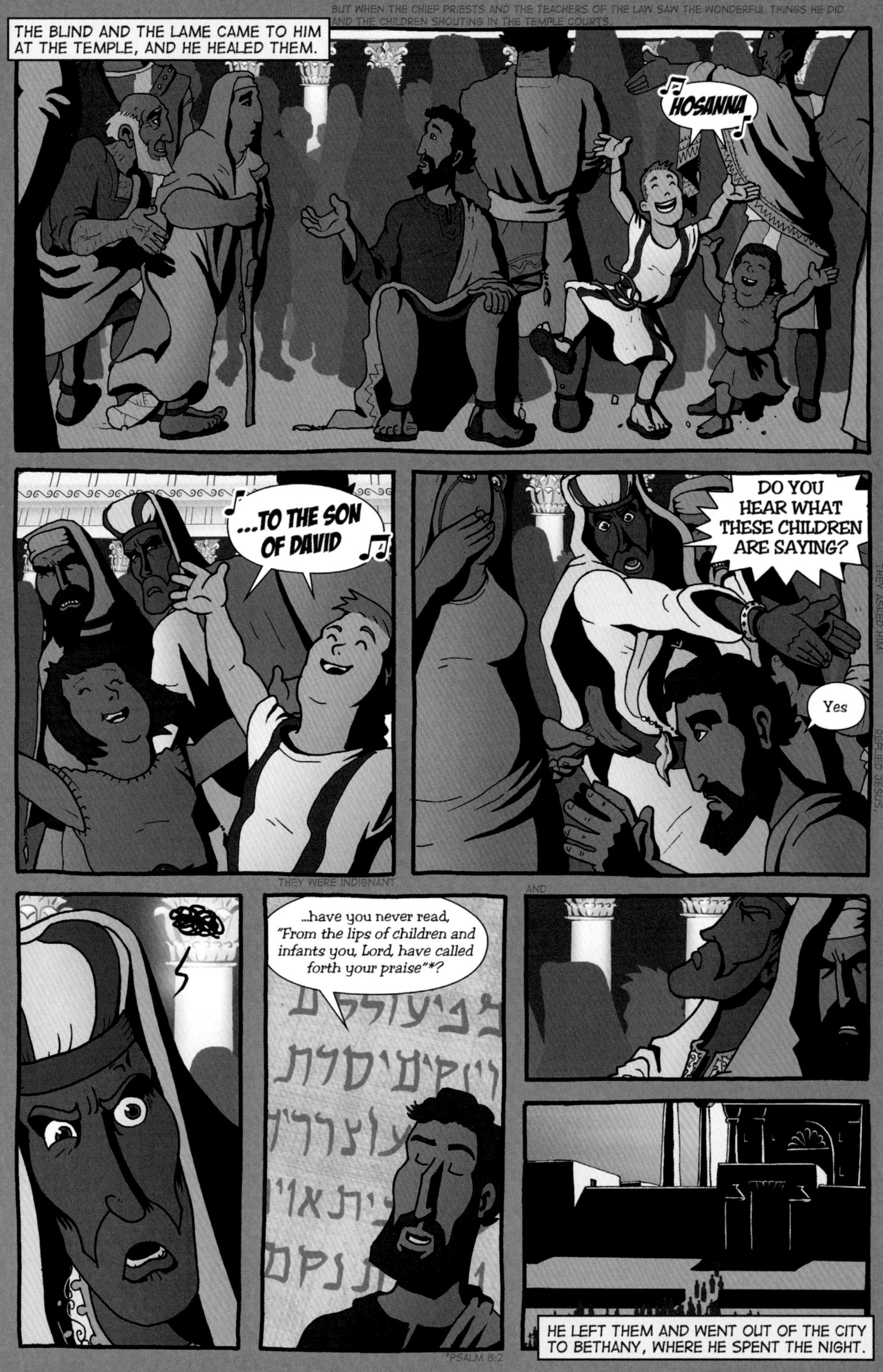

THE BLIND AND THE LAME CAME TO HIM AT THE TEMPLE, AND HE HEALED THEM.
BUT WHEN THE CHIEF PRIESTS AND THE TEACHERS OF THE LAW SAW THE WONDERFUL THINGS HE DID AND THE CHILDREN SHOUTING IN THE TEMPLE COURTS,
HOSANNA
...TO THE SON OF DAVID
THEY WERE INDIGNANT.
DO YOU HEAR WHAT THESE CHILDREN ARE SAYING?
THEY ASKED HIM.
Yes
REPLIED JESUS,
AND
...have you never read, "From the lips of children and infants you, Lord, have called forth your praise"*?
*PSALM 8:2
HE LEFT THEM AND WENT OUT OF THE CITY TO BETHANY, WHERE HE SPENT THE NIGHT.

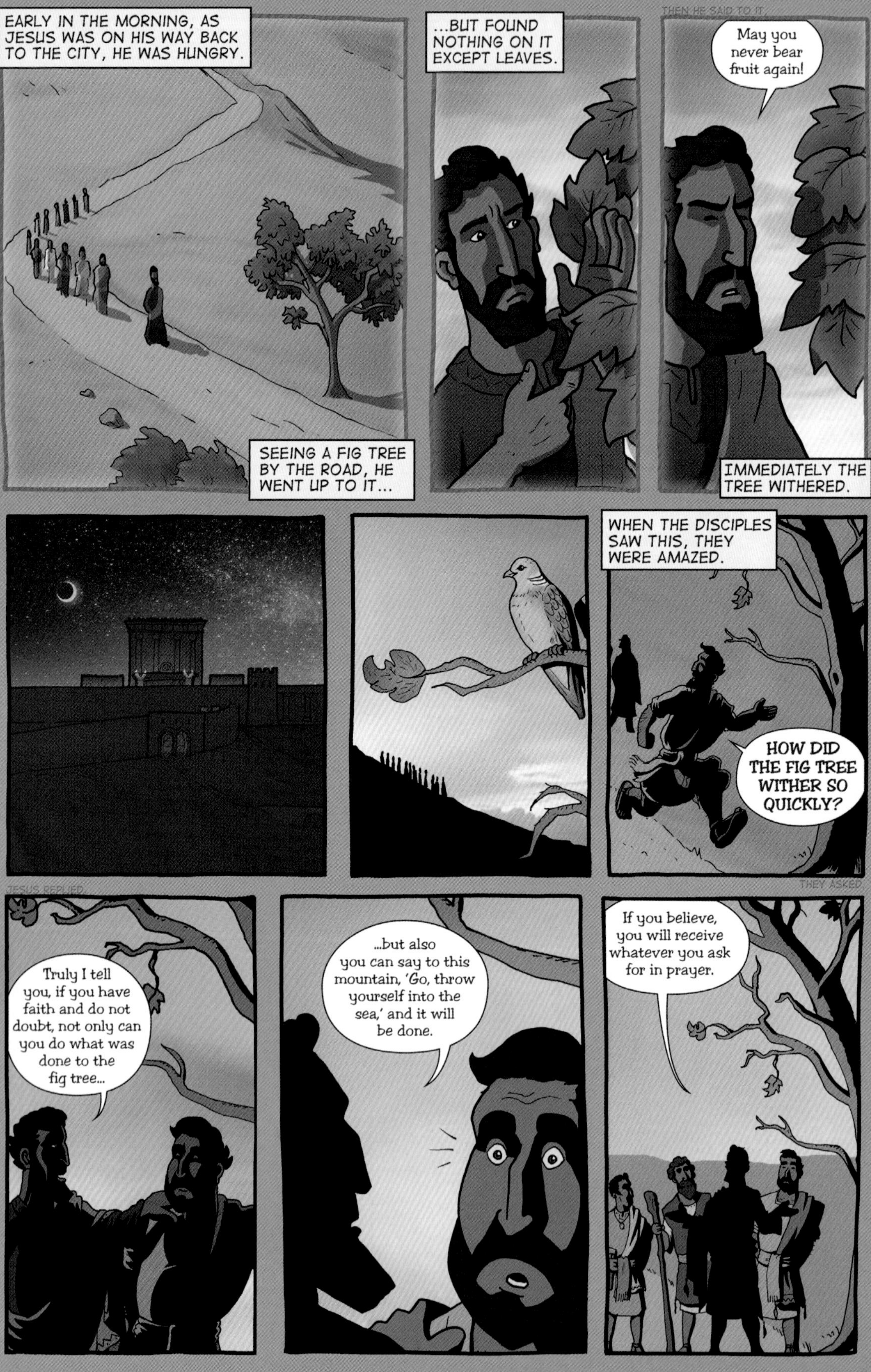
EARLY IN THE MORNING, AS JESUS WAS ON HIS WAY BACK TO THE CITY, HE WAS HUNGRY.
SEEING A FIG TREE BY THE ROAD, HE WENT UP TO IT...
...BUT FOUND NOTHING ON IT EXCEPT LEAVES.
THEN HE SAID TO IT,
May you never bear fruit again!
IMMEDIATELY THE TREE WITHERED.
WHEN THE DISCIPLES SAW THIS, THEY WERE AMAZED.
HOW DID THE FIG TREE WITHER SO QUICKLY?
THEY ASKED.
JESUS REPLIED,
Truly I tell you, if you have faith and do not doubt, not only can you do what was done to the fig tree...
...but also you can say to this mountain, 'Go, throw yourself into the sea,' and it will be done.
If you believe, you will receive whatever you ask for in prayer.

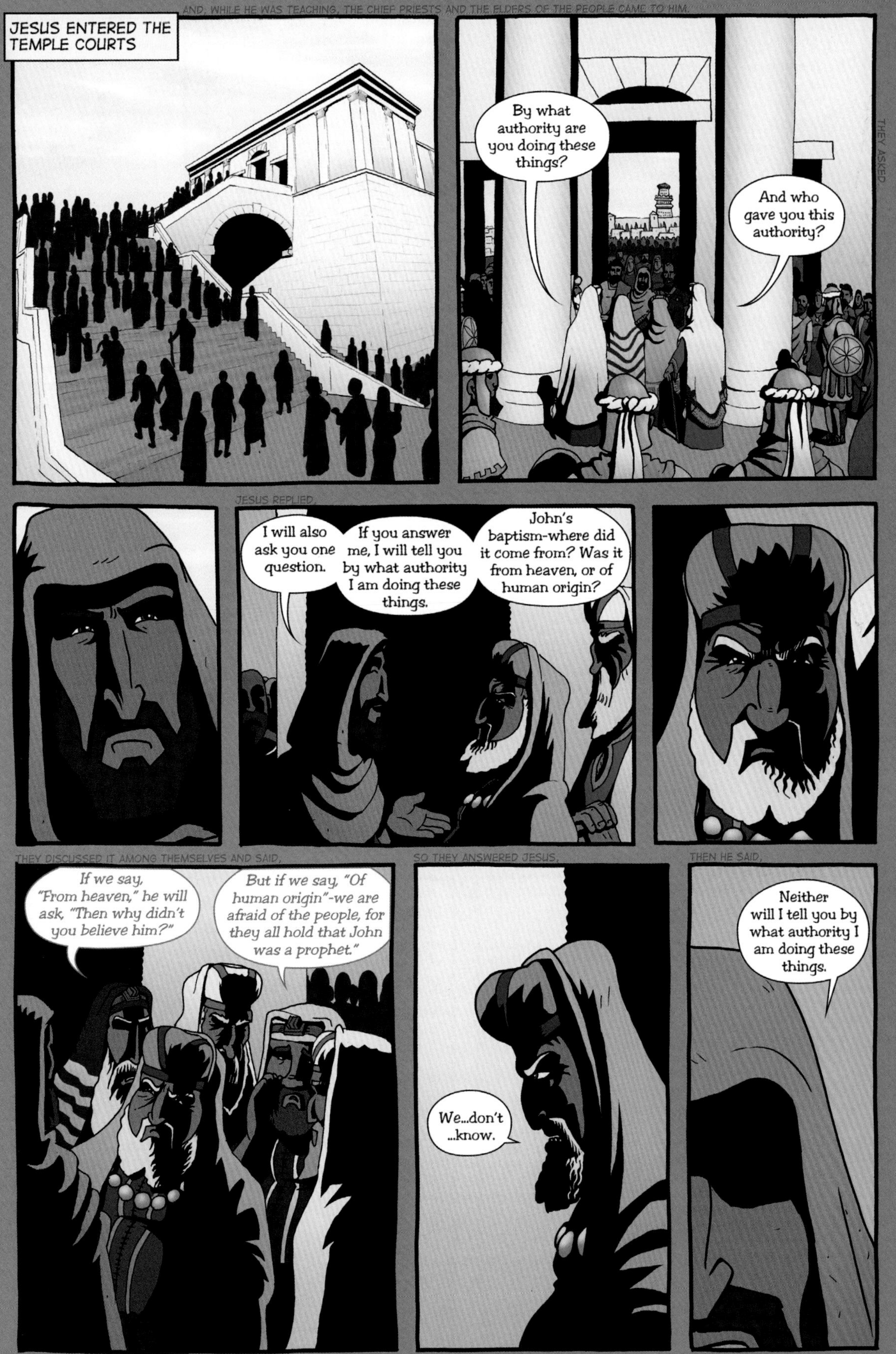
JESUS ENTERED THE TEMPLE COURTS
AND, WHILE HE WAS TEACHING, THE CHIEF PRIESTS AND THE ELDERS OF THE PEOPLE CAME TO HIM.
THEY ASKED,
By what authority are you doing these things?
And who gave you this authority?
JESUS REPLIED,
I will also ask you one question.
If you answer me, I will tell you by what authority I am doing these things.
John's baptism-where did it come from? Was it from heaven, or of human origin?
THEY DISCUSSED IT AMONG THEMSELVES AND SAID,
If we say, "From heaven," he will ask, "Then why didn't you believe him?"
But if we say, "Of human origin"-we are afraid of the people, for they all hold that John was a prophet."
SO THEY ANSWERED JESUS,
We...don't ...know.
THEN HE SAID,
Neither will I tell you by what authority I am doing these things.

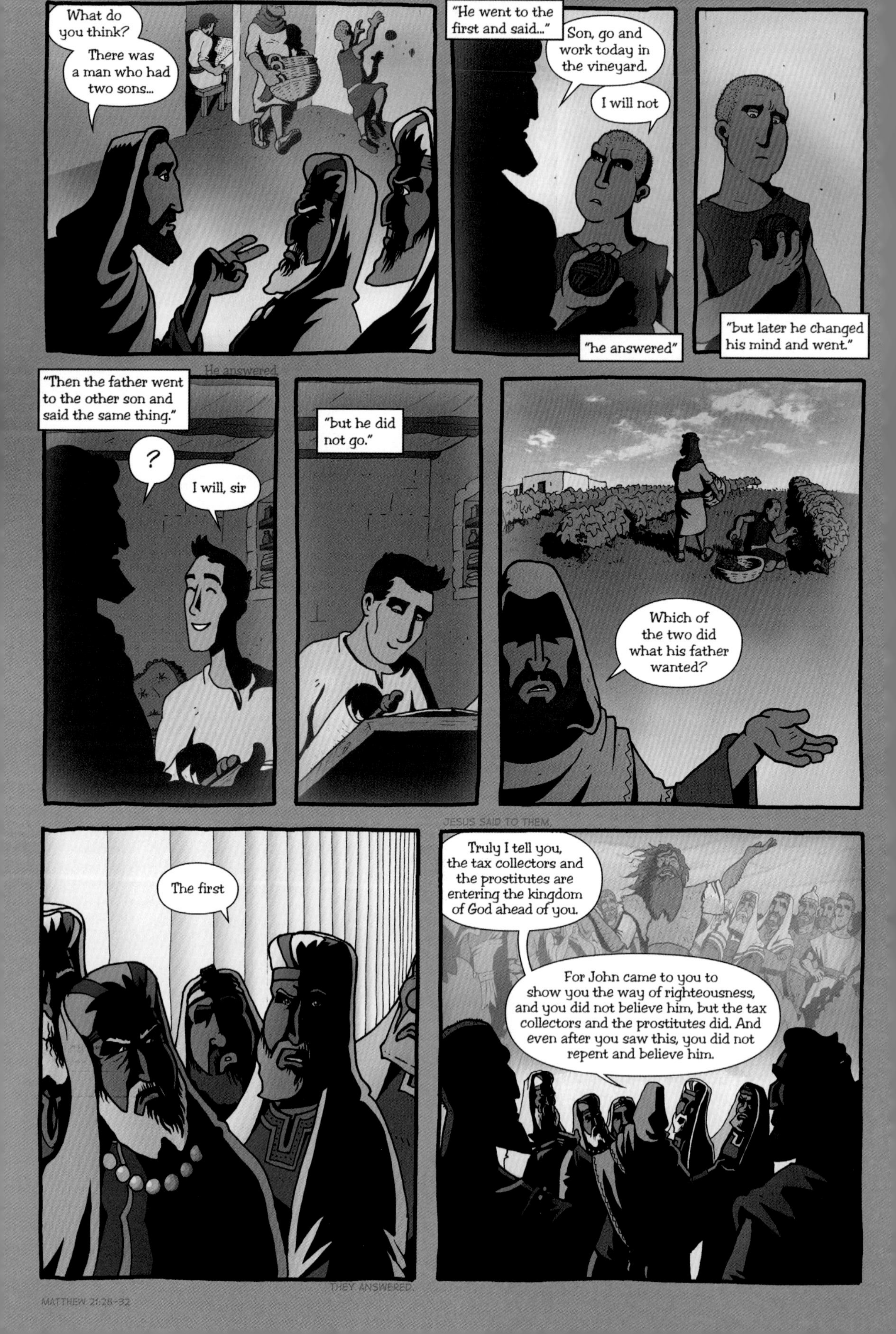

What do you think?
There was a man who had two sons...
"He went to the first and said..."
Son, go and work today in the vineyard.
I will not
"he answered"
"but later he changed his mind and went."
He answered,
"Then the father went to the other son and said the same thing."
?
I will, sir
"but he did not go."
Which of the two did what his father wanted?
JESUS SAID TO THEM,
The first
Truly I tell you, the tax collectors and the prostitutes are entering the kingdom of God ahead of you.
For John came to you to show you the way of righteousness, and you did not believe him, but the tax collectors and the prostitutes did. And even after you saw this, you did not repent and believe him.
THEY ANSWERED.

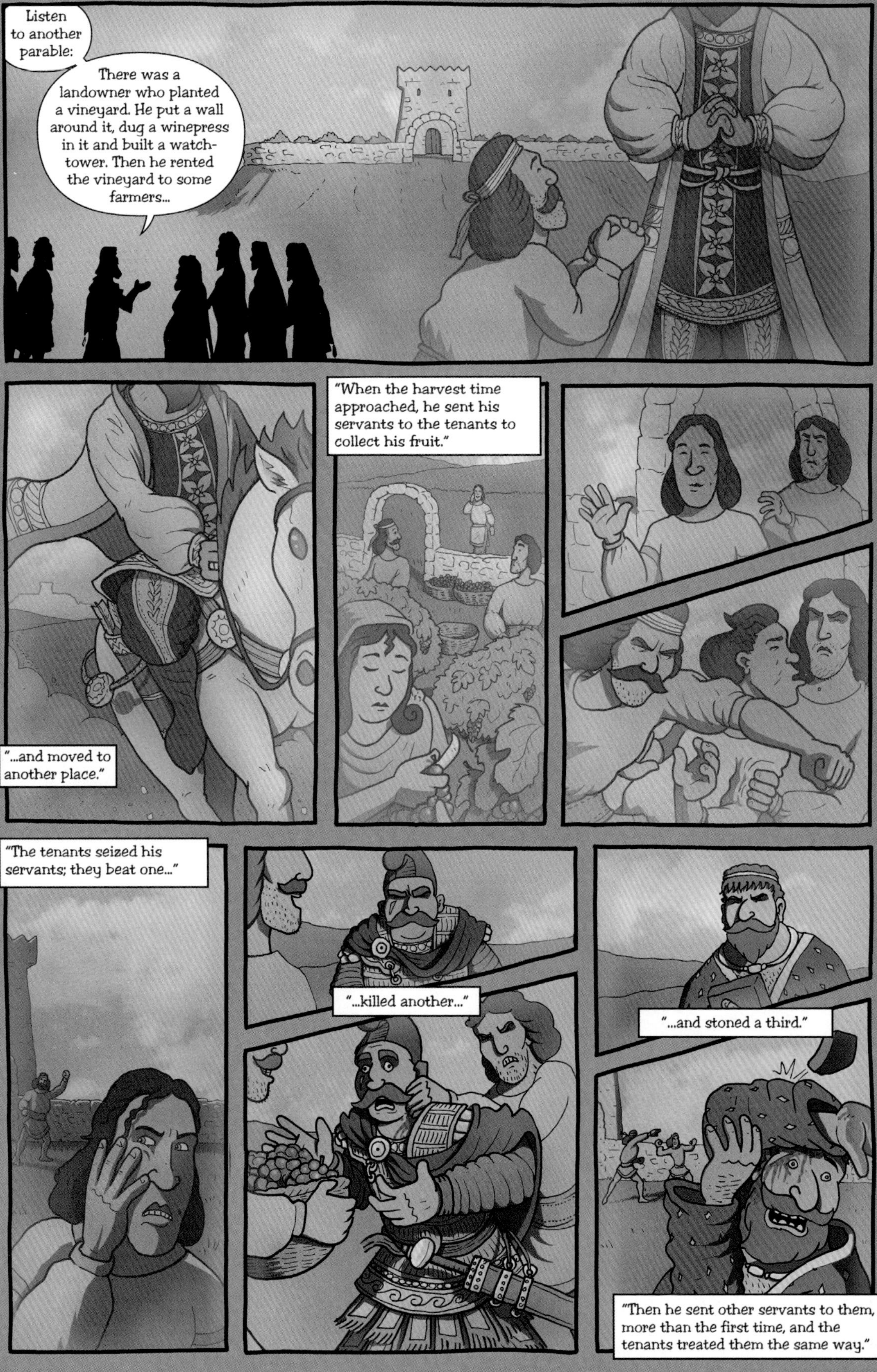
Listen to another parable:
There was a landowner who planted a vineyard. He put a wall around it, dug a winepress in it and built a watch-tower. Then he rented the vineyard to some farmers...
"...and moved to another place."
"When the harvest time approached, he sent his servants to the tenants to collect his fruit."
"The tenants seized his servants; they beat one..."
"...killed another..."
"...and stoned a third."
"Then he sent other servants to them, more than the first time, and the tenants treated them the same way."

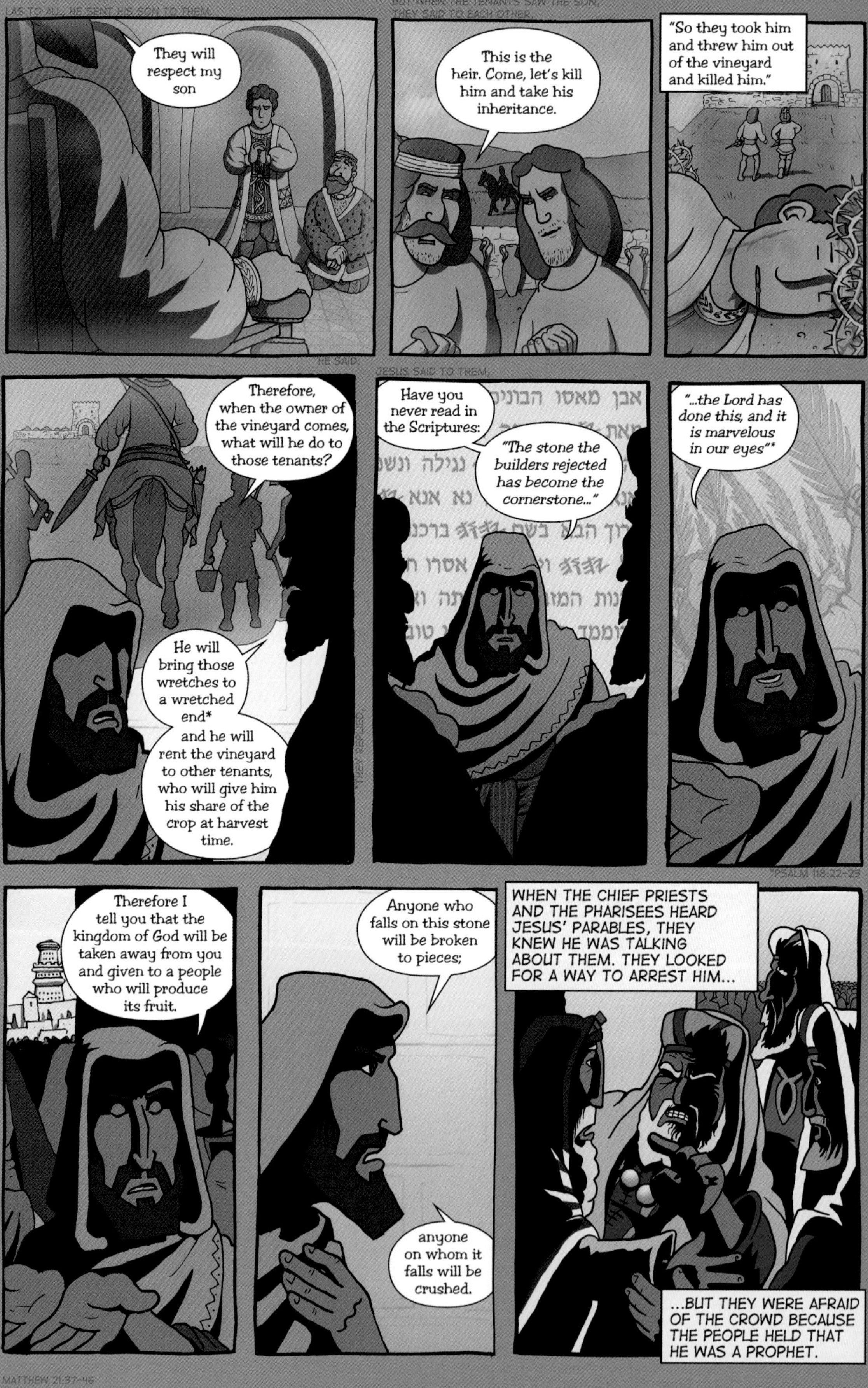
LAS TO ALL, HE SENT HIS SON TO THEM.
They will respect my son
HE SAID.
BUT WHEN THE TENANTS SAW THE SON, THEY SAID TO EACH OTHER,
This is the heir. Come, let's kill him and take his inheritance.
"So they took him and threw him out of the vineyard and killed him."
Therefore, when the owner of the vineyard comes, what will he do to those tenants?
He will bring those wretches to a wretched end*
and he will rent the vineyard to other tenants, who will give him his share of the crop at harvest time.
*THEY REPLIED.
JESUS SAID TO THEM,
Have you never read in the Scriptures:
"The stone the builders rejected has become the cornerstone..."
"...the Lord has done this, and it is marvelous in our eyes"*
*PSALM 118:22-23
Therefore I tell you that the kingdom of God will be taken away from you and given to a people who will produce its fruit.
Anyone who falls on this stone will be broken to pieces;
anyone on whom it falls will be crushed.
WHEN THE CHIEF PRIESTS AND THE PHARISEES HEARD JESUS' PARABLES, THEY KNEW HE WAS TALKING ABOUT THEM. THEY LOOKED FOR A WAY TO ARREST HIM...
...BUT THEY WERE AFRAID OF THE CROWD BECAUSE THE PEOPLE HELD THAT HE WAS A PROPHET.

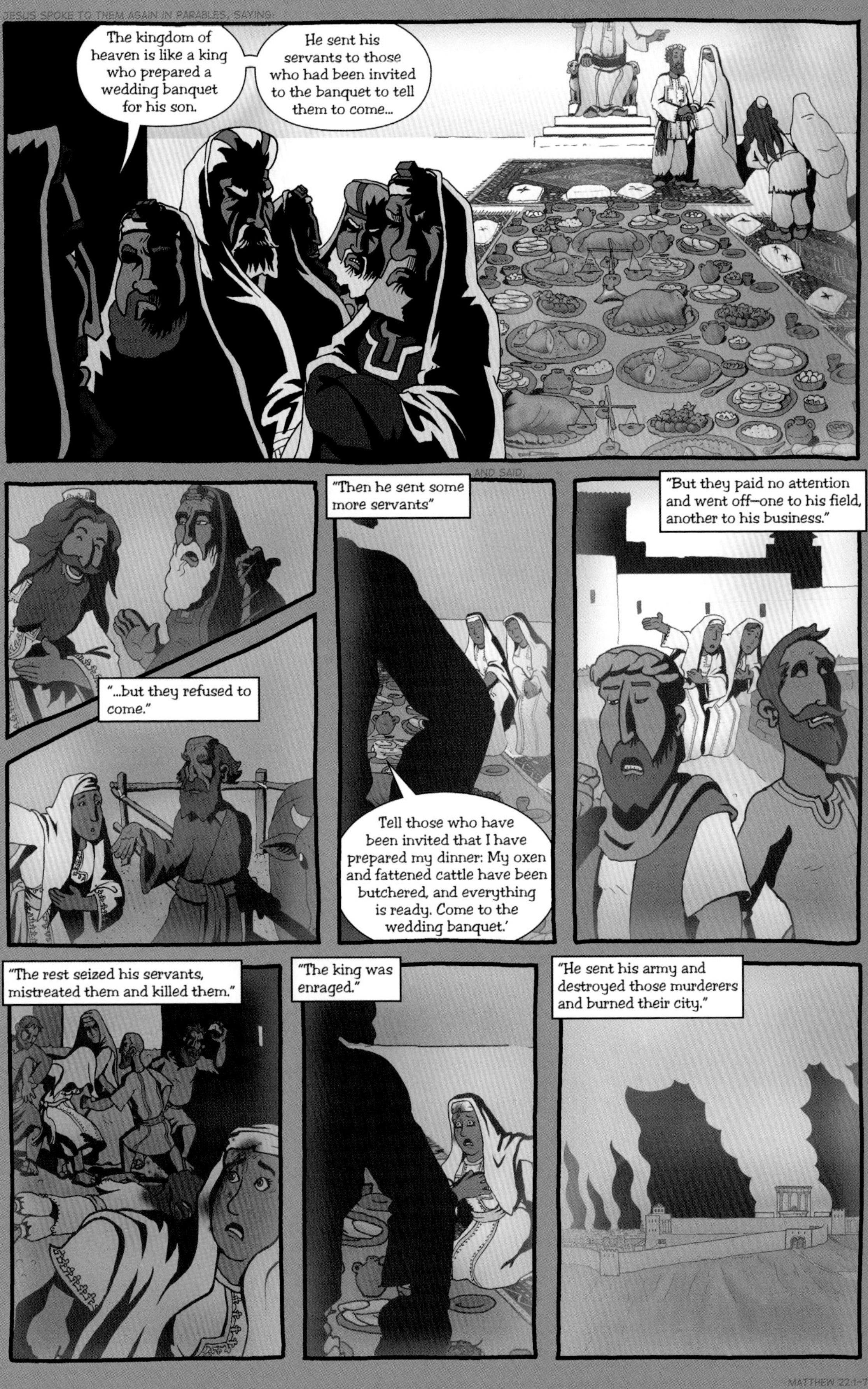
JESUS SPOKE TO THEM AGAIN IN PARABLES, SAYING:
The kingdom of heaven is like a king who prepared a wedding banquet for his son.
He sent his servants to those who had been invited to the banquet to tell them to come...
AND SAID,
"...but they refused to come."
"Then he sent some more servants"
Tell those who have been invited that I have prepared my dinner: My oxen and fattened cattle have been butchered, and everything is ready. Come to the wedding banquet.'
"But they paid no attention and went off—one to his field, another to his business."
"The rest seized his servants, mistreated them and killed them."
"The king was enraged."
"He sent his army and destroyed those murderers and burned their city."

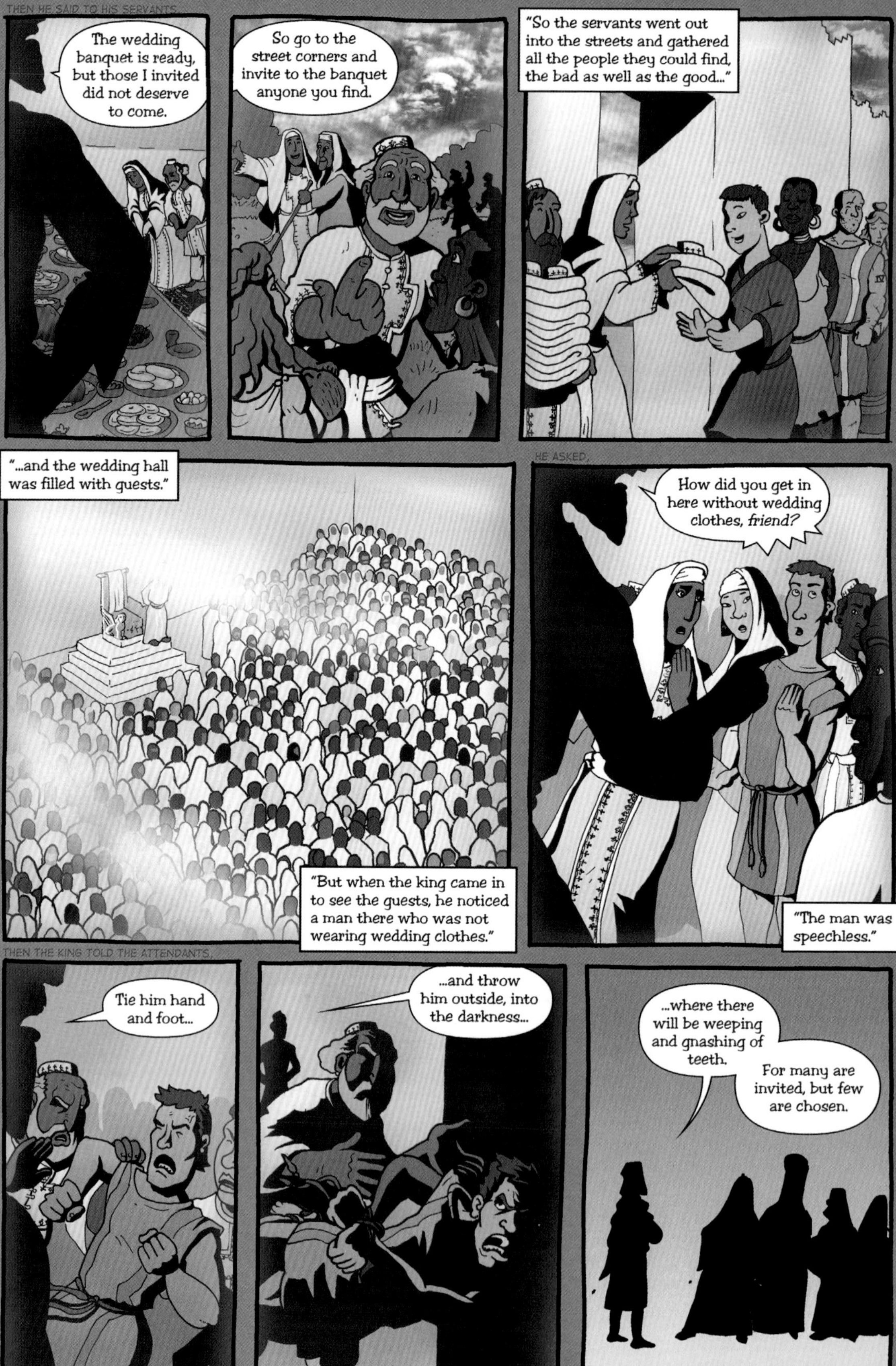
THEN HE SAID TO HIS SERVANTS...
The wedding banquet is ready, but those I invited did not deserve to come.
So go to the street corners and invite to the banquet anyone you find.
"So the servants went out into the streets and gathered all the people they could find, the bad as well as the good..."
"...and the wedding hall was filled with guests."
"But when the king came in to see the guests, he noticed a man there who was not wearing wedding clothes."
HE ASKED,
How did you get in here without wedding clothes, *friend?*
"The man was speechless."
THEN THE KING TOLD THE ATTENDANTS,
Tie him hand and foot...
...and throw him outside, into the darkness...
...where there will be weeping and gnashing of teeth.
For many are invited, but few are chosen.

MATTHEW 22:8-14

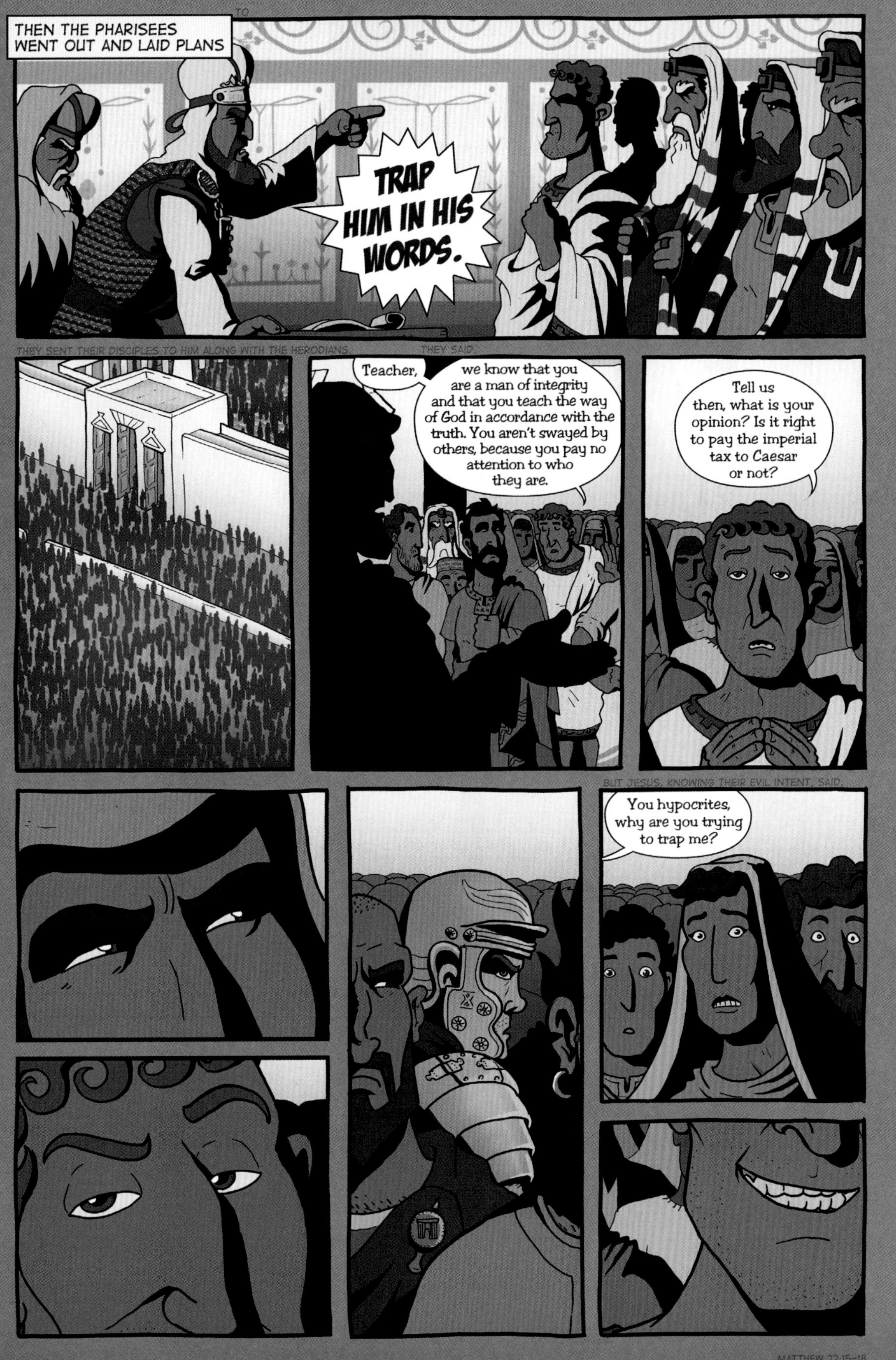
THEN THE PHARISEES WENT OUT AND LAID PLANS
TO
TRAP HIM IN HIS WORDS.
THEY SENT THEIR DISCIPLES TO HIM ALONG WITH THE HERODIANS.
THEY SAID,
Teacher,
we know that you are a man of integrity and that you teach the way of God in accordance with the truth. You aren't swayed by others, because you pay no attention to who they are.
Tell us then, what is your opinion? Is it right to pay the imperial tax to Caesar or not?
BUT JESUS, KNOWING THEIR EVIL INTENT, SAID,
You hypocrites, why are you trying to trap me?

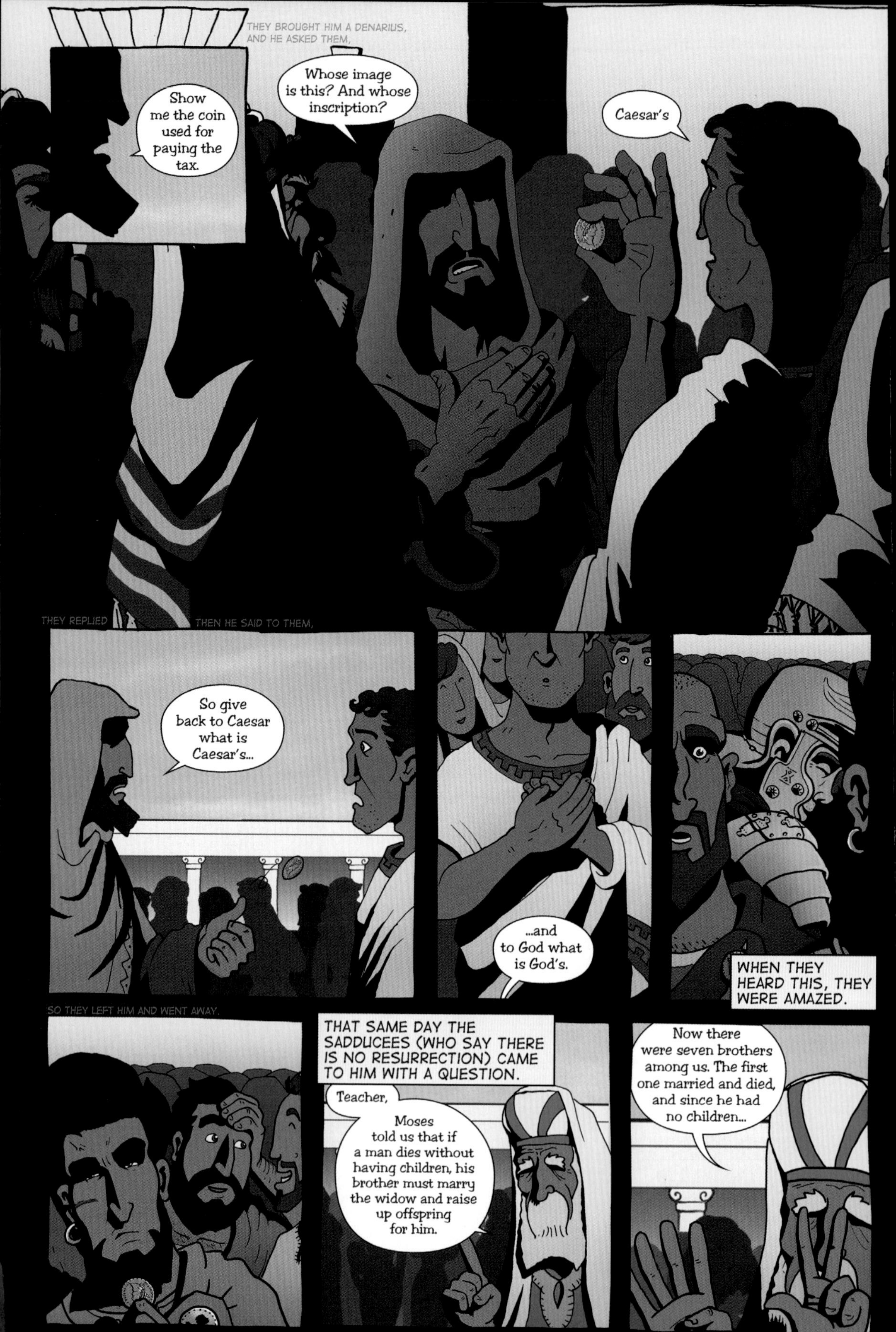
THEY BROUGHT HIM A DENARIUS, AND HE ASKED THEM,
Show me the coin used for paying the tax.
Whose image is this? And whose inscription?
Caesar's
THEY REPLIED
THEN HE SAID TO THEM,
So give back to Caesar what is Caesar's...
...and to God what is God's.
WHEN THEY HEARD THIS, THEY WERE AMAZED.
SO THEY LEFT HIM AND WENT AWAY.
THAT SAME DAY THE SADDUCEES (WHO SAY THERE IS NO RESURRECTION) CAME TO HIM WITH A QUESTION.
Teacher,
Moses told us that if a man dies without having children, his brother must marry the widow and raise up offspring for him.
Now there were seven brothers among us. The first one married and died, and since he had no children...

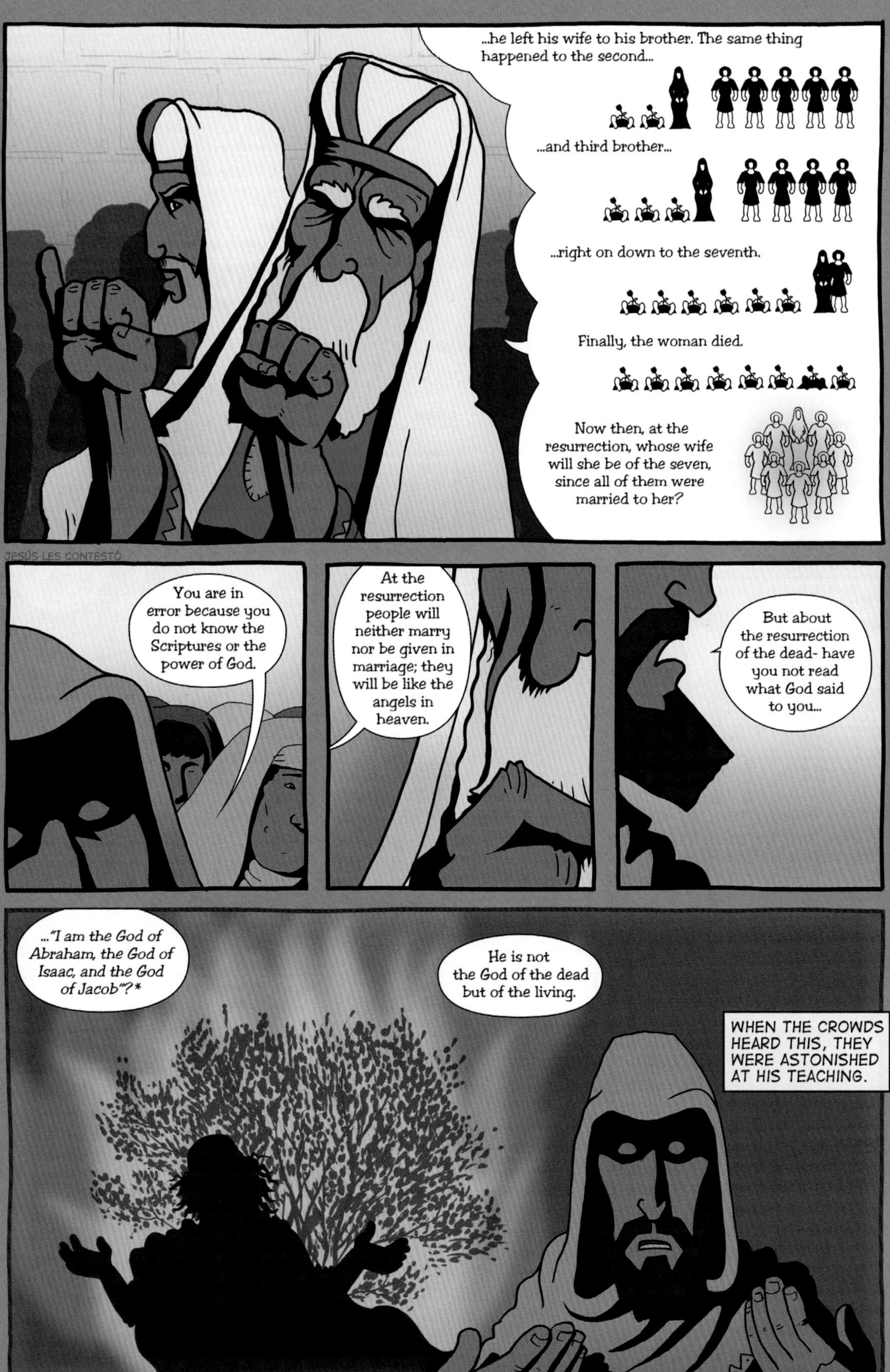
...he left his wife to his brother. The same thing happened to the second...
...and third brother...
...right on down to the seventh.
Finally, the woman died.
Now then, at the resurrection, whose wife will she be of the seven, since all of them were married to her?
JESÚS LES CONTESTÓ
You are in error because you do not know the Scriptures or the power of God.
At the resurrection people will neither marry nor be given in marriage; they will be like the angels in heaven.
But about the resurrection of the dead- have you not read what God said to you...
..."I am the God of Abraham, the God of Isaac, and the God of Jacob"?*
He is not the God of the dead but of the living.
WHEN THE CROWDS HEARD THIS, THEY WERE ASTONISHED AT HIS TEACHING.

*EXODO 3:6

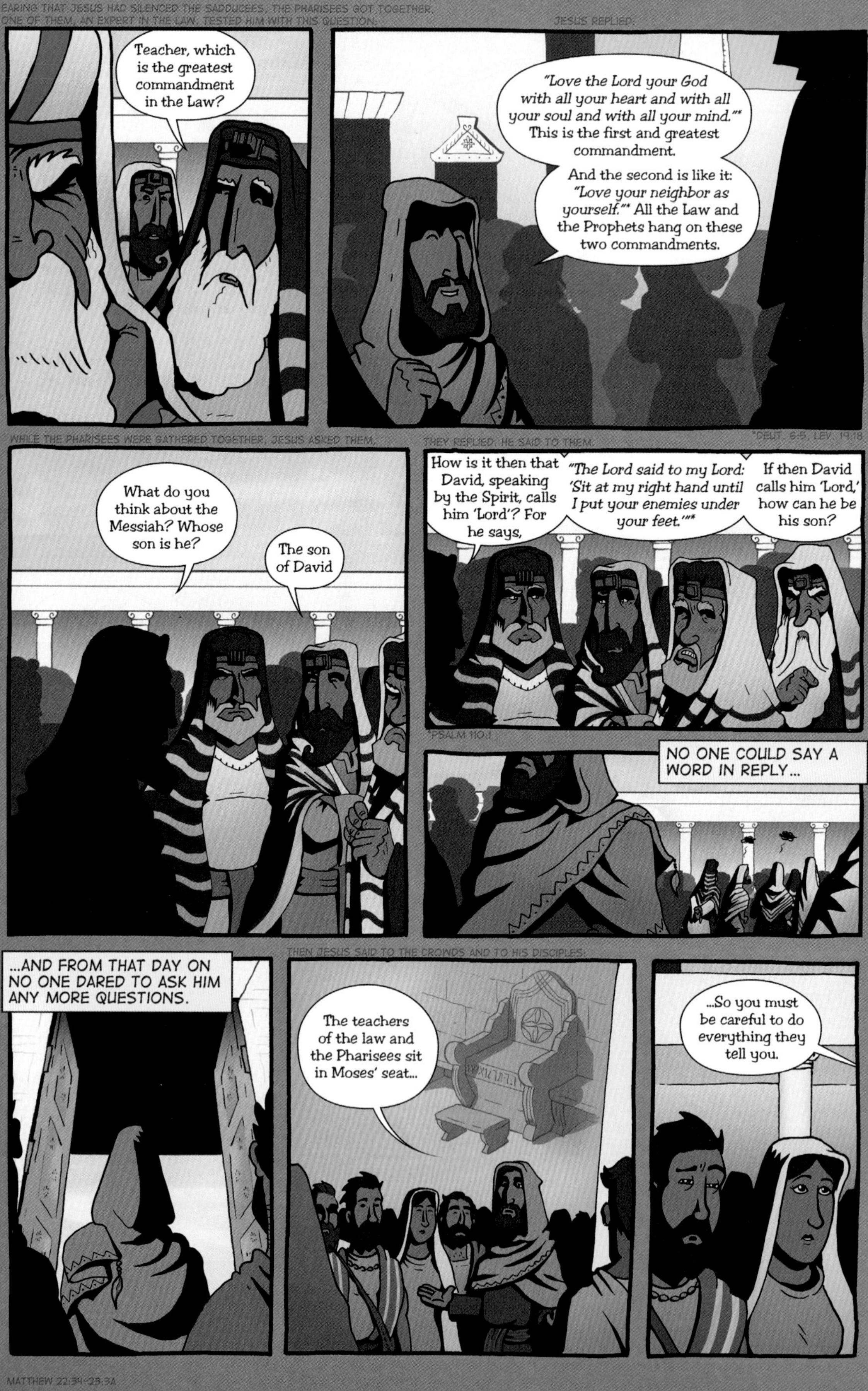
EARING THAT JESUS HAD SILENCED THE SADDUCEES, THE PHARISEES GOT TOGETHER. ONE OF THEM, AN EXPERT IN THE LAW, TESTED HIM WITH THIS QUESTION:
Teacher, which is the greatest commandment in the Law?
JESUS REPLIED:
"Love the Lord your God with all your heart and with all your soul and with all your mind."* This is the first and greatest commandment.
And the second is like it: "Love your neighbor as yourself."* All the Law and the Prophets hang on these two commandments.
*DEUT. 6:5, LEV. 19:18
WHILE THE PHARISEES WERE GATHERED TOGETHER, JESUS ASKED THEM,
What do you think about the Messiah? Whose son is he?
The son of David
THEY REPLIED. HE SAID TO THEM,
How is it then that David, speaking by the Spirit, calls him 'Lord'? For he says,
"The Lord said to my Lord: 'Sit at my right hand until I put your enemies under your feet.'"*
If then David calls him 'Lord,' how can he be his son?
*PSALM 110:1
NO ONE COULD SAY A WORD IN REPLY...
...AND FROM THAT DAY ON NO ONE DARED TO ASK HIM ANY MORE QUESTIONS.
THEN JESUS SAID TO THE CROWDS AND TO HIS DISCIPLES:
The teachers of the law and the Pharisees sit in Moses' seat...
...So you must be careful to do everything they tell you.

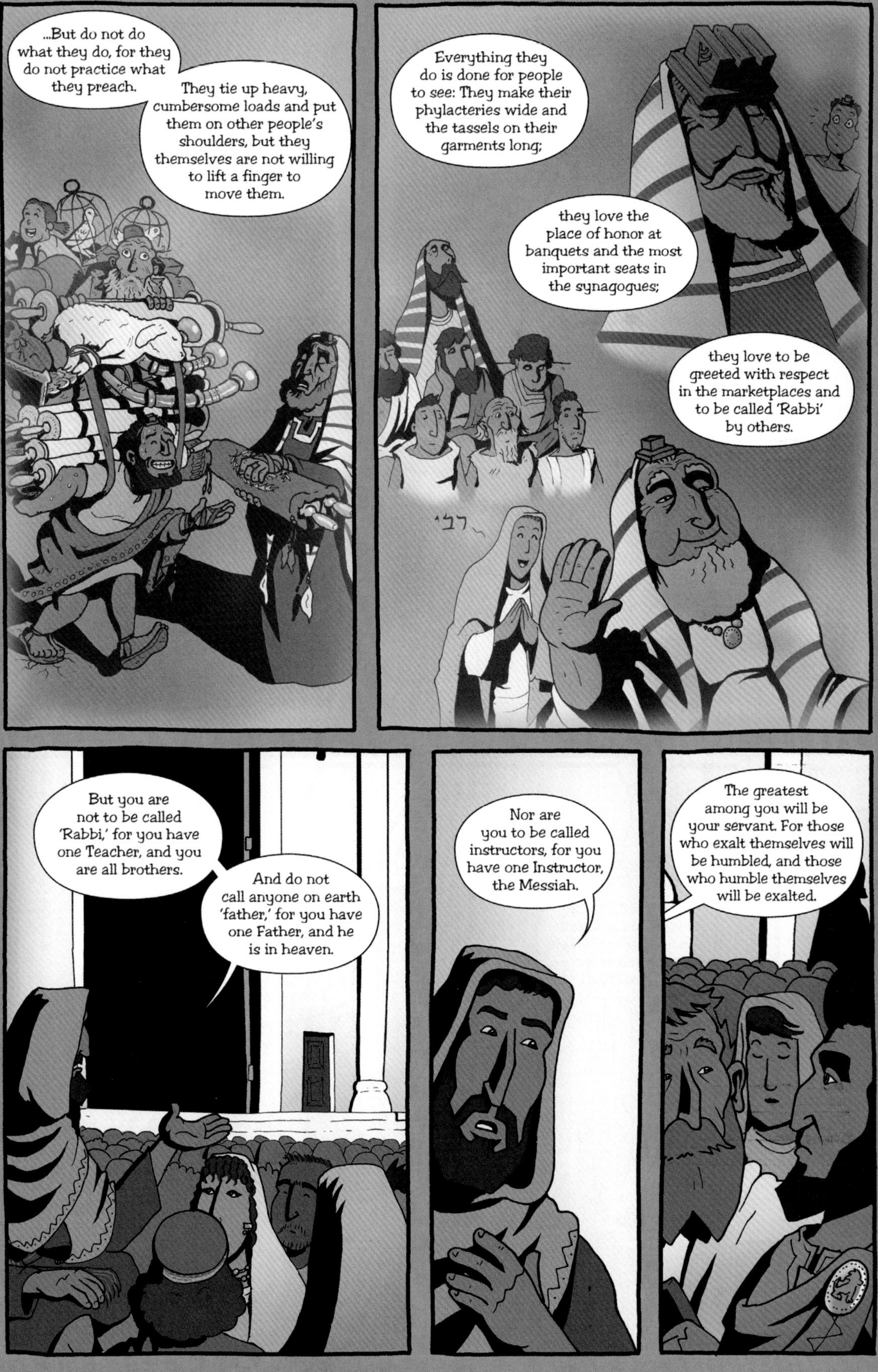
...But do not do what they do, for they do not practice what they preach.
They tie up heavy, cumbersome loads and put them on other people's shoulders, but they themselves are not willing to lift a finger to move them.
Everything they do is done for people to see: They make their phylacteries wide and the tassels on their garments long;
they love the place of honor at banquets and the most important seats in the synagogues;
they love to be greeted with respect in the marketplaces and to be called 'Rabbi' by others.
רבי
But you are not to be called 'Rabbi,' for you have one Teacher, and you are all brothers.
And do not call anyone on earth 'father,' for you have one Father, and he is in heaven.
Nor are you to be called instructors, for you have one Instructor, the Messiah.
The greatest among you will be your servant. For those who exalt themselves will be humbled, and those who humble themselves will be exalted.

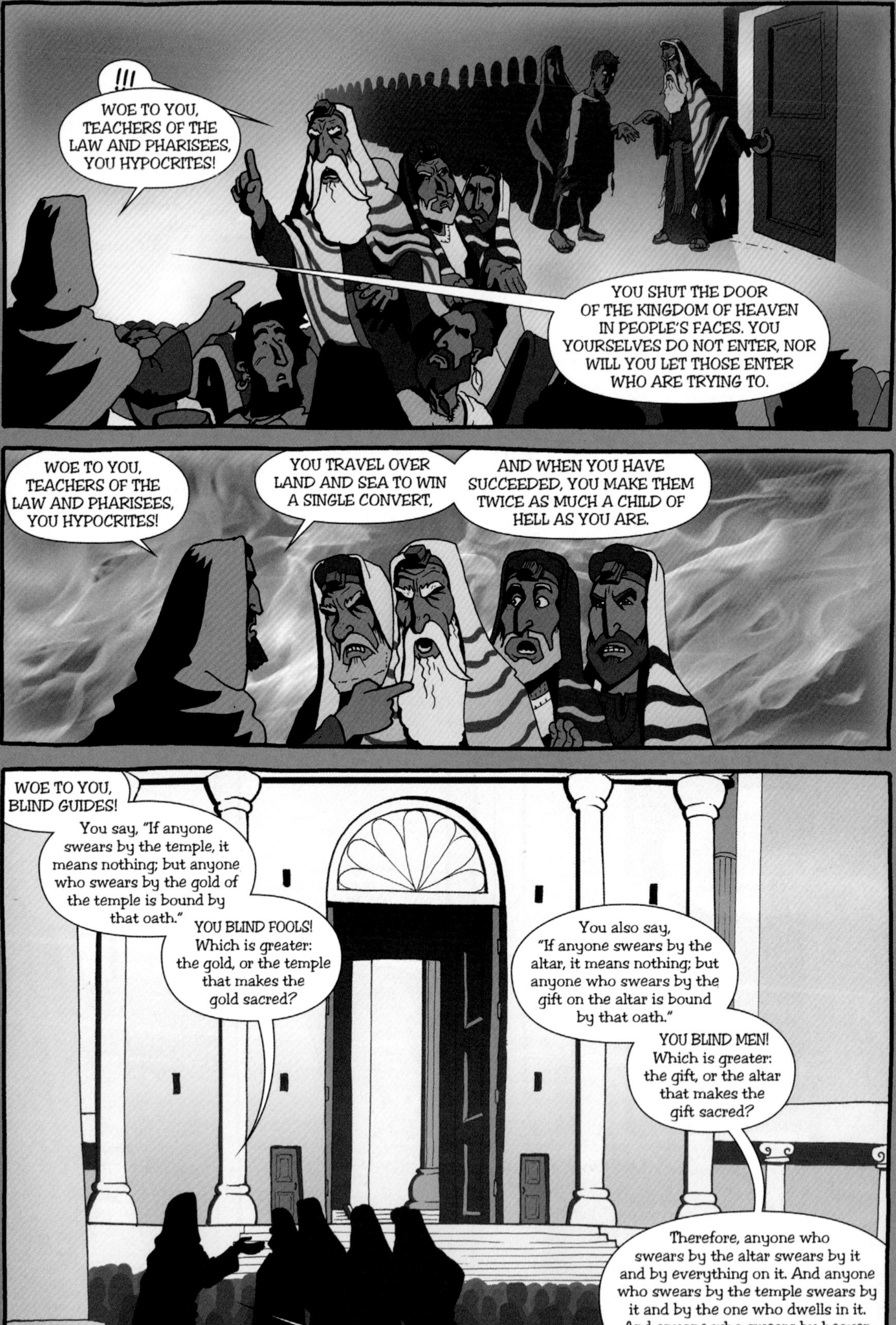
!!!
WOE TO YOU, TEACHERS OF THE LAW AND PHARISEES, YOU HYPOCRITES!
YOU SHUT THE DOOR OF THE KINGDOM OF HEAVEN IN PEOPLE'S FACES. YOU YOURSELVES DO NOT ENTER, NOR WILL YOU LET THOSE ENTER WHO ARE TRYING TO.
WOE TO YOU, TEACHERS OF THE LAW AND PHARISEES, YOU HYPOCRITES!
YOU TRAVEL OVER LAND AND SEA TO WIN A SINGLE CONVERT,
AND WHEN YOU HAVE SUCCEEDED, YOU MAKE THEM TWICE AS MUCH A CHILD OF HELL AS YOU ARE.
WOE TO YOU, BLIND GUIDES!
You say, "If anyone swears by the temple, it means nothing; but anyone who swears by the gold of the temple is bound by that oath."
YOU BLIND FOOLS! Which is greater: the gold, or the temple that makes the gold sacred?
You also say, "If anyone swears by the altar, it means nothing; but anyone who swears by the gift on the altar is bound by that oath."
YOU BLIND MEN! Which is greater: the gift, or the altar that makes the gift sacred?
Therefore, anyone who swears by the altar swears by it and by everything on it. And anyone who swears by the temple swears by it and by the one who dwells in it. And anyone who swears by heaven swears by God's throne and by the one who sits on it.

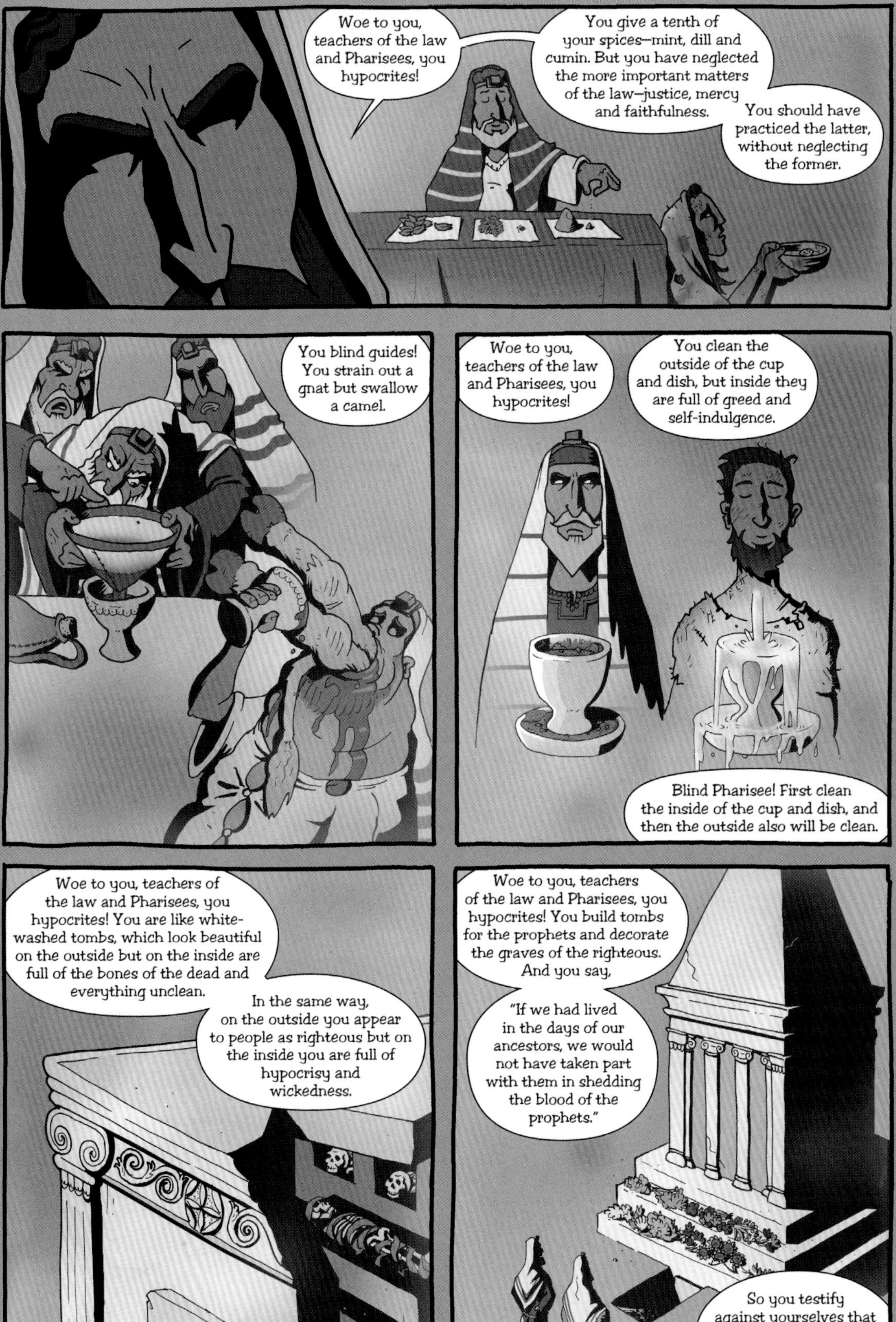
Woe to you, teachers of the law and Pharisees, you hypocrites!
You give a tenth of your spices—mint, dill and cumin. But you have neglected the more important matters of the law—justice, mercy and faithfulness.
You should have practiced the latter, without neglecting the former.
You blind guides! You strain out a gnat but swallow a camel.
Woe to you, teachers of the law and Pharisees, you hypocrites!
You clean the outside of the cup and dish, but inside they are full of greed and self-indulgence.
Blind Pharisee! First clean the inside of the cup and dish, and then the outside also will be clean.
Woe to you, teachers of the law and Pharisees, you hypocrites! You are like white-washed tombs, which look beautiful on the outside but on the inside are full of the bones of the dead and everything unclean.
In the same way, on the outside you appear to people as righteous but on the inside you are full of hypocrisy and wickedness.
Woe to you, teachers of the law and Pharisees, you hypocrites! You build tombs for the prophets and decorate the graves of the righteous. And you say,
"If we had lived in the days of our ancestors, we would not have taken part with them in shedding the blood of the prophets."
So you testify against yourselves that you are the descendants of those who murdered the prophets.

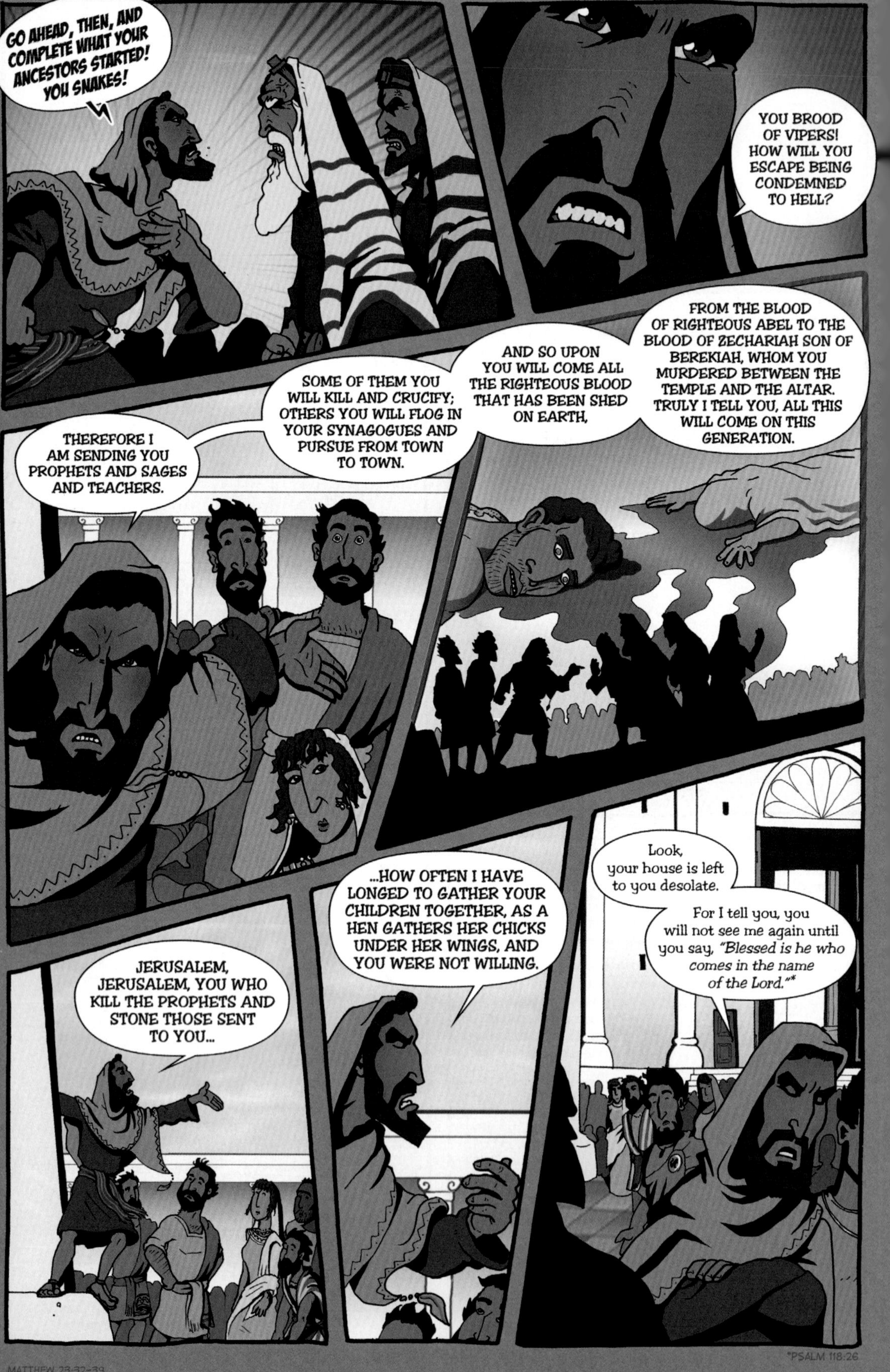
GO AHEAD, THEN, AND COMPLETE WHAT YOUR ANCESTORS STARTED! YOU SNAKES!
YOU BROOD OF VIPERS! HOW WILL YOU ESCAPE BEING CONDEMNED TO HELL?
THEREFORE I AM SENDING YOU PROPHETS AND SAGES AND TEACHERS.
SOME OF THEM YOU WILL KILL AND CRUCIFY; OTHERS YOU WILL FLOG IN YOUR SYNAGOGUES AND PURSUE FROM TOWN TO TOWN.
AND SO UPON YOU WILL COME ALL THE RIGHTEOUS BLOOD THAT HAS BEEN SHED ON EARTH,
FROM THE BLOOD OF RIGHTEOUS ABEL TO THE BLOOD OF ZECHARIAH SON OF BEREKIAH, WHOM YOU MURDERED BETWEEN THE TEMPLE AND THE ALTAR. TRULY I TELL YOU, ALL THIS WILL COME ON THIS GENERATION.
JERUSALEM, JERUSALEM, YOU WHO KILL THE PROPHETS AND STONE THOSE SENT TO YOU...
...HOW OFTEN I HAVE LONGED TO GATHER YOUR CHILDREN TOGETHER, AS A HEN GATHERS HER CHICKS UNDER HER WINGS, AND YOU WERE NOT WILLING.
Look, your house is left to you desolate.
For I tell you, you will not see me again until you say, *"Blessed is he who comes in the name of the Lord."**

*PSALM 118:26

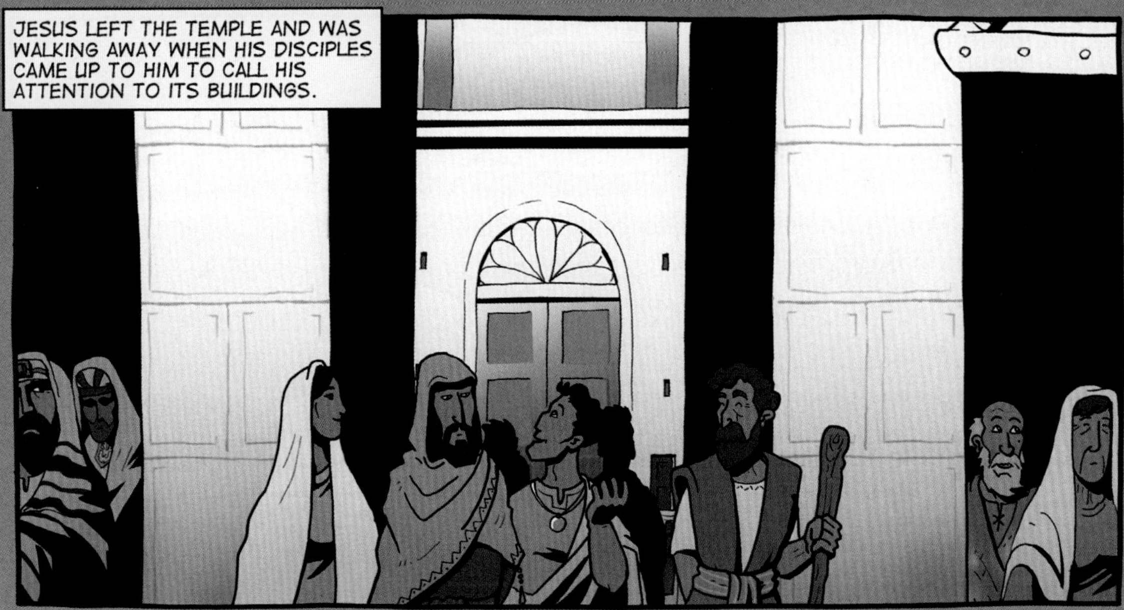
JESUS LEFT THE TEMPLE AND WAS WALKING AWAY WHEN HIS DISCIPLES CAME UP TO HIM TO CALL HIS ATTENTION TO ITS BUILDINGS.

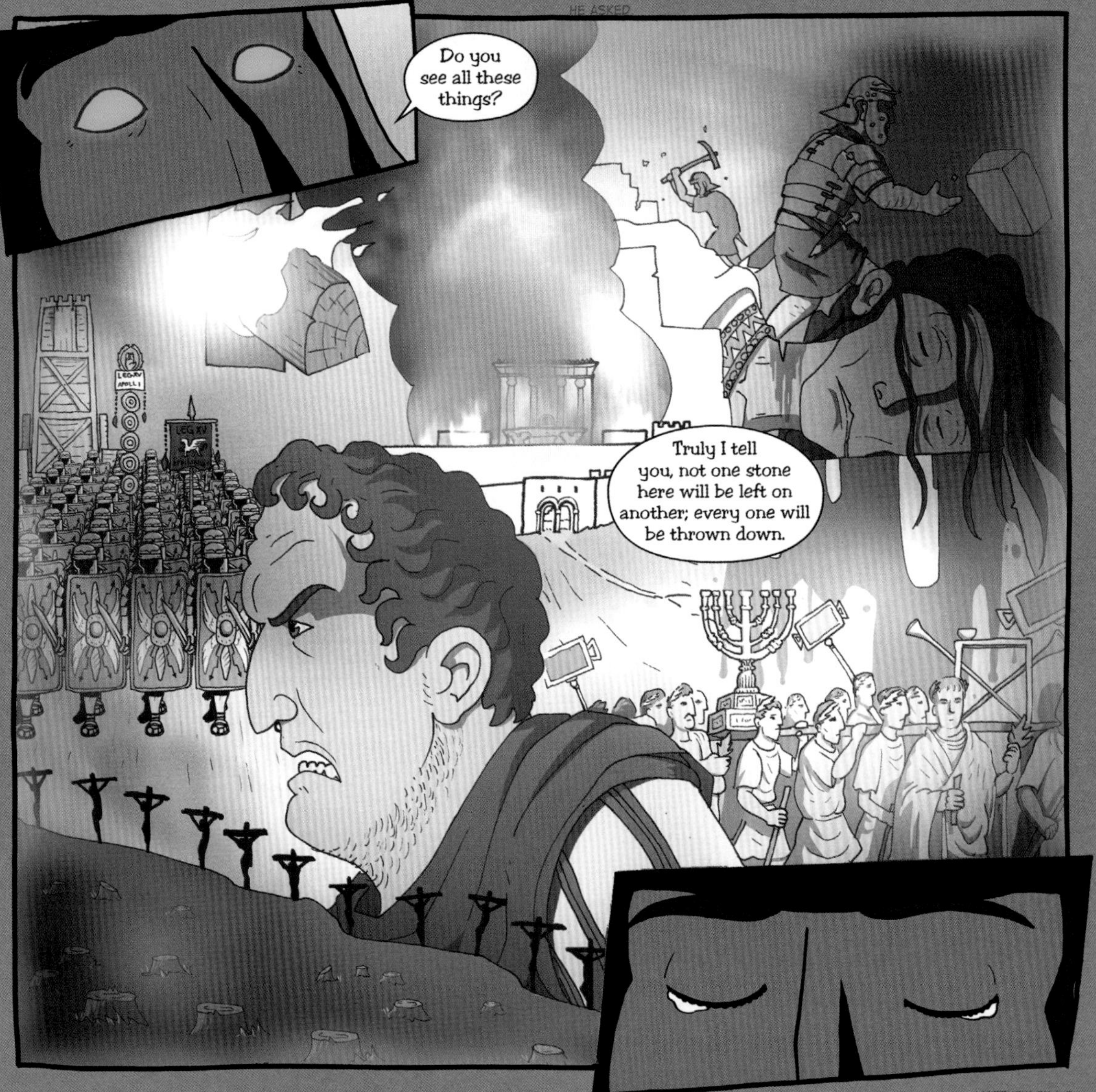
Do you see all these things?
Truly I tell you, not one stone here will be left on another; every one will be thrown down.

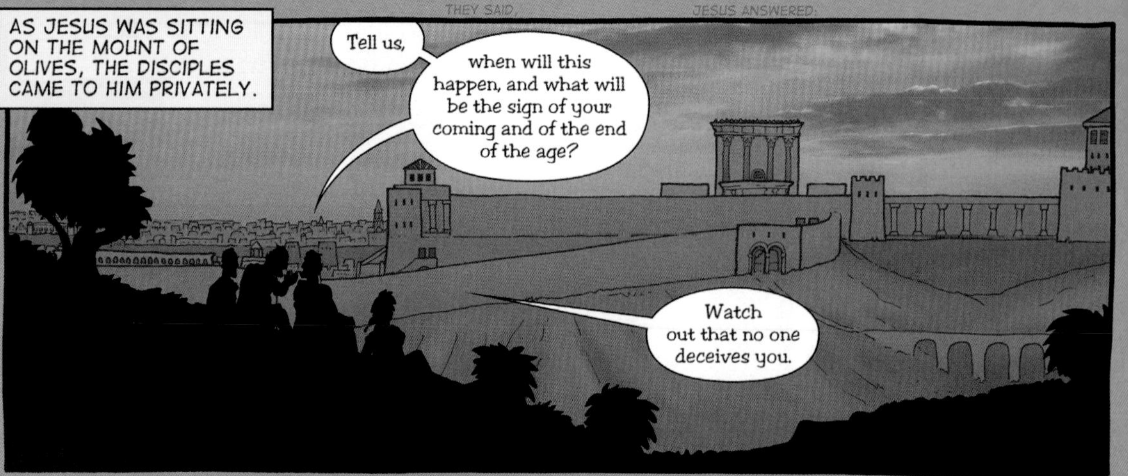

THEY SAID,
JESUS ANSWERED:
AS JESUS WAS SITTING ON THE MOUNT OF OLIVES, THE DISCIPLES CAME TO HIM PRIVATELY.
Tell us,
when will this happen, and what will be the sign of your coming and of the end of the age?
Watch out that no one deceives you.

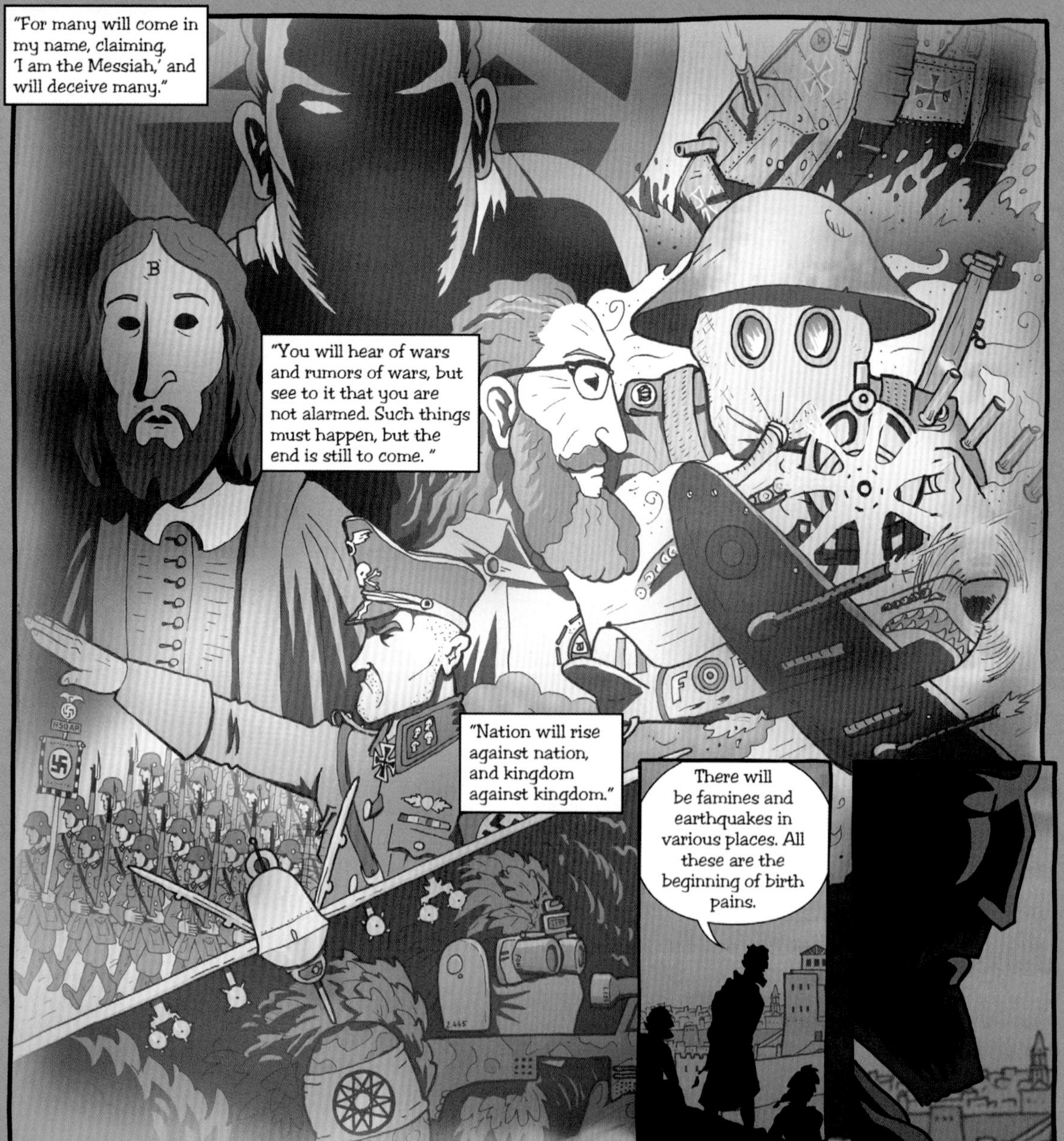

"For many will come in my name, claiming, 'I am the Messiah,' and will deceive many."
"You will hear of wars and rumors of wars, but see to it that you are not alarmed. Such things must happen, but the end is still to come."
"Nation will rise against nation, and kingdom against kingdom."
There will be famines and earthquakes in various places. All these are the beginning of birth pains.

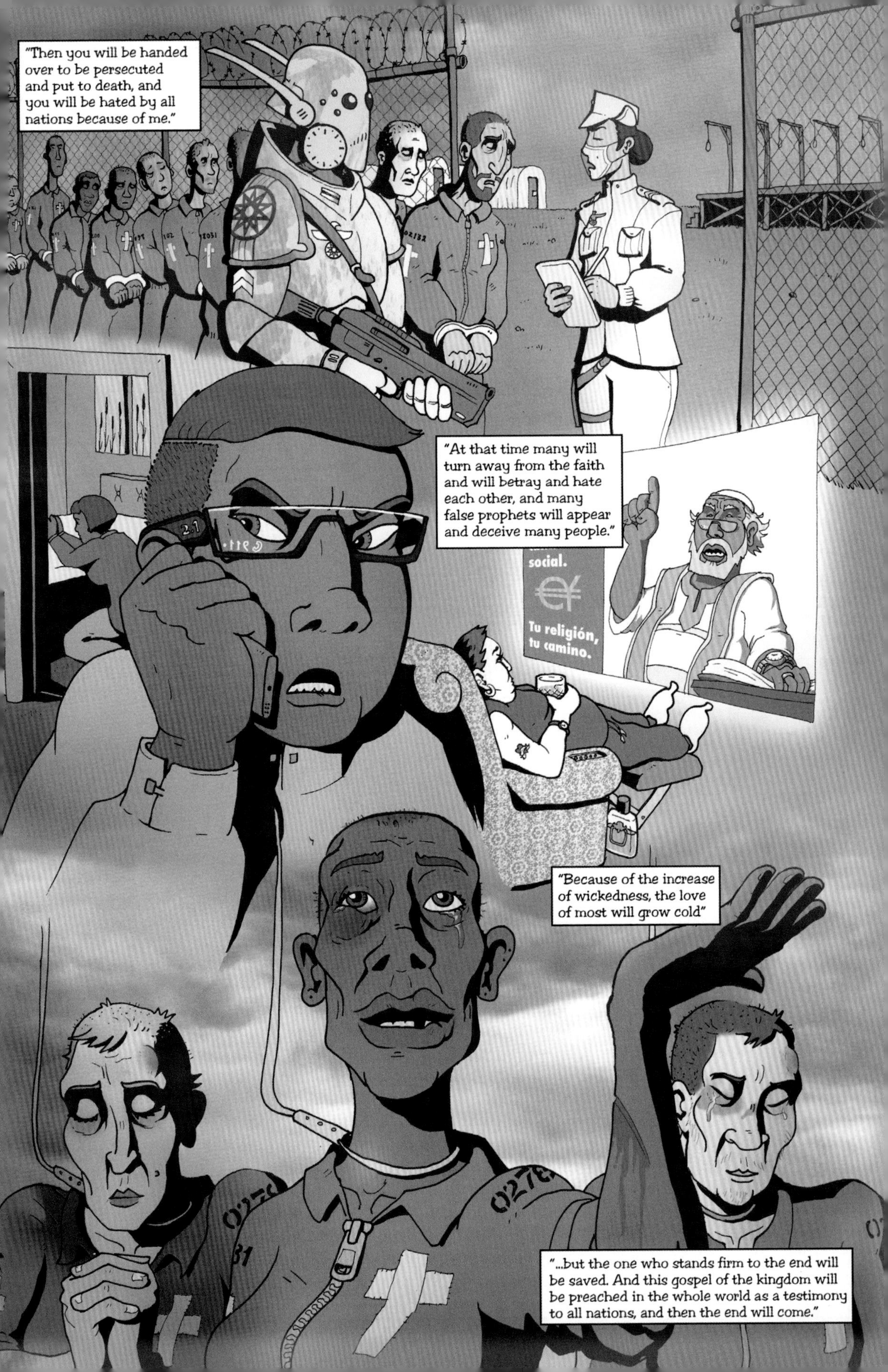
"Then you will be handed over to be persecuted and put to death, and you will be hated by all nations because of me."
"At that time many will turn away from the faith and will betray and hate each other, and many false prophets will appear and deceive many people."
social.
Tu religión, tu camino.
"Because of the increase of wickedness, the love of most will grow cold"
"...but the one who stands firm to the end will be saved. And this gospel of the kingdom will be preached in the whole world as a testimony to all nations, and then the end will come."

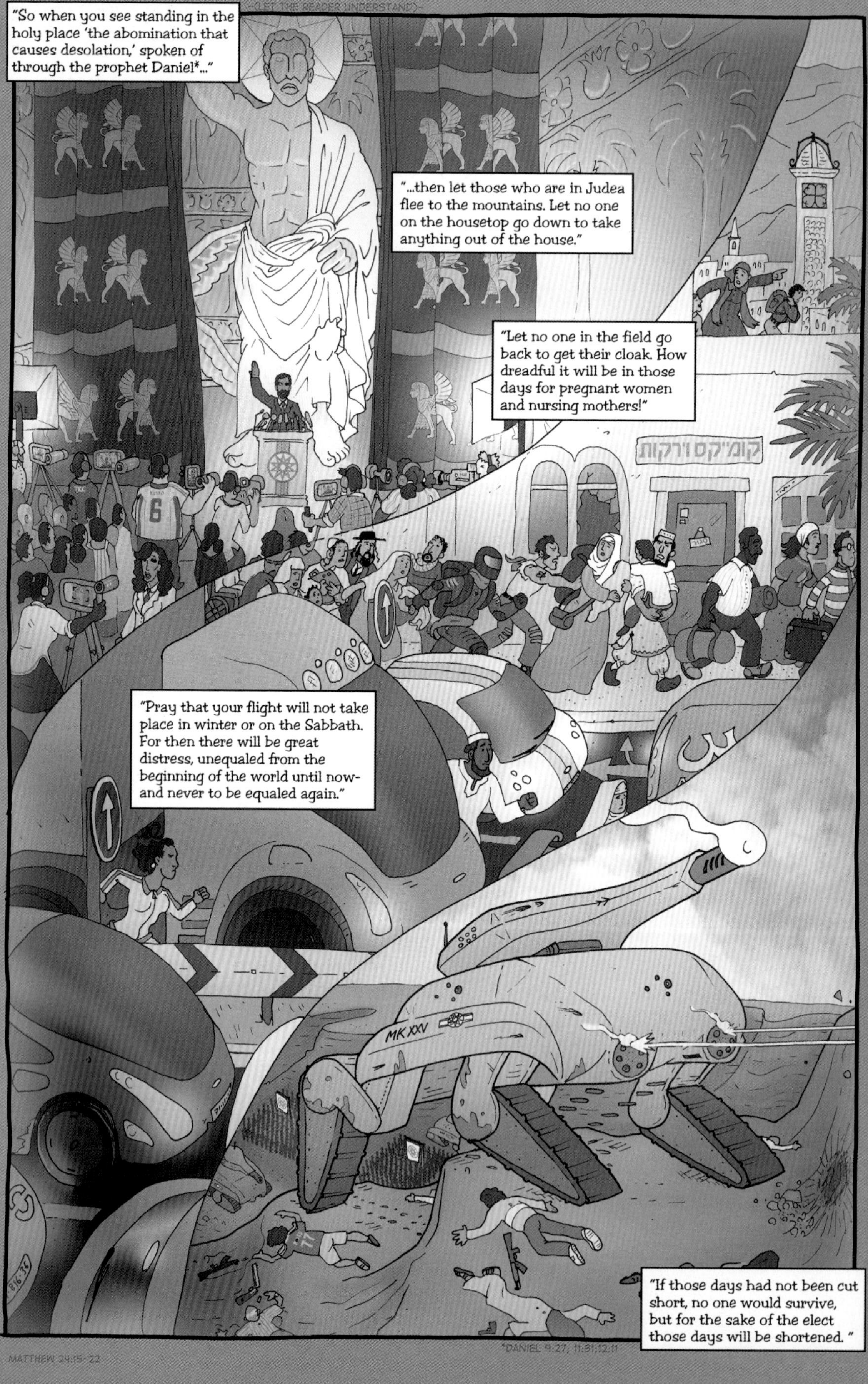
—(LET THE READER UNDERSTAND)—
"So when you see standing in the holy place 'the abomination that causes desolation,' spoken of through the prophet Daniel*..."
"...then let those who are in Judea flee to the mountains. Let no one on the housetop go down to take anything out of the house."
"Let no one in the field go back to get their cloak. How dreadful it will be in those days for pregnant women and nursing mothers!"
קומ״קס וירקות
"Pray that your flight will not take place in winter or on the Sabbath. For then there will be great distress, unequaled from the beginning of the world until now– and never to be equaled again."
MK XXV
"If those days had not been cut short, no one would survive, but for the sake of the elect those days will be shortened."

*DANIEL 9:27; 11:31;12:11

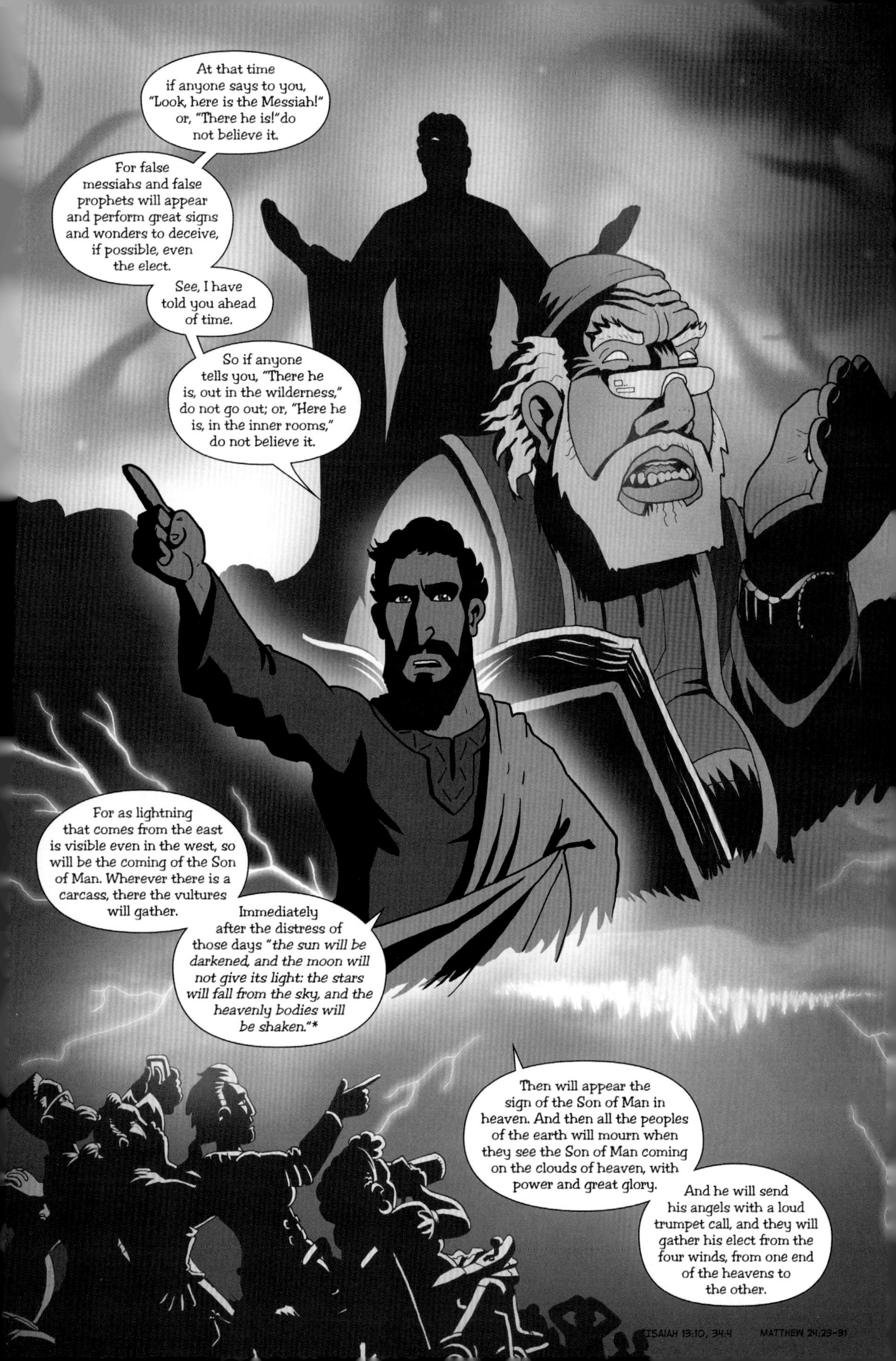

At that time if anyone says to you, "Look, here is the Messiah!" or, "There he is!" do not believe it.
For false messiahs and false prophets will appear and perform great signs and wonders to deceive, if possible, even the elect.
See, I have told you ahead of time.
So if anyone tells you, "There he is, out in the wilderness," do not go out; or, "Here he is, in the inner rooms," do not believe it.
For as lightning that comes from the east is visible even in the west, so will be the coming of the Son of Man. Wherever there is a carcass, there the vultures will gather.
Immediately after the distress of those days "*the sun will be darkened, and the moon will not give its light; the stars will fall from the sky, and the heavenly bodies will be shaken.*"*
Then will appear the sign of the Son of Man in heaven. And then all the peoples of the earth will mourn when they see the Son of Man coming on the clouds of heaven, with power and great glory.
And he will send his angels with a loud trumpet call, and they will gather his elect from the four winds, from one end of the heavens to the other.
*ISAIAH 13:10, 34:4
MATTHEW 24:23-31

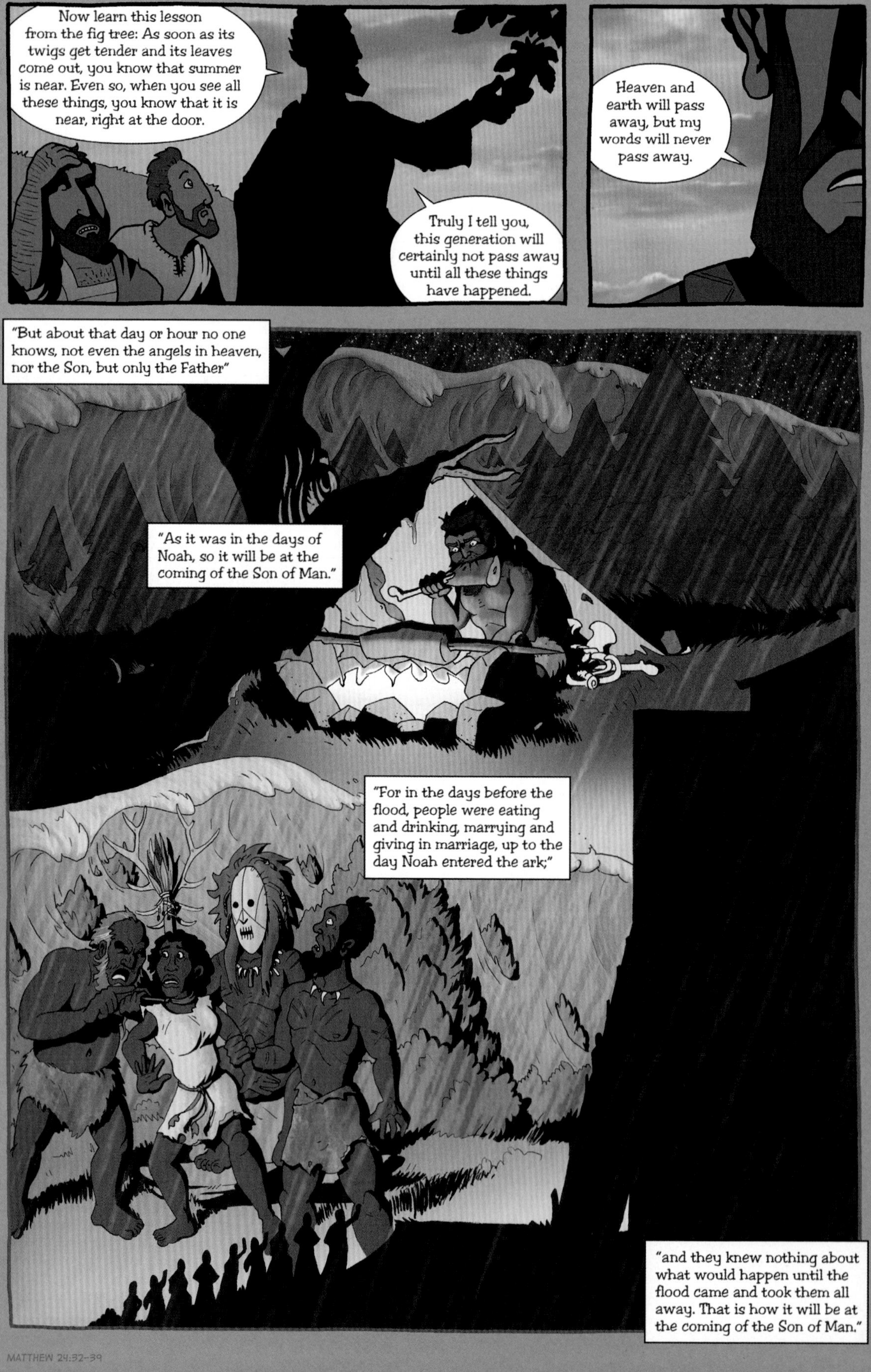
Now learn this lesson from the fig tree: As soon as its twigs get tender and its leaves come out, you know that summer is near. Even so, when you see all these things, you know that it is near, right at the door.
Truly I tell you, this generation will certainly not pass away until all these things have happened.
Heaven and earth will pass away, but my words will never pass away.
"But about that day or hour no one knows, not even the angels in heaven, nor the Son, but only the Father"
"As it was in the days of Noah, so it will be at the coming of the Son of Man."
"For in the days before the flood, people were eating and drinking, marrying and giving in marriage, up to the day Noah entered the ark;"
"and they knew nothing about what would happen until the flood came and took them all away. That is how it will be at the coming of the Son of Man."

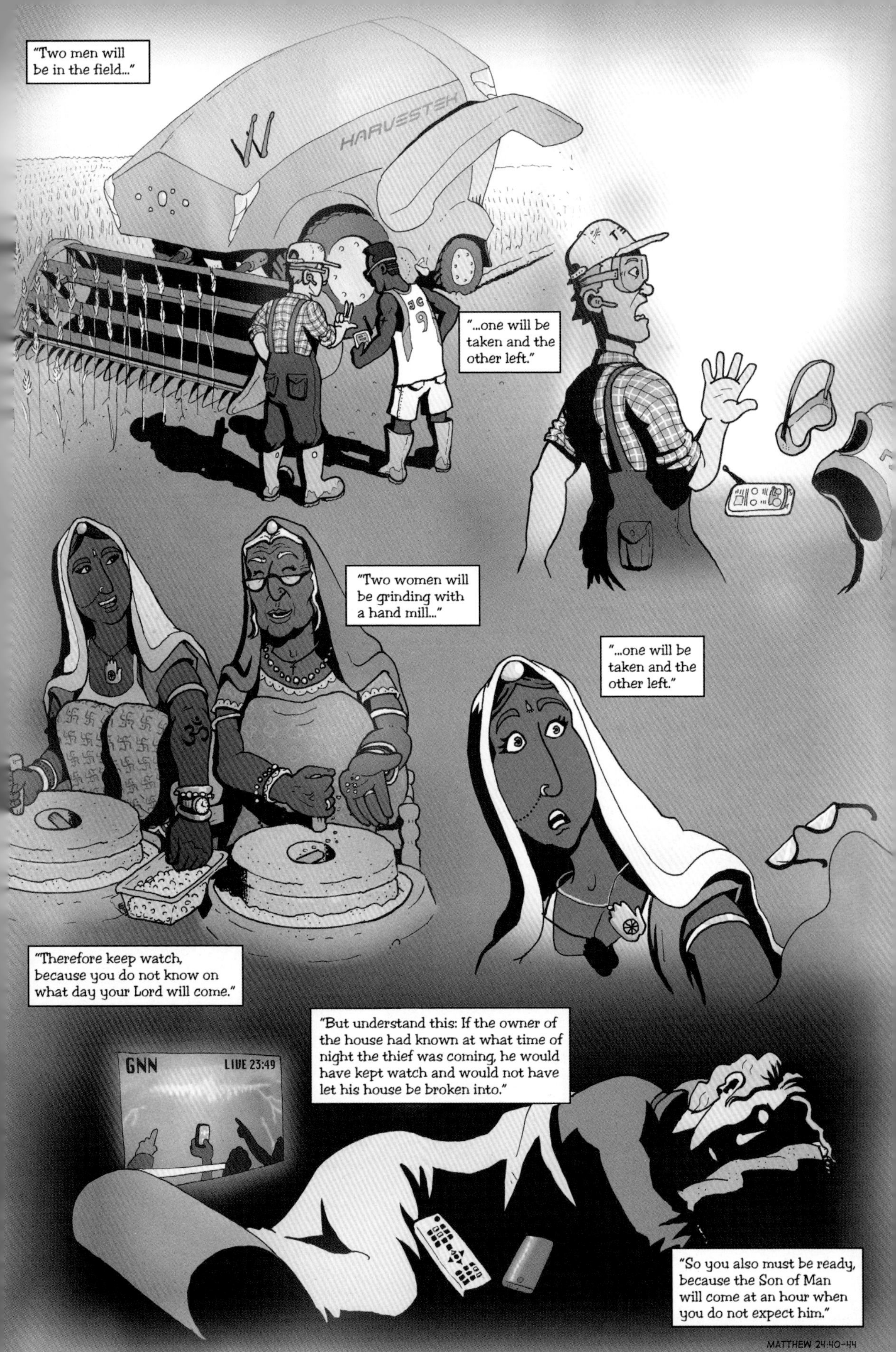
"Two men will be in the field..."
HARVESTEH
"...one will be taken and the other left."
"Two women will be grinding with a hand mill..."
"...one will be taken and the other left."
"Therefore keep watch, because you do not know on what day your Lord will come."
"But understand this: If the owner of the house had known at what time of night the thief was coming, he would have kept watch and would not have let his house be broken into."
GNN
LIVE 23:49
"So you also must be ready, because the Son of Man will come at an hour when you do not expect him."
MATTHEW 24:40-44

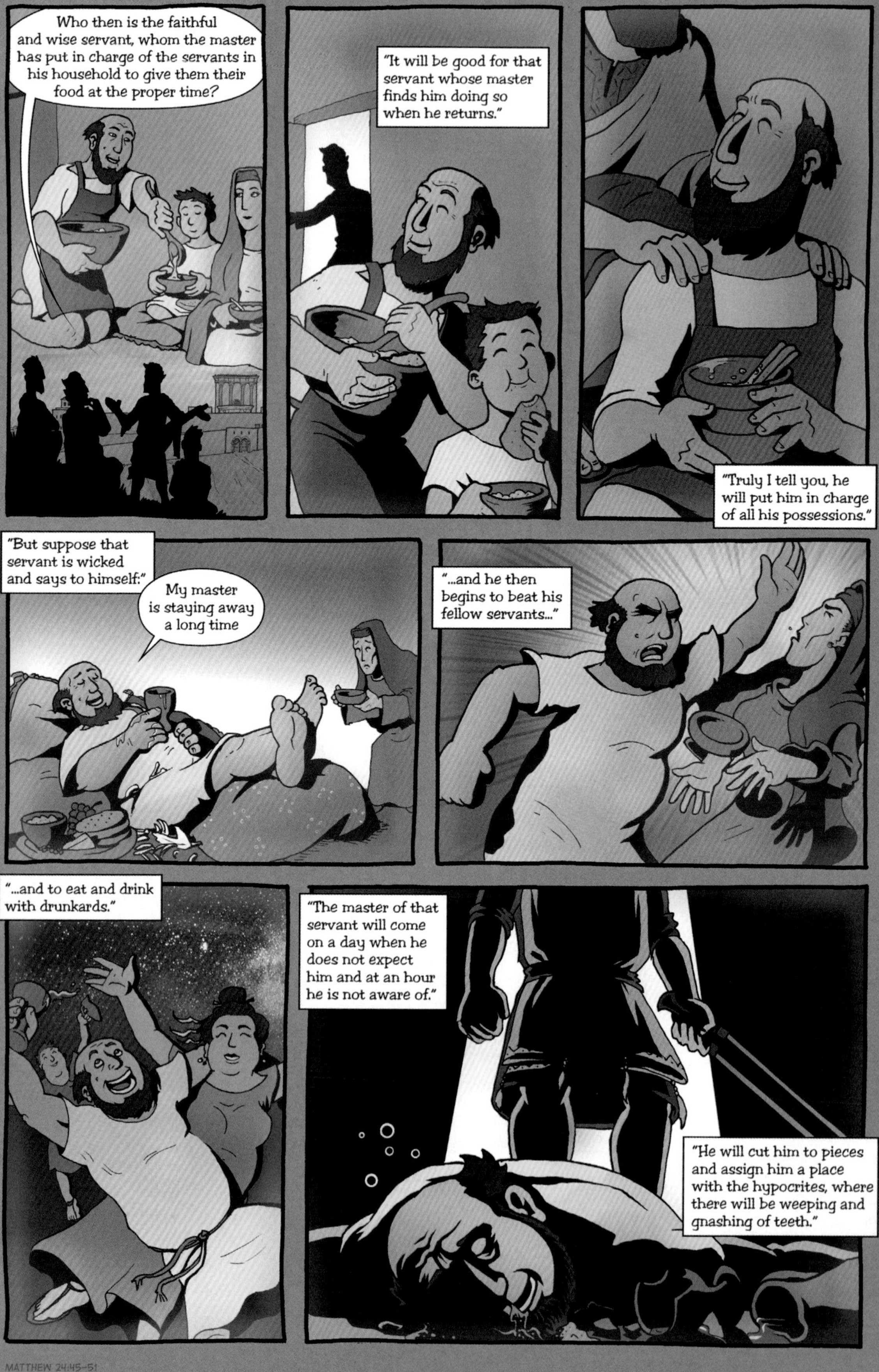
Who then is the faithful and wise servant, whom the master has put in charge of the servants in his household to give them their food at the proper time?
"It will be good for that servant whose master finds him doing so when he returns."
"Truly I tell you, he will put him in charge of all his possessions."
"But suppose that servant is wicked and says to himself:"
My master is staying away a long time
"...and he then begins to beat his fellow servants..."
"...and to eat and drink with drunkards."
"The master of that servant will come on a day when he does not expect him and at an hour he is not aware of."
"He will cut him to pieces and assign him a place with the hypocrites, where there will be weeping and gnashing of teeth."

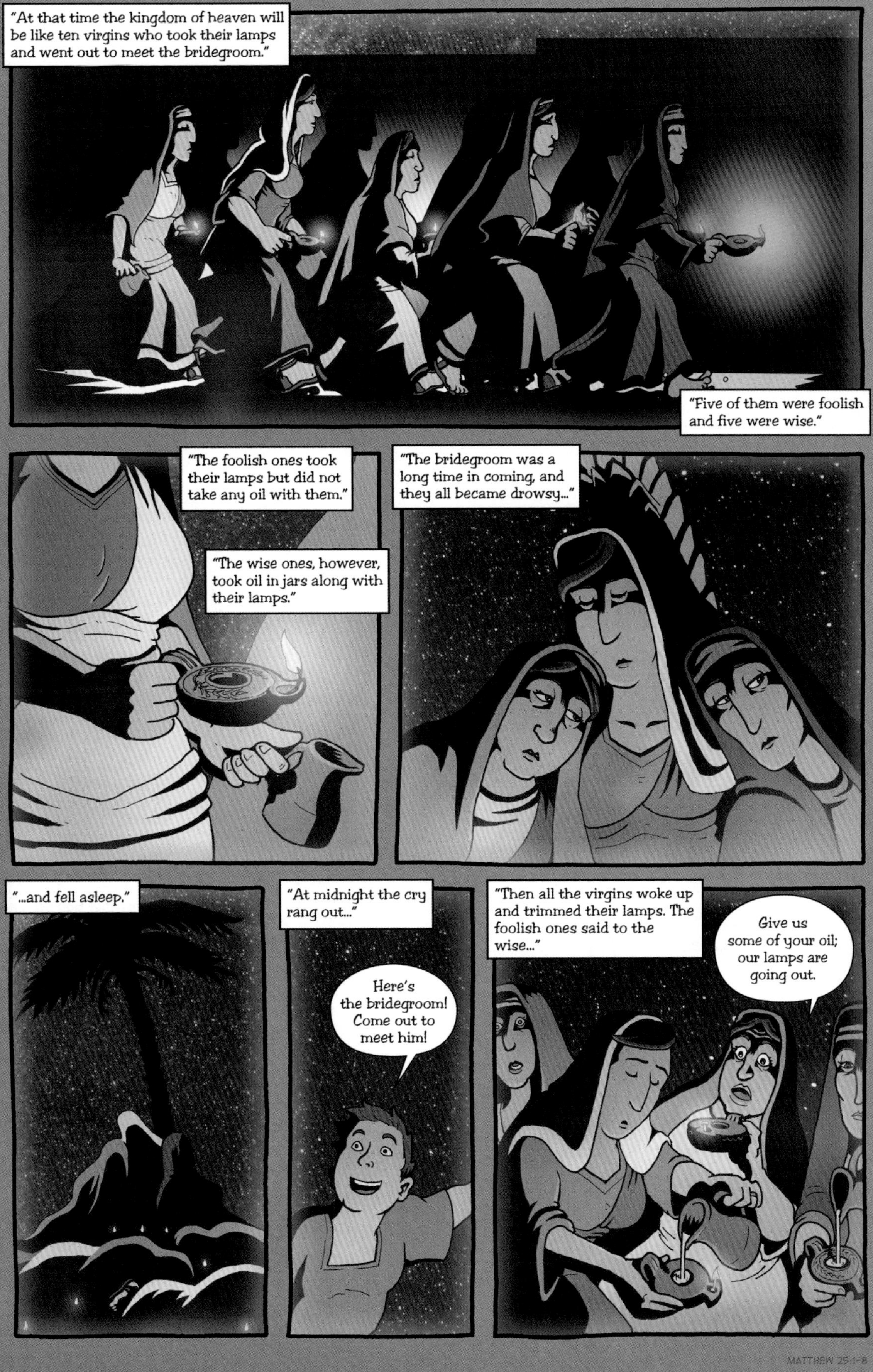
"At that time the kingdom of heaven will be like ten virgins who took their lamps and went out to meet the bridegroom."
"Five of them were foolish and five were wise."
"The foolish ones took their lamps but did not take any oil with them."
"The wise ones, however, took oil in jars along with their lamps."
"The bridegroom was a long time in coming, and they all became drowsy..."
"...and fell asleep."
"At midnight the cry rang out..."
Here's the bridegroom! Come out to meet him!
"Then all the virgins woke up and trimmed their lamps. The foolish ones said to the wise..."
Give us some of your oil; our lamps are going out.

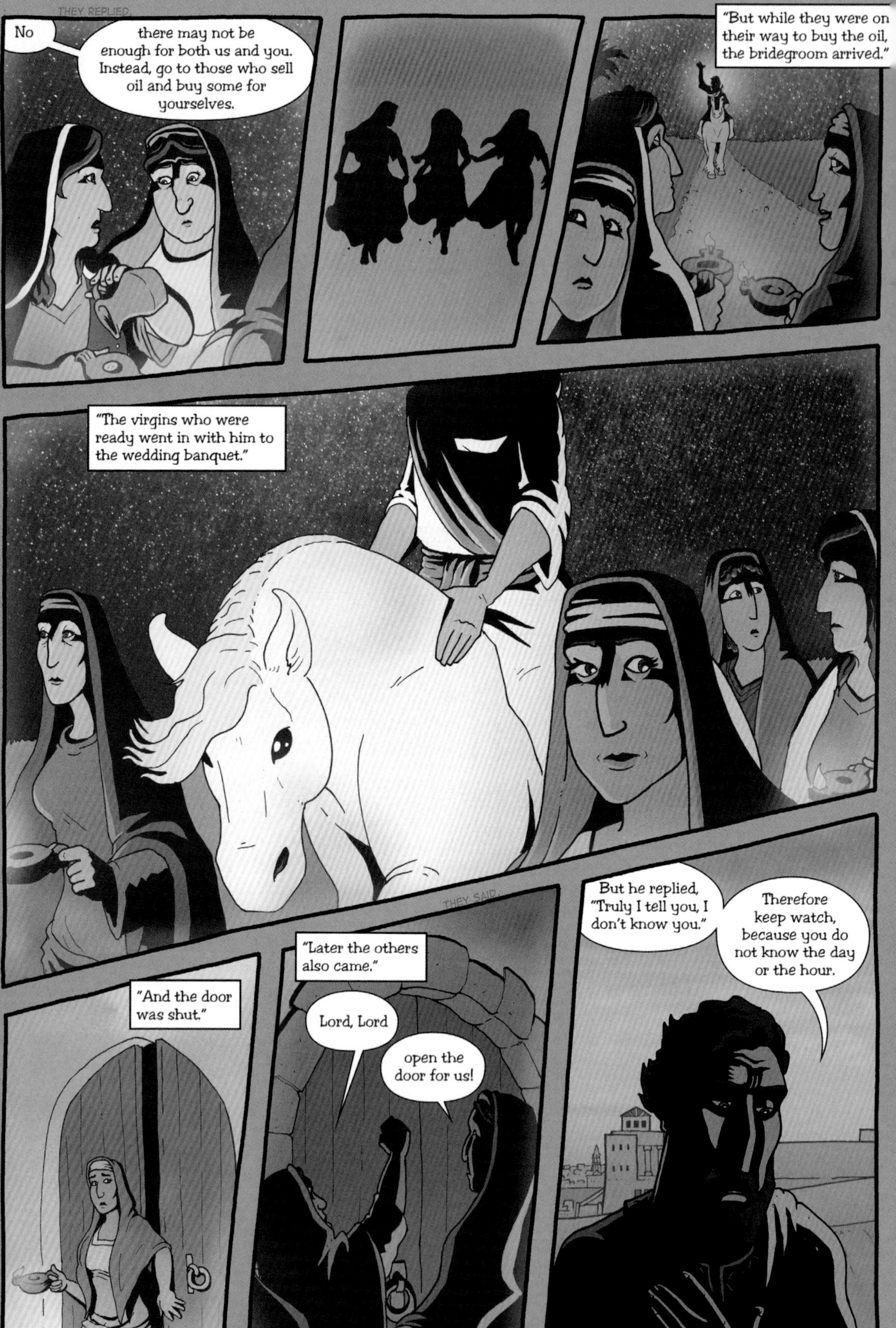
THEY REPLIED,
No
there may not be enough for both us and you. Instead, go to those who sell oil and buy some for yourselves.
"But while they were on their way to buy the oil, the bridegroom arrived."
"The virgins who were ready went in with him to the wedding banquet."
"And the door was shut."
"Later the others also came."
THEY SAID,
Lord, Lord
open the door for us!
But he replied, "Truly I tell you, I don't know you."
Therefore keep watch, because you do not know the day or the hour.

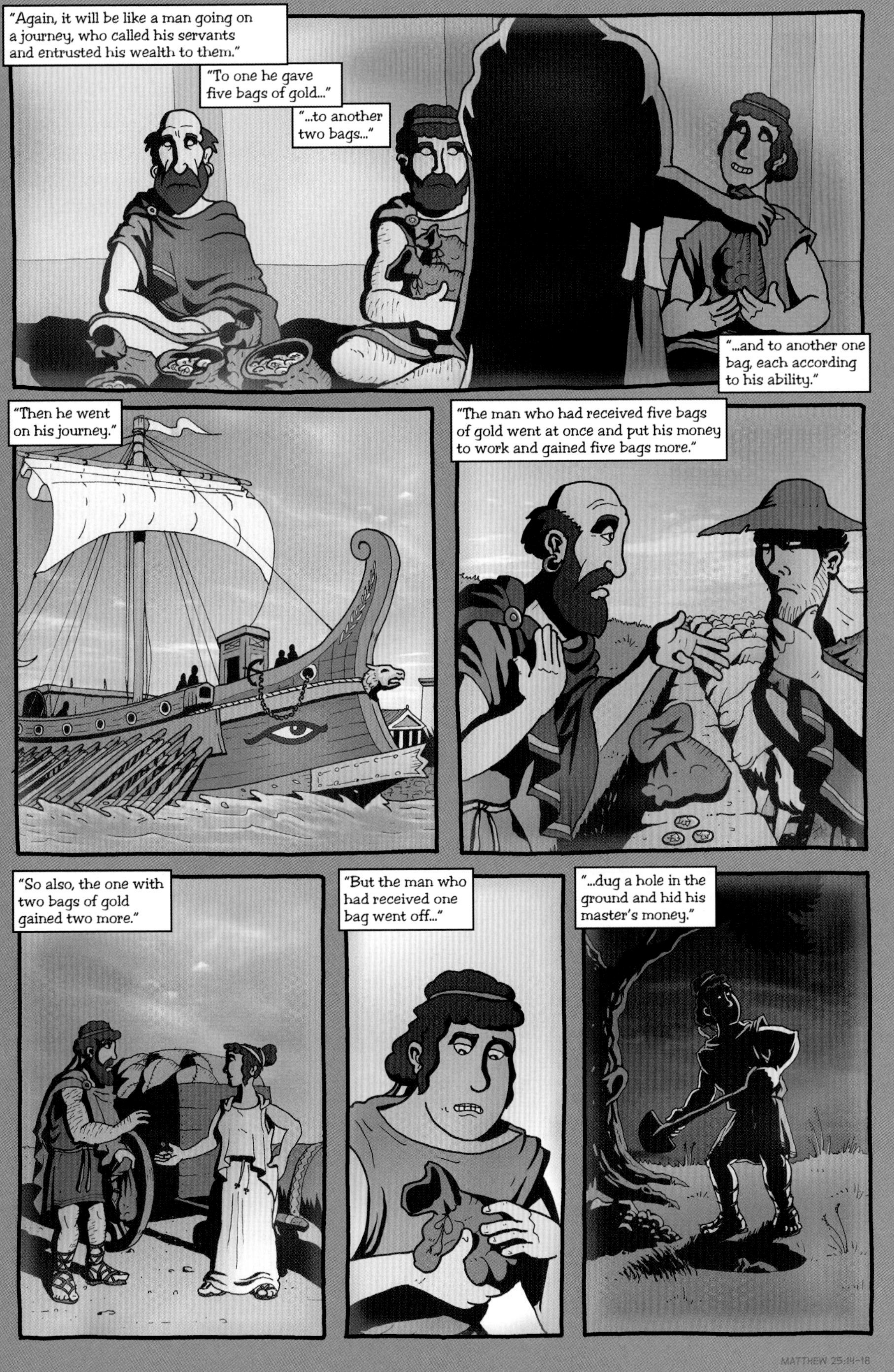
"Again, it will be like a man going on a journey, who called his servants and entrusted his wealth to them."
"To one he gave five bags of gold..."
"...to another two bags..."
"...and to another one bag, each according to his ability."
"Then he went on his journey."
"The man who had received five bags of gold went at once and put his money to work and gained five bags more."
"So also, the one with two bags of gold gained two more."
"But the man who had received one bag went off..."
"...dug a hole in the ground and hid his master's money."

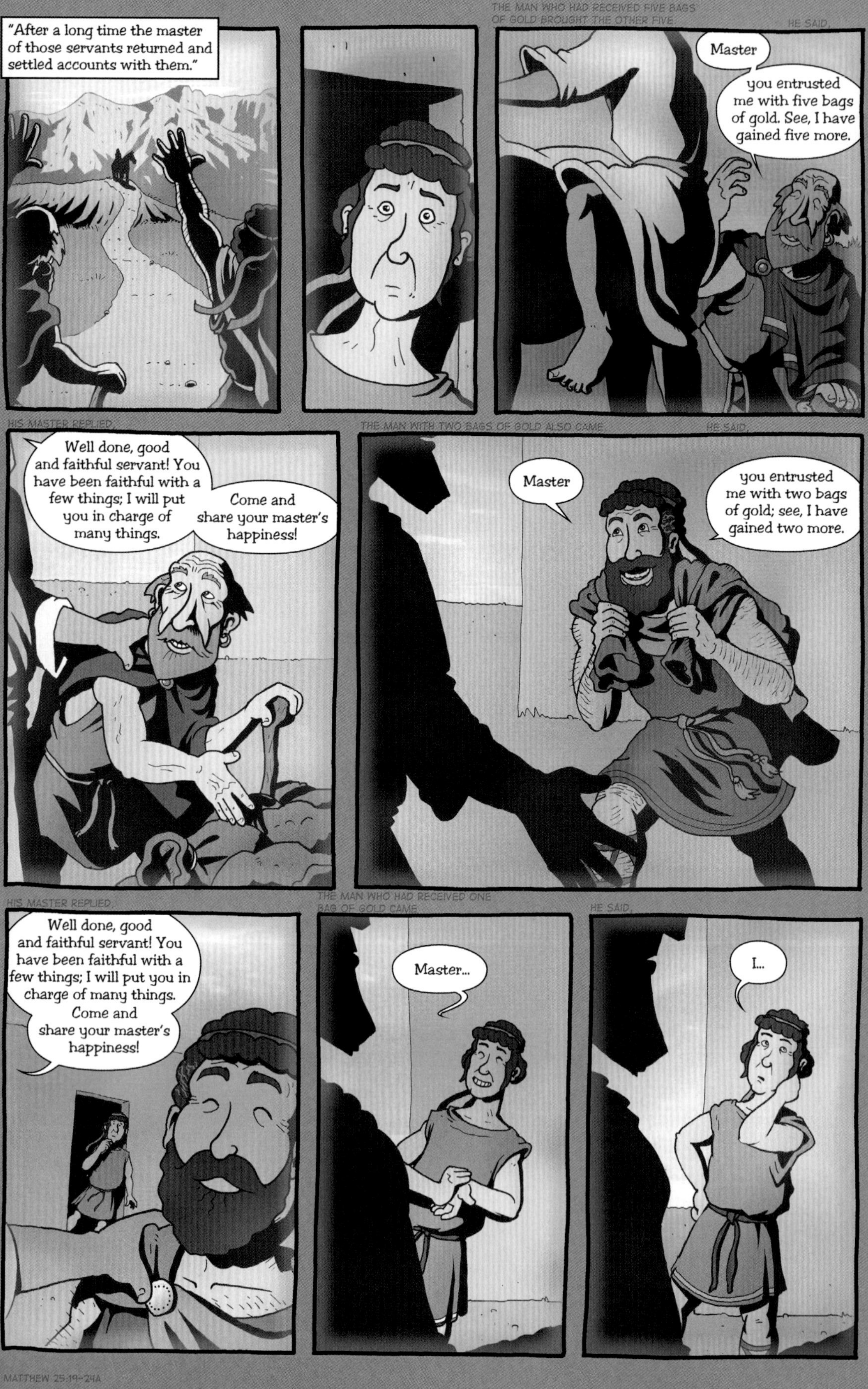

"After a long time the master of those servants returned and settled accounts with them."
THE MAN WHO HAD RECEIVED FIVE BAGS OF GOLD BROUGHT THE OTHER FIVE.
HE SAID,
Master
you entrusted me with five bags of gold. See, I have gained five more.
HIS MASTER REPLIED,
Well done, good and faithful servant! You have been faithful with a few things; I will put you in charge of many things.
Come and share your master's happiness!
THE MAN WITH TWO BAGS OF GOLD ALSO CAME.
HE SAID,
Master
you entrusted me with two bags of gold; see, I have gained two more.
HIS MASTER REPLIED,
Well done, good and faithful servant! You have been faithful with a few things; I will put you in charge of many things. Come and share your master's happiness!
THE MAN WHO HAD RECEIVED ONE BAG OF GOLD CAME
Master...
HE SAID,
I...

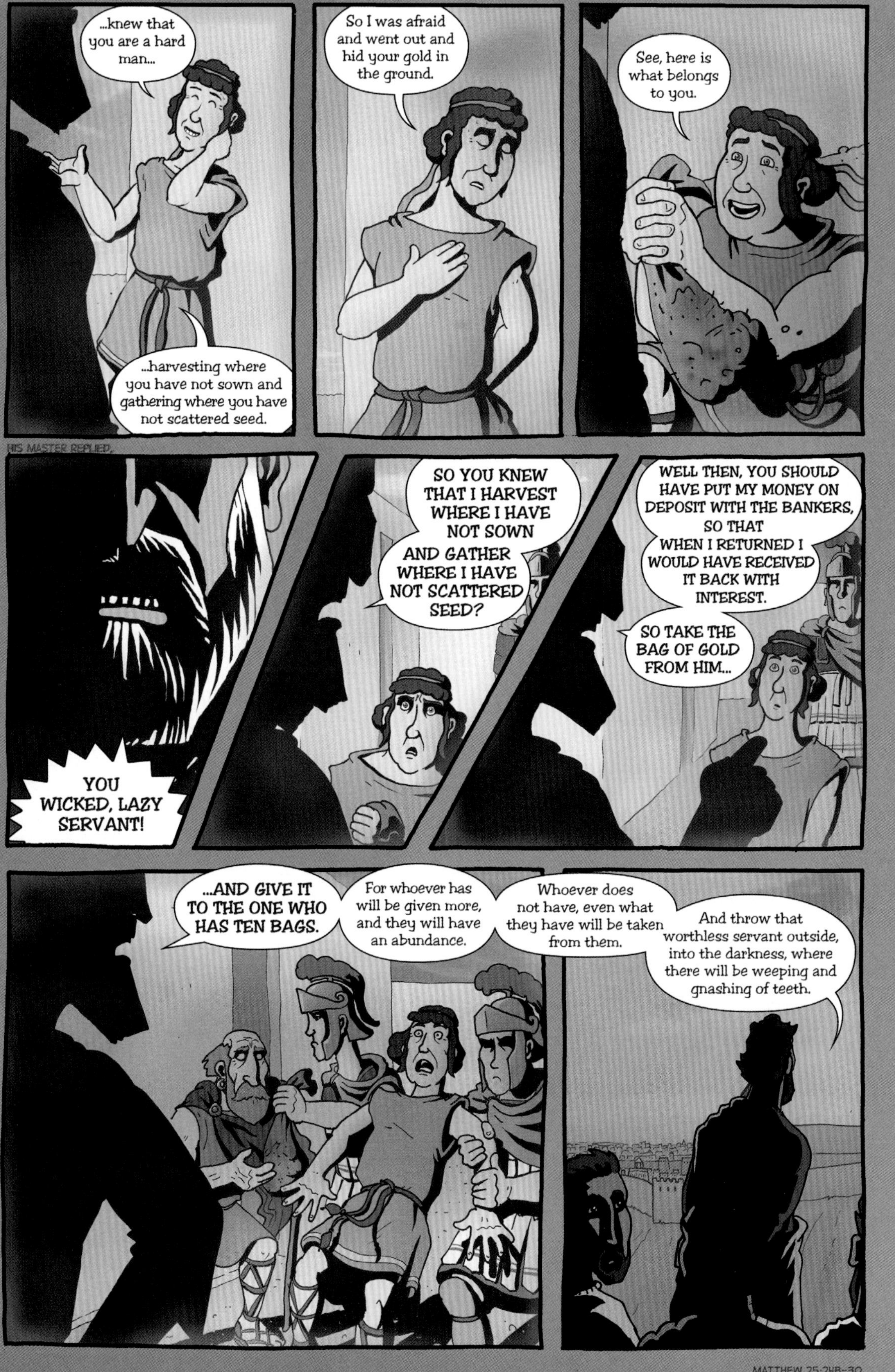
...knew that you are a hard man...
...harvesting where you have not sown and gathering where you have not scattered seed.
So I was afraid and went out and hid your gold in the ground.
See, here is what belongs to you.
HIS MASTER REPLIED,
YOU WICKED, LAZY SERVANT!
SO YOU KNEW THAT I HARVEST WHERE I HAVE NOT SOWN
AND GATHER WHERE I HAVE NOT SCATTERED SEED?
WELL THEN, YOU SHOULD HAVE PUT MY MONEY ON DEPOSIT WITH THE BANKERS, SO THAT WHEN I RETURNED I WOULD HAVE RECEIVED IT BACK WITH INTEREST.
SO TAKE THE BAG OF GOLD FROM HIM...
...AND GIVE IT TO THE ONE WHO HAS TEN BAGS.
For whoever has will be given more, and they will have an abundance.
Whoever does not have, even what they have will be taken from them.
And throw that worthless servant outside, into the darkness, where there will be weeping and gnashing of teeth.

MATTHEW 25:24B-30

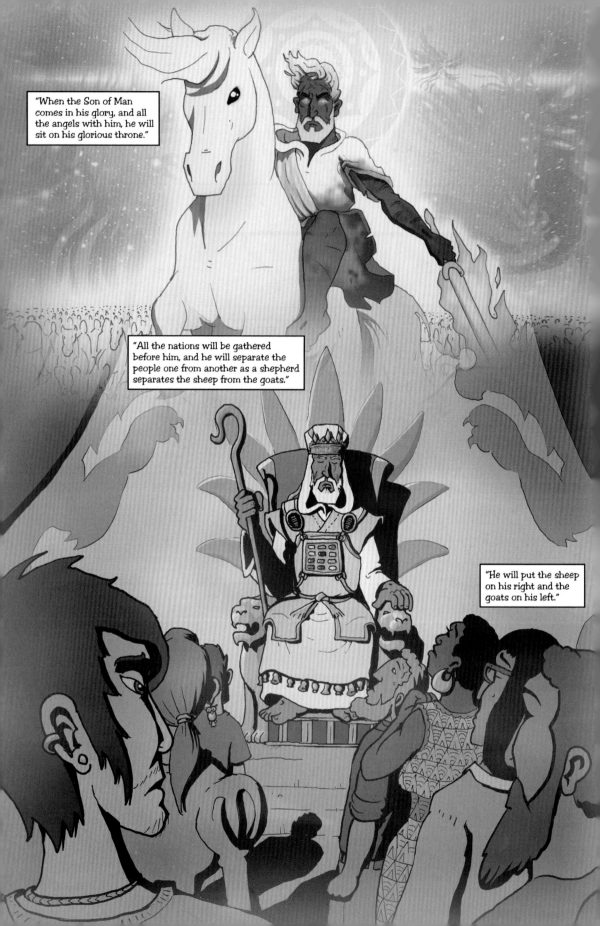

"When the Son of Man comes in his glory, and all the angels with him, he will sit on his glorious throne."

"All the nations will be gathered before him, and he will separate the people one from another as a shepherd separates the sheep from the goats."

"He will put the sheep on his right and the goats on his left."

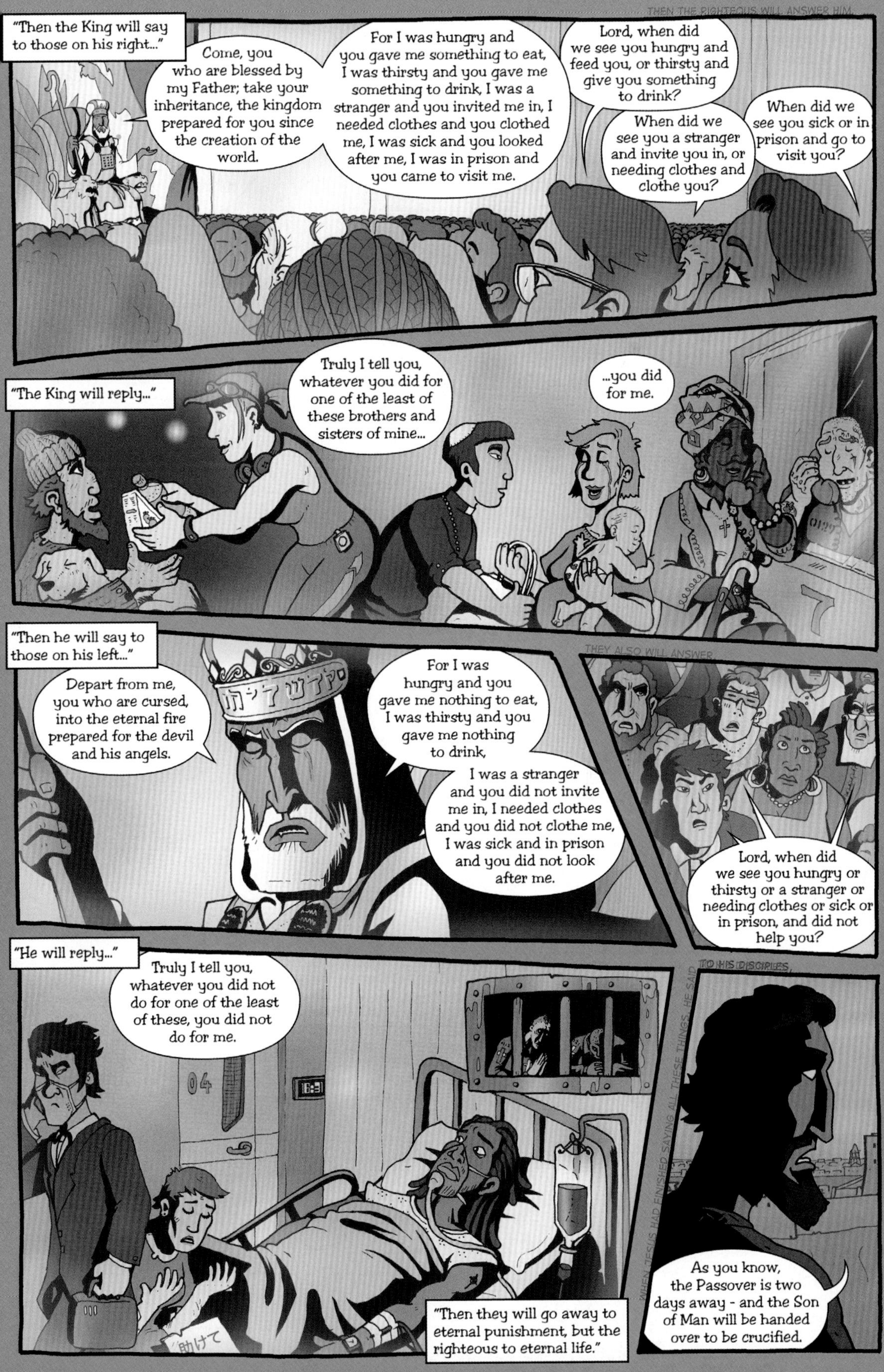
"Then the King will say to those on his right..."
Come, you who are blessed by my Father; take your inheritance, the kingdom prepared for you since the creation of the world.
For I was hungry and you gave me something to eat, I was thirsty and you gave me something to drink, I was a stranger and you invited me in, I needed clothes and you clothed me, I was sick and you looked after me, I was in prison and you came to visit me.
THEN THE RIGHTEOUS WILL ANSWER HIM,
Lord, when did we see you hungry and feed you, or thirsty and give you something to drink?
When did we see you a stranger and invite you in, or needing clothes and clothe you?
When did we see you sick or in prison and go to visit you?
"The King will reply..."
Truly I tell you, whatever you did for one of the least of these brothers and sisters of mine...
...you did for me.
"Then he will say to those on his left..."
Depart from me, you who are cursed, into the eternal fire prepared for the devil and his angels.
For I was hungry and you gave me nothing to eat, I was thirsty and you gave me nothing to drink,
I was a stranger and you did not invite me in, I needed clothes and you did not clothe me, I was sick and in prison and you did not look after me.
THEY ALSO WILL ANSWER,
Lord, when did we see you hungry or thirsty or a stranger or needing clothes or sick or in prison, and did not help you?
"He will reply..."
Truly I tell you, whatever you did not do for one of the least of these, you did not do for me.
"Then they will go away to eternal punishment, but the righteous to eternal life."
WHEN JESUS HAD FINISHED SAYING ALL THESE THINGS, HE SAID TO HIS DISCIPLES,
As you know, the Passover is two days away - and the Son of Man will be handed over to be crucified.

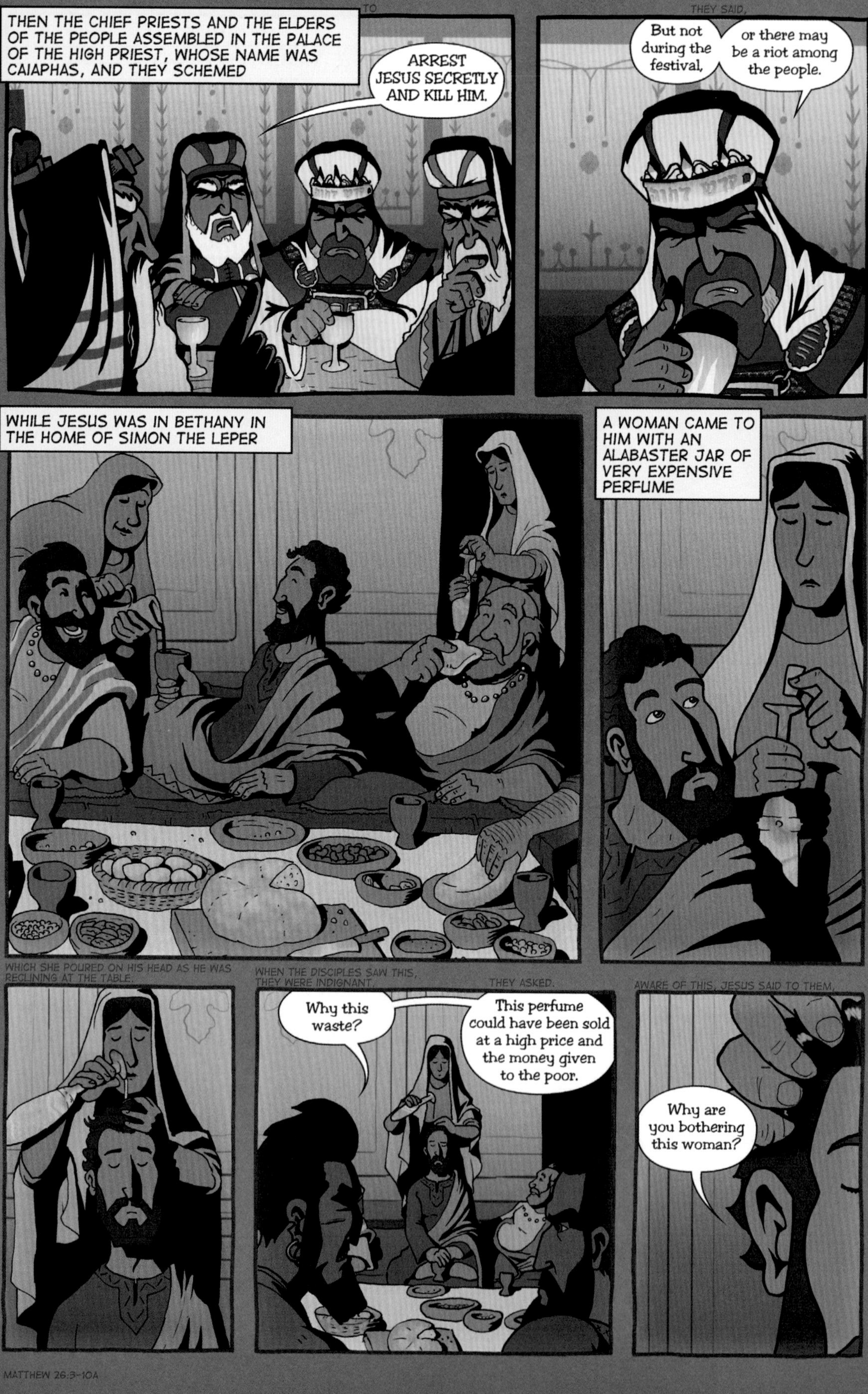

THEN THE CHIEF PRIESTS AND THE ELDERS OF THE PEOPLE ASSEMBLED IN THE PALACE OF THE HIGH PRIEST, WHOSE NAME WAS CAIAPHAS, AND THEY SCHEMED
TO
ARREST JESUS SECRETLY AND KILL HIM.
THEY SAID,
But not during the festival,
or there may be a riot among the people.
WHILE JESUS WAS IN BETHANY IN THE HOME OF SIMON THE LEPER
A WOMAN CAME TO HIM WITH AN ALABASTER JAR OF VERY EXPENSIVE PERFUME
WHICH SHE POURED ON HIS HEAD AS HE WAS RECLINING AT THE TABLE.
WHEN THE DISCIPLES SAW THIS, THEY WERE INDIGNANT.
THEY ASKED.
Why this waste?
This perfume could have been sold at a high price and the money given to the poor.
AWARE OF THIS, JESUS SAID TO THEM,
Why are you bothering this woman?

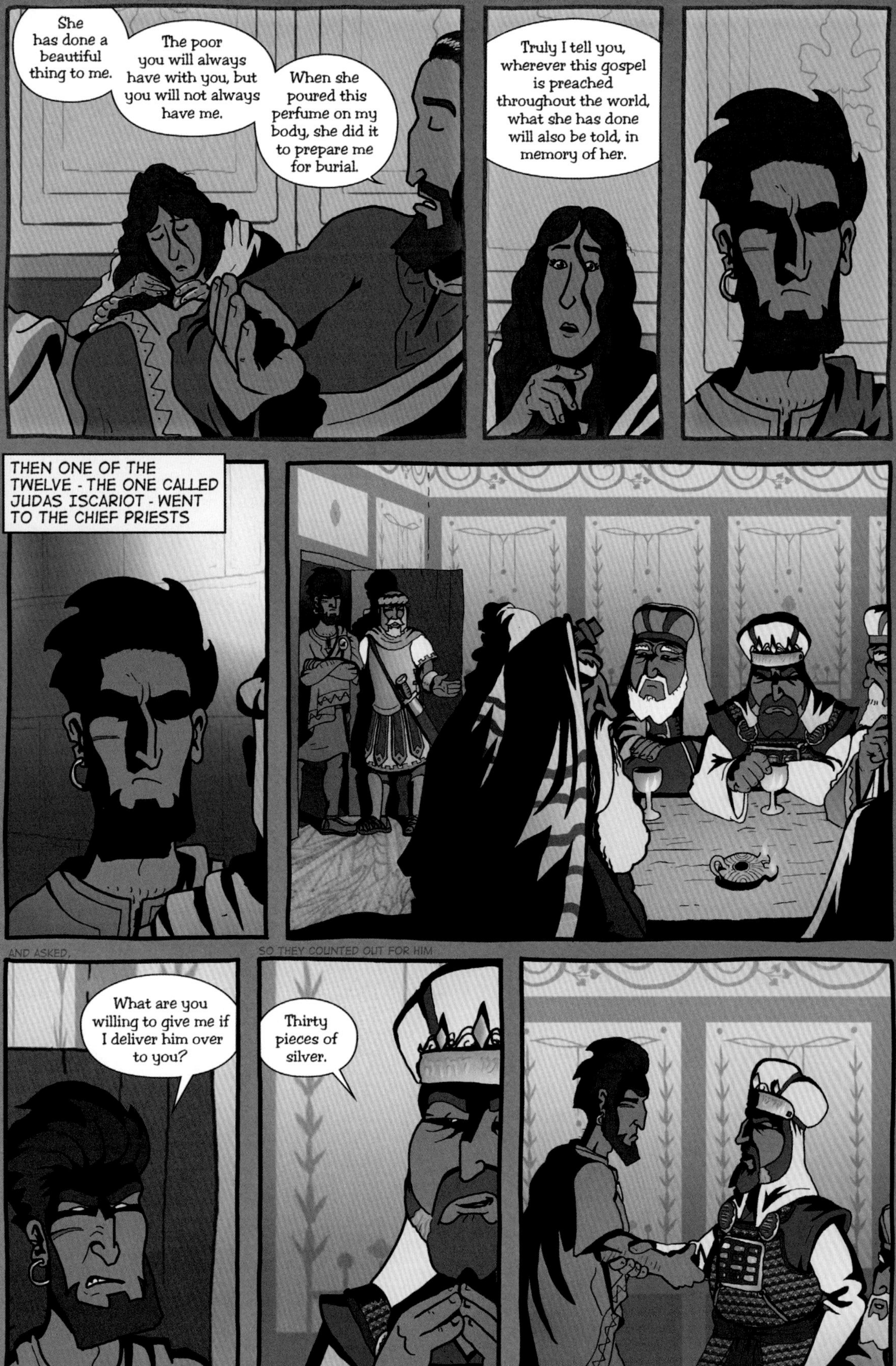

She has done a beautiful thing to me.
The poor you will always have with you, but you will not always have me.
When she poured this perfume on my body, she did it to prepare me for burial.
Truly I tell you, wherever this gospel is preached throughout the world, what she has done will also be told, in memory of her.
THEN ONE OF THE TWELVE - THE ONE CALLED JUDAS ISCARIOT - WENT TO THE CHIEF PRIESTS
AND ASKED,
What are you willing to give me if I deliver him over to you?
SO THEY COUNTED OUT FOR HIM
Thirty pieces of silver.

THE DISCIPLES CAME TO JESUS AND ASKED

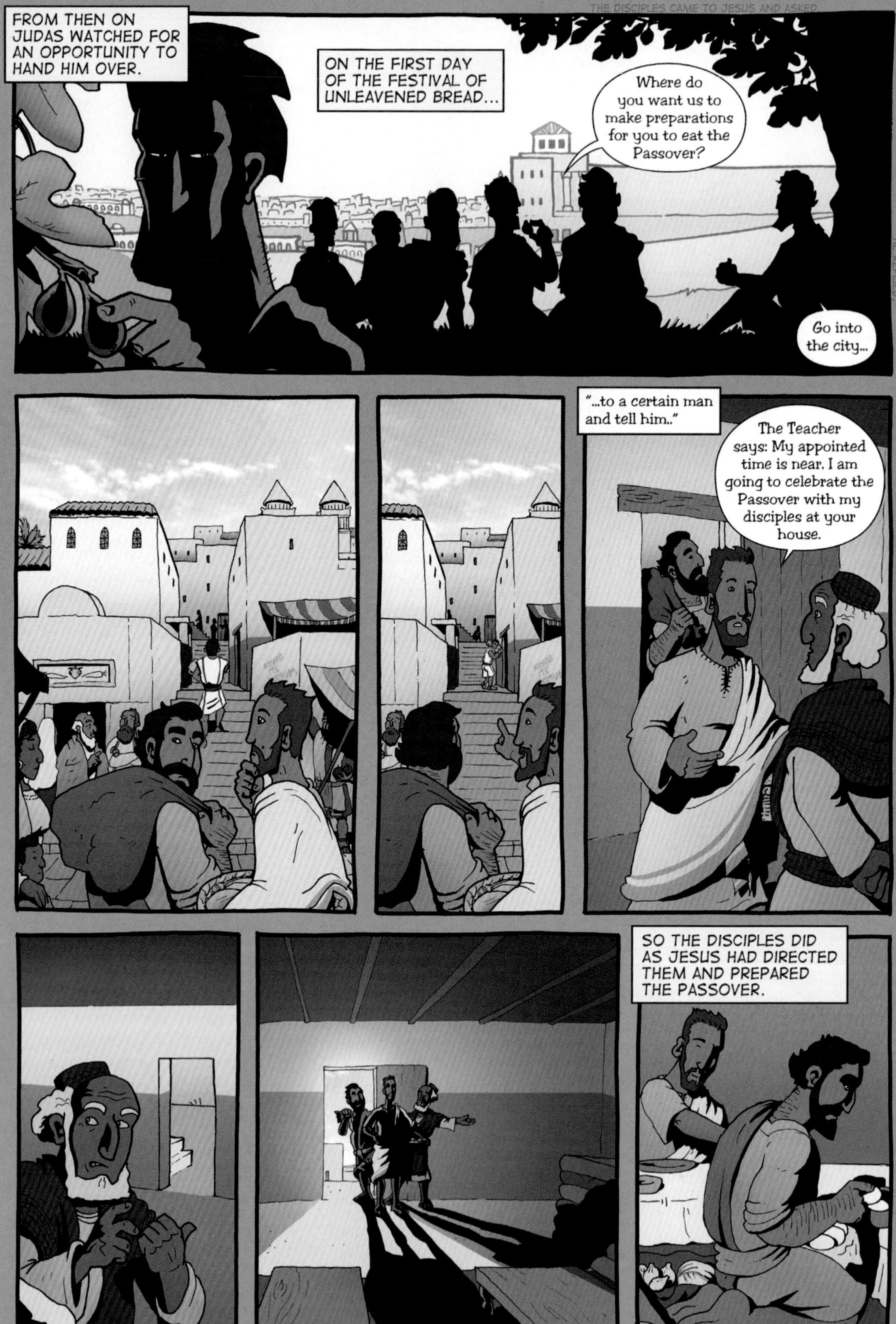
FROM THEN ON JUDAS WATCHED FOR AN OPPORTUNITY TO HAND HIM OVER.
ON THE FIRST DAY OF THE FESTIVAL OF UNLEAVENED BREAD...
Where do you want us to make preparations for you to eat the Passover?
Go into the city...
"...to a certain man and tell him.."
The Teacher says: My appointed time is near. I am going to celebrate the Passover with my disciples at your house.
SO THE DISCIPLES DID AS JESUS HAD DIRECTED THEM AND PREPARED THE PASSOVER.

HE REPLIED

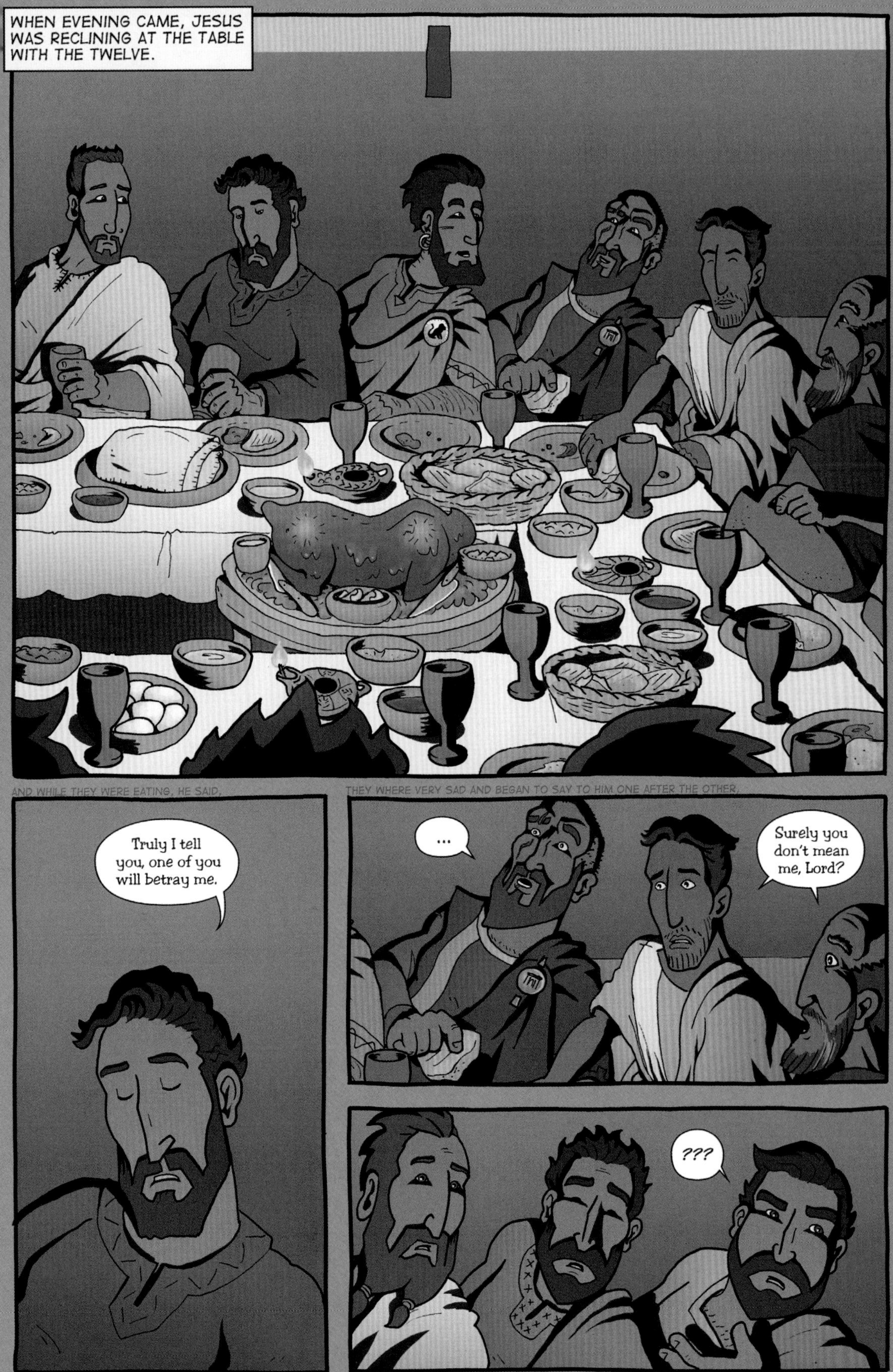
WHEN EVENING CAME, JESUS WAS RECLINING AT THE TABLE WITH THE TWELVE.
AND WHILE THEY WERE EATING, HE SAID,
Truly I tell you, one of you will betray me.
THEY WHERE VERY SAD AND BEGAN TO SAY TO HIM ONE AFTER THE OTHER,
...
Surely you don't mean me, Lord?
???

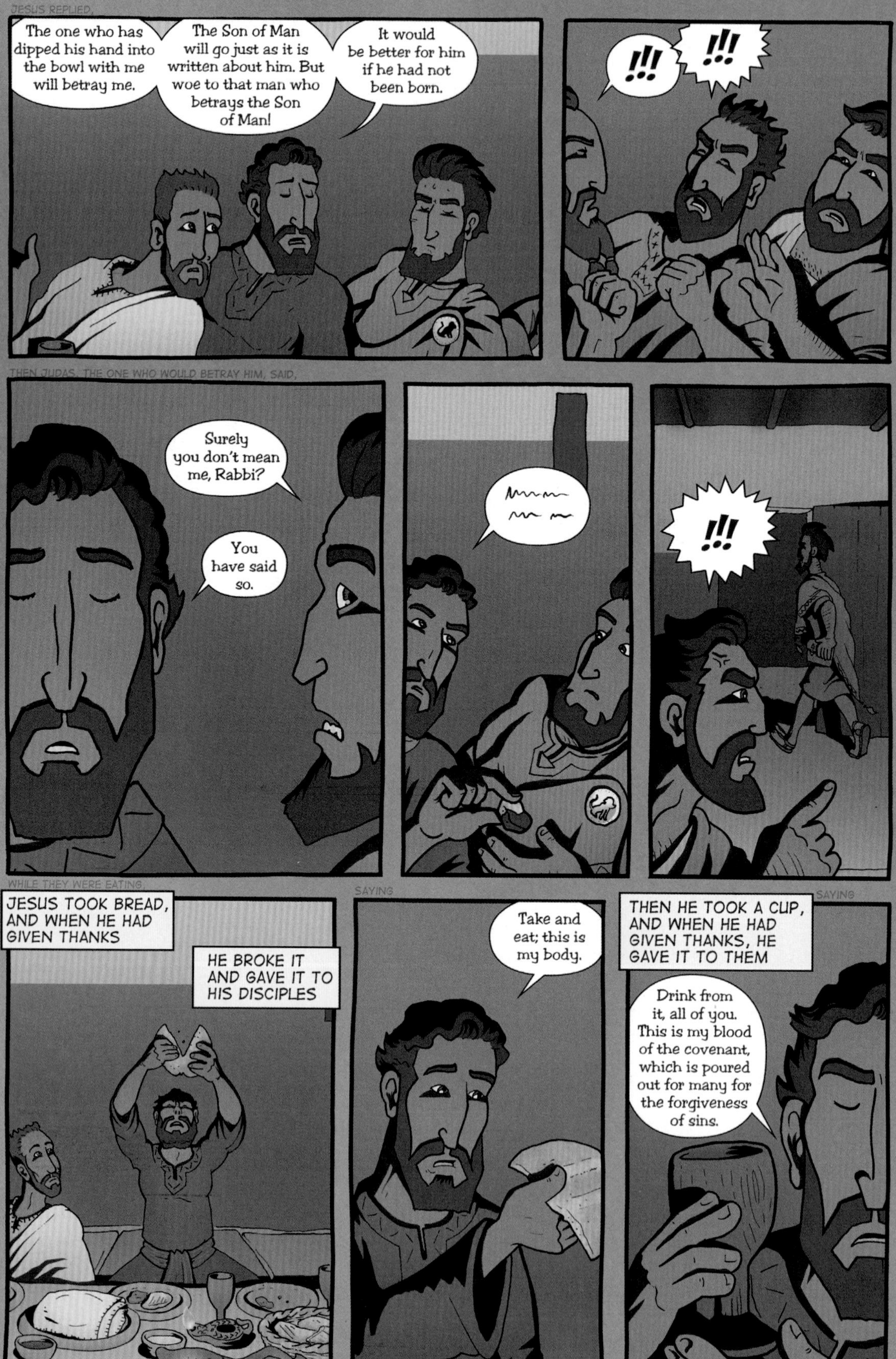
JESUS REPLIED,
The one who has dipped his hand into the bowl with me will betray me.
The Son of Man will go just as it is written about him. But woe to that man who betrays the Son of Man!
It would be better for him if he had not been born.
!!!
!!!
THEN JUDAS, THE ONE WHO WOULD BETRAY HIM, SAID,
Surely you don't mean me, Rabbi?
You have said so.
!!!
WHILE THEY WERE EATING,
JESUS TOOK BREAD, AND WHEN HE HAD GIVEN THANKS
HE BROKE IT AND GAVE IT TO HIS DISCIPLES
SAYING
Take and eat; this is my body.
THEN HE TOOK A CUP, AND WHEN HE HAD GIVEN THANKS, HE GAVE IT TO THEM
SAYING
Drink from it, all of you. This is my blood of the covenant, which is poured out for many for the forgiveness of sins.

MATTHEW 26:23–28

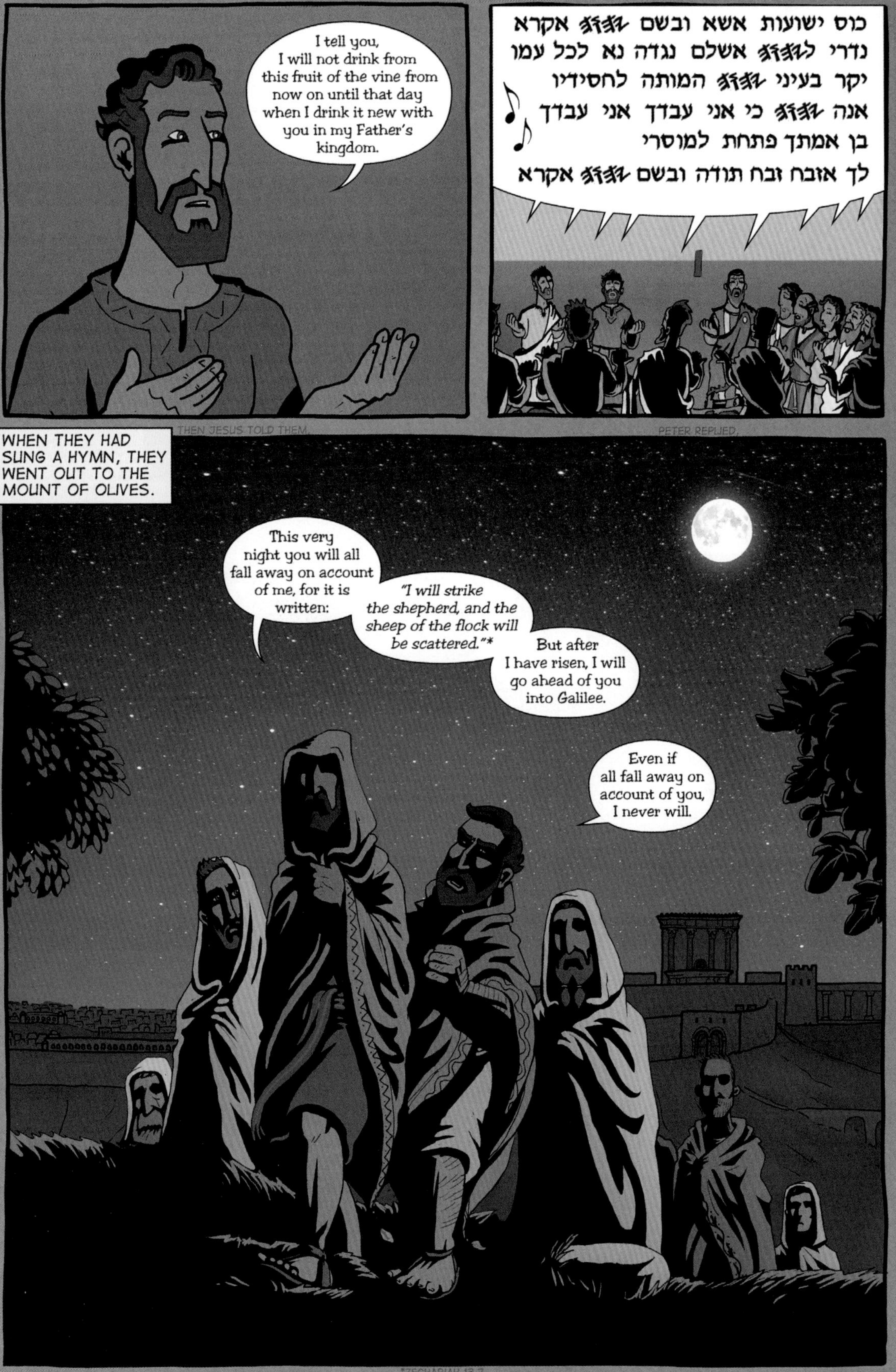
I tell you, I will not drink from this fruit of the vine from now on until that day when I drink it new with you in my Father's kingdom.
כוס ישועות אשא ובשם 𐤉𐤄𐤅𐤄 אקרא
נדרי ל𐤉𐤄𐤅𐤄 אשלם נגדה נא לכל עמו
יקר בעיני 𐤉𐤄𐤅𐤄 המותה לחסידיו
אנה 𐤉𐤄𐤅𐤄 כי אני עבדך אני עבדך
בן אמתך פתחת למוסרי
לך אזבח זבח תודה ובשם 𐤉𐤄𐤅𐤄 אקרא
THEN JESUS TOLD THEM,
PETER REPLIED,
WHEN THEY HAD SUNG A HYMN, THEY WENT OUT TO THE MOUNT OF OLIVES.
This very night you will all fall away on account of me, for it is written:
"I will strike the shepherd, and the sheep of the flock will be scattered."*
But after I have risen, I will go ahead of you into Galilee.
Even if all fall away on account of you, I never will.

*ZECHARIAH 13:7

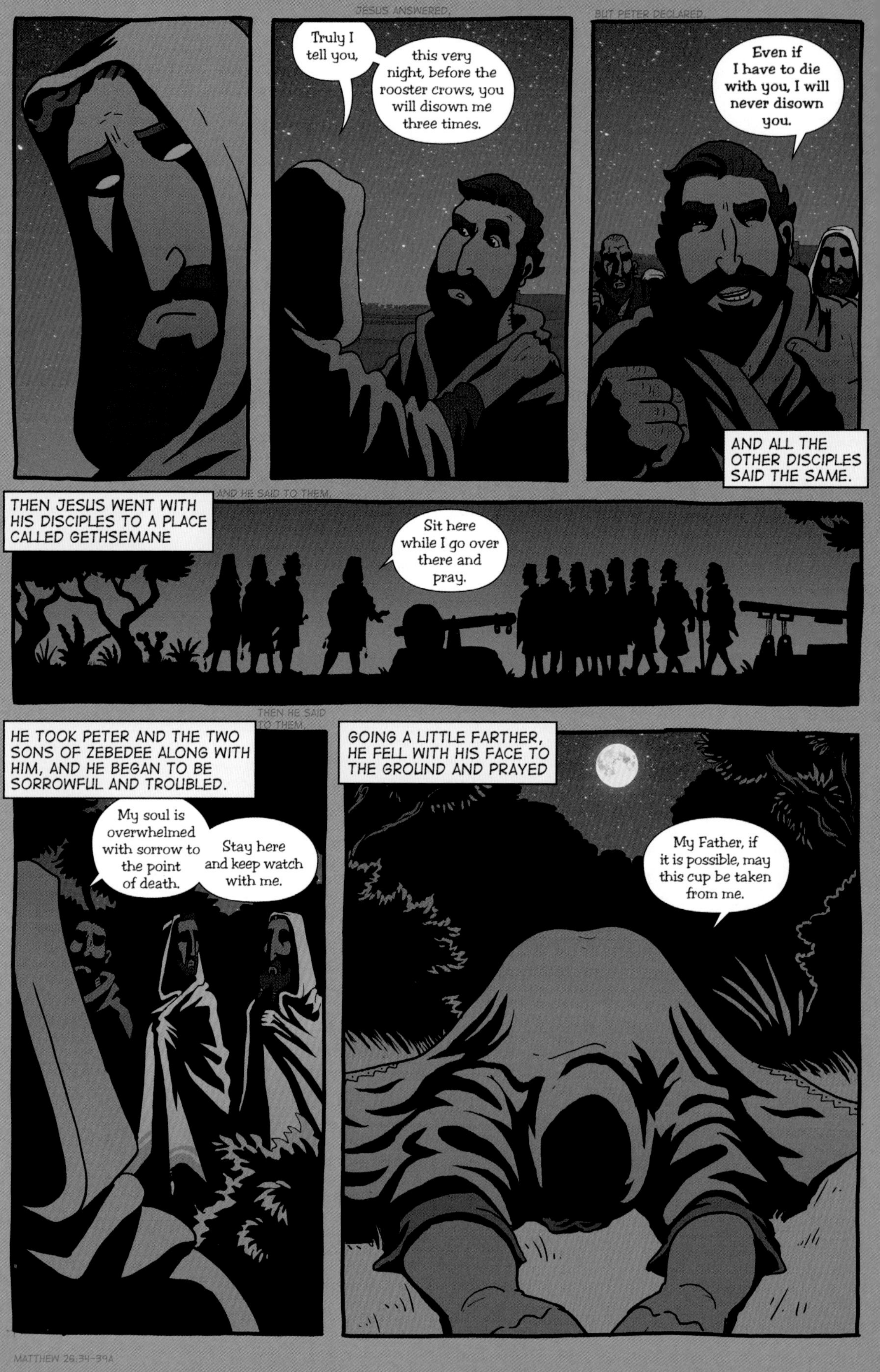
JESUS ANSWERED,
Truly I tell you,
this very night, before the rooster crows, you will disown me three times.
BUT PETER DECLARED,
Even if I have to die with you, I will never disown you.
AND ALL THE OTHER DISCIPLES SAID THE SAME.
THEN JESUS WENT WITH HIS DISCIPLES TO A PLACE CALLED GETHSEMANE
AND HE SAID TO THEM,
Sit here while I go over there and pray.
HE TOOK PETER AND THE TWO SONS OF ZEBEDEE ALONG WITH HIM, AND HE BEGAN TO BE SORROWFUL AND TROUBLED.
THEN HE SAID TO THEM,
My soul is overwhelmed with sorrow to the point of death.
Stay here and keep watch with me.
GOING A LITTLE FARTHER, HE FELL WITH HIS FACE TO THE GROUND AND PRAYED
My Father, if it is possible, may this cup be taken from me.

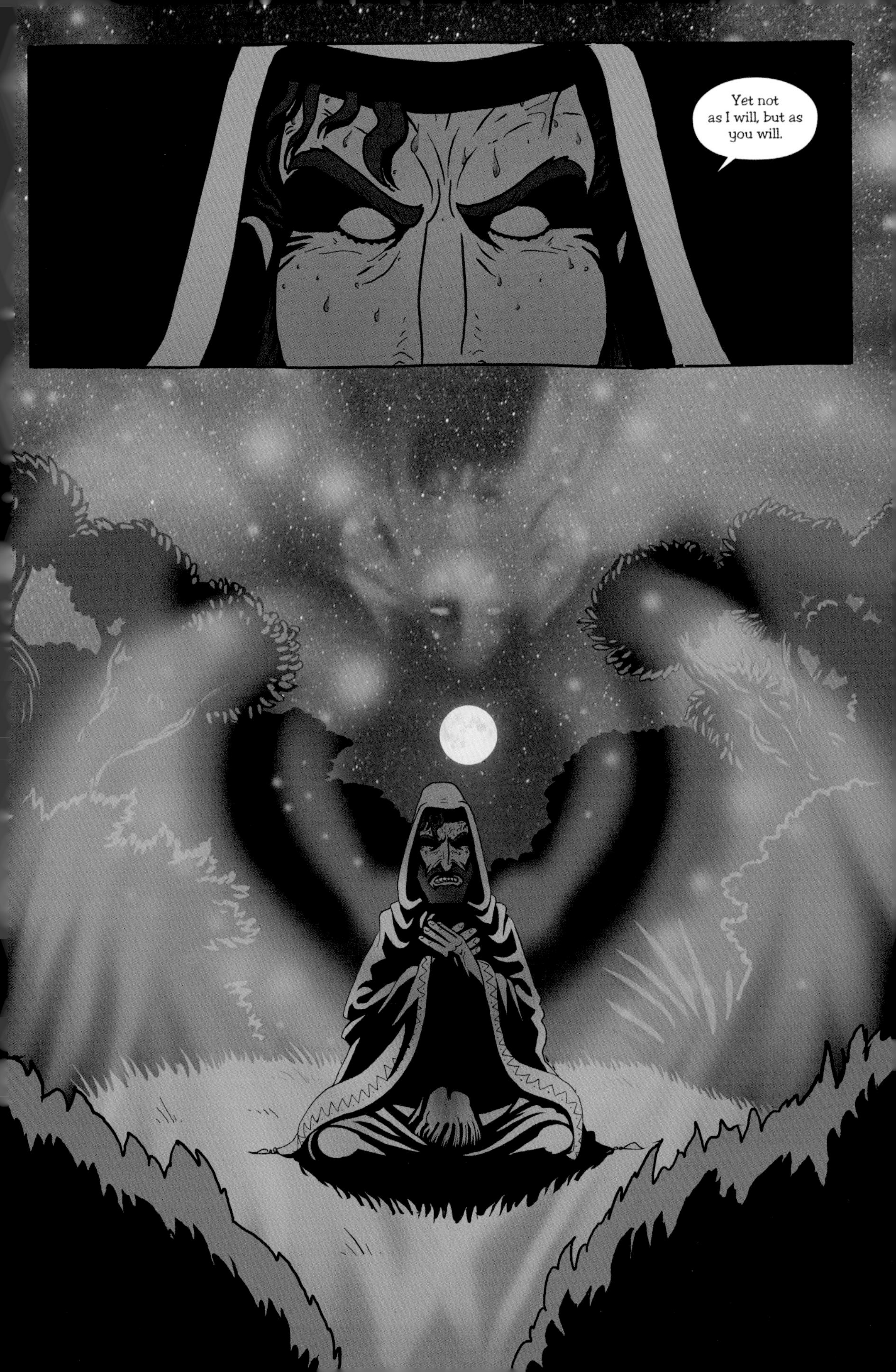
Yet not as I will, but as you will.

THEN HE RETURNED TO
HIS DISCIPLES AND
FOUND THEM SLEEPING.

Couldn't you men keep watch with me for one hour?

Watch and pray so that you will not fall into temptation.

HE ASKED PETER.

The spirit is willing, but the flesh is weak.

HE WENT AWAY A SECOND TIME AND PRAYED

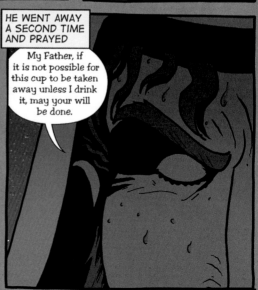

My Father, if it is not possible for this cup to be taken away unless I drink it, may your will be done.

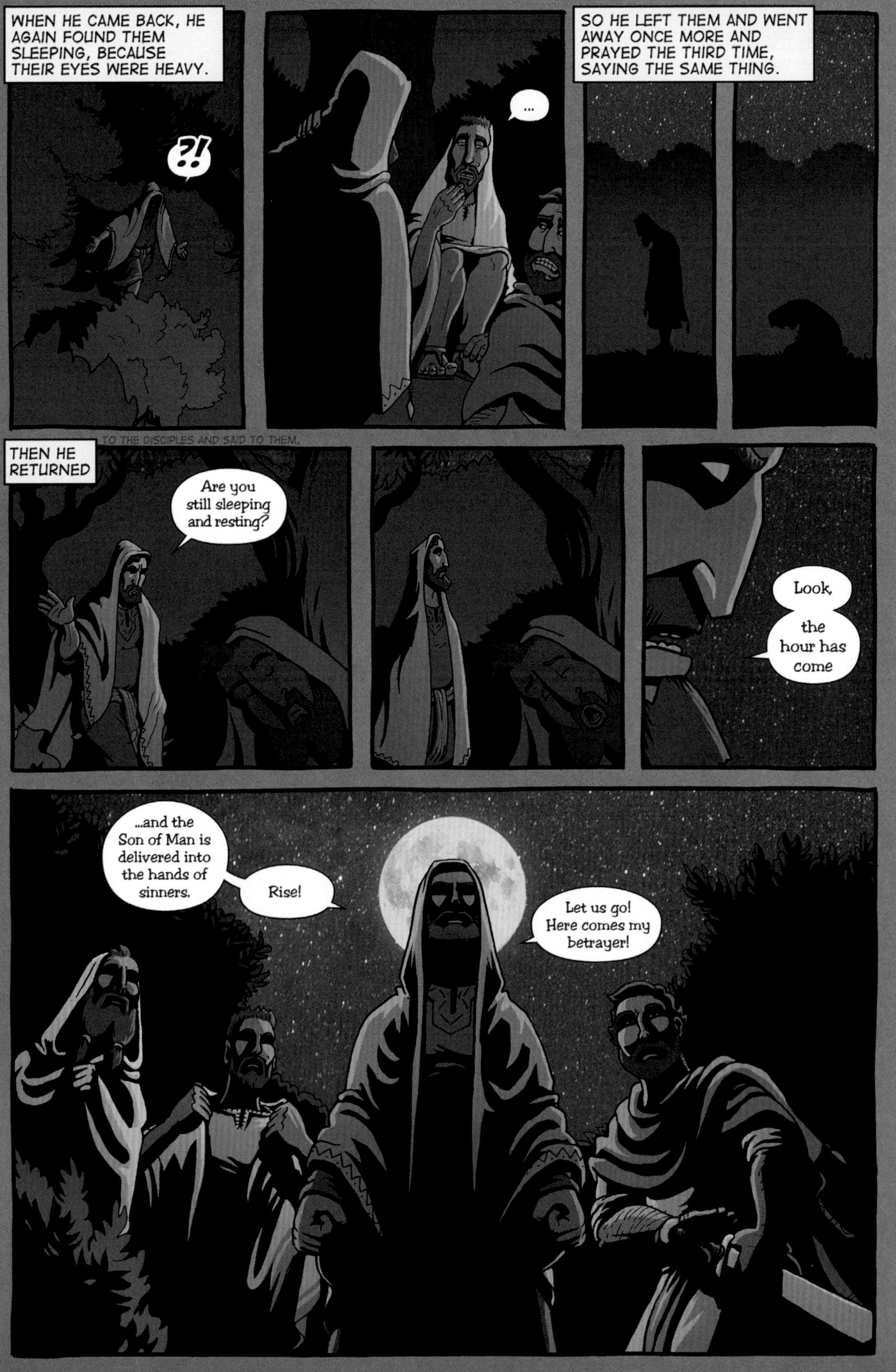
WHEN HE CAME BACK, HE AGAIN FOUND THEM SLEEPING, BECAUSE THEIR EYES WERE HEAVY.
?!
...
SO HE LEFT THEM AND WENT AWAY ONCE MORE AND PRAYED THE THIRD TIME, SAYING THE SAME THING.
THEN HE RETURNED
TO THE DISCIPLES AND SAID TO THEM,
Are you still sleeping and resting?
Look,
the hour has come
...and the Son of Man is delivered into the hands of sinners.
Rise!
Let us go! Here comes my betrayer!

MATTHEW 26:43-46

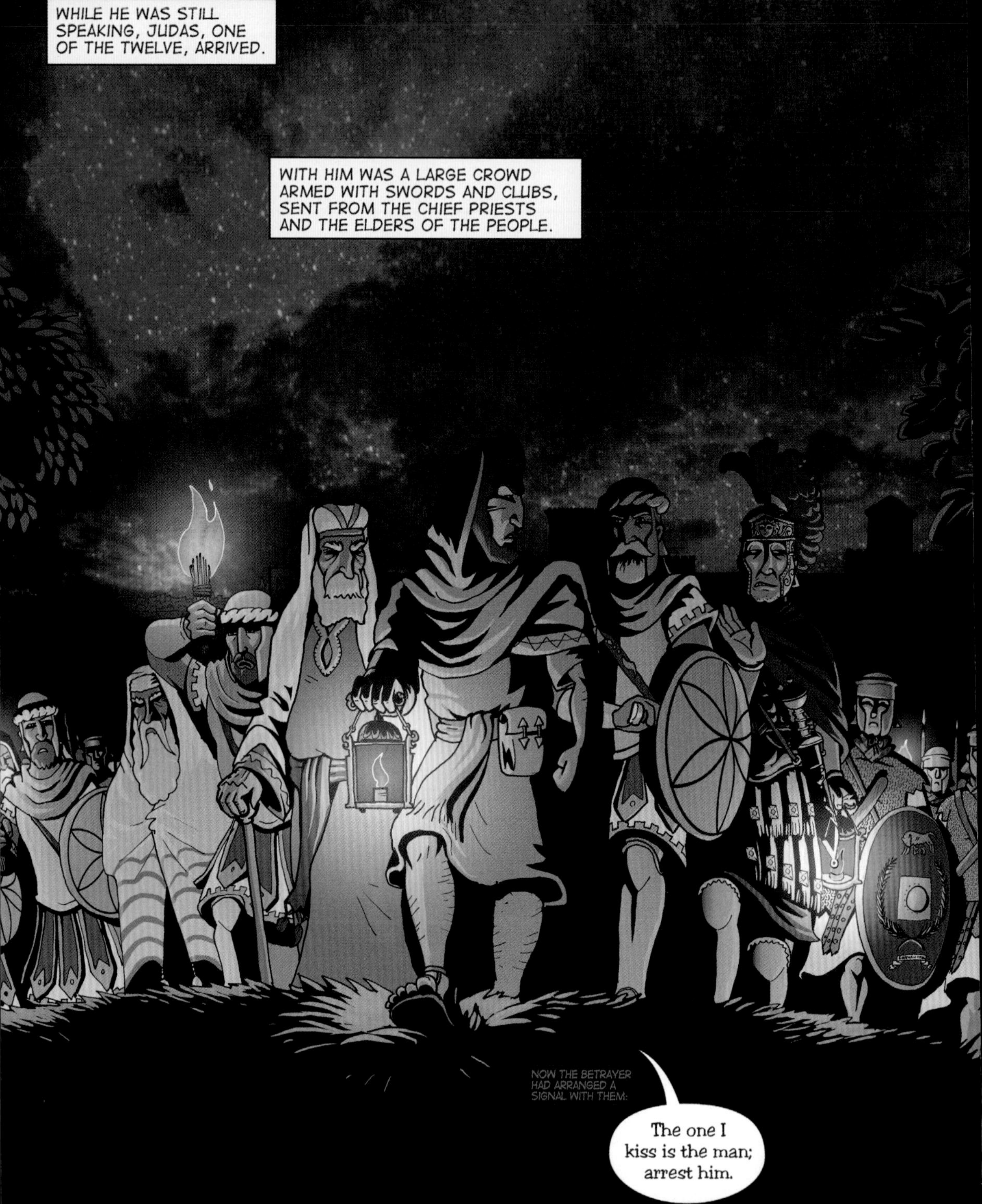
WHILE HE WAS STILL SPEAKING, JUDAS, ONE OF THE TWELVE, ARRIVED.
WITH HIM WAS A LARGE CROWD ARMED WITH SWORDS AND CLUBS, SENT FROM THE CHIEF PRIESTS AND THE ELDERS OF THE PEOPLE.
NOW THE BETRAYER HAD ARRANGED A SIGNAL WITH THEM:
The one I kiss is the man; arrest him.

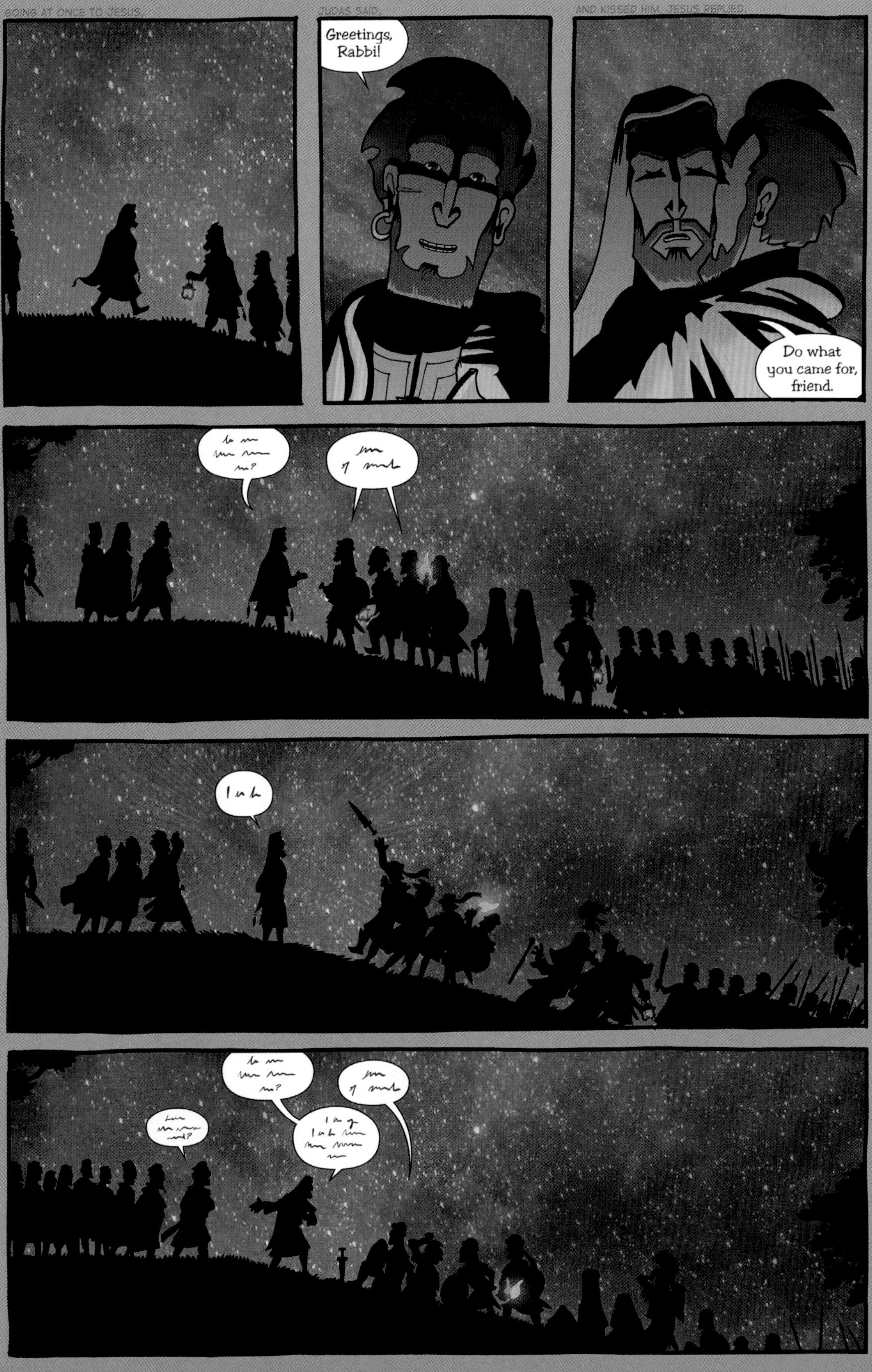
GOING AT ONCE TO JESUS,
JUDAS SAID,
Greetings, Rabbi!
AND KISSED HIM. JESUS REPLIED,
Do what you came for, friend.

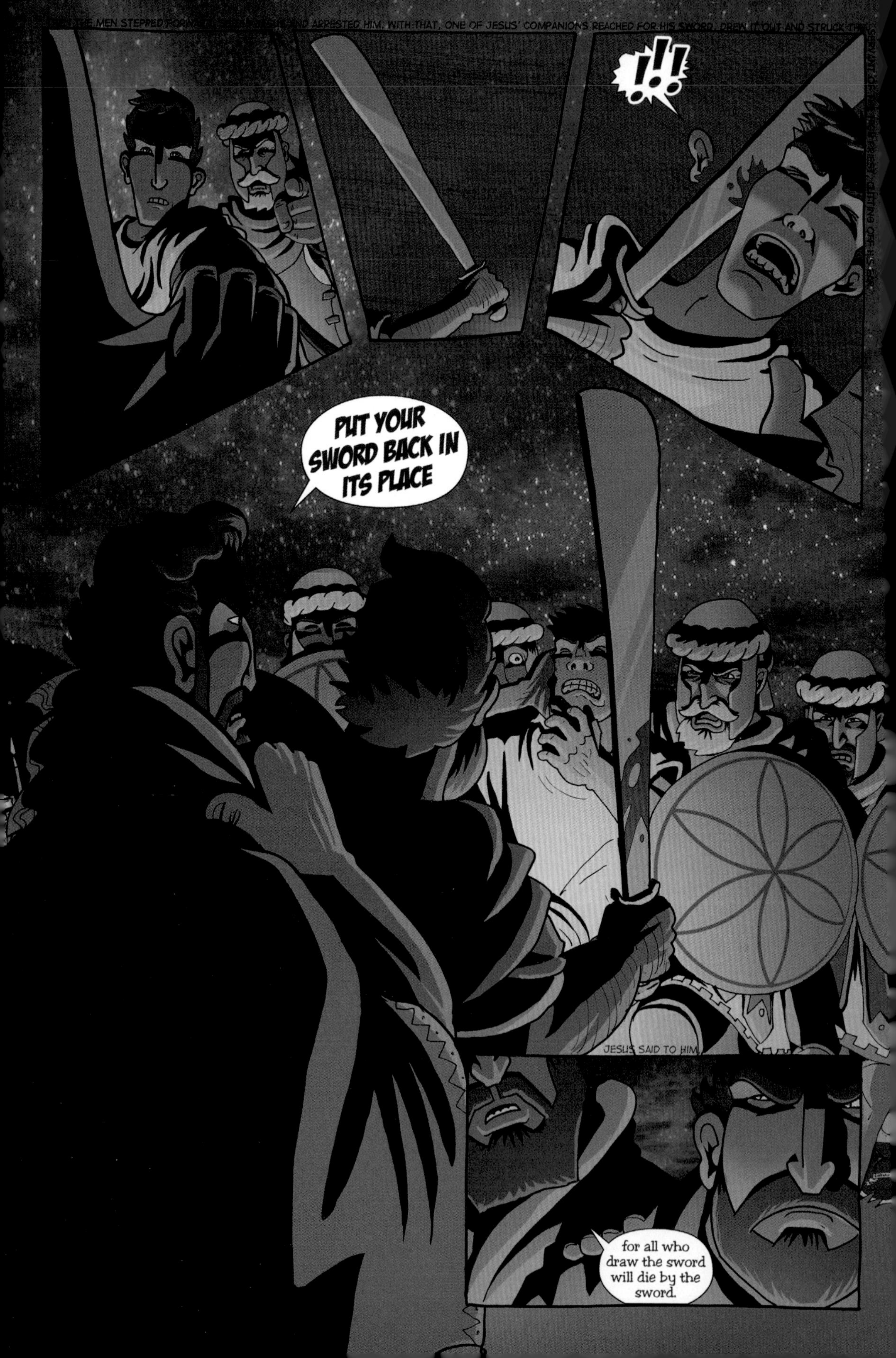
THE MEN STEPPED FORW… AND ARRESTED HIM. WITH THAT, ONE OF JESUS' COMPANIONS REACHED FOR HIS SWORD, DREW IT OUT AND STRUCK THE
SERVANT … PRIEST, CUTTING OFF HIS EAR.
!!!
PUT YOUR SWORD BACK IN ITS PLACE
JESUS SAID TO HIM.
for all who draw the sword will die by the sword.

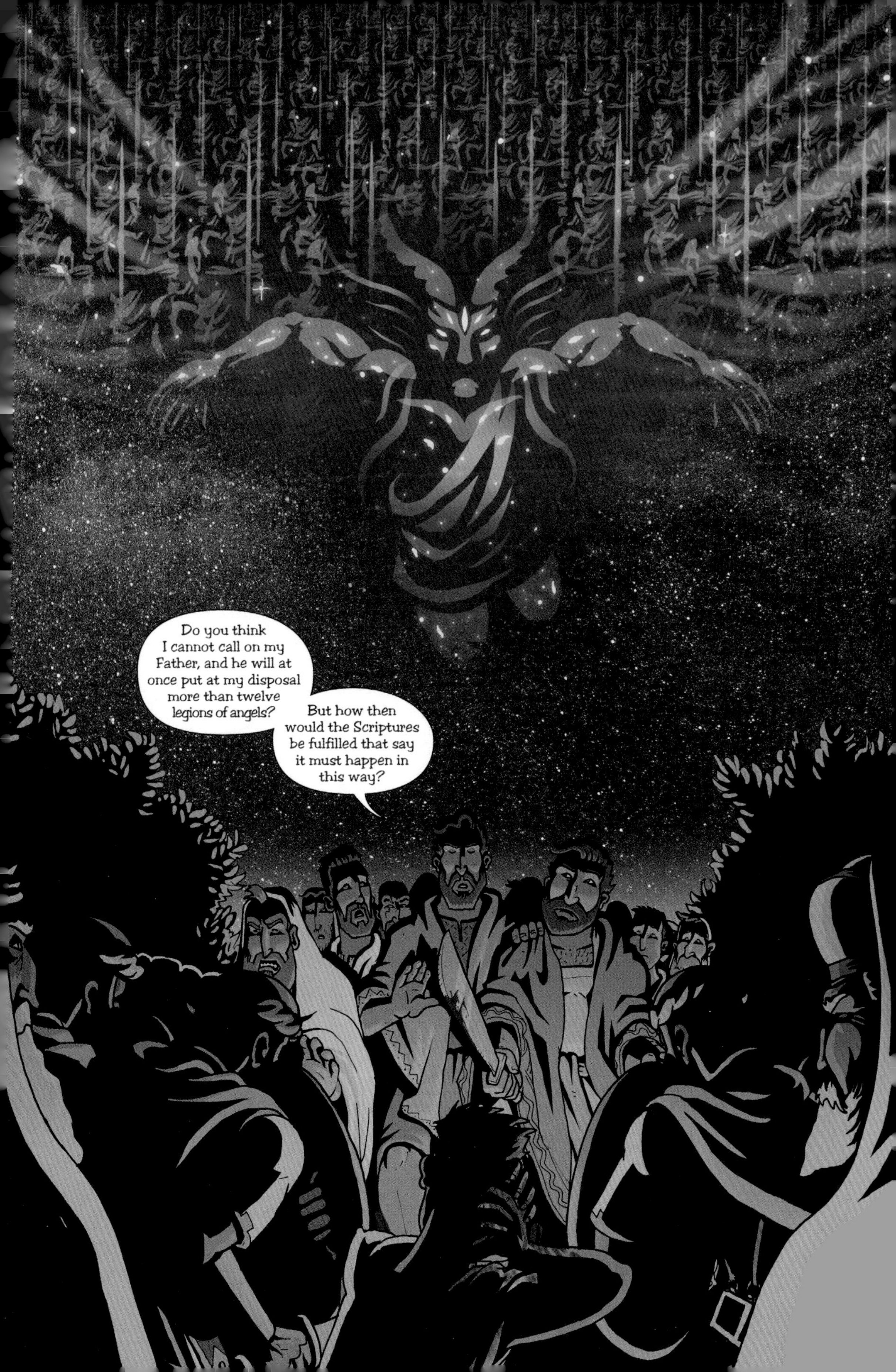

Do you think I cannot call on my Father, and he will at once put at my disposal more than twelve legions of angels?
But how then would the Scriptures be fulfilled that say it must happen in this way?

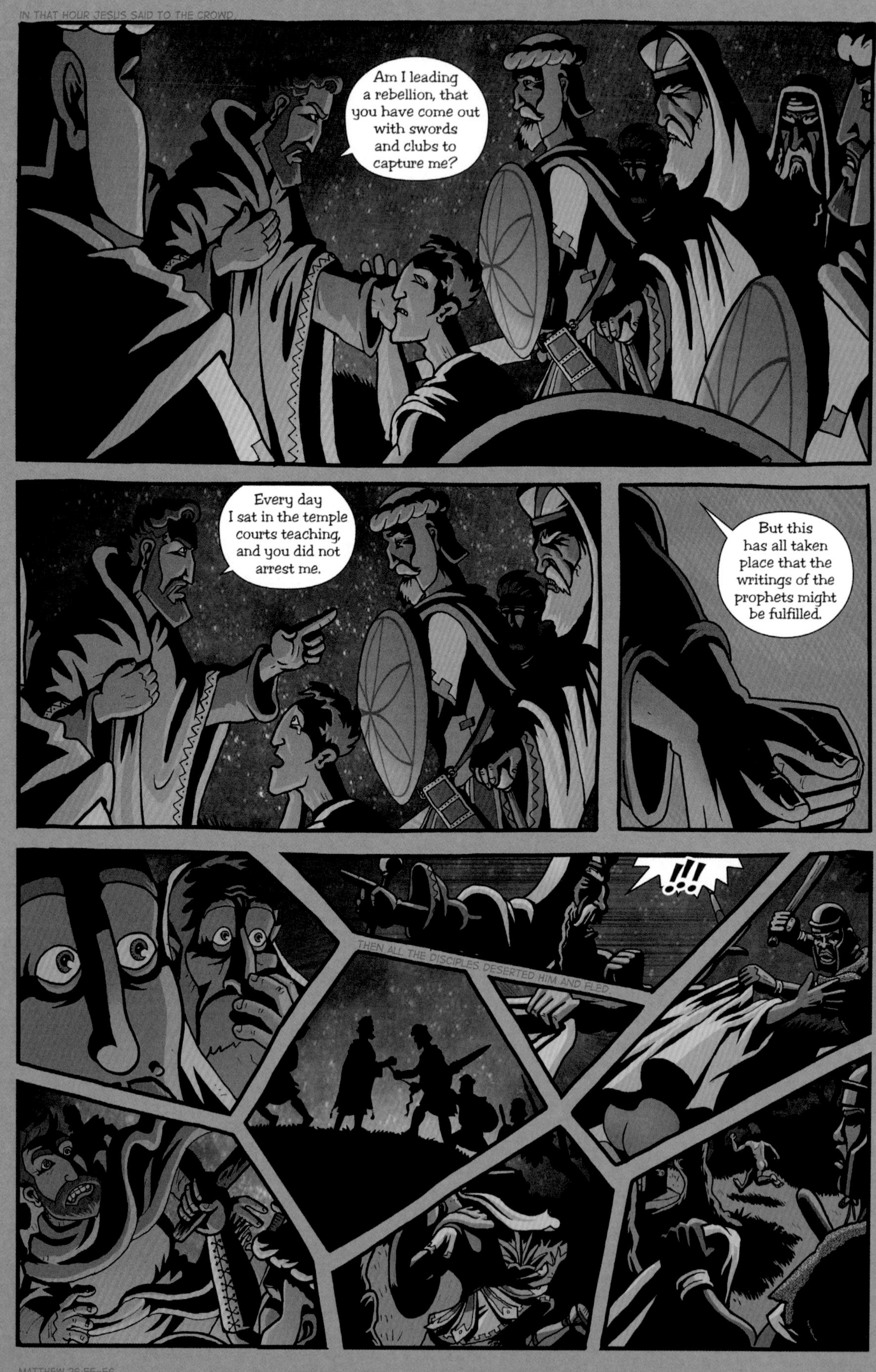
IN THAT HOUR JESUS SAID TO THE CROWD,
Am I leading a rebellion, that you have come out with swords and clubs to capture me?
Every day I sat in the temple courts teaching, and you did not arrest me.
But this has all taken place that the writings of the prophets might be fulfilled.
!!!
THEN ALL THE DISCIPLES DESERTED HIM AND FLED.

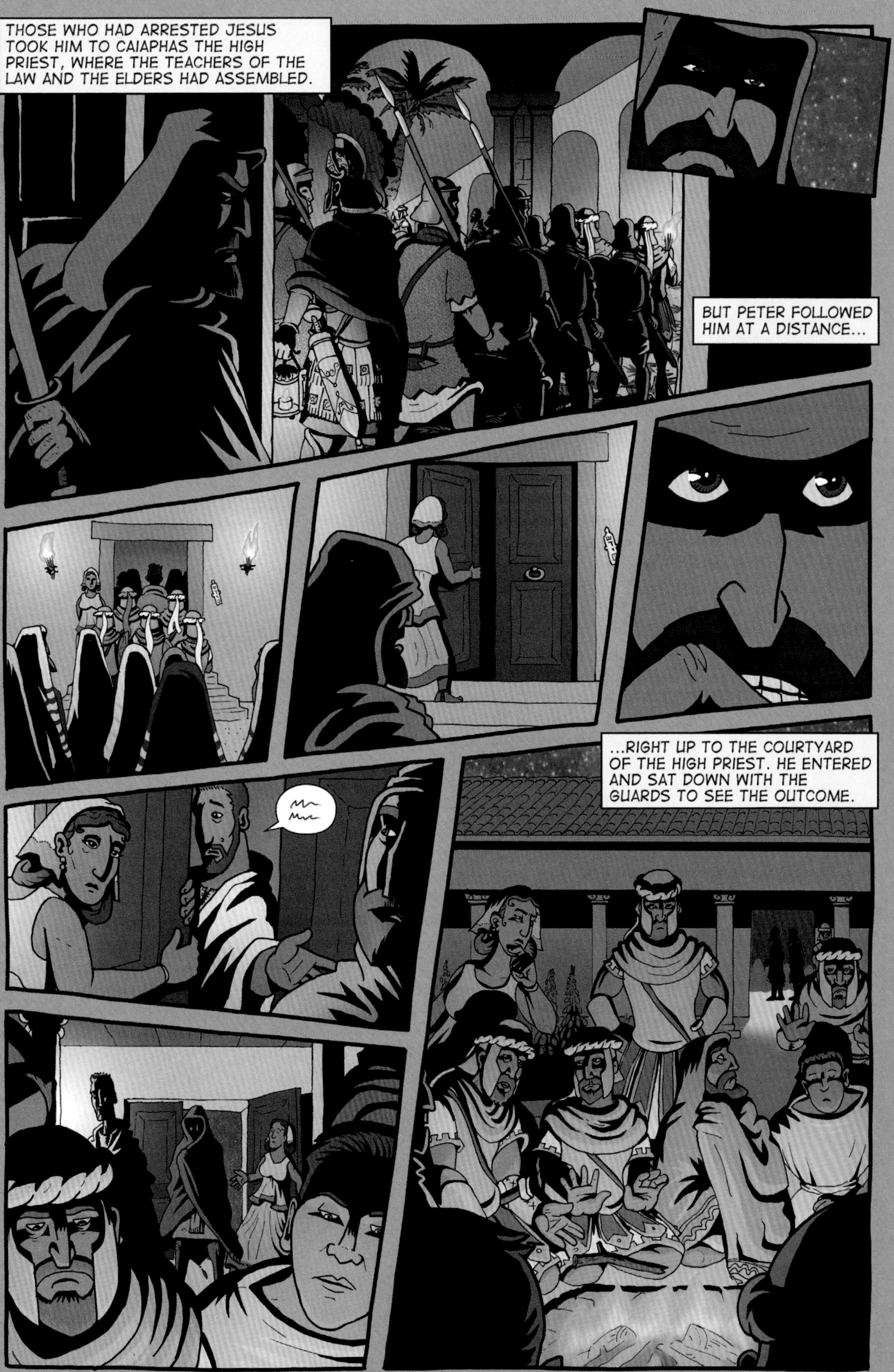
THOSE WHO HAD ARRESTED JESUS TOOK HIM TO CAIAPHAS THE HIGH PRIEST, WHERE THE TEACHERS OF THE LAW AND THE ELDERS HAD ASSEMBLED.
BUT PETER FOLLOWED HIM AT A DISTANCE...
...RIGHT UP TO THE COURTYARD OF THE HIGH PRIEST. HE ENTERED AND SAT DOWN WITH THE GUARDS TO SEE THE OUTCOME.

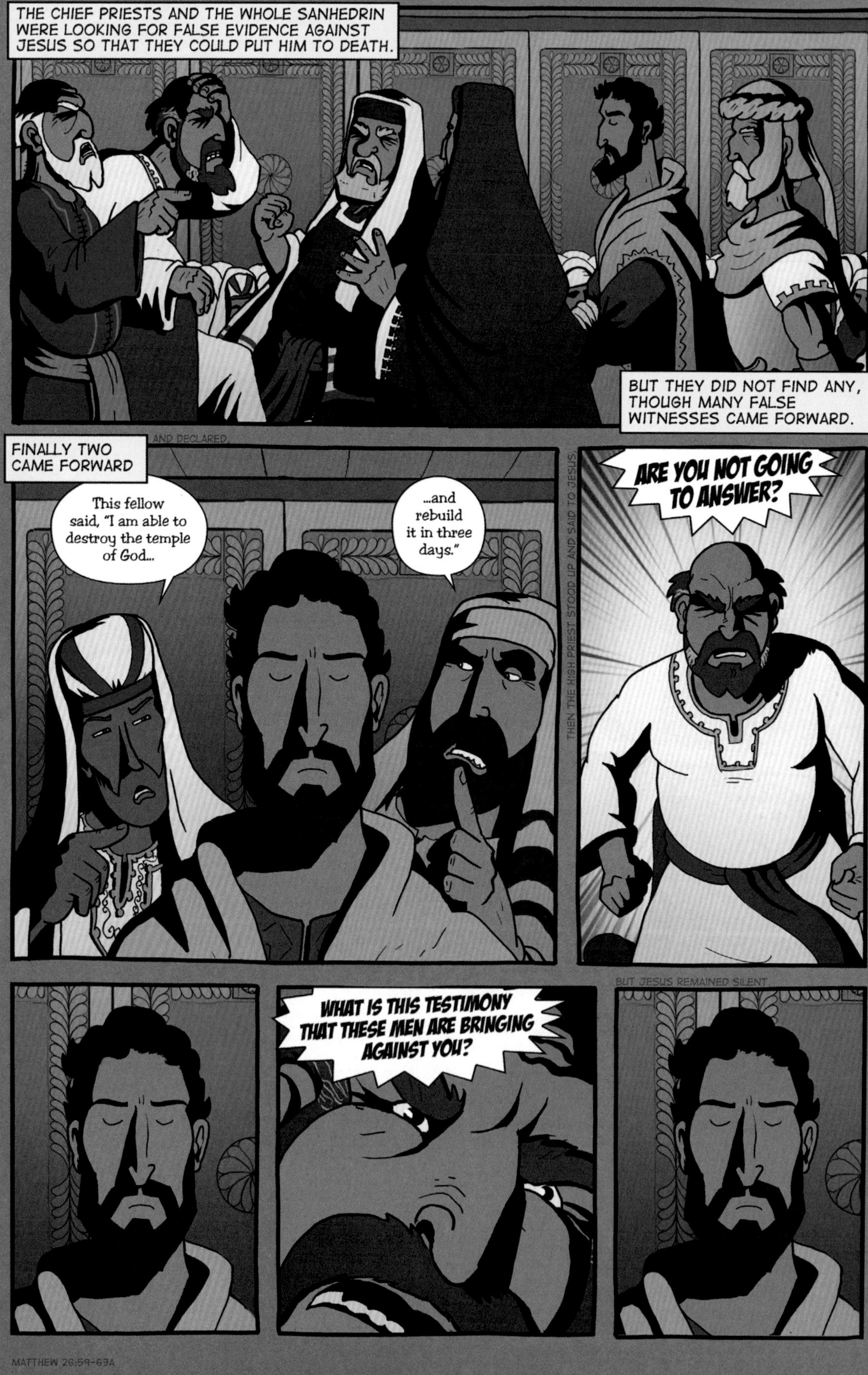
THE CHIEF PRIESTS AND THE WHOLE SANHEDRIN WERE LOOKING FOR FALSE EVIDENCE AGAINST JESUS SO THAT THEY COULD PUT HIM TO DEATH.
BUT THEY DID NOT FIND ANY, THOUGH MANY FALSE WITNESSES CAME FORWARD.
FINALLY TWO CAME FORWARD
AND DECLARED,
This fellow said, "I am able to destroy the temple of God...
...and rebuild it in three days."
THEN THE HIGH PRIEST STOOD UP AND SAID TO JESUS,
ARE YOU NOT GOING TO ANSWER?
WHAT IS THIS TESTIMONY THAT THESE MEN ARE BRINGING AGAINST YOU?
BUT JESUS REMAINED SILENT.

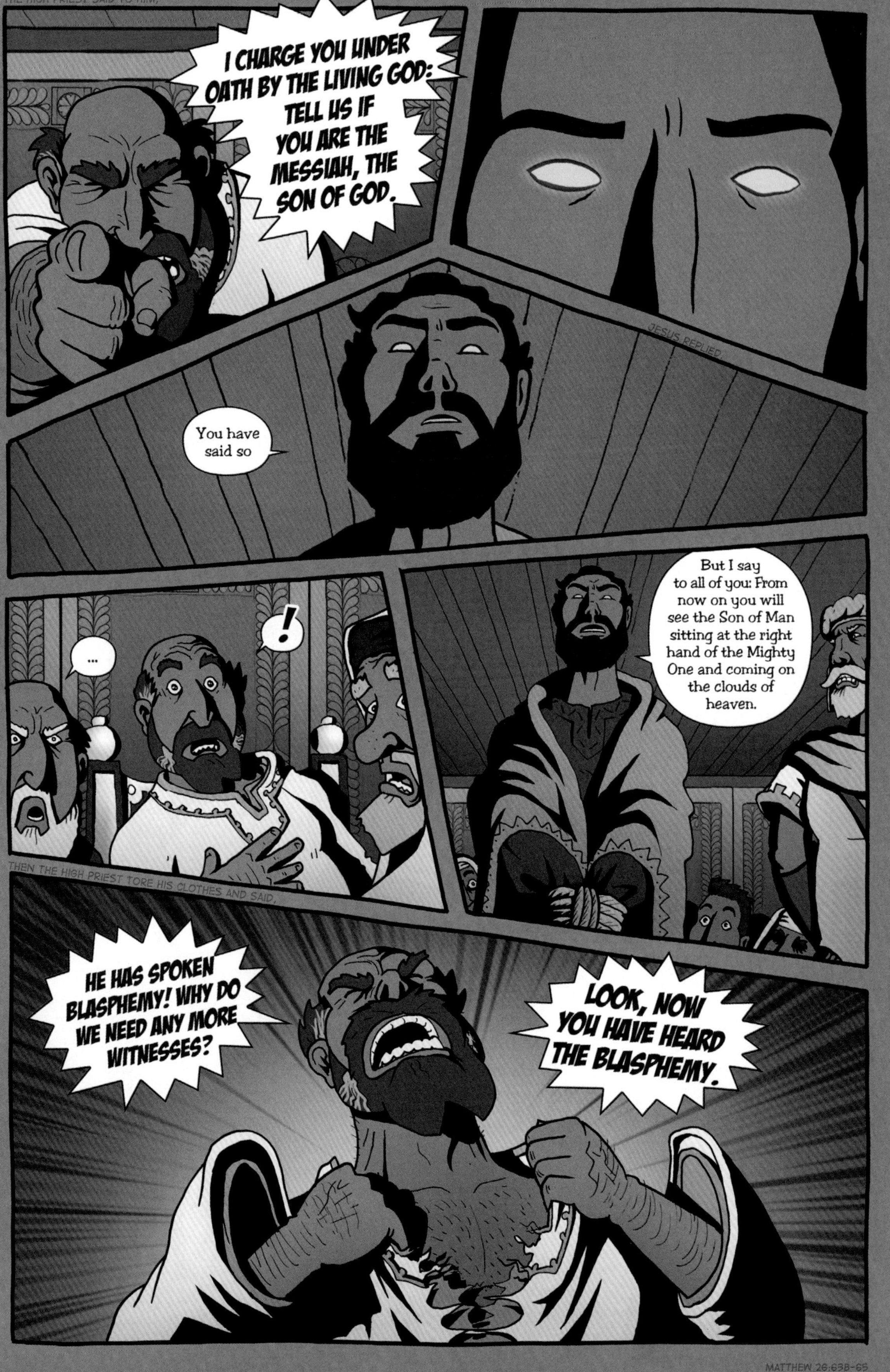
THE HIGH PRIEST SAID TO HIM,
I CHARGE YOU UNDER OATH BY THE LIVING GOD: TELL US IF YOU ARE THE MESSIAH, THE SON OF GOD.
JESUS REPLIED,
You have said so
But I say to all of you: From now on you will see the Son of Man sitting at the right hand of the Mighty One and coming on the clouds of heaven.
...
!
THEN THE HIGH PRIEST TORE HIS CLOTHES AND SAID,
HE HAS SPOKEN BLASPHEMY! WHY DO WE NEED ANY MORE WITNESSES?
LOOK, NOW YOU HAVE HEARD THE BLASPHEMY.

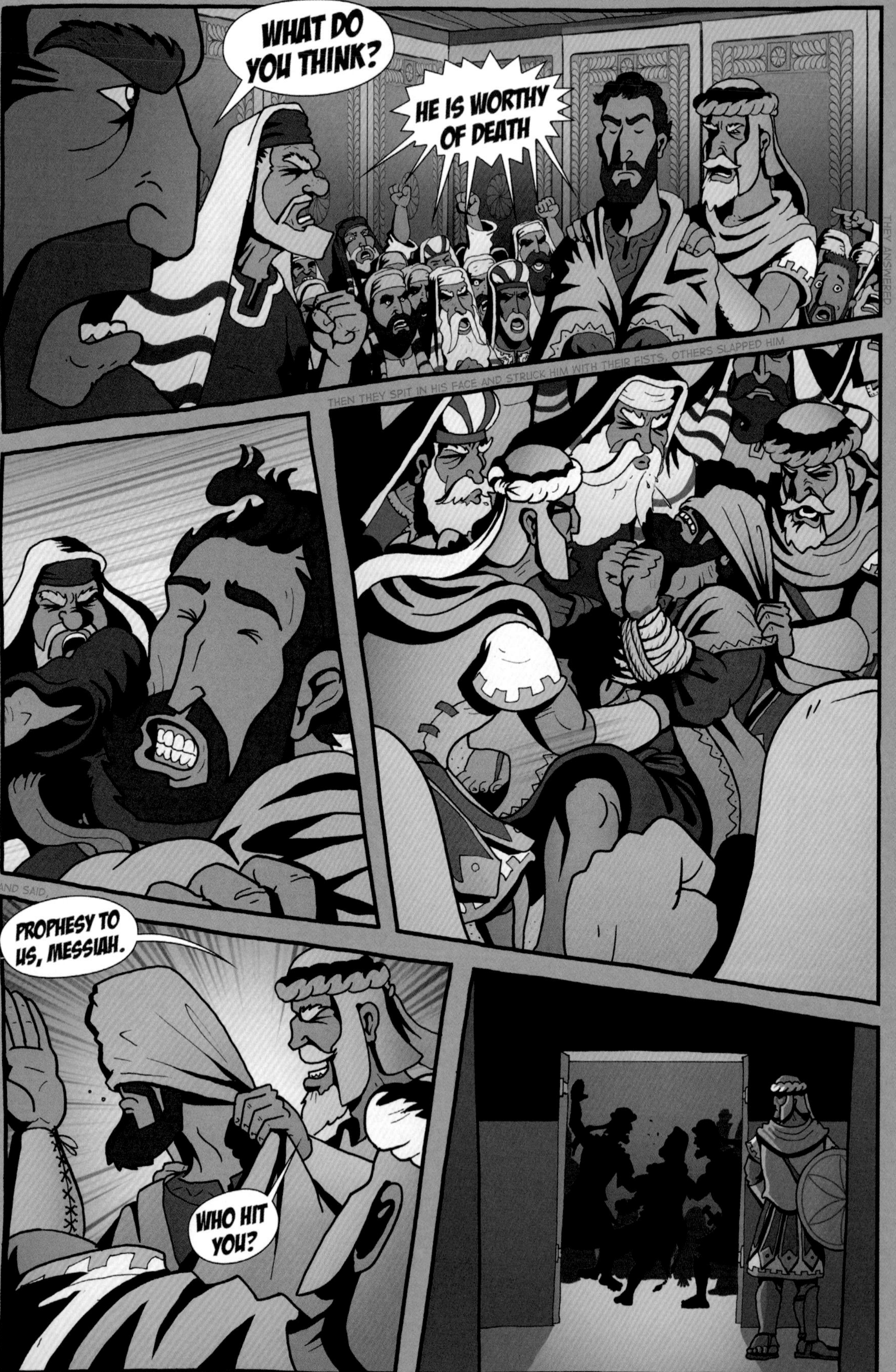
WHAT DO YOU THINK?
THEY ANSWERED,
HE IS WORTHY OF DEATH
THEN THEY SPIT IN HIS FACE AND STRUCK HIM WITH THEIR FISTS. OTHERS SLAPPED HIM
AND SAID,
PROPHESY TO US, MESSIAH.
WHO HIT YOU?

WORD FOR WORD
BIBLE COMIC

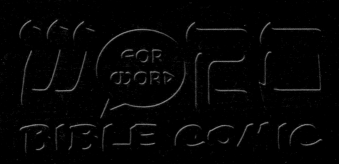

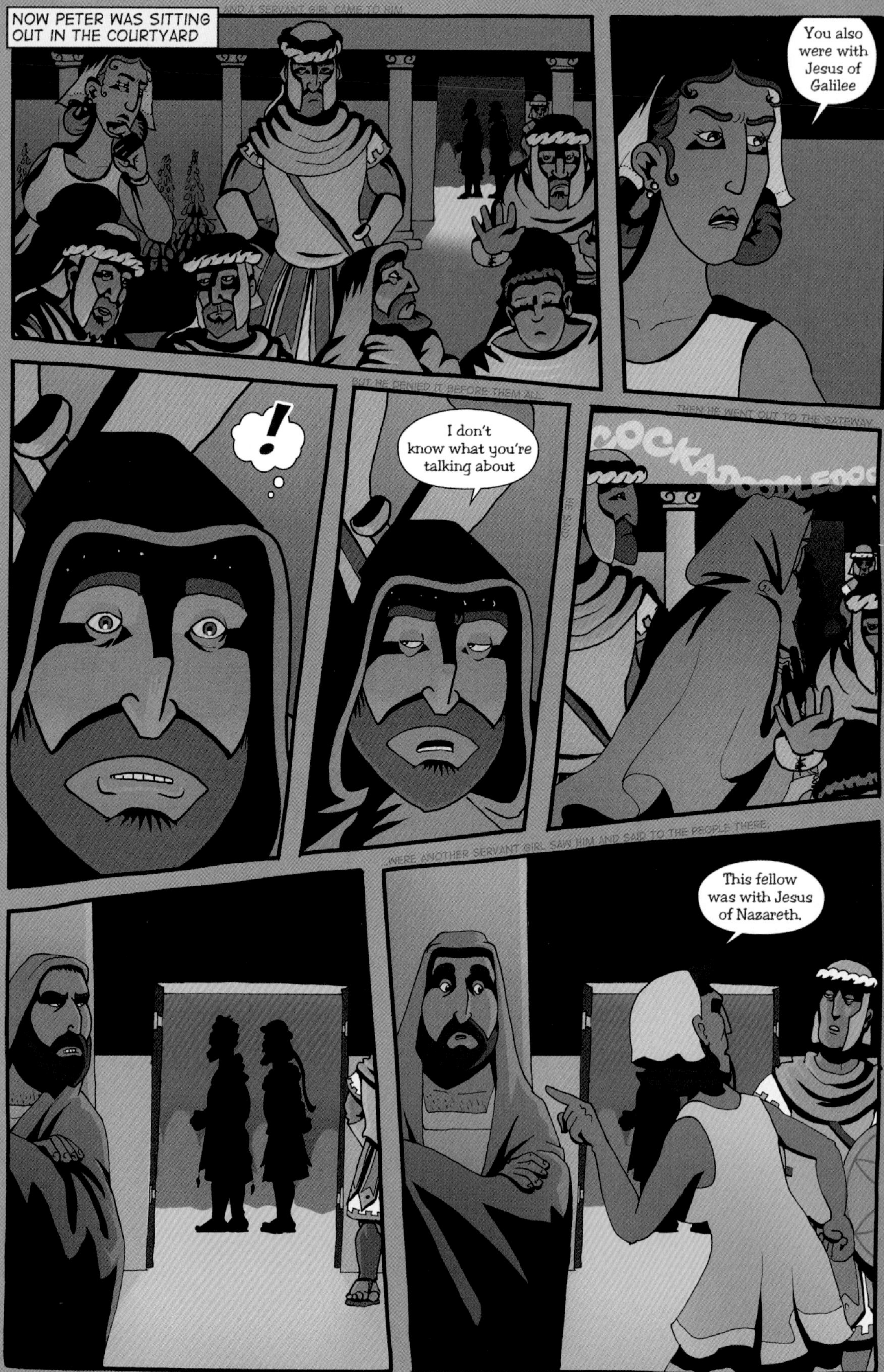

NOW PETER WAS SITTING OUT IN THE COURTYARD
AND A SERVANT GIRL CAME TO HIM.
You also were with Jesus of Galilee
SHE SAID.
!
BUT HE DENIED IT BEFORE THEM ALL.
I don't know what you're talking about
HE SAID.
THEN HE WENT OUT TO THE GATEWAY
COCKADOODLEDOO
...WERE ANOTHER SERVANT GIRL SAW HIM AND SAID TO THE PEOPLE THERE,
This fellow was with Jesus of Nazareth.

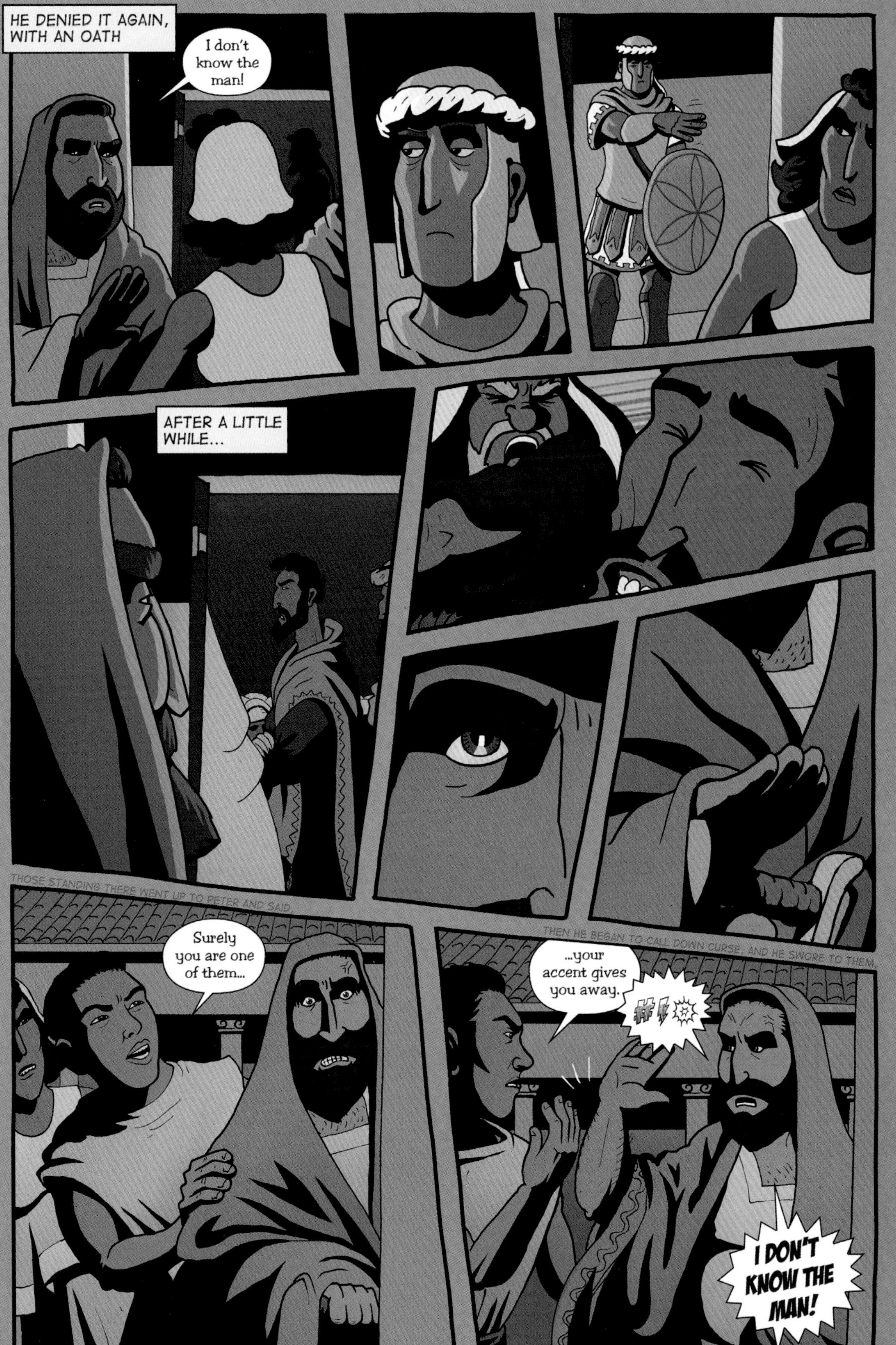

HE DENIED IT AGAIN, WITH AN OATH
I don't know the man!
AFTER A LITTLE WHILE...
THOSE STANDING THERE WENT UP TO PETER AND SAID,
Surely you are one of them...
...your accent gives you away.
THEN HE BEGAN TO CALL DOWN CURSE, AND HE SWORE TO THEM,
I DON'T KNOW THE MAN!

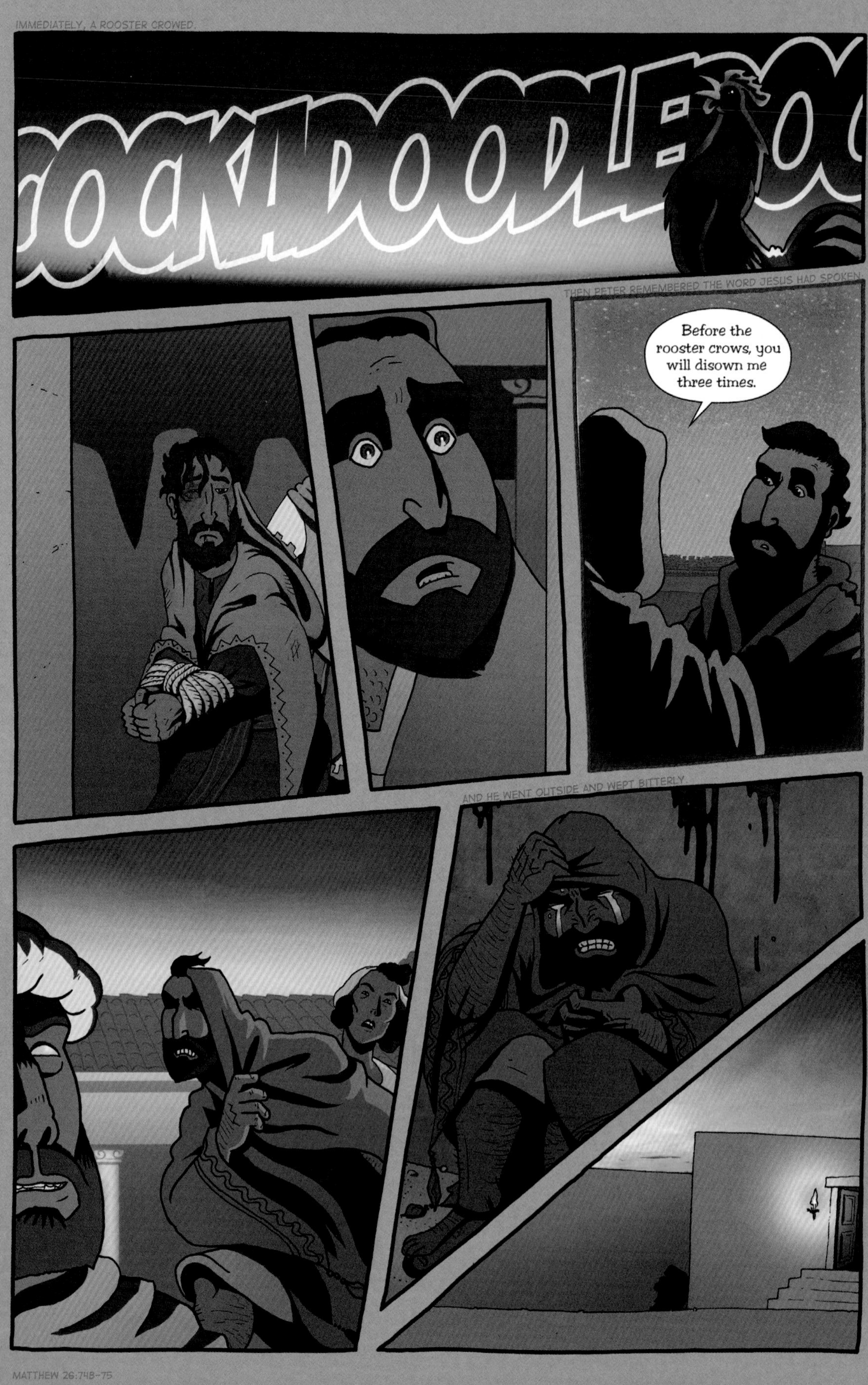
IMMEDIATELY, A ROOSTER CROWED.
COCKADOODLEDOO
THEN PETER REMEMBERED THE WORD JESUS HAD SPOKEN:
Before the rooster crows, you will disown me three times.
AND HE WENT OUTSIDE AND WEPT BITTERLY.

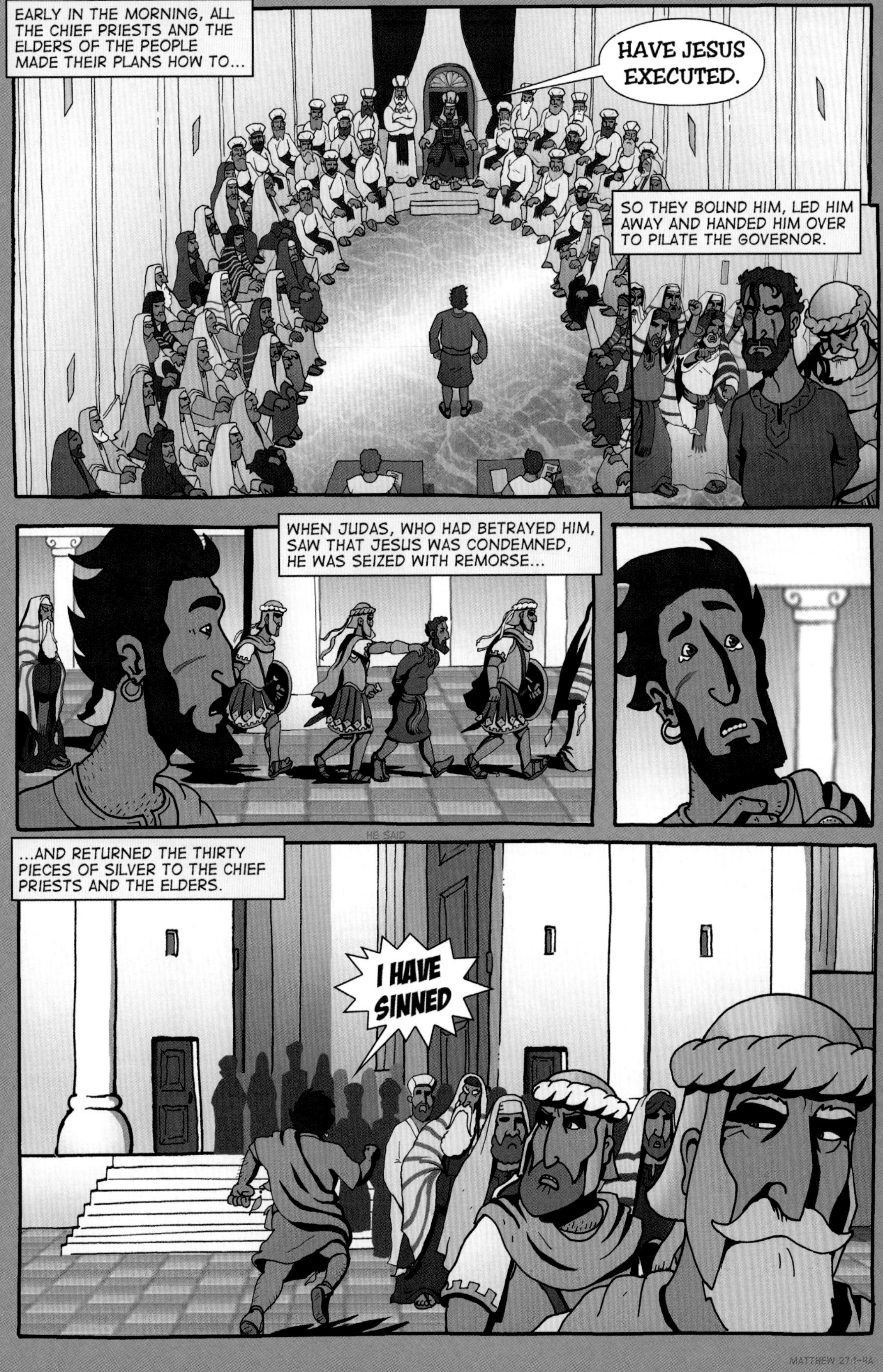
EARLY IN THE MORNING, ALL THE CHIEF PRIESTS AND THE ELDERS OF THE PEOPLE MADE THEIR PLANS HOW TO...
HAVE JESUS EXECUTED.
SO THEY BOUND HIM, LED HIM AWAY AND HANDED HIM OVER TO PILATE THE GOVERNOR.
WHEN JUDAS, WHO HAD BETRAYED HIM, SAW THAT JESUS WAS CONDEMNED, HE WAS SEIZED WITH REMORSE...
HE SAID
...AND RETURNED THE THIRTY PIECES OF SILVER TO THE CHIEF PRIESTS AND THE ELDERS.
I HAVE SINNED

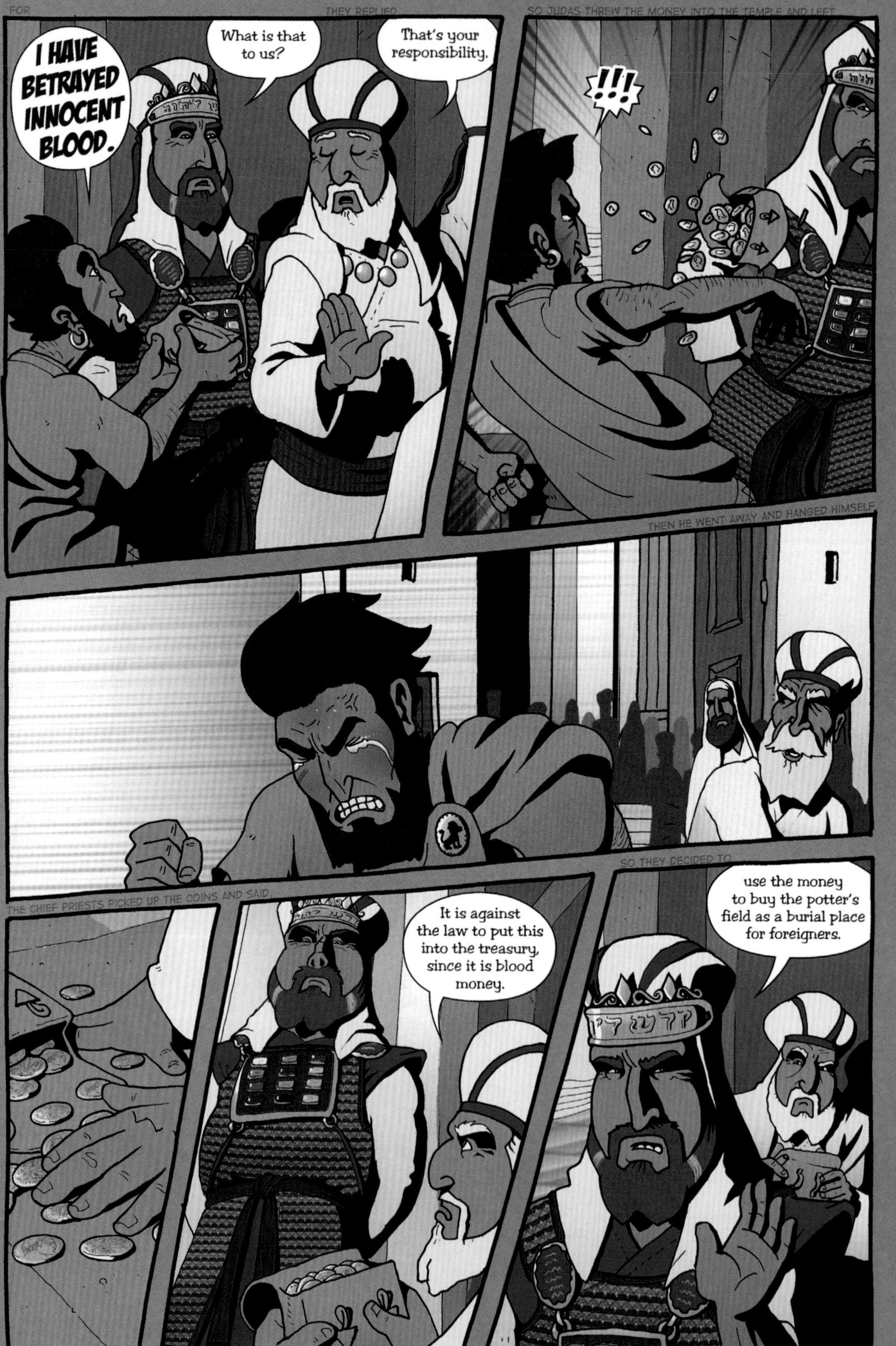
FOR
I HAVE BETRAYED INNOCENT BLOOD.
THEY REPLIED
What is that to us?
That's your responsibility.
SO JUDAS THREW THE MONEY INTO THE TEMPLE AND LEFT.
!!!
THEN HE WENT AWAY AND HANGED HIMSELF.
THE CHIEF PRIESTS PICKED UP THE COINS AND SAID,
It is against the law to put this into the treasury, since it is blood money.
SO THEY DECIDED TO
use the money to buy the potter's field as a burial place for foreigners.

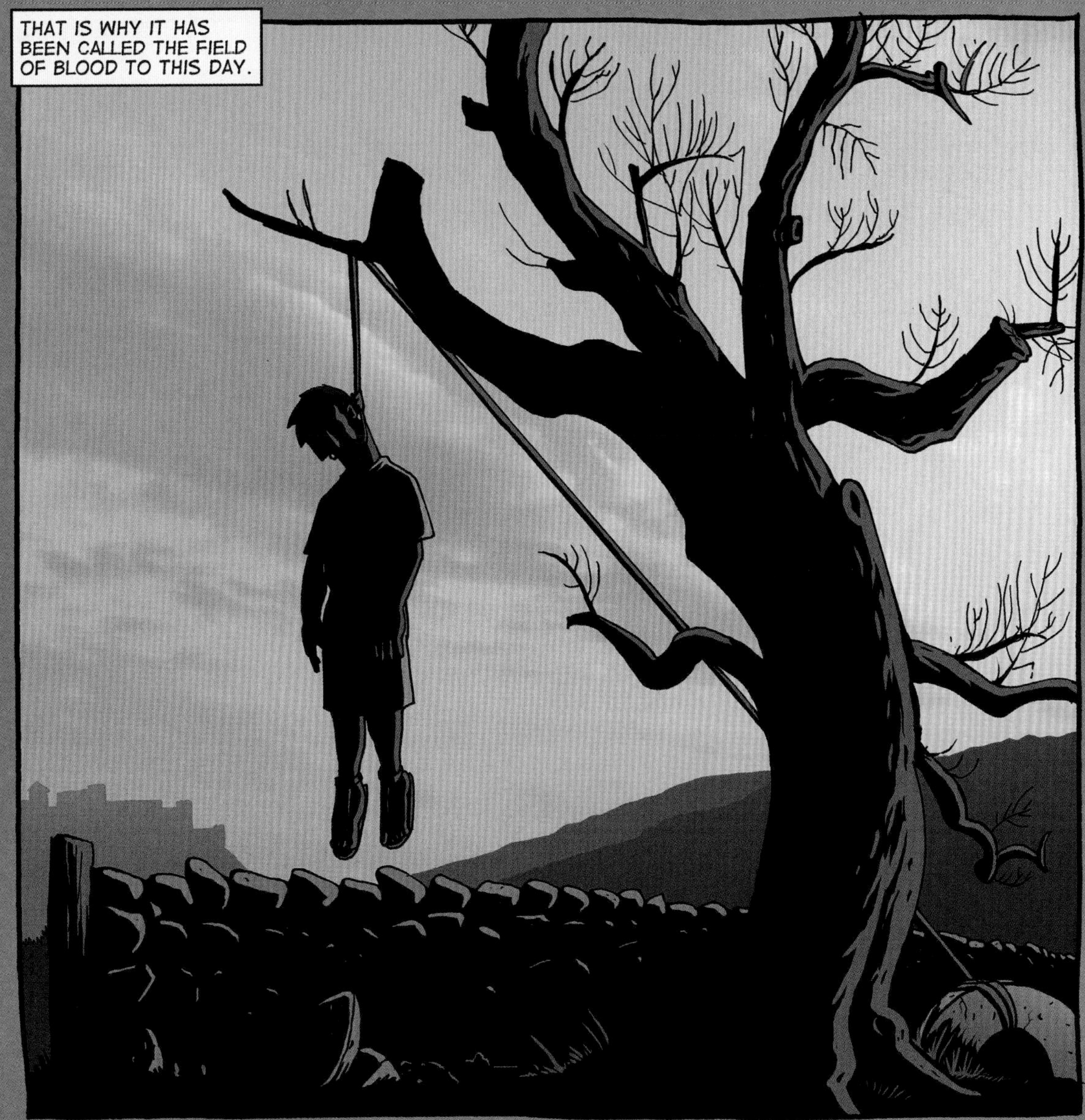
THAT IS WHY IT HAS BEEN CALLED THE FIELD OF BLOOD TO THIS DAY.

THEN WHAT WAS SPOKEN BY JEREMIAH THE PROPHET WAS FULFILLED: "THEY TOOK THE THIRTY PIECES OF SILVER, THE PRICE SET ON HIM BY THE PEOPLE OF ISRAEL, AND THEY USED THEM TO BUY THE POTTER'S FIELD, AS THE LORD COMMANDED ME."

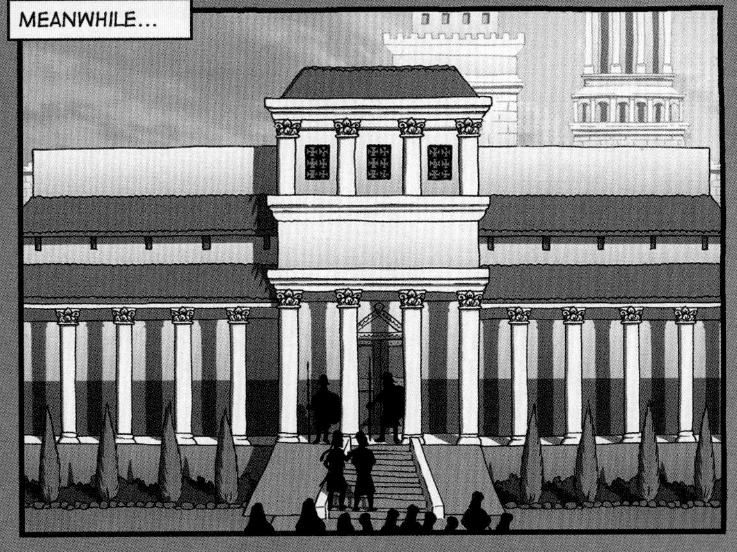
MEANWHILE...

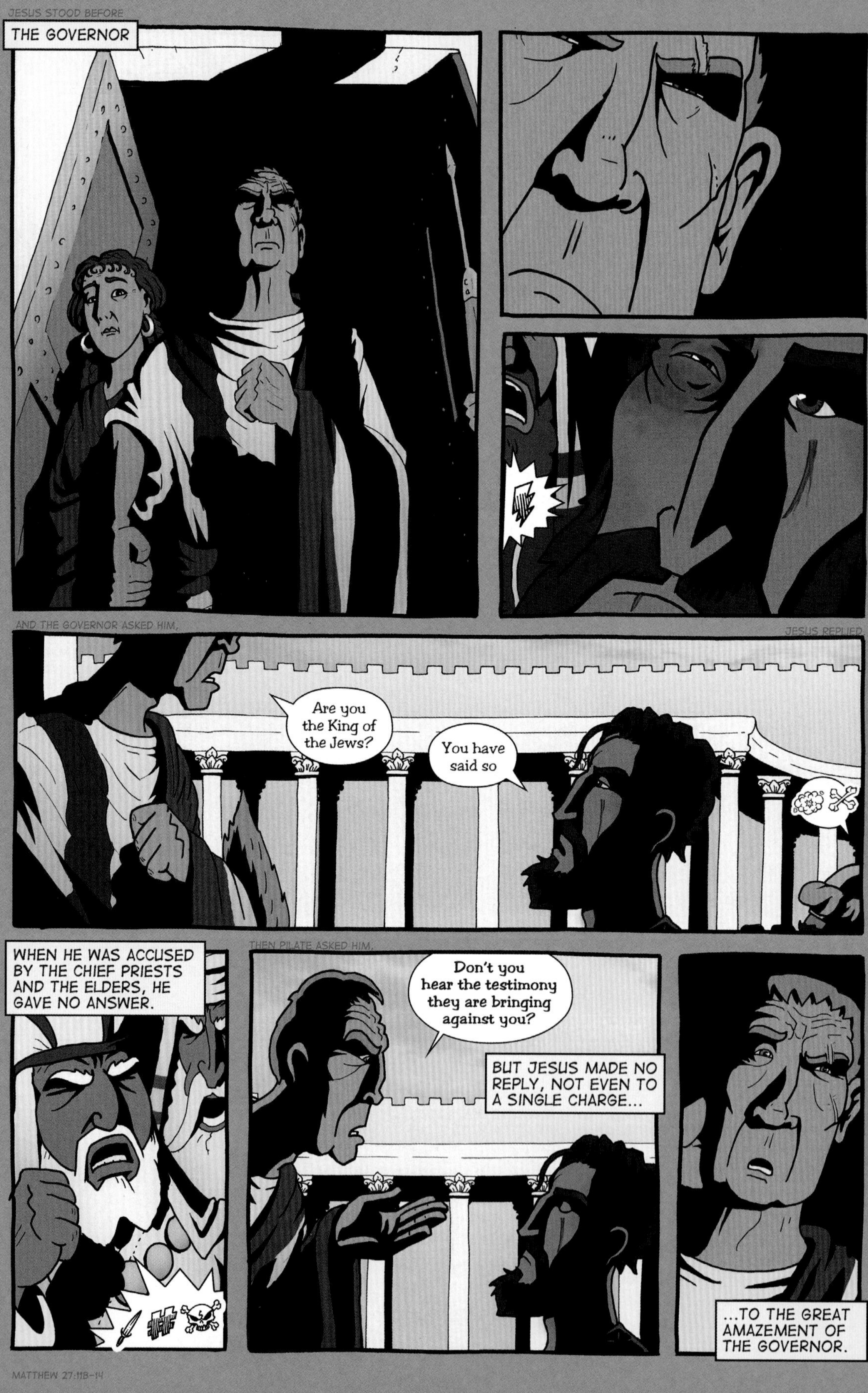

JESUS STOOD BEFORE
THE GOVERNOR
AND THE GOVERNOR ASKED HIM,
Are you the King of the Jews?
JESUS REPLIED
You have said so
WHEN HE WAS ACCUSED BY THE CHIEF PRIESTS AND THE ELDERS, HE GAVE NO ANSWER.
THEN PILATE ASKED HIM,
Don't you hear the testimony they are bringing against you?
BUT JESUS MADE NO REPLY, NOT EVEN TO A SINGLE CHARGE...
...TO THE GREAT AMAZEMENT OF THE GOVERNOR.

NOW IT WAS THE GOVERNOR'S CUSTOM AT THE FESTIVAL TO RELEASE A PRISONER CHOSEN BY THE CROWD.

AT THAT TIME THEY HAD A WELL-KNOWN PRISONER WHOSE NAME WAS JESUS BARABBAS.

SO WHEN THE CROWD HAD GATHERED, PILATE ASKED THEM

WHICH ONE DO YOU WANT ME TO RELEASE TO YOU: JESUS BARABBAS, OR JESUS WHO IS CALLED THE MESSIAH?

FOR HE KNEW

IT WAS OUT OF SELF-INTEREST THAT THEY HAD HANDED JESUS OVER TO HIM.

WHILE PILATE WAS SITTING ON THE JUDGE'S SEAT, HIS WIFE SENT HIM THIS MESSAGE:

"DON'T HAVE ANYTHING TO DO WITH THAT INNOCENT MAN, FOR I HAVE SUFFERED A GREAT DEAL TODAY IN A DREAM BECAUSE OF HIM."

BUT

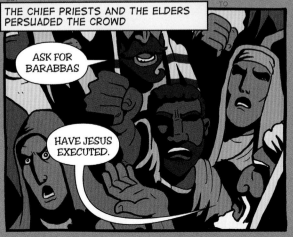

THE CHIEF PRIESTS AND THE ELDERS PERSUADED THE CROWD TO

ASK FOR BARABBAS

HAVE JESUS EXECUTED.

WHICH OF THE TWO DO YOU WANT ME TO RELEASE TO YOU?

ASKED THE GOVERNOR.

MATTHEW 27:15-21A

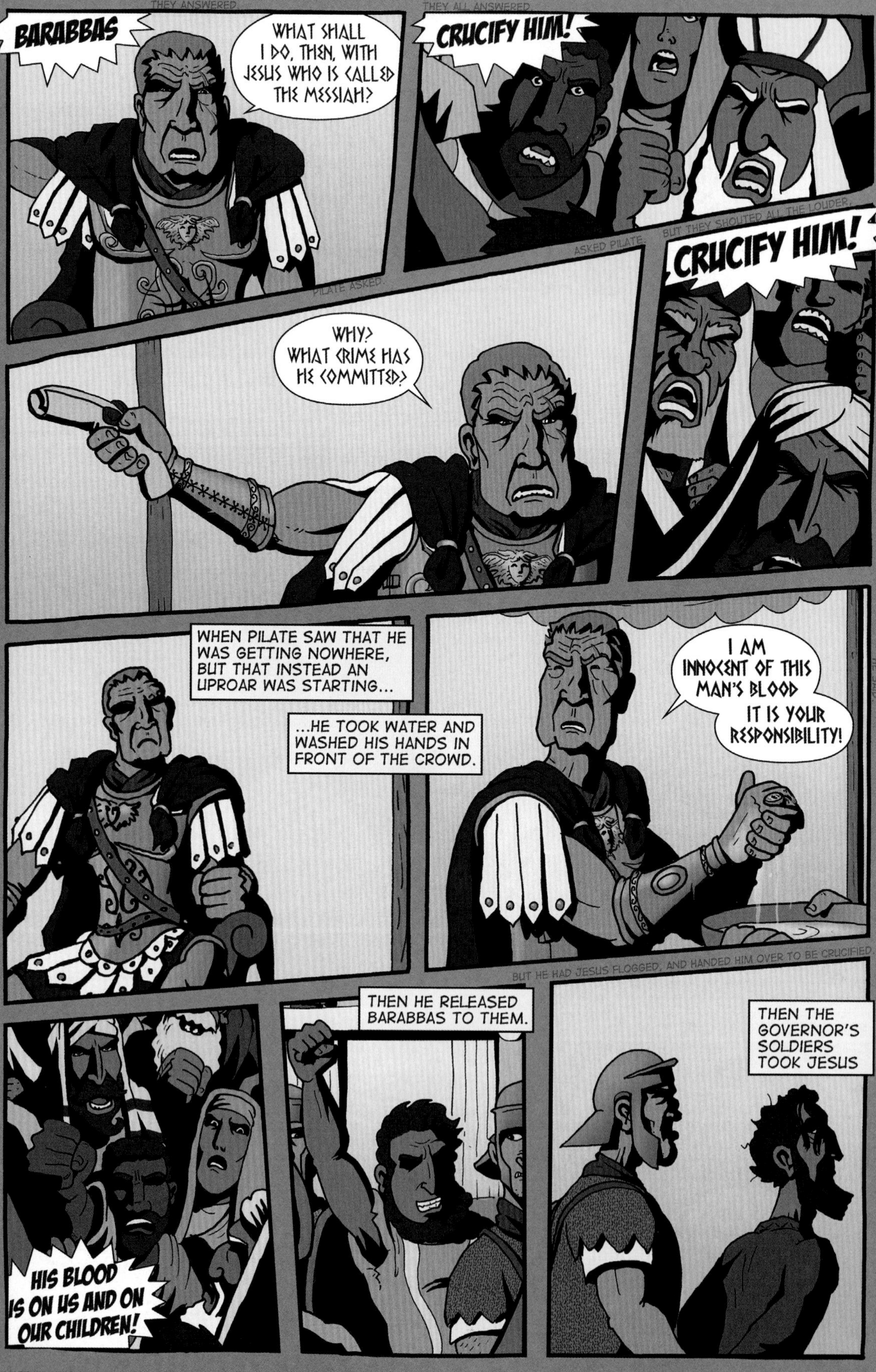
THEY ANSWERED,
BARABBAS
WHAT SHALL I DO, THEN, WITH JESUS WHO IS CALLED THE MESSIAH?
PILATE ASKED.
THEY ALL ANSWERED,
CRUCIFY HIM!
WHY? WHAT CRIME HAS HE COMMITTED?
ASKED PILATE.
BUT THEY SHOUTED ALL THE LOUDER,
CRUCIFY HIM!
WHEN PILATE SAW THAT HE WAS GETTING NOWHERE, BUT THAT INSTEAD AN UPROAR WAS STARTING...
...HE TOOK WATER AND WASHED HIS HANDS IN FRONT OF THE CROWD.
I AM INNOCENT OF THIS MAN'S BLOOD
IT IS YOUR RESPONSIBILITY!
HE SAID.
HIS BLOOD IS ON US AND ON OUR CHILDREN!
THEN HE RELEASED BARABBAS TO THEM.
BUT HE HAD JESUS FLOGGED, AND HANDED HIM OVER TO BE CRUCIFIED.
THEN THE GOVERNOR'S SOLDIERS TOOK JESUS

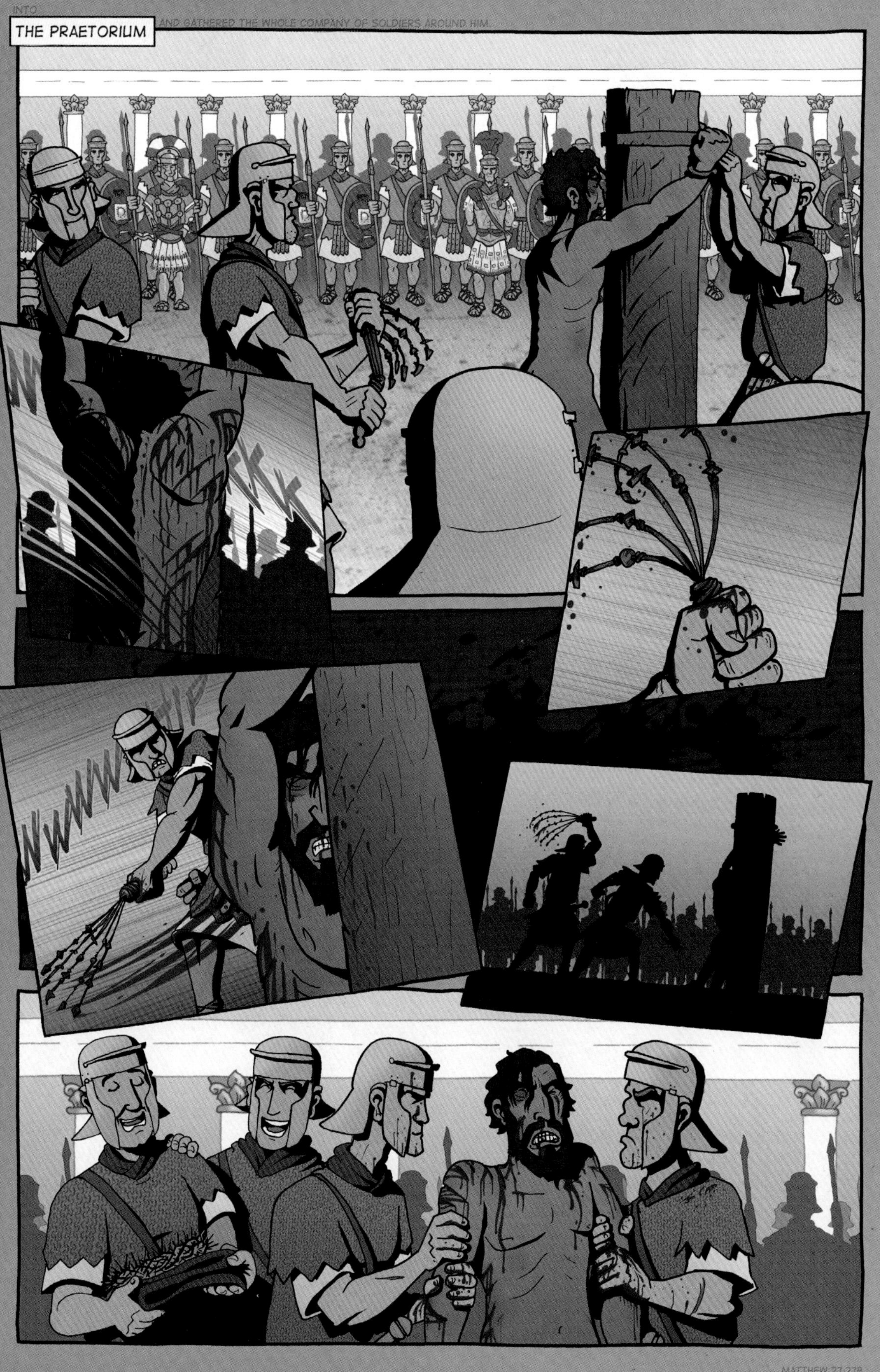
INTO
THE PRAETORIUM
AND GATHERED THE WHOLE COMPANY OF SOLDIERS AROUND HIM.

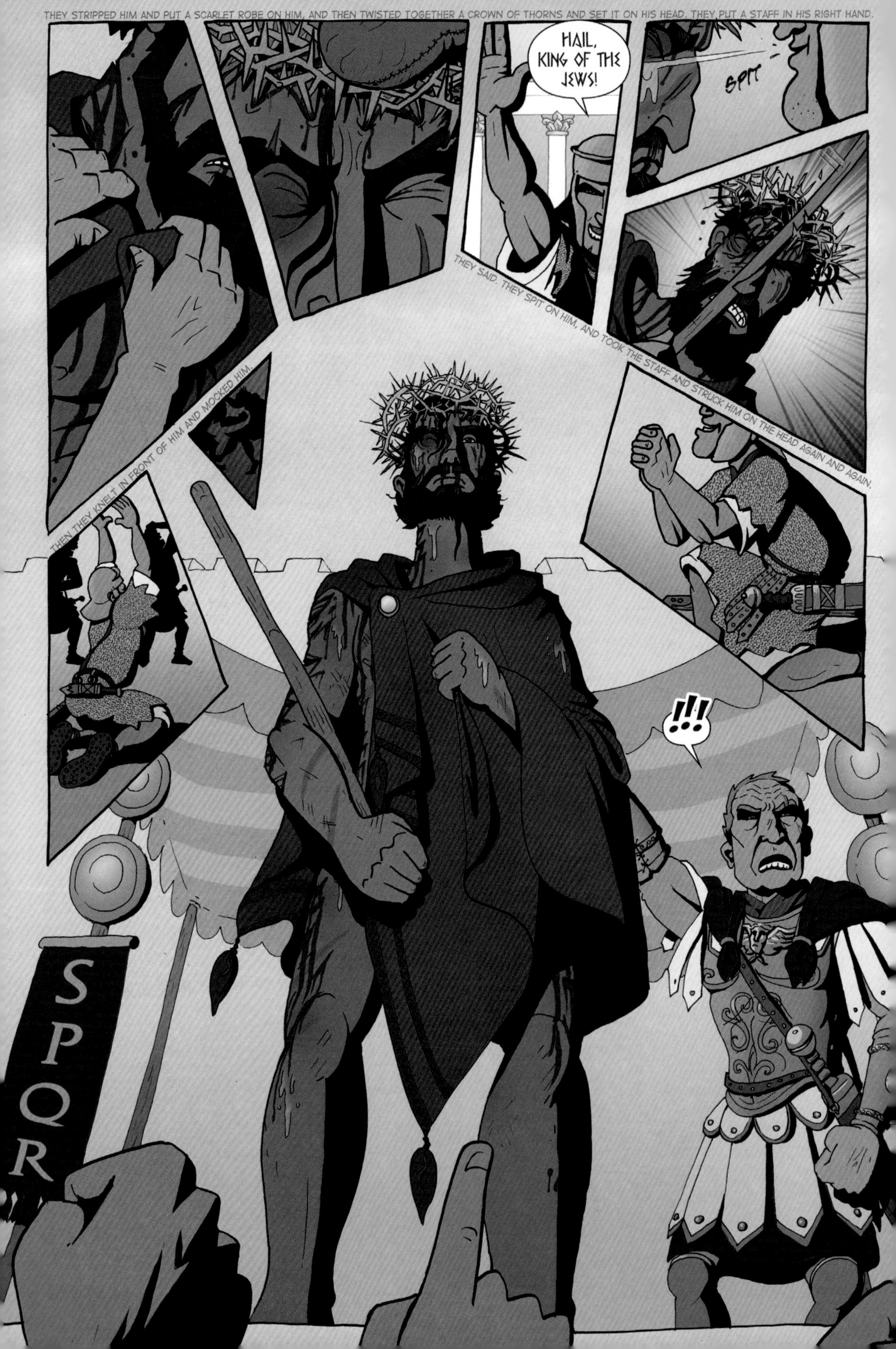
THEY STRIPPED HIM AND PUT A SCARLET ROBE ON HIM, AND THEN TWISTED TOGETHER A CROWN OF THORNS AND SET IT ON HIS HEAD. THEY PUT A STAFF IN HIS RIGHT HAND.
HAIL, KING OF THE JEWS!
SPIT
THEY SAID. THEY SPIT ON HIM, AND TOOK THE STAFF AND STRUCK HIM ON THE HEAD AGAIN AND AGAIN.
THEN THEY KNELT IN FRONT OF HIM AND MOCKED HIM.
!!!
SPQR

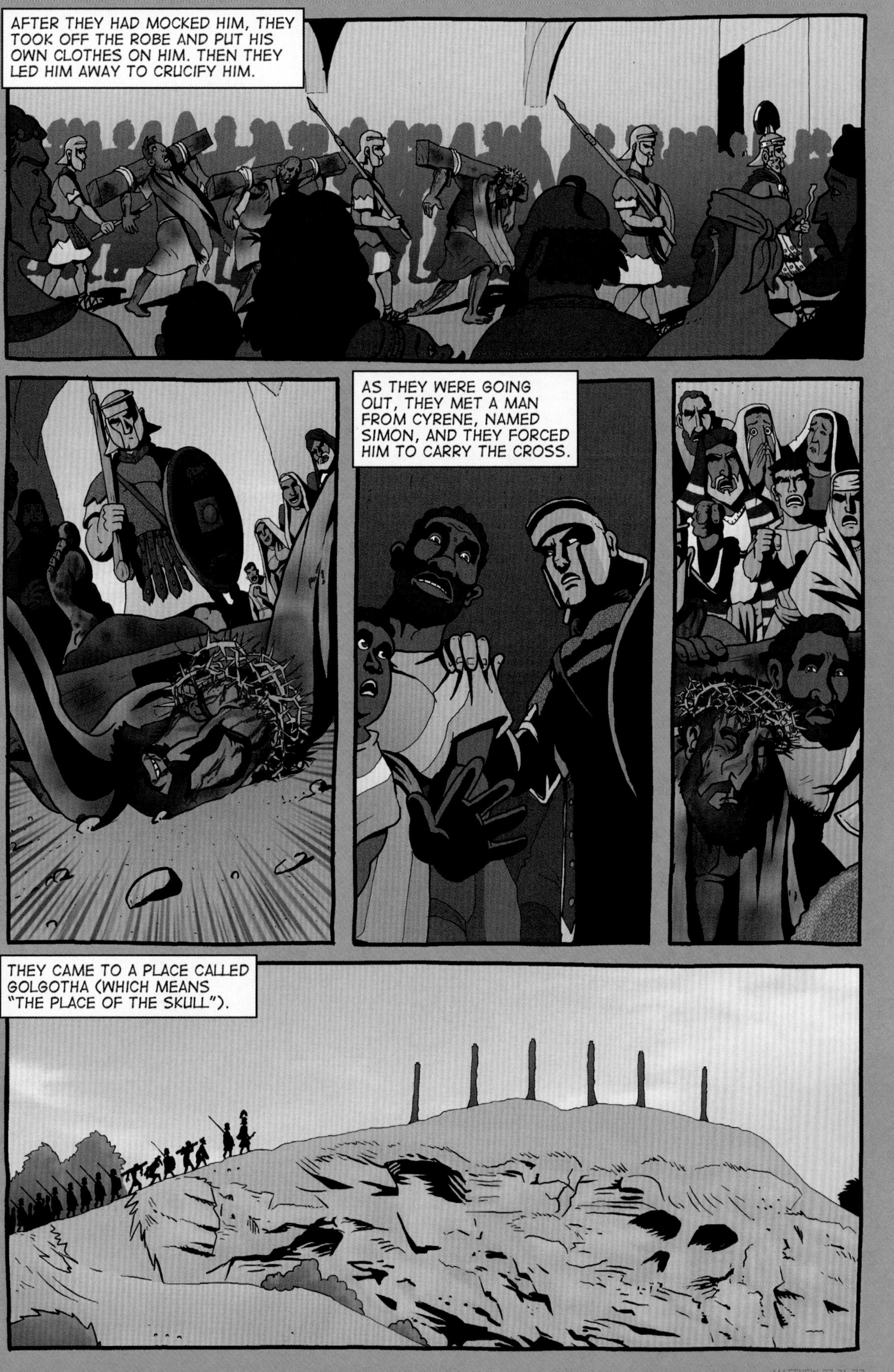
AFTER THEY HAD MOCKED HIM, THEY TOOK OFF THE ROBE AND PUT HIS OWN CLOTHES ON HIM. THEN THEY LED HIM AWAY TO CRUCIFY HIM.
AS THEY WERE GOING OUT, THEY MET A MAN FROM CYRENE, NAMED SIMON, AND THEY FORCED HIM TO CARRY THE CROSS.
THEY CAME TO A PLACE CALLED GOLGOTHA (WHICH MEANS "THE PLACE OF THE SKULL").

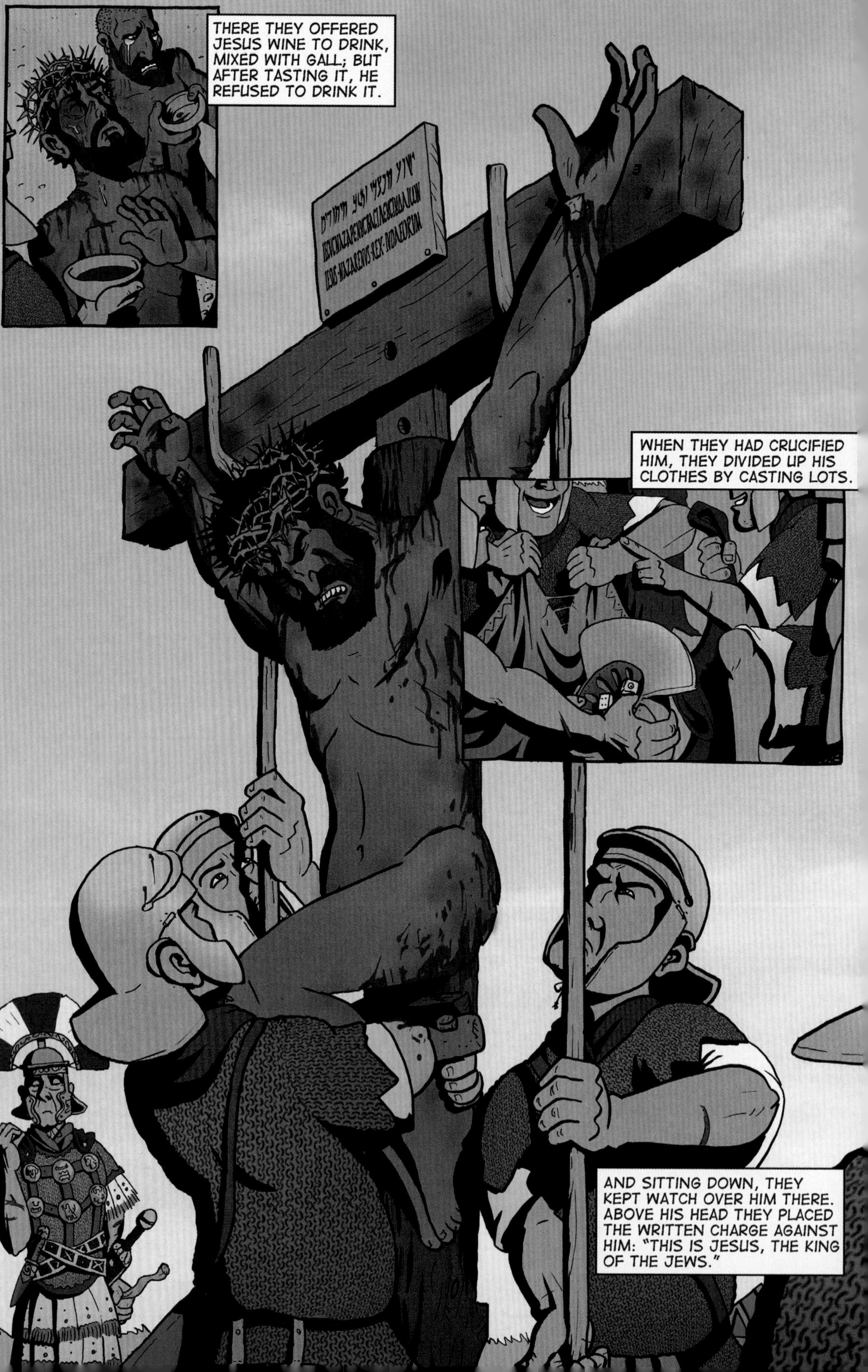
THERE THEY OFFERED JESUS WINE TO DRINK, MIXED WITH GALL; BUT AFTER TASTING IT, HE REFUSED TO DRINK IT.
IESVS·NAZARENVS·REX·IVDAEORVM
WHEN THEY HAD CRUCIFIED HIM, THEY DIVIDED UP HIS CLOTHES BY CASTING LOTS.
AND SITTING DOWN, THEY KEPT WATCH OVER HIM THERE. ABOVE HIS HEAD THEY PLACED THE WRITTEN CHARGE AGAINST HIM: "THIS IS JESUS, THE KING OF THE JEWS."

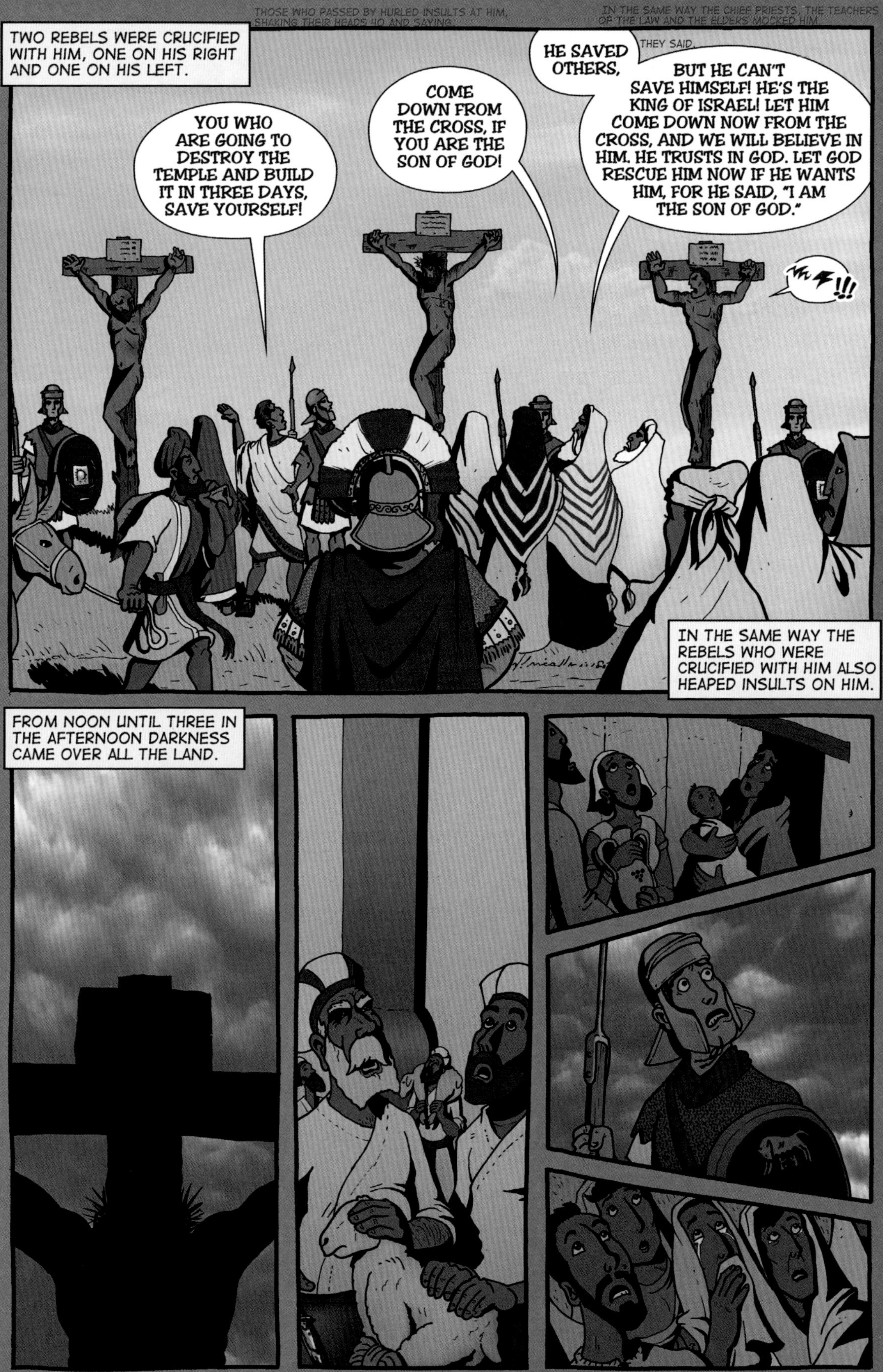
TWO REBELS WERE CRUCIFIED WITH HIM, ONE ON HIS RIGHT AND ONE ON HIS LEFT.
THOSE WHO PASSED BY HURLED INSULTS AT HIM, SHAKING THEIR HEADS 40 AND SAYING
YOU WHO ARE GOING TO DESTROY THE TEMPLE AND BUILD IT IN THREE DAYS, SAVE YOURSELF!
COME DOWN FROM THE CROSS, IF YOU ARE THE SON OF GOD!
IN THE SAME WAY THE CHIEF PRIESTS, THE TEACHERS OF THE LAW AND THE ELDERS MOCKED HIM
HE SAVED OTHERS,
THEY SAID,
BUT HE CAN'T SAVE HIMSELF! HE'S THE KING OF ISRAEL! LET HIM COME DOWN NOW FROM THE CROSS, AND WE WILL BELIEVE IN HIM. HE TRUSTS IN GOD. LET GOD RESCUE HIM NOW IF HE WANTS HIM, FOR HE SAID, "I AM THE SON OF GOD."
!!!
IN THE SAME WAY THE REBELS WHO WERE CRUCIFIED WITH HIM ALSO HEAPED INSULTS ON HIM.
FROM NOON UNTIL THREE IN THE AFTERNOON DARKNESS CAME OVER ALL THE LAND.

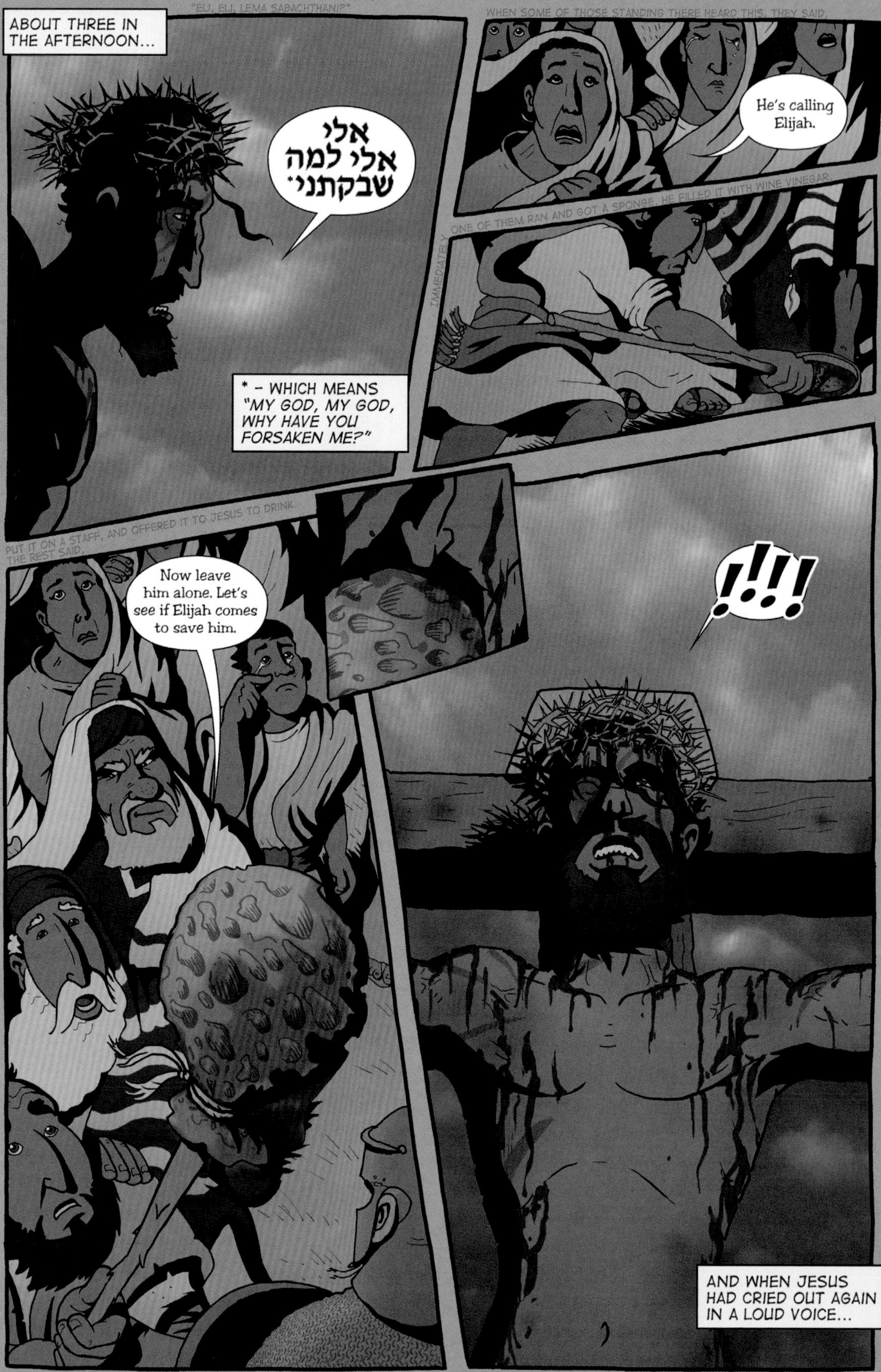
ABOUT THREE IN THE AFTERNOON...
JESUS CRIED OUT IN A LOUD VOICE, "ELI, ELI, LEMA SABACHTHANI?"
אלי אלי למה שבקתני*
* – WHICH MEANS "MY GOD, MY GOD, WHY HAVE YOU FORSAKEN ME?"
WHEN SOME OF THOSE STANDING THERE HEARD THIS, THEY SAID,
He's calling Elijah.
IMMEDIATELY ONE OF THEM RAN AND GOT A SPONGE. HE FILLED IT WITH WINE VINEGAR,
PUT IT ON A STAFF, AND OFFERED IT TO JESUS TO DRINK.
THE REST SAID,
Now leave him alone. Let's see if Elijah comes to save him.
!!!
AND WHEN JESUS HAD CRIED OUT AGAIN IN A LOUD VOICE...

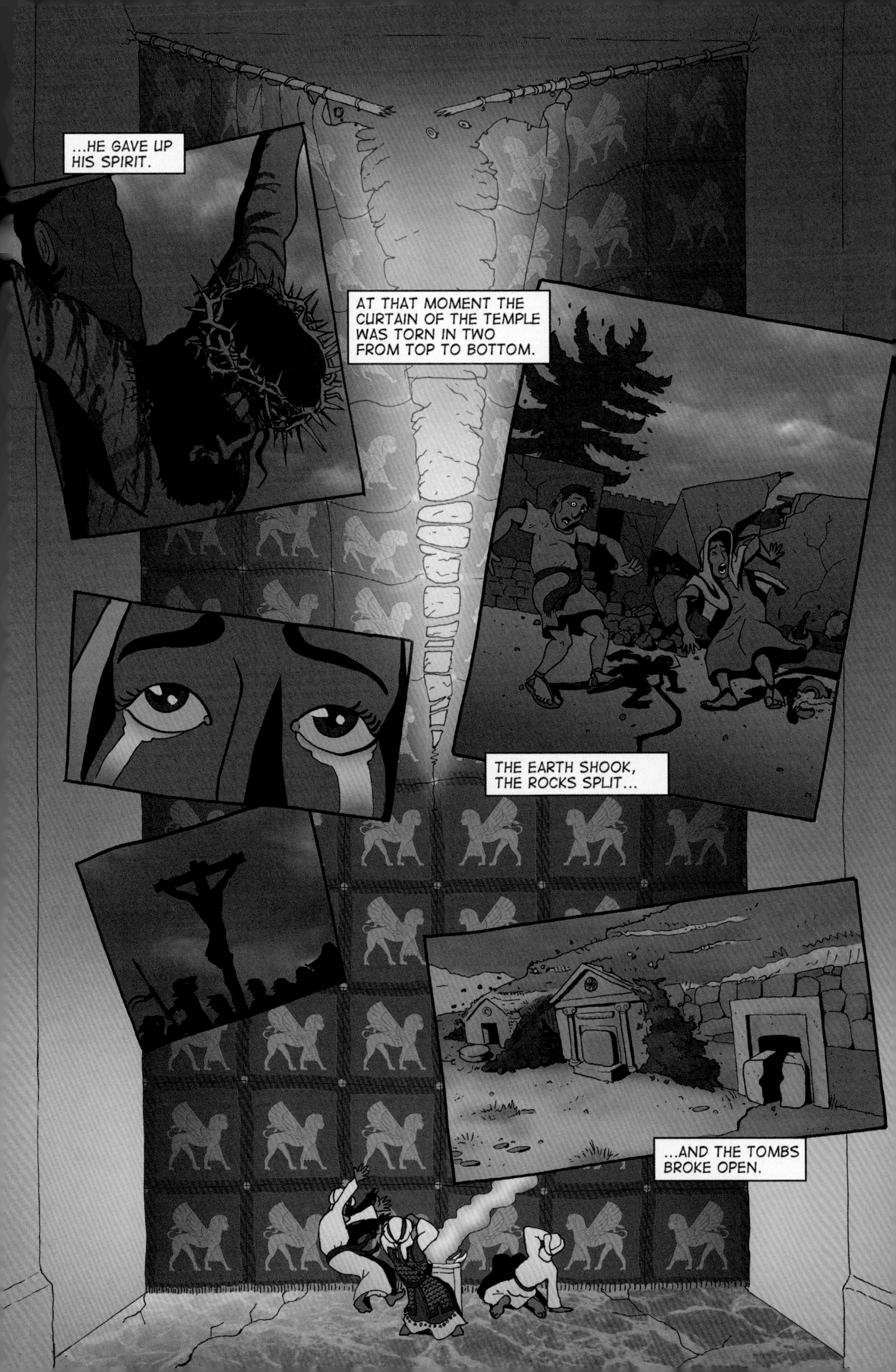
...HE GAVE UP HIS SPIRIT.
AT THAT MOMENT THE CURTAIN OF THE TEMPLE WAS TORN IN TWO FROM TOP TO BOTTOM.
THE EARTH SHOOK, THE ROCKS SPLIT...
...AND THE TOMBS BROKE OPEN.

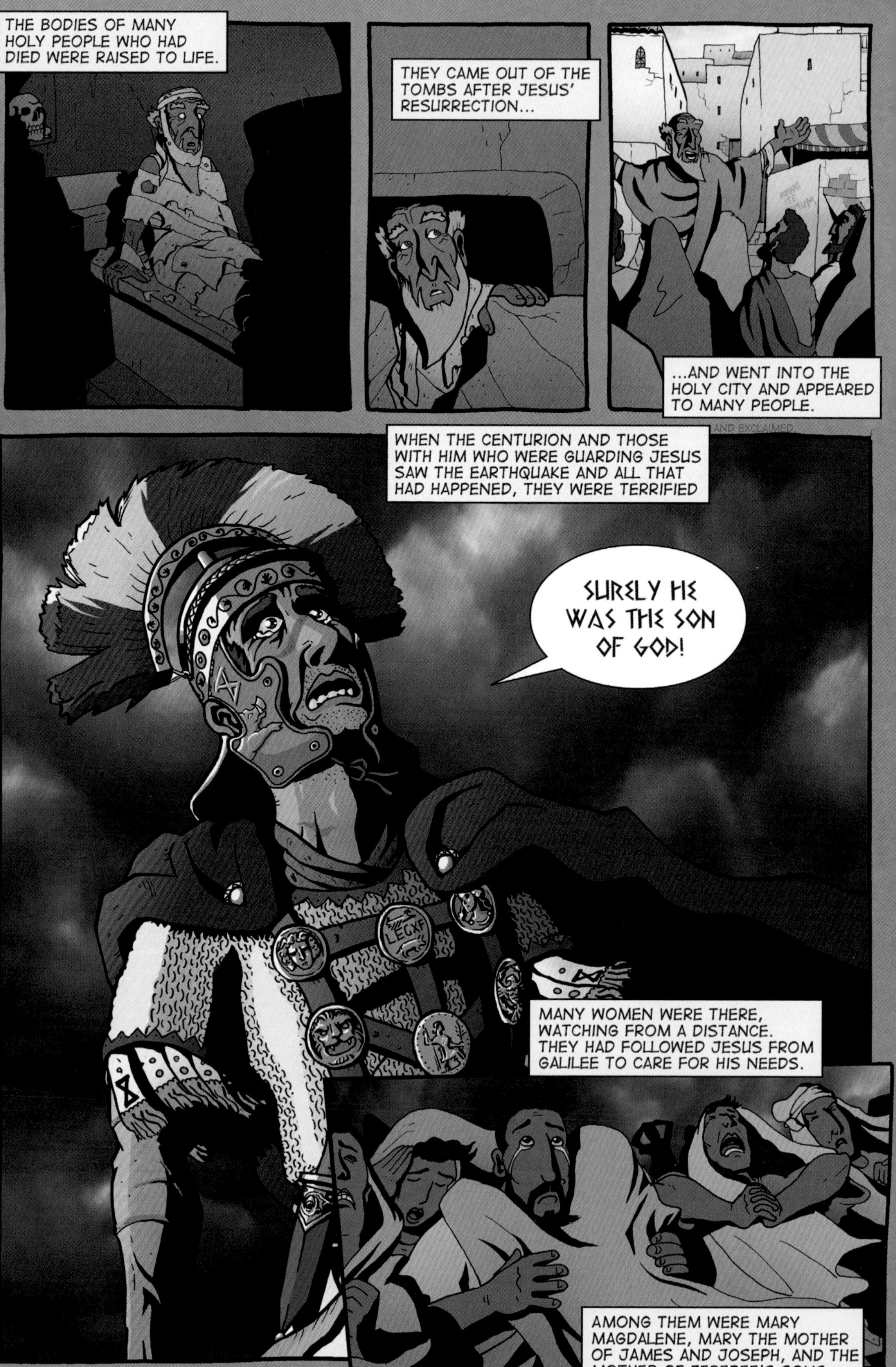
THE BODIES OF MANY HOLY PEOPLE WHO HAD DIED WERE RAISED TO LIFE.
THEY CAME OUT OF THE TOMBS AFTER JESUS' RESURRECTION...
...AND WENT INTO THE HOLY CITY AND APPEARED TO MANY PEOPLE.
WHEN THE CENTURION AND THOSE WITH HIM WHO WERE GUARDING JESUS SAW THE EARTHQUAKE AND ALL THAT HAD HAPPENED, THEY WERE TERRIFIED
AND EXCLAIMED,
SURELY HE WAS THE SON OF GOD!
MANY WOMEN WERE THERE, WATCHING FROM A DISTANCE. THEY HAD FOLLOWED JESUS FROM GALILEE TO CARE FOR HIS NEEDS.
AMONG THEM WERE MARY MAGDALENE, MARY THE MOTHER OF JAMES AND JOSEPH, AND THE MOTHER OF ZEBEDEE'S SONS.

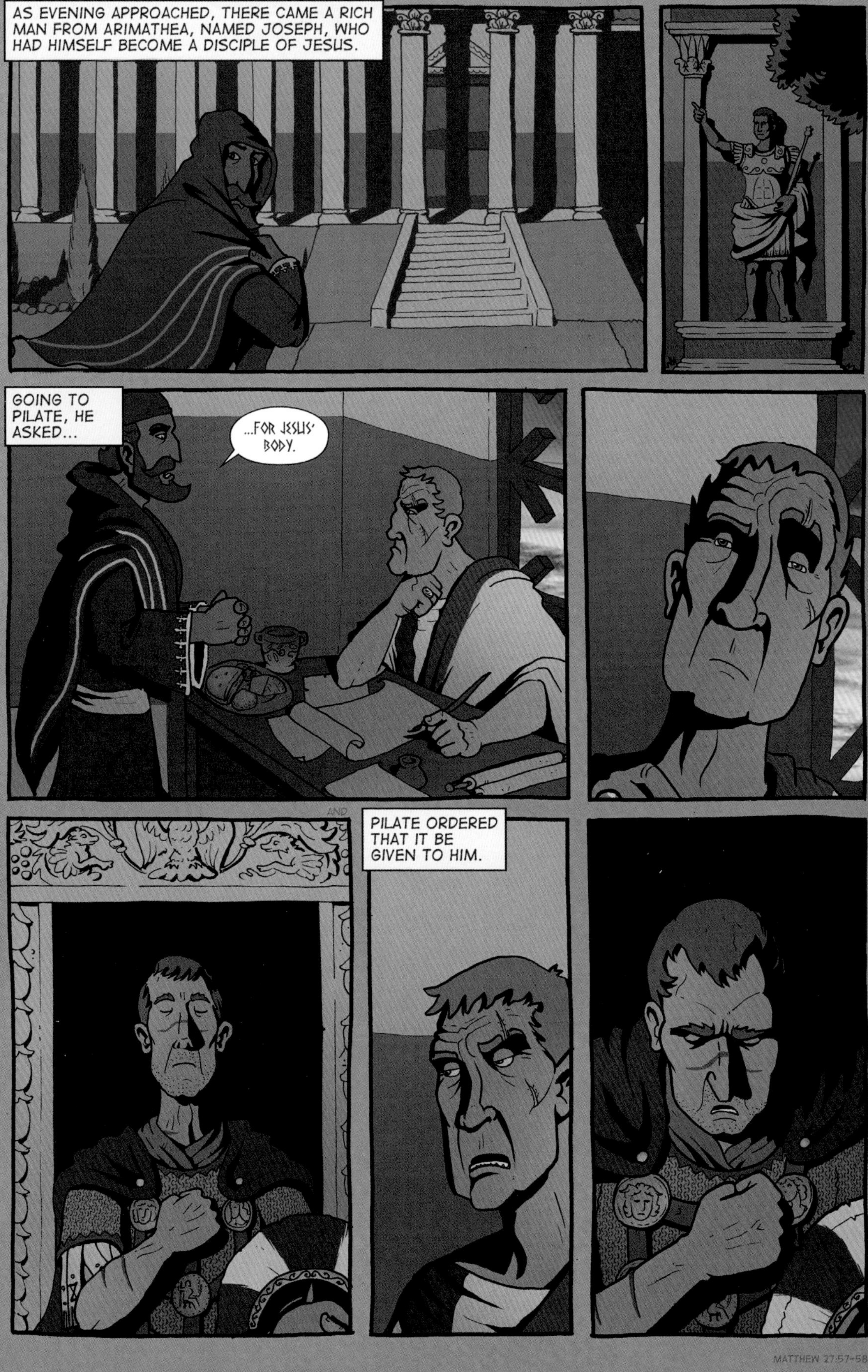
AS EVENING APPROACHED, THERE CAME A RICH MAN FROM ARIMATHEA, NAMED JOSEPH, WHO HAD HIMSELF BECOME A DISCIPLE OF JESUS.
GOING TO PILATE, HE ASKED...
...FOR JESUS' BODY.
AND
PILATE ORDERED THAT IT BE GIVEN TO HIM.

JOSEPH TOOK THE BODY, WRAPPED IT IN A CLEAN LINEN CLOTH...

על שחל ופתן תדרך תרמס כפיר ותנין

...AND PLACED IT IN HIS OWN NEW TOMB THAT HE HAD CUT OUT OF THE ROCK.

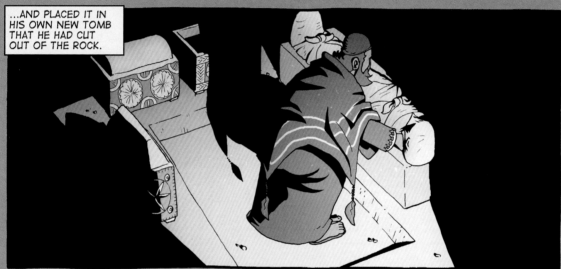

HE ROLLED A BIG STONE IN FRONT OF THE ENTRANCE TO THE TOMB AND WENT AWAY.

MARY MAGDALENE AND THE OTHER MARY WERE SITTING THERE OPPOSITE THE TOMB.

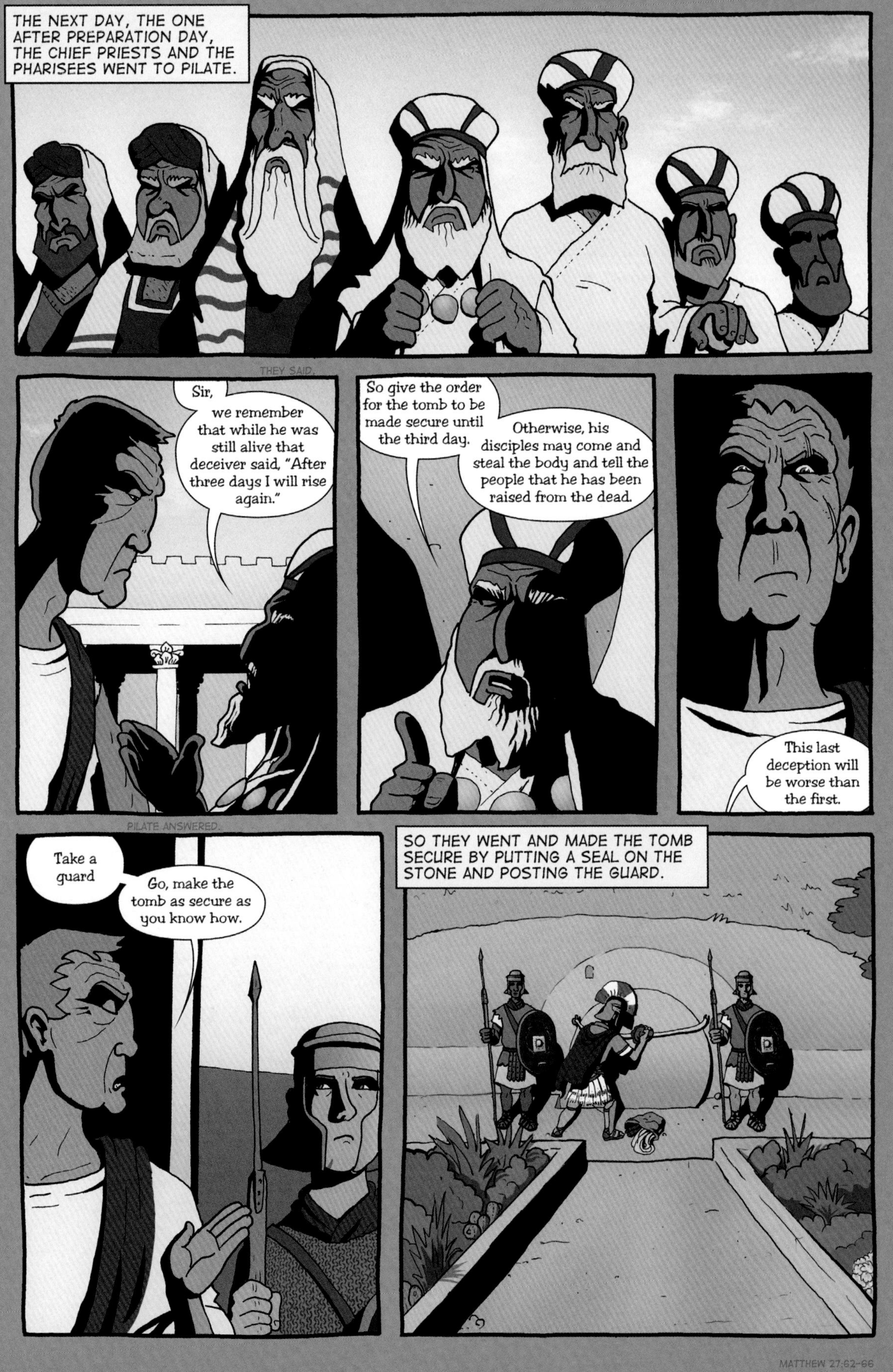
THE NEXT DAY, THE ONE AFTER PREPARATION DAY, THE CHIEF PRIESTS AND THE PHARISEES WENT TO PILATE.
THEY SAID,
Sir,
we remember that while he was still alive that deceiver said, "After three days I will rise again."
So give the order for the tomb to be made secure until the third day.
Otherwise, his disciples may come and steal the body and tell the people that he has been raised from the dead.
This last deception will be worse than the first.
PILATE ANSWERED,
Take a guard
Go, make the tomb as secure as you know how.
SO THEY WENT AND MADE THE TOMB SECURE BY PUTTING A SEAL ON THE STONE AND POSTING THE GUARD.

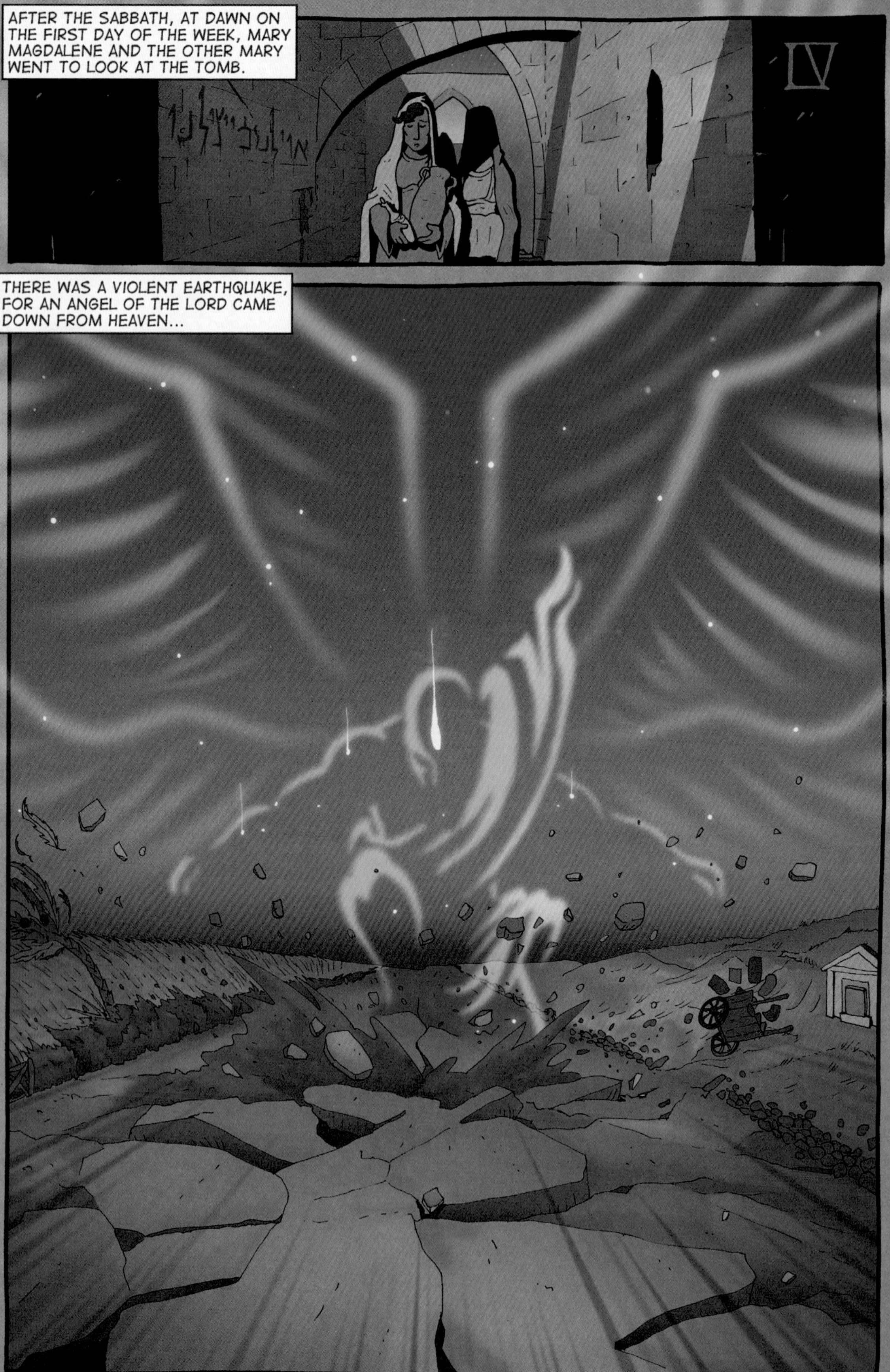
AFTER THE SABBATH, AT DAWN ON THE FIRST DAY OF THE WEEK, MARY MAGDALENE AND THE OTHER MARY WENT TO LOOK AT THE TOMB.
IV
THERE WAS A VIOLENT EARTHQUAKE, FOR AN ANGEL OF THE LORD CAME DOWN FROM HEAVEN...

MATTHEW 28:1-2A

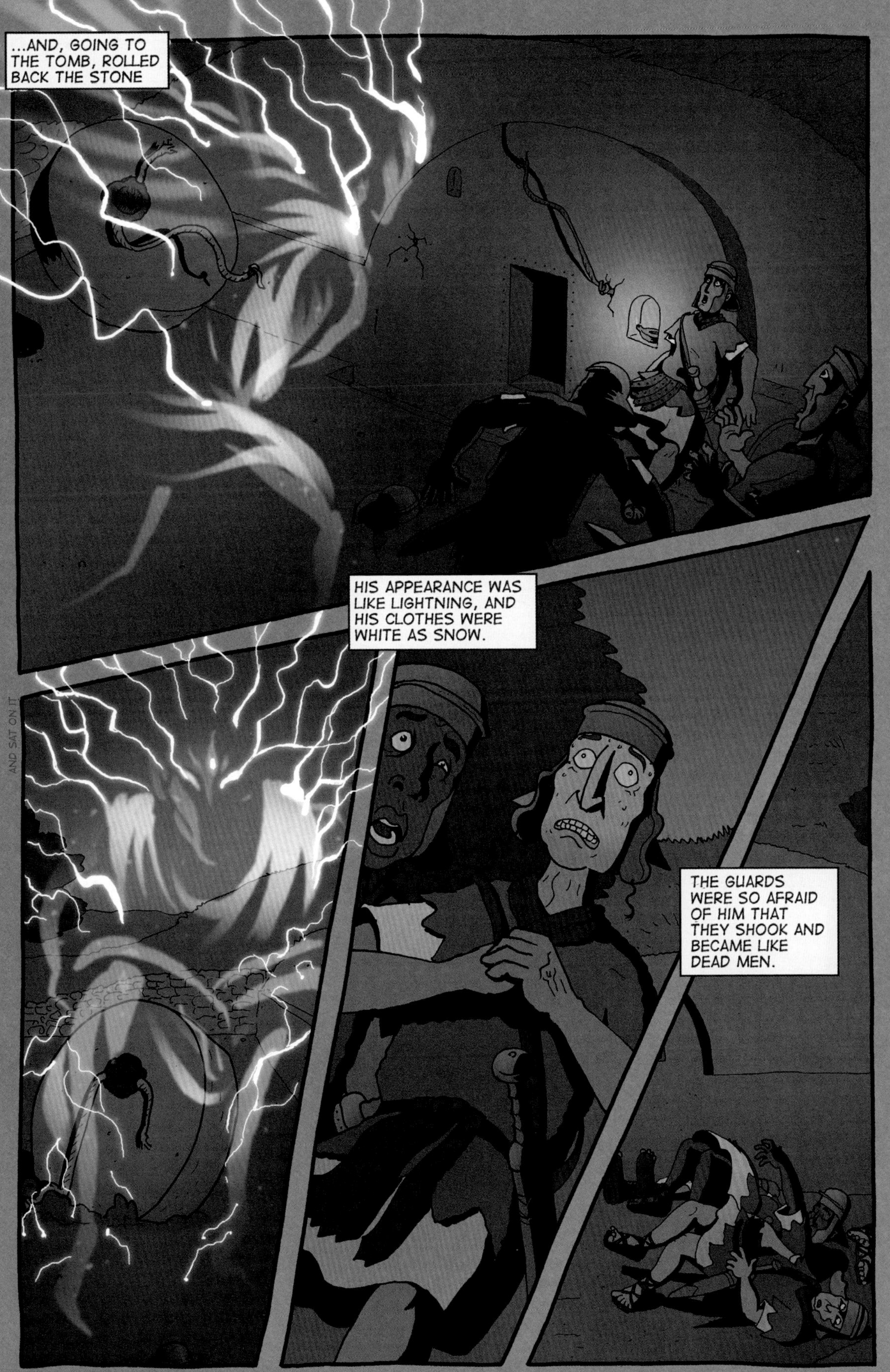
...AND, GOING TO THE TOMB, ROLLED BACK THE STONE
AND SAT ON IT
HIS APPEARANCE WAS LIKE LIGHTNING, AND HIS CLOTHES WERE WHITE AS SNOW.
THE GUARDS WERE SO AFRAID OF HIM THAT THEY SHOOK AND BECAME LIKE DEAD MEN.

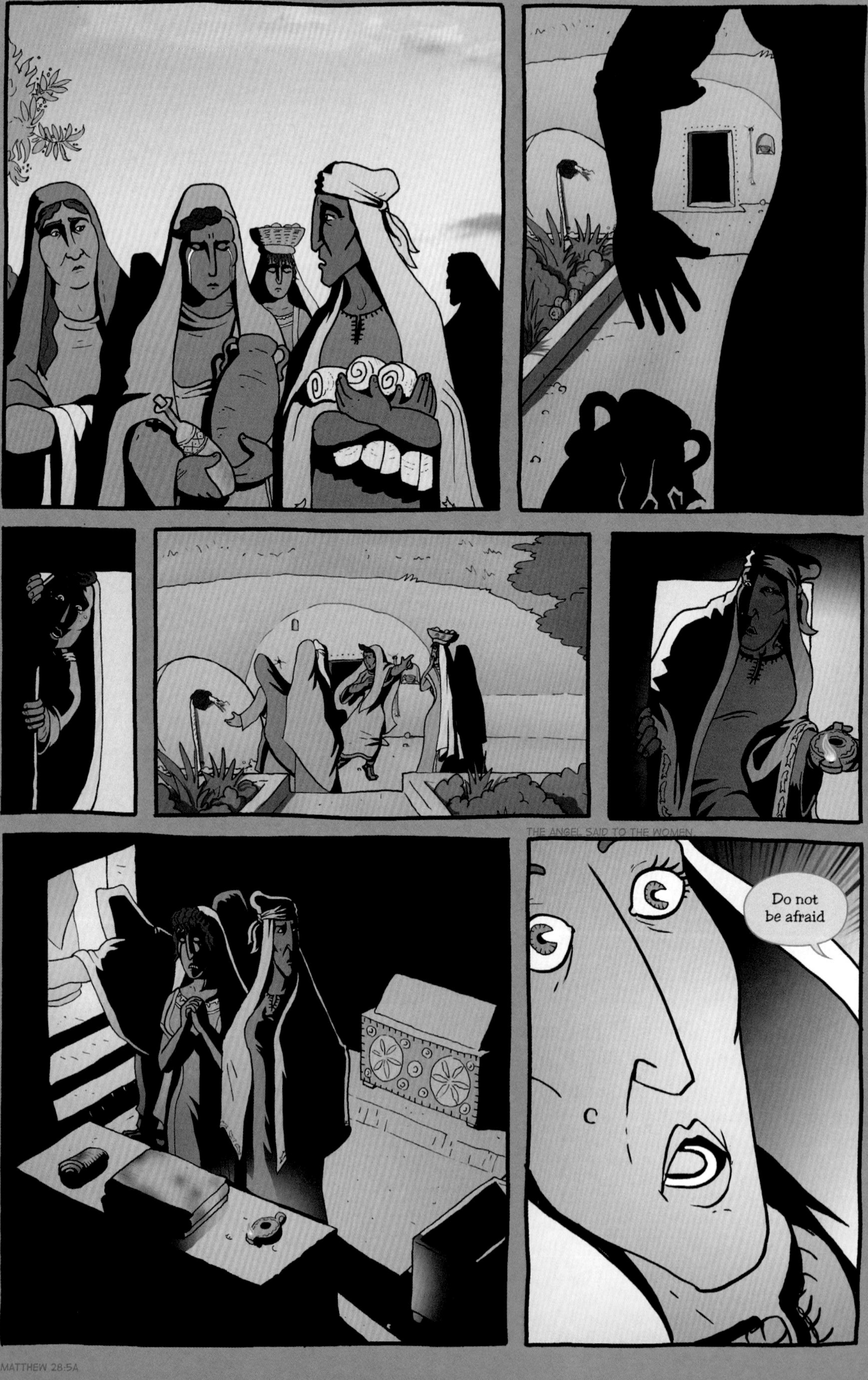
THE ANGEL SAID TO THE WOMEN
Do not be afraid

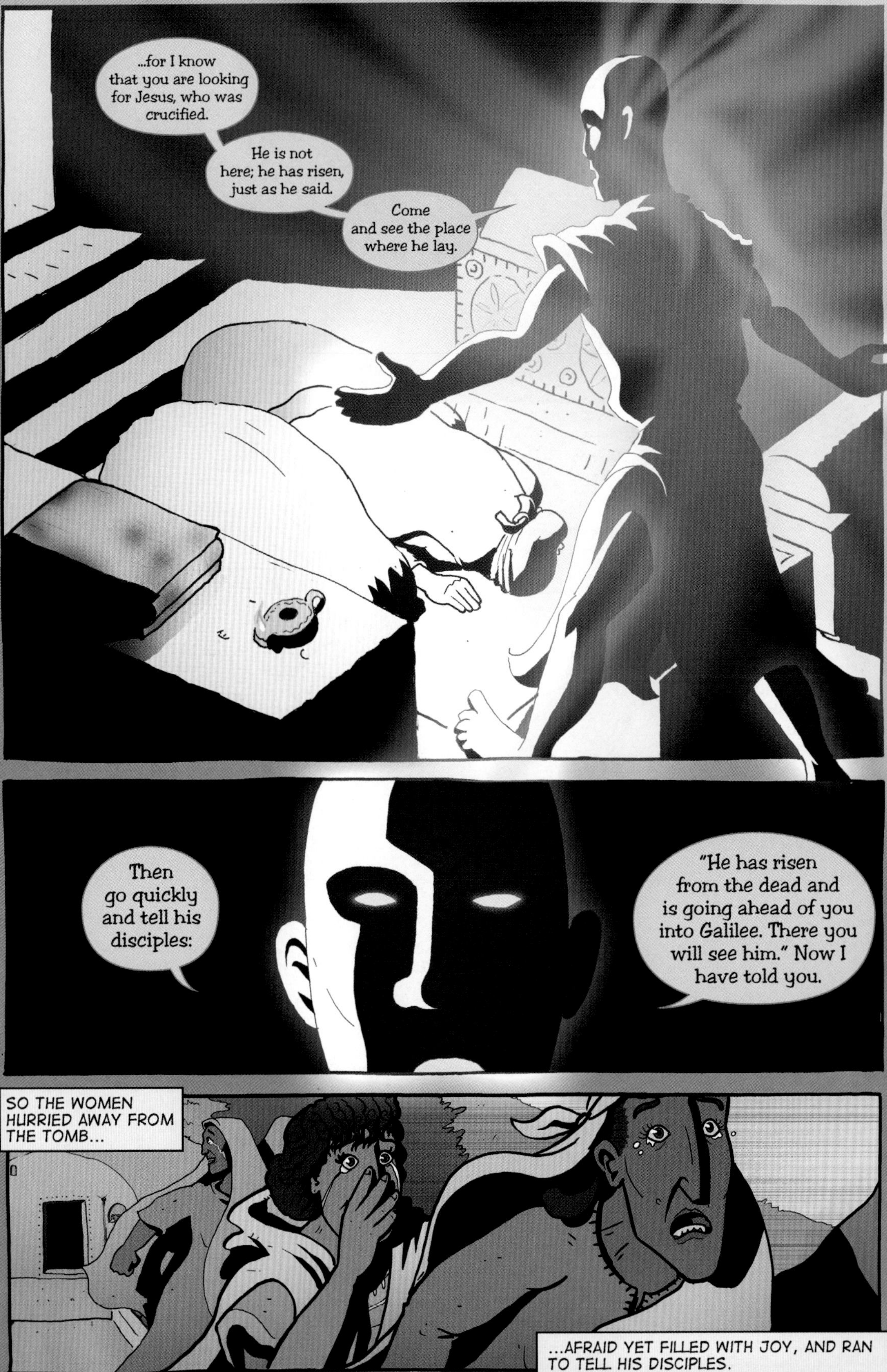
...for I know that you are looking for Jesus, who was crucified.
He is not here; he has risen, just as he said.
Come and see the place where he lay.
Then go quickly and tell his disciples:
"He has risen from the dead and is going ahead of you into Galilee. There you will see him." Now I have told you.
SO THE WOMEN HURRIED AWAY FROM THE TOMB...
...AFRAID YET FILLED WITH JOY, AND RAN TO TELL HIS DISCIPLES.

MATTHEW 28:5B–8

JESUS MET THEM.

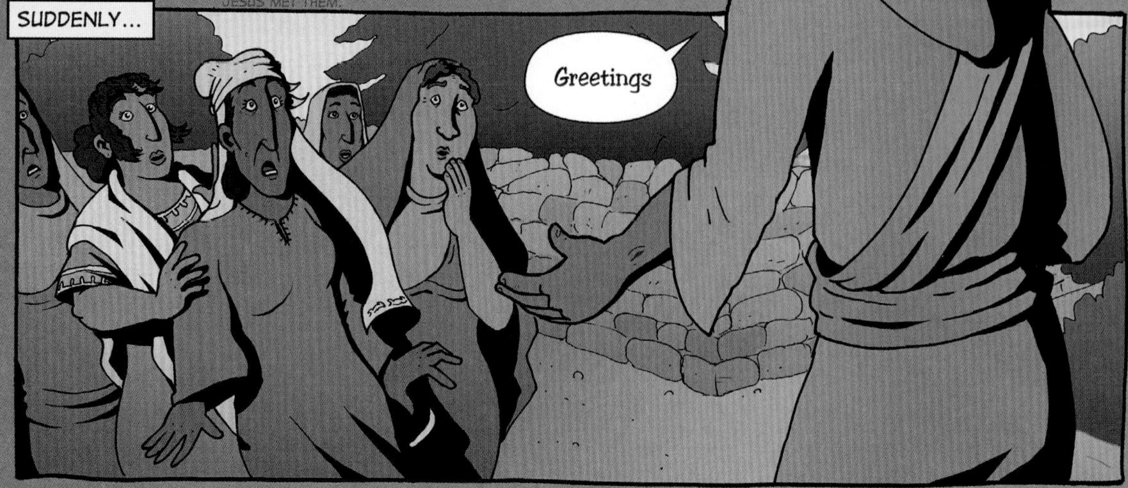
SUDDENLY...
Greetings

HE SAID. THEY CAME TO HIM, CLASPED HIS FEET AND WORSHIPED HIM. THEN JESUS SAID TO THEM,

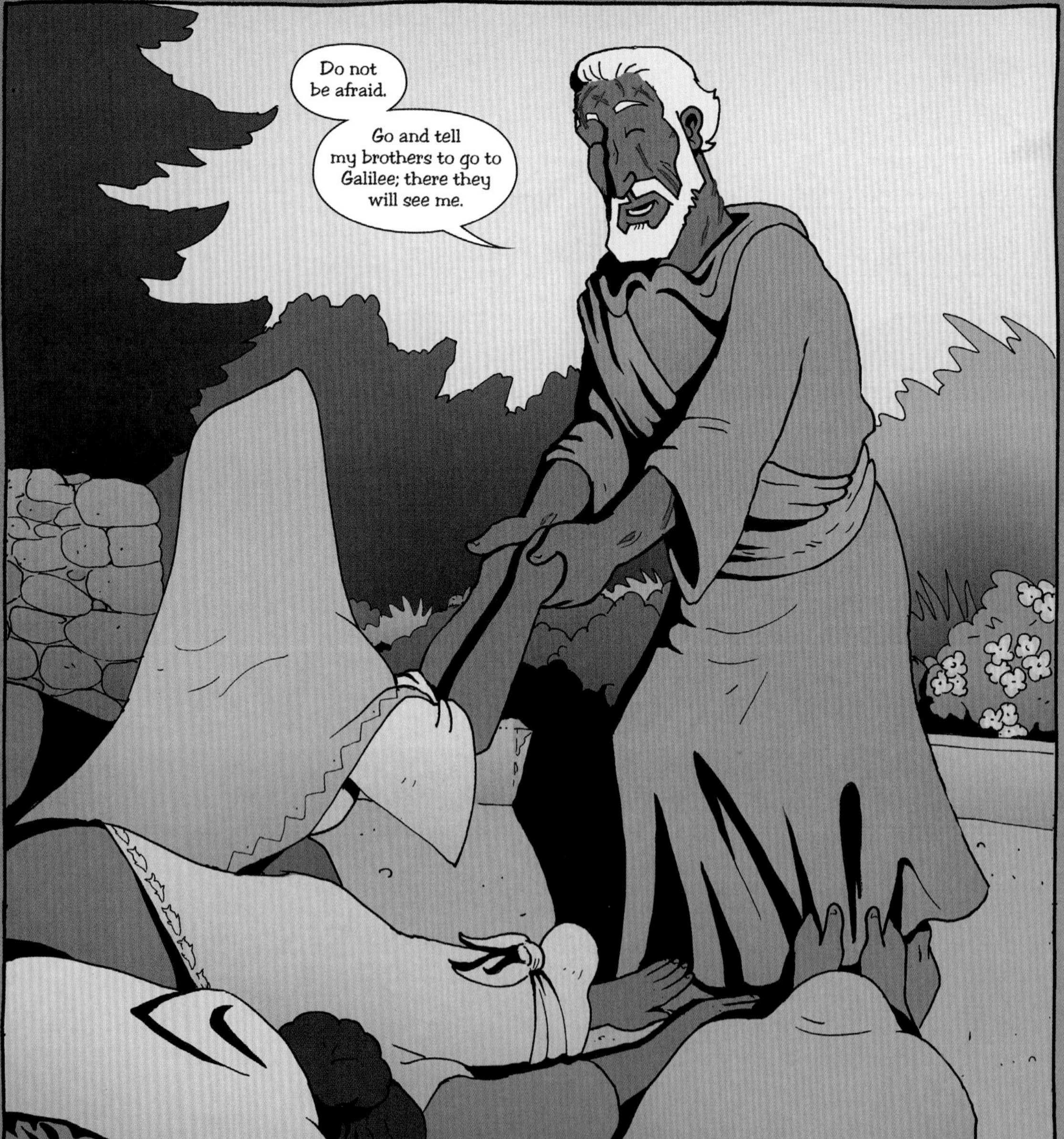
Do not be afraid.
Go and tell my brothers to go to Galilee; there they will see me.

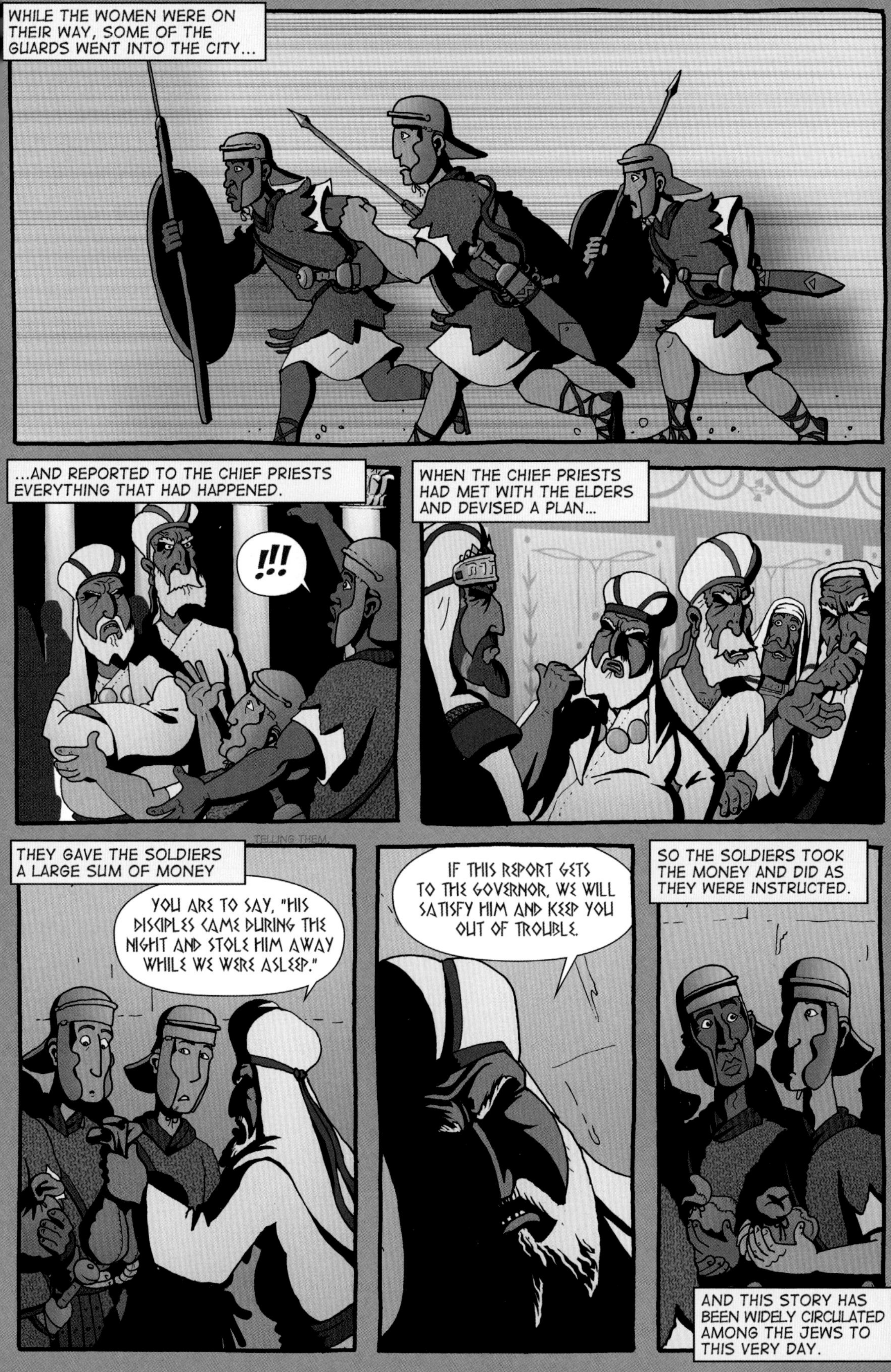
WHILE THE WOMEN WERE ON THEIR WAY, SOME OF THE GUARDS WENT INTO THE CITY...
...AND REPORTED TO THE CHIEF PRIESTS EVERYTHING THAT HAD HAPPENED.
!!!
WHEN THE CHIEF PRIESTS HAD MET WITH THE ELDERS AND DEVISED A PLAN...
TELLING THEM,
THEY GAVE THE SOLDIERS A LARGE SUM OF MONEY
YOU ARE TO SAY, "HIS DISCIPLES CAME DURING THE NIGHT AND STOLE HIM AWAY WHILE WE WERE ASLEEP."
IF THIS REPORT GETS TO THE GOVERNOR, WE WILL SATISFY HIM AND KEEP YOU OUT OF TROUBLE.
SO THE SOLDIERS TOOK THE MONEY AND DID AS THEY WERE INSTRUCTED.
AND THIS STORY HAS BEEN WIDELY CIRCULATED AMONG THE JEWS TO THIS VERY DAY.

WORD FOR WORD
BIBLE COMIC

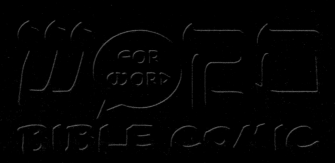

THEN THE ELEVEN DISCIPLES WENT TO GALILEE, TO THE MOUNTAIN WHERE JESUS HAD TOLD THEM TO GO.

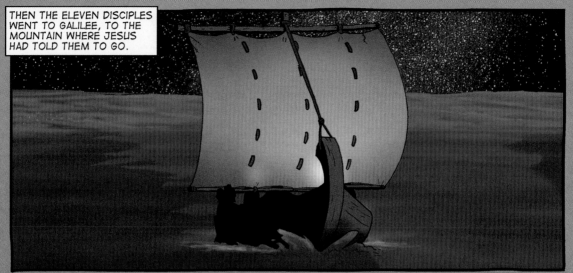

WHEN THEY SAW HIM, THEY WORSHIPED HIM; BUT SOME DOUBTED.

THEN JESUS CAME TO THEM AND SAID;

All authority in heaven and on earth has been given to me.

Therefore go and make disciples of all nations, baptizing them in the name of the Father and of the Son and of the Holy Spirit,

and teaching them to obey everything I have commanded you.

And surely I am with you always, to the very end of the age.

WHO WAS MATTHEW?

From the Gospels, we know that Matthew worked in Capernaum as a tax collector. It is possible that he grew up there. But since he was an employee of the Roman empire and Galilee was a cosmopolitan area (the Jews of the day called it "Galilee of the Gentiles"), it is also equally possible that he was stationed there by a central administration. He was a Jew, but it is not clear how old he was when he met Jesus.

Name

This man was known by two names. In the Gospels, he is called both "Matthew" and, in Mark and Luke, "Levi." Some believe that Levi may have been his original name and that Jesus renamed him Matthew, the way he gave Simon the new name Peter. *Matthew* is a shortening of the name Mattathias, which means "Gift of YHWH." *Levi* means "Joined In Harmony." In the illustration, I have depicted Matthew as a Levite in appearance and dress due to this connection, with the supposition that the name Levi may be more common among Levite families, or that the variation in names was a nickname due to his heritage.

In Mark's Gospel, this man is called Levi Son of Alphaeus. This is interesting. Since both Matthew and James the Lesser are called the "son of Alphaeus," this could indicate that they are brothers. Eastern Orthodox Church tradition supports this theory. However, nowhere in the Bible are the two explicitly called brothers, even in the lists of the twelve disciples where John and James, and Peter and Andrew, are described as brothers. In the comic, I have drawn Matthew and James the Lesser with a family resemblance, to hint at this possible connection.

Tax Collector

The most significant thing about Matthew is that he was a tax collector/customs official (Matt 9:9), also known as a publican (Matt 10:3). The system he worked under is sometimes referred to as "Tax Farming." Private individuals contracted with the government, in this case, the Roman "oppressors," for the right to collect taxes from a defined territory. The contractor had to remit a certain value, and he pocketed any money he collected beyond this (as seen with Zaccheus in Luke 19). Those who became rich in this way could bid for additional contracts and get even richer by adding to their portfolio. So you can see that corruption was built into the very fabric of the system. In addition, these tax collectors could call upon the Roman military to enforce their demands, so they were rarely refused. It was essentially an institutionalized protection racket.
[Continued on next the page]

One would imagine that even citizens of Rome would chafe under such an unscrupulous system in their own country. But the Jewish people were an occupied nation under oppressive foreign rule. Therefore, tax collectors like Matthew were considered not only venal and money-grubbing, but traitors to their own people and to God.

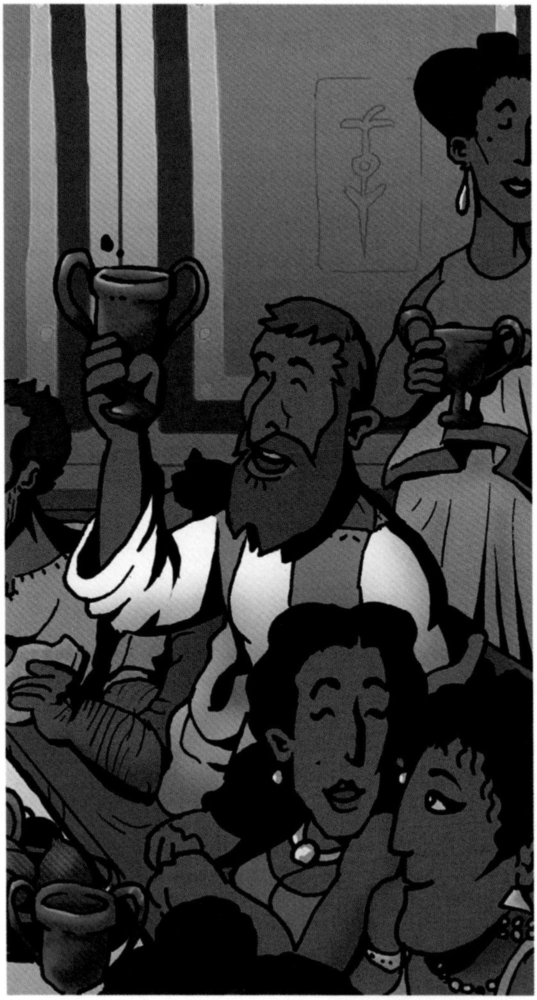

Matthew's story, therefore, displays one of the most radically changed lives in response to Jesus. When Jesus called him, he did not hesitate to follow. On a moment's notice, he walked away from his booth and left behind a lucrative profession for a life of hardship and financial uncertainty (Matt 9:9). He abandoned the pleasures of riches to become a disciple of Christ.

Ministry

Early Church Fathers such as Irenaeus (c. ad 130– 202) and Clement of Alexandria (c. ad 150-215) state that Matthew brought the good news about Jesus to the Jewish community in Judea before going to other countries, including Syria. It seems he was an apostle to the Jews, illuminating from the Old Testament Scriptures that Jesus was the fulfillment of God's promises about the Messiah. In his Gospel alone, he uses the word "fulfilled" 82 times! There is an interesting parallel when one considers this Ministry in light of God's appointment of Paul as the apostle to the Gentiles. On paper, Paul/Saul the Pharisee would seem like a good choice for a Jewish mission, but anathema to the Gentiles. In the same way, Matthew might seem a good choice to reach Romans and Greeks, but he would be reviled by the Jewish community. *"But God chose the foolish things of the world to shame the wise; God chose the weak things of the world to shame the strong. God chose the lowly things of this world and the despised things—and the things that are not—to nullify the things that are, so that no one may boast before him. ... Therefore, as it is written: 'Let the one who boasts boast in the Lord.'"* (1 Corinthians 1:27- 31)

Death

An uncertain legend says that Matthew died as a martyr. *The Roman Martyrology* of the Catholic Church suggests that Matthew was martyred in Asiatic "Ethiopia," south of the Caspian Sea.

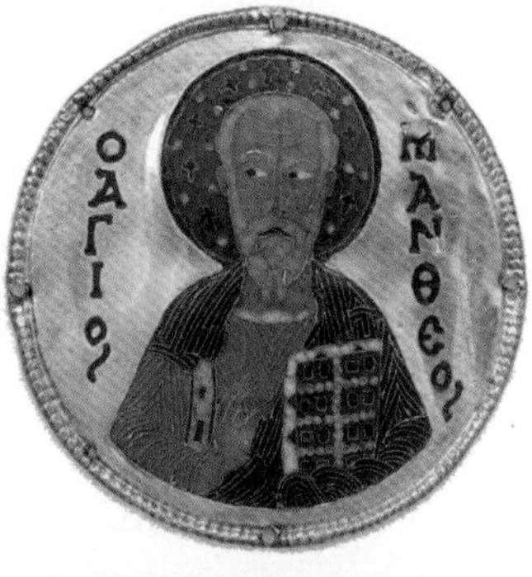

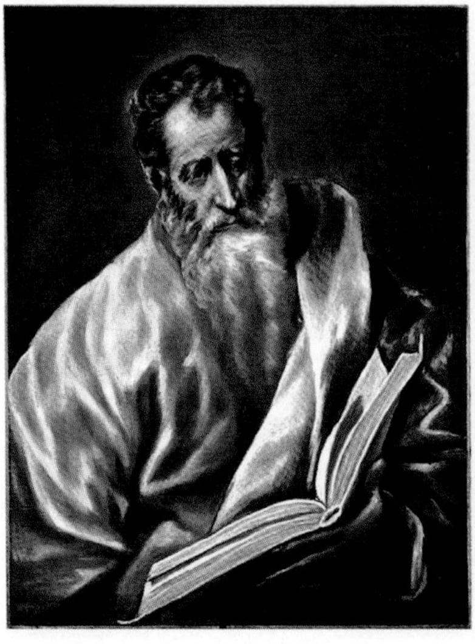

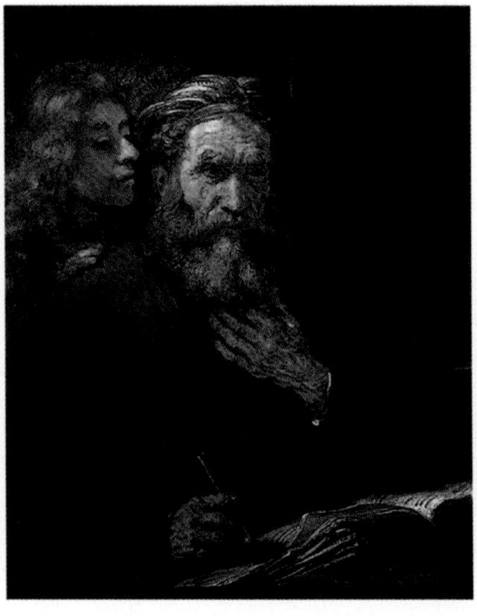

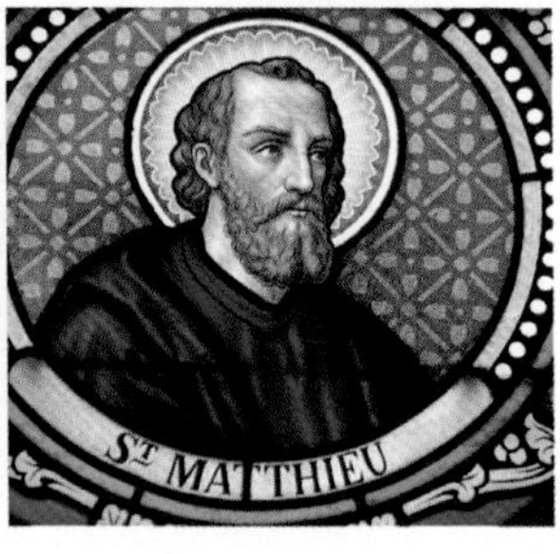
ST MATTHIEU

It's interesting how Matthew has been portrayed in a similar way throughout history. I didn't design his look with these images in mind, but perhaps the Holy Spirit is inspiring artists with his real appearance throughout the ages. (Images by El Greco, Rembrandt and two unknown artists).

WRITING JESUS' WORDS

Tachygrphos

One of the qualifications of many professionals in the Greco-Roman world was that of tachygraphy- the ability to write in shorthand. The word comes from the Greek, *tachys* (swift/speedy) and *graphos* (writing).

The use of the term oxygrphos (a synonym for tachygrphos) is used by the compliers of the Septuagint (e.g. Psalm 45:1 LXX) which indicates that the skill was already common three centuries before Christ.

As a tax collector, Matthew would have been required to have the skill of tachygraphy. As a result, he would have been able to transcribe the many words and sermons of Jesus verbatim, just as Tertius the scribe did for Paul the Apostle when he dictated his letters (Roman 16:22). That is why the Gospel of Matthew includes so many more longer discourses than the other Gospels. This gives us extra confidence in the reliability of the text.

Source: The Bible in Shorthand? The Hyperetai, Chuck Missler 2000
https://www.khouse.org/articles/2000/196/#notes

Wax Tablet

It might surprise you to learn that in the ancient world there was an ingenious way for people to take notes without using up expensive paper/papyrus and inks. This invention was the wax tablet.

Called a Deltos (δέλτος) in Greek or a Daleth in Hebrew, the way it worked was that the wooden tablet with a lip around the edge was filled with a thin layer of wax. The user would scratch the writing into the wax and it would remain there until they decided to reset their tablet) . They would do this by gentle warming up the whole tablet and the wax would melt and then set perfectly smooth again.

A stylus – a pointed shaft typically made from wood, bone, ivory, or metal - was used to inscribe the words and some even had a flat straight - edged spatula - like implement that could be used to flatten down the wax like an eraser.

These wax tablets were used in a variety of ways, from children learning to write to scribes taking down dictation in shorthand. They were also used to record business accounts including tax and customs figures as Matthew did.

The earliest example discovered is believed to date to the 14th Century BC and was recovered from a Phoenician shipwreck off the coast of Turkey. By the time of Christ, the use of such tablets was well established throughout the Roman Empire.

In this image Matthew writes the notes, "No bag, no bread, no money" Mark 6:8

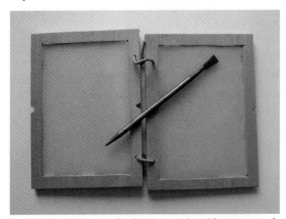

Attribution: "Tablet with wax and stylus Roman times" by Peter van der Sluijs licensed by (CC BY-SA 3.0) cropped and resized
https://commons.wikimedia.org/wiki/File:Table_with_was_and_stylus_Roman_times.jpg

Roman scribe with his stylus and tablets on his tomb stele at Flavia Solva in Noricum.

AUTHORSHIP OF THE GOSPEL

Was the Gospel of Matthew written by Matthew the Disciple?

As with the other synoptic gospels (Mark, Luke, and John), the Gospel of Matthew includes no claim of authorship or author's biography so how do we know who actually wrote it? Although the text itself makes no comment on the writer's identity, the early "Church Fathers" Papias (c. 60- 130 AD), Irenaeus's (c. 130-202 AD), Origen (c. 184- 253 AD), and Pantaenus (c. 180 AD) all accepted Matthew the disciple as its author. Their universal acceptance of Matthean authorship is thus a compelling case for accepting that the gospel was from the hand of Jesus' disciple. Significantly, despite the ancient and medieval manuscripts recording a wide variety of titles for the Gospel (for example, "According to Matthew", "Gospel According to Matthew", "Holy Gospel According to Matthew" or even "Divine Beginning of the Gospel According to Matthew") the identification of Matthew as the author is found on every New Testament fragment or manuscript that includes a title. Strikingly, this uniformity of opinion is not restricted to just one region of the Roman Empire but is actually found throughout, including North Africa, Egypt, and Asia Minor.

Another compelling reason to accept that the Gospel of Matthew was actually written by Matthew the disciple, is the numerous references to money or tax-collecting. For instance, gold and silver are recorded 28 times in the Gospel of Matthew whereas they are only mentioned once in Mark and four-times in Luke. The author of Matthew also uses very precise, and at times very technical, money-related terms. So, for example in chapter 17 verse 24 he talks about the two-drachma temple tax whilst in the following verse he uses the Greek word "stater" when describing the "four-drachma coin" that Jesus tells Peter he will find in the mouth of a fish. The author's interest in financial issues is also reflected in his choice of subject matter and in the way that he frames his narrative. For instance, the parable of the talents is only found in Matthew (25:14–30) whilst in the Lord's Prayer Matthew records "And forgive us our debts, as we have forgiven our debtors (Matthew 6:12), whereas Luke says " Forgive us our sins, for we also forgive everyone who sins against us" (Luke 11.4). This overt and obvious interest in financial matters, something that we would expect from an ex-tax collector, is therefore another indication that the disciple Matthew was the author of the gospel that bears his name.

When was it written?

As none of the original manuscripts have survived, it has been incredibly difficult for scholars to date when the synoptic gospels were initially composed. The Gospel of Matthew itself has been ascribed a range of dates spanning the first century AD with the earliest being 37 AD and the latest 100 AD. Despite this divergence of opinion, however, there is plenty of reason to believe that the Gospel of Matthew was composed in the author's own lifetime, most likely sometime during the late 50s or early 60s AD. Perhaps the most persuasive reason for accepting a date in the mid-first century is the fact that the gospel makes no mention of the execution of Jesus' brother James (62 AD), Nero's persecution of the early church (64 AD and following), or the cataclysmic Jewish revolt against Rome (66-70 AD) which culminated with the destruction of Jerusalem (Chuck Missler, The Gospel of Matthew: A Most Provocative Study, 2010). The monumental impact and significance of these events mean that Matthew would almost certainly have mentioned them had they occurred prior to the composition of his gospel.

BECOME A PATRON!

WHAT LANGUAGE WAS THE GOSPEL WRITTEN IN?

As strange as it may seem to us today, modern scholars believe that the Gospel of Matthew was written in Greek, rather than in Hebrew/Aramaic, as might be expected. However, this may not be as surprising as we first think. By the time that Matthew was writing (mid-first century ad), the vast majority of Christians were Greek-speaking, not Aramaic-speaking. Moreover, the majority of the literate population in Israel were better at reading Greek than they were at reading Hebrew. This was a situation that greatly concerned the religious and political leaders, and which had already led to the creation of the Septuagint a few hundred years earlier. (The Septuagint is a translation of the Old Testament into Greek.)

The widespread use of Greek, in both everyday writing and in public records and inscriptions, indicate, that by the time of Jesus, Greek had replaced Aramaic/Hebrew as the dominant form of writing in Israel. By composing his gospel in Greek, therefore, Matthew ensured that it would reach the widest number of people. Moreover, since Greek functioned as a *lingua franca* in many regions of the ancient Mediterranean world, Matthew's decision to write in Greek meant that his text could be used as an evangelistic tool for missionaries venturing beyond the borders of Israel. That Matthew had this use in mind when composing his gospel is perhaps indicated by his decision to write in *Koine*, a much less formal and far more accessible form of Greek than its classical counterpart.

However, the early church historian Eusebius of Caesarea (c. 260–340 AD), writes that "Matthew collected the oracles (*logia*: sayings of or about Jesus) in the Hebrew language/fashion and each one interpreted/translated them as best he could" (*History of the Church* 3.39.14–17).

Eusebius also tells us that the writings of Matthew existed in a Hebrew form in the early years of the church.

He writes that Pantaenus (c. 180 AD), "a man highly distinguished for his learning, [who] had charge of the school of the faithful in Alexandria," came across some examples. The following is Eusebius's report of Pantaenus's discovery: "It is reported that among persons there who knew of Christ, he found the Gospel according to Matthew, which had anticipated his own arrival. For Bartholomew (one of the apostles) had preached to them, and left with them the writing of Matthew in the Hebrew language, which they had preserved till that time" (*History of the Church*).

Lastly, Irenaeus (c. 180 AD) states, "Matthew also issued a written Gospel among the Hebrews in their own dialect" (*Against Heresies*, Book III, Chapter 1).

I believe Matthew's own transcriptions of Jesus' sermons were written shorthand in Aramaic, as it is not very logical to translate the language of the one speaking when one is trying to take down dictation in shorthand. Therefore, these quotes and sermons would likely have been written out in Aramaic or Hebrew first.

When it comes to compiling the whole story together we can see, even in English, that Matthew's gospel is essentially a revision and expansion of the brief and earlier Gospel of Peter's amanuensis, Mark. Mark's gospel is known to have been written directly in Greek, as it was intended for Gentiles, so these elements likely came to Matthew in that way.

Therefore, to me it does not seem unreasonable that Matthew could have compiled two versions of his Gospel from the outset, one in Koine and the other in Hebrew/Aramaic, especially when we consider that he could speak Aramaic, Hebrew and Greek and that it seems he had half of the story in one language and half of it in another as his starting points.

Right: Image of an early Koine manuscript of Matthew's Gospel called the Magdalen Papyrus (c.200 AD)

WHO WERE THE MAGI?

The prevailing understanding of who the Magi are is that they were a social caste of men learned in "magic," astrology, alchemy, medicine, dream interpretation and many related disciplines. Their caste seems to have arisen during the time of the growing affluence of the early empires of the Medes and Persians. When a nation or empire becomes rich, it has the resources to support people exploring art, science, and many other forms of academia. With time to study and understand the world, these learned and "wise" men were relied upon by kings and satraps as advisors and diviners. In this way, they gained political power and with this political power, they consolidated their position as sacerdotal mediators between men and the magical and divine.

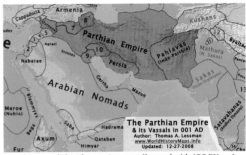

There is a connection to the between Magi and the Zoroastrian religion. It is believed that they fulfilled a multitude of roles including that of priests. However, the presence of Magi is not limited to Zoroastrian nations. Robert Charles Zaehner writes in The Dawn and Twilight of Zoroastrianism, "We hear of Magi not only in Persia, Parthia, Bactria, Chorasmia, Aria, Media, and among the Sakas, but also in non-Iranian lands like Samaria, Ethiopia, and Egypt. Their influence was also widespread throughout Asia Minor."

Armenia
Cappadocia
Kushans
Parthian Empire
Pahlavas
(Indo-Parthia)
Mathura
(N. Sakas)
Agraci
Scinites
Nabatae
Persia
Sakas
Arabian Nomads
Gerrha
Mazun
Meroe
(Nubia)
Blemmyes
Saba
Bega
Axum
Hadrama
Qataban
Himyar
Fur
Satavahanas
The Parthian Empire
& its Vassals in 001 AD
Author: Thomas A. Lessman
www.WorldHistoryMaps.info
Updated: 12-27-2008
"Parthia 001ad" by Thomas Lessman licenced with (CC BY 3.0) Resized, cropped https://commons.wikimedia.org/wiki/File:Parthia_001ad.jpg)

Why would a Magi care about a king of the Jews?

The key to this mystery is found in the Book of Daniel. Daniel interpreted the undisclosed dream of King Nebuchadnezzar (Daniel 2:48) and was given the title Rab-mag, the Chief of the Magi. (Daniel 4:9; 5:11).

During the first year of the reign of King Ahasuerus, the angel Gabriel (yes, that angel Gabriel) visited Daniel and told him when the Anointed One would come (Daniel 9:25-26). For nearly 500 years, this sect of Magi held onto this prophecy and its implied connection with Jerusalem. Waiting for this time, and apparently cued by the appearance of the star, they came to find this promised Messiah.

Finally, considering all that happened with Daniel in Babylon and then Esther as queen and Mordecai as prime minister of Persia it's entirely possible that a number of Magi positions were held by Jews. As Christopher R. Smith writes in his blog *Good Question*, "Not all of the Jews who were taken into exile by the Babylonians returned under the Persians. For many centuries afterwards, there was a flourishing Jewish community in Mesopotamia. For example, that's where the so-called Babylonian Talmud originated in Late Antiquity (though the term 'Babylon' was archaic by then)."

From Dura-Europos, individual in Parthian dress—trousers topped by a tunic—and a 'Phrygian' cap. (c.210 AD)

What did the Magi look like?

At the time of Jesus birth, much of the lands east of Jerusalem, as far as the borders of China, were under the dominion of the Parthian Empire. The earliest surviving images of the Magi date to the 2nd-3rd Century, which is 100 or so years later than Jesus' birth, but I was fascinated to discover that their attire was very much consistent with the dress of contemporaneous Parthians. This convinces me that these images were handed down from people who knew their appearance and origin.

Looking at the length of the journey the Magi would have had to make, and considering their social status, I thought it was more likely that they would have used horses rather than ride on camels. However, they also have camels in the caravan as pack animals. White horses were apparently considered sacred and were used to pull the chariots that conveyed priests. Therefore, I used white horses here to suggest the high status, wealth, and priestly caste of the Magi.

Panel from a Roman Sarcophagus, 4th Century AD. From Musée Lapidaire d'Art Chrétien, Arles, France (Attribution: "Sarcophagus relief: Holy Family with the Adoration of the Magi (EC048)" by Allan T. Kohl licenced with (CC BY 2.0) Resized https://www.flickr.com/photos/69184488@N06/11965834363)

FOCUS ON JOSEPH

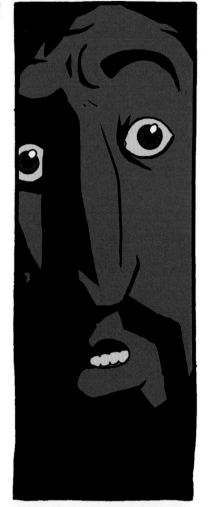

In Matthew's Gospel, the nativity story focuses on Joseph and his experience of Jesus' conception, birth and naming. This is in contrast to the way Luke focuses on Mary's side of things.

Genealogy

The genealogy that Matthew presents shows us that Joseph was a direct descendant of King David. His bloodline goes through Solomon and all the kings until Jeconiah. Joseph is the legal father of Jesus, according to Jewish Law, and this makes Jesus a legal heir to the throne of David. Joseph is not Jesus' father by blood, however, but that is a good thing, because in Jeremiah 22:30, God curses the bloodline of Jeconiah. He says, "None of his offspring will prosper, none will sit on the throne of David or rule anymore in Judah." In Luke's gospel, we get a different genealogy. It is believed to be that of Mary. From King David, it takes a different route that does not follow the line of kings but goes through descendants another of David's sons, Nathan. As a result, Mary's genealogy sidesteps the curse of Jeconiah but retains the direct bloodline to David. Therefore, Jesus' virgin birth and legal adoption by Joseph means he is the heir to David's throne both legally and by blood, but crucially he avoids the curse of Jeconiah. (For a more extensive explanation if this, go to https://www.khouse.org/articles/1998/73/)

Divorce

In ancient Israel, an official engagement to marry was as binding an arrangement as it was after the wedding ceremony was complete. This is why Joseph considers "divorcing" Mary, despite the fact they are only engaged and the union is not consummated (Deuteronomy 24:1). The only earthly explanation for his betrothed being pregnant was adultery. We learn a lot about Joseph's character from these few verses. We learn that he is righteous, since he decided he must divorce Mary to show that he does not condone her infidelity. Not doing so would bring her shame upon him. Under the Law of the Torah, Joseph had the right to have Mary stoned. However, under Roman rule, capital punishment could only be sanctioned with Roman approval. According to the Mishnah, the normal procedure would be to publically accuse her in the local village and have her tried before the Great Sanhedrin in Jerusalem (Sotah 1:4). If she were found guilty, a priest would expose her before the crowds at Nikanor Gate in the Temple. The priest would tear her dress, revealing her bosom, unbraid and expose her hair, and bind a rough rope over her breasts (Sotah 1:5-6). The society was built on a culture of shame, so a woman thus disgraced would become a social pariah and never be able to marry again. In Mary's case, she would be raising a child as an outcast.

But Matthew tells us that even before his encounter with the angel, Joseph wished to divorce Mary "quietly" in order to protect her from this pubic shaming. Also, by foregoing a public trial, Joseph also forfeited the right to be reimbursed the bride price that he would have given Mary's father at their betrothal. This shows us that he was compassionate and forgiving, and I believe it implies that he truly loved Mary.

In the comic, when Mary gives Joseph the news about the pregnancy, you can see her father there as a chaperone. I do not believe they would have been able to be alone in private before their wedding.

Profession

In the gospels, Joseph is described as a *tektōn* (τέκτων). While carpenter is a good translation for one type of tekton, the Greek term can actually refer to an artisan of wood, iron or stone. In English, the word is preserved in the word architect (arch-tektōn). However, the association with carpentry is a constant in Early Christian tradition. Justin Martyr (c. ad 100-165), for example, suggested that Jesus made yokes and plows (Fiensy, 68–69).

From the gospel narrative, we learn that Joseph's family hailed from Bethlehem, but that he was living in or around Nazareth (Mary's home town). As a result, many scholars have speculated that he may have been working as a builder and carpenter in the nearby city of Sepphoris, which was being rebuilt at the time of Jesus' birth and thereafter. In the comic I draw him with an adze, a classic wood-crafting tool.

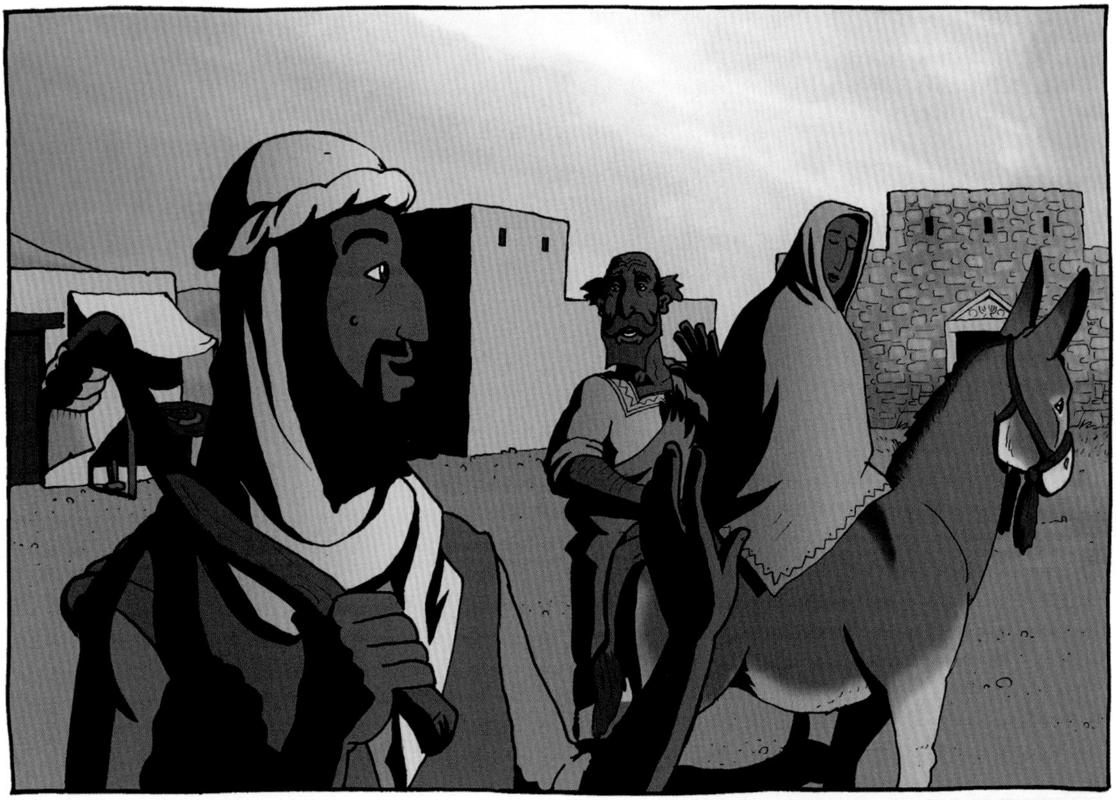

Other Children

From the Scriptures, we learn that Jesus had several siblings (Matthew 13:55-56). Some traditions, for example, the Catholic doctrine of the Perpetual Virginity of Mary, assert that Joseph and Mary never had sexual relations and therefore these were children from an unmentioned first wife of Joseph who had died. A more straightforward understanding, however, is that Jesus was the eldest child, with these several other children subsequently being born to Joseph and Mary.

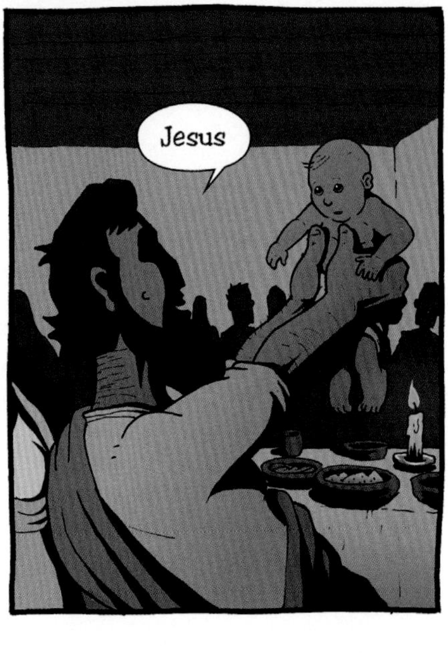
Jesus

Death

We know little about what happened to Joseph or how he died, but from the Gospels, we can see that he was alive when Jesus was twelve and was lost in Jerusalem (Luke 2:41-52.) By the time Jesus' ministry began, however, it seems that Joseph had passed away. It is implied at Jesus' first public miracle at the wedding in Cana that he was absent, as it was Mary who turned to Jesus for help. Also in Matthew 12:46-47 it was Mary who came to Capernaum to speak to Jesus as tensions began to rise, and at the cross Jesus asked the disciple John to look after Mary. As a result, we can see that as the eldest son, Jesus may have been the head of the household for many years before he left the family to travel as an itinerant rabbi.

KING HEROD I

Herod took the throne in 43 BC with the blessing of Rome after his predecessor died. "This appointment caused a lot of resentment among the Jews. After all, Herod was not a Jew. He was the son of a man from Idumea; and although Antipater (his father) had been a pious man who had worshipped the Jewish God sincerely, the Jews had always looked down upon the Idumeans as racially impure. Worse, Herod had an Arab mother, and it was commonly held that one could only be a Jew when one was born from a Jewish mother. When war broke out between the Romans and the Parthians (in Iran and Mesopotamia), the Jewish populace joined the latter." [1]

Herod always considered himself "a friend of Rome." After fleeing the Parthian invasion of 40 BC, he was restored to his throne by Octavian after Mark Anthony and the Roman forces drove the Parthians out of Judea.

Later Herod navigated his way through political acumen out of being on the wrong side of a civil war between Mark Anthony and Octavian. He was dubbed "the Great" for his many building works and long reign.

"He continued his building policy to win the hearts of his subjects. ... In Jerusalem, the king built a new market, an amphitheater, a theater, a new building where the Sanhedrin could convene, a new royal palace, and last but not least, in 20 BCE he started to rebuild the Temple." [1] He built several palaces and fortresses, including Masada on top of a 1,300-foot-high mesa-like plateau. One of Herod's greatest achievements was a massive port that he built in honor of the emperor and called Caesarea.

Coin of King Herod I reign. Featuring a helmet with long cheek pieces, surmounted by a star.

Obverse inscription "ΗΡΩΔΟΥ ΒΑΣΙΛΕΟΣ" (Of King Herod)

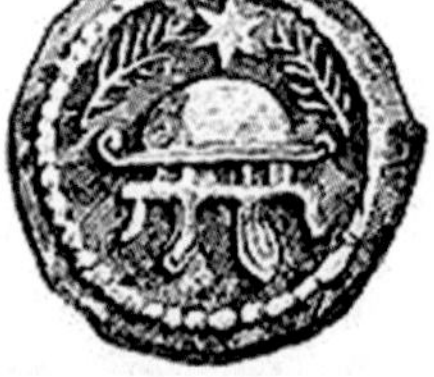

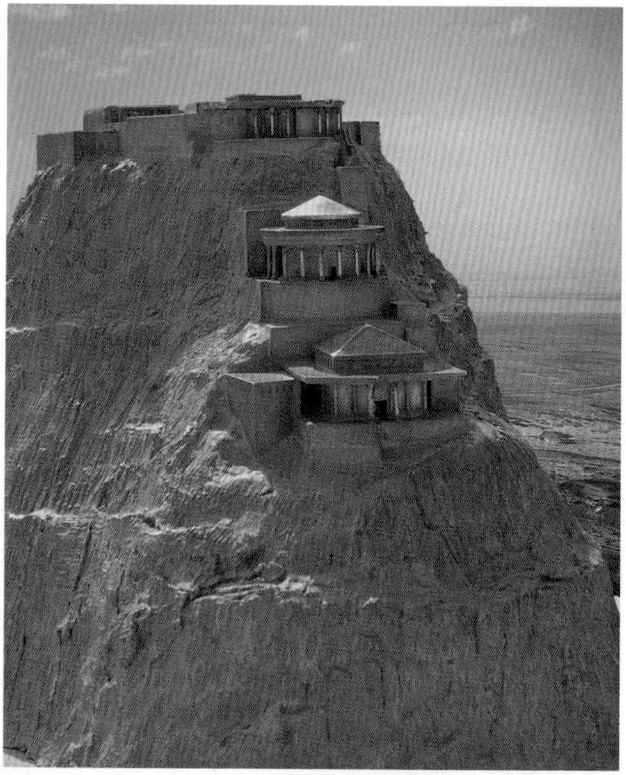

Masada: Model of the northern palace

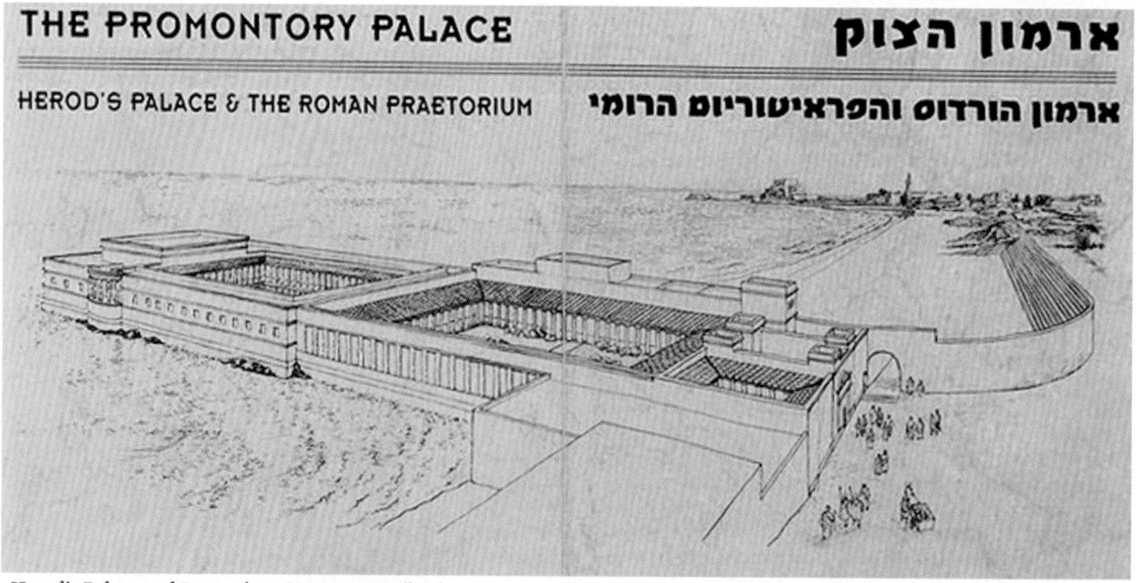
THE PROMONTORY PALACE
ארמון הצוק
HEROD'S PALACE & THE ROMAN PRAETORIUM
ארמון הורדוס והפראיטוריום הרומי

Herod's Palace and Praetorium Caesarea. Attribution: "Caesarea Maritima (3457257684)" by Random Exposure licenced with (CC BY 2.0) Transformed and cropped. https://commons.wikimedia.org/wiki/File:Caesarea_Maritima_(3457257684).jpg

“However, many of his projects won him the bitter hatred of the orthodox Jews, who disliked Herod's Greek taste—a taste he showed not only in his building projects, but also in several transgressions of the Mosaic Law.

“The orthodox were not to only ones who came to hate the new king. The Sadducees hated him because he had terminated the rule of the old royal house to which many of them were related; their own influence in the Sanhedrin was curtailed. The Pharisees despised any ruler who despised the Law. And probably all his subjects resented his excessive taxation. ... It comes as no surprise that Herod sometimes had to revert to violence, employing mercenaries and secret police to enforce order.” [2]

Herod's tenure ended in a reign of terror. In the last few years of his life, the king became ill with what is believed to be a cancer-like affliction called Fournier's gangrene. Whether it was the necrosis of his body or his impending death that caused it, Herod seems to have become paranoid and dangerously insane at this time.

For example, he burnt rebellious Jewish teachers and their pupils alive for removing a golden eagle from the entrance of the Temple. He arranged for a large number of people to be executed or assassinated including two of his wives, three of his sons, and his mother-in-law when he suspected them too of conspiracy. According to the Macrobius, Emperor Augustus quipped, “It is better to be Herod’s pig than a son” (Saturnalia 2:4:11 c.431 AD)

“As a final act of vengeance against his contemptuous subjects, he rounded up leading Jews and commanded that at his death they should be executed. His reasoning was that if there was no mourning for his death, at least there would be mourning at his death! (At Herod’s death, the order was overruled and the prisoners were released.)” [3]

Bearing in mind this unbridled psychosis and Herod's lineage, we can begin to understand a lot more about his encounter with the Parthian Magi. "It would seem as if these Magi were attempting to perpetrate a border incident which could bring swift reprisal from Parthian armies. Their request of Herod regarding the one who ‘has been born King of the Jews’ (Matt 2:2) was a calculated insult to him, a non-Jew who had contrived and bribed his way into that office.” [2]. This helps to contextualize the slaughter of the innocents (Matt 2:2) and explain why the Magi took a different way when they returned to the East.

[1] https://www.livius.org/articles/person/herod-the-great/
[2] Who were the Magi https://www.khouse.org/articles/1999/142/
[3] https://www.biblegateway.com/blog/2017/12/who-was-herod/

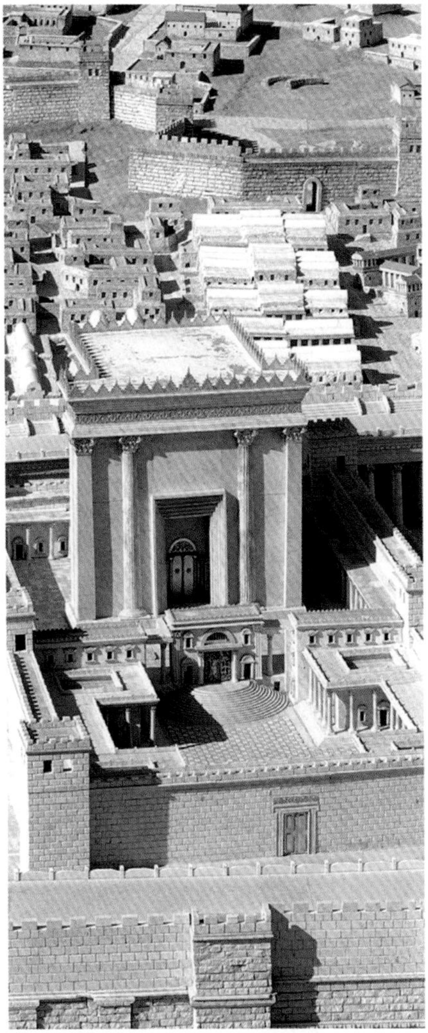

Model of Jerusalem and Herod's Temple, Israel Museum

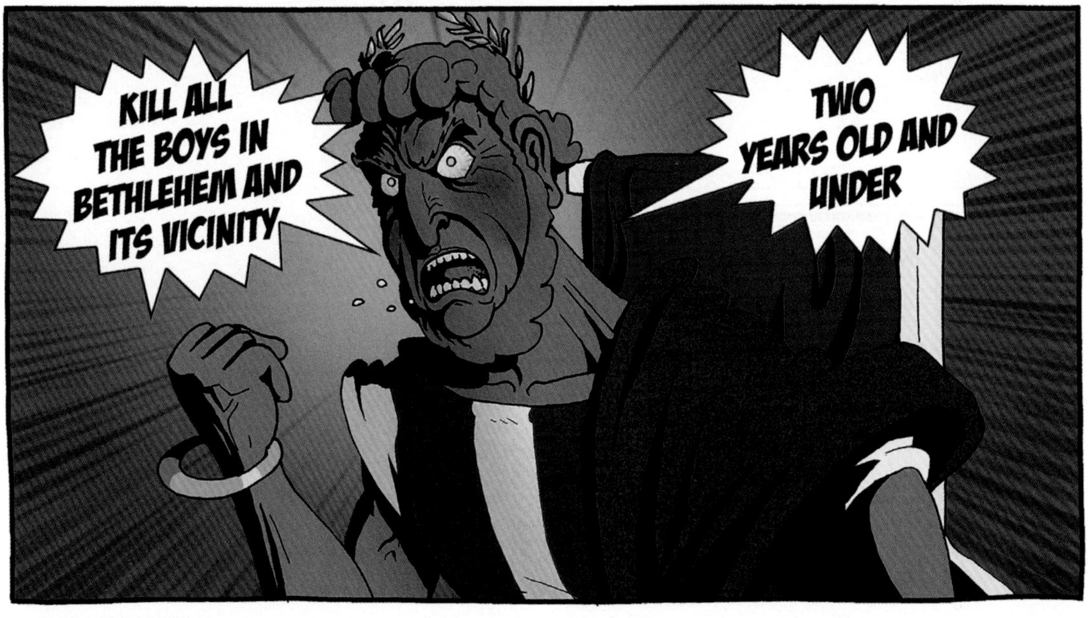
KILL ALL THE BOYS IN BETHLEHEM AND ITS VICINITY
TWO YEARS OLD AND UNDER

THE TEMPLE

I spent a great deal of time researching the Temple. After finding its descriptions and dimensions in the writings of Josephus, the Mishnah and other sources, I discovered the most reliable models of the temple had been created by Leen Ritmeyer.

I was excited to discover the images of the Temple on coins and when I cross referenced them with the images of the Temple from Dura Europus I found they were very similar. As these items were from within about a few decades of the Temple's destruction it seems likely that there were other images around and people who may have seen it themselves.

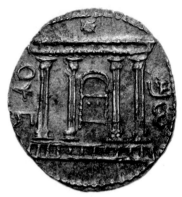

Bar Kochba Revolt Coin 132-135 AD (Right)
(Attribution: CNG Coins, Creative Commons 3.0)

Court of the Gentiles
Chamber of Hewn Stone
Altar and Laver down here
Chamber of Oils
Chamber of Nazerites
Gate of Nicanor
Court of Israelites
Chamber of Lepers
Court of Women
Chamber of Wood
Beautiful Gate
The Soreg (Wall)

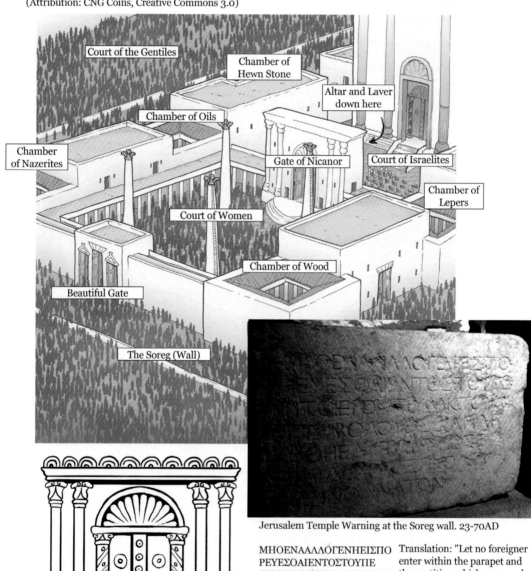

Jerusalem Temple Warning at the Soreg wall. 23-70AD

ΜΗΘΕΝΑΑΛΛΟΓΕΝΗΕΙΣΠΟ
ΡΕΥΕΣΘΑΙΕΝΤΟΣΤΟΥΠΕ
ΡΙΤΟΙΕΡΟΝΤΡΥΦΑΚΤΟΥΚΑΙ
ΠΕΡΙΒΟΛΟΥΟΣΔΑΝΛΗ
ΦΘΗΕΑΥΤΩΙΑΙΤΙΟΣΕΣ
ΤΑΙΔΙΑΤΟΕΞΑΚΟΛΟΥ
ΘΕΙΝΘΑΝΑΤΟΝ

Translation: "Let no foreigner enter within the parapet and the partition which surrounds the Temple precincts. Anyone caught [violating] will be held accountable for his ensuing death."

Trace from an image found at Dura-Europos of the Temple (c. 144)

WHAT IS THE GOSPEL?

The word gospel literally means "good news" and occurs 93 times in the Bible, exclusively in the New Testament. In Greek, it is the word euaggelion, from which we get our English words evangelist, evangel, and evangelical. The gospel is, broadly speaking, the whole of Scripture; more narrowly, the gospel is the good news concerning Christ and the way of salvation.

The key to understanding the gospel is to know why it is good news. To do that, we must start with the bad news. The Old Testament Law was given to Israel during the time of Moses (Deuteronomy 5:1). The Law can be thought of as a measuring stick, and sin is anything that falls short of "perfect" according to that standard. The righteous requirement of the Law is so stringent that no human being could possibly follow it perfectly, in letter or in spirit. Despite our "goodness" or "badness" relative to each other, we are all in the same spiritual boat—we have sinned, and the punishment for sin is death, i.e. separation from God, the source of life (Romans 3:23). In order for us to go to heaven, God's dwelling place and the realm of life and light, sin must be somehow removed or paid for. The Law established the fact that cleansing from sin can only happen through the bloody sacrifice of an innocent life (Hebrews 9:22).

The gospel involves Jesus' death on the cross as the sin offering to fulfill the Law's righteous requirement (Romans 8:3–4; Hebrews 10:5–10). Under the Law, animal sacrifices were offered year after year as a reminder of sin and a symbol of the coming sacrifice of Christ (Hebrews 10:3–4). When Christ offered Himself at Calvary, that symbol became a reality for all who would believe (Hebrews 10:11–18). The work of atonement is finished now, and that's good news.

The gospel also involves Jesus' resurrection on the third day. "He was delivered over to death for our sins and was raised to life for our justification" (Romans 4:25). The fact that Jesus conquered sin and death (sin's penalty) is good news, indeed. The fact that He offers to share that victory with us is the greatest news of all (John 14:19).

The elements of the gospel are clearly stated in 1 Corinthians 15:3–6, a key passage concerning the good news of God: "For what I received I passed on to you as of first importance: that Christ died for our sins according to the Scriptures, that he was buried, that he was raised on the third day according to the Scriptures, and that he appeared to Cephas, and then to the Twelve. After that, he appeared to more than five hundred of the brothers and sisters at the same time, most of whom are still living." Notice, first, that Paul "received" the gospel and then "passed it on"; this is a divine message, not a man-made invention. Second, the gospel is "of first importance." Everywhere the apostles went, they preached the crucifixion and resurrection of Christ. Third, the message of the gospel is accompanied by proofs: Christ died for our sins (proved by His burial), and He rose again the third day (proved by the eyewitnesses). Fourth, all this was done "according to the Scriptures"; the theme of the whole Bible is the salvation of mankind through Christ. The Bible is the gospel.

"I am not ashamed of the gospel, because it is the power of God that brings salvation to everyone who believes: first to the Jew, then to the Gentile" (Romans 1:16). The gospel is a bold message, and we are not ashamed of proclaiming it. It is a powerful message, because it is God's good news. It is a saving message, the only thing that can truly reform the human heart. It is a universal message, for Jews and Gentiles both. And the gospel is received by faith; salvation is the gift of God (Ephesians 2:8–9).

The gospel is the good news that God loves the world enough to give His only Son to die for our sin (John 3:16). The gospel is good news because our salvation and eternal life and home in heaven are guaranteed through Christ (John 14:1–4). "He has given us new birth into a living hope through the resurrection of Jesus Christ from the dead, and into an inheritance that can never perish, spoil or fade. This inheritance is kept in heaven for you" (1 Peter 1:3–4).

The gospel is good news when we understand that we do not (and cannot) earn our salvation; the work of redemption and justification is complete, having been finished on the cross (John 19:30). Jesus is the propitiation for our sins (1 John 2:2). The gospel is the good news that we, who were once enemies of God, have been reconciled by the blood of Christ and adopted into the family of God (Romans 5:10; John 1:12). "See what great love the Father has lavished on us, that we should be called children of God! And that is what we are!" (1 John 3:1). The gospel is the good news that "there is now no condemnation for those who are in Christ Jesus" (Romans 8:1).

To reject the gospel is to embrace the bad news. Condemnation before God is the result of a lack of faith in the Son of God, God's only provision for salvation. "For God did not send his Son into the world to condemn the world, but to save the world through him. Whoever believes in him is not condemned, but whoever does not believe stands condemned already because they have not believed in the name of God's one and only Son" (John 3:17–18). God has given a doomed world good news: the Gospel of Jesus Christ! -- Article by www.GotQuestion.org

A huge thank you to all Kickstarter backers and patrons!

Without the trusting support of all the backers and the ongoing support of the Patreon patrons, we would not be able to create this comic. Thank you and God bless you all! If you'd like to back the next Kickstarter follow us at kickstarter.com/profile/word4wordbiblecomic

A SOLER
AARON PLATTNER
AARON TRANES
ADAM FARLOW
AIDAN BOWES
ALASTAIR BLACK
ANDREW KRANS
AW
BAILEY NELSON
BALE FAMILY
BECKY LUQUE
BEN GREEN
BEN NICHOLS
BILL LOWRY
BJÖRN ZEIGER
BRADBROOK
BRANDON CLEAVER
BRANNON-POLLEY FAMILY
BRIAN HUISMAN
BRIAN TURNER
C WILLIS
CAMARA FAMILY
CHARLES GOODEN
CHARLOTTE BRAMLEY
CHOOI OH
CHRIS JOYCE
CHRISTOPHER DAVIS
CJ MONROE
CM LOWRY
COOMBES FAMILY
CUNNINGHAM FAMILY
D ANTHONY
D RISSE
D.MARTIN GODDARD
DAN COE
DANIEL CARPENTER
DANIEL M. PEREZ
DAVE HOLETS
DAVE METCALFE-CARR
DAVID ARINGTON
DAVID ARKEMA
DAVID HELLAM
DAVID NUNNS
DAVID PLATER
DAVID REES
DEAD TO SELF RADIO
DINO NOWAK
DORIAN WESTACOTT
DOWNIE FAMILY
ELEANOR STIRLING
ERIC DOBBS
FANT FAMILY
GARY SHIPMAN
GEOFF KNOTT
GEORGE KIRKE

GIBBS FAMILY
GRAHAM PALMER
GRAYSON S
H SHELLARD
HALFORD FAMILY
HUNNISETT FAMILY
J&J ARINGTON
JACOB THOMAS
JAKE HATCHER
JAMES B. AJIDUAH
JAMES SHARPE
JAMIE MOORCROFT-SHARP
JAVID YUNUS SULEMAN
JEREMIAH NIEVES
JESSE FAMILY
JESSICA ELLIS
JETAUN FRAZIER
JIM K.
JJ WHITE
JODY L. SELLERS
JOEL WATT
JOHANN TAMBAYAH
JON BROTHERHOOD
JON MCQUERY
JS
JUSTIN ONG
KEITH BURNETT
KM
LAETITIA GUY COURONNÉ
LEANN EMERY
LEE SHAPIRO
LIAM CAMPS
LOUISE GLENN
LUKER FAMILY
M RENYARD
MA
MAGNESS FAMILY
MARINA SIRYANA
MARSHALL WILLIAMS
MARTIN BRIDGWATER
MARTIN WADLOW
MATTHEW CHRISTJANSEN
MAX & EMMA RANDALL
MEAGEN FARRELL
MICHAEL WEILMEIER
MICHAELA BAKER
MICHELLE ARINGTON
MIKE BARLOTTA
MIKE HEITKEMPER
NATE HENDON
NAVARRETE FAMILY
NEIL KEARSLEY
NELSON FORSTER
NICK HARRIS
NIGEL AGYEMANG

PARSONS FAMILY
PATCHIN FAMILY
PATRICK BÄCHLI
PAUL MAZUMDAR
PAUL PHILBIN
PEACOCK FAMILY
PETEY MAINARDI
PETRETTA
PHIL DUNCALFE
PJOJR
QUINTEN BLACK
RANDALL WAGNER
RANDIMAN ROGERS
REAL LIFE CHURCH
RICHARD ERIC ESCOBEDO
RICHARD HUDSPETH
RICHARD TAN A KIAM
ROBERT EARLY
ROBERT L VAUGHN
ROBIN SEYMOUR
ROGER MILES
ROLANDO RODRIGUEZ
ROUND FAMILY
RYAN PRESTON
SIAN MORGAN
SCOTT GROW
SCOTT STEUBING
SEAN DORSEY
SEM BRYS
SETH SECOR
SITAL-SINGH FAMILY
SPEARMAN FAMILY
STACY FLUEGGE
STEFFI WHITEHEAD
STEPHEN FERGUSON
STEVE "THE BARD" LATOUR
STEWART WALKER
STOUFFER FAMILY
SUFFER ALEXIS DIAZ
SUNSHINE
T+M+J FÄSSLER
THE AIRHART FAMILY
THORP FAMILY
TOM FOSTER
TREY COMSTOCK
VASBY-BURNIE FAMILY
VINNEY & RACH BROWN
WESLEY SMIT
WILSON FAMILY
WISKNORT
WOLFRAM FAMILY
WOODS FAMILY
XAVIER L
YAROSLAV PLATASH
YEUNG FAMILY

BEHEMOTH & LEVIATHAN SCALE BACKERS

ADRIAN STEAD - BEN AND REBEKAH RANDALL - BILL RITTER - BROOKING FAMILY - BRUCE NICOLE
CHRIS WATTS - CHRISTOPHER WATKINS - DALZIEL FAMILY - DAN MORRICE - DANIEL GREGORY
DAVE HOLETS - DESMOND T H LIM - FERGUSON FAMILY - HEATHER GILMORE - JB
KATLYNN G. BENNETT - KELTZ FAMILY - LUCAS BRANDON - M. MONTGOMERY - MARK DARBY SLATER.
MATTHEW KIM - MICHAELA BAKER - MIKE PEPPER - NATHANIEL J MCLEGGAN - P YEO - PHIL LOUCH
RICHARD TAN - ROUND FAMILY - SEM BRYS - SIMON AND CLARIE MILES - STEPHEN AND ANNIE SELLS
TIM COX - TONY RUSSELL - TONY WILLIAMS - WILLDIG FAMILY - WILLIAM L'HOMMEDIEU - ZEN VAYDA